SUBCOMMANDER MARCOS

SUBCOMMANDER MARCOS

The Man and the Mask

NICK HENCK

Duke University Press

Durham and London

2007

Duke University Press gratefully
acknowledges the support of
Keio University, through the Keio Gijuku
Fukuzawa Memorial Fund, which provided
funds toward the production of this book.

For my parents

Marcos without the ski mask is inadmissible, is
not photogenic, is not a living legend.

—CARLOS MONSIVÁIS

Q. If everyone knows who you are, why the mask?
A touch of coquetry. They don't know who I am,
but it doesn't matter to them anyway. At stake
is what Subcomandante Marcos is, not who he
was.

—SUBCOMANDANTE MARCOS interview with
Gabriel García Márquez and Roberto Pombo

He wears a mask, and his face grows to fit it.

—GEORGE ORWELL, "Shooting an Elephant"

Put off that mask of burning gold,
With emerald eyes.
O no, my dear, you make so bold
To find if hearts be wild and wise,
And not yet cold.

*

I would but find what's there to find,
Love or deceit.
It was the mask that engaged your mind,
And after set your heart to beat,
Not what's behind.

*

—W. B. YEATS, *The Mask*

CONTENTS

ILLUSTRATIONS

ACHNOWLEDGMENTS

It has long since become the convention to preface a work with a page or two of acknowledgments. Indeed, so standard is this practice that one could be forgiven for thinking that it has become somewhat of an empty ritual. Nothing, however, could be further from the truth. We now live in an age where academics labor under a system which places on them tremendous pressure to publish, and yet one which at the same time denies them much of the time needed to do so. Thus, those academics who take the time to proofread the work of their colleagues stand to risk delaying their own research and publications, thereby harming their own careers through this sacrifice of time. It is therefore all the more commendable and heartening to find academics who are prepared to read over one's work. It is with this in mind that I extend my fullest appreciation to Professor John F. Drinkwater for his constant help, advice, and friendship over the past decade, and in particular concerning this book. I would also like to thank Professor Neil McLynn, a colleague and a friend, for all that he has done for me in terms of my career in general and this book. In addition, professors Gregory Hadley, William Snell, and Charles De Wolf, all busy academics with careers of their own, are deserving of my sincerest gratitude for devoting what precious little time they have to spare to proofreading my manuscript. (Needless to say, any remaining errors are entirely my own responsibility.)

A second group of people without whom this book could not have been completed is the librarians at various institutions I have visited. It was my privilege to work for two years at Oxford University's Bodleian Library and to have been a reader there for more than a decade now. Like that other great British institution, the National Health Service, it too is constantly asked to perform miracles while being underfunded and understaffed. Both institutions are currently called upon to function on a scale far beyond that which they were originally designed and intended for, and both face criticism on the few occasions they fail yet receive scant praise for their many successes. Finally, both institutions owe these successes to the dedication of those who staff them. With this in mind I would like to thank specifically Robert McNeil (Bodleian's Hispanic/Latin American Section), Laura Salinas (Oxford University's Latin American Centre), and Amanda Peters (Taylorian Institute) as well as others too numerous to mention for their professional advice and kindness.

At certain stages, the following people have contributed in no small way to this work: Mark Lewis (at its inception); Dr. Robert Ovetz (for supplying a CD of his interview with Subcommander Marcos); Yasunori Kasai (for his general support and his help with obtaining resources); Ms. Tamaki and Ms. Arai (for helping to obtain research materials); Laura and Emma Pros Carey and Philippe del Giudice (for their translation help); Martin Gili at Dolphin Books (for managing to get hold of several rare and obscure books); photographer Scott Sady for allowing me to use so much of his excellent work; Aurora Trejo at *Proceso* for her help obtaining photographs; and my anonymous readers at Duke. I would also like to thank Reynolds Smith and Mark Mastromarino at Duke, for their hard work on, and faith in, this project.

In terms of institutions, I would very much like to thank Keio University for a very generous grant enabling me to publish this research. Niigata University and Keio University must also take credit for providing excellent environments in which to conduct research.

In a more general way, mention should also be made both of the Irish group "irlandesa," who have done so much to make the communiqués of the EZLN and Subcommander Marcos widely accessible by translating them into English, and of the journalist Hermann Bellinghausen, whose dedication and sincere reporting continues to keep the world informed of the Zapatista project.

Finally, but by no means least, I would like to thank those around me for their time, patience, support, and encouragement. First and foremost among these are my parents of course, but also my fiancée, Yasuko, and my friends—all of them long-suffering, having been forced to share my interest in the Subcommander.

Keio University, Japan
January 2006

ABBREVIATIONS AND ACRONYMS

ANCIEZ Alianza Nacional Campesina Independiente Emiliano Zapata/ Emiliano Zapata Independent National Peasant Alliance

ARIC Asociación Rural de Interés Colectivo/Rural Association of Collective Interests (an umbrella organization under whose name various Uniones de Ejidos have grouped together)

Banamex Banco Nacional de México/National Bank of Mexico

Banrural Banco Nacional de Credito Rural/National Rural Credit Bank

CCRI Comité Clandestino de Revolución Indígena/Clandestine Indigenous Revolutionary Committee (the executive body of the EZLN)

CEOIC Consejo Estatal de Organizaciones Indígenas y Campesinas/ State Council of Indigenous and Peasant Organizations (established in 1994 in the aftermath of the January rebellion)

CIOAC Central Independiente de Obreros Agrícolas y Campesinos/ Independent Confederation of Rural Workers and Peasants

CNC Confederacíon Nacional Campesina/National Peasant Confederation (government sponsored)

CND Convencíon Nacional Democrática/National Democratic Convention

CNDH Comisión Nacional de Derechos Humanos/National Commission for Human Rights (established by the Mexican government in 1990 to monitor Human Rights abuses)

COCOPA Comisión de Concordia y Pacificación/Conciliation and Pacification Committee (a cross-party body established in response to the renewed government offensive of February 1995, which aims at negotiating a workable and dignified peace)

CONAI	Comisión Nacional de Intermediación/National Intermediation Commission
CONPAZ	Coordinadora de Organismos No Gubernamentales por la Paz/Coordinating Committee of Nongovernmental Peace Groups
DESMI	Desarrollo Económico Social de los Mexicanos Indígenas/ Social-Economic Development of the Indigenous Mexicans
EPR	Ejército Popular Revolucionario/Popular Revolutionary Army
ERPI	Ejército Revolucionario del Pueblo Insurgente/Revolutionary Army of the Insurgent People
EZLN	Ejército Zapatista de Liberación Nacional/Zapatista Army of National Liberation
FARC	Fuerzas Armadas Revolucionarias de Colombia/Revolutionary Armed Forces of Colombia (Colombia's largest guerrilla group)
FLN	Fuerzas de Liberación Nacional/Forces of National Liberation
FMLN	Frente Farabundo Martí de Liberación Nacional/Farabundo Marti National Liberation Front (El Salvadoran coalition of guerrilla movements)
FOBAPROA	A Mexican Savings Protection Banking Fund that got heavily into debt due to mismanagement and/or corruption. The Mexican government proposed a bank bailout using public funds in 1998. The PRD called a referendum to ask if ordinary Mexicans—whose taxes would pay for this—agreed to the government's proposal.
FSLN	Frente Sandinista de Liberación Nacional/Sandinista National Liberation Front (Nicaraguan guerrilla group that succeeded in taking power in 1979)
FZLN	Frente Zapatista de Liberación Nacional/Zapatista National Liberation Front
IFE	Instituto Federal Electoral/Federal Electoral Institute
ILO	International Labor Organization
IMF	International Monetary Fund

INI	Instituto Nacional Indigenista/National Indigenous Institute (a government agency established to address the problems facing indigenous peoples in Mexico)
Inmecafe	Instituto Mexicano del Café/Mexican Coffee Institute
ISA	Ideological State Apparatus
MLN	Movimiento de Liberación Nacional/National Liberation Movement
NAFTA	North American Free Trade Agreement (tripartite agreement between the United States, Canada, and Mexico to lower or abolish trade tariffs that came into effect on 1 January 1994)
NEA	National Endowment for the Arts
NGO	Nongovernmental organization
OCEZ	Organización Campesina Emiliano Zapata/Emiliano Zapata Peasant Organization
PAN	Partido Acción Nacional/National Action Party (traditionally conservative, anti-Communist, pro-Catholic, pro-business political party founded in 1939 and at the time of writing headed by Vicente Fox, president of Mexico)
Pemex	Pétroleos Mexicanos (the Mexican national oil company)
PGR	Procuraduría General de la Repúblic/Procurator General of the Republic (an office akin to the U.S. Justice Department)
PRD	Partido de la Revolución Democrática/Party of Democratic Revolution (center-left party that came into being in 1989 as a reaction to the electoral fraud of 1988)
PRI	Partido Revolucionario Institucional/Party of Institutionalized Revolution (the political party that arose after the Mexican Revolution and dominated Mexican politics until 2000)
ProCampo	Programa de Apoyo Directo al Campo/National Program for Direct Aid to the Countryside
PROCUP	Partido Revolucionario Obrero Clandestino–Unión del Pueblo/Clandestine Revolutionary Workers Party–Union of the People

Pronasol	Programa Nacional de Solidaridad/National Solidarity Program (a governmental financial aid program)
PSUM	Partido Socialista Unificado de México/Unified Socialist Party of Mexico
Quiptic	A predominantly indigenous peasant organization that had been established in 1975 in the wake of the National Indigenous Council of the previous year
RAP	Regiones Autónomas Pluri-étnicas/Pluri-ethnic Autonomous Regions
RAZ	Regiones Autónomas Zapatistas/Zapatista Autonomous Regions
RSA	Repressive State Apparatus
Sedesol	Secretaría de Desarrollo Social/Ministry of Social Development
Slop	"Root" in Tzeltal. A peasant organization that Bishop Ruiz had helped to create in 1980 in order to offset the Maoists' influence in the region, which at that time was strong.
UAM	Universidad Autónoma Metropolitana/Autonomous Metropolitan University (a radical university founded in Mexico City in 1974)
UE	Unión de Ejidos/Union of Ejidos
UNAM	Universidad Nacional Autónoma México/National Autonomous University of Mexico (Mexico City's oldest and traditionally most prestigious university)
URNG	Unidad Revolucionaria Nacional Guatemalteca/Guatemalan National Revolutionary Union (a coalition of revolutionary movements)
UU	Unión de Uniones Ejidales y Grupos Campesinos de Chiapas/ Union of Ejido Unions and Peasant Solidarity Groups of Chiapas

CAST OF MAIN CHARACTERS

This is a list of members (past and present) of the FLN and EZLN, ranked in approximate order of seniority, when they joined the FLN and/or the EZLN, and their importance within it.

FLN

Comandante Germán Fernando Yáñez Muñoz (a.k.a. Leo). Founding member of the FLN in the late 1960s in the aftermath of the Tlatelolco student massacre. After the death of his brother, César Germán Yáñez Muñoz (Pedro), at the hands of the security forces in Chiapas (1974), he took his brother's real name (Germán) for his own nom de guerre. He was one of the original six who established the EZLN *foco* in Chiapas (November 1983). He trained Marcos in guerrilla warfare. He is the husband of Lucía, whom he married during the same ceremony that Marcos married Yolanda/Ana María (1987). He was captured by security forces in October 1995, but was later released without charge. He is now an advisory editor of *Rebeldía*, the EZLN magazine.

Pedro César Germán Yáñez Muñoz, brother of Fernando Yáñez Muñoz. He was shot dead by security forces in February 1974 while undertaking guerrilla activities in Chiapas.

Roger Margil Yáñez Muñoz. The oldest brother of César and Fernando. He did the groundwork for guerrilla activity in Chiapas during the mid-1970s, distributing medical supplies there in an attempt to win over the local population. Like his father, whom he was named after, he became a doctor.

Comandante Rodrigo Javier Ramírez (a.k.a. Juan). Brother of Gabriel Ramírez (Dr. Carlos) and husband of Silvia Fernández (Gabriela, a.k.a.

Sofía). He was second-in-command of the FLN. He left the organization in January 1993 after an internal coup within the FLN.

Comandanta Elisa   María Gloria Benavides Guevara (a.k.a. Ana). She studied at the University of Nuevo León where she had met the two Yáñez brothers, Fernando and César. She joined the FLN as a teenager in the early 1970s. She was one of the original six (and the only woman) who comprised the *foco* that went to Chiapas (November 1983) and called itself the EZLN. In 1983 she was dating (and recruiting) Jorge Santiago (alias Jacobo), the head of DESMI, a regional development agency. She traveled to Nicaragua. Elisa ran the main headquarters camp, La Cueva (the cave) in Chiapas for several years before returning to Mexico City permanently to conduct FLN operations there (around 1988). She had previously (around 1985) fallen in love with Javier Elorriaga (Vicente), with whom she had a son, named Vicente after his father's nom de guerre. After the internal coup (January 1993) she and her husband were put in charge of the FLN's ideological commission, editing and publishing internal documents. She was seized in the government's February 1995 offensive, but the case was thrown out amid allegations of torture and irregularities concerning due process.

Lucía   Gloria Muñoz. The wife of Germán. She had been at Tlatelolco Plaza during the massacre of the students in 1968. She helped train and politically educate indigenous recruits in a safe house in the Tuxtla Gutiérrez. She received the post of secretary of the masses during the January 1993 Prado meeting, thus becoming (with Marcos and Germán) one of the three cornerstones of the FLN and EZLN. She is currently an advisory editor for the EZLN's *Rebeldía* magazine.

Gabriela   Silvia Fernández (a.k.a. Sofía), wife of Comandante Rodrigo, in charge of editing and publishing the FLN's publications, and possibly Rafael Guillén's (and Daniel's) recruiter at UAM. She left the movement at the same time as her husband, after the January 1993 internal coup.

Rodolfo   Real name unknown. A native of Chihuahua and one of the initial six founding members of the EZLN who arrived in Chiapas in November 1983. Around late 1984 or early 1985 he was relocated to his home state of Chihuahua where he took command of the newly implanted Villa Front—the FLN's northern counterpart to its southern wing, the EZLN.

Dr. Carlos   Gabriel Ramírez. Rodrigo's brother and husband to Mercedes (Rocío Casariego), Marcos's former girlfriend. He frequently traveled to

Nicaragua and worked in EZLN camps in Chiapas. He left the organization after the January 1993 internal coup.

Mercedes   Rocío Casariego. Formerly Rafael Guillén's girlfriend while they were at UNAM, she later went on to marry Dr. Carlos and to work in Nicaragua and Chiapas. She left the organization after the January 1993 internal coup. She named her daughter Mercedes, after her own nom de guerre.

"Marcos"   Adelaido Villafranco. Rafael Guillén took Villafranco's nom de guerre for himself following Villafranco's death (26 May 1983) at an army checkpoint in Puebla. Rafael had accompanied "Marcos" on long journeys, during which he had been impressed by the latter's knowledge of Mexican history.

EZLN

Subcomandante Pedro   Héctor Ochao. He was from Mexico City. Although not one of the six FLN members who established the *foco* in Chiapas (November 1983), he arrived very soon afterward (probably late 1983 or early 1984). It was he who scouted the La Pesadilla (the nightmare) camp. He was very close to Marcos. He remained in Chiapas all the time (from his arrival to his death a decade later), leaving only once, briefly, for hospital treatment. He too, like Marcos and Daniel, commanded a camp of his own. He was shot dead in January 1994 while leading an attack on Las Margaritas.

Subcomandante Marcos   Rafael Sebastián Guillén Vicente (the subject of this biography).

Subcomandante Daniel   Salvador Morales Garibay. A native of Michoacán, he was a teaching assistant in Rafael Guillén's department at UAM. He joined the FLN and EZLN and spent some time briefly in Chiapas in 1985 before working for three years (1985–88) under Germán in Mexico City. There he was promoted to Subcommander and later returned to Chiapas and put in charge of his own camp. He and Marcos frequently disagreed and this, plus general disillusionment with the cause, led Daniel to distance himself from the movement. He left it in 1993 and, allegedly fearing reprisals, fled to the United States. In 1994, from his self-imposed exile, he began making contact with the Mexican government's intelligence services. He made a statement giving details about the movement to the intelligence services in February 1995.

Yolanda/Ana María   Real name unknown. A Tzotzil from Sabanilla. She joined the EZLN early on, in December 1984, at age fourteen. Marcos led her on her first training mission that month. She was soon placed in charge of recruitment in the north of the region. She subsequently worked undercover as an auxiliary nurse at a hospital in San Andrés Larráinzar. She married Marcos in 1987. She rose to the rank of major and led the attacks on San Cristóbal and Rancho Nuevo in January 1994.

Jacobo   Jorge Santiago. Head of DESMI, a regional development agency started by Bishop Ruiz and funded by international nongovernmental organizations. He had been romantically involved with Elisa during the early 1980s. He helped recruit Tzotzils in the region of Sabanilla and diverted DESMI funds to the EZLN.

Mario   Real name unknown. A Tzotzil from Sabanilla, he joined the EZLN very young in December 1984 along with Yolanda/Ana María. He soon rose to the rank of major and was put in charge of the Baby Doc camp (around 1986). After Subcommander Daniel left the organization in 1993 Mario was put in charge of Daniel's former camp, La Calabazas (the pumpkins) at the Sierra Corralchén. He also led the attack on Ocosingo in January 1994.

Tacho   Humberto Trejo. A Tojolabal and leader of the region's *campesino* unions, the Unión de Ejidos de la Selva. In the 1970s, he had been sent to the Marists in San Cristóbal to attend bible study workshops in which he was also taught arithmetic, first aid, Mexican history, agrarian rights, and how to establish cooperatives. He rose to the rank of comandante. He came to the front of the EZLN as Marcos attempted to step back out of the limelight. He was a central figure, for example, in the Encuentro (1996), and negotiated and signed (along with David) the San Andrés Accords.

David   Real name unknown. A Tzotzil and former catechist. Like Tacho, he became a central figure in the EZLN after Marcos decided to take more of a back seat. He negotiated and signed (along with Tacho) the San Andrés Accords.

Moisés   Real name unknown. A Tzeltal who often acted as translator between Marcos and the indigenous during the early years. He rose to the rank of major and led the attack on Comitán in January 1994.

Hugo Francisco Gómez. A Tzeltal from Las Cañadas, who had been president of Quiptic in the late 1970s, secretary of the Unión de Uniones/ARIC in the late 1980s and then one of the leaders of the ANCIEZ during the early 1990s. He rose to the rank of capitán and headed the arm of the movement devoted to the organization of masses, before being killed in Ocosingo during the uprising. Marcos carried a photograph of Hugo around with him after his death and even dedicated several verses of Paul Eluard's poem "El Castillo de los pobres" ("The Castle of the Poor") to him in one of his communiqués.

Jesús Lázaro Hernández. He had worked as a catechist attending the Chiapas Indigenous Council (and so was known to Samuel Ruiz), and was simultaneously the secretary of Quiptic. He helped to introduce the EZLN into indigenous communities and peasant organizations. In January 1986 he organized the First Worker-Peasant Meeting of the FLN, designed to forge links between Chiapan peasants and workers from cities in the north of Mexico. He became the president of ARIC (1991), helping the EZLN to control the organization and steer its members into the guerrillas' ranks.

Vicente Jorge Javier Elorriaga Berdegué. He joined the FLN and EZLN at some point during the 1980s, later becoming a comandante. He fell in love with Comandanta Elisa (mid-1980s) and they had a son together (named Vicente after his father's nom de guerre). His duties were concerned with the FLN's ideological commission. During 1994 he distributed the EZLN's communiqués to the press and acted as a liaison between the EZLN and the government. He was arrested during the government's February 1995 offensive. He was tried and sentenced to thirteen years in prison for terrorism. He was released on 6 June 1996 and shortly after was made head of the FZLN, which he worked to publicize.

Old Antonio Initially thought by many to be a literary construct of Marcos, it appears he was a real person. He and Marcos met while the latter was leading a training mission in December 1984. It was Old Antonio who invited the EZLN into his village, thus giving the guerrillas their first foothold in the communities. Former Subcommander-turned-informer Daniel insists that Old Antonio was an assassin who had fled into the jungle to escape justice. He died in May or June 1994. Marcos often includes him in his communiqués, with Old Antonio acting as the dispenser of indigenous wisdom.

Castelán Francisco López. A Chol from Sabanilla who was the Unión de Uniones president. He recruited for the EZLN.

OTHERS

Avendaño, Amado Coeditor of San Cristóbal's *el Tiempo* newspaper and PRD gubernatorial candidate for the state in 1994.

Camacho Solís, Manuel Mayor of Mexico City in 1988, he was a potential PRI presidential candidate in the 1994 elections. However, he was passed over in favor of Luis Donaldo Colosio, and was instead made peace commissioner in charge of negotiating a peace with the EZLN after the uprising.

Cárdenas, Cuauhtémoc Son of President Lázaro Cárdenas (1934–40). He broke from the PRI and ran for the 1988 presidential election. Despite being widely perceived as the victor, electoral fraud resulted in Salinas being declared the winner. He then co-founded the PRD.

Colosio, Luis Donaldo The 1994 PRI presidential candidate before his assassination on 23 March 1994.

Fox Quesada, Vicente PAN President of Mexico (2000–2006). He boasted prior to taking office that he could solve the Chiapas problem in fifteen minutes.

Madrazo Cuellar, José Manuel Camacho Solís's replacement as peace commissioner.

Robledo, Eduardo 1994 PRI gubernatorial candidate for Chiapas.

Ruiz, Samuel Bishop of the San Cristóbal Diocese from 1960–2000. He was influenced by liberation theology. The EZLN nominated him as an official mediator between it and the government. He founded the Fray Bartolomé de las Casas Human Rights Center and formed the CONAI mediation body.

Salinas di Gortari, Carlos President of Mexico (1988–1994). He earned a doctorate from Harvard. He was secretary of budget and finance (1982–87), during which time the government implemented a severe economic austerity program. He was declared president in the 1988 election despite blatant electoral fraud. He initiated a policy of mass privatizations.

Zapata, Emiliano Mexico's most famous and much-loved peasant leader in the Mexican Revolution. He fought tirelessly and uncompromisingly for agrarian reform. In 1919 he was tricked into meeting with the government to discuss peace and was treacherously assassinated at a place called Chinameca.

Zedillo, Ernesto President of Mexico (1994–2000). He earned his doctorate in economics from Yale. He had been the education minister and was only nominated as the PRI presidential candidate because its first choice, Luis Colosio, was assassinated.

Key to states

1 DISTRITO FEDERAL
2 MORELOS
3 TLAXCALA
4 ESTADO DE MÉXICO
5 QUERÉTARO
6 AGUASCALIENTES
7 COLIMA

MAP 1: MEXICO.

SUBCOMMANDER MARCOS

INTRODUCTION

At dawn on 1 January 1994 Subcommander Marcos made his debut on the world stage. From the balcony of San Cristóbal's town hall he addressed the crowd that had gathered below, informing them that the Zapatista Army of National Liberation (EZLN in Spanish) had seized four towns in the southeastern state of Chiapas and was holding them in revolt from the Mexican government. By the time that dusk fell on that same town square about twelve hours later Marcos was on his way to becoming the most famous guerrilla leader since Che Guevara. In the weeks and months that followed, through a succession of interviews, communiqués, and public spectacles, the Subcommander acted as a conduit through which the rebelling indigenous peasants under his command articulated their grievances and demands to Mexican society and the government. Also during this period, through a combination of his charisma, media savvy, and the mystique attending him, a cult of celebrity swiftly attached itself to Marcos to the extent that he has become today a world-recognized revolutionary icon and the champion of the anti-neoliberal-globalization movement.

More than a decade has now elapsed since those early days of Zapatismo, and much ink has been spilled by myriad authors (historians, novelists, journalists, essayists, anthropologists, and others) concerning almost every aspect of the Zapatista uprising in Chiapas: its origins, course, and results, and their implications. However, despite this considerable interest in the Zapatista movement in general, and in Marcos in particular—to the extent that he has enjoyed a high media profile and has seen the publication and translation of numerous collections of his communiqués (six in English alone)[1]—incredible as it may seem, after more than ten years there still remains no biography in English of the rebellion's main protagonist. Of course, of the plethora of books treating Chiapas to have appeared over the last decade many devote a chapter (or two) to discussion of the man the world has come to know as "El Sup."[2] However, there exist only two works, both in Spanish, of a biographical nature focusing on the man himself.

Of these, the first to appear was César Jacobo Romero's *Marcos: ¿Un profesional de la esperanza?*, described on its front cover as a *"biografía unofficial."*[3] It is at times an astute work that attempts to piece together a profile of the Subcommander and his background from snippets of Marcos's own writings and interviews with him. Ultimately, however, Romero was laboring under the disadvantage of not knowing Marcos's real identity—this had yet to be revealed by the Mexican authorities as Rafael Sebastián Guillén Vicente—and so all he had to work on were the frequently self-contradictory hints Marcos threw out, often with the aim of misleading the security forces and the media, both of which were determined to ascertain his true identity.[4] Indeed, Romero quotes Marcos as saying "the only sure thing about what I have said about my identity is that it's false—mere repartee with the press."[5]

The second work, *Marcos: la genial impostura* by Bertrand de la Grange and Maite Rico, took full advantage of the information provided by Marcos's unmasking by Mexico's Procuraduría General de la Republic—an office akin to that of the U.S. Justice Department—in February 1995.[6] Unfortunately, the book, although well researched, is a prejudiced and polemical work[7]—it is so hostile, in fact, that the Zedillo government bought up thousands of copies of it to distribute as anti-Zapatista propaganda—while de la Grange's continued denigration of Marcos and the Zapatistas, especially in the aftermath of the Acteal massacre, led to his replacement as *Le Monde*'s Chiapas correspondent in 1998.[8]

Little justification is therefore necessary for attempting to produce an objective biography in English of the Subcomandante. Prior to writing such a biography, however, and given that *Marcos: la genial impostura* is the only major biographical work treating both Marcos and Rafael Guillén, it is perhaps as well to devote some space to discussing the criticisms it raises. The authors' jaundiced views on Marcos are obvious throughout the work. The Subcommander's motives are consistently brought into question, and he is never given the benefit of the doubt where this may reflect positively on him. Although the authors are honest in that they do not attempt to conceal their animosity toward Marcos, they are not wholly candid concerning the origins of their animosity. A less well-informed reader may think that de la Grange and Rico dislike Marcos purely because they believe him to be a self-promoting, middle-class, doctrinaire Marxist disguising himself as a liberal champion of Mexico's indigenous people. However, at least part of the reason for their prejudice perhaps derives from a personality clash between de la Grange and Marcos that resulted in the former being denied access to Zapatista information and excluded from participation in the Intercontinental Encuentro (summer 1996).[9] Indeed, already by the spring of 1996 de la Grange had been accused by fellow journalists of treating the Zapatistas with contempt and mocking Marcos.[10]

Once the source of this hostility is understood, de la Grange's and Rico's criticisms of Marcos's racial profile (i.e., mestizo), his bourgeois origins, his Marxist past, and his self-aggrandizement can be easily dismissed. That Marcos is not himself indigenous seems to me irrelevant. Quite why de la Grange and Rico should think that Marcos's credentials as the military leader of a movement that aims at the improvement of the rights and conditions of indigenous people should be questioned on the grounds that he himself is mestizo escapes my comprehension.[11] This is an especially lame criticism when applied to a man who has spent nearly twenty years living with indigenous people and learning their languages and culture. (It should be remembered that many anthropologists who are considered academic authorities on various peoples have spent considerably less time in the field with their subjects.) Moreover, if one objects to a mestizo being a prominent member of an indigenous uprising, what can one say about whites having held prominent positions in the black civil rights movements in the United States during the 1960s or in South Africa during the 1980s? The argument that a revolutionary who aims at the empowerment of the impoverished must belong to this social class is puerile. It is possible to be a man *for* the people, without being a man *of* the people; and therefore it is also possible to be a man *for* the indigenous, without being *of* the indigenous. Moreover, at least one professor of anthropology and Latin American studies has argued, conversely, that Marcos's white, middle-class background is indeed relevant, but that this was a contributing factor to his being accepted by the indigenous as their spokesperson. Gary H. Gossen rejects the image of Marcos as the unscrupulous Subcommander who has duped a weak and docile indigenous people and is manipulating them for reasons of self-aggrandizement and the furthering of Marxism.[12] Rather, after noting that "Mayan ethnicity, cosmology, historical reckoning, and political legitimacy have always drawn freely from symbolic and ideological forms of other ethnic and political entities—particularly those perceived to be stronger than themselves—in order to situate and centre themselves in the present,"[13] he concludes that "*Subcomandante Marcos* is utterly plausible as a spokesperson for an Indian cause precisely because he is outside of, extrasomatic to, the Indian community."[14]

Concerning Marcos's Marxist past, I am not sure precisely what Rico and de la Grange are objecting to. If they are objecting simply to Marcos having had a Marxist past, this would lead to the dismissal of countless politicians (both in Mexico,[15] and also in Latin America and Europe). If, however, they object to Marcos having changed his political stance from one of orthodox Marxist (when he joined the FLN in 1979 at about age twenty-two) to less orthodox Leftwinger (as he was by 1994 at age thirty-seven), on the grounds that this makes him shallow or fickle, one ought perhaps to recall the words of Muhammad Ali, to the effect that a man who thinks the same thing at forty as he had at twenty has wasted twenty years of his life. Carlos Monsiváis contrasts what he sees as Marcos's flexibility with the rigidity of those who oppose him, noting: "The fact is that the proposals of Marcos and the EZLN have changed radically. Frankly, those of their adversaries have not."[16] If de la Grange and Rico believe that Marcos has deliberately attempted to conceal his Marxist past, a cursory glimpse at the Subcommander's interviews with Castillo and Brisac or Yvon Le Bot show him to be quite candid about the Marxist leanings of the initial project: he admits to attempting to establish an armed group (*foco*) whose ideology and tactics were those espoused by Che Guevara.[17] (Elsewhere, he is equally as candid about the failure of this venture, in particular the imposition of Marxist and Maoist doctrine on the indigenous population.)[18] Rather, I agree with Lorenzano, who observes:

> Any attempt to understand—or sanitize—the EZLN as a mere extension of the [Marxist] guerrilla movements of the 1960s and 1970s would be not only useless but sterile and ill-intentioned or even reactionary. . . . It is also the attitude assumed by intellectuals close to neo-liberalism (such as Octavio Paz and Héctor Aguilar Camín) and by certain would-be ex-radicals who regret their past.[19]

The only other possibility is that de la Grange and Rico remain unconvinced that Marcos has transformed himself from a doctrinaire Marxist into a pro-democracy Zapatista. If so, they are not alone. Tello Díaz also remains doubtful, while Oppenheimer argues that the Subcommander's "political history should at least raise questions about the sincerity of his moderate, post-insurrection rhetoric."[20] Indeed, Luis Lorenzano is compelled to devote time and space to the condemnation of those "political analysts . . . of the right," who "maintain that the EZLN's expressions in favor of democracy represent a sudden, opportunistic maneuver to conceal their terrible miasmas of archaism, dogmatism and totalitarianism."[21] Likewise, Mexico's leading novelist, essayist, and former ambassador to

France, Carlos Fuentes, also addresses the interpretations of such right-wing political analysts. In his letter to the Subcommander himself, he writes of the EZLN:

> A few years ago all these demands would have been stamped with the red-hot branding iron of anti-Communism. You are the first post-Communist actors on the stage of the Third World. Your aspirations can no longer be concealed or perverted as part of a Soviet world conspiracy. Only the shipwrecked of the cold war, bereft of Manichean enemies, can still believe that.[22]

It is, of course, certainly possible that Marcos is merely pretending to have undergone this transformation in an attempt to court the popularity of a world that has largely rejected orthodox Marxism. However, such an assessment assumes that Marcos has also managed to deceive his indigenous supporters, with whom he lived side by side for ten years preceding the uprising,[23] not to mention a host of academics from around the world who have interviewed him. Rather, I would point to the many eminent former doctrinaire Marxists who have modified their stances with age, especially since the fall of the Berlin Wall, and am prepared to accept (with the at least 5,000 indigenous who follow him) Marcos's claim that the cross-pollination of Marxism with indigenous ideology and social structures produced a new thought system.[24]

With regard to Marcos's alleged self-aggrandizement, there is no doubt that he has a strong sense of self-worth that borders on the supremely egotistical. However, it is also worth pointing out that inspection of the lives of people who have become significant leaders seems to reveal this as being a necessary character trait.[25] Régis Debray, who interviewed both Che Guevara and Subcommander Marcos clandestinely in the jungle, talks of the latter's "indispensable megalomania—necessary, I imagine, to endure 'the long voyage from suffering to hope,' of 11 years of mosquitoes, black beans and clandestine work, of a decade with damp feet, without chocolates [the thing Marcos confesses to missing most from his former urban life] or press conferences."[26] True, the Zapatista movement has from the start been inextricably caught up with the personality cult of Marcos, but it is perhaps an unpalatable truth that the vast majority of humanity finds it easier to identify with a single individual (even if he is masked) than a committee. De la Grange and Rico simply go too far in this charge—though not as far as Juan Miguel de Mora, who writes of Marcos's "megalomania" and sometimes implies that Marcos undertook the Zapatista uprising entirely out of the desire to be famous.[27] Marcos could not have known during those ten long years in the jungle that he would become famous; he did however run the risk of dying in obscurity, as did many other Chiapans and not a few Latin American guerrillas. Even Enrique Krauze, himself no great friend of Marcos, is prepared to concede that "his commitment to altering the social reality of Chiapas and Mexico is authentic (his democratic convictions less certain). He has been in the jungle with the Indians since 1983. It is a real and some would say admirable life choice."[28] The essayist, journalist, and novelist Elena Poniatowska echoes this, writing "he has lived according to his ideas, which seems a lot to ask in our country . . . he stayed in the jungle for eleven years, he has shared and continues to share the Indian's living conditions."[29] Even Octavio Paz, who is positively hostile toward Marcos, declares that the Subcommander's "capacity to establish quite profound links with the Indian groups is admirable."[30]

In short, *Subcomandante Marcos: la genial impostura* is deeply flawed, not in its research but in its interpretation. The eminent social anthropologist George A. Collier criticized the book because "in emphasizing the non-indigenous leadership of the EZLN [it fails to] succeed in explaining how the movement built up such a powerful indigenous base."[31] The award-winning Spanish poet, essayist, and novelist Manuel Vázquez Montalbán makes a sustained and prolonged attack on *Subcomandante Marcos: la genial impostura* in a collection of interviews with Marcos that Montalbán published as *Marcos: El señor de los espejos*. In it, he denounces *Subcomandante Marcos: la genial impostura* as "the most ferociously anti-Marcos book to have been published to date," and he goes on to attack it at length for its bias[32]; for the abuse it heaps upon Marcos, Samuel Ruiz, and anyone (such as Danielle Mitterrand, Carlos Monsiváis, and Oliver Stone) who has anything to do with them; for its failure to allow for even the possibility that Marcos has based some of his life choices on conscience; for the services it renders the Mexican government's anti-Zapatista propaganda machinery; and for its lack of humor and appreciation of Marcos's own humor. De la Grange's and Rico's censure of Marcos for having a secret past life Montalbán dismisses as "a puerile indignation."[33]

In this book I present an alternative view of Marcos, assembled from more than twenty interviews (most published, some filmed, tape-recorded, or posted on the Internet) that the Subcommander has granted since 1 January 1994; from more than two hundred communiqués explicitly signed by him and nearly two hundred others signed by the EZLN's Clandestine Indigenous Revolutionary Committee (a significant proportion of which were probably his work); from numerous speeches he has made during conventions, "*encuentros*," marches, and rallies; from an extensive number of press releases; and from a wealth of secondary material, including the published testimonies of family members, friends, acquaintances, and colleagues, and books and articles written by journalists and scholars.

I have also, of course, visited Chiapas, and more recently I attended a large rally and two smaller, more intimate, gatherings addressed by Marcos. However, I have not interviewed the Subcommander. By 1998, when I began writing this book—stimulated by the publication that year of the work of de la Grange and Rico—Marcos was already granting fewer interviews on the grounds that the media were tending to focus on him personally rather than the Zapatista movement. I therefore decided to concentrate on the considerable body of material already collected by others— the methodology employed by biographers of historical figures.

Indeed, it may be argued that, though a contemporary figure, Marcos is best considered at a distance. He has pursued a policy of deliberate obfuscation when dealing with interviewers, and it would have been naïve of me to expect any more candid treatment from him. Marcos has consistently demonstrated great skill in dissembling during interviews, a predilection to some extent forced upon him by the fact that he is leading an armed movement in an area in which paramilitary groups proliferate—unconsidered honesty could cost the EZLN popular support and even lives—but one which also, and perhaps in equal measure, is studiously contrived by him for his own purposes. Pulling the wool over the eyes of eager questioners is very much part of his technique in projecting a mysterious image of himself; one suspects that it has even become part of his character. As journalist John Ross observes, "Marcos tells many reporters many different stories":

> At various moments, Marcos informs us that the Zapatistas put their ski masks on (a) because they could be identified by the authorities if they didn't, (b) because it was cold, (c) because the Zapatistas are too handsome to walk around unprotected, and (d) because being masked promotes egalitarianism among the EZLN leaders, and thwarts the germination of a "caudillo."[34]

Nor is Ross alone in this observation. Joel Simon states that Marcos "tells different stories about his past during each interview."[35] Indeed, the Subcommander gave the *Miami Herald* journalist Andres Oppenheimer a candid insight into his method of deception:

Look, what happens is that when a Chilean comes to see me, I tell him I visited Chile. When somebody comes from Los Angeles, I tell him I was in Los Angeles. When a Frenchman comes, I tell him I was in France . . . When people start asking me personal questions, I ask them, Where are you from? Oh, from Veracruz? I was in Veracruz. You are from Monterrey? Ah, I've been in Monterrey. You are from San Francisco? I've been there; I've even worked at a gay bar there. Whatever they ask me, I've been there.[36]

In this respect it is remarkable how Marcos steadfastly refuses to cooperate even with those interviewers whom he greatly admires. For example, the following exchange took place between the Subcommander and Carlos Monsiváis, of whom Marcos is a self-confessed "avid reader":[37]

CM: As I assume you have an academic past, I would like to ask you to do an exercise . . .

M: My academic past is one of the myths . . .[38]

Gabriel García Márquez, whom Marcos describes as "special" among those writers who influenced him,[39] enjoyed no more candor from the Subcommander:

GGM: In passing you mentioned that there were swivel chairs when you were young. How old are you?

M: I am 518 years old [laughter] . . .

CGM: If everyone knows who you are, why the mask?

M: A touch of coquetry. They don't know who I am, but it doesn't matter to them anyway. At stake is what *Subcomandante Marcos* is, not who he was.[40]

Thus I fully concur with Oppenheimer's appraisal (1998 [1996]:75): having interviewed the Subcommander as early as 23 July 1994, he concluded that

I had intended to ask him whether his name was one of about half a dozen that Interior Ministry intelligence officials were periodically leaking to the press, but I decided it would be of no use: he would have lied anyway. His standard response was that he had been born when he arrived in Chiapas ten years earlier, that his parents were the Indians who accepted him as one of them, and that his real name was *Marcos*.[41]

My purpose throughout is not to judge Marcos, to condemn or condone his actions, but rather to try to comprehend and contextualize him—hence the structure of the work, with the first two parts treating "Marcos the man" and the third part dealing with the almost legendary figure he has become since donning his mask. This partitioning is not arbitrary, since the Subcommander himself told interviewer Saul Landau: "There are three *Marcoses*: *Marcos* of the past who has a past, the *Marcos* of the mountains before the first of January, and post January 1 *Marcos*."[42] Any judgment of Marcos, if one must be made, ought to focus on the virtue or merit of his aims and the efficacy and integrity with which he has pursued them. As for Marcos's character, it is as well to turn to Jorge Castañeda's nuanced and astute appraisal of Che Guevara, which I believe has a significant bearing upon the way we should view Marcos. His analysis of Guevara helps us to understand Marcos far better than do such labels as "first post-modern guerrilla hero,"[43] "professional of violence,"[44] a jungle "Fitzcarraldo,"[45] and "classic *caudillo* refreshed by postmodern humor and the reading of Cortázar,"[46] and certainly more than such descriptions as anachronistic utopian idealist, orthodox Marxist, or manipulator of gullible Indians. Of Che Guevara, Castañeda writes:

> He symbolizes an intellectual middle class outraged by an intolerable estrangement from the society it lives in and the abyss separating that class from the vast, undifferentiated universe of the poor . . . But Guevara also represents the heroism and nobility of myriad middle-class Latin Americans who rose up in the best way they could find, against a status quo they eventually discovered to be unlivable. If ever there was an illustration of the anguish evoked in sensitive and reasonable, but far from exceptional, individuals at being affluent and comfortable islands in a sea of destitution, it was Guevara. He will endure as a symbol, not of revolution or guerrilla warfare, but of the extreme difficulty, if not the actual impossibility, of indifference.[47]

The key point concerning Marcos, as of Che, is not who he is or what he has done previously, but rather what he symbolizes. When one hears the name Guevara, one does not think of "Ernesto," the Argentine doctor, for he transcended his personal identity and became "Che," the revolutionary icon. The same is true, although at present to a lesser extent, with Marcos. (In Tom Hayden's eyes, for example, Marcos "stands for the principle that we each must know what we would risk dying for in order to know what we live for.")[48] For men such as Marcos and Guevara, and many others, Marxism was the intellectual solution to a moral or sentimental problem with which they could not reconcile themselves: namely, how can you live with yourself comfortably when the overwhelming majority of those around you are intolerably destitute? Indeed, this is what Marcos himself tells us, only more succinctly, in one of his communiqués: "The owner of the voice [i.e., Marcos] confesses that, facing the choice between comfort and responsibility, he always chose responsibility."[49] Similarly, in an interview he gave in March 1994, in which he explained the roots of his own personal road to rebellion, Marcos commented that "understanding that there is injustice, then trying to understand the roots of this injustice . . . invariably leads you to ask yourself: and you, what are you going to do about it?"[50] Elsewhere he elaborates on this a little, telling another interviewer: "I imagine everyone has to choose at some point. We either kept living a comfortable life, materially comfortable, or we had to be consistent with a certain type of ideals. We had to choose and be consistent and so . . . here we are."[51] In these lines are the keys to understanding not only Marcos's motivation but also his popularity, since many other people share these sentiments concerning the impossibility of indifference to social injustice and the answer to the current debate concerning the future of revolutions.[52] Glaring social inequalities will continue to fuel revolution, since it would appear that even among people not suffering directly from these ills, there are some for whom the pain of witnessing them renders indifference impossible. There will thus, in my view, undoubtedly be other revolutions, but they will be different in form, both from those coming before and from each other (depending on the social context). What we see in the pages which follow is the life of a leader of one of these future revolutions, a leader born during the Cold War and who thus owes something to his Marxist-Leninist and Maoist predecessors, but who is also maturing in a postmodern age of globalization and is therefore experimenting with fresh, new concepts and methods.

PART I

---　✳　---

Rafael

1. Birth and Family

Rafael Sebastián Guillén Vicente was born in Tampico on 19 June 1957 into a family that neighbors have described as "part of [Tampico] society though not high society."[1] Tampico is in the state of Tamaulipas—famous for its seafood and its cyclones—on the Gulf of Mexico.[2] In the 1950s it was a bustling tropical port; in the early part of the twentieth century it had been the busiest oil port in the world. In hindsight it seems ironic that in the 1930s government money had been diverted away from public building projects (such as reservoirs) in Chiapas and toward Tampico: the consequential stunting of Chiapas's development would provide Rafael, a middle-class scion of the beneficiary city, with a setting and support base for his career as a revolutionary.[3]

Rafael's date of birth is highly significant, coinciding with the emergence of left-wing guerrilla insurgency based on the *foco*.[4] The year 1957 saw Che Guevara and Fidel and Raul Castro fighting their way through the Sierra Maestra toward Havana in neighboring Cuba. (They had arrived on Cuban soil on 2 December 1956, having sailed from Tuxpán, only 94 miles [151 km] down the coast from Tampico.) One month after Rafael's birth, on 21 July, Guevara became the first combatant to be promoted to comandante and was given command of the second column (called Column 4 in order to confuse the enemy). Rafael's most impressionable years (ten to eighteen) witnessed the death of Guevara (October 1967); the year of revolution (1968), including the Paris student uprising and the massacre of students in Mexico City at Tlatelolco (2 October 1968); and the severe repression unleashed by the Echeverría government against left-wing militant groups (the early and mid-1970s).[5] It is not hard to imagine the impact of such events on the media and thus, consequently, on a politically minded family. Marcos states that as a family, "We learnt to read, not so much in school, as in the columns of newspapers."[6] These happenings probably resulted in Rafael's first exposure to and participation in intense political discussion. Such family debate must have formed a lasting impression on him.

Significantly, in the immediate aftermath of Tlatelolco, the student leader Eduardo Valle prophesied:

> I think the Movement will have its effect on the children. . . . In genera-tions that lived it . . . seeing their older brothers move . . . into action, hearing stories of the days of terror, feeling them in their blood . . . *the government of this country will have to be very wary of those who were ten or fifteen in 1968 . . . they will always remember the assaults upon, the murders of their brothers.*[7]

Rafael, at that time aged eleven, proved to be just such a child, going on later to fulfill this prophecy by becoming the greatest thorn in the sides of the Salinas and Zedillo governments.

The impact of Tlatelolco on Rafael is made explicit in Marcos's commu-niqué *Tlatelolco: Thirty Years Later the Struggle Continues,* dated 2 October 1998 and addressed "to the Generation of Dignity of 1968." It was written to commemorate the thirtieth anniversary of the massacre, and, in addition to saluting those who died or felt the pain of 1968 and demanding "that the whole truth be told, that yesterday's and today's crimes no longer go unpunished," Marcos lays claim to being part of the same tradition as those who rebelled in 1968, the tradition of resistance. While admitting that the Zapatistas are "different and distinct" from those who resisted thirty years previously, the enemy is portrayed as the same, with the free-standing line "1968.1998," designed to highlight the fact that nothing had changed, com-prising four of the final fifteen lines of the communiqué.[8] Further evidence of the impact of Tlatelolco on Rafael can be seen in a February 1994 inter-view with *La Jornada* correspondents. The journalists asked him, "Genera-tionally speaking, are you a product of '68?" Marcos replied: "I'm definitely post-'68, but not the core of '68 . . . I was a little kid. But I do come from everything that followed, especially the electoral frauds, the most scandal-ous one in 1988, but others as well."[9]

Ten days after the student massacre, Mexico hosted the Olympic Games (12–27 October 1968). Marcos subtly plays on the near coincidence of these two occurrences in his *Tlatelolco* communiqué, where he talks of the "olym-pic astonishment and shame that beheld the [Tlatelolco] massacre." The Games, no doubt, also impacted on Rafael, who later enjoyed sports, espe-cially basketball. The 1968 Olympics also proved memorable politically for the discussion provoked by the controversial Black Power salute made by the U.S. athletes Tommie Smith and John Carlos.

Just as people are partly a product of the era into which they were born, so they are also partly a product of the families in which they were raised. Rafael, like Lenin, was the fourth of eight children.[10] He had six brothers and one sister, all of whom went on to attend university. His sister, Mercedes del Carmen Guillén Vicente, also known as "Paloma," obtained a degree in law and economics. Alfonso earned a degree in business management and subsequently became a professor of Mexican history at Universidad Autónoma de Baja California Sur. Héctor also earned a degree in business management. Carlos obtained a degree in sociology at Mexico City's National Autonomous University (UNAM), and he later went on to become a federal government accounting officer. He died of asphyxia in July 1994 at age thirty-eight; he had had epilepsy from childhood. Rafael also obtained his degree, in philosophy and arts, at UNAM. David's degree was in agricultural engineering, Sergio's was in mathematics, and Fernando's was in public finance and accountancy.

The fact that Rafael was the fourth of eight children is perhaps of some consequence. Much research has been undertaken recently on the effect birth order has on personality. The eminent sociologist Frank J. Sulloway has studied birth order for twenty years and recently finished a study in which he used more than half a million data points mined from tens of thousands of biographies relating to the lives of 6,000 individuals.[11] He concluded that "some people, it seems, are born to rebel."[12] Sulloway argues that birth order (whether you are the firstborn child or a later-born child) greatly shapes your propensity to rebel. He argues that "siblings become different for the same reason that species do over time: divergence minimizes competition for scarce resources."[13] Elaborating on this, he adds:

> Siblings compete with one another in an effort to secure physical, emotional, and intellectual resources from parents. Depending on differences of birth order, gender, physical traits, and aspects of temperament, siblings create differing roles for themselves within the family system. These differing roles in turn lead to disparate ways of currying parental favor. . . . As children become older and their unique interests and talents begin to emerge, siblings become increasingly diversified in their niches. One sibling may become recognized for athletic prowess, whereas another may manifest artistic talents. Yet another sibling may be good at mediating arguments and become the family diplomat.[14]

According to Sulloway, "Revolutionaries owe their radicalism to competition for limited family resources—and to the niches that characterize such competition—not to class consciousness."[15]

Of direct relevance to Marcos, Sulloway argues that "laterborns are more likely to identify with the underdog and to challenge the established order" and that "their hearts and souls are most thoroughly identified with radical changes that defy the status quo."[16] They characteristically possess an "openness to experience, a dimension that is associated with being unconventional, adventurous, and rebellious." They tend "as family underdogs . . . to empathize with other downtrodden individuals and generally support egalitarian social changes . . . to be more adventurous than firstborns . . . [and] to question authority and to resist pressure to conform to a consensus."[17] In his conclusion, Sulloway states: "In Western history, laterborns have been eighteen times more likely than firstborns to champion radical political revolutions."[18] He points out that Marx, Lenin, Trotsky, and Castro were all laterborns, although interestingly Guevara, a firstborn, was not. Firstborns, on the contrary, "identify more strongly with power and authority [since] they arrive first within the family and employ their superior size and strength to defend their special status."[19] It is interesting to note that the Guilléns' second child, their only daughter, Paloma, conforms to this pattern, having become a deputy and delegate of the PRI (Partido Revolucionario Institucional) XV district in 1984 and marrying José María Morfín (advisor to the governor for the state of Puebla) in 1993. She and her husband were subsequently awarded the certificate of good conduct by the governor of Puebla, Manuel Bartlett, for their services to the PRI.

Sulloway's findings concerning middle children—to which category both Marcos and Fidel Castro belong—are even more pertinent.[20] He argues that "when they rebel, they do so largely out of frustration, or compassion for others, rather than from hatred or ideological fanaticism," and that "middle children make the most 'romantic' revolutionaries."[21] This second assertion concerning romanticism had earlier been made by two other scholars, Rejai and Phillips, who reviewed the lives of 135 political leaders forged in 31 rebellions.[22] Rafael's romanticism clearly owes much to his father, Alfonso, who appears to have had the same Quixotic disposition as Che Guevara's father, although as a successful entrepreneur he was clearly blessed with greater business acumen and possibly better fortune, since at its height his furniture business had eight outlets and twenty employees. Alfonso had been a dreamer and a lover of poetry, but after marriage and having a large family he had to attend to the more practical matter of making money to provide for them. He lived out his utopianism vicariously through his son, Rafael, in whom he inculcated "a love of poetry and noble causes" and through whom his idealism lived on.[23] Indeed, his father claims that Rafael, as Marcos, "has restored to me the joy of living, my second youth."[24]

The work by Rejai and Phillips is particularly interesting since it identifies features common to most revolutionaries. They argue, for example, that

> revolutionary elites are typically of legitimate birth . . . from relatively large families, with over 65 percent having three to nineteen siblings . . . are urban born . . . tend to enjoy "tranquil" family lives . . . [are] middle class [and] of mainstream variety in respect to ethnicity and religion . . . [are] well educated (nearly 70 percent have college or professional education) . . . have impressive publication records . . . [and] are cosmopolitan in many senses; they speak foreign languages, travel far and long . . . [and] do not follow either their fathers' profession or the profession for which they were originally trained.[25]

Rafael, as we will see, conforms to this revolutionary elite pattern on every count.

It is perhaps also worth noting that Rafael also conforms to the findings of a recent study on birth order that concluded: "Middleborns seldom name their parents as their closest interactants."[26] The same study also found that when asked "to whom would you turn for emotional support," "middleborns were more than five times as likely to name a sibling than were firstborn or lastborn respondents."[27] This perhaps helps to explain Rafael's especially close relationship with his brother Carlos, with whom he lived at university for three years. The tendency to turn to family members other than parents for emotional support perhaps also explains why, like Che, Rafael was particularly close to his maternal grandmother, Antonia González. She had moved from Veracruz to live with the Guillén family when her husband died. She would often look after the children while their mother worked alongside Rafael's father in the family furniture store. Apparently she was an affectionate woman and Rafael grew profoundly attached to her.

Like many high achievers Rafael was a precocious child, his parents having given him a head start by educating him themselves before he went to school. Marcos claims, "I learned to read in my house, not at school; so when I went to school I had a great advantage, because I was already well read."[28] This, however, conflicts with what his father tells us, namely that "before the age of five, *without having even learned to read,* he already knew how to recite."[29] (He claims to have taught Rafael to recite from memory "El Sembrador," the 495-word poem by Marcos Rafael Blanco Belmonte.)[30] Whatever the truth about Rafael's reading capabilities, it is clear that he was exposed at a young age to learning. This ought not to surprise us, given that his father had worked as a rural teacher for seven years, prior to building his furniture empire. When asked by Gabriel García Márquez where his "considerable literary education of the traditional kind" came from, Marcos replied:

> From childhood. In our family words had a very special value. Our way of approaching the world was through language . . . Early on, my mother and father gave us books that disclosed other things. One way or another, we became conscious of language—not as a way of communicating, but of constructing something. As if it were a pleasure more than a duty.[31]

He then outlines his boyhood literary diet:

> The Latin American boom came first. . . . My parents introduced us to García Márquez, Carlos Fuentes, Monsiváis, Vargas Llosa (regardless of his ideas), to mention only a few. They set us to reading them. *A Hundred Years of Solitude* to explain what the provinces were like at the time. *The Death of Artemio Cruz* to show what had happened to the Mexican Revolution. *Días de guardar* to describe what was happening in the middle classes. As for *La cuidad y los perros*, it was in a way a portrait of us, but in the nude. All these things were there. . . . Next came Shakespeare . . . then Cervantes, then García Lorca, and then came a phase of poetry. . . . We went straight from the alphabet to literature and from there to theoretical and political texts, until we got to high school.[32]

Marcos believes that as a result of this parental encouragement:

> We went out into the world in the same way that we went out into literature. I think this marked us. We didn't look out at the world through a news-wire but through a novel, an essay or a poem. That made us very different. That was the prism through which my parents wanted me to view the world, as others might choose the prism of the media, or a dark prism to stop you seeing what's happening.[33]

In addition to introducing their children to literature, Rafael's parents provided them with a firm grounding in Mexican history. Marcos informs us in one interview that "my parents taught me a lot about Mexican history," adding, "my main influences were Villa, Zapata, Morelos, Hildago, Guerrero: I grew up with these heroes."[34]

As well as developing their children's intellects, Rafael's parents also imbued their offspring with a strong sense of morality. In an interview given in March (but published in June) 1994 Marcos tells us:

> My parents taught us that, whatever path we chose, we should always choose *el camino de la verdad*—the path of truth—no matter how hard it might be, whatever it might cost. That we shouldn't value life over the truth. That it was better to lose your life than to lose truth . . . we were taught that all human beings had rights, and it was our duty to fight against injustice.[35]

2. School Years

When he was six Rafael began his primary education. He attended the Colegio Félix de Jesús Rougier (as its name suggests, a Jesuit school run by monks) from 1963 to 1969. Two of his elder brothers, Alfonso and Carlos, and his elder sister Paloma also attended the school. Their mother, being a teacher and a cultured woman, carefully supervised all her children's homework.

Rafael's school, even now, is characterized by its strictness, but it was even stricter during the period he attended it. In addition to fostering academic achievement the school also closely monitored other aspects of the students' conduct and behavior, notably cleanliness, responsibility, and discipline. (For example, pupils were checked daily for whether they had clean nails, had washed behind their ears, had brought a clean white handkerchief with them, had cleaned their shoes, and had a uniform on that was complete and in order.) Rafael distinguished himself by his hard work and good conduct. Indeed, according to one teacher, the Guillén children "were excellent and noble . . . oratorical types."[1]

However, it is evident that Rafael was to some extent overshadowed academically by his eldest brother Alfonso. While Rafael regularly obtained grades of nine or ten out of ten, Alfonso was a straight ten student. Thus, although Rafael was undoubtedly a bright pupil, as one of his teachers stresses, "he was no child prodigy, his intellectual capacity developed later."[2] Although Rafael strove to emulate his brother's achievements he could not; he failed, for example, to obtain the Ribbon of Honor that his brother had succeeded in earning. Alfonso's academic superiority in primary school may well help to explain why Rafael chose to develop his creative side in secondary school, writing poetry, acting, and directing movies. In terms of Sulloway's theories, Rafael's creative efforts may represent a subconscious attempt to carve himself a new niche, thereby avoiding direct competition in the academic sphere with a brother whose intellectual capabilities thus far seemed vastly superior. Rafael, for his part, "won awards for perseverance, conduct and application."[3]

Despite attending a Jesuit school, it is clear that Rafael lost his religion in these years. Indeed, when interviewed decades later as Marcos, he revealed that "the last religious service I attended was when I took my First Communion. I was eight years old."[4] One must infer that Rafael did not proceed to Confirmation, a traditional affirmation of one's faith in Catholic countries, commonly undergone at around twelve years of age. This perhaps ought not to surprise us since he reveals in one of his interviews that in his family, "We were very independent of religion. It was a very humanist tradition, and not attached to any particular line."[5]

In 1969, Rafael moved to secondary school, attending the Jesuit Instituto Cultural de Tampico. The establishment's motto was *Duc in Altum*, taken from Luke 5:4 where Jesus goes to the shores of Galilee and exhorts the fishermen "to *put out into the deep* and let down your nets for a catch." Here it is perhaps best rendered "*Delve Deep* [inside yourself spiritually]." According to his then friends and peers it was here that his personality became more complex. He was serious yet jocular, sociable yet reserved, and frequently showed solidarity with others while at the same time being a rather solitary individual who retained a strong independent streak. It was during his secondary school education (1970–73) that Rafael began to develop his creative side, becoming a good sketcher and acting in Samuel Beckett's *Waiting for Godot*.

It was also during this period that Rafael discovered Cervantes. As he tells us in one interview, "I was given a book when I turned twelve, a beautiful cloth edition. It was *Don Quixote*. I had read it before, but in those children's editions. It was an expensive book, a special present which must still be out there somewhere."[6] His passion for *Don Quixote* can be seen from the fact that it was one of the books he took with him to Chiapas when he began his guerrilla work there.[7] Moreover, this passion evidently remains with him even today, for he tells us that "*Don Quixote* is always by my side . . . [it] is the best book of political theory."[8] It is worth remembering that the stories in which Marcos's alter ego, the fictional beetle called Don Durito, appears, are very much in the style of *Don Quixote*. Interestingly, Rafael's childhood hero, Che Guevara, was also a lover of *Don Quixote*, identifying himself with this patron saint of lost causes in his farewell letter to his father (dated 2 January 1967): "Don Ernesto, amid the dust kicked up by the heels of Rocinante,[9] with my lance at the ready to do battle with enemy giants, I send you this brief note."[10]

Rafael also admired the poetry of Pablo Neruda (1904–73), again like Che.[11] Rafael included the Chilean poet's *Canto General* among the few books he took with him to Chiapas,[12] named him first in his list of poets who had impressed him most,[13] and quoted part of his "The Liberators" in one of his communiqués.[14] Rafael's fondness for both Cervantes and Pablo Neruda appear to have been inherited from his father and perhaps his paternal aunt, who had written poetry under the pen name Perla Mar.[15]

Marcos's comments concerning his schooling are scant. He merely tells us: "In High School I read about Hitler, Marx, Lenin, Mussolini—history and political science in general . . . [and] learned English."[16] When asked, "Did your classmates believe that you were or might be a Communist?," he replied, "No, I don't think so. Perhaps the most they called me was a little radish: red outside and white inside."[17]

3. High School College

In 1973 at age sixteen Rafael entered the school's college (the Instituto Cultural de Tampico), having decided to stay on at the same institution. It was a coeducational college; women comprised more than 50 percent of the students in many classes. It is no surprise that the Jesuits maintained close supervision of their students, restricting their conduct in numerous ways. One former female pupil recalls: "If we had boyfriends at the school we were never allowed to hold hands, it was like a sacrilege."[1]

Being a Jesuit institution, value was placed not just on academic studies but also on students' character development. It is therefore not surprising that Rafael's sixth-grade teacher, Refugio Marín, should recall that: "He always helped his compañeros, he always shared what he had, always, always, always. He saved his pocket money and any compañero who didn't have any money he would buy a cake or a drink. He was a good compañero. He always helped the needy."[2]

The school, as part of this ethos, promoted pupil participation in local community-welfare projects. Accompanied by a teacher, Rafael and others would visit the impoverished Pescador housing estate nearby and offer their labor. Decades later, as Marcos, Rafael would answer the question "What were the roots of your personal rebellion?" by stating: "It's a process . . . you begin to take steps—first becoming interested in a situation, then understanding that there is injustice, then trying to understand the roots of this injustice. . . . You begin by helping out in small ways, taking logical steps."[3] It is tempting to think that his realization of injustice in the world and those first small steps were derived from his social work in Pescador when he was sixteen or so. In any event, a former female friend of Rafael's, who also attended the college and participated in its welfare projects, recollects: "There I saw men bricklaying and doing the washing. We learned to live with people and share tacos. It was part of our formation, learning to live with all types of people, to do the best thing and to learn the things which they had to teach us."[4] Arguably, it was this hands-on experience

in the alleviation of poverty and the betterment of local society that imbued Rafael with an appreciation of the importance of practical solutions
to problems. This was to continue even through his university education
in philosophy, which tended then to be concerned with the predominantly
theoretical (as opposed to the practical), and was to remain with him for
the next thirty years.

It was also at this time that Rafael began demonstrating a liking for
theatre and movies. As one of his contemporaries at the school puts it,
"He was one of the principal people involved in every activity, but above all
in cultural activities. . . . He was a promoter of theatrical events, [and] of
poetry."[5] His passion for acting was encouraged in literature class, where
pupils were required to act out important scenes from major works of literature. In addition, there were extracurricular opportunities which allowed
Rafael to indulge his cinematic and theatrical whims. A fellow pupil at this
time, Jorge Nieto, recalls a movie the students made entitled *Bubblegum*.
The plot was about the theft of a secret formula for a chewing gum bomb,
and it was shot in a style similar to that employed a decade later in *The
Untouchables*. Rafael, using a Super 8 camera he had, was the cameraman.
Apparently, Rafael and others had also wanted to perform Jodorowsky's *El
juego que todos jugamos* [*The Game We All Play*], but the teachers forbade it
because it contained obscene language, involved some actors showing their
buttocks, and entailed a rat being thrown into the audience.

In the second year of college, he starred in Carlos Fuentes's play *El tuerto
es rey* (*The One-Eyed Man Is King*). He apparently chose the play, thereby
revealing his developing passion for Fuentes. The plot, according to its
author, involves a Duke (el Duque) and a woman (Donata) who are both
blind "but each believes that only they are blind; each one believes that
the other is their guardian and guide."[6] Rafael, then eighteen, played the
Duke, who in the final climactic scene is killed by five guerrillas who burst
into his home. The whole scene is symbolic; the Duke represents God, and
the question of The Creation (of both man and the universe) is played out
in the dialogue between him and the guerrillas. The director of the play,
Rubén Núñez de Cáceres, Rafael's literature teacher at the time and now
principal of Monterrey's Technical College (Preparatoria del Tecnológico
de Monterrey), describes Guillén's performance as "brilliant" (buenísima).[7]
Jorge Nieto confirms this, stating that Rafael "was a very good actor and
had an eye for scenery."[8] Rafael would frequently exercise his natural flair
for theatricals years later as Subcommander Marcos, leading one author to
dub him "the Subcomandante of performance."[9]

When talking of Rafael generally, Núñez notes that "he was always very special, rebellious, different from the bulk of the boys."[10] However, Núñez also remarks that although Rafael was "an anti-establishment student, he had not yet developed a politically coherent philosophy."[11] One of Rafael's fellow students at the college further attests to Guillén's antiestablishment outlook at this time. Guillermo Heredia Niño notes: "He appeared to swim against the current. He was not the classic sheep, he was always questioning things. He was famous among the teachers for telling them facts and information in class. He would say, 'I think there is another option.' He was a deep person. He was a leader of opinions."[12]

This is confirmed by Jorge Nieto, who tells us:

> He was a leader, but not because people trailed behind him, but because of his ideas. He didn't aim at being the protagonist. He expressed his opinions, but not because he wanted to win applause. Like Voltaire, he was not able to agree with what we said to him, but he respected our right to say it. He went around with everyone, but walked alone. He looked you in the eye, but not to assert himself or intimidate you, but rather to pay attention to you. He was frank. One time he said to me, "You disappoint me," but after we had finished the discussion he said, "Don't worry," and smiled; he would continue being your friend, making jokes and telling funny stories, like in his communiqués, with his at times sarcastic humor.[13]

Another former fellow student comments less charitably:

> Rafael already had very radical political convictions. He felt he was predestined to make the revolution, like Fidel Castro, but at the same time he was a pacifist. He spent from twelve to eighteen going around calling us the guilty bourgeois; and when we told him, although he would never admit it, that he was just such a bourgeois, like us, he would be offended and get very angry. It was impossible to discuss things with him. He believed he held a monopoly on reason.[14]

Rafael's oratorical prowess was finely honed during his time in college. His Jesuit teachers placed a great deal of emphasis on rhetorical training in general and declamation in particular. One of them, Father José Quesada, who taught ethics, remembers Rafael as "a good student, intellectually inquisitive, but never first class," adding that "Rafael was like the others, but he wanted to know more."[15] Father Quesada would divide the class into two groups of students and have one group propose a motion and the other oppose it. Subjects for discussion included contraception, abortion, capitalism, socialism, and communism. A friend of Rafael's at the time, who also attended this class, assures us that "Rafael beat us [in these debates] because he was very analytical."[16] Another fellow student, Max García Appedole, tells us "Guillén was an excellent orator, he was very cultivated," adding that "we competed various years in competitions organized by the Jesuits . . . [which Rafael] would always win; already by then he hated to lose." Max also asserts that Rafael "had a great capacity for writing."[17] Father Quesada's classes were unorthodox but effective; as the same student recalls, "instead of giving us a lesson on Miguel Hernández, he would order us to listen to the songs of Joan Manuel concerning his poems."[18] In this way, Father Quesada would pass onto his students his enthusiasm for a particular author. One of his favorites was León Felipe, his liking for whom he passed on to Rafael who, years later, took a copy of his poems to Chiapas,[19] and as Subcomandante quoted him in some of his communiqués.[20] (Interestingly, Tomás Borge, the sole surviving founding member of the FSLN [Frente Sandinista de Liberación Nacional, the Sandinista National Liberation Front] in Nicaragua and later that country's minister of the interior, notes in his memoir that Che Guevara would "recite poems by . . . León Felipe.")[21]

The college also provided other extracurricular opportunities for Rafael to exercise his creative talents. He entered an essay competition; the subject, which he himself chose, was Efraín Huerta's poem *Declaración de Odio*. Rafael came second to García Appedole, who insists that years later the Subcommander used part of the young Rafael's essay in one of his first communiqués. In addition to essay competitions and poetry recitals Rafael, following in the footsteps of Nicaragua's guerrilla leader Carlos Fonseca, created and edited a college magazine which ran for a single issue (May 1976).[22] It was called *La Raíz Oculta* (*The Secret Root*), and Rafael wrote the introduction, an essay, a story, and an untitled poem for it.

Despite being rather theatrical and literary—to the extent that he walked around perpetually carrying a book—Rafael was by no means exclusively intellectual. He had a girlfriend named Iliana and played basketball for the college team, even teaching it to the girls at his school. Indeed, Rafael appears to have had a fondness for basketball, as did his brother Carlos. Their father assures us that they "were stars"; not so, apparently, with baseball, at which both brothers "were fairly bad."[23] (Fortunately for Carlos and Rafael, as their father points out, "as the [family] furniture firm sponsored the [baseball] team, nobody dared to drop them from it.")[24] Despite this exercise, Rafael's physique at the time has been described as "fragile,"[25] although he was by no means effete. Indeed, Heredia Niño tells how, one Navy Day (1 June), when the naval cadets came to the school with buckets and balloons in order to soak the students who were sitting in the courtyard, all of Rafael's peers fled. He, however, sat motionless while they exhausted themselves by dousing him repeatedly.

During this period Rafael began to hero-worship Che Guevara. His admiration for Che was to remain with him for the next twenty years. In an interview he gave as Subcommander Marcos in 1997, he stated: "Che is closer to us than many people think," adding, "He is still around and alive thirty years on from his death . . . one way or another, all rebel movements in Latin America are the heirs to Che's rebellion."[26] Similarly, in a message he sent to those at the inaugural ceremony of the American Planning of the Intercontinental Meeting for Humanity and Against Neoliberalism (6 April 1996), Marcos declared his debt to Che, mentioning Guevara's name eleven times and claiming that "time and again the image of El Che, dreaming in the school at La Higuera, claimed its place between my hands."[27] So too, in an interview with Yvon Le Bot published the same year, the Subcommander talked admiringly of "the Che who continued to struggle, who chose to continue being a rebel, who decided to abandon everything and begin anew . . . with all the difficulties that this represents . . . who went, against all odds, to raise a dream, a utopia."[28] We know that the young Rafael even went so far in his hero-worship as to wear Che's trademark beret. Elia Esther Hoz Zavala, a friend of the Guillén family for more than twenty years, who studied with Rafael at college and at university, and whose sister, Blanca, dated Rafael's brother, Carlos, attests to the impact Che made on her, Rafael, and indeed their entire generation: "He was our idol twenty years ago. . . . We considered Che to be a leader because of the way he was, because of his ideals."[29]

It was almost certainly from Che that Rafael acquired his fondness for a habit that would become his trademark: pipe smoking. Elia Esther says that Rafael had "a mania" for pipes. She continues, "he had a collection of them, he would carry one around in order to recite a poem or give an exposition," adding, however, that "at that time he did not smoke [it]."[30] If Rafael used his numerous pipes only as props, his fondness for carrying them around, like his fondness for wearing a beret, arose from pure affectation—a common trait among adolescents. Che had on occasion smoked a pipe and had even recommended doing so to would-be guerrillas; during his later missions in the Congo and Bolivia, he frequently smoked a pipe, since the cigars he had smoked in Cuba were in short supply. During these impressionable years, Rafael was no doubt exposed to numerous photographs of Che in Africa and Bolivia, puffing on his pipe, and chose to emulate him.[31]

Núñez, Rafael's literature teacher, assures us that on leaving college to go to university, Rafael turned to him and said, "Now I am going to make the revolution."[32]

Rafael spent the few months between leaving college and enrolling at UNAM working in the family business and traveling. All the sons helped out in their father's furniture stores, running errands and making deliveries. Rafael did so too and, in addition, wrote some advertising slogans for the business. One read "Visit us and revive the old pleasure of giving." He also went to Paris for two months to learn French. He had apparently been to France once before, accompanying his father on a business trip. His father recollects: "We went to France and Spain. He was like the Lone Ranger. He went to the opera instead of coming with us to parties. He didn't join in with the group." Being bright and witty at times, Rafael could appear gregarious sometimes; however, at other times he could also appear somewhat aloof.[33]

4. UNAM

On leaving the Jesuit Instituto Cultural de Tampico, Rafael entered the Faculty of Philosophy and Arts (Filosofía y Letras) at Mexico's National Autonomous University (UNAM) in 1977. This move from Tamaulipas to Mexico City must have represented quite a break for him. Provincial, industrial Tampico was very different from the gigantic, sprawling cosmopolitan capital. Moreover, psychologically Rafael would now have to make the transition to being a small fish in a very large pool. However, he appears to have risen to the challenge. Indeed, there are indications that Rafael welcomed the move to the capital, deeming Tampico to be too cloistered. In two separate interviews given six years apart, Marcos indicates that in some ways Rafael had outgrown Tampico. In the first, he describes Tampico as having "a very provincial atmosphere," continuing, "It was very closed culturally; if you wanted to know about cultural things, or what was happening in the rest of the world, you had to go to Mexico City," and finally adding, "To go to the theatre, the movies, to get good books, magazines like *Penthouse* and *Playboy*—only in Mexico City."[1] In the second interview, when talking about his childhood and in particular his love of books, he states: "All of this was in the provinces, where the society pages of the local newspaper are the cultural horizon. The outside world was Mexico City and its bookshops—the great attraction of coming here."[2] Of course, although Tampico was somewhat of a cultural backwater, Marcos himself recognizes that "occasionally there would be provincial book fairs, where we could get hold of something interesting,"[3] but he does note its limits, stating that "in the provinces, politics either came with [the political cartoonist] Rius,[4] or it didn't come at all."[5]

The shock of being away from home, however, would have been eased to some extent by the fact that Rafael's older brother Carlos was already studying at UNAM. Carlos tells us that the two of them shared a small apartment near the campus and "were together three years, because Rafael reached the end of his course in six semesters instead of the stipulated ten."[6] Further-more, Elia Esther Hoz Zavala, the long-standing family friend mentioned in the previous chapter, also went to UNAM in 1977 to study biology.

During that first year there was a long strike by the university union on behalf of both administrative and academic staff over contracts. Rafael threw himself into the affair. As one administrator and veteran union leader, Ruth Peza, informs us: "Rafael made our strike posters and wrote our an-nouncements. We gave him the central idea and he drafted the words. We liked what he did a lot."[7] Peza notes, for example, that during the strike Rafael coined the phrase that he would later employ with great effect as Marcos, namely *¡Muera el mal gobierno!* ("Death to bad government").[8] She adds that the Trotskyites comprised a highly vociferous and influential core of support for the strikers and that Rafael went around with them, although he never became a fully integrated member of their group. These activities surrounding the union played a role in Rafael's political develop-ment, one he himself appears to have acknowledged when two years later he recommended that his junior colleague and newly recruited member of the Fuerzas de Liberación Nacional (FLN, Forces of National Liberation), Salvador Morales Garibay, should observe union debates. Morales tells us that "Guillén said to me, 'watch and listen, watch how they fight, some against the others, and watch how some say this and others say something different'; this was my first participation in politics."[9]

In the end, the strike was broken when police stormed the campus. This resort to violence by the authorities perhaps helps to explain Marcos's un-compromising stance toward the negotiations in the 1999–2000 UNAM dispute between students and the university authorities in response to a proposed increase in undergraduate tuition fees from a few cents to 680 pesos (US$65) per semester. He issued numerous communiqués urging the students not to back down.[10] Not only that, but in summer 1999 the Subcommander redirected money raised for the benefit of Zapatista com-munities by the Workers Union at Mexico City's other major university, Universidad Autónoma Metropolitana (UAM, Autonomous Metropolitan University), back to striking UNAM students.[11]

Indeed, as early as 6 February 1994 Marcos had established a corre-spondence with his alma mater's student body. He issued a communiqué "To the University Student Council (CEU) of the National Autonomous University of Mexico (UNAM)," thanking them for a letter of support he had received from them and taunting the Procuraduría General de la Republic (PGR) with a nostalgic postscript:[12]

When I was young (Hello? PGR? Here comes more data), there used to be a lightly wooded place between the main library, the Faculty of Philosophy and Letters, the Humanities Tower, Insurgentes Avenue, and the interior circuit of the University Campus. We used to call that space, for reasons obvious to the initiates, the "Valley of Passions," and it was energetically visited by diverse elements of the fauna who populated the University Campus beginning at 7 P.M. (an hour when those of good conscience drink hot chocolate and the bad ones make themselves hot enough to melt); they came from the humanities, sciences, and other areas (are there others?). At that time, a Cuban (Are you ready, Ambassador Jones? Make a note of more proof of pro-Castroism) who used to give lectures seated in front of piano keys the color of his skin, and who called himself Snowball, would repeat over and over: "You can't have a good conscience and a heart."[13]

Despite this detailed account of UNAM's campus and student life, which is tantamount to an admission that he attended the university, Marcos nonetheless denies outright having been a UNAM student. In a videotaped interview, he was asked directly: "How did your politicization begin, as a student at the UNAM?" Marcos responded: "Well, I was not a student at the UNAM, but yes at some other university [cough]."[14] A behavioral psychologist would perhaps make much of this cough, the only one Marcos emits in an interview that lasted twenty-six minutes.

The strike in Rafael's first year at university meant that many of his classes were cancelled, leaving him much free time to explore the capital and watch the newscasts and read the newspapers, which were full of accounts of daring guerrilla actions performed by La Liga 23 de Septiembre (23 September League). As one UNAM professor from that era put it, "Every day the actions of the White Brigade and the September the 23rd League appeared in the newspapers . . . at this time the armed struggle was a daily news item."[15] Indeed, political life in the capital was highly polarized between left-wing activists and guerrillas and repressive government forces. As one contemporary activist reminds us: "In 1977, [left-wing intellectual and political activist] Alfonso Peralta was shot dead in front of his students as he left his classroom in Mexico City." He continues, "I narrowly escaped a couple of kidnapping attempts in 1978. Others who did not were brutally tortured or assassinated."[16]

In his first year, Elia Esther tells us, Rafael made few friends at UNAM. No doubt his reserved and sometimes aloof character accounts for some of this. Like many charismatic individuals, Rafael flourished in small circles where his charm and humor had a direct impact, but he was less influential in large, impersonal environments such as UNAM. Living with his brother, with whom he was close, Rafael may not have felt pressured to make new friends.

Elia Esther also informs us that while at UNAM Rafael had a girlfriend named Rocío Casariego who he took back to Tampico to meet his family.[17] Rocío shared Rafael's revolutionary fervor and, in August 1981, under the alias Mercedes,[18] she accompanied Comandanta Elisa to Nicaragua. Around this time, however, the couple separated, although they did not lose contact completely. She went on to marry FLN Comandante Rodrigo's brother, Gabriel Ramírez (alias Doctor Carlos), who accompanied her back to Nicaragua again for two months in 1987. They both spent the best part of a decade helping out in various Chiapan EZLN camps with medicine and literacy campaigns—a decade in which they surely must have come into contact with Marcos. Reflecting on her relationship with Rafael in an interview she states: "Guillén was a good orator, but only one of many. He wasn't the most outstanding personality in the universe [personalidad más chingona del universo]. . . . Like everyone around then, he had a thin beard. And, like all northerners—and everyone in general—he was sexist."[19] Rocío recalled an occasion when she had agreed to give Rafael and some of his friends a lift in her car, but had run out of gas. According to her he annoyed her the whole journey by asking "how is it possible?" and "why did you agree to bring us then?" This, however, contradicts Elia Esther's assertion that Rafael was "respectful toward whoever he was going with."[20] The discrepancy may be explained either by Elia Esther's not being party to everything that occurred between the couple, or by simple disenchantment with a former partner.

In class, Rafael is remembered by one professor as being "an outgoing young man who was always making jokes and who, unlike most philosophy students, was also into sports: he was a pretty good basketball player."[21] (His love of basketball, as we have seen, was shared by his brother, Carlos; at university they continued to play it and also enjoyed games of soccer and volleyball together.) The professor continues:

> It is clear that in spite of the seriousness that Rafael Guillén was able to adopt when speaking about philosophy, he always had a witty character, which led him to nickname himself *El Cachumbambé*. . . . He always exercised this witty irreverence inherited from '68. If there was anybody

who embodied this irreverence and who gave it meaning it was Rafael Guillén. This wit he possessed made him particularly outstanding and gave him relative independence. He was very different from the others, who were very serious.[22]

One example of Rafael's irreverence can be found in an anecdote dating to this time relating to a statement Castro made about Cuba's revolutionaries: "Yesterday, we were a handful of men; today, we are an entire people conquering the future." Rafael coined the trope (concerning Mexico's revolutionaries): "Yesterday, we were an entire people conquering the future; today, we are a handful of men."[23]

Not everyone held Rafael's irreverent humor and habitual questioning in such high regard. One contemporary describes Rafael and his set as follows: "There were eight or nine of them; a really irritating group. Rafael was a very ironic student, arrogant, aggressive, like in the communiqués of Marcos. But they were all like this. They did not blush in the least to call some professors ignorant. They were a tremendous nuisance."[24] Rafael, for his part, clearly was frustrated by some of the classes he took and by some of his peers, which may help explain his irreverence. Nearly two decades later, as Subcommander Marcos, he looked back at his student days and stated: "In the end, we did not study and were not shaped to know and to work as we wanted to, but in what society and the Power demanded that we become. . . . University was a large corral for the domestication of youth."[25] And although he went on to add that "It was also a place where the youth refused to be domesticated and there was a lot of rebellion and organization," Marcos would also note that for many students "their horizon was the classroom, they could be very rebellious in the classroom and very conformist in the family, for example, or in outside politics."

Certain professors with whom he came into contact and the schools of thought developing in the university at that time nevertheless did stimulate Rafael and helped him to define himself. Marxism held intellectual sway, to the extent that students protested when an internal analysis of the courses being offered by the philosophy faculty showed a predominant concern with positivism, with "only" 20 percent of the classes being devoted to Marxist authors.

Among these, the French Marxist school of philosophy, influenced by Louis Althusser and Michel Foucault, held sway. For example, Cesáreo Morales, who directed Rafael's thesis, had in 1977 recently returned from Paris where he had been greatly influenced by Althusser, and Alberto Híjar, professor of aesthetics and art criticism and president of the judging panel of Rafael's thesis, had been the first professor in Mexico to promote Althusser's theories. Moreover, at the time Rafael entered UNAM, a former economics professor from the university, Adolfo Orive, who had studied in France under the Maoist academic Charles Bettelheim and who had been present in Paris during the May 1968 student demonstrations, began to form a Maoist group in Chiapas.[26] As Casariego puts it, "This was the period of the deification of French philosophy."[27]

Althusser is comparatively little regarded these days, except by the Amherst school, but during the 1960s and 1970s his interpretations and elaborations of Marxism were debated in universities throughout Europe. Althusser was a Marxist and a member of the French Communist Party. In the 1960s, he had attempted to rehabilitate Lenin as a philosopher in his work *Pour Marx*, which was also strongly influenced by Mao. During the 1970s, Althusser developed Antonio Gramsci's theories on "state apparatuses"—the means of control exercised by bourgeois governments. Althusser divided state apparatuses into two categories: repressive state apparatuses (RSAS), represented by the army, police, judiciary, etc.; and ideological state apparatuses (ISAS), represented by education systems, the mass media, the family, etc.—"institutions which are all unified by the dominant ideology."[28] It was discussion of the latter category that came to the foreground during the 1970s, so much so that one academic has referred to the period 1969–79 as "the ISAS Decade."[29] Althusser began to examine the subtle means of control exercised by bourgeois governments and came to the conclusion that as western Europe transformed itself from a feudal to a capitalist society there had been an accompanying change in what constituted the predominant ISA, namely from the "family-church apparatus" to the "family-education apparatus." Althusser, however, never drew the conclusion that revolution was necessary to counter bourgeois ISAS. He was in no way an advocate of revolution. Not only did he not participate in the student demonstrations in Paris in 1968, but he also criticized Régis Debray's *Revolution in the Revolution*, saying, "In your writings the validity of guerrilla warfare is demonstrated less by its own merits than through the defects or drawbacks of past forms of struggle that you examine; it is supported less by its positive qualities than by the negative aspects of other forms of struggle."[30]

Althusser's philosophy was the prevailing school of thought at UNAM during the period Rafael studied there. That he was very much a product of this school of thought can be seen in some of the seminar papers he pre-

sented and the conferences he attended,[31] and most notably in his graduation thesis, a 121-page work entitled *Philosophy and Education*,[32] which was
classic Althusser.

In one chapter, Rafael examined the family as an example of a form of
ISA and concluded that the family represented a primary source of capitalist oppression, arguing that "as a unit of consumption and reproduction
of the labor force, the family in the capitalist system is also the basic unit
of reproduction and transformation of the dominant ideology."[33] He went
on to provide a quintessentially Althusserian analysis of how ISAS operate:
"Ideology thus conforms to practices that support forms of domination,
which in turn support forms of capitalist production, which amount to
forms of exploitation."[34]

In another section of his thesis, discussing education, Rafael did not
restrict himself to Althusserian generalizations concerning the educational
apparatus employed by Western bourgeois states. Instead, he specifically
analyzed the primary school textbooks used in Mexico's schools and argued that school formed part of the ISA by which the PRI government inculcated obedience and conformism in the people during their most impressionable and formative years.

In a chapter dealing with philosophy and philosophers, Rafael reaffirmed
Althusser's critique—inherited from Lenin—of certain types of academic
philosophers who, far from fulfilling the role of liberal, critical educators,
uphold the predominant bourgeois ideology by indoctrinating their students in it. Rafael took up this theme, arguing that through these academic
philosophers "philosophy is thus articulated in such a way as to justify the
repressive politics and education of the capitalist state system."[35] Moreover, Rafael (following Marx) argued that philosophy as taught by these
academic philosophers as a means of making sense of the world was a
capitalist diversion, deflecting philosophy from its true purpose, that of
changing, not interpreting, society.[36] Rafael had even less time for many
of the university's Marxist philosophers, who, he observed, tended to shun
all attempts at any practical application of philosophy. He described them
as "Coffee-table Marxists . . . [who] look at political activism with Olympic
disdain. They shake their heads with disapproval when presented with a
pamphlet talking about the struggle in a given factory, farm workers here
or peasants there. Political activism, rallies, assemblies and street protests
are petty things for them."[37] What was required, he believed, was "a new
philosophical praxis: philosophy as a revolutionary weapon."[38]

Rafael was clearly reacting against the academic world in which he found himself. Marxism, to most of his contemporaries—faculty and students alike—was a means of interpreting society, not rebuilding it. Instead of reading Lenin on the political practicalities of establishing a Marxist state, everyone's attention was turned to authors like Foucault, who were more interested in analyzing the bourgeois states in which they lived. Rafael, having participated in practical social welfare projects, had developed a taste for something more concrete. There exists evidence that points toward Rafael's disillusionment at this time with the intellectual Left's doctrinaire, self-serving condescension. In a later communiqué from him as Marcos, he states:

> When I was young and beautiful, intellectuals tended to group themselves around a single publication, entrench themselves, and from there tell the truth to the ignorant world of mortals. In those days they were called "elite intellectuals" and there were many of them, since magazines and ideological tendencies were all the fashion. They were publications to be read by those who published them. "Editorial masturbation," says Lucha. If you, innocent earthling, wanted to touch their ivory towers, you had to go through a field of thorns.[39]

Despite exhibiting his deep Marxist convictions and appreciation of the practical application of Marxist philosophy, Rafael's thesis in no way pointed to his becoming a guerrilla leader, as both Alberto Híjar and Cesáreo Morales are quick to stress.[40] Rafael's thesis was exceptional in its academic rigor and execution, but not in its basic premises, its views on the state, or because it pointed to a future career as a professional revolutionary. In some respects, however, the thesis is at least the stylistic forebear of Marcos's communiqués. For example, he ended it by signing it "en algún lugar muy cerca de la Ciudad Universitaria" ("somewhere very close to the university campus"); Marcos, possibly imitating the Nicaraguan guerrilla leader Carlos Fonseca,[41] signed one of his first communiqués "desde algún lugar de las montañas del Sureste Mexicano" ("from somewhere in the mountains of Southeast Mexico"),[42] shortening this to "desde de las montañas del Sureste Mexicano" ("from the mountains of Southeast Mexico") in his later communiqués. Marcos's appreciation of the power of words, which is illustrated in many of his communiqués and which, as we have seen, Rafael learned in childhood from his parents, is also reflected in his thesis, which he headed with a quotation of Michel Foucault: "Discourse is not simply that which translates struggles or systems of domination, but is the thing for which and by which there is struggle, discourse is the power which is to be seized."[43]

Rafael's thesis was very much a product of its time and of the prevailing trend in philosophy at UNAM during these years. Certainly the adjudicating panel, headed by Alberto Híjar, lapped it up, and Rafael won the Gabino Barreda Award for the most distinguished university student of his generation.[44] Híjar, commenting on the award, states that in the oral examination Rafael's "answers were brilliant, the thesis also."[45]

Ironically, by the time Rafael submitted his thesis in October 1980, Althusser had already withdrawn his theories concerning ISAs.[46] A month later, in November, Althusser was institutionalized for killing his wife, Hélène; he died in 1990. Thus, the Althusserian ripples were continuing to influence thought in Mexico even as the philosopher himself was sinking from view.

While at UNAM, Rafael also developed his linguistic skills: "At the university I learned French, Portuguese, [and] Italian." This linguistic training later stood him in good stead for acquiring various indigenous languages as well as for enabling him to keep abreast of world events—he tells us, for example, that he listened to Radio France International while in the Chiapan jungles during the 1980s.[47] He impressed numerous foreign members of the press and visitors, in particular Danielle Mitterrand, whom he charmed by greeting in French with the words "Good evening, madame, I am but a paper knight and all I can offer you is a paper rose."[48] However, Mitterrand's account of this meeting reveals that for the remainder of their time together she and the Subcommander communicated through an interpreter named Anita.[49] Indeed, the British journalist Kirsty Lang, having interviewed Mitterrand about this encounter, states: "Marcos, she [Mitterrand] said, later confessed to hardly speaking any French and admitted he had spent the whole day practicing those few words."[50] Needless to say, this casts into doubt the extent of Marcos's proficiency in spoken French.

Rafael, like most students, was preoccupied during his time at university by what he was going to do upon graduation. Almost two decades later, as Marcos, he would give one interviewer an insight into his thinking at that time: "In the end the question is: 'After university, what?' Yes work, but work for what? In which society? At what cost? At what social cost and at what cost as a person?"[51]

For the young Rafael, just as for Che Guevara, Carlos Fonseca, and many other middle-class Latin Americans who found the status quo in

their highly inequitable societies intolerable, joining a revolutionary movement seemed the natural, perhaps even the only, choice. Thus we come to
the most important question with regard to Rafael's time at UNAM; namely,
whether it was here or later that Rafael began his career as a guerrilla. We
know he mixed with radical left-wing individuals from his very first year
there, associating with Trotskyites during the strike of 1977. We also know
that certain members of the FLN had direct links with UNAM. It would
seem, for example, that Javier Elorriaga, who later joined the FLN, adopting
the alias Vicente, and who was first put in charge of editing the organization's in-house magazine *Neplanta*, had also been recruited while he was
studying at UNAM's faculty of philosophy and arts.[52] Moreover, we have seen
that Rafael was a student of Híjar who had previously been involved with
the FLN, the guerrilla group of which Rafael was a member before splitting
from it and taking the Chiapas branch of the organization, called the EZLN,
with him in the early 1990s. Híjar had edited at least one of the FLN's documents and was incriminated by having been photographed alongside five
hooded members of the guerrilla group. As a result he had been seized by
security forces and tortured. All of this led to his being brought in again
for questioning by the Mexican security forces in February 1995, as soon
as the true identity of Marcos was discovered. It is therefore possible that
Híjar introduced Rafael into the ranks of the FLN while he was still an
undergraduate at UNAM, recommending him to his former FLN associates
who were still in the movement. Yet Híjar, having been questioned in 1995
about his connection with Rafael, was allowed to go free. Furthermore,
Tello Díaz, who drew extensively on sources within the Mexican security
forces for his *La rebelión de las Cañadas*,[53] nowhere suggests that Híjar put
Rafael in contact with the FLN. Perhaps Híjar played an indirect role in
Rafael's recruitment, merely recommending him for a teaching post at
UAM, where he himself taught and where, whether known or unknown to
Híjar, several faculty members were recruiting for the FLN.

In short, the question of whether Rafael came into contact with other
revolutionaries through his UNAM connection is, currently, impossible
to answer and represents the most significant gap in our knowledge, and
therefore understanding, of Rafael's transformation into Marcos. We know
Rafael was already working in the FLN movement by the end of 1979, since
Salvador Morales Garibay, the former Subcommander Daniel before he left
the organization, tells us that Rafael "began to have contact with the FLN
when he arrived at UAM: by the end of 1979 he was already helping in
the safe houses."[54] Moreover, in a communiqué of September 2002, Sub-

commander Marcos relates how he first met Comandante Germán and his partner Lucía in 1980:

> I'm remembering when I met you, 22 years ago, you and *Lucía*, in the house we called *La Mina* ("The Mine"). And it was *La Mina* not because it contained treasure, but because it was dark and damp as a cave. At that time *Lucía* was determined to make me eat, and you were determined to teach me so many things which, you said, would be useful someday. I believe that I was not a good guest nor a good student, but I well remember the little figure of Che you gave me on my birthday, and on which you wrote, in your own hand, those words of José Martí that go, more or less: "The true man does not look at which side lives better, but on which side duty lies."[55]

However, given the almost two-year overlap between the date Rafael started his teaching career at UAM (16 January 1979) and the completion of his dissertation at UNAM (October 1980), it is impossible to tell which of the capital's two prestigious universities introduced the future Subcommander to the clandestine world of the FLN.

The nineteenth of July 1979 witnessed the triumph of the Sandinista revolution in Nicaragua. Less than four months later, Rafael may have journeyed to the scene of what was then the most recent and successful Latin American revolution. According to the testimony of one Nicaraguan, whose community Rafael allegedly visited, this took place "between October and November 1979."[56] This date is far from secure, however, since all the other Nicaraguans interviewed could be no more precise than to date the visit between 1979 and 1982.[57] De la Grange and Rico date it to August 1981,[58] although they nowhere specify their sources, simply citing "the testimonies of his own *compañeros*."[59] Indeed, the evidence for any trip Rafael made to Nicaragua is entirely circumstantial, although this does not mean it should be discounted. When photographs of a young Rafael (in his early to mid-twenties) were released by the Mexican government in February 1995 as part of its campaign to "unmask Marcos" and were subsequently published by the Mexican weekly magazine *Proceso*,[60] people from the village of San Juan de Río Coco in the mountains of northern Nicaragua contacted their local press to claim they had seen this man in their locality around fifteen years earlier. *Proceso* then sent reporters to Nicaragua to obtain their testimony.[61] As *Proceso* points out, "All the people who were shown the photograph of Rafael Guillén said they recognized him; nobody, however, saved any photograph, cards, or objects that would prove his presence in this village.[62] This throws up another element of doubt. It appears that reporters showed local inhabitants a photograph of Rafael Guillén and asked them if they recognized him. A much sounder methodology would have been to ask them to pick out the man they had seen fifteen years before from a batch of photographs. Likewise, their descriptions of Rafael, although occasionally specific and accurate—for example, the statement that he did not drink alcohol—are by and large general and would fit most Mexicans (e.g., that he liked eating chilies, barbecued meat, and rice).[63]

In addition, no official immigration record mentions Rafael Guillén.[64] As both *Proceso* and de la Grange and Rico observe, during this period many people entered the country under aliases,[65] which perhaps accounts for why the real names of Comandantes Elisa and Germán do not feature in Nicaragua's official immigration records either, despite the fact that we know they entered the country.[66] However, as de la Grange and Rico emphasize, the Nicaraguan immigration records do record the entry of Salvador Morales (the future Subcommander Daniel), Rocío Casariego (Rafael's then girlfriend), and Gabriel Ramírez (Doctor Carlos),[67] and we know from the Nicaraguan villagers that Rafael appears to have used his real name, not a pseudonym, when interacting with them.[68] This led de la Grange and Rico to ask if whether "Marcos, like Elisa and Germán, utilized a false identity in order to enter Nicaragua, or whether the old Sandinista leaders, who despite their electoral defeat in 1990 still control the intelligence services, made the archives containing traces of compromising relations disappear?"[69] Interestingly, Luz Marina, secretary to the then Nicaraguan minister of culture, Ernesto Cardinal, claimed, on being shown the same photographs the *Proceso* reporters showed the San Juan de Río Coco villagers, that Rafael had participated in the first cultural promotion course organized by the new Sandinista ministry.[70]

Finally, Marcos's own words on the matter, given during an interview with Yvon Le Bot prove interesting.[71] Having asked the Subcommander if the Zapatistas had been to El Salvador and Nicaragua and having received a categorical negative,[72] Le Bot asked Marcos specifically if he himself had participated "in the Sandinista literacy campaign in 1980."[73] The Subcommander replied evasively: "Ah! Yes, perhaps there have been *compañeros* of ours who were conducting solidarity work . . . but as for the whole notion that we were trained in Cuba, in Nicaragua, it is a lie."

A further problem is the nature of Rafael's supposed visit. On one hand, the Nicaraguans talk of Rafael conducting literacy and vaccination campaigns in remote mountain areas; on the other hand, the Mexican sources evidently utilized by de la Grange and Rico and Tello Díaz describe him conducting "a workshop for the design of communication directed by a union which belonged to the Sandinista Liberation Front."[74] (None of the sources mention a military element to the visit, and all the Nicaraguans asked about this flatly reject the notion that Rafael received military instruction while in Nicaragua.)[75] This apparent disparity can be reconciled only by postulating either a trip that encompassed two quite distinct aspects, each remembered separately by the Mexicans and the Nicaraguans, or a second, later visit to Nicaragua. If we accept a subsequent trip, the problem arises as to when this took place. De la Grange and Rico point to the six-month period of unpaid leave Rafael took from teaching at UAM between May and October 1982 and appear to postulate—although they nowhere state it explicitly—a second journey to Nicaragua during this time.[76] (So, too, *Proceso* states that Rafael had been to Nicaragua "various times," although it only offers two sets of dates—"the first between December 1979 and January 1980" and again "in August 1987.")[77] However, Tello Díaz, who evidently enjoys privileged access to Mexican intelligence services information, flatly rejects this, stating that "between May and October of 1982 . . . [Rafael] did not leave Mexico."[78] Of course, Tello Díaz or his source may be wrong; perhaps a trip did take place, either then or during one of the long vacations at the end of each academic year at UAM. If, however, one accepts that Rafael traveled to Nicaragua in late 1979 or early 1980, that visit was possibly the only one he made there, and included both the elements of urban work with FSLN-affiliated unions and social organizations and rural literacy and vaccination campaigns.

Whatever the precise date, nature, and number of any alleged trip(s) to Nicaragua, or even whether such a trip took place, Rafael, in the immediate aftermath of the Sandinista victory, concentrated on finishing his studies at UNAM and continuing in his post as a lecturer in the capital's other major university, UAM, which he had begun on 16 January 1979.

5. The Graduate

UAM (Universidad Autónoma Metropolitana) had been founded in 1974 and at the time enjoyed a reputation for being highly radical. Its early atmosphere has been described by Raul Velasco Ugalde, one of UAM-Xochimilco's ideological leaders, as one of "permanent effervescence."[1] He states that its foundation constituted "an experience absolutely unheard of in the history of the Mexican university system," adding that it proved to be

> a hotbed of conflicting ideas, vanguardist initiatives, enthusiastic excesses, and important innovations; a knot of contradictions; a manifestation of the Mexican political schizophrenia that ephemerally escaped from the control of its promoters; a formidable attempt at redefining the university, its consciousness, both its own and in its relation to society. It was all this and much more.[2]

One distinguished contemporary student goes even farther:

> Well-known as an incubator for Marxist, pro-Cuba, pro-Sandinista activity . . . when Xochimilco opened, it immediately superseded UNAM in antigovernment militancy. It became a magnet for subversive artists, would-be guerrilla fighters, and sharp-tongued political thinkers. The place was known for its unorthodox educational methods, and fields of study often lost their boundaries. Professors not only sensitized us to the nation's poverty and injustice, they encouraged us to take action.[3]

As a result, according to another UAM contemporary, now a deputy with the Partido Acción Nacional (National Action Party), "UAM attracted an army of teachers, the majority of them militant leftists."[4] It was into this "climate of creativity, of initiative, of enthusiasm, of frank discussion"[5] that Rafael plunged on 16 January 1979, remaining immersed in it until 3 February 1984.[6]

Teaching at UAM was carried out in three departments: Biological Sciences, Social Sciences, and Sciences and Arts for Design. Topographically,

UAM was spread over three campuses: Xochimilco, Azcapotzalco, and Iztapalapa. Rafael taught in the Department of Sciences and Arts for Design at the UAM-Xochimilco campus. As one former colleague comments, "We [teachers] were all radicals, particularly those of us in the Sciences and Arts for Design Department."[7]

The underlying philosophy of the university was to promote interdisciplinary studies and to be strongly connected to society at large. For inspiration it looked to the Swiss child-psychologist Jean Piaget, who stressed the importance of exposure to "reality" in the development of children. It attempted to dispense with the theoretical and to concentrate on the practical application of theories devised for the betterment of society. Indeed, as Raul Velasco Ugalde observes, "The university ideologues insisted on the necessity of breaking with the tradition of teaching exclusively theory . . . the university, they emphasized, should do practical work . . . its teaching should be fixed in reality."[8] Another former UAM teacher from the period of Rafael's attendance declares, "We wanted to put the emphasis as much on practice as on theory, and we understood that it was our duty to give back to the community what we received from it."[9] Of the three departments, Biological Sciences and Sciences and Arts for Design were most preoccupied with practice over theory and its relevance to society. Such an emphasis, as we have seen, was close to Rafael's heart.

Another factor that would have endeared UAM to Rafael was the university's promotion of an egalitarian structure. One example of this was that UAM's union (SITUAM) was the first Mexican university union to represent simultaneously both its academic and its administrative staff. On a smaller point of detail, there was no hierarchical separation of UAM-Xochimilco's administrators: high-ranking functionaries did not have offices apart from other staff members.

It is hardly surprising that Rafael should have been drawn to an innovative, egalitarian institution that shared his disdain for the purely theoretical. Moreover, in the company of colleagues such as Alberto Híjar, he throve in this environment. As one contemporary colleague from the same department comments:

> No one was more radical than a group of young, brilliant, serious, and hardworking teachers in the Department of Science and Art for Design. Guillén and Silvia were in the middle of that group. I thought we were sectarian, but they beat us. They kept strictly to themselves, like a little family. But they came up with very original, very creative projects.

They were big on Althusser, on his theories of ideology and communication, and on something they called *gráfica monumental*. Before they left the school, they did a wonderful mural for the auditorium—it's still there.[10]

The singling out of Silvia, in addition to Rafael, is highly significant. Silvia, whose nom de guerre was Gabriela, was the wife of Rodrigo (Javier Ramírez), the FLN's second-in-command after Germán, and was in charge of editing, printing, and publishing the FLN's numerous publications.[11] It was apparently she who made contact with Salvador Morales, then a teaching assistant in the same department as Rafael, and who later joined the EZLN in Chiapas under the pseudonym Daniel.[12] Morales informs us that he and Rafael "entered into the organization [the FLN] in the same period,"[13] and one is left with the strong possibility that this was also through Silvia, who acted as the guerrillas' liaison officer and urban contact. Morales himself had "begun his revolutionary career . . . doing the layout for the in-house leftist magazine *Proletarian Conscience* . . . [which had] Marxist militants behind it, people like Commander in Chief *Germán* and other members of the National Liberation Forces, [who used it as] an important tool for promoting political consciousness and recruiting new militants."[14] Undoubtedly one of the magazine's Marxist backers would have been Silvia, whose job within the FLN was closely connected with editing and publishing the organization's revolutionary material. Indeed, many of the FLN members who later appeared in Chiapas seem to have been connected with either UNAM or UAM, or both.[15] Years later, as Marcos, Rafael would tell one interviewer, "The majority of the members of this organization [the FLN] were from the middle class; university professors, professionals, engineers, medics," adding that "It was a very, very small group: I am talking of ten or so, perhaps twenty people."[16]

In this regard, Mexico fits in well with what was happening elsewhere in Latin America during this era, given that its major universities were hotbeds of left-wing activism. McClintock states "as in almost all Latin American revolutionary experiences, in both El Salvador and Peru the university was the key place where the guerrilla leadership formed," adding, "the vast majority of the FMLN leaders were university-educated and came from the middle class or upper middle class; the entire original Shining Path leadership was also from such a background."[17] Mexico's guerrillas were no different. The original FLN cell, comprising the two Yáñez brothers, Fernando and César, and Elisa, centered on the University of Nuevo León.

The higher echelons of the Chiapas wing of the FLN, later called the EZLN, comprising Subcommanders Marcos and Daniel and their veteran liaison officer, Gabriela, all came together at UAM.[18]

In addition to Mexico's homegrown left-wing radicals, some of whom—for example, Gilberto Guevara Niebla, Roberto Escudero, and Miguel Sandoval—had gained hands-on experience of practical politics as participants in the 1968 student demonstrations, Rafael would also have come into contact with many intellectuals, most of them left wing, from elsewhere in Latin America. Foreigners, it should be noted, made up 20 percent of the faculty at UAM-Xochimilco. Many of these had experienced firsthand left-wing attempts at building more equitable societies and the right-wing response (e.g., Salvador Allende's attempt to create a Socialist Chile). Ilan Stavans, a former UAM student, sums up the situation in the early eighties: "Our teachers were dissatisfied middle-class Mexican Leftists, exiled Argentine intellectuals, and other Latin American émigrés. Our idols were Che Guevara, and Herbert Marcuse. Wealthy professors urged us to agitate among peasants in the countryside."[19]

Both within Mexico itself and in Latin America at large, the general climate for those on the political left was one of great excitement. When Rafael started teaching in 1979, Cuba had reached its zenith, with Castro chairing the Sixth Summit of the Movement of Non-Aligned Countries in Havana. The same year witnessed, as already noted, the victory of the Sandinistas in nearby Nicaragua on 19 July. Moreover, during the early 1980s Grenada and Jamaica briefly looked as if they might become socialist, while the governments of neighboring Guatemala and El Salvador were engaged in life-and-death struggles for survival against left-wing guerrilla movements. For Rafael and many of his contemporaries, hopes of a continent-wide left-wing conflagration were high: in Washington, fears of precisely this brought about urgent, determined, and often decisive U.S. interference in all of these countries.

Courses at the university were organized on a modular basis. Each course began with a general module for all the students. After this, students took certain modules run by their specific department in addition to the more general courses. They began specializing in a subject only at the end of their second year. Each module lasted three months. In the term devoted to theory, Guillén prescribed the reading of works by Michel Foucault, Karl Marx, Louis Althusser, Poulantzas, Armand Matelart, and Mao. This was no doubt baffling for many of the students enrolled in his class, which formed part of the graphic design for communication course, the more so since this course tended to attract the "beautiful people." His course on design, which he dubbed "Design with a Social Character," proposed "locating design within the context of the modes of production."[20] He was not alone in this; rather, a good number of the faculty involved in the graphic design for communication course as a whole emphasized "design committed to social movements."[21] Indeed, the Department of Sciences and Arts for Design was split between two factions of professors: the more traditional ones who proposed that the emphasis should be placed on design for publicity and those like Rafael who attempted to incorporate a social element into the course, namely, the dissemination of an alternative propaganda to that espoused by the dominant culture. There was no animosity between the two schools of thought, since they differed not on basic pedagogical principles but on the nature and extent of their application. This division appears to have in fact worked well, producing a creative tension resulting in a well-rounded course being offered to the students.

As for Rafael's classes, several of his former students and colleagues have been interviewed by the Mexican weekly *Proceso* and have left on record their views on him as a teacher. According to one of them, he was a man of "sharp and accurate intelligence, very good humored, and unaffected."[22] Another concurs, "remarking on his sharp intellect and infectious verbosity . . . bright and articulate."[23] Bearded and perpetually gesticulating with his pipe in his hand, in between puffing away at it, he earned the affectionate, paternal nickname of Guillomas (in addition to his other nickname, Cachumbambé).

From the testimony of his students it would appear that Rafael was one of those teachers who was popular with students but who also managed to get a lot of work out of them. One, Víctor Soler, who was one of Rafael's first students and who went on to become a designer and a teacher himself, recollects that Guillén was "a brilliant guy, responsible, who managed a class very well [and] didn't let us down."[24] He adds that "you had to work, he didn't just talk on and on like a parrot and hand-out materials, you had to sweat and hand-in assignments."[25] According to Soler, in the fourth term the students had to present an audiovisual piece complete with photographs, text, and sequences which, if it did not come up to Rafael's expectations, resulted in a severe scolding. Salvador Morales, who worked as a teaching assistant in the same department as Rafael and who later joined the FLN and rose to the rank of Subcomandante, tells us that Guillén would tell students from more well-to-do families, "I am going to instruct you like your parents exploited the Mexicans"; in other words, he was going to work them hard! Morales also adds that Rafael "was a showman who from even then knew what he wanted, and had the capacity to control his own actions as well as the people."[26]

He was clearly popular with some of the female students, several of whom remember him as being "extremely attractive." One, Lourdes Balderrama, who studied under Rafael during his first year of teaching at UAM and who to this day has retained a photograph of him, claims "he had a lot of charisma, but I never knew him to have a girlfriend." She continues, "with a great sense of humor he would sometimes say that he was very handsome and other times say he was very ugly." She adds, "to me he never appeared much of a tough-guy but rather a friendly character."[27] (Rafael was to retain this ambivalent perception of his own physical attractiveness even after he transformed into Marcos. In some interviews he jokingly claims to don a ski-mask in order to conceal his handsomeness.[28] However, in at least one other interview, he claims that his indigenous compañeros tease him that he has to wear a mask because his ugliness would disillusion women if they could see his face.[29]) Balderrama, who later went on to become a graphic designer in a publicity agency, recalls that Guillén's classes were dynamic and placed great emphasis on class struggle. She relates how students were taught to question absolutely everything and that Guillén's class in particular encouraged students to reflect upon themselves and their relationship to the surrounding environment. She goes on to say that often in class Rafael "was tremendously serious, but at the same time, as we were advancing through the analysis of texts . . . he made marvelous jokes."[30]

Another female student, Marcela Capdevila, who was helped by advice from Guillén in completing her final piece of work, a kind of graduation thesis, claims to have identified "spiritually" with this professor who was "clearly formed in the humanistic tradition."[31] During the three months Rafael advised her on her thesis, Capdevila claims he always showed himself to be "discreet in all his affairs, very prudent, very respectful, but also with a great sense of humor."[32] Concerning his style of argumentation, she states:

He was always more convincing than the rest, although he never went so far as to impose his views on anyone, he was not overbearing. . . . He was radical in his propositions, but not so as to be inflexible. He was radical because he had training, because he had concepts, because he had a very extensive theoretical framework. . . . But he was not intolerant or arbitrary in this way.[33]

That Guillén could be easygoing and relaxed at times is to some extent corroborated by Víctor Soler's testimony. He writes that although Rafael stressed certain elements in his classes, he always emphasized in the end that the students "should draw our own conclusions and define our own function and our role according to the characteristics of each of us. . . . It always interested him that we were not a homogeneous group."[34]

Of his colleagues, Mauricio Gómez Morín Fuentes, with whom Guillén enjoyed a friendly working relationship, describes Rafael as affable and approachable. He describes Guillén as "having cordial relations with the world," continuing, "he was outgoing and chatty."[35] He also noted that Guillén "stood-out" among the other teachers "on account of his sharp, cryptic intelligence."[36]

Rafael's lifestyle while at both UNAM and UAM appears to have been somewhat spartan. His girlfriend from UNAM, Rocío, tells us that, "he was austere . . . one pair of trousers and three shirts constituted his entire wardrobe."[37] So, too, we are told Rafael was nicknamed *Patas verde* (green feet) at UAM on account of his "always wearing green training shoes."[38] Marcos recalls that on leaving for Chiapas, "I left behind in the city, a metro ticket, a pile of books, a broken pencil, a notebook full of poems. . . . I don't recall having left anything else . . . no music records nor tape cassettes."[39]

Interestingly, given his involvement in the UNAM strike in 1977, Rafael never openly involved himself in university politics during the time he was at UAM. There is no evidence that he participated directly in either the faculty and administrative union or the student union, and this despite his recommendation to Salvador Morales, his junior colleague and new recruit to the FLN, to observe union politics in order to become more politicized. Víctor Soler states that although Guillén did "participate and involve himself above all in the problems of the course," he "had no links with the union."[40] Lourdes Balderrama supports this, saying "I don't think he sympathized much [with the union]." Indeed, *Proceso*, after interviewing many of Rafael's students, friends, and colleagues, comes to the conclusion that, "he gave the impression, his friends of that time say, that he was not even interested in unionism, despite the fact that his class was eminently political and the dynamic of both the course and his group was one of continual and heated debates."[41] Given that Rafael had embroiled himself to some extent in UNAM's strike in 1977 and that he again involved himself (albeit from afar) in the industrial action at UNAM in 1999/2000 through his communiqués on the subject, his apparent lack of interest in UAM's union requires explanation. The most plausible hypothesis is that because Rafael was already involved clandestinely in the FLN he did not wish to draw attention to himself or his activities by getting embroiled in union matters, and so elected to exercise his influence "from the wings." This is to some extent supported by the testimony of Salvador Morales who tells us that at UAM "there were very important strikes, with which Guillén had much to do because from behind the scenes and without participating in meetings, he would say 'it is necessary to do this' and people did it."[42]

Guillén was certainly not the only individual from UAM who left the university during this era, having distilled his or her counter-culture ideologies and honed his or her revolutionary skills, in order to improve what they perceived as the sick society in which they lived. Some went to work for trade unions; others forged links with local urban or rural community action groups. Still more went to Nicaragua to help build what they hoped would prove a socialist utopia. Ilan Stavans, a former student at UAM in the early 1980s, tells how "friends would take time off to travel to distant rural regions and live with the indigenous people," adding, "most eventually returned, but many didn't—they simply vanished, adopting new identities and new lives."[43] In 1982, another UAM professor, Benjamín Berlange, went to the rugged Eastern Sierra Madre and founded a school, the Centre for Rural Training and Development (CESDER), to teach the local population land management, animal husbandry, and the establishing of local craft cooperatives. Today Berlange is also an advisor to the EZLN. He notes:

> Marcos and I are of the same generation. At the same time that he went to Chiapas, we came here with a very different perspective having nothing to do with the armed struggle. When the Zapatistas emerged in Chiapas, for a moment we wondered whether we should have been armed revolutionaries and fought here, for example, in the Sierra. Marcos did it, why didn't we? Maybe we've been mistaken for the last ten years. But the possibility of this armed group—this new discourse—only appeared after years of working from below with local organizations.[44]

In their own small way several of those whom Rafael had taught attempted to put into practice the knowledge and techniques they had acquired. Víctor Soler worked on Cuauhtémoc Cárdenas's election campaign placards and went on to design the mathematics textbook for fifth-grade primary school students; Balderrama produced thirty-two silk-screen posters that were sent to Nicaragua's Atlantic zone as part of the literacy campaign there; and Capdevila participated in courses on "political graphics" at the Autonomous University of Puebla and produced the poster for the market in the village of San Salvador Cuautenco, in Xochimilco.

By the time Rafael finally left UAM for good, on 3 February 1984, the university was entering a very difficult period. Raul Velasco Ugalde points to a general decline in conditions there from 1980 onward. Small concrete buildings now housed the faculty, but their design meant that artificial light was required even in the daytime. The faculty felt incarcerated in these impersonal dingy buildings, apart from one another; the atmosphere was no longer convivial. Also in this period, UAM, and particularly the union, became very short of funds. Staff began to leave. Eventually, those who had initially been the most ardent supporters turned into the institution's fiercest critics.[45] Rafael left behind him an institution that was, according to Ugalde, a shadow of its former glory as he embarked on a new career as a professional revolutionary. However, he did take something of UAM with him. His written style was given its final shape at UAM. Stavans, a student at UAM during Guillén's time there and only about five years his junior, claims that on reading Subcommander Marcos's communiqués over a decade later he was "struck by the similarities between his postmodern tongue and the often hallucinatory verbiage at Xochimilco, full of postscripts and qualifications and references to high and low, from modernist literature and academic Marxism to pop culture." He continues:

> *El Sup* said his idols were the nationally known "new journalists" Carlos Monsiváis and Elena Poniatowska, whom my whole intellectual generation deeply admired and whose works trespass intellectual boundaries with glee. . . . His speeches, like the authors we studied at UAM, seamlessly mix fiction with reality becoming masterful self-parodies, texts about texts about texts.[46]

In addition to teaching at UAM, Rafael also spent the three years between graduating from UNAM and his permanent departure for Chiapas in perfecting his practical revolutionary skills. For example, he helped out in the FLN safe houses in the capital, went on errands to other parts of the country with other FLN cadres to visit the FLN's other fronts (such as the Villa Front in the Sierra Tarahumara) and its safe houses in Yanga (Veracruz), and so on.[47] Tello Díaz writes:

Between May and October 1982, in effect, Rafael Guillén asked for permission to take unpaid leave from UAM's Xochimilco, but he did not leave Mexico. *Daniel*, his comrade in arms, asserts that during these months, he [Rafael] put his name forward to represent the urban militants before the Political Bureau of the FLN. After, he took under his charge the Monterrey network, and recommenced also his classes in UAM.[48]

It would appear that Rafael even visited Chiapas on occasions in preparation for his immersion into guerrilla life there. Oppenheimer, a journalist who enjoys access to sources within the Mexican intelligence services, asserts that Rafael, employing his first nom de guerre, Zacarías, had even run "a 'first aid' training course in the Chiapas jungle . . . [that] was a thinly disguised guerrilla training course run by the National Liberation Forces."[49] One of a small number of faculty and students who participated in this course was Rafael's fellow UAM staff member, Salvador Morales, later to become Subcommander Daniel.[50] No doubt Rafael had begun by visiting Chiapas for a few weekends at a time and had then progressed to spending increasingly lengthy periods there during the long university vacations.

Regrettably, little else is known for certain about these important three years of Rafael's life. We know from interviews with his family that Rafael had told them a complex cocktail of truth and fiction. For example, he told them that he had got a job as a UAM professor, which was true; that he had spent time studying at the Sorbonne in Paris, which appears to have been false, or at least has nowhere been corroborated; that he had lived for some years in Nicaragua, which he appears to have visited, but only briefly and that back in 1979; and that he had worked for Mexico City's Route 100 bus union, first as a driver and then as a labor organizer, which appears plausible, but nothing more.[51] We also have the claims of de la Grange and Rico, who cite two sources whose anonymity and identity they protect by calling them just Antonio and Mauricio. According to Antonio, Rafael "at the start of the eighties had made several trips in order to make contact with the Chicanos of Los Angeles and Texas, who controlled the arms black market and sold them to us."[52] This seems plausible enough given the hints Subcommander Marcos would later drop concerning time spent in the United States, although, given our complete ignorance concerning the source of this information and the Subcommander's tendency of intentionally giving interviewers the false impression that he had visited the countries they came from, we cannot test its veracity.[53] Conversely, the claim of a certain Mauricio that he met Rafael in a military training camp at Punto Cero just outside Havana between May and October 1982 appears far less credible.[54] For although de la Grange and Rico describe Mauricio as "an old *compañero* of *Marcos*," and although Mauricio's portrayal of Rafael as "truly obsessed with Che [Guevara]" fits well with what we know of Guillén then, there is no supporting evidence.[55] Moreover, Tello Díaz, a man who appears to enjoy an especially privileged access to sources, flatly rejects the suggestion, stating that "there are no indications to suppose that *Marcos* had trained in Cuba," adding "[he] did not leave Mexico" during this period (May to October 1982).[56] Instead, Tello Díaz prefers the "more trustworthy" (*más confiables*) testimony of former-Subcommander-turned-informer Daniel, who states that Rafael at this time was busy representing the urban militants before the political bureau and then assumed responsibility for the Monterrey network of the FLN.[57] Moreover, in a recent communiqué Marcos himself discusses this period, making no mention of any foreign trip, but rather emphasizing jungle training in Chiapas. He writes: "we selected those persons who would form part of the EZLN. This was around 1982. Practices were organized for one or two months in the *selva*, during which the performance of those in attendance was evaluated in order to see who would 'make the cut.'"[58]

RAFAEL SEBASTIÁN
GUILLÉN VICENTE IN A
SUPER 8 MOVIE MADE AT
HIGH SCHOOL COLLEGE
(1976). ARCHIVO *PROCESO*.

RAFAEL GUILLÉN
IN PROFILE (1980).
ARCHIVO *PROCESO*.

RAFAEL GUILLÉN
TEACHING A CLASS
AT UAM SOME TIME
BETWEEN 16 JANUARY
1979 AND 3 FEBRUARY
1984. ARCHIVO *PROCESO*.

RAFAEL GUILLÉN
IN HIS OFFICE AT
UAM. ARCHIVO
PROCESO.

PART II

Marcos the Guerrilla

MAP 2: CENTRAL AND EASTERN CHIAPAS.

6. Chiapas

Chiapas, the world in which Rafael in 1984 was about to immerse himself for twenty years, was an ideal setting for the implantation of a left-wing guerrilla *foco* that sought to grow clandestinely by harnessing popular discontent among the local peasantry.[1] Its dense jungle provided cover, and its numerous waterways (such as the Negro, Lacanjah, Lacantún, Santo Domingo, and Jataté rivers) aided movement and communication. Chiapas's proximity with Guatemala also meant that there was an easy escape route which the Mexican Federal Army could not close in its pursuit of the guerrillas.[2] Indeed, the ex-Subcommander, Daniel, tells us that "Chiapas was not chosen for its revolutionary potential, but on account of its geography," adding, "[it] was an apt place for guerrillas, the Lacandón in particular, since it was closed off, difficult to access . . . [and] there were no soldiers there so that it was possible to practice shooting without problems."[3] Marcos confirms this; when asked by one interviewer "Why Chiapas?" he replied, "You need geographic conditions of isolation, security, depopulated zones, places where you won't be detected."[4]

Terrain and geographical location had, in the late 1960s, been what previously prompted Mario Payeras and his guerrilla *foco* to choose the area for their training base and subsequently as their springboard from which they launched a guerrilla insurgence in Guatemala. (In this way, and in many others, Payeras was a precursor to Marcos; indeed, the similarities are striking. In addition to installing a guerrilla *foco* in Chiapas, he, like Marcos, was one of the very first to emphasize indigenous participation, amassing over a period of years an indigenous and *campesino* support base that emerged later to wage a local guerrilla war and simultaneously a more widespread public relations war in order to gain international support and recognition.)[5]

However, it was not only terrain and geography that made Chiapas fertile ground for rebellion in 1984; the socioeconomic and political landscape also contributed significantly. Centuries of neglect by those in power in

Mexico City, who were prepared to allow first the conquistadors and priests and then local elites and landlords free rein in the region, had meant that the Enlightenment ideals of liberty, equality, fraternity, and democracy— let alone the more modest ideals of the Mexican Revolution[6]—had almost completely passed Chiapas by. After visiting Chiapas in 1938, Graham Greene described the plight of the indigenous population there: "In bad years they say hundreds starve to death, but no one knows—they retire like wounded animals into the mountains and forests, eating berries, lasting as long as they can, seeking no pity." He continues, "The trouble was, Chiapas was so poor [and] . . . forgotten in Mexico City; it was so far away Mexicans didn't know it existed."[7] It is fair to say that fifty years on, little had changed—indeed, many Chiapans continued to die from starvation[8]—and that which had, had changed for the worse.

Cynthia McClintock recently noted:

> The cause of a revolutionary movement cannot be something that has not changed in some way; if something had always been present or had not changed, then it cannot explain the timing of the emergence of the movement . . . in other words the cause of the revolutionary movement . . . must be something different from previous years . . . or else, in the logic of the social sciences, a similar revolution would have occurred earlier. . . . For social scientists, causation requires that something different happened.[9]

She focuses her study on Peru's Sendero Luminoso and El Salvador's Frente Farabundo Martí de Liberación Nacional (FMLN, Farabundo Marti National Liberation Front) and comes to the conclusion that this new variable was economic crisis in the case of the former, and political exclusion and repression in the latter.[10] In Chiapas, I would argue, all of these factors were present and proved significant.

In economic terms, 1982 had been a disastrous year for Mexico in general and for Chiapas in particular, and it marked a turning point in Mexico's economic policy. At the national level, as a *NACLA Report on the Americas* observes, prior to this

> four components had guided Mexican economic policy: a high degree of state participation in the economy; a strategy of "stable development" which attempted to keep prices, interest rates and the exchange rate under control; the protection of domestic industry with high tariff and non-tariff barriers to international trade and investment; and an at-

tempt to provide a relatively high degree of social security to Mexican citizens. [However,] beginning with the reforms of President Miguel De la Madrid in 1983—reforms dictated in large part by the international lending agencies which were "helping" the country emerge from its moratorium on international debt payments—economic policy took a 180-degree turn. Embarking on the "free-market" path pioneered by the "Chicago boys" employed by the Chilean dictatorship, Mexico reversed all four directions and entered into a period of reform that privatized and deregulated the economy, opened it to international investment and trade, and cut loose the workforce—especially the peasantry—from its traditional protections and supports.[11]

James Petras puts it even more starkly, identifying a "transition from an authoritarian state-capitalism to a police-state kleptocracy which dubs itself 'free-market liberalism' and describes its electoral reforms and the assassination of opponents as a 'transition to democracy.'"[12] Oil prices plummeted, and consequently Mexico began defaulting on its foreign debt, thereby threatening to bring down the world banking system. Mike González describes the consequences:

> The result was a collapse in the value of wages close to 40 percent, cuts in social spending of over 40 percent, a rise in unemployment of 15 percent (from 9 percent to 24 percent of the economically active population) and a rampant program of privatization. The overall outcome was a dramatic redistribution of wealth toward the rich—with labor's share of GDP falling from 41 percent to 29 percent.[13]

All this, of course, had an effect at the local level. As James Stephenson observes, these cuts "forced the Government to halt large oil exploration and hydroelectric projects, which had been a major source of jobs in the state [of Chiapas]." So, too, the agricultural subsidies given to co-opt the more dangerous and militant peasant organizations came to an end. In Chiapas, Guatemalan refugees started flooding in over the border from the south, attempting to escape fearsome repression from their own military which was conducting a bloody counterinsurgency campaign. As a result, "the Guatemalan refugee problem doubled the population in certain parts of Chiapas and brought in cheap labor to compete successfully for many farming jobs.[14] To compound the problem there was a considerable influx of perhaps as many as 14,000 Zoque Indians from the north, escaping the damage wreaked by the March 1982 eruption of the Chichonál volcano.[15]

Concerning the second factor, political exclusion, there was little change in the highlands and jungles of Chiapas. The only change possible was one for the better, and this had not taken place. Local landlords or elites (*caciques*) monopolized political and economic power in the region, receiving the full support of the federal government, and therefore the judiciary, the army, and the police in return for ensuring continued PRI victories in elections.[16] (No better proof of this need be cited than the fact that in the 1991 congressional elections, at a time when the EZLN was experiencing a period of rapid growth in recruitment and support in the region, Oxchuc, located deep within the Zapatista's sphere of influence, witnessed the PRI supposedly winning 100 percent of the 11,073 votes cast there.)[17] In short, the local state and party apparatus, inextricably linked as they were, could direct PRI and government funds to those who voted for the party or could unleash the full weight of the law and the military against those who refused to acquiesce in this travesty of democracy.

Repression, unlike political exclusion, had not remained a constant; indeed, it escalated considerably during the early 1980s.[18] As in the case of El Salvador's FMLN, this also proved a significant factor in Chiapas and is what lent the guerrillas their initial legitimacy, since they offered to provide much needed self-defense services.[19] Peaceful mobilizations were being met with increasingly brutal opposition; landowners were responding to land takeovers by employing paramilitaries; and governors were becoming increasingly hard-line, culminating in the choice of a retired army general, Absalón Castellanos Domínguez, as state governor (1982–88).[20] In 1984 he enacted a severe penal code that significantly broadened the definition of "crimes against internal security" to include many activities Western liberal democracies would consider forms of legitimate popular protest.[21] (As one Chiapan would comment despairingly, "When we try to organize and fight back, they call us agitators and throw us in jail. Who can we complain to? The cattle ranchers are the mayors, judges, and the PRI officials. We have no place to turn."[22] In time, the EZLN would end up providing this "place to turn" to.) According to one recent publication, Domínguez's term of office saw the assassination of 102 *campesinos*; the disappearance of 327; the imprisonment of 590 and the kidnapping and torture of 427; the expulsion of 407 families from their homes; and the overrunning by security forces of 54 communities.[23] (Things were to deteriorate under his successor, González Garrido. Michael Tangeman notes: "Not only did rights abuses increase under [President Salinas's] cousin González Garrido in Chiapas, but the Jesuits' Pro center noted a nationwide 50 percent increase in political murders and torture and a 1,000 percent increase in other rights abuses in some parts of the country during Salinas's first year in office."[24] Roger Burbach observes that "just months after he [Garrido] took office, two of the principal *campesino* leaders in the state were assassinated.")[25]

Moreover, concerning political exclusion, Domínguez had sided completely with the landowning elite, of which he was a member, owning ten estates totaling 20,800 hectares (twenty-six times the area permitted by law).[26] Certainly he inherited a bad situation, since in 1983, "30 per cent of Chiapan lands were . . . controlled by *latifundistas* while at least 100,000 peasants were landless."[27] However, not only did the general not attempt to remedy this situation, he exacerbated it. In just six years:

> He issued more documents of nonaffectability (*certificados de inafecta-bilidad*) than all the previous state governors combined . . . the main beneficiaries were the private ranchers, who were issued with 4,714 *certificados*,[28] equivalent to 95 percent of the total number distributed in the state since 1934. By the end of his administration at least 70 percent of the area used by cattle ranchers was legally beyond the reach of agrarian reform.[29]

It is hardly surprising then, that "almost thirty percent of Mexico's outstanding land claims (*rezago agrario*) are in Chiapas."[30] Moreover, what little land Domínguez did distribute to peasants went to *campesino* groups aligned with the PRI. For example, while the PRI affiliated Confederacíon Nacional Campesina received some land, "of 493 major land grants made in the state, only 27 [i.e., 5.47 percent] went to communities of *ejidos* aligned with militant peasant organizations."[31] This PRI practice of rewarding loyal peasants and co-opting others left very few options open to those unwilling to sell out. Worse still, often the land granted was of poor quality, a factor that, when compounded by the lack of government investment in the state's infrastructure, resulted in it being far less productive than other areas of Mexico.[32]

The state also witnessed significant militarization during this period, a circumstance overlooked by those like de la Grange and Rico who blame the Zapatistas for increased militarization in the region. This process began in 1981, when sizeable military maneuvers were conducted near the Guatemalan border. Upward of 40,000 federal troops remained in the area, and in 1983 a second Chiapan military zone was created, two new airstrips were built in Comitán and Tonalá, and the Terán airport at Tuxtla Gutiérrez, the Chiapan state capital, was transformed into a military hanger.[33] More-over, as Thomas Benjamin observes, under Domínguez, "The two state police forces, the Public Security Police and the Judicial Police, were placed under the command of military officers."[34] Thus, as early as 1985, when *Proceso* sent reporters to interview chiapanecos, two men from Soconusco (in Southern Chiapas) could be quoted as saying: "Chiapas lives under a state of siege. General Absalón Castellanos Domínguez tries to solve the region's problems by the least adequate means: repression."[35] In March 1987 one reporter wrote that "Chiapas has been turned into another one of the principal operations of the armed forces."[36] (It was for all these reasons that Marcos had the general kidnapped on New Year's Eve 1994, imprison-ing him for six weeks and having him tried for crimes against the *campesi-nos* by the Justice Tribunal of the EZLN. The tribunal, unsurprisingly, found him guilty, passing a life sentence of hard, manual labor, which it later commuted.)[37] Thus, as in the case of El Salvador's guerrillas, Marcos and his *foco* flourished as a result of repression practiced against the *campesino* population.[38]

In short, the lot of the chiapaneco peasant was analogous to the pitiable plight of the Cuban peasantry that Marcos's hero, Che Guevara, had de-picted nearly a quarter of a century earlier:

> The situation of the peasants in the rugged mountain zones was noth-ing less than frightful. The peasant, having migrated from afar with a yearning for freedom, had put all his efforts into squeezing out an existence from the newly cleared land. Through a thousand and one sacrifices he had coaxed the coffee plants to grow on the craggy slopes where creating anything new entails sacrifice. All this he did by his own sweat. . . . Suddenly, when the coffee plants were beginning to blossom with the fruit that represented his hope, the lands were claimed by a new owner. It might be a foreign company, a local land-grabber, or some other speculator taking advantage of peasant indebtedness. The political bosses and local army chieftains worked for the company or the land-grabber, jailing or murdering any peasant who was unduly rebellious against these arbitrary acts.[39]

However, in Marcos's case, unlike Che's, much of the political groundwork had already been done for him. The chiapanecos had been politicized by various groups from the 1970s onward, including the Catholic Church and the Maoists.[40] The former Subcommander Daniel tells us, "These people were already more or less formed politically."[41] The only thing they had not received was military instruction; there was thus a role for Marcos to fill when he arrived. While the people's spiritual needs had been sustained by the Church and their political needs had been provided for by various political groups, including the Maoists, the military training required simply in order for them to protect themselves and survive was wanting. Marcos tells us: "It was when we arrived that the military question began. There was no military organization before I arrived, we initiated it."[42] Needless to say, the guerrillas were only too pleased to step into this gap immediately. As Marcos puts it:

> When we first came here we talked about the issue of armed struggle. And the indigenous people said, "Yes, we have to take up arms and defend ourselves." So we began to train for self-defense, not for how to attack. That's how the Zapatista National Liberation Army was born, as a self-defense force. And that's how we grew.[43]

Elsewhere, Marcos expands on the need for self-defense at this time, saying: "As far as the peasants are concerned, the EZLN arose as a self-defense group to defend against ranchers' hired gunmen, who try to take their land and maltreat them, limiting the social and political advancement of the Indians. So they took up arms so as not to be defenseless."[44] If any doubt exists as to the genuineness of the chiapaneco *campesinos'* need for self-defense at this time, one only need consider a study cited by Thomas Benjamin: "Of 115 serious agrarian disputes in Chiapas during the 1970s . . . 87 [i.e., 75 percent] had been caused by the takeover of ejidal lands by cattle ranchers,"[45] land which, Marcos observes, "has cultural, religious and historic connotations."[46] The case of Monte Libano, in Ocosingo municipality, is especially illustrative of the peasants' need for self-defense. State police had burned down the hamlet no less than three times since its establishment, in 1976, again in 1979, and most recently in 1982.[47] Little wonder then that a decade later this municipality was to become Zapatista heartland.

In sum, the terrain, the geography, and the socioeconomic and political climate in Chiapas were pregnant with revolutionary potential when Marcos arrived there in 1984 with precisely the intention of fomenting revolution. Roger Burbach observes, during the previous year, "The situation had become so explosive that in early 1983 President Miguel de la Madrid, just months after taking office, made an emergency trip to Chiapas. His efforts were aimed at containing and controlling the growing social upheaval."[48] This emergency trip, and the president's subsequent announcement of the six-year, 300 million dollar "Plan Chiapas" aid package for the state,[49] was no doubt spurred by a report in *Proceso* that year which had stated that Chiapas was only "one step from guerrilla war . . . because of worsening injustice."[50] In time, Marcos, witnessing this injustice (and the attendant repression) year in, year out, at first hand (rather than merely through the pages of Mexico City–based news publications), would accompany Chiapas this step further.

7. Guerrilla Inception

Marcos's arrival had, according to the ex-Subcommander Daniel, been preceded the previous year (1983) by that of six Mexicans, three ladinos (Germán, Elisa, and Rodolfo), and three indigenous men (Javier, Jorge, and Frank), who had set up camp in the jungle on 17 November 1983.[1] Marcos, well acquainted with these protagonists and therefore to some extent party to this event, recently wrote:

> Twenty years ago, in 1983, a group of people were preparing, in some safe house, the tools they would need to be taking to the mountains of the Mexican Southeast. Perhaps twenty years ago, the day went by in checking on the impedimenta, gathering reports on roads, alternative routes, weather, detailing itineraries, orders, devices. Twenty years ago, perhaps at this very hour, they would have been getting into a vehicle and beginning the trip to Chiapas. . . . Let us assume, then, that they started their trip on November 10, 1983. A few days later, they reached the end of a dirt road, got their things out, said goodbye to the driver with a "hasta luego" and, after adjusting their knapsacks, began the ascent of one of the sierras, sloping to the west, which cross the Selva Lacandona. After walking for many hours, with some 25 kilos of weight on their backs, they set up their first camp, right in the middle of the sierra.[2]

This group, headed by Germán (Fernando Yáñez Muñoz) and seconded by Elisa (María Gloria Benavides Guevara) had arrived, presumably by *colectivo*,[3] or perhaps by truck, at La Sultana, which lies two-thirds of the way along the road southeast from Ocosingo to San Quintin, at the confluence where the Rio Chajuil and the Rio Tezanconejo meet to become the Rio Jataté. It was probably there that they said goodbye to the driver and began their trek, dressed in Pemex uniforms to avoid suspicion, east until they hit the Montes Azules biosphere reserve about 25 km away.

In 1992, Marcos was to describe the terrain and sights that one encounters on precisely this journey in his *The South East in Two Winds, a Storm and a Prophecy*. He, too, had presumably taken this same route, which had brought Elisa and Germán to the jungle. He writes:

> Pass by Cuxulja and instead of following the detour to Altamirano, drive on till you reach Ocosingo . . . follow the road that goes to San Quintin, in front of the Montes Azules Reserve . . . go to where the Jatate and Perlas Rivers join . . . walk for three eight-hour days . . . to see San Martin . . . it is a very poor and small community . . . [with] groups of children riddled with tapeworms and lice, half-naked.[4]

The group of six immediately began clandestine training. Their plan was to found a southern wing of the FLN, to be called the EZLN, to complement the Villa Front, which it had opened in the north of the country.[5] This represented a return to the area by the FLN which, in the 1970s, had had a cell in Ocosingo,[6] a former EZLN subcommander relating: "It [Chiapas] was a place already known; the group formed by César Germán Yáñez ["Pedro"], the founder of the FLN, had already been there from the start of the seventies."[7] Indeed, César Germán Yáñez (from whom "Germán," his younger brother, took his nom de guerre) had been killed in a shootout with security forces in February 1974 while undertaking guerrilla activities there under the pseudonym "Pedro." "Germán" and "Pedro's" older brother, Margil Yáñez (alias Roger), had also laid the groundwork for guerrilla activity in Chiapas during the mid-1970s, distributing medical supplies in the zone in an attempt to win over the local population. More recently, in particular in the region of Sabanilla, where the FLN had operated during the 1970s under first "Pedro" and then Roger, contact was made in March 1980 with a respected Tzotzil known to the FLN as Paco, who then facilitated the recruitment of Tzotzil cadres such as Yolanda, Frank, and Mario.[8] Elisa was also no stranger to Chiapas. She must have been making shorts trips there during the early 1980s for training purposes, since by the time of her arrival in autumn 1983 she was dating (and recruiting) Jorge Santiago (alias Jacobo), the head of Desarrollo Económico Social de los Mexicanos Indígenas (DESMI, Social-Economic Development of the Indigenous Mexicans), a regional development agency started by Bishop Ruiz and funded by international NGOs.

On 17 November, the first Zapatista camp was founded by the six-person *foco*,[9] deep in the Lacandón jungle just north of Lake Miramar near the source of the Río Negro. By "camp," one must assume a very temporary affair since according to Elisa, "we were fairly nomadic;[10] we had only plastic sheets, hammocks and rucksacks, sometimes just a simple sack with shoulder straps."[11] In the weeks that followed however, a camp of sorts was fixed, since Marcos tells us that:

> One day they [the six-person *foco*] sent an insurgent to explore a site in order to see if it was suitable for encampment. The insurgent returned, saying that the place "was a dream." The *compañeros* marched in that direction, and, when they arrived, they found a swamp. They then told the *compañero*: "This isn't a dream, it's a nightmare." Ergo, the camp was then called "The Nightmare."[12] It must have been in the first months of 1984. The name of that insurgent was Pedro.[13]

In setting up camp in the Lacandón jungle, "The idea," according to former Subcommander Daniel, "was to arrive in the jungle, to install themselves, to train themselves, to control the jungle, or at least be 'accepted' by the jungle, and having done that to leave to go make contact with the people: in short to practice there, to train as guerrillas, so that after they would be able to attack anywhere in the country."[14]

Marcos elaborates further on the group's outlook and overall strategy:

> The EZLN was born having as points of reference the political-military organizations of the guerrilla movements in Latin America during the 60s and 70s: that is to say, political-military structures with the central aim of overthrowing a regime and the taking of power by the people in general. . . . When the first group of the EZLN arrived here, in the jungles of Chiapas, it was a very small group with this political-military structure that I am talking about.[15]

Just how little the EZLN's outlook had changed from its guerrilla predecessors of the 1960s and 1970s is borne out by Marcos's own writings from this time. In December 1984, he wrote in *Neplanta* that "the EZLN is installing itself in the mountains of Mexico in order to prepare for initiating the guerrilla offensive against the bourgeois army."[16] How could the EZLN be anything else when the organization was headed by Yáñez (alias Germán), in his forties and a veteran of the guerrilla movements of the 1960s and 1970s? However, from the outset Marcos maintained a somewhat more flexible approach than had some of his more dogmatic predecessors; and this flexibility, borne of pragmatism and realism, would be what allowed the EZLN to adapt and grow: "From the start, we have seen armed struggle as one in a series of processes or forms of struggle that are themselves subject to change; sometimes one is more important and at times another is more important." The Subcommander adds, "Of course we were thinking about armed struggle. But not as the only strategy, not as the only way to bring all this together, but rather as part of something broader that had to be prepared, integrated."[17]

Very soon into their endeavors, the group of six suffered a setback—one of them (possibly Jorge) was accidentally shot and killed during a training exercise. He was left-handed and it is said that today he is commemorated in the Zapatista left-handed salute.[18] As Marcos himself observed, "If I remember correctly, the EZLN had seven support-base members when I arrived, and two others who 'went up and down' to the city with mail and for supplies."[19] Indeed, former Subcommander Daniel notes that although "other groups of three, four or five began to arrive . . . they came for a visit of no more than fifteen days during their vacations, and when they had seen and got to know the jungle, they returned."[20]

In May 1984, Germán returned to Mexico City to continue organizing and orchestrating the FLN from there. He left Elisa in charge in Chiapas to supervise the training of future new recruits, amongst whom would soon be a dedicated and enthusiastic Marcos. With hindsight, it is easy to see that Germán's departure left a power vacuum that Elisa could not fill. Extremely experienced and capable though she was, Elisa was a woman in a male-dominated and macho society. In the years to come, the EZLN would become a progressive force that promoted gender equality, but in 1984 this still was a long way off. Tomás, a veteran indigenous Zapatista, informs us that, at this time, "*Comandanta* Elisa was in charge, but as she was a woman she wasn't taken very seriously."[21] Indeed, Subcommander Daniel confirms this, stating that "Elisa was a big zero . . . she was third-in-command of the FLN, but really nobody took her into account."[22] In time, the gap would come to be filled by Marcos.

Prior to embarking for Chiapas, while he was assisting in the FLN's safe houses in Mexico City, Rafael had been known by the nom de guerre Zacarías. On his arrival in the jungle, he soon changed this to Marcos, perhaps as an added security measure. If contacts in Mexico City had known him as Zacarías, the name change would ensure that if these contacts subsequently defected or were seized and tortured by security forces, no connection could be made between Zacarías and Marcos. Rafael was not alone in inventing a new identity at this time: previously, the FLN's first-in-command, Germán, had been known as Leo; its second-in-command, Rodrigo, had been known as Juan; Comandanta Elisa had used the pseudonym Ana; and the EZLN's liaison officer (and Rodrigo's wife), Gabriela, had employed the nom de guerre Sofía. In short, the entire upper echelon of the FLN now assumed new noms de guerre in preparation for their campaign in Chiapas.[23] The name Marcos, like so many noms de guerre used by guerrillas,[24] was taken by Rafael from a fellow FLN guerrilla, Adelaido Villafranco (alias Marcos), who he knew personally and who had been killed recently (26 May 1983) at an army checkpoint in Puebla.[25] Rafael had accompanied "Marcos" when they had traveled "the very long journeys by road . . . from one side to the other of the Republic"—no doubt from the Villa Front in the north to San Cristóbal in the south—during which Rafael had been impressed by his companion's "highly impressive authority" and his "encyclopedic knowledge of Mexican history, above all military history," which he recounted to Rafael "so as not to fall asleep at the wheel."[26]

Perhaps in order to mark this new stage of his life, namely his entry into the world of the rural guerrilla, Rafael wrote a poem in which he paid homage to those who like him had joined the FLN and who in 1979 had signed the organization's declaration affirming their commitment to its principles.[27] It runs:

"ACCOUNT OF THE EVENTS"
Today, the sixth day of the month
of August of the year
nineteen hundred and seventy-nine,
as history forewarned,
the coffee bitter,
the tobacco running out,
the afternoon declining
and everything in place for conspiring
against the shadows and darkness
which obscure the world and its sun,
the below signed appear
in front of me, the patria, in order to
declare the following.

First.—That the below signed
renounce their homes, work,

family and studies and all the
comforts which have been
accumulated in the hands of the few
upon the misery of the many.

Second.—That the below signed
renounce a future,
paid on time, of
individual enjoyment.

Third.—That the below signed
also renounce the shield
of indifference in the face of the suffering
of others and the vainglory of a
place among the powerful.

Fourth.—That the below signed
are prepared for all the sacrifices
necessary in order to fight silently
and without rest in order to make me,
the patria, free and true.

Fifth.—That the below signed
are prepared to suffer persecution,
calumny and torture, and even
to die if it is necessary, in order to achieve
what was noted in the Fourth point.

Sixth.—That I, the patria, will know
to keep your place in history
and to watch over your memory
as they watch over my life.

Seventh.—That the below signed
will leave enough space under their
names so that all honest men
and women may sign this
document, and, when the moment comes,
the entire people shall sign it.
There being nothing left to be said,
and very much to do, the
below signed leave their

blood as example and
their steps as guide.

Valiantly and Respectfully,

LIVE FOR THE PATRIA OR
DIE FOR LIBERTY.
Manuel, Salvador, Alfredo, Manolo, María Luisa,
Soledad, Murcia, Aurora, Gabriel, Ruth, Mario,
Ismael, Héctor, Tomás Alfonso, Ricardo. . . .
And the signatures will follow
of those who will have to die and
of those who will have to live
fighting, in this
country of sorrowful history
called Mexico, embraced
by the sea and, soon,
with the wind in its favor.

When Rafael left Mexico City for Chiapas, he brought along with him those personal possessions he treasured most, mainly books. The Subcommander tells us:

> Of the twelve books that I carried with me to the jungle, one was Pablo Neruda's *Canto General*; another was a selection of poems by Miguel Hernández; also poems by León Felipe; Cortázar's *Historía de Cronopios y Famas*; the *Memoirs* of Francisco Villa; *Don Quixote* . . . I did not plan this or reflect on it much before taking them. They said to me, "Okay, you're going to leave now, get your stuff together," and I grabbed those books which came to hand, the ones that I read most often or consulted most. I had many more, but they were left behind. The ones I brought I just chucked into my rucksack.[28]

These treasured volumes, Marcos explains, proved cumbersome in the short run:

> I used to carry books around in the mountains, and was scolded for it: why was I carrying them around? It was really suicide. When you first come, you want to bring your whole library, right? But the load of ammunition, food and everything else is divided equally, and on top of that you're carrying books. You end up getting rid of them, because no one is about to say: "Well, since you're carrying so many books, I'll give you

less ammunition." No, you carry the same amount. . . . And I got rid of them gradually in the different camps.[29]

However, as it turned out, gradually Marcos's comrades began to appreciate his bringing books to the jungle, until a point came when, as the Subcommander relates, "Every time I left a book behind, someone would offer to carry it for me. . . . 'A story is going to come out of that,' they would say."[30]

Both Tello Díaz[31] and de la Grange and Rico[32] give the month of Marcos's arrival in Chiapas as May. However, these authors do not cite their sources for this date,[33] and there appears ample testimony from Marcos himself that he in fact arrived in August. For example, in his communiqué entitled "The Retreat Is Making Us Almost Scratch the Sky" (dated 20 February 1995), he states that Marcos, "was born in the guerrilla camp . . . in the Lacandón Jungle, Chiapas, early one morning in August 1984."[34]

Indeed, I believe it is possible to fix the date of Marcos's arrival in Chiapas as 6 August. For, in his communiqué entitled "To Open a Crack in History" (dated September 1999), there appears a postscript headed "Fifteen Years Ago," the first paragraph of which states:

> In this August of the end of the millennium, the calendar pointed to the sixth day when this dawn appeared. And with the swaying moon came back a memory of another August and another sixth, fifteen years ago, when I began my entry into these mountains that were and are, like it or not, home, school, road, and door. I began my entry in August, and I didn't complete it until September.[35]

In the postscript's final paragraph Marcos reaffirms this, writing: "That was fifteen years ago. Since then . . . every 6 August keeps giving birth to a special dawn."[36]

This date, I would argue, was not chosen at random. Marcos, as we will continually observe, has a strong sense of occasion; he would not have simply left the date of his entrance onto the guerrilla stage to pure chance. Instead, he chose to commence his life as a guerrilla on the fifteenth anniversary of the founding of the FLN.[37] (In doing so, he was fulfilling to the highest degree possible his commitment to "always commemorating 6 August" as stipulated by article 13, section l of the FLN statutes.)

It is evident from his "To Open a Crack in History" communiqué that Marcos greatly respected his predecessors in the FLN. He pays homage to them, writing:

Thirty years ago [i.e., in 1969], a few people scratched history, and knowing this, they began calling to many others so that by dint of scribbling, scratching, and scrawling, they would end up rending the veil of history, so that the light would finally be seen. That, and nothing else, is the struggle we are making.[38]

In the same communiqué, Marcos provides us with a detailed description of his initial experience of guerrilla life in the summer of 1984:

I should confess something to you. When I laboriously climbed the first of the steep hills that abound in these parts, I was sure it would be my last. I wasn't thinking of revolution, of high human ideals or a shining future for the disposed and forgotten of always.[39] No, I was thinking I'd made the worst decision in my life, that the pain that squeezed my chest, more and more, would end up totally closing off my increasingly skimpy airway, that the best thing for me would be to go back and let the revolution manage itself without me, along with similar rationalizations. If I didn't go back, it was only because I didn't know the way back. All I knew was that I had to follow the compañero preceding me who, judging by the cigarette he was smoking while effortlessly negotiating the mud, seemed to be merely out for a stroll. I didn't think that one day I'd be able to climb a hill while smoking and not feel as if I was dying with each step, or that a time would come when I'd be able to manage the mud that was as abundant underfoot as the stars are overhead. No, I wasn't thinking at all then. I was concentrating on every breath I was trying to take.

What finally happened is that at some point we reached the highest crest of the hill, and the man in charge of the meager column (we were three[40]) said we would rest there. I let myself fall in the mud that seemed closest and told myself that perhaps it wouldn't be so hard to find the way back, that all I would have to do would be to walk down for another eternity, and that someday I would have to reach the point where the truck had dropped us off. I was making my calculations, including the excuses I would give them and give myself for abandoning the beginning of my career as a guerrilla, when the compañero approached me and offered me a cigarette. I refused with a shake of my head, not because I didn't want to talk but because I'd tried saying, "No thanks," and only a groan had come out.

After a bit, taking advantage of the fact that the man in charge had gone off some distance to satisfy what is referred to as a basic biological need, I used the .20 caliber rifle that I was carrying more like a walking stick than a combat weapon, and pulled myself up as best as I could. That was how I was able to see something from the top of that mountain that had a profound impact on me . . .

I looked upward. I saw a sky that was a gift and a relief—no, more like a promise. The moon was like a smiling nocturnal swing, the stars sprinkling blue lights, and the ancient serpent of luminous wounds that you call the Milky Way seemed to be resting its head there, very far away.[41]

I stayed looking for a time, knowing I'd have to climb up that wretched hill to see this dawn, that the mud, the slips, the stones that hurt my flesh inside and out, the tired lungs incapable of pulling in the necessary air, the cramped legs, the anguished clinging to the rifle walking-stick to free my boots from the imprisoning mud, the feeling of loneliness and desolation, the weight I was carrying on my back (which I came to know later, was only a token, since in reality there would always be three times that or more; anyway, that "token"! weighed tons to me), that all of that—and much more that would come later—is what had made it possible for that moon, those stars, and the Milky Way to be there and no other place . . .

Perhaps you are asking what happened to my intention to turn back and abandon the guerrilla life, and you might suppose that the vision of that first dawn in the mountains made me abandon my idea of fleeing, lifted my morale and firmed my revolutionary conscience. Well, you are wrong. I put my plan into operation and went down the hill. What happened is I mistook which side to go down. Instead of going down the slope that would take me back to the road and from there to "civilization," I went down the side that took me deeper into the rain forest and that led me to another hill, and another and another . . .

That was fifteen years ago. Since then I have kept mistaking which side to go down, and every August 6 keeps giving birth to a special dawn.[42]

Of course, one cannot take this account completely at face value. Marcos, in places, is clearly indulging in rhetorical license. Although the going must indeed have been very tough[43]—I have climbed Chiapan hills carrying a loaded rucksack and found it grueling despite being relatively young (30) and fit—it is nonetheless unlikely that a dedicated revolutionary, who had been in physical training precisely to prepare himself for this moment,[44] and whose hero from childhood had been Che Guevara, would have felt more than the merest twinge of doubt as to whether he was cut out for guerrilla life. (There may, however, be a kernel of truth in Marcos' claim that he went down the wrong side of the hill since one of his former comrades maintain that "Marcos was a bad explorer: if he didn't carry a compass or if nobody accompanied him, he got himself lost.")[45] Rather, Marcos is here playing the antihero, attempting to re-create the candid self-mocking, occasionally philosophical, accounts of guerrilla life provided by Guevara.[46] What separated Marcos from other cadres sent from the capital to Chiapas for their jungle training was that he remained there, whereas the vast majority of the others just did the basic minimum and returned almost immediately to city life. As former Subcommander Daniel observes, "Those that held up stayed, those that didn't were able to go back."[47] Marcos not only stayed and persevered, he flourished, making the mountains and jungle his home, "learning how to hunt, handle weapons, march, sleep in a hammock—nobody could sleep in a hammock—and practice the military training Gérman had taught him."[48]

It is evident that the transition from an urban, intellectual lifestyle in the capital to that of a rustic, *guerrillero* existence was not easy for Marcos. He concedes that "for a *ladino*, the Lacandón jungle is the worst thing that can happen to you."[49] In a video interview, he confides:

> It was a nightmare. Imagine a person who comes from an urban culture, one of the world's largest cities, with a university education, accustomed to city life. It's like landing on another planet. The language, the surroundings are new. You're seen as an alien from outer space. Everything tells you: "Leave. This is a mistake. You don't belong in this place." And, it's said in a foreign tongue, but they let you know: the people, the way they act; the weather when it rains; the sunshine; the earth, when it turns to mud; the diseases; the insects; homesickness. You're being told: "You don't belong here." If that's not a nightmare, what is?[50]

Daniel tells us that the FLN's second-in-command, Rodrigo, "never imagined that Guillén could endure the jungle, he was too bourgeois, but he surprised everyone."[51] Prior to Marcos, Che Guevara[52], Mario Payeras,[53] and Tomás Borge[54] had described the rigors of rural guerrilla life: heat and thirst, hunger, insects, snakes, disquieting nocturnal sounds, diarrhea, the sense of total isolation, intermittent downpours, arduous physical exertions, etc.[55] As Marcos succinctly put it: "Life in the mountains is a bitch, a real bitch."[56]

8. The Wilderness Years

Initially the guerrillas lived in the remote mountain regions. Even when Marcos arrived they led a largely itinerant life; Marcos echoes Elisa's words, describing the *foco* as "a type of nomadic guerrilla."[1] At this stage they shunned all contact with local people both from fear of being betrayed by them and because they felt that they were not themselves ready politically and militarily to offer the skills required by the locals. This keeping apart from the indigenous communities had the effect of making the *La Pesadilla* camp even more of a "nightmare." As Marcos tells us: "Really, it was a nightmare . . . with only this small politicized group, which did not even amount to ten indigenous, without any possibility of support from the communities."[2] The mountains were perceived as magical by indigenous Chiapans, who seldom ventured into them from fear of encountering wild beasts or ghosts, and were thus an ideal location in which to undertake clandestine activities. And yet, at the same time came certain costs. Marcos tells us that "This first stage, was a very difficult stage, very solitary . . . At this stage this uninhabited mountain sector was still a place of death, a place of ghosts."[3] He reiterates the theme of solitude in his interviews with Le Bot[4] and later with Avilés and Minà, in which he confessed that in the mountains they experienced "great solitude, in which we were all pushed to as far as we could go: bodily, emotionally, and intellectually."[5]

Elsewhere, Marcos comments on the physical privations of life in *las montañas*: "The mountain was rejecting us. The mountain made us hungry, sick. It pushed rain and cold on us. The aggression of animals, insects, all of this was saying: 'Go, get out of here, you have no business here.'"[6] It also appears that the mountains tested Marcos and the others psychologically: "The only thing that allowed you to survive was the hope that something would come from everything we were doing. It was an irrational expectation, totally loony, because there was nothing, absolutely nothing, that would validate what we were doing—not world news, nor anything."[7] Indeed, the mountains appear to have made a big impact on Marcos. A collection of his utterances compiled by Marta Durán de Huerta and published under the title *Yo, Marcos* contains an entire chapter dedicated to and entitled *La montaña*.[8]

This early but crucial time in the mountains was when the guerrillas, from necessity, acquired their survival skills. As Marcos recollects:

> We had to undertake exploration, locate places where there was game, where there was water, a type of nomadic guerrilla that seeks more than anything to make itself part of the terrain. . . . We learned how to live there, to identify animals, to hunt them, to dress the meat, to prepare it for cooking, also to eat it . . . and we became part of the mountains.[9]

He continued the theme in a subsequent interview, stating:

> When we arrived in the mountains we had no support in the villages, you finished the food and you were screwed. Then, we ate everything: opossums, rodents and vipers, we learned how to eat snake. . . . We also ate rats. We took urine when the routes we walked were very long. . . . This is the part no reporters ask about, truly. They don't ask us about this epoch in which we were guerrillas.[10]

(The failure of journalists to focus on this initial stage is something that Marcos evidently feels strongly about. It is important, because if one ignores it, it is too easy to dismiss him, as do de la Grange and Rico, as a self-aggrandizing adventurer.[11] As Marcos takes pains to reiterate: "The journalists that come ask you: 'What did you say to Camacho, and what about Salinas,' 'How did you attack San Cristóbal,' 'What does it feel like to be a starlet?' and other such rubbish along these lines. But nobody asks about the time when we didn't have ski-masks, when we didn't have anything."[12])

Marcos admits he learned his survival skills from the three indigenous *campesinos* (Javier, Jorge, and Frank) who formed part of the initial group of six which had arrived in November 1983: "They taught me everything. . . . They taught me to live in the mountains; to hunt; to track animals; to recognize them; to recognize poisonous plants and edible ones, ones which store water—because there are places where there is no water and you have to get water out of the plant; and about the noises of the night."[13]

One of the biggest problems in the mountains was food. Simply getting hold of it was difficult and time-consuming. First an animal had to be located, tracked, hunted, and killed. Then the carcass had to be butchered and the meat cleaned, prepared, and cooked, a slow process over a small wood fire. Frequently once eaten such food caused attacks of diarrhea, and any food left over and stored ran the risk of being eaten by rodents.[14] There was also the problem of sugar craving. The body burns many calories in extreme physical exertion and in trying to stay warm during the freezing highland nights. It then begins to crave the "quick fix" that sugar provides. Marcos recollects how "in the mountains we talked a lot about sugar, it's what we spoke of most . . . the physical toll requires much sugar . . . it was an obsession for those of us who came from the city."[15] He then recounts conversations and dreams about ice cream and other unobtainable sweet-tasting snacks.

Another major problem was the way in which the mountains dictated the guerrillas' daily routine. As Marcos observes: "You come from the city accustomed to being able to manage your time with relative autonomy. You are able to extend the day well into the night, to read, to study, to do many activities when night has already fallen. But not in the mountains."[16] Darkness descends in the mountains as early as 5 P.M. and tends to be all encompassing. It puts an end to all activities and can seem endless, with daybreak as much as twelve hours away. There is little constructive to do and frustration and boredom set in.

Finally, there was the problem of isolation, not just from one's friends and family back home or from the local inhabitants, but from the world at large.[17] In terms of access to information, Marcos relates: "When we were in the mountains . . . we couldn't find out about anything. We could only get hold of short-wave radios, Radio Havana, The Voice of America, Radio Exterior of Spain, Radio France International. These were the stations we listened to; we did not know well what was happening at large."[18] Elsewhere Marcos reiterates this, adding, "And at the national level we had almost no news; the little that we did know was that which filtered down to us from the foreign news, and that was very little."[19] This is perhaps somewhat of an exaggeration; after all, we know the guerrillas had an urban contact in Mexico City, Silvia Fernández (alias Gabriela),[20] through whom they liaised with Germán. So, too, as noted above, Marcos elsewhere tells us that the guerrillas had two "runners" "who 'went up and down' to the city with mail and for supplies."[21] Contact would have been kept to a minimum for the sake of security, and Marcos himself tells us that "as the logistical line came from the city we had to wait months for things to arrive,"[22] but it existed. (A few years later, as we shall see in chapter 10, the guerrillas were able to gain much greater access to news when they established fixed base camps and installed televisions in them.) It is, however, likely that the guerrillas deliberately cut themselves off from the rest of the world, choosing to cocoon themselves and any new recruits in a revolutionary atmosphere in order to boost morale by convincing themselves that what they were doing was not anachronistic or atypical of the region. Rather, restricted information was a choice, not a necessity, as former Subcommander Daniel observes: "In the jungle the only thing we heard was short-wave radio, especially Radio Havana, and also Radio Sandino from Nicaragua and the Farabundo Martí from the Salvadoran guerrillas. At that time the idea of socialism was not so distant, even less so with Radio Havana on all day."[23]

Thus, the initial stage of the *foco*, as Marcos notes, was spent in the mountains "training, carrying out military practice, studying, discussing politics, preparing food, doing guard duty at night and resting by day";[24] in short, preparing the *foco*, transforming it from a small group of mainly urban intellectuals, their heads full of political and military theory, into a disciplined guerrilla group inured to the hardships of guerrilla life. Marcos notes, "We began to learn about weapons . . . the first stage was pure survival . . . we had to learn how to survive in the mountains, to get the mountains to accept us."[25] So, too, Marcos tells us, in these early days, "The political work was above all internal, we did not work outside [of the group]."[26] Only later would the *foco* have the moral authority to approach local communities and ask to be heard by them; and only then would they themselves have acquired the practical experience necessary to have something to offer the indigenous population.

Ideologically, the guerrillas had a very clear idea of what was required of them, Marcos recounting that "we kept repeating to ourselves all day, all night, 'We are good. This is what we have to do,'" adding "there was nothing outside of us to confirm that what we were doing made sense."[27] Elsewhere he notes, "Our conception was . . . what is necessary is a group of strong men and women, with ideological and physical strength, with the resistance to carry out this task"; adding, "Our conception was that we were few but of high quality. . . . Well, I'm not saying that we were that high quality, but we sure were few."[28] The size of the group must indeed have been small—less than ten. Of the six who had originally arrived in November 1983, one had died in a shooting accident (possibly Jorge) and one (Germán) had returned to Mexico City in May 1984. Pedro had joined the initial six soon on, since he had scouted the "Nightmare" camp in the early weeks of 1984, as had an indigenous Chol recruit called Benjamín. Marcos then joined the *foco* in August, along with a female Chol (Cecilia) and an (unidentified) male Tzotzil (possibly Josué or Paco). Thus, Marcos tells us: "The first time we celebrated the anniversary on 17 November, 1984 . . . there were nine of us."[29]

Marcos rose rapidly through the ranks of this tiny group, becoming sub-lieutenant, lieutenant, and first captain in rapid succession. In less than three months between his arriving in Chiapas and the celebration of the *foco*'s first anniversary in November, he had risen to the rank of second captain.[30] In October, no doubt in line with his new rank, Marcos, dressed in civilian clothes so as to pass himself off as a tourist to Lake Miramar,[31] had attended a meeting at the *ejido* of Las Tazas with other FLN members, most notably Panchón (an agronomist from the Monterrey cell), in order to discuss agricultural techniques and the need for political organization with a handful of local community leaders.[32] Present at the meeting, for example, was Lázaro Hernández. He had worked as a catechist attending the Chiapas Indigenous Council (and was therefore known to Bishop Samuel Ruiz), and was simultaneously the secretary of Quiptic, a predominantly indigenous peasant organization that had been established in 1975 in the wake of the National Indigenous Council of the previous year.[33] Hernández would go on to have close relations with the guerrillas, helping to introduce them into indigenous communities and peasant organizations and even joining their ranks under the nom de guerre Jesús.[34]

It was also around this time that Marcos, again as part of the duties attached to his higher rank, began to take charge of training new recruits. He briefly describes what must have been one of his first training exercises: "Ana María and Mario are with me on this expedition, ten years before the dawn of January. The two have just joined the guerrillas. I am an infantry lieutenant,[35] and it is my turn to teach them what others taught me: to live in the mountains."[36] Given that Marcos informs us in a later communiqué that Ana María joined the guerrillas "in December 1984,"[37] we can date this training exercise to around this time.

This training mission proved highly significant since it was now that Marcos was first to encounter "Old Antonio." (Some have doubted the authenticity of Old Antonio, claiming that he is one of Marcos's literary constructs, but his existence is confirmed by the former Subcommander-turned-informer Daniel, who, true to form in never missing an opportunity to denigrate Marcos, informs us that Old Antonio was "an assassin . . . [who] arrived in the last community, in the furthest reaches of the jungle, because he was fleeing after having assassinated someone.")[38] Relating how he led an expedition in which he was teaching Ana María and Mario "to live in the mountains," Marcos tells us that "on the preceding day" he "had bumped into 'Old Antonio' for the first time."[39] They had lied to one another as to their true purposes in being in that spot in the jungle— Marcos claimed to be hunting, Old Antonio that he was going to check his maize field—and had then quickly parted. The next day both Marcos and Old Antonio doubled-back on themselves and reappeared at the same spot. They soon began to chat, discussing Emiliano Zapata, Pancho Villa, the Mexican Revolution, and indigenous folklore. Old Antonio then told Marcos "The Story of Questions" and made him a present of a very old photograph of Zapata. This was to mark the start of a close and important relationship between these two men. The first village to open its arms to the Zapatistas was Antonio's, the old man having smoothed the way for their acceptance (see chapter 9). He was also to feature in many of Marcos's communiqués after the 1994 uprising, in particular those containing folk-loric or didactic tales.

9. First Contact

Throughout 1985 the guerrillas, whose ranks Marcos informs us stood at eight in January,[1] attempted to make contact with local communities. This reaching out to local communities was perhaps spurred on by fear of what Marcos years later described as "the ghost of Che," and in particular "the ghost of Ñancahuazú."[2] Che died isolated and betrayed by a local *campesino*, in a corner of Bolivia, having utterly failed to win over the region's local inhabitants. A similar occurrence had even taken place within the FLN's own recent history when, in early 1974, it had sent a cell to the Chiapas jungle to establish a *foco* which subsequently failed to win any local support and was betrayed by the *campesinos*. The memory of this was no doubt fresh in Germán and Elisa's minds and they would have taken pains to inform Marcos of this earlier failure and the reasons behind it. Evidently Che's fate, and that of the earlier FLN *foco*, was not lost on Marcos, who explains in one interview, "If we had continued with that form of organization we would still be deep in the rain forest with 15 or 20 guerrillas."[3] In a later interview he expands on this theme, arguing that:

> If we didn't manage to enter into contact with the communities, with the indigenous of the region, we would not be able to survive, although we could maintain ourselves in material terms, by means of hunting wild animals, we would have been practicing a sort of absurd revolutionary interbreeding. We had to be in contact with the neighboring population, not only out of logistical considerations but also for political ones, because when it came to it we were seeking to be a revolutionary movement of all these people.[4]

Thus, some influential indigenous leaders were approached and were impressed at what they heard, subsequently pledging to offer their support. Several among them belonged to the militant *campesino* group the Unión de Uniones. Its president, Francisco López, a Chol from Sabanilla, threw in his support, and it was perhaps through him that Yolanda (also known as Ana María), who was also from Sabanilla, and several other indigenous recruits joined Marcos in the mountains two months later in December. A special relationship was established between the guerrillas and the Sabanilla Chols. As one veteran indigenous Zapatista observes, "First they [the guerrillas] gained [the *ejido* of] Tierra y Libertad: it was easy because they were all Chols from Sabanilla."[5] This strategy whereby the ladinos in the group relied more heavily on their indigenous comrades who were able to forge personal and family links in the local communities, would in time yield great dividends.[6] As Marcos later explained:

> The indigenous of this intermediary group chatted with their families, who were also indigenous, Tzeltals, Tzotzils, Chols, Tojolobals, and these families decided to send their youngest sons and daughters to the mountains to become guerrillas. There we had this political-military group with an indigenous ingredient within it.[7]

At this stage, however, "everything was very secretive."[8] Fortunately for Marcos and the others, their desire to incorporate the *campesinos* into a military command structure coincided with the populace's desire to arm in order to protect itself from governmental repression and the "White Guards" (paramilitaries) of the more extreme bourgeoisie. Marcos candidly explains this relationship in some detail:

> The group which . . . acts as the intermediary between the Zapatista army and the communities, this group of politicized indigenous, begins to speak with some leaders of the indigenous communities who they know about armed struggle. This coincided with an expansion in "White Guards" and their repressive actions, above all in the Jungle and the North of Chiapas, where the indigenous are naturally setting up self-defense groups. . . . It was a very practical, very immediate interest, one of survival, that allowed this first contact between the indigenous communities and the political-military group. . . . There is a kind of exchange: "we teach them to fight and they help us to obtain supplies"— that was our difficulty—"and to transport these things." . . . We gave them training and military instruction in exchange for them helping to transport food or them selling us maize, beans, rice, sugar, batteries, things that we needed. We gave them money and they bought these things for us. This gave rise to a kind of relationship of exchange which also began to have a political and cultural exchange.[9]

Thus there was no need to cajole a reluctant population into bearing arms since the needs and desire of both the *campesinos* and the guerrillas were fully complementary. Of course, Marcos and the other cadres always had an eye to the future when they would need to convince this self-defense force to become more active and more aggressive. As the Subcommander freely admits:[10]

> On the one hand, there were those [within the EZLN] who hoped that armed action would bring about a revolution and a change of power, in this case the fall of the governing party and the ascension of another party, but that in the end it would be the people who took power. On the other hand, there were the more immediate expectations of the indigenous people here. For them, the necessity of armed struggle was more as a form of defense against groups of very violent, aggressive, and powerful ranchers. And thus we tried to convince them of the necessity of a broader political struggle.[11]

However, this change from defense to offense was a bridge that could be crossed later; for the present, there was no need to reveal to the local communities the *foco*'s grand design of taking on the Mexican Federal Army and seizing power through violent revolution. In short, these local self-defense forces could be formed within a rigid military command structure into a well-armed, well-trained, body of fighters capable of going on the offensive, without its members realizing that this was the ultimate aim of its leadership. All the while Marcos and the others would be politically educating the recruits so as to more easily sell them the idea of becoming an aggressive force in the future. The political and military groundwork was being laid well in advance. All that was required was for the threat of repression by the government or the "White Guards" to be maintained, and maintained it was. The year 1985 saw shootings and other attacks on Enrique Vázquez, a Tojolabal leader of the Unified Socialist Party of Mexico (PSUM); Florentino Pérez, a *campesino* leader; Margarito Ruiz, secretary general of the Independent Confederation of Rural Workers and Peasants (CIOA) peasant organization; and Andulio Gálvez, state deputy for the PSUM. Moreover, on 11 August alone four communities were evicted by state police.[12] So numerous and blatant were these and other attacks on leading indigenous or *campesino* figures—there were at least twenty instances—that Amnesty International published a bulletin on them in 1985 and a more extensive follow-up report the following year.[13]

As well as politicizing and militarizing the local inhabitants, the *foco* also undertook public health works in the region. As Marcos tells us in one of his early communiqués, "We saw many people die, including many children.[14] They died in our arms while we were carrying out the health campaign that the government didn't undertake, and we had to do ourselves."[15] An indigenous Zapatista paints a similar story, telling us that Marcos and the others "helped the population with medicine and advice."[16] Just as the Cuban guerrillas had won over rural communities in the Sierra Maestra by giving them haircuts, dental checks, and medical treatment, so now the EZLN sought to win chiapaneco hearts and minds. Where Castro had been aided in this endeavor by the Argentine doctor, Che Guevara, with whom he would develop a close friendship, Marcos was aided by a young indigenous nurse from Sabanilla called Yolanda or sometimes Ana María, who had joined the guerrillas as early as December 1984 (see chapter 8) and whom Marcos would later marry in a jungle ceremony in 1987 (see chapter 11).

The year 1985 also saw the arrival in the guerrilla camp of another FLN cadre using the nom de guerre Daniel.[17] He was none other than Salvador Morales, a former teaching assistant in Rafael's department at UAM. He had joined the FLN's ranks shortly after Rafael while at UAM. Indeed, Morales himself tells us that "from the end of 1979 he [Guillén] was helping in the safe houses, while I had scarcely begun [in the movement]."[18] He arrived at a crucial time, one in which, as he observes, the guerrillas "began to leave [the jungle] to make political contacts in the communities."[19] (Initially at least, he remained in Chiapas only briefly, going back to Mexico City in 1985 to work alongside Germán, before returning, with the rank of Subcommander, to Chiapas three years later during a special anniversary parade held in the jungle in November 1988.)[20] This increased and sustained contact with select local communities is attested to by Marcos himself,[21] who informs us that "in 1985,[22] for the first time, we took over a village," adding modestly that this consisted of, "a few plots of corn, some seedlings, a couple of banana trees, a small coffee plantation, and several little *champada* trees." Marcos tells us that "this was the village of 'Old Antonio,' who had invited us to visit his *ejido*."[23] Marcos, at that time a Second Captain, recorded the details of this first visit in his logbook, dating the encounter to the last week of September. He notes how he gave a talk to the villagers, which either Mario or Moisés (the entry simply reads "M.") translated. After, he and the other cadres carried out military instruction, talks on politics, and medical consultations, before finally sitting down together with the villagers to eat tortillas and beans and to drink coffee.[24] This strategy of approaching the communities indirectly through a respected indigenous elder was to prove very effective.

The EZLN was beginning to extend its influence in the region. In an internal FLN publication of November 1985 Marcos writes: "We left the *Comandancia* [headquarters] with the task of undertaking an exploration with the object of planting a group of combatants in a new zone,"[25] elaborating elsewhere: "I was Second Captain, we were in the 'Sierra del Almendro,' and the mother column had stayed in another mountain range."[26]

Nearly two decades on, looking back to that November, and in particular the celebration of the EZLN's second anniversary, Marcos recollects:

> I had three insurgents under my command. If I have my math right, there were four of us in that camp [called Watapil]. We celebrated the anniversary with tostadas, coffee, *pinole* with sugar and a *cojola* we'd killed that morning.
>
> There were songs and poems. One of us would sing or recite, and the other three applauded with a level of boredom worthy of a better cause. When it was my turn, I told them—in a solemn speech, without any arguments other than the mosquitoes and solitude which surrounded us—that one day there would be thousands of us, and that our word would go around the world. The other three agreed that the tostada was moldy and that it had most certainly sickened me and that was why I was delirious. I remember it rained that night.[27]

Meanwhile, far away in the capital an event occurred which had a profound effect on Mexican society at large. At 7:17 A.M. on 19 September 1985, an earthquake measuring 8.1 on the Richter scale struck Mexico City, killing at least 10,000 people and injuring 50,000. Faced with such overwhelming destruction not even the seemingly omnipotent PRI state government, hamstrung as it was by inefficiency and corruption, could offer an effective response. An NACLA *Report on the Americas* noted:

> Neither the government nor the community organizations of the ruling PRI proved capable of organizing rescue actions, post-earthquake relief or housing construction. All these tasks were left to non-governmental organizations, informal neighborhood groups and the parish. In the process, community organizations—both church groups and the spontaneously created groups of victims—forged new links with international relief donors.[28]

Monsiváis concludes that "the experience of the earthquake gave the term 'civil society' an unexpected credibility."[29] It was "civil society" that was to come to the rescue of the Zapatistas in January 1994, compelling the government to pursue a peaceful solution to the uprising and to which Marcos would appeal throughout the rest of the 1990s. His communiqué entitled "Civil Society That So Perturbs" (19 September 1996) pays homage to civil society and recounts the part played by the earthquake in its formation:

> It's been eleven years since a new political and social force emerged as a result of the government's inability to confront the problems of the earthquake that shook the capital. This new force proved that it could respond to destruction with creativity, to chaos with organization, to death with life. . . . While the government vacillated between false promises and stealing humanitarian aid, Civil Society organized itself, by itself, to revive and rebuild a city that, amid all the pain, quickly reminded itself that it's nothing without its inhabitants. . . . This new strength . . . of Civil Society that so perturbs the government leaders, today gives hope that it's possible to rebuild the country.[30]

In Chiapas, cause for hope was scant. In October, a demonstration in the state capital, Tuxtla Gutiérrez, by the peasant organization Coordinadora de Luchas de Chiapas was violently dispersed by police;[31] and Andulio Gálvez, an advisor to the CIOAC peasant organization who had recently been elected to the local congress as a deputy for the Unified Socialist Party of Mexico, was assassinated.[32] Unsurprisingly, the same month saw the publication of an article stating: "The Chiapas area is considered especially vulnerable to insurrection."[33]

10. Promotion and Expansion

In January 1986, Marcos, aided by Lázaro Hernández (alias Jesús), organized the First Worker-Peasant Meeting of the FLN, designed to forge links between local Chiapan peasants and workers from cities in the north of the country. The topic for discussion was how the two could unite to overthrow their common oppressor, the bourgeois government. The meeting lasted for three days. In addition to the workers and local *campesinos* the meeting was attended by Comandantes Elisa and Rodolfo who came down from Mexico City. It was housed deep in the jungle in a new compound that contained an assembly hall with two platforms capable of holding almost a hundred people, named "the *Compañero* César Yáñez Hall" after Germán's brother "Pedro." There was also an adjoining dining hall. After the delegates had left, the compound became a new camp for the guerrillas, called *El Encuentro* ("The Meeting") in honor of this event. In its construction and its staging, this event would stand Marcos in good stead for the hosting years later of the Zapatistas's National Democratic Convention in Aguascalientes (6–9 August 1994) and the Intercontinental Encuentro for Humanity and against Neoliberalism (1996). As Tello Díaz notes, "It was the first time that Marcos revealed his sense of theatre on the Jungle stage."[1]

The start of 1986 also appears to have witnessed the FLN approaching El Salvador's guerrillas for aid. Drawing on an interview with the former Salvadoran guerrilla leader, Ana Guadalupe Martínez (on 5 May 1995, in Cartagena, Colombia), Oppenheimer writes:

> In early 1986, a group of Mexicans who identified themselves as members of a new Zapatista rebel movement in southern Mexico had approached El Salvador's Farabundo Martí National Liberation Forces in search of military training and logistics support. A meeting with two top officers of the Salvadoran guerrilla group was arranged to take place in Managua, Nicaragua.[2]

This overture, and one to Cuba, however, was rebuffed. As Ana Guadalupe explains:

> We told them it was crazy, that there was nothing we could do for them. We would not help a rebel movement in the only country with which we had good relations. From there they went on to Cuba. A few weeks later [Communist Party America's department head Manuel] Piñeiro told us at a meeting in Havana that the Mexicans had gone to them, and that he had turned them down as well. For Cuba, messing up with Mexico would amount to committing a political hara-kiri, Piñeiro told us.[3]

It would be interesting to know whether or not Marcos formed part of these delegations to the El Salvadorans and Cubans, but unfortunately nothing of any certainty can be said on the matter. Possibly Marcos was still too low ranking at this stage to have been sent on such a mission—he probably was not promoted to Subcommander until later in the year. More likely is that higher-ranking, veteran leaders, such as Germán, Rodrigo, Gabriela, and Elisa were chosen as the FLN's ambassadors. In any event, the El Salvadorans's and Cubans's reluctance to sponsor an insurgency in the only country in Latin America whose government looked favorably on revolutionaries abroad may have been irksome in the short term, but it did allow Marcos years later to claim proudly in one of his first communiqués that the EZLN had received no foreign backing and therefore was, contrary to what the government was then asserting, a truly homegrown, Mexican revolutionary movement.[4]

However, despite the FLN's efforts to nationalize (and perhaps even internationalize) their operations, at this time the Chiapan branch of the organization was still by and large moving and training clandestinely, avoiding direct contact with the majority of neighboring communities. Marcos reflects on a mission he undertook on 31 December 1985: "I waited for a connection to help me cross some settlements where there were no compañeros. The crossing had to be by night. With dawn came January and 1986. It was still a time to be hidden, to conceal ourselves from those we would become part of later."[5]

By this time the *foco's* ranks had been increased to around twelve by new recruits and other FLN cadres from the cities. Marcos tells us that morale at this time was high within the *foco*: "We felt invincible . . . that with our pure conviction we could defeat any army."[6] Elsewhere he elaborates on the *foco's* confidence, relating that "in 1986 we had already grown to twelve, and we could conquer the world, or so we told ourselves. We were able to eat the world like it was an apple."[7] However, this dozen suffered erosion, Marcos informing us that "the twelve quickly became ten; two died; five are elsewhere."[8] This claim, made in two interviews given nine months apart,[9] that the guerrillas numbered "twelve," is of particular importance for those intent on attempting to ascertain the *foco*'s composition at this point in the Zapatistas's development. The Subcommander claims that "of the first six, three were *mestizo* and three were indigenous; of the twelve from 1986, one was *mestizo* and the other eleven were indigenous. Only I remained of the *mestizos*. Later two others came up."[10] However, Marcos is almost certainly not telling us the whole story here. What, for example, had happened to Elisa and Pedro? Elisa did not leave Chiapas permanently until 1988. There are two possible explanations. One is that Elisa spent some of her time traveling to and from Mexico City liaising with Germán and staying at a safe house in San Cristóbal[11] training cadres, allowing Marcos to count himself as the only mestizo permanently stationed in the jungle. (It should be noted that even Marcos sometimes traveled outside the region going on arms runs, meeting with cadres from the Villa Front in the Sierra Tarahumara, and even on rare occasions visiting his family in Tampico.) The other explanation is that Marcos is deliberately omitting mention of Elisa in order to bolster his image as the only mestizo who had stuck it out in Chiapas and to obscure the fact that he was not the local commander but rather the subordinate of a woman. Marcos's claim also fails to take into account Pedro, "who along with Marcos and Daniel was one of the three *ladinos* [non-indigenous] who formed the nucleus of the EZLN."[12] According to Tello Díaz, Pedro remained permanently stationed in the jungle, leaving only once for a very brief trip to Mexico City almost at the start of his days in the jungle to receive treatment for a skin disease (leishmania) he had contracted from parasites.[13] Moreover, Major Moisés informs us that he met Pedro in a safe house in the capital where the latter was recuperating from his skin disease, but that Pedro had already returned to Chiapas by the time that Moisés himself went back there in 1985.[14] In 1986, then, Pedro appears to have been in Chiapas. Marcos's omission of Pedro is curious given the latter's importance and also that, as we shall see, he was very close to and fond of Pedrito ("[dear little] Pedro"), as he called him.

Most of the eleven indigenous guerrillas had been recruited from friends or family members of the original three indigenous guerrillas, who in turn recruited other relatives and acquaintances.[15] As Marcos says, "Initially we began to go down the family line: the father recruited his children, the children their brothers and sisters, then to the cousins and to the uncles, and in this way it flowed."[16] From then on there was a fairly steady acceleration of membership. As Lieutenant Norma points out, "There are times when there are three siblings who join, four siblings, six or eight siblings who join up."[17] However, these extended family members and friends were frequently of a different nature to the initial members of the group. The first three indigenous members of the original *foco* and the eleven members Marcos refers to above were all highly politicized,[18] with many of them either belonging to Slop—a peasant organization whose name means "root" in Tzeltal, which Bishop Ruiz had helped to create in 1980 along with the Ocosingo parish priest Pablo Iribarren, in order to offset the Maoists's influence in the region which at that time was strong—or at least coming from the Avellanal Canyon where Slop was most influential. Many of the new recruits, on the other hand, were *campesinos* pure and simple and had not been politicized in any way. The FLN set about remedying this and, in addition, broadening their experiences and horizons by teaching them trades that would be useful to their communities and the guerrilla group (such as agronomy, tailoring, soldering, radio operation, cobbling, etc.). Adolescent indigenous recruits were frequently sent to San Cristóbal, the state capital Tuxtla Gutiérrez, and even to Mexico City to receive political, military, medical, and technical training. One of de la Grange's and Rico's sources, identified simply as Antonio, relates his own experience:

> [When] I was fourteen . . . some Tzeltal *campesinos* came to speak with us. They approached the more playful among us. We went to the river to bathe with them. One day they offered to take me to study cobbling in Mexico City. To others they spoke of studying agronomy, radio operating, soldering, tailoring and medicine. They gave us free food and board. We went in their van a few days later. We were ten boys from different regions.[19]

He continues his story, telling us that the boys first spent a brief time in a safe house in Tuxtla Gutiérrez, being instructed physically and politically by Germán's wife Lucía, who he describes as "in her fifties, [who] had been in Tlatelolco Plaza in 1968 when the students had been massacred . . . [and who] carried a 9mm pistol and explained how to arm and disarm it."[20] According to Antonio, Lucía told him "that they were preparing us to help the indigenous communities."[21] He remembers that his time there "was very good"; he recollects how "they taught us to make dinner and called us their little sons and took care of us."[22] They were then asked if they wanted to continue their studies and, after a positive reply, the boys spent seven months in Mexico City, moving to three different safe houses during that time. There, in the capital, Comandante Germán, a Chol Lieutenant Jorge, Paula, and others, instructed them in unarmed combat, economics, Mexican history, leftist politics, and many other disciplines. While there they also visited workshops to learn certain practical trades and were taken to Mexico City's museums in order to learn Mexican history and culture.

So, too, more local venues were employed for the instruction of promising (part-time) militia members and for the preparation of selected local inhabitants for guerrilla life. In one communiqué Marcos tells of a safe house which was used to prepare cadres politically that was constructed in Tojolabal territory at the site which was later named "Aguascalientes."[23] Marcos writes, "That little house was built far from anyone, so no one would see those first clandestine Tojolabales who joined the EZLN. There they held meetings, they studied, and they stored the tortillas and the beans they would send into the mountains to nourish the insurgents."[24]

Secrecy remained of paramount importance since nonrecruited members of nearby communities continued to pose a potential security risk and therefore still had to be treated with caution. As Marcos points out:

> We had sympathizers in different villages, but clandestine, they did not say publicly that they supported an armed group because there was already a rumor in the villages of the jungle that there was an armed group, but for some they were bandits, for others they were part of the ghosts stories and lost gods that they have in the mountains.[25]

These sympathizers in the villages predominantly provided information and food. As one former Zapatista puts it, "When you had gained a community they helped you with food, and so little by little we were expanding until we gained the canyons of the Lacandón jungle."[26] However, because this all took place clandestinely, initially it caused frictions within the communities, since many thought the rebels were engaged in witchcraft or other practices harmful to the community. Why else, the other villagers asked, would these individuals be acting suspiciously, moving around at night, journeying into the mountains, forever acting in secrecy?

This tension evaporated as more and more *campesinos* were taken into the sympathizers' confidence and the Zapatistas became common knowledge. Comandante Tacho describes the process and, in particular, the importance of women in it. He notes: "We trained women who were like political delegates . . . we would come into town with them and have secret meetings with them . . . then, when we had two, or three, or four *compañe-ras* in one town, we would put them in charge of seeing who else they could get to work with us, and little by little we would grow, until finally a whole town was with us."[27] In time, as Marcos notes, these new recruits "began to speak more and more, and they managed to become a majority in some villages, and in others, all of them were Zapatistas."[28] As the guerrillas entered villages, the *campesinos* began to see with their own eyes what had only been rumored: myth was revealed as reality, Marcos asserting: "The first reaction of the villagers was one of respect: 'These [guerrillas] sleep where I do not dare to sleep, and live worse than I.' And yes, all the villagers knew that the guerrillas live worse than any impoverished *campesino* in the region. And this allowed them to listen to what we had to say."[29] Marcos's fellow Zapatistas concur. For example, Tomás, a veteran indigenous Zapatista, tells us "to be in the mountains is to be in the shit, and Marcos endured the same as us."[30] Two other indigenous Zapatistas, Lieutenant Avelino and Sublieutenant Nicodemo, agree, explaining: "Marcos is not poor, but he sees and realizes the problems of the indigenous. He has a clear conscience, walking for days in the rain, eating the same as us, and if there is no food, he doesn't eat either. He suffers like us."[31] This is echoed by a female Zapatista supporter in La Realidad, who comments: "Whatever the poor eat, he eats. When he is here, is he going to eat better food? What we eat, he eats. If we eat [only] vegetables, he does too. We don't believe he is from the city."[32]

Unfortunately, what the guerrillas had to say was at first literally incomprehensible to the predominantly indigenous villagers. A significant proportion of Chiapas's indigenous people do not understand Spanish, speaking only their own language. The guerrilla leadership, for its part, did not speak the indigenous languages. As Elisa herself admits, "Before going to the jungle I had intended to learn Tzotzil but I dropped it as a student. So, I spoke in Spanish and asked someone to translate for me. At times it wasn't easy. For example, they had no equivalent for the word Liberty."[33] So, too, initially at least, Marcos was ignorant of these languages and found having to confront them something of a shock.[34] As he confessed to one interviewer, in the early days he would encounter indigenous *campesinos* who would "start saying all sorts of crap about me. They would just start laughing in front of me, making fun of me, and it was real tough not knowing what they were saying."[35] This spurred him into learning at least some words and phrases. As he observes, "The first thing you gotta learn are the cuss words, for survival's sake."[36] There is considerable debate even now as to the extent of Marcos's acquisition of indigenous languages. His detractors claim that Marcos speaks almost no Tzeltal, Tzotzil, or Chol, instead relying on his indigenous comandantes to translate for him. The former Subcommander Daniel, for example, insists that Marcos merely "learned to express himself imitating the Tzeltal language: [Major] Moisés translated."[37] This testimony should be set against the fact that Marcos is clearly fairly capable linguistically, possessing a superb command of his own language, a by no means inconsiderable ability in English,[38] and a modicum of French. Is it really plausible that such a man, who had a very real incentive to study these indigenous languages and who has spent two decades interacting with indigenous peoples in their own surroundings, would have picked up no more than a smattering of their tongue?

The guerrillas' message was rendered more unintelligible by the choice of references it employed, being highly charged with Marxist rhetoric. Marcos relates:

> Imperialism, social crisis, the correlation of force with opportunity, these things were not understood. . . . They were very honest. You asked them, "Do you understand?," and they told you, "No." They said to you that they didn't understand any of it, that they couldn't understand your words, that you should search for other words: "Your words are too hard, we don't understand."[39]

Having hit a brick wall, Marcos instead had to adapt, "to transform our message" to local conditions.[40] Marcos tells us he came to "realize that we had to learn to listen, and, afterwards, to speak,"[41] something that the Left, particularly in Latin America, has traditionally not been very good at. All too often the Left talks and expects everyone else to listen and be converted by force of its eloquence and reason. Marcos had to stop merely spouting an alien (Marxist) dogma in an alien (Castilian) tongue and to learn the languages of the indigenous and also their cultural reference points. "In order to survive we had to translate ourselves using a different code . . . this language constructed itself from the bottom upwards."[42] Marcos elaborates further, stating: "It became necessary to assimilate, to resolve, to learn the language, but also to learn something more than the language itself: the *use* of language, of the symbol in communication, all that."[43] Moreover, the cultural references, icons, and symbols had to be exchanged for those of the region and in particular of the indigenous: "They have a different substratum, a complex prehistory of uprisings, so we modified our approach interactively."[44] Messages were now explained in simple parables of direct relevance to everyday *campesino* life. Indigenous myths, legends, and folklore were incorporated and utilized in these fables. As a result, the guerrilla's message became comprehensible, palatable indeed, and this in turn boosted recruitment.

All this took time, however. The guerrillas did not abandon their Marxist rhetoric readily, and their conversion from speakers to listeners was a slow process. However, by 1986 this process was well under way:

> How long did it take us to realize that we had to learn to listen, and, afterwards, to speak? I'm not sure, not a few moons have passed now, but I calculate some two years at least. Meaning that what had been a classic revolutionary guerrilla war in 1984 . . . by 1986 was already an armed group, overwhelmingly indigenous, listening attentively and barely babbling its first words with a new teacher: the Indian peoples.[45]

Recruitment throughout 1986 was no doubt also accelerated by the events of that year. On 17 January corn producers had blocked the Pan American highway near Ixtapa, between Tuxtla and San Cristóbal, protesting against a recent government pledge that it would raise the guaranteed price for corn by 32 percent, but only in northern states. (In all likelihood the government was trying to ensure continued support for the PRI in areas where opposition parties were making significant headway: Chiapas, thanks to the PRI caciques, was never in danger of falling to the PRD or PAN and so was not seen as needing shoring up.) Chiapas governor Absalón Castellanos Domínguez sent in troops to break up the demonstrations, jailing even mere onlookers and newspaper reporters covering the event. Some of those arrested spent the next two years in jail. This incident, and the pervading atmosphere of state repression in the region as detailed in Amnesty International's report on human rights violations in Chiapas and Oaxaca,[46] did much to drive the local *campesinos* into Marcos's arms.

This event, coupled with the persistence of the EZLN, had made many see the need for self-defense training on a grand scale with improved co-ordination and cooperation between communities. Naturally, Marcos depicts the expansion and development of the military organization as being initiated by the *campesinos*: "The comrades saw it wasn't enough to do self-defense of a single *ejido* or community but rather to establish alliances with others and to begin to make up military and paramilitary contingents on a larger scale, still for the purpose of self-defense."[47] However, at this stage the *campesinos* never saw themselves as constituting the vanguard of a left-wing revolution.

By June 1986 local recruitment had really taken off, with "ten new recruits a day" coming to join the guerrillas' ranks, which now numbered some "200 insurgents."[48] Tzeltal support was strongest. These new recruits swelled the EZLN's numbers to the extent that new camps had to be built. Hitherto, there had been a series of small camps. Marcos, for example, tells us of four: one called the Stove, "because that was where we built the first one" [that is, stove]; another called De la Juventud, "because that was where the first group of insurgent youth, called 'Rebel Youth of the South,' was formed"; another called Margaret Thatcher, "because we had hung a hog there, which, I swear, was the clone of the 'Iron lady'"; and another named Watapil, "because that was the name of the plant whose leaves we used to make a shed for storing food."[49] Moreover, *compañero* Raúl tells us of two further camps, one called Fogón (cooking ring or burner) and another El Maleficio (the curse or spell), while Comandante Abraham mentions yet another two called Zapata and Puma.[50] Elisa ran the main headquarters camp, La Cueva (the cave), while Marcos had been put in charge of the newly constructed El Recluta (the recruit) camp.

Marcos had recently been placed in charge of training new recruits, which duty, and the new training camp, may well have followed his promotion to Subcommander. (The exact date of his promotion is not known, but he had gained it by the end of this eventful and productive year.[51] Marcos himself dates his command to this period, telling one documentary video interviewer, "I've been in command since 1985 or 1986 . . . yes, 1986.")[52] In addition, Marcos oversaw the construction of a provisional base that he called Cama de Nubes (the bed of clouds), which was located less than 100 km as the crow flies from San Cristóbal. (Some years later this became Marcos's headquarters, capable of holding forty to fifty people and with a sturdy, rain-proof, two-room domicile for the Subcomandante, complete with television[53] and shelves of books and FLN documents, from where he would broadcast Zapatista Hour daily by radio to the other camps and to support communities.)[54]

Of the other camps, one, under Subcomandante Pedro, was called La Loma (the hillock) and was situated close to the Jataté river in the Colmena sierra, a predominantly Tojolobal area. Another was under the command of Major Mario and was called the Baby Doc camp, after his detachment's mascot, a pig, which they had named after the Haitian dictator Jean Claude Duvalier who had been overthrown that year. As Marcos relates:

Another camp was called "Baby Doc," in honor of the one who terrorized, with the blessings of the United States, Haitian lands. It so happened that we were on the move, with a column of recruits, in order to set up camp near a village. We ran into a pair of *jabali*, a ton of wild pigs, along the road. The guerrilla column deployed with discipline and skill. The one who was in the front yelled "pigs," and, fuelled and driven by panic, he climbed a tree with a skill we've never seen since. Others ran bravely . . . but to the opposite side from where the enemy, the wild boar, were. Some took aim, and they realized there were two wild boars. During the enemy retreat—when the pigs left—a piglet, barely the size of a domestic cat, was left abandoned. We adopted him, and we named him "Baby Doc," because Papa Doc had died at that time, bequeathing the slaughter to his offspring. We encamped there, in order to dress the meat and eat.[55]

A medical base was also established in Morelia, a village in the Alta Mirano valley on the south slopes of la Corralchén, with an ambulance and two doctors.

The newfound independence from Elisa and other more senior FLN cadres that Marcos now enjoyed through his new command and through being in charge of his own camp was highly significant for his development from Rafael to the Marcos we know today. Now he could enjoy some autonomy and give full expression to his personality.

Marcos was of a very different temperament from the others. They tended to be older, in Germán's case by more than a decade, and were very much a product of the 1970s. They had been molded by a decade of widespread, clandestine guerrilla activity, internecine fighting, betrayals, and the dirty war unleashed against them by the government's extra-judicial security force, the notorious Brigada Blanca (White Brigade).[56] As a result, they were doctrinaire, uncompromising, and authoritarian. Germán appears to have been especially severe. One Zapatista source cited by de la Grange and Rico tell us that "he was hard and dictatorial . . . he reacted very forcibly when faced with errors, he was very strict with us."[57] Another former Zapatista tells us Germán "is very hard line; he never pardons anyone anything." Even Elisa, his comrade of long standing, is on record as saying "he is a violent man."[58] It has even been alleged that he was responsible in 1984 for the only known execution of a Zapatista. Benjamín, a Chol from Sabanilla, had misappropriated funds given him to buy arms and had been known on occasion to get drunk and talk about the EZLN to anyone who would listen.[59] For Germán, the cause, and even the organization, was more important than any single individual who participated in it. He and Rodrigo were deadly serious about the FLN and their Marxist beliefs, expressing the latter in a quintessentially left-wing vocabulary.[60] Conversely, Marcos had been spared the 1970s and the decimation that decade brought to so many guerrillas. He had not experienced the personal loss of family and loved ones in shootouts with security forces as had Germán and Elisa, nor had he been seized by the police and tortured as had Germán,[61] and therefore his outlook and temperament tended to be lighter, even jocular, displaying the irreverence that had characterized Rafael in his youth. In a 1985 issue of *Neplanta*, the FLN's in-house magazine, Marcos specifically states, "My company was famous in the battalion for joking. . . . I don't see it as a bad thing, I limit myself to watching that this good humor is not converted into aggression and to avoid someone feeling offended by some comment."[62] This is not to say, however, that Marcos was any less earnest than the others. Elisa perhaps sums him up best when she tells us, "He was very fond of joking, he laughed about everything. . . . In reality everything was very important to him, but he didn't let it be known."[63] As for Marxist vocabulary, Marcos's language is not peppered with references to "bourgeois acts of repression," "vile imperialists," "overthrowing the capitalist oppressors," or "establishing a Socialist state."

In an introduction written for a collected edition of his communiqués, Marcos gives a detailed account of a training exercise he undertook that year:

> It was 1986. I left our base camp with a column of combatants on a short exploratory march. All my boys were novices; the majority of them had been with us for less than a month and they were still arguing about what was the worst part of trying to adapt: the diarrhea or the nostalgia. The two "veterans" in the group had been with us for two and three months, respectively. So there I was, sometimes dragging them, sometimes pushing them, through their political and military training. Our mission was to open a new route for military maneuvers and to train the recruits in the tasks of exploration, marching, and setting up camp. The work was hard because there was not enough water and we had to ration what we had taken with us from the base camp. So survival practice was added to the training, as the lack of water made cooking difficult. The maneuvers were to last four days, with approximately one liter of water per person, per day, and only *pinole* with sugar to eat. An hour after we

left the base we found that our route took us through some steep, difficult hills. The hours passed and we ascended and descended hills on paths that would frighten the most experienced mountain goats.

Finally, after seven or eight hours of non-stop up and down, we arrived at the top of a hill where I decided to set up camp, as the afternoon was beginning to give way to twilight shadows. The water ration was distributed, and most of the recruits, despite my warnings to save a little liquid for the *pinole*, "burned their boats" and immediately chugged down their whole ration, as they were very thirsty, and the psychological effect of knowing the water was rationed only made their anxiety worse. When the time came to eat, they saw the consequence of their foolishness: no matter how much they chewed, they were unable to swallow—without water they were not able to get the *pinole* with sugar to go down their throats. There were two hours of such silence that we could clearly hear the crunching between their teeth, and the sounds from their throats when they finally managed to swallow a piece of the sugared corn dust. The next day, having learned their lesson, they all saved part of their water ration for their morning *pinole*. That day we left on the maneuver at 09:00 hours and returned at 16:00, so it was seven hours of walking and cutting paths, going up and down hills, without any water except what we sweat.

We spent three days like that; on the fourth, the weakness of the whole group was evident. During the meals (?), the sado-masochism that seems to characterize insurgents appeared: between bites of *pinole* and little sips of water, we began to talk about *taquitos, tamales*, cakes, steaks, soft drinks, and other things that could only make us laugh because our bodies didn't have enough water to cry. To top it off, the day we were going to return to our base, we found a nearby river, and that night the mountain mischievously honored us with a strong downpour which soaked us before we managed to get under cover. We did not lose our good humor and we swore endlessly at the roof, the rain, and the jungle, and all their respective kin. But really this was all part of the training and was not surprising. The work was completed, in general the people responded well, although one person nearly fainted carrying his load up a particularly difficult hill.[64]

It is quite clear that this mission was not exceptional but rather represented a regular occurrence, with Marcos frequently leading new recruits on such training exercises. Indeed, a little later in the same text he tells us that "on one of these explorations, we returned to the camp, as always, completely wiped out."

New local recruits to the EZLN formed three distinct categories. If they joined as full-time guerrillas who lived year-round in the camp they were "insurgents." Those pledging their allegiance to the EZLN, but continuing to live outside the camp, pursuing their former occupations, but attending camp on a part-time basis for regular training, were "militia." Finally, there were "supporters": villagers who provided food and provisions for the guerrillas who acted as a support base.

As in other Latin American guerrilla forces (such as the Sandinistas, Sendero Luminoso, Guatemala's EGP [Ejército Guerrillero de los Pobres, Guerrilla Army of the Poor], and El Salvador's FMLN), women made up a significant proportion of these new recruits.[65] As Marcos explains:

> When the EZLN entered the communities it let women into the force and they could become officers because the only conditions required to become a soldier were commitment to an ideal and a code of regulations. This meant a step forward for women. . . . I'm not saying that the conditions of women in the EZLN are optimum, but they are definitely better than in their communities. The quantitive composition of the EZLN includes many women, more than half. Let's say the amount of women is about a third or a quarter of the whole army, like about 25 or 30 per cent are women in the regular force.[66]

As Marcos freely admits, this is not to say that camp life was paradisiacal. It was incredibly arduous, but so was life in the communities, and at least in the camp the women were respected, taught to read, received good meals, and could reach the age of twenty without being married and having already borne and lost children. Conversely, in the villages they would typically be uneducated, malnourished, maltreated, pregnant, and surrounded by sick and hungry offspring. Marcos's then *compañera*, Ana María, notes how "among twelve-year-old girls . . . none presents a normal nutritional condition, while for boys of the same age the percentage is 39.4," adding, "life expectancy [for women] in the indigenous communities is 44 years, as compared with a national average of 70 years."[67] Another indigenous woman talks of women being bartered as brides:

> Sometimes in the communities they force us to get married; sometimes they trade us for cows. The way they treat us isn't fair. It is mistreatment when they force us to marry. They should respect their daughters' de-

cisions and marriage should be voluntary. When a woman is married against her will, the couple fights and the man is more likely to mistreat her. The parents are the ones to blame for forcing her to marry. That's part of our tradition. Sometimes the father-in-law wants to take the bride as his woman for a while, and does not want her for the bridegroom.[68]

Yet another indigenous woman, Soledad, describes daily life in the communities:

When I was in my community, I got up every day at 4am to make the tortillas and prepare breakfast. I had to go out to get water, because the community has no running water, so you have to carry it. Then I'd take the sheep out to pasture and on the way back I'd carry wood. When I got back, I would embroider or weave. That's the way the days would go, every day.[69]

Lieutenant Amalia perhaps sums up best the condition of indigenous women:

When I was fifteen, I realized that there was an armed organization in the sierra. I knew how to read and write, but I did not speak Spanish when I entered the [guerrilla] army. The army taught me, and in the army I studied Mexican history and combat strategies. It was very hard, but no harder than life at home. When you've carried heavy loads of wood ever since you were ten, everything becomes easy. In my own home, I don't have much more than what I have here. The same mud hut and the same food. For me, it is preferable to die in combat than to die of cholera or of parasites.[70]

Marcos tells us that some of the indigenous village women asked the female insurgents how they were treated in the guerrilla camp and were astounded by the contrast:

"If you don't want to be 'taken' do they punish you?" [The answer was] "No, they can't 'take' you if you don't want to be taken." [Then they asked] "If you don't love a man can you refuse to marry him?" "Yes [they answered]. If you don't want to, you don't get married." Then a shitload of women started coming to us.[71]

Other indigenous village women, though perhaps not as repressed as those quoted above, certainly felt they could fulfill their potential better in the guerrilla camp than in their communities. Isidora, a twenty-year-old Tzeltal woman, tells how she had heard of the guerrilla army and how women there had equal rights and were taught how to read, and so "I wanted to be free, free as all the *companeros* who lived there in that army . . . I wanted to learn what they knew—to read and write."[72]

Of course, a significant influx of new recruits required not only more camps and training and medical facilities, but also more arms. The EZLN was winning over local people to its cause by offering itself as a means of defense against the military, local security forces, and the White Guards; such a stance would have been thoroughly unconvincing had it lacked a reasonable arsenal. This required a comparatively sudden and massive increase in arms supplies. Marcos tells us that he obtained weapons:

> From three sources. A small portion comes from the "work of ants," of buying arms here and there. Another important source is the Mexican police and army involved in the anti-drug battle. When they arrest traffickers, they seize their weapons, but they only turn over small portion of the weapons to their superiors, the rest are sold on the black market. That's how we bought AK-47s, M-16s, and other arms. They thought they were selling to other drug traffickers and that they would soon enough arrest them and resell the weapons. The third source was the *guardias blancas* of the ranchers, trained by the security forces and the army. They had good weapons and last year began to receive Uzis. Finally, there are the weapons of the peasants themselves, shotguns and rudimentary things.[73]

But Marcos is again not telling the whole story. First, although he acknowledges the peasants as a source of arms, he is not giving us all the details. It is clear from former Subcommander Daniel that the *campesinos* were made to contribute money for the purchase of arms by selling produce. They gave this money to Marcos, who sent it to Germán, who in turn bought the weapons and sent them down to Marcos to distribute among the troops. The FLN was simply not wealthy enough to provide arms from its own funds.[74] (Maoist philosophy may also have been a factor: It stipulates that by having the peasants make sacrifices such as purchasing their own weapons this strengthens their identification with the cause and ultimately therefore their commitment to it, while in addition ensuring that they take good care of the arms.) Second, many of the guns came from Chicano contacts Germán and Marcos had made in the United States,[75] the latter when he perhaps visited the country precisely to establish these contacts in the early

1980s. These weapons, and others from elsewhere (in particular, neighboring Guatemala), were then modified (for example, the barrels shortened or the firing mechanisms transformed from semi-automatic to fully automatic, etc.) or rearmed (after they had been de-activated by U.S. law enforcement agencies upon initial confiscation from criminals) in workshops in Mexico City and Yanga (Veracruz). The guns were driven to Chiapas by a three-ton truck, hidden in compartments in the front, rear, and sides of the vehicle obscured by heavy metal fenders. Third, and more surprising, Daniel informs us that the peasants used money from two government aid agencies, Sedesol and Solidaridad, to buy arms. Initially, the EZLN leadership had told the *campesinos* to reject government aid, believing that it was a hollow attempt by the PRI at buying their silence and obedience, "but, the time came when they were told to accept the money, and part of it went to buy arms."[76]

As a result, the weapons that arrived in the Chiapan jungle were by all accounts a real hotchpotch, everything from modern U.S. M-16s, AR-15s and Ruger Mini-14s, Russian SKS Siminov's and AK-47s, and Israeli UZIs, to the older British Sten-guns and 303 Savages, U.S. M-1s, and German Commando 45s. The weapons were distributed among the EZLN cadres on the basis of whether they were insurgents or militia. The insurgents received the best weapons, and they received them free. The militia received poorer weapons and had to pay for them out of their own pockets. One source of revenue was the community funds set aside for communal fiestas, much of which had previously gone on alcohol. As Marcos states: "We began to make work collectives and the money that before was used for the fiestas, for alcohol (because there was much alcoholism) or for community costs, we began to dedicate to the buying of weapons."[77] (The consequent abolition of alcohol consumption had the added benefit of ensuring secrecy and therefore security, since alcohol all too often loosens the tongue. Marcos states that alcohol also played a part in recruitment. Initially teetotalers were chosen above all others, with those who promised not to drink in the future being favored next.)[78] In any case, unlike other Latin American guerrilla groups, the EZLN, as Marcos proudly boasts, never resorted to kidnapping, extortion, or robbery in order to fund its purchase of arms, a factor which perhaps explains why it was so poorly armed compared with other guerrillas. Possibly Marcos was aware of Che Guevara's warning to the Argentine guerrilla Ciro Bustos, that "if you start out by robbing banks you end up as a bank robber."[79]

Interestingly, despite all these potential sources of arms, the number of firearms the EZLN held was clearly limited and continued to be so. The defector Subcomandante Daniel tells us that at the Votán military parade, in August 1988, although some 1,400 EZLN combatants were present, only 500 carried guns.[80] Even as late as the January 1994 uprising, for which the EZLN had been preparing for over a year, many EZLN troops had to enter into combat carrying wooden replica rifles.

The issue of arms purchases by Marcos is an important one, since it generated a cloud which hangs over the Subcommander's head. It has been alleged that Marcos overcharged *campesinos* for the weapons they purchased from him. The accusation is reported in de la Grange and Rico, where they quote Antonio as saying:

> At the start of the 80s Marcos had made various journeys to make contact with Chicanos in Los Angeles and Texas, who controlled the arms black market and they sold them to us. They cost from 1000 to 2000 pesos (between 300 and 600 dollars according to the current rate of exchange) but with transportation and all the expenses Marcos sold them for double that to the militia. If the people did not have sufficient money in order to buy them, they used loans from *Banrural* which the government gave them in order to buy livestock.[81]

The validity of this accusation has, however, yet to be proved.

Another controversy surrounding Marcos at this time, which may possibly be linked to weapons, concerns an alleged visit to Nicaragua. Again, as in the case of Marcos's alleged profiteering from weapon deals, de la Grange and Rico cite Antonio as their source. (Indeed, the bulk of the material used by de la Grange and Rico in their attacks on Marcos comes from him. Unfortunately, we have no idea as to Antonio's reliability since his name is a pseudonym designed to shield his identity and the only other thing we are told is that "he has devoted ten years of his life to the cause."[82] We do not know, for example, whether Antonio was a high-ranking Zapatista and therefore knew Marcos intimately or what were his motivations for providing this information. Does he, for example, like Daniel, have a grudge against Marcos?) Antonio claims, "I recollect a visit that he made to Nicaragua, I believe this was in 1986. He stayed for two months."[83] De la Grange and Rico make much of this, and Marcos's alleged earlier trip to Nicaragua while he was teaching at UAM in the late 1970s and early 1980s, as well as a possible visit to Cuba. Clearly, for them this confirms their suspicions that Marcos is really a die-hard Communist who is merely pretending to have changed his spots by adopting the guise of a less doctrinaire and more liberal individual bent on furthering indigenous rights. This picture of Marcos's character and the development of his political thought is for me overly simplistic, clumsy, and fundamentally erroneous; furthermore, it should be offset against Marcos's own vehement denial, when asked candidly by Le Bot if he had received training in Nicaragua or had participated in the literacy program there.[84]

Of course, the possession of weapons does not make an effective guerrilla force, and one wonders where Marcos, a former university professor, learned to handle them. Questioned by one interviewer about how he learned military tactics, Marcos replied:

> Pancho Villa, as far as regular army tactics are concerned, and Emiliano Zapata, with respect to the interchange between guerrilla and peasant. We got the rest out of a manual of the Mexican army that fell into our hands, and a small manual from the Pentagon, and some work by a French general whose name I can't remember.[85]

Did these manuals also provide instruction in the handling of firearms? Certainly the image of a self-taught intellectual combating state forces using army textbooks is a romantic one, but one doubts whether it represents the whole truth. It is more likely that Marcos received much of his training from Germán and other veteran members of the FLN. Indeed, Daniel tells us that it was in Chiapas that "Guillén . . . began to learn how to . . . handle weapons . . . and perform the military practices that Germán taught."[86]

In order to inculcate a feeling of professionalism among the new cadres, uniforms had to be acquired. The main source of shirts and trousers was Pemex, Mexico's nationalized oil company. Precisely how a vast amount of clothing was stolen from the company remains a mystery; perhaps uniforms went missing bit by bit over a protracted period all over the country, or perhaps several major incidents of thefts accounted for them.[87] These too were modified (the indigenous of Chiapas often being of slighter build than average Mexicans) in the same workshops and in safe houses in San Cristóbal. As for footwear and headgear, Antonio states:

> The boots were of leather and the soles we made with remnants of tires. They were very good for walking. *Captain Eduardo*, who was in Veracruz, sent us some 200 other pairs of boots moreover. His father had a footwear factory and helped us in this way. The material of the uniforms and caps were bought in Tuxtla or San Cristóbal, in stores around the

market. The black material in one shop, the green material in another and the coffee colored in another, so as not to arouse attention. In the secure house in San Cristóbal there were four persons working with sewing machines.[88]

The increased numbers also caused problems concerning provisions. Local communities provided much of the food for the guerrilla camps, but there were logistical problems that became even more acute whenever large-scale training exercises took place. As Marcos relates:

> Making a meal took much time; you had to carry water far because the camps were not close to streams or rivers. You had to cut the firewood and wash the plates well. . . . Cooking with firewood took a lot of time, because in addition to carrying the firewood there were many other things to do besides. It took three or four hours to make a meal for twenty or thirty combatants, and another hour-and-a-half to wash the pots and dry them, because we had to go down to the river carrying them. . . . [Therefore] in the mountains we only had two meals: an early breakfast and a meal very late.[89]

While Marcos was wrestling with logistical problems, economic and social conditions in Mexico were deteriorating. Camín and Meyer note:

> In order to satisfy their basic needs, workers earning the minimum wage had to work 50 hours per week in 1982; to buy the same basket of goods, people had to work 85 hours in 1986. . . . Once the figures are estimated for the purchasing power of wages with respect to the eight basic food items—corn tortillas, beans, beef, sugar, coffee, eggs, milk and lard—the purchasing power of the minimum wage in 1986 was the same as in 1940. . . . In 1986, public expenditure on health was the lowest it had been in twenty years: 35 million Mexicans remained outside the health system of the country.[90]

11. A Jungle Wedding

The following year, 1987, was an important one personally for Marcos. At a guerrilla encampment located in thick jungle he married a Tzotzil woman known by two noms de guerre, Yolanda and Ana María.[1] She was from Sabanilla, a Zapatista stronghold from the movement's inception, so the ceremony took place near the *ejido* of Pichucalco, located only 60 km north west of Sabanilla, on federal highway 195 linking Tuxtla Gutiérrez and Villahermosa. Marcos tells us that Ana María/Yolanda had joined the *foco* in December 1984 and that he had led her into the mountains on her first training exercise that month. Yolanda was interviewed by a reporter from *La Jornada* (7 March 1994) who described her as "the twenty-six year old infantry major."[2] She was, by her own admission, "very young" when she first joined the guerrillas,[3] and about nineteen years old when she married Marcos (who was then thirty) in 1987. (It perhaps ought to be emphasized, however, that even by the age at which Ana María/Yolanda joined the ranks of the EZLN, a considerable percentage of Tzotzil girls are married and have at least one child.) Marcos writes in his "Twelve Women in the Twelfth Year"[4] admiringly of her entry into the guerrillas' ranks three years previously:

> In December 1984, not yet twenty years old, she arrives in the mountains of the Lacandón Jungle, carrying the marks of the whole history of indigenous humiliation on her body. In December 1984 this brown woman says, "Enough is enough!" so softly that only she hears herself. In January 1994 this woman and several thousand indigenous people do not just say, but yell, "Enough is enough!" so loudly that all the world hears them.[5]

Given that Ana María/Yolanda joined the guerrillas so early in their formation, just four months after Marcos, it is a reasonable conjecture that her family had strong connections with one or more of the FLN's "point men" in Chiapas. Probable candidates for these initial points of contact in and around Sabanilla include Paco, a respected Tzotzil known to the FLN, who had facilitated the recruitment of numerous Tzotzil cadres, among them his own nephew, Frank;[6] Jacobo (Jorge Santiago), the head of DESMI, who had contacts in Sabanilla and who, because of his relationship with Elisa, provided logistical support under the cover of DESMI for the establishment of Germán's and Elisa's *foco*;[7] and the Unión de Uniones president, a Chol also from Sabanilla, Francisco López, who was well connected with the FLN, later becoming a militant within the EZLN under the alias Castelán.[8] In any event, Ana María states:

> Since the age of eight I've participated in peaceful struggles, in marches and meetings.[9] Everyone in my family is a fighter, everyone has been organizing themselves to have a more dignified life . . . we were in an organization—I won't say which—with other people, other towns.[10] We were all together, including the children. . . . My family, before I was born, was already in the struggle.[11]

Thus, Ana María's experience highlights the importance of what Kampwirth terms "family traditions of resistance," arguing that "families are probably the most important socializing networks because of their universality and intimacy."[12]

Ana María evidently responded well to guerrilla training, since she was soon placed in charge of recruitment in the north of the region. Before and after joining the guerrillas she worked as an auxiliary nurse at the hospital of Las Hermanas de San Vicente de Paul at San Andrés Larráinzar, less than 50 km due south of her hometown.[13] The northern part of Chiapas appears to have been politicized long before Marcos and the FLN arrived. Many of the guerrillas' ranks would be filled, initially at least, by *campesinos* from this area, and in particular from Sabanilla. (Interestingly, neighboring Tila—less than 20 km to the north east—later became the headquarters of the infamous right-wing paramilitary organization Peace and Justice, established by ranchers to counter what they perceived as growing left-wing militant activism in the region.) Ana María had been one of the first local people to join the guerrillas, as she told *La Jornada* reporters in March 1994:

> When I joined, there were only two women out of a total of eight or nine people in the mountains. The *compañeros* taught us to walk in the mountains, to load the guns, to hunt. They taught us combat exercises and

when we learned that, they taught us politics. Then we went out into the communities to talk to our people, to tell them about our struggle and how we could solve things, and many people began to join us, men, women and children.[14]

On the same day—the date and the month or season are unknown—as Marcos and Ana María tied the knot, Germán married Lucía. Elisa, we are told, acted as a witness, and some forty *insurgentes* also attended this revolutionary wedding ceremony.[15]

A revolutionary wedding appears not to have been the exclusive preserve of Marcos and Germán. Within the ranks of the guerrillas many opted for such a wedding instead of a traditional indigenous or Catholic ceremony. Usually, the betrothed would pass under an arch of rifles presented by two squads of guerrillas.[16] Their fellow comrades would be present, and Marcos generally presided over the ceremony as a kind of revolutionary registrar, with authority invested in him not by the Church but by the Revolution. (Such a role was not without precedent: Tomás Borge, the sole surviving founder member of the FSLN, tells how the Sandinistas' leader, Carlos Fonseca, had, while undertaking a guerrilla campaign in the countryside, "assumed public administrative functions, marrying the guerrilla couple Francisco Rivera and Celestina López.")[17] The wedding contract derived its legitimacy not from the Bible but from the guerrillas' Revolutionary Laws.[18]

Following the uprising in January 1994, several references to Ana María can be found in the communiqués of Marcos. One communiqué, for example, centers on a domestic scene in which Marcos describes talking to Eva and Heriberto, some of the children in a Zapatista community:

> In this climate of curiosity and with a surprising coherence for her four-years-almost-five-or-six, Eva asks, "What about my present?" The word "present" provokes identical reactions in Beto, Toñita, and Heriberto. They all start yelling, "Where's my present?" I'm trapped and on the point of being sacrificed. But in walks Ana María, who saves my life, as she did in San Cristóbal almost one year ago (under very different circumstances). Ana María has an enormous bag of candy with her. "Here's the present the Sup has for you," she says, while giving me that I-don't-know-what-you-men-would-do-without-women look.[19]

There is some evidence to suggest that in 1987, Marcos, as well as getting married, also undertook a trip to Nicaragua. This is far from certain, however, and in fact hinges predominantly on the testimony of a newspaper reporter, Oliver Bodán, who refuses to divulge his source.[20] However, if Bodán is to be trusted, Marcos, employing the alias Jorge Narváez, received military instruction as part of a group of Mexicans and Argentineans in la Brigada de Defensa Local 368 de Jinotega. Sometimes, according to the first newspaper report (17 February 1995), these men would come down from their training camp in the hills and go to the local town to let off steam at the disco there. There, while the others would dance and have a drink, Jorge Narváez kept himself apart, never drinking or dancing, but rather possessed of an almost "priestly air," reserved, cultured, and softly spoken. He was "a man of the utmost austerity, who never spoke of his own ideas but was rather absolutely devoted to the Sandinista cause and dazzled by the course of the revolution." The second newspaper story (18 February 1995) quoted an anthropologist, an expert on indigenous issues and a dissident Sandinista, who had met this group of Mexicans in Nicaragua in August 1987 and then claimed to have seen Jorge Narváez again in 1991 during a meeting with some guerrillas in Chiapas to which he had been invited following a congress in Cuernavaca (Mexico) in which he had spoken on his field of expertise. (These guerrillas supposedly had wished to discuss indigenous issues.) The two men remained silent, feigning not to recognize each other. After the meeting, the anthropologist declined the guerrillas' request for his help and advice, and they went their separate ways.

It is far from implausible that Marcos might have visited Nicaragua at this time, and a visit is attested to by Antonio, although he dates it to the previous year. The matter of whether he received military training there, however, is more doubtful. (Nicaragua's former minister of the interior, Tomás Borge, has repeatedly gone on record as denying the military training of foreigners on Nicaraguan soil.)[21] Without knowing Bodán's sources we have no way of assessing their reliability, despite his insistence that they are "absolutely trustworthy." Even if we take Bodán's reports at face value, how likely is it that his witnesses were able to accurately recollect the faces of people they saw only briefly eight years previously? And, in the case of the anthropologist, even if his memory was correct, his identification could be faulty; it is perhaps possible, for example, that Jorge Narváez was not Marcos but was in fact Rodrigo's brother, Gabriel Ramírez (alias Doctor Carlos), who we know spent two months in Nicaragua in 1987 and who had been a frequent visitor both there and to Zapatista camps in Chiapas.[22] The confused memories some Nicaraguans have of the particularly tumultuous period of the early years of the Sandinista regime has been highlighted by Susan Meiselas's documentary film *Pictures from a Revolution*.

If Marcos did journey to Nicaragua in August 1987, he would have been there during a very important period which may have helped him to formulate his own vision of an issue that would be of prime relevance for Mexico from the mid-1990s onward—that of indigenous autonomy. As Mattiace observes:

> In Nicaragua . . . on September 2, 1987, the Autonomy Statute was passed by the Sandinista legislature, which established two multi-ethnic Atlantic coast regions. . . . This statute included guarantees of equal citizenship for Atlantic coast indigenous peoples, as well as protection of their special rights. Under the agreement, the state recognized communal forms of landownership and indigenous people's right to "provide themselves with their own forms of social organization and to administer their local affairs according to their traditions."[23]

Interestingly, two of the chief architects of this regional autonomy agreement were the Mexican anthropologists Héctor Díaz-Polanco and Gilberto López y Rivas. Eight years later, the Subcommander would specifically request these two men as advisors for the EZLN's negotiation team at the San Andrés talks on indigenous autonomy. It should be noted, however, that throughout his communiqués Marcos nowhere cites the Sandinista government's legislation on indigenous autonomy as an example of what the Zapatistas were seeking—indeed, he does not mention Nicaragua at all in this context.

Meanwhile in the country at large, as Castañeda has observed, "even according to official figures renowned for their cosmetic treatment, the number of poor grew from 32.1 million and 45 percent of the population in 1981 to 41.3 million and 51 percent in 1987."[24] Indeed, the years 1982 to 1987 saw Mexico undergoing zero percent economic growth. Aguilar Camín and Meyer note that "between 1982 and 1987 the minimum wage had undergone a reduction of more than 40 percent."[25] Economic conditions in Chiapas at the time were well in line with this trend. Moreover, in the same year, a report by the Academia Mexicana de Derechos Humanos declared that the Chiapas governorship of General Castellanos was characterized by corruption and repression.[26] Indeed, 1987 ended with seven people being killed when security police dispersed demonstrations undertaken by independent peasant organizations in Simojovel and La Independencia.[27] All of this served to add fuel to the guerrillas' fire.

12. An Election, Exponential Growth, and a Rift

The year 1988 started with a potentially serious incident for the guerrillas. In February a twenty-eight man military patrol found wooden practice rifles and a shelter near the *ejido* of San Francisco, 55 km south of San Cristóbal.[1] Fortunately for Marcos and his *campañeros*, for reasons still unclear, the patrol did not penetrate deeper into the jungle. A Zapatista eyewitness, Salvador, provides the details:

> [The soldiers] fell down on the ground with blisters and stopped to rest about a kilometer from one of our camps, which was called El Camarón [the shrimp]. Marcos gave the order to prepare an ambush. We dug trenches and obstructed the road that led to the camp with felled trees. The military had discovered a little earlier a shelter where we kept wooden rifles for training. They should have suspected something, but they preferred to act like they suspected nothing. It was better for them. If they had approached a little closer we would have killed them all.[2]

Salvador acknowledges, however, that such an encounter would have sounded the death knell for the EZLN, since reinforcements would have been drafted in and "We would not have been able to resist for long; it would have been our final adventure."[3]

Curiously, the army failed to follow up this find, and so the round-ups, interrogations, increased patrols, house-to-house searches, aerial reconnaissance, and so on, which usually follow such a discovery, never happened. Possibly the lack of real arms and live ammunition led the soldiers to conclude that the culprits were simply high-spirited, bored local youths playing at being soldiers.

On 6 July 1988 there was a general election in Mexico. This election has become infamous as the grossest and most blatant example of the kind of electoral fraud commonly experienced in Latin America. In the middle of a televised computerized counting of the votes, which was presaging a PRD victory over the PRI for the first time in almost sixty years, there was a power blackout lasting several hours. After it had been repaired, the count showed a complete reversal of the trend exhibited only hours before, and Carlos Salinas of the PRI was declared victor.

At a local level, in Ocosingo (one of the country's largest municipalities) the extent and blatancy of electoral fraud would have been comic if it had not been so tragic. The PRI claimed to have received approximately 102,000 votes, with its nearest rival, PSUM, said to have polled a mere 3,000. However, given that the government's own statistics numbered the municipality's total population (that is, voters and nonvoters) at only 110,000, a vote tally exceeding 100,000 is surely impossible.[4] (In Chiapas as a whole the vote for the PRI was, according to government figures, 39 percent above the national average.)[5] Such naked disregard for democracy appears to have greatly boosted Zapatista membership, with many *campesinos* now utterly convinced that all peaceful and legitimate means of changing their plight had been exhausted. As Marcos puts it, "The compañeros saw that voting didn't matter either because there was no respect for obvious, basic things."[6]

Also tied to Salinas's fraudulent election victory was the matter of neoliberal economics. True, the North American Free Trade Agreement (NAFTA) was not being seriously discussed yet, nor was the rescinding of article 27 of the Mexican constitution; these would not take place until the early 1990s. However, there was no mistaking the cut of Salinas's cloth. He was a U.S.-educated technocrat who believed almost religiously in neoliberalism. (He was not a voice crying out in the wilderness: the Chicago school of economics, with its emphasis on extreme neoliberal policies, was being given carte blanche to run the economy in Pinochet's Chile; in Peru, President Fujimori would soon be applying his own austere neoliberalism—"the Fuji-shock"; while Argentina under Carlos Menem, Bolivia under Víctor Paz Estenssoro, and Venezuela under Carlos Andrés Pérez all embraced neoliberalism.) Thus, as Marcos observes:

> In 1988, by means of the electoral fraud, president Salinas was imposed on us and with him the whole neo-liberal project. In these moments many people began to arrive, many compañeros, and the dream that the EZLN would become a regular army with great potential was realized. In the period 1988 to 1991 we gathered together thousands of combatants. In 1992 we had 50 thousand[7] in arms, hidden, silent, dedicated to preparing themselves. The principal recruiter was the neo-liberal model, that opened people's eyes: "Yes, now it's arms or death."[8]

In another interview he states, "We Zapatistas passed from tens to thousands in a short time; I am speaking of a single year, 1988–9. We passed from being eighty combatants to 1,300 in less than a year."[9] Elsewhere, Marcos insists that "of the various ingredients that explain the massive growth of the EZLN . . . one was the fraud against Cardenas, which signified the cancellation of a possibility of a peaceful transition for a certain sector of the indigenous, the most politicized, above all those from the [peasant organizations] Union of Unions, ARIC."[10]

On 6 August 1988 fell two important anniversaries: the nineteenth anniversary of FLN and the fourth anniversary of Marcos's permanent immersion into Chiapas and guerrilla life. To celebrate the former, a military parade code-named Votán (after the Mayan deity) was organized in Chiapas by Germán. Vivid descriptions of the parade have come down to us in accounts published in the FLN's *Neplanta*, written by Germán's new wife, Lucía, and in an interview with the EZLN defector Subcomandante Daniel. The inhabitants of around seventy villages and *ejidos* were present. The parade lasted forty minutes and included 1,000 troops, consisting of numerous detachments. First came the insurgents wearing brown uniforms and then the militia dressed in green uniforms. There was a cavalry regiment, infantry battalions, and a machete regiment. Finally there was a detachment of boys around ten or eleven years old, displaying banners proclaiming their community of origin and the names of various Mexican and international revolutionary heroes. (The parade must have looked very much like the one choreographed by Marcos at the National Democratic Convention in Aguascalientes on 6–9 August 1994 — again, complete with youths — that was filmed and released on video.)[11] These troops all saluted and then presented arms to Germán. There then followed a further salute in the form of a volley of gunfire and shouts from the troops. After this, three hours of military maneuvers were conducted that included mock battles staged against enemy installations. Marcos presided over a five-stage "attack" on an army barracks situated between two hills. Afterward, there were speeches. Marcos spoke first, emphasizing the need for unity among *campesinos* and communities and stressing the need for militia members not simply to wear the EZLN's uniform but to participate actively in furthering the movement. Then Germán spoke, recollecting the names, deeds, and dreams of comrades who had already perished for the cause. The ceremony ended with the shout of "Live for the fatherland or die for liberty"; there then followed a massive feast in which a cow was slaughtered and eaten and a hundred kilos of beans, rice, salt, and sugar were consumed.[12]

The leadership used this unusual gathering of communities to discuss important issues concerning the local *campesinos* and the FLN as a whole. Problems in the communities (such as drunkenness), security, and the shadowing of police, army, and paramilitary movements were addressed, and a reassertion was made of the FLN's claim to be a nationwide organization poised to overthrow the government.

The occasion also witnessed the promotion of certain EZLN cadres, among them captains Yolanda and Mario, who both became majors. The Votán military parade also witnessed the return to Chiapas of Daniel, who had initially come to the jungle as a guerrilla shortly after Marcos and who had stayed there for about a year before being transferred to the capital for three years to work alongside the FLN's high command there. He now returned having been raised to the rank of Subcommander, like Marcos, and was given his own camp in the woodlands of the Sierra Corralchén called Las Calabazas (the pumpkins). One wonders how Marcos must have felt about the return and promotion of this part-time guerrilla. He and Daniel had never enjoyed an easy personal relationship. Indeed, Daniel is on record as saying, "As *compañeros* we never got along. His style of imposing himself on you sickened me: he did it in a subtle way and I resisted. There had always been a distance between us."[13] Marcos had joined the FLN first, helping in the safe houses before Daniel joined the movement. Moreover, where Marcos had been a professor at UAM, Daniel had been a teaching assistant there, helping with everyday practical tasks such as ordering office materials and stationery, doing photocopying, and conducting general maintenance. In short, politically and intellectually (or at least professionally) Marcos must have felt Daniel to be his inferior. Now, one may guess, the jealousy and rivalry between the two was exacerbated by what Marcos must have perceived as Daniel's strolling into a top position within the EZLN after having spent three years in a comparatively comfortable post in the capital and having done almost none of the back-breaking, foot-slogging groundwork in Chiapas. Thus, although they both shared the same title, Marcos must have felt Daniel's revolutionary, or at least guerrilla, credentials were far inferior to his own. Moreover, Daniel's arrival on the scene was a threat to the relatively free hand Marcos had been enjoying in Chiapas. (Although Elisa was nominally Marcos's superior—largely based on the fact that she had been a member of the FLN since 1972—she was only two years older than him and female, which resulted in her not being taken as seriously as Marcos by some of her comrades in Chiapas.) One example of how Daniel's presence limited Marcos's freedom of action, and the tension this caused, concerns finances. Daniel was supposed to be in charge of EZLN funds. However, as he explains, "There were a series of incidents and disagreements in the handling of the accounts because Marcos never gave explanations concerning the use of resources."[14] Marcos, as the senior in years, education, and experience within the organization, no doubt felt scant obligation to inform Daniel of how he was spending funds, and the personal animosity that existed between them would only have strengthened his reluctance to do so.

It seems likely, given the timing, that Daniel was intended to replace Elisa.[15] Certainly, it is about now that Gloria Benavides (alias Elisa) fades from view in our picture of the EZLN in Chiapas. Marcos, Daniel, and Pedro feature prominently as the local Subcommanders, each with his own camp and his own theatre of operations,[16] but there is no mention anymore of Elisa. We know that she married Jorge Javier Elorriaga Berde-gué (alias Comandante Vicente) in 1988,[17] and perhaps went to join him in Mexico City to undertake FLN duties there, nearer her new husband. She had, after all, just spent five years in the jungle during which time Vicente had made several visits to her camp in Chiapas. (Tello Díaz, usually a highly trustworthy source of information given his close connections with Mexico's security forces, tells us that Elisa was pregnant in 1988,[18] which could help explain her recall. There is a problem here, however. Elisa's only known child—a son, named Vicente after his father's nom de guerre— was aged only eighteen months in February 1995 when she was identified and detained by the Mexican Justice Department. Either Tello Díaz has been wrongly informed on this matter then, and a child was not indeed conceived in 1988, or we must suppose that Elisa did become pregnant in 1988 but subsequently lost the baby.)[19] The arrival of Subcomandante Daniel perhaps represents a deliberate attempt on Germán's part not to create a power vacuum with Elisa's reassignment.

The anniversary celebration was no doubt held in Chiapas because this was the theatre where the FLN was enjoying greatest success. (Adolfo Gilly, who interviewed Marcos, tells us that "between 1988 and 1989" the EZLN's "membership increased from fewer than 100 to 1,300.")[20] This newfound success in recruitment and spreading the revolutionary word contrasted strongly with the poor headway being made on other fronts. In an October

1988 edition of *Neplanta*, Germán reveals that the FLN leadership was becoming increasingly disillusioned with politicizing the urban proletariat:

> We have failed in our project of incorporating the workers into being professional revolutionaries. . . . It is no use idealizing the working class, thinking that by approaching them this assures the future of the revolution. Only by employing Leninist-Marxist theory and practice will we manage to get the working class to develop a consciousness and convert itself into a class in itself, for itself.[21]

As a means of remedying this lack of political consciousness, the same edition of *Neplanta* announced the FLN's founding of Las Escuelas de Cuadros (Schools of Cadres). One of these, probably the main one, was a safe house near Mexico City's international airport, where as many as twenty or thirty *campesinos* would gather from all over the country, but particularly Chiapas, Chihuahua, Puebla, and Veracruz, to receive instruction (mainly from UNAM and UAM professors, who appear to have formed the central pillar of the organization). The cadres would remain there for one month, receiving political education and taking general courses in anthropology and history (complete with trips to various museums) and even classes in art and music. These studies were directed by the medic Carlos and his wife Mercedes (alias Rocío, Marcos' ex-girlfriend), who specialized in historical materialism; a Russian called Boris, who specialized in Marxist economics; an Italian, Natalia, who specialized in material dialectics; and others (a professor called Luis, a woman known as Rosita, and a Salvadoran).

By the end of 1988 a pronounced and potentially damaging division arose between the Catholic Church in the region, represented by Bishop Samuel Ruiz, and Marcos. It would appear that previously the EZLN and the diocese had enjoyed a symbiotic relationship. The EZLN benefited from the clergy's endeavors to politicize, organize, educate, and establish contact between the various communities living in Chiapas.[22] Lázaro Hernández, who was first a deacon, then a Zapatista and president of ARIC (1991), and finally a PRI deputy, tells us that "Marcos didn't organize anything here; when he came the people were already organized by the Church and the [peasant organization] ARIC and *el Sup* used this."[23] One priest has commented that "the Church was not behind the Zapatistas: it went before them." Even Bishop Ruiz has conceded as much, declaring that "these people [the EZLN] have arrived to mount a saddled horse"—the horse was armed rebellion, and it was Ruiz himself and his catechists who had saddled it.[24] At the very least, as Kampwirth observes, "The church's advocacy of basic human rights had the effect (in a state where basic human rights were often ignored), of preparing some indigenous people for later mobilization in the Zapatista army."[25] The clergy, for its part, benefited from the military know-how supplied by the EZLN that was required to form the self-defense forces so urgently desired by local communities. The Church itself acknowledged the need for self-defense, having been informed of its importance by men like Javier Vargas who it had sent to Nicaragua precisely in order to learn about organizing the peasantry politically and militarily, but they lacked experience in it and perhaps also the heart for it. (Indeed, as late as June 1992, with the Sandinistas democratically ousted from power and the FMLN sitting down with the El Salvadoran government to discuss peace, Ruiz stated, "The Kingdom of God is able to pass through a political channel, as in the case of Nicaragua.")[26] Perhaps initially then Don Ruiz had hoped that the EZLN would work alongside the Church in Chiapas in order to facilitate the transition to the Kingdom of God and became opposed to Marcos only when he realized that the EZLN would not respect the Church and work alongside it as guerrillas had done in Nicaragua, El Salvador, and Guatemala. In this respect, there are those sympathetic to the bishop who liken him to the sorcerer's apprentice who set in play forces that rapidly grew beyond his control. Daniel, the ex-Subcommander, argues that Ruiz seriously underestimated Marcos and the EZLN:

> I believe he never imagined the EZLN had the capacity to make contact with the people and to convince them. I believe that Samuel Ruiz thought that the same thing was going to happen as had happened with the Maoists who had arrived earlier and who had carried out the same things but had been thrown out by the communities at the point when they began to meddle in their problems.[27]

In any event, by the end of 1988 the betrothal of convenience between the EZLN and the Church appeared well and truly over.

The rift, when it came, was due to several factors. Marcos's revolutionary weddings were breaking the Church's monopoly on matrimonial services, and the Subcommander's presiding over them was perceived by the diocese as both an encroachment on Church prerogatives and as a sacrilege. Marcos and the bishop were diametrically and vehemently opposed on certain issues, in particular birth control. Marcos believed whole-heartedly in it. The guerrillas were issued contraceptive devices at a clinic in Morelia which the movement had helped found and fund. Nor was the encouragement and distribution of contraceptives restricted to the guerrillas themselves. Marcos believed that one of the major contributing factors to the hardship and poverty of Chiapas was its overpopulation. Finally, according to one source at least, Marcos was becoming increasingly intolerant regarding questions of faith, even going so far as to preach atheism.[28] (In Europe, Communism had a long tradition of atheism; however, in Latin America religion and revolution had frequently been less mutually exclusive, as is shown by the role played by Catholic priests in the guerrilla struggles in El Salvador, Guatemala, and Nicaragua—not to mention Colombia's guerrilla priest, Camilo Torres.)[29] This claim has not been corroborated and so is far from certain. It directly contradicts Marcos's assertion that "we are not religious, nor are we against religion. . . . We respect beliefs";[30] and it ignores the fact that many Zapatistas were or had been catechists, including some high-ranking cadres such as Tacho, who went on to become a Comandante.[31] However, if true, it is not difficult to see why the diocese might have been even more resentful of Marcos's attitude and actions.[32] Marcos and the other members of the EZLN had initially benefited from the work of the Church in the region, and now they were turning around and biting the hand that had fed them.

In 1988, Ruiz, with the help of Hernández, decided that the Church should, to some extent, distance itself from the guerrillas and go its own way by resurrecting Slop. Not only did Slop provide an alternative organization to the EZLN, but it also attempted to arm itself and present itself to the people as a rival community self-defense force for those who wanted protection from landowners, the police, and the army, but who were not interested in fomenting a revolution. Slop's efforts, in this respect, were soon thwarted by a combination of Marcos's swift and direct action and by the incompetence of some of Slop's own members.[33] However, a number of EZLN members deserted to join Slop,[34] which generated great tension between the two organizations.

In order to arrive at some sort of modus vivendi, Marcos "asked *Rodrigo* to go and tell Samuel [Ruiz] to calm his people down," and so there followed "various meetings in Tuxtla between Samuel, his chief deputy Gonzalo Ituarte and *Rodrigo*, in one of which Marcos participated."[35] According to former Subcommander Daniel, "*Rodrigo* was the only one who defended the clergy . . . he asked Samuel to understand the political work of the organization, and tried to smooth over the rough patches"; whereas Marcos, on the other hand, only "respected religion in public—his motto being, 'it is necessary to use Samuel Ruiz,' [and so] he used him when he was able to and hid information from him, and when the bishop hindered him, he sent him to speak with *Rodrigo*."[36] After several such meetings a pact was made in Lázaro's house in Ocosingo whereby Slop, ARIC, and the EZLN agreed to a nonaggression pact and promised not to encroach on each other's territory and to respect each other and their constituencies. More specifically, Slop promised to abandon its commitment to self-defense and to dismantle the training camps and bases it had established for this purpose in return for the EZLN allowing those individuals and communities that chose to secede from the guerrillas to do so freely and without future molestation.[37] Daniel puts it even more starkly: "In the final meeting which they held in Ocosingo they arrived at an accord whereby the other group [that is, Slop] would disarm themselves and Marcos agreed not to take reprisals against their organizers."[38] However, this was something of an uneasy truce. Daniel also tells us that "this led, however, to communities beginning to divide among themselves."[39] Some priests would not baptize pro-Zapatista supporters or permit them to receive Communion, while the Zapatistas frequently made life uncomfortable for those within a community who were opposed to violence, claiming that such people posed a serious security risk.

De la Grange and Rico make much of this split between Bishop Ruiz and Marcos, and in the short term it did indeed lead to a considerable exodus from the guerrillas' ranks in certain areas. However, in the long run, the rift does not appear to have been permanent. The recent history of the Catholic Church in Chiapas was inextricably linked to the EZLN. Hernández claims that "a third part of the catechists were with the EZLN."[40] As Marcos himself states, "There are catechists among us, also *sabáticos* [Seventh-Day Adventists]."[41] Whatever Ruiz and Marcos thought about each other personally, discord did not lead to bitter feuding. On the contrary, Ruiz appears to have abstained from criticizing the guerrillas or Marcos in his pastoral messages and interviews. The most he ever says on the subject is that he believes the Zapatistas's cause to be just, but does not concur with their methods.[42] Perhaps Krauze best expresses Ruiz's attitude toward Marcos and the EZLN when he writes:

> He [Ruiz] broke with the Zapatistas at this time (and only for a time) around the issue of the armed revolt as a tool, but not as a possibility to be totally dismissed. The Zapatistas were moving toward a tactical decision with which he did not agree and they were moving toward it independently, expanding their power partly at the expense of the diocese.[43]

Marcos, for his part, requested that the bishop act as mediator in the February 1994 peace negotiations[44]—not an obvious or wise choice had there been any acrimony between them—during which the two men appeared to have enjoyed a fairly cordial relationship. Moreover, in an interview he gave to Le Bot in 1996, Marcos took great pains to stress that "the friction (roce) [had been] with the authorities of the local church, with the indigenous church, not with the diocese," adding when pushed further on the matter, "I am speaking of the local authorities, or the *tuhuneles* [indigenous catechists], the deacons, the catechists: I am not referring to the external Church, the diocese, the bishop, the priests, the parish, but to the Church at the interior of the community—it was a struggle for local power."[45]

Indeed, I would argue that although mere conjecture, it is not implausible the two men felt some kind of affinity based on their common experiences in Chiapas. Marcos had originally come to Chiapas with a good deal of Leftist baggage and rhetoric and the intention imposing a revolutionary agenda and doctrine on the indigenous communities, but had finally, from living side by side with them, adjusted his original views to be more in line with their perspective. The same could be said of Bishop Ruiz, who writes of his similar experience years earlier: "Our first actions, years before Vatican II, were destructive of the culture. We had only our criteria with which to judge the traditional customs, shaping our judgment with ethnocentrism and moralism, attitudes that regrettably were very common at that time."[46]

The year ended with Patrocinio González Garrido, President Salinas's cousin by marriage, taking up office as state governor in December. His predecessor, Absalón Castellanos, as one of his final, outgoing actions, "leveled a community" in what was rapidly becoming a climate of "very selective violence towards indigenous people" in which "people were disappeared near Palenque."[47] Garrido promptly set about enacting revisions to the penal code which, so one human rights group has argued, "filled [Chiapas's] prisons with political prisoners."[48] As Hernández Navarro observed:

> Article 8 of the State Penal Code punishes the intellectual authors of an alleged crime and article 135 punishes the occupation of public squares. Under the first statute, it is an easy matter to identify a person as a suspect and to jail them for months without a trial. While the second discourages protest of these actions . . . Practically all democratic *campesino* organizations active in the state have some members in prison.[49]

Similarly, Minnesota Advocates for Human Rights published a report on the recently revised code entitled *Codificando Represion: El Codigo Penal para el Estado de Chiapas* in which it stated that "the provisions [of the code], taken together . . . create broad categories of political crimes which embrace every conceivable form of political protest, with the possible exception of the printed word."[50] The report ends by recommending fundamental changes in the penal code so that the legal standards governing the state conform to international principles of human rights ratified by Mexico. The new governor also, according to one female Chiapan activist, increased repression and "started to strike at [peasant] leaders . . . it was very serious and very selective."[51] This is corroborated by Harvey:

> The first three months of his [Garrido's] administration saw the assassination of several members of independent organizations, including two of the principal leaders in the state: Sebastián Pérez Núñez of the CIOAC and Arturo Albores Velasco of the OCEZ. González Garrido denied government involvement but human rights activists criticized the impunity of these and other actions.[52]

When coupled with the electoral fraud of the same year and the fall of the price of coffee the following year, "this . . . boom in assassinations by White Guards, above all in the north of Chiapas and in the Jungle," Marcos argues, was one of "the various ingredients that explain the massive growth of the EZLN" during 1988–89.[53]

Chiapas was not alone in its suffering. As Castañeda observes, "In Mexico, human rights organizations of all stripes and colors have sprung up across the country since 1988, as the human rights situation deteriorated and various Church groups, from Dominicans to Jesuits, and regional associations from Chihuahua to Chiapas, devoted part of their energy to this issue."[54] As part of this trend, and in response to the new governor's revision of the penal code, in March of the following year Bishop Samuel Ruiz established the Fray Bartolomé de las Casas Human Rights Center. As Gary MacEoin notes:

> The first issue of the center's bulletin had demonstrated the need for such a watchdog. Assembling only materials available on the public record, it listed 4,732 cases of repressive actions between January 1974 and July 1987 to which public authority was a party: assassinations, tortures, imprisonments, theft of titles to land, repression of protest marches.[55]

Economically, in the country at large, "Mexico's per capita consumption of rice, black beans, corn and wheat—the poor's basic staples—was halved between 1981 and 1988":[56] the poor were experiencing severe malnutrition. According to one source, "The proportion of maize producers operating at a loss jumped from 43 percent in 1987 to 65 percent in 1988"[57]—a statistic that is particularly significant considering that Chiapas is one of Mexico's major maize-cultivating states.

13. Bust and Boom

Although both the EZLN and the Catholic Church attempted to give the outward appearance of abiding by the 1988 pact, each worked secretly to extend its influence and undermine that of the other. Marcos spent much of his time and effort in the period 1989 to 1993 attempting to counter Bishop Ruiz's pacifying influence in the region. Despite this rift, or possibly as an attempt at healing it, Germán proposed that on 4 February 1989 Ruiz should bless the opening of a clinic that "1200 [EZLN] combatants had come together to construct" at Ibarra near Ocosingo.[1] Ruiz appears to have accepted the olive branch, possibly calculating that this would provide excellent publicity for the Church, demonstrating to both the local and the international community the commitment of the diocese to improving the physical as well as the spiritual well-being of the indigenous chiapanecos. The EZLN no doubt benefited by having the bishop bless the clinic: it would make it appear to the authorities that the clinic was a legitimate Church project and so dissuade them from prying too deeply into its true founders, constituency, and purpose, and it would also generate the appearance of harmony between the Church and the EZLN to local people, who may have felt troubled by the recent tensions between these two powerful local organizations. Money for the clinic had come from a number of sources, among them FLN fund-raisers in Mexico City; from contributions and levies on local, nearby communities; from international aid agencies; and from the diocese. (Two other small clinics were also established in Oventic and Morelia, and all three were in Zapatista heartland and served EZLN communities. Indeed, Major Moisés tells us that as the Zapatistas grew in numerical strength "they began to construct clinics in each region.")[2] This peace offering between the head of the FLN and the head of the diocese, however, did not work in the long run; among the disputes the clinic caused was, for example, the bishop's offense at its distributing contraceptives to Zapatista insurgents and militia.

To compound the problems arising from this local, temporary feud between the Church and the EZLN, other international forces were at work undermining the Zapatistas's position in Chiapas. For example, in October 1989, the government of the People's Republic of China had to roll tanks over "the People" in order to keep them in line, and in November, the fall of the Berlin Wall and the consequent collapse of the Soviet Socialist system (and its attendant ideology) also had a knock-on effect on the EZLN and the FLN, both of which lost frontline cadres and supporters behind the lines. Marcos himself is on record as saying, "Everything we had prepared came crashing down. When we heard that all this [the fall of the Wall] was happening, we said to ourselves: 'We are going to lose people. They are going to start to leave.'"[3]

These fears proved ill founded. Certainly, not everything was all doom and gloom in the EZLN camp. In November, the Zapatistas celebrated their six-year anniversary with military maneuvers while listening on Radio Venceremos to the "brilliant military actions" of the Salvadoran FMLN in seizing the country's capital, San Salvador.[4] (Indeed, the success of the FMLN, the EZLN's heroes and partial role models,[5] perhaps to some extent encouraged the Zapatistas to believe that Central America might yet remain a bastion of revolutionary ardor.) Within six years the EZLN had arrived at a point where they had enough trained combatants to conduct military maneuvers. Moreover, as Marcos informs us, whereas up until and including 1988, "contact with the communities was still sporadic . . . not intimate . . . rather, very much from time to time," this changed in 1989, "when contact became very close, when already in the mountains there were more than a hundred, hundreds of combatants, professional guerrillas who were dedicated purely to this."[6] He notes that although the Zapatistas still did not at this point control entire villages, nor could they move openly and freely among them, as of 1989 "people from the villages would begin to come to the mountains, to the camps, for *fiestas*, on 10 April, on 17 November and on 16 September, the historic *fiestas* of Mexico or of the EZLN."[7]

As a further counterweight to the bleak news from Eastern Europe and China, the Mexican government was continuing to drive Chiapan *campesinos* into the EZLN's arms. For example, the appointment in December 1988 of the pro-landowner and Draconian state governor, Patrocinio González Garrido, did much to aggravate tensions in the countryside. As already noted, he introduced excessively severe legislation that prohibited most forms of legitimate demonstration. This was only part of the story however. As the assistant director of the *Diario de Chiapas* newspaper later told *Proceso*: "Terror was only a pretext to build an economic empire. Using terror, and under the guise of respect for the law, Don Patrocinio accumulated his inexplicable wealth."[8] In addition, he was responsible for imposing a ban on forestry, which consequently removed a source of income for many chiapaneco *campesinos*. According to an anonymous peasant leader of the Emiliano Zapata Campesino Organization: "Right now we are dealing with a law that was passed when Patronicio González was governor of Chiapas that prohibits cutting wood in the forest. This law affected the communities in the region a great deal because many compañeros make their living from wood."[9] Hinting at the inequities and corruption that allowed large international companies to log considerable expanses of forest but that would lead to the long imprisonment of an indigenous person for cutting enough timber for subsistence and petty retail, he adds: "It's not true that when they passed that law they stopped deforestation; it goes on. It's not possible to save the life of a tree and deny the life of the people in the indigenous communities. That did a lot of damage."[10] The extent of the "damage" caused to chiapanecos by this law may be noted from the fact that "in Altamirano, 93 percent of homes use firewood for cooking," while "in Ocosingo, 89 percent use firewood, and in Las Margaritas, 92 percent do."[11] Little wonder that these three municipalities became Zapatista strongholds.

Furthermore, at the same time: "The international price of coffee fell from $120 to 140 to an average of $60 to 70 per 100 pounds, leading to a 65 percent decrease in producers' incomes . . . [while] the closure of the government-controlled *Inmecafé* company eliminated channels of commercialization and technical support in the region."[12] Rosalva Aída Hernández Castillo details what this meant for coffee-producing *campesinos*: "In 1989 a small-scale coffee grower with a minimum of two hectares (the average for Mam peasants) that yielded a crop of five hundred pounds would obtain in the market a sum equivalent to 369 days of minimum-wage labor: by 1995 the same producers obtained only 195 days of minimum-wage labor."[13] Chiapas's economy was heavily dependent at this time on coffee. As Marcos states: "Chiapas bleeds coffee. Thirty-five percent of the coffee produced in Mexico comes from this area. The industry employs 87,000 people.[14] More than 100,000 tons of coffee are taken from this state to fatten the beast's bank accounts."[15] While the Mexican government cannot be blamed for an international fall in coffee prices, the abolition of Inmecafé, undertaken in preparation for participation in NAFTA or motivated by more general neoliberal trends which were sweeping the continent at that time, represented the government's complete abandonment of the Chiapan peasantry to the vicissitudes of the world market.[16] Many chiapanecos interpreted this as the government reneging on its duty to protect them from outside forces.[17] Van Cott perhaps sums it up best, writing:

> Coffee is the most important agricultural product of Chiapas, representing 46 percent of national production, 70 percent of which is cultivated by small growers. . . . In 1989, however, international coffee prices fell to half their prior level. Because the Salinas administration had dismantled a system of agricultural supports that previously had sustained peasant growers during times of hardship, the coffee growers were left with mounting debts and few alternatives. As the main source of cash income for Indians in eastern Chiapas, the crisis experienced by the coffee-growers cooperatives and the insensitivity of the government to their pleas for assistance fueled political unrest and opposition to the Salinas administration.[18]

Marcos himself listed "the fall in the price of coffee" as "one of the various ingredients that explained the massive growth of the EZLN."[19]

To make matters worse, a political blow accompanied the economic one caused by the collapse of coffee prices. Previously in indigenous communities, local authorities had been granted the power to preside over non-felony (civil) disputes among community members in accordance with indigenous custom. A township would elect its own president, who would resolve such disputes in addition to undertaking functions similar to those of a town mayor. As communities became more and more divided during the 1970s between PRI and opposition members, townships which were most divided elected a magistrate for each faction. Thus, each faction's house could be kept in order without the involvement of magistrates from the opposing side. Although divisive, as a modus vivendi this arrangement proved fairly effective. However, in 1989 the Chiapas governor, González, ruled that only one magistrate per community would be permitted and that each one must hold an official appointment from the governor. A staunch PRI man, he tended only to grant such appointments to pro-PRI individuals. Thus, many anti-PRI factions in indigenous communities now had to submit themselves to their opponents if they wanted recourse to customary law.

Finally, the Mexican government began accelerating the militarization of Chiapas. As Van Cott observes, "In order to subdue the increasing opposition political activity that had surrounded the 1988 elections, in 1989 the Salinas administration beefed up the military presence in Chiapas."[20]

The net impression given by the government to the chiapanecos was one of total neglect followed by legislative and military repression unleashed against any expression of sentiment this engendered.

Meanwhile, in Mexico at large the economic climate deteriorated further. Castañeda notes, "The ancestral injustice of Mexican society attained alarming proportions [by 1989], making citizens unequal even in the face of death: according to the World Bank, life expectancy for the poorest 10 percent of the population was twenty years less than for the richest 10 percent."[21] Thus, far from subsiding due to the demise of the Socialist bloc, the potential for revolution continued to grow in Mexico, since although the fall of the Berlin Wall made a Socialist or Communist revolution improbable, the prerequisite conditions for a revolution flourished with each passing year. As Paco Ignacio Taibo II, Mexico's detective novelist and author of a biography of Che Guevara, commented on 10 October 1990:

> The fact that the [old-style, Soviet Socialist/Communist] revolution is impossible does not make it morally less necessary, nor the reasons for revolt less urgent, even without an alternative. The PRI are still scum, and the country they propose is still a mixture of economic misery for many, social misery for the majority, and moral misery for all.[22]

Thus, when the FLN celebrated its twentieth anniversary in August, its Chiapas wing, the EZLN, could muster several thousand militants for its march in Galeana.[23] Indeed, Marcos notes that "in this period, from 1989 to 1990, we went being from several hundred to thousands of combatants . . . it was a boom in Zapatismo, a phenomenal expansion, out of all proportion."[24]

14. Fallout

In 1990 the shockwaves resulting from the fall of the Berlin Wall began to be felt throughout the world. The early nineties represented a major crisis for the Left and led to its demoralization at all levels. The FLN and the EZLN were no exception. The FMLN accepted dialogue in 1989, and Colombia's M-19 (19th of April Movement) followed suit in March 1990—its subsequent gains in the 1991 general election, after it had converted into a political party, caused many Latin Americans to think that armed struggle was now obsolete. February 1990 saw the Sandinistas being voted out of power in Nicaragua—a huge blow for Marcos, who, as we have seen, was an ardent admirer of Nicaragua's Socialist revolution. Almost exactly a year later, in February 1991, Ecuador's "Alfaro Lives, Dammit!" guerrillas also came to the negotiating table. Meanwhile, Sendero Luminoso was dealt a severe blow on 12 September 1992 when its leader, Abimael Guzmán, was arrested by police. Added to this, Maoists suffered a blow from reforms undertaken in China which caused a huge crisis of confidence and identity in revolutionary groups worldwide.

As a result, almost overnight many renounced an ideology they had been inspired by and had suffered for all their lives. For example, in August 1991, Volodia Teitelboim, the president of the Chilean Communist Party, once a persecuted group, decided to drop all reference to Marxism and Leninism in the party's statutes. Conversely, others reacted vehemently against being told that their doctrine was a false one and had always been so—they refused to concede this, for conceding it would have robbed them of their past and present raison d'être and their future dreams. It would have also rendered their sufferings and losses meaningless, something which many could not even bear to contemplate. The armed Left either had to recant its revolutionary ways and sit down at peace talks in order to follow a democratic path or adopt a hard-line Maoist stance, claiming moral and ideological superiority over what they perceived as Soviet and Chinese revisionism.

To some extent, Marcos's skill, and perhaps his major success, lies in the fact that he found another way, neither reverting to a fossilized doctrine, nor completely renouncing his revolutionary heritage and beliefs. Such clear flexibility of mind, which contradicts de la Grange's and Rico's assertion that Marcos's character was always doctrinaire and uncompromising, may be attributed to the fact that he had been spared much of the persecution, suffering, and loss of others on the Left. Whatever Marcos's personal thoughts on the matter, however, publicly the FLN and EZLN at this time maintained a traditional Marxist-Leninist stance. As we shall see, the aims and language of the FLN and EZLN remained explicitly Socialist down to and including the January 1994 uprising. Marcos's mind may have been flexible, but Germán was still in overall command, and he remained staunchly doctrinaire. Moreover, given that Socialist ideology had sustained the guerrillas during many hard years in the jungle; that its promise of improving the living conditions of the peasants had attracted many chiapanecos to the EZLN; and that once they had joined the organization these cadres had been extensively schooled in Socialism, renunciation of Marxism-Leninism at this stage would have precipitated a dangerous crisis of identity and purpose. As Tello Díaz observes: "The project that the rebels defended in secrecy—Socialism—had been of course necessary in order to survive the years in the jungle. It was impossible for them to renounce it: they had nothing else."[1] Marcos to some extent confirms this in an interview with Oppenheimer.[2] When asked why the EZLN's statutes, laws, and other writings remained staunchly Socialist in their outlook and vocabulary, he replied that the Zapatista troops had become accustomed over the years to formulating and articulating their ideas using Marxist rhetoric and that any change in this language, let alone in the content of these concepts, would have resulted in ideological confusion.

Marcos received considerable encouragement in the form of the continued success the EZLN had in drawing the indigenous to its banner. And, in Ecuador, in June 1990, the indigenous gave ample demonstration of what Indian power could achieve by bringing the capital, Quito, to a halt for a week.[3] Left-wing groups elsewhere in the world, and particularly in Eastern Europe, had nothing to encourage or comfort them in their moment of disillusionment, whereas the EZLN's isolation protected it from this tide of gloom. The experience of the Zapatistas in bucking the world trend was considerably aided by the continuing economic depression in Mexico. As Weinberg observes, "A 1990 World Bank study found that 41 million (nearly half) of the population lived in poverty; 17 million in extreme poverty."[4] In

Chiapas, the government's criminal neglect of the state's population was reflected in official statistics. "Data for 1990 from the National Population Council show that out of a population of over 3.5 million, 30.1% were illiterate, while 62% did not complete their primary education . . . 30% of all dwellings had no electricity, 40% lacked piped water."[5] The previous year's coffee crisis, impacting upon an already impoverished peasantry, meant that "nineteen percent of the working population receive[d] no income and nearly forty percent receive[d] less than the minimum wage [11 pesos, roughly $3.00 per day]."[6] In addition to falling incomes, a rising birth rate put further pressure on land and resources, a problem that Marcos had identified and over which he had clashed with Bishop Ruiz. "From 1980 to 1990, Chiapas reported an average growth rate [in live births] of 5.4 percent annually, twice the average annual rate for the whole country, which was 2.15 percent during the same period."[7]

As if neglect were not enough to drive indigenous *campesinos* into the EZLN's waiting arms, this period witnessed a significant escalation in state repression. Violence erupted in Comitán when the army attempted to evict peasants from a plot of land that had been granted them by presidential decree decades earlier. According to one indigenous chiapaneco interviewed in 1994:

> Way back in 1940, a president had promised the Indios there a piece of land (*un paraje*) for each Indio. But three years ago [in 1991], the promise had been erased when their land was forcibly taken by the Mexican Army. A minor rebellion had taken place and a group known as the Organización Campesina Emiliano Zapata was formed.[8]

In the communities of Paso Achiote, Emiliano Zapata, and Unión y Progreso, police and hired gunmen working for ranchers evicted over a hundred families from land they were occupying there.[9] In addition, as Harvey observes, "Several settlements in Chiapa de Corzo were destroyed by state police and landowners on two separate occasions in April 1990 and April 1991."[10]

On 14 March, the first major open confrontation between the state government and the diocese's new human rights center took place. State police violently evicted farm workers from land in the municipality of Ocosingo. Ruiz publicly denounced such police repression. No doubt in retaliation, the police then arrested two workers from the Human Rights Center and accused Marcelo Rotsaet, a Belgian priest working for the diocese, of being the intellectual author of land takeovers and of inciting Guatemalan refugees to join the Guatemalan guerrilla movement. Although the charges were never proved, Rotsaet's migration papers were confiscated, and he was sent to Mexico City and held incommunicado for forty hours before being expelled from the country.

Human rights violations grew apace in Chiapas (and throughout Mexico) during the early 1990s and were documented by Human Rights Watch America, Amnesty International, and Minnesota Advocates for Human Rights.[11] It is therefore hardly surprising to learn that of the seventy-two reported land invasions undertaken by peasants during the period from November 1986 to 1990, sixty-nine ended in the forcible expulsion of the *campesinos*.[12]

15. From the People's Guerrilla to a Guerrilla People

The increased militarization of the state, coupled with continued neglect (compounded by a cholera epidemic[1]) and an increase in repression, more than offset the calls for peace of Bishop Ruiz and resulted in a local reversal of the continental trend away from guerrilla warfare. As Marcos notes:

> When everything in the world was saying no to armed struggle, because the option of communism had disappeared, we thought that people here would also say no to change, and particularly to armed struggle. It was logical, there was tremendous ideological bombardment. But the opposite happened in the communities. That was when more people joined us, when more people joined the Zapatista Army militia, when more towns declared: "we are being left with no other choice." When everything internationally was saying no to armed struggle, indigenous *campesinos* in Chiapas were saying yes, yes, yes.[2]

Marcos even asserts that he and the rest of the leadership tried to dissuade the lower ranking cadres from pushing for action by pointing to the less than encouraging signs coming from the international arena, to which, the Subcommander claims, they replied: "We don't want to know what's happening in the rest of the world. We are dying and we have to ask the people. Didn't you say that we must do what the people say? . . . Well, let's ask them."[3]

The increasing desperation of the indigenous, which manifested itself in their clamoring to join the ranks of the EZLN, also meant that Marcos was insulated from much—though not all[4]—of the global demoralization felt by many of those on the Left. As more and more young indigenous cadres were recruited, the percentage of Zapatistas in each community rose. Given that recruitment frequently took place through family members and along kinship lines, stretching even to friends of the family, soon entire communities became Zapatista. This in turn meant that the guerrillas could approach communities directly and move freely among them.

As the communities and the EZLN interacted they were forced to adapt themselves in order to fit with each other. As Marcos put it, "There began the process of transformation for the EZLN, from an army of the revolutionary vanguard to an army of the indigenous communities, an army that is part of the indigenous resistance movement."[5] It is clear that the coming together of the EZLN and the indigenous communities was not a smooth process. Marcos tells us that "there was a certain amount of clashing while we made the adjustment from our orthodox way of seeing the world in terms of 'bourgeois and proletarians' to the community's collective democratic conceptions, and their world view."[6] In another interview he elaborates further on this culture clash:

> Once the EZLN has come closer to the communities, it can't make decisions without first giving the communities notice of what's to be done, and through a slow process we ended up asking them permission. That's when the collision happened, and the political-military organization stopped making decisions vertically and started making collective decisions horizontally. This is the first defeat (*derrota*) of the EZLN and starts to be known massively . . . this was around 1990–91.[7]

That Marcos allowed the EZLN to be "defeated" by the communities is, I believe, another example of the Subcommander's flexibility of mind and to some extent of his genius. Many previous guerrilla insurgencies in Latin America had failed due to the inability of their leaders—usually young, white, educated, middle-class, Marxist/Maoists, like Marcos—to submit themselves to the will of their potential peasant and/or indigenous recruit base. These leaders traditionally perceived their role as instilling or raising the class consciousness of the peasantry in order to wage a guerrilla war, in short, as a one-way process whereby they were the bestowers of knowledge and the peasants were its recipients. Marcos, to his credit, was able to alter his perception of this role, eventually going so far as to invert it.[8] That the Subcommander would effect such a complete turnaround was anything but a certainty. While Kampwirth is correct in observing that "being a multi-ethnic, dual-gender movement, the EZLN could not have been doctrinaire if it wanted to hold that coalition together," and that therefore necessity to some extent forced the EZLN to become less doctrinaire if it wanted to succeed in Chiapas, she is equally correct in her observation that its leadership "did not have to accept the new agenda and strategies. It could have refused to take the lead of the locals, either trying to impose its agenda on the jungle residents or leaving in search of a new place to organize."[9] That the leadership "instead . . . stayed, becoming less Marxist and more indigenous in the process"[10] was never a foregone conclusion and is what distinguishes the EZLN and Marcos from so many other Latin American guerrilla insurgencies.

In any case, this "defeat" brought about a massive swelling of the EZLN's ranks. Marcos himself talks "about an increase from dozens of combatants to thousands in a few months"[11] and elsewhere concludes: "I think that we were absolutely on target when we surrendered, when we said that it would be better to do what they said. That is when the EZLN spread and grew explosively."[12]

Since the communities were unwilling to submit themselves totally to the dictates of the outsiders, each organized a local militia which, though trained by Marcos, was under the direct orders of the local community. In some ways this weakened the EZLN since its military power now became decentralized, dispersed, and fragmented. Rapid, full mobilization or military action became impossible, since each local unit had to receive orders from the local community leaders. However, in other ways it was a great strength, since under the previous *foco*-style structure communities were seldom prepared to submit themselves completely to outsiders. Now, whole communities were prepared to become Zapatista since they retained autonomy. As Marcos puts it: "We gave military action second place to organization of the population: as a result, it's very difficult to draw a line between the combat force and the support population. We say here that even the hens are Zapatistas."[13] This politico-military federation of communes eventually became an integrated network through the establishment of interregional commands, the culmination of which was the creation of the Comité Clandestino de Revolución Indígena (CCRI, Clandestine Indigenous Revolutionary Committee) in 1993.

Its increased size and its emergence as a more community-integrated "people's army"[14] meant that the EZLN could now model its structure on that of a regular army.[15] Instead of operating in small units like most guerrilla forces, the EZLN was now able to establish a fully integrated command structure. Within this, the three Subcommanders, Marcos, Daniel, and Pedro, each commanded a regiment comprising approximately 1,500 combatants.[16] Directly under them were eight majors, Alfredo, César, Javier, Josué, Mario, Moisés, Rolando, and Yolanda, each in charge of a battalion of 40 *insurgentes* and 500 *milicianos*. Subordinate to the majors were the captains, each leading a company of fifteen soldiers. Finally, each captain had three lieutenants, who were responsible for a section of five combatants.[17] Thus, the EZLN was made up of a basic kernel of about 320 highly trained cadres—the *insurgentes*—around which were the *milicianos*, part-time troops, less well-trained, armed, or disciplined than the insurgents. Though it was small, its fixed units and established chain-of-command meant that the EZLN, unlike most of the guerrilla groups calling themselves *ejércitos* (armies), actually deserved this description. To mark this new status, Marcos tells us that in 1991 the EZLN held military "maneuvers with four thousand men, designed to cover all entrances into the jungle."[18]

Throughout 1991, Marcos also sought to extend the EZLN's influence even further in the region by infiltrating the Asociación Rural de Interés Colectivo (ARIC, Rural Association of Collective Interests), its largest peasant organization. He had previously managed to gain control of another of the region's *campesino* unions, the Unión de Ejidos de la Selva, through its leader, Humberto Trejo, and through Francisco Gómez, a Tzeltal from Las Cañadas who had been president of Quiptic in the late 1970s, secretary of the Unión de Uniones/ARIC in the late 1980s, and then one of the leaders of the Alianza Nacional Campesina Independiente Emiliano Zapata (ANCIEZ, Emiliano Zapata Independent National Peasant Alliance) during the early 1990s. Both Trejo and Gómez were members of the EZLN, bearing the noms de guerre of Tacho and Hugo respectively. (ARIC had grown considerably during the 1980s, representing the culmination of a unification process whereby several Uniones de Ejidos, including Quiptic, had come together. The Unión de Uniones added ARIC to its name in 1988.) Marcos hoped that he could use the ARIC Unión de Uniones to boost recruitment,[19] organize the peasants, and create a legitimate front for the EZLN. Initially, at least, he was successful in this venture. Leyva Solano observes that "in the Las Cañadas region of the *municipios* of Ocosingo and Altamirano, the population that participated in both the *Unión de Uniones* and the EZLN in 1990 came to approximately 23,300 and controlled 60,757 hectares of *ejidal* property and 7,751 hectares of private property."[20] Marcos even managed to have a long-serving Zapatista cadre, Lázaro Hernández (alias Jesús), elected to the presidency of ARIC in 1991, although by now the organization had polarized, dividing itself into two opposing factions: that supporting the EZLN and that rejecting the armed struggle; Lázaro's victory in the election for president had been a very close run thing. However, for a while, indeed up to the outbreak of hostilities in January 1994, Lázaro proved invaluable to the Zapatista cause. As a catechist of many years standing he had close ties with Ruiz and with many members of Slop, and so he served to bridge the gap between Marcos and the bishop. His example also demonstrated that belonging to the EZLN and being a friend of the bishop (and a good Catholic) were not necessarily mutually exclusive. In the long run, however, Marcos was to lose his grip on ARIC after the uprising in 1994, when Lázaro decided that the best way to improve the lot of its members was to reject the EZLN and instead to court the favor of the government. Humberto Trejo (alias Tacho), on the other hand, stayed with the EZLN, rising to the rank of Comandante, while Francisco Gómez (alias Hugo) went on to become *capitán* before dying in Ocosingo during the uprising.

In February 1991 Germán made another visit to Chiapas. This time however, he brought with him the ashes of his recently deceased mother, whose dying wish had been to have her remains scattered at Laguna Ocotal where her son, Germán's brother, César (Pedro), was reportedly last seen alive. Again, this event highlights the difference in revolutionary experience between Germán and Marcos, and helps in no small way to explain why Marcos was able to free himself from the doctrinaire constraints of the Socialist cause that continued to bind Germán. Marcos had not invested as much emotionally in the cause as Germán, nor had he sacrificed as much.

Also early in the year, the Federal Army discovered a cache of guerrilla equipment, including uniforms, wooden practice rifles, and such, in the *ejido* of Quintana Roo, near Sabanilla. Although, as in the 1988 discovery, none of the items discovered pointed directly to a specifically Mexican guerrilla group, other evidence was found that incriminated a local priest, Felipe Toussaint, in dealings with the EZLN. Felipe, or Oscar as he was known to the guerrillas, had had frequent contact with the EZLN from its inception in 1983, holding Communion in nearby villages, many of which were pro-Zapatista. This alerted the Federal Army to the involvement by some clerics in insurgent activities and helped to increase tension between the diocese and the military in Chiapas. Less than six months later, Joel Padrón, the parish priest of Simojovel, was arrested on charges related to guerrilla activity.

The year 1991 also saw the further militarization of the state. Rancho Nuevo, the headquarters of the 83rd Infantry Battalion, was built near San Cristóbal on federal highway 190, which leads to Comitán and ultimately the Guatemalan border, 120 km to the south. According to the government, it was constructed in order to police the movement of Guatemalans entering Mexico from across the border. No doubt the United States had

brought pressure to bear on this matter, with Mexican control of the border with Guatemala having the additional benefit of hindering the passage
of illegal immigrants into the United States from Central America,[21] and
assisting in the war on drugs. De la Grange and Rico argue that Rancho
Nuevo was created because the Mexican government had been tipped off
by the Guatemalan security forces as to the presence of Mexican guerrillas in Chiapas.[22] (Previously the only guerrilla forces operating in Chiapas
had been Guatemalan, which, like that of Mario Payeras and his *foco*, had
trained in Chiapas and then used it as a springboard to launch themselves
back into their national fray. These were to some extent tolerated by the
Mexican government since they posed no real threat to Mexico's internal
security.) Whatever the motivation behind it, the establishment of this new
base was perceived by the Indians as an unwelcome imposition. In particular, it was built on an old Tzotzil graveyard. Locals had tried to dissuade the
government from siting it there, and there was even a campaign against the
site by *El Tiempo*, the San Cristóbal newspaper.

There were other signs of increasing militarization in the region. The
American journalist and author Worth H. Weller recounts the experience
of Dr. Lucila Vargas from the department of journalism and mass media
communication at the University of North Carolina at Chapel Hill who, in
1991, was a radio journalist in Las Margaritas, near Comitán. As Weller
points out, "One of the first things that happened to her was that four
truckloads of heavily armed troops turned up in front of her radio station
to see what 'this light-skinned journalist was up to.'" Weller quotes Vargas
as saying:

> To believe that Chiapas wasn't heavily militarized before the 1994 up-
> rising is simply a false assumption. The Zapatistas did not cause the
> militarization of Chiapas. When I was there it was already much more
> heavily militarized than any other area of Mexico. This is simply how
> Mexico has always treated its indigenous people.[23]

This is corroborated by veteran anthropologist George A. Collier:

> Although Mexico has always used the carrot and stick to win political
> support, the drying up of state economic resources has weakened the
> government's capacity for retaining loyalties other than by policing
> them . . . militarization was significant in Chiapas in the wake of the
> 1994 rebellion, but it actually began in the late eighties. (I vividly re-
> member the arrival in 1989 of a contingent of troops in Zinacantán

to persuade the municipal authorities there to acquire arms to defend against rogues and dissidents.)[24]

The summer of 1991 saw midterm elections in Mexico, in which the PRD officially received a mere 9 percent of the vote. Electoral fraud was again widely suspected at home and abroad, with the *New York Times* running the story "The Missing Reform in Mexico," in which it lumped Mexico with Cuba, Guyana, and Suriname as the four countries in the hemisphere where free and fair elections did not occur.[25] Moreover, as had been the trend for decades, electoral fraud was even more pronounced and extreme in Chiapas than in the rest of the country. MacEoin observes, for example, that "Chiapas had more municipalities that voted 100 percent PRI than any other state," and goes on to cite the example of San Juan Cancuc, "where 102 percent of the inhabitants were registered to vote."[26] Oppenheimer wrote scathingly: "Some districts in Chiapas reported official results that could have been included in the *Guinness Book of Records* if anybody had believed in their fairness: In La Trinitaria, for instance, the PRI scored 18,114 votes, the opposition, 0."[27] So too, Russell observes how "in Oxchuc, the PRI obtained not 99.9 percent of the 11,073 votes cast, but 100 percent." Moreover, Russell goes on to note: "In 1991, the opposition Party of the Democratic Revolution (PRD) claimed it had won mayoral elections in Ocosingo and Las Margaritas (two municipalities later occupied by the rebels). . . . Nevertheless, Gov. González Garrido awarded these mayoralties to the PRI candidates and jailed 153 PRD supporters."[28] (This no doubt did much to strengthen Marcos's argument that all legitimate democratic attempts at opposing the government were futile.) In short, the result was that after the 1991 elections the governor was PRI, the city mayor was PRI, 110 out of 111 of the state's municipalities were PRI ruled (thereby also ensuring that the state congress was more than 99 percent PRI controlled), and all the judicial and military authorities were PRI.

Meanwhile, on 20–21 July, Marcos created a legitimate front for the EZLN in the form of a peasant organization called ANCIEZ.[29] This organization allowed the EZLN to conduct marches, demonstrations, and protests in public under a legitimate guise. Frank was chosen to head ANCIEZ. He was a veteran guerrilla, having formed part of the group, headed by Germán and Elisa, that had first established the EZLN in Chiapas in 1983. From Chiapas he had moved to Puebla, spending many years organizing the peasant communities around Coxcatlán between the Sierra Negra and the Tehuacán valley, before returning to Chiapas again. ANCIEZ began its activities near the *ejido* of San Isidro el Ocotal, in predominantly Tzotzil-dominated Zapatista heartland. (Less than two years later this *ejido* would be held responsible by the Federal Army for the killing of two of its intelligence operatives in the region; thirteen members of the community were rounded up and tortured into confessing to the murder; see chapter 17.) ANCIEZ soon spread its influence throughout the Altamirano municipality. (Needless to say, the movement also enjoyed a close working relationship with ARIC, given that both organizations at this time were headed by long-standing Zapatista cadres.) Unsurprisingly, its professed aims were almost exactly the same as the EZLN's (that is, to struggle for more and better land, clean water, schools, credit, etc.), and to this end it created workshops and funded clinics in the area. Bishop Ruiz and his diocese were no longer necessary to provide a legitimate front to such projects.

In the beginning of September, Bishop Ruiz gave a press conference in Mexico City in which he declared that Chiapas was the worst state in the whole country for human rights violations. He cited in particular the recent case whereby state police had detained 129 members of the Union of Ejiditarios who had been on their way to Mexico City to seek redress from President Salinas. Among those detained were eighteen women and four children, all of whom were brutally beaten, the former being made to strip naked as an additional humiliation.[30] *La Jornada* subsequently published the bishop's denunciations nationwide.[31] This caused a very tense atmosphere between the diocese and the state government. On 18 September, police arrested Joel Padrón, the parish priest of Simojovel, accusing him of robbery, threatening behavior, illegal possession of firearms, and "gang-making." One must conclude that this represented a warning by state authorities to Ruiz that if he continued to draw attention to the poor human rights record of Chiapas, the state authorities would make life hard for him, his colleagues, and subordinates. Padrón was held in the notorious Cerro Hueco jail in Tuxtla Gutiérrez. Meanwhile, Ruiz and the diocese mobilized demands for his release, which was achieved the next month (6 November) following a large demonstration in the state capital and a report by Amnesty International. However, this victory came at a cost, as Marcos observes:

> While thousands of *campesinos* marched in Tuxtla Gutiérrez to demand Padrón's freedom, ranchers in Ocosingo sent their paramilitary forces to clear out property-owning *campesinos*. Four hundred men, armed by the ranchers, destroyed and burned houses, beat indigenous women

and murdered a *campesino*, Juan, by shooting him in the face. After the expulsion, the paramilitary forces . . . drove along the region's roads in pick-up trucks provided by their masters. Ostentatiously displaying their arms, drunk and intoxicated, they shouted: "Ranchers are number one!" and warned everyone that it was only the beginning. Undaunted, municipal authorities in Ocosingo and soldiers stationed in the region looked passively on the gunmen's triumphant parade. In Tuxtla Gutiérrez, almost 10,000 *campesinos* marched in favor of Father Padrón's release. In a corner of Ocosingo, Juan's wife buried her husband, victim of the proud ranchers. There was no march or protest petition for Juan's death.[32]

On 21 September, the Mexican army stumbled on one of the guerrilla training camps near Sabanilla in the north of Chiapas. However, as in February 1988 and earlier in 1991, it again failed to follow up on its discovery. This is perhaps not as surprising as one might at first think, since the security forces were well aware that for the past decade Guatemalan guerrillas had been training in Chiapas with an eye to launching themselves over the border; they probably concluded that this camp was one of theirs, and so no threat to Mexico's internal security.

The same month saw the distribution among senior U.S. State Department and National Security Latin American specialists of a classified fifteen-page report by the Central Intelligence Agency entitled *Mexico's Troubled South: Being Left Behind*, which stated that "high level corruption, reportedly including the governor of Chiapas, was undermining local authorities and contributing to sporadic violence." It concluded that because of declining living standards and increasing frustration in the face of government intransigence and corruption, political discontent would rise. It also noted that "southern states have a tradition of tumultuous local politics," although it (wrongly) dismissed any threat of "a cohesive region wide threat to the ruling party" because local grassroots organizations limited their activities to purely "parochial interests."[33]

In October, at Quetzaltenango, in neighboring Guatemala, the first international meeting of indigenous people took place. (San Cristóbal, it should be remembered, is closer to Quetzaltenango than it is to Mexico City, and almost as easy to reach.) This meeting marked the beginning of what would emerge in the following year as a rapidly growing spontaneous indigenous movement within the region. For now, however, in late 1991, the contrast between Guatemala and Chiapas could not have been starker.

On 28 December at Palenque, when members of the Committee for the Defense of Indigenous Liberty assembled to demonstrate against corruption, state interference in the life of their communities, and deleterious national economic policies, they were violently dispersed and more than a hundred of them were incarcerated, beaten, and tortured by the state police.[34]

16. Indigenous Indignation

The year 1992 was marked by two crucial developments, both linked to amendments in the Mexican constitution, which resulted in a further swelling of the EZLN ranks. The first concerned an increase in indigenous pride. The year 1992 was the Year of the Indigenous and saw Rigoberta Menchú, an indigenous Guatemalan female activist and author, being awarded the Nobel Peace Prize—the first indigenous person ever to receive it.[1] In neighboring Mexico, as part of this general, hemisphere-wide movement, in January 1992 article 4 of the Mexican constitution was revised to recognize Mexico's indigenous for the first time as a distinct ethnic group (as opposed to members of a particular social class, that is, *campesinos*). As George A. Collier observes, the way had been paved for this amendment back in 1990 when "Mexico ratified additions to the International Labor Organization (ILO) charter, including Conventions 107 and 169, which accord specific collective rights to cultural and ethnic minorities and require nation states to protect their indigenous communities." He adds, "Convention 169 has provided a strong legal basis for indigenous groups in Guatemala to demand protection of cultural rights after the Guatemalan war ended in the 1980s."[2] Now, as Mattiace says, "Convention 169 gave Indian activists a leg to stand on as they pressured the Mexican state to recognize native peoples as peoples, with rights accorded them by international law."[3] The revision of article 4 was certainly a step in the right direction by the Mexican government. However, in order to be in any way effective it had to have corresponding state legislation to support it and a strong commitment to indigenous rights on the part of the state legislators and bureaucrats; needless to say, both were significantly lacking.

As the year progressed, this movement gathered force throughout the continent, finding its ultimate expression in the myriad demonstrations organized in October against the "celebration" of the 500th anniversary of Christopher Columbus's arrival in the Americas in 1492. As Van Cott notes:

Organizing to counter state-sponsored celebrations of the "discovery" of the Americas, which began in earnest in 1989, was one of the most important catalysts to indigenous mobilization in the hemisphere, and this was also the case in Mexico. Not only did the quincentenary mobilizations politicize Indians, it raised awareness of indigenous communities among other sectors of society and engendered sympathy for their problems.[4] This change in attitude toward Indians in Mexico made possible the widespread sympathy later expressed for the EZLN.[5]

This is supported by what Marcos himself tells us of this period:

> In 1992 . . . there was a lot of organizing in the indigenous communities about to commemorate the five hundred years of resistance since the landing of Christopher Columbus in the Americas. That's when the indigenous people of this region said, "We've already been struggling for five hundred years. It's time to say 'enough.'"[6]

In sum, it was only natural that many indigenous people saw the EZLN as an attractive vehicle for promoting their interests, asserting their identity, and pressurizing the government for recognition of their basic rights. Marcos's astuteness is shown by the rapidity with which he grasped the importance of this new movement and the skill with which he harnessed its power.

The second factor that contributed greatly to EZLN recruitment and that was also linked to a change in the Mexican constitution concerned the amendment of article 27 of the constitution a few weeks later, in February 1992. Article 27 dealt specifically with the question of land ownership. In order to pave the way for NAFTA, and in an attempt to encourage investment (especially foreign) in impoverished rural areas,[7] article 27 was changed to allow the sale of communal, *ejido* land, while at the same time the government declared an immediate end to any further state redistribution of land. This ultimately had two major detrimental consequences for chiapaneco *campesinos*. First, they could now lose this land, either by being pressurized by neighboring *latifundias* to sell it or being subject to dispossession by the banks following default on a loan.[8] Second, it crushed all remaining hope of any extra land being granted to them by the government. (Land, as one anthropologist noted, "was more than simply material—it was closely tied to the spiritual, material, and symbolic life of the larger community.")[9] The revision of article 27, in addition to having concrete consequences, also entailed a symbolic one. As García de León points out,

Salinas and his technocrats had dismissed opposition to the law "as mere sterile nostalgia for the past, a simplistic longing for the restoration of a failed utopia . . . [since] today it is said, with some truth, that the original Article 27 was dead and didn't respond to the needs of the present."[10] However, for the chiapaneco *campesinos*, the revision of article 27 represented the repudiation of one of the very few reforms that the Revolution had brought to Chiapas, even if these had taken decades longer to reach that state than many others. Psychologically, it was akin to exhuming Zapata's corpse and scattering the remains to the four winds. Moreover, it saw the government renege on one of the few promises of the Revolution. In short, it was an affront to a national hero and a rebuttal of one of the principles that the modern Mexican State was founded upon. In this way, the government proved unusually insensitive to the importance of revolutionary symbolism; not so the EZLN, which proved far more astute in realizing the importance of symbolism and infinitely more adept at harnessing the imagery of Zapata and the Revolution which it would wrest from the government.[11]

The government was not only insensitive to symbolism; in typical fashion, the PRI ran roughshod over any opposition to the amendment, be it from peasant groups or any other political opponents.[12] Again, García de León notes:

> The presidency rejected the concrete proposals of the majority of the organizations of the CAP [Permanent Agrarian Council], and . . . threatened and bribed legislators for the approval of this law, with no legitimate foundation nor sufficient discussion with the affected sectors of the population. The law was basically approved . . . to make the national agrarian structure compatible with powerful foreign interests, an unequal and increasingly unjust effort which today is called "globalization." If the Salinista reform had been the product of a consensus, as some functionaries have asserted, and not merely the imposition of a reform suggested by the World Bank in 1988, it would not be rejected by a majority of the *campesino* organizations now, as it is being implemented.[13]

Unsurprisingly, one of the peasant organizations most vehemently opposed to the reform was the newly created legitimate front of the EZLN, the ANCIEZ. On 19 January, the same month as the reform was passed, ANCIEZ, in conjunction with ARIC, which was also headed by an EZLN veteran, conducted its first mass mobilization to demonstrate against the reform of article 27 and the NAFTA proposals. Four thousand *campesinos* marched to the central park of Ocosingo and held a rally in which speakers from the organization lambasted not only the article 27 reform and the NAFTA proposals but also the increased militarization of the state. ANCIEZ then sent delegates to the Chamber of Deputies in Mexico City to express their grievances.

Marcos later summed up the *campesinos'* reaction to this steamrollering of their livelihoods and way of life in January 1994:

> [The government] really screwed us, now that they destroyed Article 27, for which Zapata and his Revolution fought. Salinas de Gortari arrived on the scene with his lackeys, and his groups, and in a flash they destroyed it. We and our families have been sold down the river, or you could say that they stole our pants and sold them. What can we do? We did everything legal that we could so far as elections and organizations were concerned, and to no avail.[14]

Similarly, not long afterward, in an interview for *La Jornada*, Marcos stated: "The thing that most radicalized our *compañeros* were the changes to article 27; that was the door that was shut on the Indian people's ability to survive in a legal and peaceful manner. That was the reason they decided to take up arms, so that they could be heard, because they were tired of paying such a high blood tax."[15] Hardly surprising then, as Lorenzano has observed, that the EZLN experienced a wave of "massive affiliations in 1992" in response to the reform.[16]

Meanwhile, also in January, in Mexico City the El Salvadoran government signed a peace treaty with the guerrillas who had been fighting to overthrow it for over a decade. The news was a bitter blow for revolutionary groups everywhere; one scholar claiming that it resulted in "a transnational loss of revolutionary élan."[17] If the FMLN, led by men of the caliber of Joaquín Villalobos and Shafik Handel and personally supported by Fidel Castro, had been forced to admit the impossibility of outright victory, what hope was there for other guerrilla movements? Morale throughout Latin America's guerrilla groups was beginning to ebb, not just because of the FMLN's inability to achieve outright victory, but also because of the ousting of the Sandinistas in Nicaragua and the failure of the Guatemalan guerrillas. Even Marcos could not hide his disappointment. De la Grange and Rico quote their usual source, Antonio, as recollecting that while previously, "Marcos said we should follow the example of the FMLN who had created the conditions necessary for unleashing the revolution in El Salvador," after January 1992 Marcos began saying "they are traitors . . . Joaquín Villalobos is a traitor . . . the *comandantes* did not consult the base. They signed the peace because they sold out. . . . If we have lost Shafik, we will follow another example."[18]

In March 1992, Marcos had to leave Chiapas for Mexico City in order to receive medical treatment for acute gastritis, which had been causing him to vomit almost every time he ate. Captain Yolanda, his wife, attended him, and shortly afterward, when he had fully recovered, they both went to visit Marcos's family in Tampico for a few days. He introduced Yolanda as his wife and told them she was Nicaraguan. He said that they both worked for the National Institute of Adult Education in Tuxtla Gutiérrez where they also owned a general store called Mi Abuela (my grandmother). While at home he also wrote and presented a paper on the consequences of Mexico's signing of the NAFTA agreement entitled "The Twentieth-Century Businessman and the Challenges of His Circumstance."[19] He delivered it on 26 March—also his mother's birthday—to Tampico's Association of Sales and Marketing Executives. Since his retirement Marcos's father had been director of the Asociación de Ejecutivos de Ventas y Mercadotecnia de Tampico, the same organization that had, in 1973, helped fund a short course in public speaking that Rafael attended. This paper bears all the hallmarks of what today we recognize as the Subcommander's style, littered as it is with references to "oblivion," "voices," "the blood of Conquest," "la Patria," "the Fourth World War," and even "having to wear a mask in order to live and love." Where did Marcos's parents believe their son had been for the last decade, during which he had very infrequently contacted them? The answer can be found in a speech his father had made to businessmen in Matamoros, up the coast from Tampico near the U.S. border, almost two weeks previously, in which he had talked of a son who was a philosopher, who had received a doctorate from the Sorbonne, and who was now giving classes in Nicaragua receiving only food and lodging in return. This, his father urged, was "a man who is congruent in his manner of thought, who is married to his principles, who lives his ideals; a Don Quixote of the twentieth century."[20]

Meanwhile, during Marcos's absence from Chiapas the state government signaled its unwillingness to heed indigenous demands by imprisoning three officials from the federal government–sponsored Instituto

Nacional Indigenista (INI, National Indigenist Institute),[21] thereby demonstrating that whereas the rest of the world may have been celebrating the Year of the Indigenous, in Chiapas the Indians would be kept firmly in their place.

Marcos returned to Chiapas in time to witness firsthand ANCIEZ members stage a massive rally in Ocosingo commemorating the anniversary of the death of Emiliano Zapata on 10 April. He describes it in *The Southeast in Two Winds, a Storm and a Prophecy* written four months later:

In the municipal seat of Ocosingo, 4,000 indigenous *campesinos* from the organization ANCIEZ march from different points of the city. Three marches converge in front of the municipal building. The municipal president doesn't know what it's all about and flees. On the floor of his office is a calendar indicating the date: April 10, 1992. Outside, Indigenous *campesinos* from Ocosingo, Oxchuc, Huixtán, Chilón, Yajalon, Sabanilla, Salto de Agua, Palenque, Altamirano, Margaritas, San Cristóbal, San Andrés and Cancuc dance in front of a giant image of Zapata painted by one of them, recite poetry, sing, and speak. Only they are listening. The landowners, businessmen, and judicial officials are closed up in their homes and shops, the federal garrison appears deserted. The *campesinos* shout that Zapata lives and the struggle continues. One of them reads a letter addressed to Carlos Salinas de Gortari in which they accuse him of having brought all of the Agrarian Reform gains made under Zapata to an end, of selling the country with the North American Free Trade Agreement and of bringing Mexico back to the times of Porfirio Díaz. They declare forcefully that they will not recognize Salinas' reforms to Article 27 of the Political Constitution. At two o'clock in the afternoon the demonstration disperses, in apparent order, but the causes persist. With the same outward appearances everything returns to calm.[22]

Marcos's presence in person to observe and supervise this demonstration, together with the choice of venue, Ocosingo's municipal building in the central plaza, and the fact that the march converged there from three different points, makes one wonder if it was not undertaken specifically as a rehearsal for the taking of Ocosingo less than two years later. At the very least it would have acquainted EZLN cadres with the town's layout, a scaled-down reconstruction of which was found when Subcommander Daniel's camp was discovered by the army in May 1993.

April also saw the arrival in Mexico City of the March for Peace and Human Rights of Native Peoples by 400 chiapanecos who had set out six weeks earlier (on 7 March) from Palenque to demonstrate against repression in the state of Chiapas. The Xi'Nich (Chol for "march of the ants"), as they called themselves, undertook their 1,106 km walk in order to petition for the state's new penal code to be reformed and to push for police officers accused of human rights abuses to be put on trial. The march received a great deal of attention in the national press, finally making the desperate plight of indigenous chiapanecos known to the public at large. The marchers even gained assurances from the government that their petition would be addressed. However, as Harvey observes:

> By the end of 1992 several of the demands had not been met. The State's Penal Code was not reformed; no police officers were ever brought to trial for alleged human rights abuses; and municipal presidents continued to impose *agentes municipales*. There were still thirty arrest orders out against CDLI [Committee for the Defense of Indigenous Liberty] members, and new public works had not begun.[23]

In May, Marcos organized a gathering of EZLN troops on the airstrip at La Sultana in order to assess the movement's strength. He writes:

> On 20 May 1992, in a village in the jungle, we assembled 5,000 armed men and women, for a party that we held for no other reason than to see if we were able to do it. On this day, we told each combatant to bring a rocket, a party firework and a firebrand of torch pine. Some were ordered to light their fireworks at the same time, others were ordered to light the firebrands. The idea was that we would be able to emit a tremendous amount of light. . . . And so we lit the firebrands and then and there we realized that we were able to fight, that we were able to join together in order to fight.[24]

Marcos's realization that the EZLN was now a sizeable combative force in turn led him to reflect on both the possibilities this afforded the movement and to contrast its success with that of its mother organization, the FLN, back in Mexico City. Recently, despite some setbacks, the EZLN had enjoyed considerable success in winning over chiapanecos to its cause. Indeed, as already noted above, the fact that the FLN's commemorative celebration in 1988 was held in Chiapas, not in Mexico City or in the area controlled by its northern front, had already signaled its preeminence. The

EZLN was flourishing; the FLN was not—on the contrary, it was struggling. As the former Subcommander Daniel puts it:

> Guillén Vicente began to see that the national and international situation was changing, and also that inside the organization. If the indigenous were financing the cities, it was because there were no militants in the cities. Then, where was this mother organization, the FLN? The safe houses of Mexico City were full of indigenous who were studying radio operating, nursing, techniques for war, but there were no people there from the city.[25]

As if to highlight the differing experiences of the mother organization and its offshoot, Daniel continues, "While Guillén was preparing for war, *Rodrigo* was considering the idea that the FLN should transform itself into a political party and abandon the armed struggle."[26] As Tello Díaz rightly observes, in the long run Marcos would in fact "opt for a variation of what *Rodrigo* had proposed,"[27] downplaying the armed struggle, establishing an unarmed, open and legitimate front (the FZLN) that aimed at unifying disparate groups sympathetic to the Zapatistas and their goals. However, Rodrigo gave, perhaps, the right advice at the wrong time. Marcos realized the incredibly detrimental effect on morale that such a volte-face would have on cadres who had been persuaded of the whole concept of a Marxist-Leninist armed struggle. Why, Marcos must have asked himself, would cadres continue to follow leaders who had suddenly turned around and rejected the philosophy that they had been espousing and teaching for over a decade? Perhaps, moreover, at a personal level, Marcos was not about to sacrifice nearly ten years of guerrilla training and recruitment in the jungle, and with it his dreams of being a guerrilla leader in the mold of Che Guevara fighting for social justice, just because the FLN in Mexico City was flagging, and especially not when he and the EZLN were experiencing such success. He therefore set about strengthening the EZLN's hand by ensuring that the indigenous chiapanecos comprising it continued to focus on military matters.

Thus, throughout the spring and early summer of 1992 Marcos toured the communities in the region canvassing the indigenous on their views about the forthcoming "celebration" of the discovery of America by Christopher Columbus. The more the issue was debated, and the more the media in Mexico and elsewhere made of this anniversary, adding insult to injury by employing the euphemistic phrase "a meeting of two worlds" to describe what the majority of indigenous perceived as a process of conquest and extermination, the more passions were inflamed. Feelings ran high in the communities, no doubt stoked up considerably by Marcos and the guerrilla leadership, and it was felt that this final insult could not go unchallenged: action of some description was required to ensure that contemporaries would not celebrate and history would not record genocide as merely an encounter between two cultures. As Marcos himself tells us, "In 1992 we perceived a question that was very important for the indigenous communities, which was the character of the Conquest, what the Discovery of America signified," adding, "inside the indigenous movement at the local level—I'm not sure of the national level—there was concern about what this signified and the necessity to have a demonstration."[28] Thus, when, in August—the same month in which he wrote his *The Southeast in Two Winds*[29]—Marcos conducted a referendum among 65,000 indigenous *campesinos* (representing roughly 60 communities) in Las Cañadas to canvas their opinions as to the form this action should take, they opted for war. Marcos described this consultation process in considerable detail in an interview with Le Bot, in which he claimed:

> This was the first consultation of what came to be a regular style of organizing the Zapatistas in the communities. This happened in the second half of 1992 and coincided with the mobilization that the indigenous peoples were making to celebrate the five hundred years, the grand march that was to happen on the 12 October in San Cristóbal. The indigenous proposed it as the last civil presentation of the indigenous movement that is already Zapatista. . . .
>
> During this time we were carrying out the consultation, with an explanation in each town about conditions in the community among the ethnic groups, about the international situation, the national situation, and asking whether or not the time was right to begin the war. In the months of September, October, and the first two weeks of November, we carried out the consultation in something like four hundred or five hundred communities, among Tzotziles, Ch'oles, Tojolabales, and Tzeltales. In the north, the highlands, and the cañadas, a majority of the people participated in this consultation . . .
>
> We made the decision by means of a kind of referendum. After the October march, we started the count. . . . The vote was approved by a majority of those inside of the EZLN. The areas where we were operating included the highlands, the North and above all in the jungle. We asked them to send us arguments about why or why not so that the authorities

(military and civil) of the EZLN could evaluate the situation. Among the Zapatistas who voted against the war [there] was the argument that the repression would be very severe, that the people were not ready, that there were divided communities and that it was better to wait. . . . These were serious arguments. In conclusion, a wide majority of people stated that they were in favor of beginning the war now.[30]

There exists, however, much controversy concerning this consultation process. For one thing, Daniel claims that only 15,000 indigenous in fact voted to commence hostilities.[31] Moreover, de la Grange and Rico state — without citing any proof or indicating their source for this information — that Marcos selected for participation only those communities he knew would be favorable to action, while ignoring those that he felt might vote against it. They therefore conclude that "in fact, the process had not been too democratic."[32] De la Grange's and Rico's skepticism is also shared by Womack, who claims that "of the 385 communities [in the cañadas] that had *ejidos* . . . the CCRI asked the ones that had shown most commitment, maybe 30, to take the final accord, to go to war." As he puts it: "Their assemblies groaned for consensus for the armed way, but it would not come," adding, "maybe 25 voted for it." He continues: "The most Zapatista community in the canyons could finally do no better than a vote of 67 for war, 21 against."[33] (However, as Stephen points out, "It should be noted that Womack cites no sources at all in his book," adding, "His account often, but not always, parallels that of Tello Díaz 1995, and I find it questionable for that reason."[34]) The question of just how representative the referendum was is surely worth making, although equally it is one that is now probably unanswerable. All I would add is that even the lowest figure of those consulted is impressively high: Daniel's figure of 15,000 voting outright for war is hardly insignificant. Moreover, popular feelings both against the "celebration" and for definite action are to some extent borne out by the fact that the EZLN was able to muster several thousand indigenous *campesinos* for an anticolonial demonstration march through San Cristóbal later that year in October.

The Subcomandante has left on record a detailed description of the process by which each individual community discussed and voted on whether to wage war. In a communiqué issued on 28 May 1994 Marcos tells of how this decision was debated and arrived at in the village of Old Antonio:

About two years ago, in 1992, when I was making the rounds of the communities calling meetings to see whether or not we were to begin the war, I arrived at "Old Antonio's" town. . . . When we arrive at the village meeting place, it is already beginning to get dark. Young Antonio comes back after a while with the Act of Agreement, which says, more or less: "The men and women and children met in the community school to examine in their hearts whether it is time to start the war for freedom and the three groups separated, that is, the women, the children, and the men, to discuss it and then later we met again in the little school and the majority had reached the point in that the war should begin because Mexico is being sold to foreigners and hunger is occurring, but it is not occurring that we are no longer Mexicans, and in the agreement 12 men and 23 women and 8 children who already have their thoughts clear came forward and those who know how signed and those who don't, put down their fingerprint."[35]

Concerning the impetus for commencing the war, Marcos himself has often testified to the indigenous communities' desire to make themselves heard:

The indigenous people of this region . . . voted in their communities, and the decision was made to go to war. . . . They told me to start the war, because I was the one in charge of military planning. I said that we couldn't, that we weren't ready. I said we needed time, because all of our training was for defense, while they now wanted to attack the cities. So I asked them for more time to organize.[36]

This was also to some extent echoed in his interview with Le Bot:

The process of radicalization had precipitated and the communities had reached a point of no return about the question of war that was expressed by the indigenous leaders of the communities and the regions that later became the Comité [Clandestine Revolutionary Indigenous Committee]. So the indigenous leaders proposed that we begin the war in 1992. . . . We told them that the conditions were not right yet, and that the international situation was not favorable, and that the national situation was also very unfavorable for any kind of attempts at change, especially for armed struggle. So we decided together that we needed to consult. . . .

   In conclusion, a wide majority of people stated that they were in favor of beginning the war now [at the end of 1992], and the communities gave a formal order to the EZLN to fight the war together with them.[37]

In these passages, it should be noted, Marcos attributes the impetus for war as coming from the indigenous people themselves. However, this interpretation of events has been strongly rejected by Marcos's detractors, who prefer to depict the Subcommander as agitating for war and manipulating the usually docile Indians into waging a suicidal conflict. For example, Daniel insists that:

> From 1992 Marcos began to prepare the people for war. With the support of *Yolanda, Rolando, Mario* and the other indigenous majors he prepared a series of meetings in order to convince the communities that they had to go to war. He gathered together those in charge and sent them to talk with their people. He told them: "*Rodrigo* wants to change the organization, and we are going to lose all these years of work." Guillén proved once again that he had a great capacity for manipulation, which I already knew from UAM. He managed to convince those in charge that the communities should vote yes to war. The arguments were of this type: they are going to die of hunger and the soldiers will repress them. These were the votes (*votaciones*) of Marcos: "Are you going to live like dogs or die like heroes? Do you want soldiers to come and violate the women? No!" It was obvious, Guillén won the vote in the communities in 1992.[38]

However, Daniel's testimony, it should be remembered, is far from impartial. Moreover, one has to ask how plausible it is. Despite his frequent assertions that "it was a trick of Guillén Vicente, something that he was able to do . . . a magic that he had for convincing people, for manipulating words,"[39] can we honestly believe that Marcos was able to trick two thousand indigenous into rising up in arms in order to take on the Federal Army, and a further few thousand to support them logistically? To postulate such a scenario one would have to believe that the indigenous people are docile and gullible.

The truth perhaps lies somewhere between these two extremes, far more nuanced than either Marcos or his detractors allow. Of course, Marcos favored armed military action. His hero from childhood was Che Guevara, the classic revolutionary guerrilla leader, upon whom he modeled himself and whose image he continued to project all the time he was in Chiapas.[40] For the past decade Marcos had been gearing himself specifically for this eventuality. There is no way he would oppose armed action; rather, it is perfectly clear that he strongly favored it. To him revolution was an (or perhaps the only) effective means of changing a status quo which he detested,[41] and being a revolutionary was the noblest profession of them all—the process and the profession together producing better human beings and a better world for them to live in. However, the desire for action was by no means limited solely to the mestizo, university-educated, high-ranking EZLN officers. In 1994 Comandante Isaac, an indigenous officer, claimed that:

> It's the people themselves who said, "enough, let's begin [the war]. We can't take it any more because we we're already dying of hunger." So the leaders, the CCRI and the Zapatista Army said, "If the people say it's time, then it's time. Let's begin." That's how the struggle began.[42]

Nor was the impetus for war limited even to the EZLN leadership: many indigenous *campesinos* were equally desirous of some form of direct, armed action and not because they had been duped into believing that they were an invincible vanguard destined to lead a nationwide revolution, as some of Marcos's detractors have claimed. On the contrary, quite the reverse appears to have taken place. Indeed, in an in-depth interview for the video documentary *Marcos: historia y palabra*, the Subcommander paints a completely antithetical picture of events: "The Indian communities demand the EZLN, which is by that time their army, not only to defend them from landlords, White Guards or possible attacks by the army or the police, but to be the way to have their demands fulfilled. They say 'If we are this poor and now we have a way to claim our rights, then let's do it!'" Indeed, this last point is conceded by Legorreta Díaz (1998, 237), who notes that "the support bases, the militia, the recruits and the insurgents were convinced that the armed movement represented the best possibility for rapidly overcoming the conditions of poverty so as to resolve all their problems and needs: land, health, food, housing, education, etc." What happened then was that the needs and desires both of Marcos and of the indigenous communities appear to have coincided: the former striving to fulfill the Guevaran ideal of commanding a rural guerrilla vanguard that would ignite a popular socialist revolution, and the latter seeing the EZLN as a way to protest effectively against an intolerable status quo. Why, many must have asked, should they spend years creating, training, and supplying what was in fact their own army and then not use it as a tool to force the government into addressing their grievances?

As Marcos explains in the same interview, although both the *Comandantes* and the communities coincided in their desire for armed action, they did not necessarily agree on the timing of it. He continues, emphasizing that this caused a tension between the indigenous communities and the FLN, and even EZLN, leadership:

> But the leading structure is still apart, the command is still within the politico-military organization and not in the communities, and this authority does not see war at a specific term, it believes in waiting, to see if a nick of time provokes it. In fact, by that time, it's noticed that the national and international conditions do not favor a confrontation, not even to start an armed struggle; and on the other hand, the communities get in motion facing the alternative of dying or fighting.

It would appear then that although Marcos and the other subcomandantes and comandantes were very much in favor of initiating the armed struggle, they were not entirely convinced that now was the time to do so; whereas the indigenous communities, armed with this tool to press home their demands on an indifferent government, did not wish to waste any more time. (Of course, as Adolfo Gilly points out, it is entirely feasible that "this divergence between the communities and the leaders of the EZLN could have been invented or exaggerated by Marcos in order to underscore the popular or democratic character of the decision-making in a movement 'from below' or in order to counterbalance official accusations that the rebellion was the product of outside agitators 'deceiving' or 'manipulating' 'the masses'"—although it ought to be noted that Gilly himself dismisses this cynical interpretation on various grounds.)[43] In fact, 1991–92 had seen a spate of desertions from the EZLN by *campesinos* who were impatient with the guerrillas' reluctance to push their claims through violent means. Why, they asked, should the communities keep sending the guerrillas food, money, and provisions, not to mention their young men and women for training, if the guerrillas were not prepared to fulfill their espoused purpose of fighting? If the guerrilla leadership continued to pour cold water on the *campesinos'* desire for direct action, or at the very least a show of military strength, there was danger of demoralization and even mass desertion. As Oppenheimer observes, Marcos "was under growing pressure from his Mayan rebel officers, who had promised their troops land seizures and greater political freedoms, and were now starting to suffer defections from Indians who had grown tired of the endless military training."[44]

In this sense, Marcos's situation was perhaps analogous to George Orwell's position as he describes it in "Shooting an Elephant." Orwell was an officer in the Indian Imperial Police in British-occupied Burma from

1922–27. One day an elephant went on the rampage and he, as the highest representative of colonial power in the region, was required to deal with the situation. Orwell writes:

> At that moment I glanced round at the crowd that had followed me. It was an immense crowd, two thousand at least and growing every minute. . . . They were watching me as they would a conjurer about to perform a trick. . . . And suddenly I realized that I should have to shoot the elephant after all. The people expected it of me and I had got to do it; I could feel their two thousand wills pressing me forward, irresistibly. . . . Here was I, the white man with his gun, standing in front of the unarmed native crowd—seemingly the leading actor of the piece; but in reality I was only an absurd puppet pushed to and fro by the will of those . . . faces behind. . . . I had got to shoot the elephant. I had committed myself to it when I sent for the rifle. A sahib has got to act like a sahib . . . to come all that way, rifle in hand, with two thousand people marching at my heels, and then to trail away feebly, having done nothing—no, that was impossible.[45]

Marcos was the "sahib," or leader. He had sent for his gun (that is, he had set himself up as a revolutionary and had armed and trained the people to be guerrillas). He was now followed by two thousand (or more) people all expecting him to do something. And he too therefore would have to use this power he wielded regardless of whether he wished to or not— there was no way he could simply turn around, do nothing and "trail away feebly." In the same passage Orwell makes a point every bit as appropriate for Marcos concerning the lot of the white man who tries to lead "natives": "he shall spend his life trying to impress the 'natives' and so in every crisis he has got to do what the 'natives' expect of him. He wears a mask, and his face grows to fit it."[46]

In any event, Marcos, armed with the impressive results of his recent referendum, immediately journeyed to Mexico City in order to convince Germán and the rest of the FLN leadership that the time was right for an uprising in Chiapas, if not countrywide. Clutching the acts of the assemblies, which contained both every individual signature and also the village seals, he pushed for a definite timescale for revolution to be put in place: the time for action had come. The leadership was not entirely convinced however. Rodrigo strongly opposed Marcos, saying that they were not yet ready militarily. (There is evidence to suggest that by this stage Rodrigo had changed his opinion concerning the validity or even desirability of armed struggle, and instead favored transforming the FLN into a mass popular pressure group of some description.)[47] Moreover, even if it was conceded that Chiapas was teetering on the brink of rebellion—which Rodrigo suspected was not the case—the Villa Front in the North and the Central Front were years behind in terms of recruitment, arms, training, winning over the local population, and even of politicizing the peasantry. The greater good of the whole body, of the FLN in its entirety, must, the leadership argued, take priority over that of a single limb, regardless of how strong that limb might be. For one branch to act prematurely, without the support of the others, was likely to render it easy to isolate and exterminate.

Marcos knew this, but he was faced with a dilemma. The El Salvadoran guerrilla war had demonstrated that the people and the guerrillas had to be synchronized. (In El Salvador they had not been, and they had ultimately failed to wrest power from the government.)[48] Marcos appreciated how narrow the revolutionary window of opportunity could be and was eager for the EZLN not to miss its chance.

In addition, the Subcommander must also have been aware that there was often a tension between the guerrillas at the front and the political cadres in the cities. His study of the Cuban Revolution would have meant he was very well versed in the sometimes contradictory exegeses of those operating in the Sierra Maestra and the citizens of the Llanos. He would also surely have been well acquainted with Debray's analysis of the Cuban Revolution, in which he warned that politicos in the cities readily succumb to "an increasing tendency to view the opening of hostilities as a somewhat sacrilegious temptation, a kind of adventurism, perennially 'premature.'"[49]

Finally, de la Grange and Rico identify a possible further factor that may have led Marcos to push for action, namely, his age. They note that Marcos would be thirty-five on 19 June 1992, and this may have made him impatient for action, fearing that he was approaching the end of his prime.[50] Marcos was surely aware of his hero Che Guevara's entry in his Bolivian diary for 14 June 1967: "I've reached my thirty-ninth birthday, and am inevitably approaching the age when my future as a guerrilla must be considered."[51] Against this, it should be remembered that Colombia's Tirofijo ("sure shot") Marulanda was still going strong in 1992 aged over sixty, and that the FLN's own Comandante Germán had established the EZLN's first camp in Chiapas in November 1983 at age forty and remained in robust health in 1992.

On 12 September Marcos returned from the meeting in Mexico City and went straight to San Cristóbal where he called a clandestine meeting of local cadres, including Subcomandantes Pedro and Daniel, eight indigenous majors, Frank (who was responsible for various *campesinos* committees), and Ana (who represented worker organizations in the north of the country). It was held in an EZLN safe house in the city, located less than 100 km as the crow flies from Marcos's Cama de Nubes camp.[52] On the agenda was "war," and more specifically whether the decision to wage it should be taken at the local level independently of the central command in Mexico City. None of the Comandantes (Rodrigo, Germán, and Elisa) were present. Indeed, this was the point, since Marcos argued at the meeting that Rodrigo was an obstacle in the way of the EZLN realizing its ambitions. He argued that Rodrigo had lost touch with the wishes and feelings of the *campesinos*, which was why he was opposing revolution in Chiapas.[53] Marcos therefore proposed that Germán and Rodrigo should be called to a meeting in Chiapas four months later, in January 1993, to hear the EZLN's arguments, and that at this meeting a proposal should be made for him to replace Rodrigo in the hierarchy of the FLN. According to one of de la Grange's and Rico's sources, Marcos even went so far as to tell those present at the meeting that Germán had already given his approval for the deposition of Rodrigo.[54] However, it is far from certain whether this version is correct: did Marcos in fact tell those attending that he had received Germán's authorization to replace Rodrigo, and if so, was this a lie or had he and Germán secretly agreed to cut Rodrigo out of the loop? The answer is, as so often in the case of the internal politicking within guerrilla groups, unknowable. In any event, Marcos's proposal was supported by the two other Subcomandantes present, Pedro and Daniel.

The question naturally arises as to Marcos's motivation for this alleged *coup de palais*. Was it simply that he was ruthlessly ambitious and wanted to usurp Rodrigo's position? This is of course possible, but it is also clear that there were other forces at play. For one thing, Marcos evidently worried that by procrastinating the *campesinos'* enthusiasm would fail, closing the window of opportunity for revolution. Clearly, Subcommanders Marcos, Pedro, and Daniel felt that because they were permanently stationed on the frontline, they were in a better position to judge the situation and were more in touch with the locals' feelings than Commanders Rodrigo and Germán, who were both far removed from events in Chiapas. There was, of course, much truth in this, but the difference in opinion between the Subcomandantes on one hand and the Comandantes on the other could be explained in terms of the difference between a tactical and a strategic perspective. The Subcomandantes clearly believed their front to be of prime importance, whereas the Comandantes had to consider the whole picture.

This meeting on 12 September 1992 was pivotal for the EZLN since it also saw the drawing-up of the Revolutionary Laws.[55] These laws at this time included the Urban Reform Law, the Labor Law, the Industry and Commerce Law, the Social Security Law, the Justice Law, and the Revolutionary Agrarian Law.[56] The majority of these laws were very much in keeping with those of other guerrilla organizations in Central and South America. For example, the Revolutionary Agrarian Law called for land redistribution, and there were also calls for fair wages to be paid by multinational corporations, and so on.[57] In them, very little specific mention is made of the indigenous; instead, the laws are couched in typically Marxist, that is, class-based, terms. Indeed, de la Grange and Rico argue that "the influence of the indigenous in the production of these documents is almost nonexistent."[58] This, however, is only half true, since although the language employed in the laws is predominantly Marxist and therefore class-based, the *campesinos* who the laws were supposed to benefit were predominantly indigenous.

On 16 September, Marcos went to observe a military parade in San Cristóbal by soldiers from the new Rancho Nuevo military base. Nearly four hundred troops participated, which unnerved locals who were unused to seeing large-scale military parades in their town. Marcos used the opportunity to assess the strength of the military force.

Meanwhile, the Mexican Center for Human Rights reported that in 1992, Chiapas was the state with the highest number of individual rights violations and that "the majority of the aggressions were against Tzeltal and Tzotzil indigenous groups, as well as *mestizo campesino* groups."[59]

A month later, on Monday, 12 October, 10,000 indigenous people swarmed into San Cristóbal to demonstrate against the 500th anniversary of Columbus's arrival. They had begun to gather on Sunday night and arrived at dawn in the sleepy colonial town. The lead group in this enterprise was the EZLN's front-organization ANCIEZ, which provided "approximately half of the 10,000 Indians who participated."[60] Marcos had been very busy throughout 1992 preparing for this day: what therefore appeared to the authorities as a demonstration by a *campesino* union was in fact a guerrilla maneuver planned by Marcos, orchestrated by Frank, and carried out by Zapatista troops. Indeed, the march was conducted with almost military organization and precision and may perhaps be viewed, like the ANCIEZ march on Ocosingo earlier that year (10 April), as a dry run for the actual taking of San Cristóbal on the 1 January 1994. Halfway through the march some indigenous people split from the main body of the procession and, led by Frank, made an attack on the town's statue of the Spanish Conquistador Diego de Mazariegos, located in the courtyard of the baroque church of Santo Domingo. (De Mazariegos had founded San Cristóbal and had directed a Spanish victory against the indigenous Chamula.) An indigenous *campesino* climbed the pedestal and toppled the statue with several blows from a sledgehammer.[61] A small group of police attempted to intervene but had to give up after being pelted by stone-throwing *campesinos*. Meanwhile, majors César and Mario were stationed at the city's gates on guard duty. Marcos was also present filming the assault on the statue by his cadres. He was caught doing so on film by a tourist; the footage came to light only after Marcos's true identity was revealed in February 1995.[62]

Finally, it is worth addressing an alleged change in Marcos's personality dating to this time. Up to this point the image of Marcos has been that of a nondoctrinaire individual, at least when compared to more senior figures within the FLN and with other Latin American guerrillas in general. De la Grange's and Rico's source, Antonio, claims that "From 1992 . . . Marcos began to be very strict . . . he had changed much. He had turned very intolerant."[63] This abrupt change in Marcos's personality is nowhere else attested. One possible explanation for Antonio's claim lies in what he cites to support this accusation, namely, that Marcos declared a prohibition on alcohol—the Subcommander himself was a teetotaler.[64] Antonio talks of incarceration and forced labor being imposed upon *campesinos* who persisted in drinking. This ban, however, was not the result of Marcos becoming a puritanical zealot,[65] but was dictated by two practical considerations. First, alcohol loosens tongues, and secrecy was more important than ever once the decision had been made to prepare for war.[66] Second, alcoholism was rife among certain of the indigenous of Chiapas.[67] Bonner convincingly demonstrates the benefits that prohibition had produced in Evangelical communities.[68] A North American evangelical who lived alongside the indigenous of Chiapas for several decades noted:

> The money formerly expended for liquor for ritual and personal consumption is now being used for buying better clothes, for building better houses, for acquiring horses and cattle, etc. In addition, freedom from galling debts incurred for liquor . . . and personal freedom from domination by alcoholism have engendered in them a new respect.[69]

Marcos was proud of the effects of this ban, the impetus for which appears not to have come from him alone. On 17 March 1995, "looking back at a year of Zapatista government," he boasted:

> We lowered to zero the rate of alcoholism. The women[70] here had become very angry, saying all that alcohol was good for was to make the men beat their women and children; they therefore gave the order that no drinking was allowed. The people who benefited most were the children and women, and the ones who suffered most were the businessmen and the government.[71]

17. An Internal Coup and the Road to War

The scheduled meeting of the FLN's highest ranking cadres took place on 23–25 January 1993 at the school hall in the small village of Prado, in Ocosingo municipality. Its purpose was of paramount importance: to discuss the future of the FLN. It was attended by all the senior members of the organization. Marcos, Lucía, Pedro, Daniel, and Vicente were present, as were Comandantes Elisa, Rodrigo, and Germán, who had traveled from Mexico City especially to attend. In addition, the EZLN was there in force, in the form of a hundred Zapatista lieutenants, some 200 Zapatista delegates, and representatives from twenty nearby indigenous communities.

On the agenda was:

1. The ratification of the Declaracion de Principios del Partido de las Fuerzas de Liberacion Nacional, which had been drafted the previous year.
2. The debating and ratification of the Revolutionary Laws drafted four months previously.
3. The creation of the Comité Clandestino de Revolución Indígena (CCRI, Clandestine Indigenous Revolutionary Committee).
4. A vote on starting the war.
5. The changing of the name of the National Directive to the Central Committee and with it the reduction of its members from six to three.

According to one eyewitness, Raul, all present were agreed on the need for struggle and on the nature of this struggle (that is, that it should be proletarian and student based, Marxist-Leninist, international, and revolutionary). The Declaracion de Principios del Partido de las Fuerzas de Liberacion Nacional was therefore approved without controversy. The declaration's preamble stated that all peaceful means of change had been exhausted and that violence was now the only alternative. Interestingly, article 58 urged

Christian progressives to join the struggle, as they had done in Nicaragua, Guatemala, and El Salvador. (In Chiapas, this represented an attempt to win over some of Bishop Ruiz's faithful who had recently distanced themselves from the EZLN on his urging.) Also significant is the point made by de la Grange and Rico concerning the similarity of expression between the aims, phrases, and symbols of the 1993 declaration, and those of the Estatutos de las Fuerzas de Liberacion Nacional written more than a decade earlier (1980). They note the declaration's "astonishing orthodoxy," and its "refusal to accept the consequences of international changes, especially the fall of the Berlin Wall, the disintegration of the USSR, the defeat of the Sandinistas in Nicaragua and the shipwreck of the Cuban revolution," concluding that after having read the two documents side by side it was as if "there had been no passage of time between the 1980 document and the 1992 one."[1] The similarity is less disturbing when one realizes that both were drawn up by Rodrigo, a diehard Marxist-Leninist veteran of the 1960s and 1970s. Moreover, Oppenheimer tells us that Marcos had explained it as resulting from the fact that indigenous and *campesino* activists in Chiapas had been fed a diet of Marxist rhetoric for the past three decades and that this was what they expected to hear from their leaders.[2] Any significant change in the EZLN's rhetoric risked ideological confusion, and ultimately a crisis of morale, which could not be countenanced in the twelve months leading up to the uprising.

The ratification of the declaration then, went smoothly. The next stage, which involved the debating and ratification of the Revolutionary Laws drafted four months previously, proved more contentious. Each law had to be translated into the various indigenous languages and then agreed in debate. Divisions soon emerged between the white, middle-class, university-educated cadres and the indigenous *campesinos*. For example, the former proposed a divorce law, but this was rejected by the latter, who perhaps felt this would have an incredibly destabilizing effect on their traditionally patriarchal communities. Eventually, however, many of these issues were resolved. This process of discussion and compromise undoubtedly proved highly instructive, helping to prepare the EZLN for future mass debates, such as whether to accept the government's peace proposal in spring 1994, and the subsequent accords arising from the San Andrés negotiations.

Next on the agenda was the formation of the CCRI.[3] (Although the structure of this committee was established at this meeting, the name CCRI was not employed until the following year, as Marcos makes clear: "In January 1993 the structure of the actual communities' power is created, and in

1994 it would be called the Clandestine Revolutionary Indian Committee.")[4] Originally at least, Daniel tells us, the CCRI "had nothing to do with the military organization of the EZLN, they were representatives from each zone," adding, "they only became commanders after January 1994."[5] Ross provides perhaps the most succinct explanation of the CCRI's composition:

> Each communal assembly selects its own officers: an organizational supervisor (*responsable*) to secure the communal safe house, education and health commissioners who meet regionally, and delegates to one of four Clandestine Revolutionary Indigenous Committees or CRRIS, each of the four Zapatista language groups having their own — each CRRI has 16 to 40 members depending on regional population. 11 delegates are chosen to sit on the ruling CCRI–General Command.[6]

There then came discussion of whether it was time to confront the Mexican government in the field. When Marcos proposed launching the armed struggle he acknowledged that not all prerequisites were satisfied, but he emphasized the words of his hero, Che Guevara, on this matter: that a revolutionary army could itself create some of the necessary conditions if these were lacking. He also pointed to the result of the recent referendum, which had returned an emphatic "yes" in favor of war. Finally, he noted that the EZLN had originally been established in Chiapas with the precise intention of eventually waging war against the Mexican government and violently overthrowing it: the moment had now come for the guerrillas to justify their existence by fulfilling their destiny. When he had concluded, Marcos was applauded loudly by most of the delegates — the vast majority of whom were members of the EZLN.

Rodrigo then took the floor and proposed a counter motion: that although he was not opposed to initiating hostilities in principle, the time was not yet ripe: "The moment has arrived for us to launch ourselves against the government, but not to do so hastily."[7] Rodrigo's arguments were more nuanced on this occasion than the ones he had used against Marcos in Mexico City the previous year, when he had categorically rejected the commencement of hostilities as being premature. Surrounded by EZLN troops and by members of the local support base communities, he probably felt that he had to sound as if he was in favor of war to prevent himself being seen as a coward or as casting aspersions on the effectiveness of the EZLN troops who filled the hall. How could he admit the unpopular truth to those present that the FLN's forces in the rest of the country were not ready to join their struggle and that they themselves were ill prepared—weaknesses for which he, as second-in-command of the organization, would have to take some responsibility. Thus, although in Mexico City in 1992 Rodrigo had won the first round of arguments against Marcos's proposal for starting hostilities, he would ultimately lose out in the second round as Marcos pressed home his advantage of being on home turf. In the end, the subtleties of Rodrigo's arguments were drowned in the war cry of the EZLN members present. Marcos proclaimed the debate over and called for a vote. Eventually, after much debate, everyone, even Rodrigo, approved the motion for war. As one indigenous *campesino* observed, "It was inevitable; we had sold all our livestock to buy arms; we were not able to turn back."[8]

The next issue was that of timing. Marcos perhaps shared Rodrigo's concerns about lack of preparedness, but he also had a more acute awareness of the need to begin operations in order to stem desertions and disillusionment. He clearly felt that many months would still be required to make the necessary preparations. As he observes, "There were logistical questions," which dictated that the uprising "had to begin just after harvest when we could get money together [and] when our food reserves would be greatest" since there was a strong possibility "that the war would be long, that we would be surrounded, that they would drive us into the mountains."[9] However, many in the communities were impatient for action. So it was that, as Marcos informs us: "In January of 1993, they said they would give me one year to make the arrangements. 'If you don't do it in a year, we'll do it without you,' they said. They told me that the latest date was December 31, 1993."[10]

Given that the meeting took place at Prado, deep in Zapatista heartland, it is hardly surprising that Marcos was able to obtain the result he wanted. Daniel tells us that Marcos spared no effort in ensuring the decision went his way:

> The meeting was prepared. The representatives from the communities had arrived three days before and been given political chats on how to vote. They were told: "When Rodrigo arrives and wants to convince you, don't let him. If you don't understand anything, there's no problem. You raise your hand when the major raises his." And this is what happened. In the end, who was going to understand Spanish, or who was going to understand all the political speeches being given there? Not many people. This is what caused the rupture with Rodrigo, he saw that when one hand was raised, the others raised theirs.[11]

It is worth asking why Rodrigo and Germán acquiesced in this choice of venue given that it would allow Marcos such a significant advantage. Certainly, the EZLN (that is, the Chiapas wing of the FLN) had enjoyed by far the greatest success in recruiting, but was that the sole reason behind the choice? It would appear that Rodrigo, like Bishop Ruiz, simply underestimated Marcos. As Daniel tells us, "Rodrigo was untroubled because he never believed that Marcos would be able to obtain a position in favor of war."[12] As for Germán, one has to conclude that this arrangement was made with his full connivance, as is to some extent confirmed by what happened next.

The final motion on the agenda involved significant changes to the National Directive's name (to that of the Central Committee) and also its composition (by cutting the number of its members from six to three). Marcos proposed that Germán should become secretary general of the party *and* secretary of the interior, in effect giving him overall command of finances, recruitment, health, communications, and information. Germán's position as *jefe* of the organization was now consolidated and confirmed. This move may be interpreted as the price Marcos had agreed to pay to have the meeting held in Zapatista heartland and to persuade Germán to acquiesce to Marcos's second proposal: that he, Marcos, should occupy the FLN's next most senior position, that of military secretary. Article 40 of the statutes now stated that Marcos commanded all EZLN troops, commandos, special units, army support units, militia, and support bases, and article 41 gave him supervision of all activities, open or clandestine, in the zones controlled by the EZLN. In addition, Marcos proposed that Pedro and Daniel be his right-hand men. Germán's wife Lucía (now age 50 and active since the 1970s) received the post of secretary of the masses. She was to be assisted by three under-secretaries, Ana (in charge of workers), Frank (in charge of *campesinos*), and Andres (in charge of popular organizations). Meanwhile, Elisa and her partner Vicente were granted responsibility for the ideological commission, which chiefly involved editing and printing party publications. (De la Grange and Rico are quick to point out that, with the exception of Frank, none of the new leaders chosen that day were indigenous or Chiapan, but this is understandable given that what was at stake were positions in the FLN movement as a whole, and not just ones within the EZLN.[13] The FLN was not limited to Chiapas, but had two other fronts, nor was its focus predominantly indigenous, given its Marxist-Leninist emphasis on the urban working class.) The result was that Marcos, Germán, and Lucía now comprised the three cornerstones of the FLN, with Rodrigo and his partner Gabriela completely cut out of the equation. It appears highly likely that a deal had been struck between Germán and Marcos, possibly with the connivance of others, such as Elisa, Lucía, Vicente, Pedro, and Daniel.

This motion clearly came as a shock to Rodrigo and Gabriela who were, after all, two of the FLN's most senior figures, both having been with the organization from its inception. Faced with this *fait accompli* Rodrigo rose to his feet in response and said, "This isn't democratic or anything,"[14] adding "I don't agree with any of this, you have deceived me; this is the last time you will see me."[15] Then he and Gabriela walked straight out of the hall, not stopping to say farewell to anyone, and got into their car and drove off, never to have contact with the organization again. One eyewitness tells us that after Rodrigo and Gabriela stormed out the hall fell uncomfortably silent: "Many of the insurgents were left feeling sad . . . I believe Marcos also felt it."[16] Rodrigo subsequently moved to Los Angeles, and Gabriela returned to Mexico City, where she taught art history. Their departure from the FLN that day had serious consequences, since Rodrigo's brother, Dr. Carlos, and his wife (and Marcos's former partner) Mercedes, also abandoned the organization. They too were long-standing veterans of the FLN and had spent much time in Chiapas. Their absence left a void in Mexico City, where formerly the FLN had been strongest, recruiting from both UNAM and UAM and instructing insurgents from all three fronts in safe houses there.

Nor was this exodus limited to Mexico City FLN cells: some members of the Chiapan EZLN abandoned the organization as a result of the putsch. One was Major César, who had been trained by Marcos personally and who now acted as his bodyguard. Even more damaging was the departure of Subcommander Daniel, who had never got on personally with Marcos and who of late had become increasingly disenchanted with both the revolution in general and the EZLN in particular. Daniel states that he had already begun "to withdraw little by little"[17] from his responsibilities the previous year, having become disillusioned with the fact that although the EZLN kept telling its *campesino* constituents that "it was a democratic organization which was going to help the people, that the enemy was the bourgeoisie and imperialism, and that these were exploiting them . . . yet we were still going and squeezing them and telling them to give us their money to buy arms."[18] Daniel adds, "The problem didn't remain at that, but rather the money arrived but the arms didn't . . . [instead] the money arrived in the cities and was shared out among the safe houses." He asked, "How is it possible that the poor, screwed indigenous who scarcely had enough to live off . . . were sustaining the urban networks?[19] Daniel felt especially aggrieved at what he perceived as Marcos's misspending on electronic gadgetry.[20] Unable to reconcile this apparent contradiction and unwilling to endure Marcos's hostile attitude toward him[21] and what he perceived as deceitful propaganda,[22] Daniel attempted to distance himself from the FLN and the EZLN. In an interview he gave in 1999, Daniel tells us, "Marcos saw that I was not the great revolutionary and he sent me to San Cristóbal in June 1992. I remained there until February 1993."[23] (Marcos was no doubt all too eager to see the back of Daniel, who he disliked intensely and who had been a thorn in his side since his promotion to subcommander and arrival in Chiapas in 1988. He now had a free hand to do what he liked in Chiapas; the only other person of his rank was Subcommander Pedro, of whom Marcos was very fond.) After the Prado meeting, Daniel was sent to work in another safe house in Jalapa, Veracruz, which he subsequently "left in July 1993."[24] Shortly afterward he visited his parents for the last time and then fled the country for the United States, allegedly fearing for his life.[25] Given that Daniel had watched Rodrigo, Gabriela, Dr. Carlos, Mercedes, and Major César simply walk out on the FLN—despite them posing a serious security risk—without incurring retribution, one wonders how realistic these fears were. In contrast to other Latin American guerrilla groups, which always preferred to err on the side of caution,[26] the FLN and EZLN made no attempt to hunt down and assassinate these potential security risks—a fact that sits uneasily against the image of a ruthless and vindictive FLN as projected by de la Grange and Rico. Moreover, Daniel's fear certainly did not deter him from returning to Mexico less than two years later and turning state's evidence against his former comrades, including revealing Marcos's true identity to the security forces. To date (more than ten years later) no retribution has been taken against him by the FLN or EZLN.

Following the Prado meeting the EZLN increased its activity in Chiapas, regularly consulting the CCRI in the villages. As Marcos tells us, the latter "gave the military leaders freedom to fix the date [of the uprising] and move people, troops and resources: the whole of 1993 was dedicated to this."[27] This had two results.

The first was that it brought Marcos and Bishop Ruiz into direct conflict. Prior to Prado, Germán and Rodrigo had been the main interlocutors with Ruiz, but henceforth the bishop's main interface with the EZLN was Marcos. Moreover, whereas previously the EZLN had contented itself with preparing for a prolonged people's war, the commencement of which would be at some unspecified point in the (perhaps distant) future, now a war led by Marcos was imminent. Thus, from this point onward, Ruiz worked feverishly to prevent the outbreak of war, making regular visits to outlying communities to preach against a conflict that he saw as suicidal. Through his Church-based peasant organization, Slop, and his subordinate clergy, he strove to counter Marcos's influence in the area.

Second, the increase in activity led to a flurry of rumors about the presence of guerrillas in the region. (Despite the massive swelling in re-cruitment to the EZLN's ranks, the guerrillas' activities had, by and large, hitherto been kept hidden from the authorities, who, being mestizos, could not speak the indigenous languages and so could not gather intelligence effectively.)[28] This in turn brought about increased military patrols of the canyons and jungle, although a serious offensive against the insurgents was not contemplated since the security forces still believed that any guer-rillas were probably Guatemalans who were merely using Chiapas to train before launching themselves back into their own country. Initially at least, Marcos, Daniel, and Pedro were able to stay one step ahead of the Mexican army thanks to an elaborate system of short-wave radios scattered through-out the jungle communities.[29] The EZLN had taken the idea, and possibly even some of the technical hardware for this communication network, from the diocese, which had used it to spread the word of God to remote parts of the interior.

However, the system was not infallible, and in March 1993 an incident occurred in which two army officers (Captain Marco Antonio Romero and Lieutenant Porfirio Millán from the military intelligence service) went missing while on duty 25 km from San Cristóbal, very near Rancho Nuevo. The two were subsequently discovered to have been killed, their badly burned bodies being found shortly afterward by security forces. The au-thorities were perplexed, not knowing if the murders were drug related, politically motivated, caused by common banditry, or indicative of guerril-las. Soon, however, security forces seized thirteen members of the nearby Tzotzil community of San Isidro el Ocotal and brought them in for interro-gation.[30] A few days later they were accused of the murder, based almost exclusively on their own confessions. The Fray Bartolomé de las Casas Human Rights Center, headed by Bishop Ruiz, interceded on the Tzotzils's behalf, arguing that they had been tortured into confessing. The center ini-tiated a vociferous publicity campaign on the men's behalf and eventually obtained their release. This incident caused great friction between authori-ties and the bishop. The Mexican military had always viewed the Church with suspicion and particularly disliked the recent establishment of the Ruiz's Center for Human Rights. Put simply, it was not accustomed to having to give account of its actions. Finally, although the judge threw out the case, ordering the Tzotzils to be released, many enemies of the bishop and the center claimed that their acquittal was secured purely on account of legal sophistries and technicalities.

On 8 March, the EZLN called another major meeting to discuss the Revolutionary Laws. Susana had been sent out to talk to women's groups about forming a women's revolutionary law. She presented her findings to this meeting, as a result of which the women's law was agreed. This law, however, represents another clash of cultures between the white, middle-class intelligentsia, headed by Marcos, Pedro, and Daniel, and their indigenous subordinates. The former had to bring considerable pressure to bear on the male-dominated and conservative, patriarchically inclined CCRI. When Susana stood up and read aloud the findings of her consultation there was much murmuring and opposition from the menfolk.[31] One man even joked that he did not care whether the law was passed because his wife could not understand Spanish. This was overheard by a female Tzotzil major who retorted, "Well, now you're fucked because we're going to translate it into all the dialects." In the end, the women's demands were accepted. "The men," Marcos assures us, "had to give in because the women bargained, saying they would only support the issues that the men wanted if the men approved these changes."[32]

Less than two weeks later, on 25 March, the communities voted on whether to start the rebellion before the end of the year. Since the meeting at Prado, where the EZLN leadership had voted for war backed by the newly created CCRI, veteran community leaders from the movement had fanned out across the jungle and highland communities arguing in favor of military action before the year's end.

Less than a month later, on Saturday 22 May, there occurred an event that was to have profound repercussions both for the EZLN as a whole and Marcos in particular. Subcommander Daniel's former camp, Las Calabazas (the pumpkins) at the Sierra Corralchén, now commanded by Major Mario, was discovered by Federal Army troops of the 83rd Infantry Battalion. They were following up on a skirmish with the guerrillas near the community of Nazaret in which two soldiers[33] and one Zapatista, Lieutenant Rafael, a Tzotzil from La Garrucha, were killed.

It is uncertain why the army sent a patrol into the area, although in recent weeks there had been a definite increase in military activity there. It is possible that there had been a security breach within the EZLN and that the Mexican military had been tipped off as to the location of a guerrilla camp in the area. However, it is far more likely that these incursions were due to the fact that the area was being secured with a view to an imminent exploitation of the region's natural resources. Drilling for oil had taken place in the Sierra at Nazaret in 1990, just above La Garrucha, where Daniel's camp was situated, but the well had been capped in 1991 after producing very little oil.[34] However, throughout 1992–93, no doubt in part at least connected with contemporary negotiations concerning NAFTA, private national (for example, Comesa, Perforadata, Compañia Mexicana de Geofisica) and international (for example, France's Général de Geophysique and the United States's Western) companies were engaged in oil exploration around Ocosingo. Moreover, the search for oil had uncovered a huge reserve of natural gas there.[35] Since it was on the road to Nazaret that the skirmish took place, it has been speculated that there was a link between the presence of Federal Army troops on that road and the presence of this highly lucrative natural resource.[36] As far as the Lacandón jungle's other resources are concerned, one article points out:

> Mexico is considered to be the third most biodiverse country in the world; most of this biodiversity is concentrated in the jungle areas in the south-east part of the country, especially in the state of Chiapas. The Lacandón Jungle, which represents only 0.16 per cent of national territory, actually contains more than twenty per cent of this biodiversity. Overall, Mexico has an immense variety of plants and animals and contains each of the 32 different ecosystems identified for the planet as a whole. In spite of the terrible devastation, the Las Cañadas region, which borders on the Lacandón Jungle, contains a third of these ecosystems.[37]

Marcos had always viewed Daniel's Las Calabazas camp as vulnerable. He had even argued that it should be dismantled, on the grounds that it lay in a region in which local communities were divided between pro- and anti-Zapatistas, making its location liable to betrayal. However, given the chronic tension between Marcos and Daniel, Daniel interpreted Marcos's proposal as a means of robbing him of his power base and countered that it was precisely because of the divided loyalties of the local population that the EZLN needed to maintain its presence and influence in the region.[38]

The army's discovery of the camp resulted in the loss of twenty-seven firearms, stores of ammunition and explosives, and the complete destruction of six wooden dormitories capable of holding 200 men, trenches, parapets, replica tanks, an electric generator, and a model of a military installation near Ocosingo. In a report he wrote to Germán on 24 June, after having inspected the camp following the army's withdrawal, Marcos wrote that the security forces "had completely cleaned out everything," adding that they must have "found . . . everything, absolutely everything . . . that was hidden . . . [including] the pits and the caves . . . and the installations [which] had been totally destroyed." Marcos must have been acutely aware of how catastrophic this discovery could prove, since he will have remembered how the discovery of Che's safe-house-cum-base-camp at Ñancahuazú in Bolivia had sealed his doom. It is also clear from the report that Marcos was troubled by the same two things that had especially perturbed Che about the army's discovery of Ñancahuazú: likely breaches of security and the guerrillas' loss of the element of surprise.

Indeed, the discovery of Daniel's camp alerted the security forces to the fact that it was not merely drug traffickers or bandits but rather a considerable and well-equipped guerrilla force that was operating in the area. The military could now give credence to the rumors they had heard of armed men operating in the area and now were aware of the approximate size and nature of this group and had a rough inkling as to its objectives. The security forces' perception of what they were up against was immeasurably sharpened by their discovery at the camp of a video shot in 1992, directed by Marcos and featuring a voice-over by him,[39] which detailed the EZLN's activities (drilling, training in the setting up of road blocks and check points, hand-to-hand combat, etc.) and even its long-term aims to move from a traditional guerrilla army to a people's army.

The loss of weapons and ammunition that had proved difficult and costly to obtain in the first place, the destruction of a major base camp, and the knowledge that the army now knew of their existence also must have seriously damaged the guerrillas' morale. In addition, the incident highlighted serious flaws in their training, communications, and command structure. Indeed, three weeks later Marcos, in keeping with general Latin American guerrilla practice[40] and the specific recommendations outlined in the FLN's statutes,[41] made a report to Germán cataloguing the errors concerned. First and foremost, Daniel's successor, Major Mario, a Tzotzil from near Sabanilla, was criticized for not having evacuated the camp in a more quick and orderly manner. Marcos also castigated the major for not destroying the incriminating evidence, including the guerrillas' future plans and in particular "the audiovisual material." It would also appear that

Mario had failed to report a flyover by an army helicopter or to rig up camouflage netting or conceal smoke from the kitchen. Daniel, who until just a few months before had been in charge of the camp, confirms Mario's negligence: "Despite being warned, he left the door open: he did not conceal the road that led to the camp, which was the most marked one and would logically therefore be followed by the soldiers."[42] So, too, Captain Gabriela testifies how she informed Mario of the soldiers' approach at 10:00 hours, but instead of evacuating the camp, destroying the important information, and simply melting away into the jungle, Mario gave orders for an ambush, the firefight beginning at 16:45.[43] As a result, the guerrillas did not return to camp until after dark and the burning of sensitive materials did not commence until 21:00 hours, after the enemy had retired. It was thus not until 23:30 that Mario and his men evacuated the camp, and by then it was pitch black, so that after 200 meters of stumbling around lost in the darkness they were forced to light lanterns, making them easy targets for enemy units left behind in ambush. The shooting cost the life of insurgent Rafael,[44] and it was a miracle, Marcos concluded, that they had not all been totally annihilated. Also criticized were majors Alfredo and Rolando, both answerable only to Subcommanders Marcos and Pedro. The first had given incorrect information about the army's movements, while the second had not followed the procedures outlined "in our manuals . . . that have been constantly repeated in courses and talks."[45]

In true Guevaran style, the Subcommander did not spare himself from critical analysis.[46] Indeed, in his report Marcos sounds very much like Che, strongly criticizing the errors the guerrillas committed but highlighting also his own failings in the venture. His main mistake, as he saw it, was that his "order to retreat given to the Fifth Regiment on the night of 22/05/93 was risky and reckless, based on partial information and my supposition, rather than on the certain knowledge, that the enemy had retired."[47] Daniel tells us that Marcos had been away in San Cristóbal that day and that "when he found out what was happening he went to Ocosingo and controlled by radio the movements of Mario."[48] It was then, according to Daniel, that Marcos "committed an error . . . and ordered that instead of leaving through San Miguel, which was known to be free from problems [Mario and his troops] should go forward."[49] This is when they fell into the Federal Army's ambush.

This error was perhaps, however, a small problem compared to Marcos's true failing, which had been strategic more than tactical. In fact, de la Grange and Rico cite a senior army official who had analyzed Marcos's handling of this incident as saying that he admired Marcos for his tactical acumen and "above all for his capacity to wait until the last moment before making a decision."[50] What the general criticizes is the lack of initiative on the part of the indigenous command and the absence of discipline among the guerrillas, for which Marcos, who trained and commanded them, must bear some responsibility. Indeed, these failings, the army chief proceeds to emphasize, were "the corollary of the excessive power exercised by Marcos . . . [who] wants to control everything and this causes him to commit errors."[51] In other words, Marcos's reluctance to delegate had the unfortunate result of stifling, or at least discouraging, initiative among his indigenous subordinates, who in turn were perhaps inclined to defer to and rely on the man who, as he put it, had "taught most of them whatever they know . . . when it comes to military affairs."[52] (Hitherto, this had not been problematic since the guerrillas had always been able to avoid contact with the army because they knew the terrain well and had a good communications system.) This desire to control everything stemmed perhaps from Marcos's own personality: his love of directing videos and staging events demonstrates his wanting to be at the center of things, supervising and controlling the people around him. One must also consider, however, whether it was based, in part, on a lack of confidence in the troops under his command. If so, we must ask the extent to which this lack of confidence was justified or misplaced. If troops feel their superiors do not think they can produce what is asked of them, they are less likely to be able to do so, since their morale will be undermined. However, if the troops under Marcos's command were genuinely of poor quality, one has to ask why, after up to ten years of training, was this so? Was it because Marcos had not allowed them to exercise initiative; was it some basic failing in the training system; was it a failing in the troops themselves; or was it a combination of all three?

This brings me to my final point related to that fateful day, concerning Marcos's temperament. In his report to Germán, Marcos expressed frankly his suspicion that the camp had been betrayed by a local called Abelardo Gómez, who lived in a village at the foot of the Sierra Corralchén and who had strong links with Slop. He stated that the man would face a revolutionary tribunal to assess his guilt. De la Grange and Rico make much of this, and the fact that the Subcommander stated that Abelardo, if found guilty, should be executed, citing this as an example of Marcos's dark side—extreme, cruel, authoritarian, merciless. However, disregarding the fact that in war treachery has to be dealt with quickly and firmly, it should be pointed out that, despite de la Grange's and Rico's noise on the issue, nothing in fact happened to Gómez, despite the fact that Marcos continued to believe in his guilt. Indeed, de la Grange and Rico quote a local priest who interceded on Abelardo's behalf as saying, "It was not easy to convince Marcos that he should pardon (*perdonara*) Abelardo"[53] — suggesting that the *campesino* had in fact been found guilty, but had escaped execution.

News of the clash, which had proved beyond a shadow of a doubt that a considerable guerrilla force was operating in Chiapas, did not immediately find its way into the national or international press. Even a communiqué issued by the secretary of defense on 31 May, giving an account of the discovery of the camp and the subsequent follow-up action, makes no mention of guerrillas, describing them instead as "a group of individuals, whose number has not yet been determined, that presumably carried out illegal activities."[54] Moreover, in an interview with *Miami Herald* reporter Oppenheimer just days after the incident, Minister of the Interior Patrocinio González — the former governor of Chiapas until a few months earlier — stated: "There is definitely no guerrilla activity in Chiapas. There are land invasions and clashes that leave injured and even dead, but that's a far cry from a guerrilla problem. These are internal conflicts, not an insurgency."[55] Some, including Marcos, have stated that the reason behind the Mexican government's suppression of the facts was its desire to avoid releasing news that would jeopardize the signing of NAFTA, which was then being hotly debated in all three member states.

May 1993 was to prove a bad month for Mexico's image since Juan Jesus Posadas Ocampo, archbishop of Guadalajara, was assassinated on 24 May. This much publicized event did nothing to inspire confidence in the country's stability.

Meanwhile, the Mexican government wasted no time in secretly following up on the camp's discovery. From 26 May to 2 June the army scoured the jungle using trucks and helicopters. It intercepted rebel radio communications and, according to military officials, had drawn a net around the guerrillas. (It would appear from an Amnesty International report of June 1993 that state security forces and ranchers used the opportunity to attack communities they perceived as hostile.)[56] Army officials claim that they were poised to tighten this net and deliver the *coup de grâce* when an order from Mexico City came through calling for their return to base. Marcos evidently believes this claim, stating in one interview:

This was not a military decision, but a political decision. In military terms they thought that our group could be exterminated. But actually exterminating it, and sending troops, would mean that the national government had to acknowledge the existence of the guerrillas. And we believe, after careful thought, that on the eve of NAFTA the withdrawal was not a mistake by the Federal Army. I'm sure that it was a top-level decision. It could have only been made by the president of the Republic.[57]

De la Grange and Rico also give credence to this interpretation, arguing that the order to retire came from the president himself and was issued for three main reasons: first, with the signing of NAFTA imminent, he did not want the U.S. Congress to know about guerrillas in his country, nor did he want any further incidents to take place as a result of which the Mexican military—always prone to extreme repression—would be scrutinized by the press in both countries; second, that the recent assassination of Bishop Juan Jesus Posadas in Guadalajara had already made Mexico look like a banana republic, and news of guerrillas operating in the south of the country would strengthen this perception; and finally, the coming twenty-fifth anniversary of the October 1968 student massacre at Tlatelolco in Mexico City meant that any military action would come under close scrutiny both at home and abroad.[58] Instead, the government opted for pumping huge amounts of money into the area through the Social Development Ministry (Sedesol) in an attempt to defuse the situation.[59]

A further factor in the military's failure to finish off the guerrillas was the part played by Bishop Ruiz, who, as in February, once again intervened to keep the army in check. As de la Grange and Rico note:

Throughout 1993 Don Samuel had lent great services to the Zapatista cause, mobilizing the human rights organizations after the assassination of 2 army officials and the discovery of a guerrilla camp in the Corralchén mountains. In both cases his intervention had moved back the federal troops, thereby avoiding a confrontation that would have been devastating for the EZLN. Condemned to co-operating against a common enemy—the authorities and the large landowners—the two messiahs [Marcos and Ruiz], allies or adversaries depending on the circumstances, contended for power in the same territory. The chief of the rebels had used the catechists in order to organize his *army*, which had annoyed the bishop. But nor did it escape Samuel either that the threat of an insurrection in his diocese would convince the Vatican to keep him in his position. And, if finally the uprising occurred, his presence would be indispensable.[60]

De la Grange and Rico further argue that for the Subcommander's part "Marcos . . . knew that the eventual translation of Ruiz to another diocese would eliminate the principal obstacle for a military operation against the Zapatista camps," and so conclude that "the destiny of Marcos and the bishop of San Cristóbal were already intertwined."[61]

Despite the best efforts of the president to conceal the existence of guerrillas in Chiapas,[62] the increased troop deployment and activity in the region brought unwanted attention from two major Mexican news publications. In rapid succession three separate reports were published by the weekly news magazine *Proceso*[63] and the Mexico City daily newspaper *La Jornada*,[64] in which various individuals openly attested to guerrilla activity in the area. In the first report, appearing in *Proceso* (in June), the government itself conceded that it "acknowledged evidence that there are guerrillas in Chiapas." In the second, from *La Jornada* (in August), a representative of a Chiapan peasant organization claimed "the existence of guerrillas is not a rumor; it has been proven that there are well-armed guerrillas operating near the Guatemalan border and it is known that they have training grounds." These publications prompted Minister of the Interior Patrocinio González, who had just left the post of governor of Chiapas, to issue (11 August 1993) his now infamous assertion that "there are no guerrillas in Chiapas." No one was convinced, however, and in the final report in *Proceso* (in September), a Jesuit priest, Mardonio Morales, from the Lacandón attested to a significant guerrilla presence in the area that dated back at least eight years.[65] Moreover, Oppenheimer observed that this issue "was even beginning to draw the attention of the international media . . . [since] the *Miami Herald* published a front-page story (28 June 1993), under the headline 'Guerrillas in Chiapas?'"[66]

Marcos, meanwhile, took advantage of the reprieve to step up preparations for war. A firsthand account from a San Cristóbal market trader tells how one Tuesday in May a Chamula girl purchased thirty ski masks and ordered a further three hundred, which she collected as agreed when she returned a few weeks later. (Marcos has stated that his own ski masks are "made of wool, knitted in Chiapas of course and purchased in the markets of San Cristóbal and Ocosingo."[67]) In June others came to the same trader and ordered green trousers, "fifty pairs of 28 inch waist, sixty 29, seventy 30." July saw massive sales of brown shirts, "two hundred size 14, three hundred size 14½, four hundred size fifteen." August saw similarly high numbers of bandana sales. "Then, in October and November, when it starts to get cold, they came for heavy shirts. I'd start out in the morning with sixty, and by afternoon they'd all be gone. It was like that every day."[68] In the six months prior to the January 1994 offensive, a total of 180 green trousers, 900 brown shirts, and a considerable number of bandanas and winter shirts had been purchased by the guerrillas in the local market.

Also as part of the preparations for war, Marcos told the EZLN troops to "choose a pseudonym."[69] Apparently in this they were allowed to use "their own reasoning," which led to some fairly interesting choices—many being biblical (*David, Moisés,* and *Josué*), some political (*Fidel Castro* and, bizarrely, *Ronald Reagan*), and others clearly deriving from the world of popular culture (*Bruce Li*).

On 11 August, Patrocinio González proclaimed the nonexistence of guerrillas in Chiapas, Bishop Ruiz handed the Pope a twenty-eight page memorandum excoriating the Mexican government's treatment of indigenous Mexicans, and over a thousand Zapatistas conducted maneuvers near Ibarra commemorating the twenty-fourth anniversary of the setting up of the FLN. The following day was no less important since it saw agreement on NAFTA being announced by the three governments concerned, who immediately set about canvassing their respective legislatures for approval. However, as Oxfam's Belinda Coote observes, "President Salinas, by defining the agreement as a treaty, denied the opportunity for a full debate on the issue in the Chamber of Deputies. It was held in the Chamber of Senators, where 61 out of 64 senators belong to the PRI."[70] The undemocratic way in which the agreement was ratified in Mexico (and the United States),[71] and the much-publicized predictions of the economic hardship it would cause,[72] did much to enhance Marcos's popularity with the general public when he publicly denounced it throughout 1994.[73]

Also in August, the prevailing atmosphere of military repression and human rights abuses which accompanied the army's actions in the aftermath of May's clashes with the EZLN resulted in a joint report by Minnesota Advocates for Human Rights and the World Policy Institute.[74] In the same month, the Jesuit Refugee Service also issued an "Urgent Call to the International Community," expressing concerns over human-rights violations in Chiapas. Meanwhile, a report by the Miguel Agustín Pro Human Rights Centre characterized Chiapas in 1993 as being again "as it was in 1992, the state with the most violations of rights of individuals and organizations," adding "the sector most affected was the Indian peasant . . . the most frequent violations [being] assaults and injuries, followed by arbitrary arrests, threats, torture and murder."[75]

In September 1993, President Salinas visited Chiapas. He opened the giant Social Security Solidarity Rural Hospital at Guadelupe Tepeyac,[76] which cost US$5 million and was situated less than 50 km from Ibarra, where the previous month the guerrillas had held massive maneuvers to commemorate the FLN's twenty-fourth anniversary. Little did he know that a considerable proportion of the five hundred Tojolabal Indians who formed his audience that day were members of the EZLN. (Less than four months later the community became Marcos's headquarters.) Salinas also pledged 670 million pesos for the state as part of his much trumpeted National Solidarity Program (Pronasol).[77] In hindsight, these measures can be seen as a desperate attempt to shore up what was rapidly becoming an unmanageable problem. Salinas realized that urgent measures were needed to rectify the years of government neglect and corruption in order to avert serious social unrest. Unfortunately, his measures were seen by many chiapanecos as too little, too late.[78] Moreover, much of this money was either misdirected—for example, by providing hundreds of basketball courts for communities in a state where 33.1 percent lack electricity, 41.6 percent lack drinking water, and 50 percent of the population suffers malnutrition[79]—or it was simply misappropriated. As Thomas Benjamin succinctly puts it:

> Money was channeled into Chiapas in the hope that it would smother conflict and purchase peace. Infusions of money, however, with no change in the intimate nexus of power and interests in the state, bought only time, an occasional truce. And in time . . . most of the money found its way into the pockets of politicians and the rich.[80]

To compound the resentment and further polarize the state, often only communities that had voted PRI in the 1988 general election or in more recent local elections benefited; the Zapatista communities that tended to abstain from voting or voted PRD received little or nothing.[81] This led Marcos to sarcastically lambaste the Solidarity program:

> Pronasol has the mentality of a son-of-a-bitch that sees the indigenous people as children, as ill-bred children. Instead of giving his kids a spanking like they deserve, the father—who is so understanding and generous—is going to give them candy after getting them to promise not to misbehave again.[82]

Finally, one should bear in mind that Solidarity funding occurred within a context of declining government spending. As Womack observes, "federal funding for 'regional development' fell (from 37 percent of total funding in 1989, 43 percent in 1990, 49 percent in 1991, 40 percent in 1992) to 29 percent in the year before the Zapatista revolt."[83] So too, Hernández Castillo observes how "opponents of the [Solidarity] Regional Funds have pointed out that they amount to between just one-third and one-fourth of all moneys [previously] granted by BANRURAL [State Bank for Rural Credit] and other commercial banks for similar agricultural projects; in addition, critics have pointed out that they are not generally handed over on time."[84] Similarly, Arturo Cano observes:

> Although "faithfully paying its debts," the Indian population of Los Altos suffered a reduction in the resources it received. In 1990, this region, now the scene of armed conflict, received 23 percent of the program's total credit; in 1993 the proportion fell to 16 percent. Something similar . . . happened in the jungle. In 1990 credit there was 17 percent of the total; in 1991, 13 percent; in 1992, 11 percent; and in 1993 it plummeted to 6 percent.[85]

As autumn 1993 approached, Marcos's preparations for war grew apace. Marcos informs us that originally the guerrillas had planned to launch their attack on 12 October, the feast of the Virgin of Guadalupe, "because there are a lot of pilgrimages that day. So we thought that we could get the troops into town as if they were civilians going to see the Virgin of Guadalupe, while they were really going to attack the cities. But we weren't ready."[86] He adds, "The army discovered our arms cache up in the mountains, a five or six hour walk from here, so we had to pull back and postpone our plans until December."[87] Given this recent setback, Marcos must have been acutely aware of the pressing need to commence hostilities. Indeed, Daniel states that the date for the uprising was "pretty much dictated since because of leaks and drunks [among the EZLN cadres and support base], everybody already knew that there was going to be a guerrilla war."[88]

On 26 October Vatican nuncio Girolamo Prigione summoned Bishop Ruiz to tell him that Pope John Paul II requested of him that he either resign or immediately rectify his stance in respect of doctrine, liberation theology, and administration. It is not clear why the papal nuncio was only now choosing to exert pressure on Ruiz to resign given that the bishop had occupied his see for nearly three decades and had not significantly changed his views on Christian doctrine, liberation, theology, or administration for at least the past twenty years. The answer probably lies in the recent rapprochement between Rome and the Mexican government, which had resulted in the first papal visit to the country on 11 August 1993. It is legitimate to suppose that a deal of some kind was struck whereby the Pope was permitted to come to Mexico provided that he rein in those bishops who had been outspoken critics of the authorities.[89] Ruiz's establishment of a human rights center that directly challenged the authorities and openly accused them of human-rights violations, his intervention following the two clashes (in February and May) between the EZLN and the army, and his recent twenty-eight-page letter which he handed to the Pope during his visit to Mexico lambasting the government's corruption, repression, torture, neglect, and racism toward the Indians, had done nothing to endear him to the authorities. Nor was Ruiz alone; other members of the Mexican clergy were also speaking out against various government policies. As Chomsky notes, on 1 November 1993,

> a "Communication of Mexican Bishops on NAFTA" condemned the agreement, along with the economic policies of which it is part, because of their deleterious social effects. They reiterated the concern of the 1992 Conference of Latin American Bishops that "the market economy . . . not become something absolute to which everything is sacrificed, accentuating the inequality and the marginalization of a large portion of the population."[90]

A papal visit was a small price for the government to pay if it resulted in the removal, or even the silencing, of vociferously critical members of the Mexican clergy. Ruiz, however, refused to go voluntarily and instead requested a public trial to establish his guilt. Moreover, he made a great deal of noise about this through his connections and supporters in foreign parliaments and European NGOs, with which he had close ties through the Fray Bartolomé human rights center. He also roused support in Chiapas. On 24 November, thousands of Indians marched through San Cristóbal in his support and held a three-hour Mass in the cathedral, refuting the accusations against him and denouncing the attempts to force him out of office. The Church, unwilling to incur such adverse publicity, backed off. For now at least, Ruiz's position was assured, and without him having to compromise his freedom of expression. However, as Womack notes, these recent ecclesiastical intrigues, though unsuccessful in removing Ruiz, "seriously distracted the bishop and his clerics from their efforts to prevent war."[91]

Also in November, almost as if to reassert its refusal to be scrutinized, the Mexican military arrested one of its own high-ranking officers, Brigadier General José Francisco Gallardo Rodriguez (an officer with an impeccable service record), following the publication of an article in which he called for the creation of an ombudsman for human rights in the armed services. (After languishing in a military jail for over five years without charge, he was sentenced on 11 March 1998 to 14 years and 8 months for corruption and bringing the army's reputation into disrepute. Human Rights Watch/America, Amnesty International, and the Inter-American Commission on Human Rights all called for his release, which was finally granted on 7 February 2002.)[92]

On 17 November, the tenth anniversary of the EZLN's arrival in Chiapas, Marcos, indigenous community leaders, and the EZLN's *insurgentes* came together in Zapatista heartland to hold a ceremony signaling the opening of hostilities in four weeks time. Marcos himself described the meeting less than a year later in a communiqué published in *La Jornada* on 22 September 1994. He writes:

> Another night, another rain, another cold. November 17, 1993. Tenth anniversary of the formation of the EZLN. The Zapatista general staff thronged around the fire. The general plans have been made and the details worked out at the tactical level. The troops have gone to sleep, only the officers with higher rank than Major, are still awake. Old Antonio is there, the only man who can breach all the Zapatista checkpoints and enter wherever he wishes without anyone impeding his passage. The formal meeting ends and now, between jokes and anecdotes, we review the plans and dreams.[93]

Since the initial date (12 October) for the EZLN to open hostilities had proved too premature, a later date for attack had to be chosen. This new date needed to be equally advantageous to the Zapatistas: it should offer cover to the troops infiltrating the towns and should be at a time when the Federal Army soldiers would be off guard. As Marcos observes, three dates were available:

> The next possible date was the night of December 24, for Christmas. But the committee decided that since it was a religious date, an attack might be interpreted as being antireligious. I only had a few days left. So I chose December 28, because the 28th is *Día de los Inocentes* [Fools' Day] and people play a lot of practical jokes on that day. I thought, "that's good. When the soldiers call and say they're being attacked, the general's going to think they're playing a trick on him, and he'll hang up." But then I thought that when the journalists reported the attack, the

same thing would happen, no one would believe them. So we decided to postpone the date again, until 31st.[94]

In another interview Marcos elaborates on the choice of the 31st, saying: "We figured people would be on vacation so there wouldn't be any civilian population. The majority of people would be at home and wouldn't be on the streets in case of a shoot-out. The officers of the Federal Army would also be on vacation."[95] Daniel also emphasizes the element of surprise in choosing New Year's Eve, noting that "Guillén decided to leave it until the last day of the year by which time nobody was going to expect anything."[96] Marcos's calculations proved right, since the commander of the military zone, General Gastón Menchaca, had granted holiday leave to many of his troops, leaving just a skeleton force at Rancho Nuevo.[97]

On 28 December 1993, the guerrillas began to position themselves for their attack on 1 January. They started to steal trucks from Pemex, local landowners, and the French Society of Geophysics, near Ocosingo and Las Margaritas. Some Zapatistas even began infiltrating in small numbers the towns to be taken over.[98] By daybreak on 31 December more and more hijackings were occurring in the Ocosingo municipality as the vast majority of the EZLN troops commandeered trucks and other vehicles to enter en masse the five towns they had targeted. Oppenheimer calls these hijackings "a shrewd diversionary tactic,"[99] but this is to misunderstand what happened. They were dictated by sheer necessity, trucks being required to transport troops from remote outlying villages and camps into the towns.[100] In fact, stealing trucks from around Ocosingo was far from diversionary, since it attracted the attention of the authorities. As Marcos relates: "A federal army helicopter was circling the town of San Miguel [Ocosingo municipality], undoubtedly alerted by the enormous number of vehicles that were concentrating in that town."[101] Also on the 31st, and more alarming for the authorities, the Zapatistas stole 1,500 kilograms of dynamite from the Pemex oil company located in the north of the state.[102]

The plan was as follows.[103] Subcommander Marcos and his wife Yolanda were to seize San Cristóbal, where he would remain while she went on to lead troops in a three-pronged attack on the army barracks at Rancho Nuevo from the north. Major Alfredo's task was to take Altamirano using the 600-strong Eighth Battalion, which formed part of the Fifth Regiment and mainly comprised Tzeltals, and then march on Rancho Nuevo from the east, en route taking Chanal, Oxchuc, and Huixtan. Major Moisés was to command the First Regiment and advance as far as Comitán, attacking the military barracks there, having already taken Las Margaritas on the way. The plan was for this force to meet up with Subcommander Pedro and then advance under his orders northward to form the southern prong of the attack on Rancho Nuevo. Unfortunately, Pedro was shot dead in Las Margaritas, leaving Moisés unexpectedly in command of the entire force (1,200 Tojolabales) of the southern flank. Major Mario's job was to take a considerable portion of the Zapatista Third Regiment, comprising some 1,500 Tzeltals, and seize Ocosingo. However, as Marcos points out, "prior to that they were, 'in passing,' going to take over the *fincas* in the area and get their hands on the armaments that belonged to the *finqueros'* White Guards."[104] Major Josué's task was to destroy the railway line at Salto de Agua, threaten the Pemex oil refinery in southern Tabasco, and ambush any Federal troops who came from Palenque to relieve Ocosingo. "In addition," as Marcos relates, "there was a battalion in the so-called 'Second Strategic reserve,' made up of Chol indigenous, in the depths of our launch bases, and three battalions were at the ready in the Tzeltal, Tojolabal and Chol regions, in the 'First Strategic reserve.'"[105] He concludes: "The EZLN came to public light with more than 4,500 combatants in the first line of fire, the Twenty-first Zapatista Infantry Division, and some 2,000 combatants remained in reserve."

During the night and early hours of the morning, numerous other minor towns and villages were also seized, including Simojovel and Larráinzar, with a group of Zapatistas getting even as far as Chiapa de Corzo, considerably to the west of San Cristóbal and only 16 km from the state capital Tuxtla. The guerrillas carried their uniforms in bundles or rucksacks on their backs. Some even trekked in from the jungle, mountains, and not too distant villages, entering the towns through the narrow and gloomy alleyways of their suburbs. (In San Cristóbal they are even said to have copied the tactic of El Salvador's FMLN[106] and made use of the sewers: "The sewer lines led them to the centre of town, and when the signal was given, they streamed up out of the manholes.)[107] In the quiet side streets of these slumbering towns, under cover of night, they changed into combat gear and converged on the towns' squares.

In a recent communiqué Marcos provides a fairly detailed account of his actions during the thirty-six hours preceding the seizure of San Cristóbal:

I remember that on the night of December 30, 1993, I found myself on the Ocosingo–San Cristóbal de las Casas highway. On that day, I had been at the positions we were maintaining around Ocosingo. I had checked by radio on the situation of our troops who were concentrating along various points next to the highway, throughout the cañadas of Patiwitz, from Monte Libano and Las Tazas. These troops belonged to the Third Infantry Regiment . . .

While still on the highway, I made a stop at one of the highest areas, making radio contact with Battalion 24 (also part of the Fifth Regiment), whose mission was to attack (in conjunction with Battalion #8) the Rancho Nuevo military barracks . . .

Upon reaching San Cristóbal, I skirted the city and headed for the position where the headquarters of the General Command of the EZLN was to be. From there, I communicated by radio with the head of the First Regiment, Subcomandante Insurgente Pedro, Chief of the Zapatista General Staff and second-in-command of the EZLN . . .

On the dawn of December 31, 1993, I confirmed the attack, the date and the hour . . . The time: midnight. The morning of the 31st was spent vacating the urban positions which were being maintained in some places. Around 2 P.M. the different regiments confirmed to the Comandancia General by radio that they were ready. The countdown was begun at 5 P.M.: That hour was dubbed "Minus 7." From that point on, all communication was cut with the regiment. The next radio contact was planned for "Plus 7," 7 A.M. on January 1, 1994 . . . with those who were still alive.[108]

What did Marcos and his army expect would be the result of this act of rebellion? What are we to make, for example, of the first point of the EZLN's Declaration of War, which stated the guerrillas' intention to "advance to the capital of the country, overcoming the Mexican Federal Army"? Did Marcos believe this was a likely prospect? Had he managed to delude himself through a combination of revolutionary fervor and an ardent desire to fulfill a destiny he had been working toward for so long?

On the contrary, I would argue it is highly unlikely that Marcos believed the defeat of the Mexican Federal Army and an advance on the capital was possible. For one thing, the Subcommander's visit to Chihuahua in February 1989 to mark the fifteenth anniversary of Neplanta had left him with no illusions as to the comparative weakness of the FLN's northern "Villa Front." This had seemed little more than a handful of cadres wandering about the mountains, leaving Marcos to comment acidly that "it would be better if they just went home."[109] In the intervening five years Germán had no doubt repeatedly made it clear to Marcos that he could not even expect the other wings of the FLN, let alone the general populace, to join the uprising. Rather, I urge that Marcos's bold intentions should be seen as rhetoric designed both to rouse his troops and to ensure that the media and the government would not simply dismiss the EZLN as an insignificant, localized phenomenon. In short, these highly unrealistic proposals should be viewed as a mixture of bravado, guerrilla posturing, morale boosting, and publicity seeking. This is why on Zapatista radio, at 13:28 on 1 January 1994, the guerrillas were still broadcasting their hopes of "advancing on to the capital, conquering the Federal Army."[110] (Months later, Marcos would place a very positive spin on this aim, claiming that metaphorically at least the Zapatistas "would take the capital" and in fact already had to some extent.)[111]

Leaving rhetoric aside, Marcos, I believe, decided to gamble on what the government's reaction to the rebellion might be. He no doubt calculated that any government in this situation has only three options. The first is to ignore the problem and claim that it is local and insignificant. The second is a military response. The final option is to begin a dialogue. Obviously, the seizure of San Cristóbal, Altamirano, Ocosingo, and Las Margaritas by guerrillas who declared themselves to be rebelling against what they called an illegitimate government, who demanded democracy (and other basic human rights), and who signaled their intention to march on Mexico City, would make the first option almost impossible. These military actions were certain to elicit some kind of response. Indeed, in an interview given on the first day of the uprising, the Subcommander told reporters: "We want to know what this event will provoke, what will move the national consciousness."[112] (It is highly significant that Marcos chooses the word "event" and not "rebellion," "revolution," or "uprising," to describe the seizure of San Cristóbal.)[113] In his eyes, the government could not ignore the Zapatistas, and so the EZLN embarked on rebellion "with only two certainties": "One was that they were going to tear us to shreds. The other was that the act would attract the attention of good persons towards a crime that was no less bloody because it was silent and removed from the media: the genocide of thousands of Mexican indigenous families." He continues:

And . . . it could sound as if we were inclined to being martyrs who sacrificed themselves for others. I would lie if we said yes. Because, even though, looking at it coldly, we had no chance militarily, our hearts weren't thinking of death, but of life, and, given that we were (and are) Zapatistas and, ergo, our doubts include ourselves, we thought that we could be wrong about being torn to shreds, perhaps the entire people of Mexico would rise up.[114]

It would thus appear that the rebellion was undertaken in the full knowledge that if the government did indeed choose to respond using the army, the Zapatistas would be crushed. (In this sense, Marcos was telling the truth when he told one interviewer: "We were prepared to die, but we didn't want to die.")[115] At the same time, however, there was hope that somehow the uprising would not be crushed outright. In the event, this hope proved justified, since world attention was turned toward Chiapas and Mexican civil society stepped in to ensure that the Zapatistas were not annihilated. The Subcommander was nonetheless still somewhat surprised when the EZLN was not destroyed by the Federal Army; more than three months later "he laughed, as if he still couldn't quite believe it," as he told one interviewer: "We went out, fought, and they didn't kill us. We're still here. Our cynical calculation was that we would be killed between January 1 and January 6."[116] As he commented to another interviewer, "There are things you can't understand until they happen."[117]

If Marcos did indeed take a gamble on how the government would respond to the rebellion, did he explain this clearly to those under his command? If not, did he employ his rhetoric deliberately to paint an unrealistic picture of the EZLN's chances of success in this quixotic endeavor, thus masking the extent of the risks from them? In short, did the Subcommander, as certain of his detractors maintain,[118] beguile the indigenous rank-and-file under his command, tricking them into embarking on a suicidal campaign with false hopes of a victory which he knew was impossible? These questions are largely unanswerable. However, certain hypotheses are worth exploring.

It is possible, for example, that the younger members of the EZLN did not see the Declaration of War for what it really was, that is, propaganda, and, in their youthful exuberance and overconfidence, may have taken it far too literally. Inexperienced, unworldly, and raised in a cocooned environment on a diet of left-wing propaganda from their leaders and radio broadcasts from Cuba, El Salvador's FMLN, and Guatemala's URNG, these youngsters perhaps had their revolutionary fervor distilled into a highly concentrated form. Youths, after all, are all too often prone to be wildly overconfident and possess an exaggerated belief in their own capacities.[119] (As former Subcommander Daniel points out, Samuel Ruiz and the curate Gonzalo Ituarte had both underestimated the EZLN, simply dismissing it as "'Marcos and these boys,' saying that it was all a fever of reckless youths and that it would pass.")[120] Certainly a high proportion of the EZLN at this time numbered youths, the average age being reckoned by Marcos as "a scandalous 22 years old."[121]

The older and wiser Zapatistas, however, who had thrashed out the decision to go to war as heads of their communities, perhaps had other thoughts on their minds. These "elders" perhaps tended to be more traditional, more conservative; possessed of the typical shrewd, canny peasant mentality that has shown itself resistant in many revolutions throughout the world to newly introduced ideologies, preferring instead to focus on securing immediate, attainable, material gains locally. Some were no doubt moved by a combination of everything from "desperation with a terrible present and an uncertain future, to anger at past defeats and humiliations, and to a utopic desire of recovering a lost Indian nation."[122] Others, Legorreta Díaz (1998, 237) argues, found "the offer made by the leaders of the EZLN very attractive: they offered a *total* change through armed struggle, not little by little, but with a single blow." Womack suggests that yet others were possibly motivated by "the prospect of restored and revived Solidarity Regional Funds in the canyons . . . this prospect/threat moved the EZLN into action."[123] For many, their uprising was a cry for global or at least national attention and a means of exerting pressure on a hitherto indifferent government. (Marcos himself, when interviewed on 1 January 1994 in San Cristóbal, described the action as "only a call of attention . . . a call of attention for everybody in the country and the world."[124] In a later interview Marcos makes much the same point, stating "We didn't go to war on January 1 to kill or to be killed. We went to war to make ourselves heard.")[125]

Finally, given so many potential motives for rebelling, it is perhaps worth considering the possibility that Marcos, although far from averse to the idea of insurrection, was to some extent put under pressure to act by his indigenous followers. Having preached for so long about the considerable rewards reaped by the Cuban and Nicaraguan *campesinos* following their revolutions, he was now compelled to lead his followers in armed rebellion and to promise them that substantial benefits would result.

In any case, after 1 January 1994 Marcos would continually portray the uprising as the only choice between passively accepting death (and so dying in obscurity) and the possibility of dying in order to make themselves heard. Such a portrayal had a double benefit. First, it was romantic and therefore highly attractive, calling to mind Zapata's aphorism that "It is better to die on one's feet than to live on one's knees." Second, it lent moral justification to the rebellion by suggesting that there was no alternative between rising up and probably dying and not rising up and still probably dying. At first glance, given that 15,000 indigenous people die every year in Chiapas from treatable diseases,[126] and given the government's indifference to and even repression of their pleas for help,[127] this claim may not seem so far-fetched. However, as Kampwirth observes, "The poorest of the poor are very unlikely revolutionaries, since they are too overwhelmed by the reality of everyday life to be able to organize to change that reality,"[128] and so the indigenous who went to make up the EZLN fighters were not likely to have come from the same section of society or the same communities as the dirt poor who tended to die in their droves.[129]

As this chapter closes, we stand on the threshold of the rebellion, with Marcos and the EZLN poised to unleash a guerrilla war against the Mexican government, expecting the worst but hoping for the best. We have witnessed the movement itself develop from a tiny, six-man *foco* at its inception into a fully fledged guerrilla organization leading a veritable People's Army. We have also charted Marcos's personal development from that of a young, inexperienced university graduate recruited to join this small *foco* to that of an experienced Subcommander of the EZLN.

FERNANDO YÁÑEZ MUÑOZ,
ALIAS COMANDANTE
GERMÁN (1995). ARCHIVO
PROCESO.

MARÍA GLORIA BENAVIDES
GUEVARA, ALIAS COMANDANTA
ELISA (1995). GERMÁN
CANSECO/*PROCESO*.

RAFAEL GUILLÉN IN 1992, PERHAPS TAKEN DURING
A PRESENTATION TO TAMPICO'S ASSOCIATION OF
SALES AND MARKETING EXECUTIVES (26 MARCH).
ARCHIVO *PROCESO*.

JORGE JAVIER
ELORRIAGA BERDEGUÉ
(ALIAS COMANDANTE
VICENTE), HUSBAND OF
COMANDANTA ELISA
(1996). SCOTT SADY.

PART III

Marcos the Star Spokesman

18. The Uprising

Not long after midnight, having changed into their combat fatigues, the Zapatistas entered the town square of San Cristóbal and hoisted their flag bearing a red five-point star on a black background.[1] The motif was that of the FLN, but underneath, instead of its initials, were those of the EZLN. At around the same time, Yolanda (also known as Ana María), Marcos's wife, seized the Mexican flag. Marcos subsequently described the scene, scarcely hiding his admiration for her:

> Although her face is wreathed in black, still one can see a few strands of hair upon her forehead, and the eyes with the spark of one who searches. Before her she holds an M-1 carbine in the "assault" position. She has a pistol strapped to her waist. Over the left side of the chest, that place where hopes and convictions reside, she carries the rank of infantry major of an insurgent army that has called itself, this cold dawn of January 1, 1994, the Zapatista National Liberation Army.
>
> Under her command, a rebel column takes the former capital of the south-eastern Mexican state of Chiapas, San Cristóbal de Las Casas. The central square of San Cristóbal is deserted. Only the indigenous men and women under her command are witness to the moment in which the major, a rebel indigenous Tzotzil woman, takes the national flag and gives it to the commanders of the rebellion, those called "the Indigenous Clandestine Revolutionary Committee." At 02:00 southeastern time, January 1 of 1994, over the radio, the major says, "We have recovered the flag. 10–23 over."
>
> For the rest of the world, it is 01:00 hours of the New Year, but for her, those words mark a decade-long wait.[2]

The guerrillas then immediately set about burning the public archives in the *palacio municipio* (town hall). Inside were thousands of petitions for land and justice, filed but unresolved; property records, falsified and authentic; law suits pending; deeds and titles; and other such documents.

(Twenty-seven percent of Mexico's pending land petitions are from the state of Chiapas, some claims dating back two hundred years.) As Juan Bañuelos, a chiapaneco and winner of the National Prize for Poetry in 1968, puts it: "It was a symbolic act: the EZLN set fire to the lies, robbery, oppression, and cynicism of the system, as represented by City Hall. It was an act of purification." Next, they turned out the prison cells, freeing 179 prisoners. Bañuelos continues:

> In the same way, the Zapatistas opened jails and released prisoners, the majority of whom were victims of unjust judicial proceedings, which had been tainted by bribery or consigned to oblivion, or they were defendants whose bodies were marked by the brutality of the police. All of this was carried out under the symbol of liberty.[3]

Meanwhile, on the outskirts of town, some of Marcos's most trusted cadres, armed with the best weaponry at the Zapatistas's disposal, were setting up roadblocks at the entrance to the city. He had stationed them there, just as he had done during the demonstration against the celebration of Columbus's discovery of America fourteen months earlier, to counter any attempt by the army to retake the city. Oppenheimer believes this was more than a prudent military precaution:

> The idea was to provoke the army into trying to recover San Cristóbal, attacking the elite rebel positions on the outskirts of the city, which would have caused large numbers of civilian casualties and would have exposed the army to charges of massive human rights violations. If the army attacked, it would lose the propaganda war.[4] If it didn't, it would lose as well: The television cameras would focus on the takeover of San Cristóbal municipal palace by a ragtag army of landless Mayans mostly armed with toy guns. And it worked exactly as planned.[5]

However, Oppenheimer is perhaps confusing tactics and strategy. Marcos placed his best troops at the routes into the city because this is a sound military tactic designed to secure access into the city and prevent the rebels inside from being surprised and surrounded should the Mexican government opt for a military solution to the rebellion. Marcos's overall strategy was to seize San Cristóbal and several other towns in order to provoke the government, not the army, into some kind of response. His roadblocks were not intended to bring down the army's wrath upon his best troops and the civilian population,[6] but were a tactic designed to meet a military response to the situation should the government choose a violent, non-diplomatic solution to the situation.

In the meantime, over 700 km to the north, almost in a different world, Salinas was celebrating New Years with a party in Los Pinos (the Mexican equivalent to the White House). He was about to embark on his final six months as president, having just had his protégé Luis Donaldo Colosio accepted as presidential candidate[7]; NAFTA had come into effect at midnight, leading *Newsweek*'s 1993 year-end "Conventional Wisdom" section to dub Mexico a "U.S. sunbelt state"; the country was about to become a member of the OECD (Organization for Economic Co-operation and Development); *Time* magazine had recently named Salinas "International Newsmaker of the Year for Latin America"; and he was now looking forward to the next stage in his career, his U.S.- and Mexico-backed candidacy as head of the World Trade Organization.[8] A phone call from his secretary of defense interrupted the festivities, telling Salinas that a guerrilla army had seized San Cristóbal, Altamirano, Ocosingo, and Las Margaritas. The shock must have been tremendous. De la Grange and Rico are correct when they observe that 1994 and Mexico were the least likely time and place for a new guerrilla group to emerge. The fall of the Berlin Wall and subsequent disintegration of the Soviet Union, the pacification of Nicaragua's Sandinistas and El Salvador's FMLN, and the defeat of Guatemala's and Grenada's leftists had made a Marxist guerrilla uprising in Central America highly unlikely. Mexico, in particular, looked the least likely country in the entire hemisphere to experience problems with guerrillas. President Luis Echeverría had systematically destroyed Mexico's guerrilla groups during the seventies by means of co-optation, infiltration, and brutal repression, while (on paper at least) Salinas's years in office had witnessed an economic miracle.[9] In short, Marxist guerrillas were a Third World phenomenon and Mexico, at least in the eyes of its president and its northern neighbor, was decidedly a First World country.

At a little before 8 A.M., Marcos arrived on the scene wearing his now customary black ski mask and driving a blue Volkswagen. He was carrying an Ingram submachine gun and a walkie-talkie. He drove around the town square accompanied by two female guerrillas and handed out weapons. The guns came from the city's police station, which Marcos and some of his cadres had just captured. As Marcos told one reporter months later, "My job was to lead the attack on the police headquarters."[10] (It is alleged that while Marcos was in the police station gathering together much needed weapons the phone rang. A concerned citizen was warning the police that he had seen many armed men entering the city. "It's okay, we know, don't worry, everything is under control," came the reply. Unbeknownst to the caller, it was the guerrillas' leader, Subcommander Marcos, and not the chief of police, who had picked up the receiver.)[11] Shortly afterward he jumped back into the blue Volkswagen and headed for the town square. As Marcos himself has explained, this was not the original plan: "One Zapatista officer whose job was to carry the weapons from the police headquarters to the central square—where our forces had the fewest weapons—got wounded. So I had to go and take his place."[12]

There, in the central plaza, on the balcony of the municipal palace, his face unmasked, Felipe, an indigenous Comandante and catechist from San Andrés Larráinzar, was busy giving orders to the troops under his command and explaining these actions to the rapidly growing crowd of concerned San Cristóbal citizens, local newspaper reporters, and foreign tourists. He, and not Marcos, had been chosen to be the public face of the EZLN. (The guerrillas' claims to be impoverished and oppressed indigenous *campesinos* fighting for basic human rights would be given far greater credence if they were put forward openly by such a person, and not by a highly educated, articulate, white, masked man sporting an accent from one of Mexico's central states.) Surrounded by fellow indigenous officers, such as Uno, Virginia, and Ovidio, he introduced himself as a member of the CCRI (Comité Clandestino de Revolución Indígena). In halting Spanish, he read from a crumpled, handwritten address: "We have come to San Cristóbal de las Casas to do a revolution against capitalism. . . . We have fought peacefully for years trying to get a solution, but the government has never cared to solve our big problems about land rights and other problems." He went on to make many of the points that Marcos had delineated in *The Southeast in Two Winds*: that Chiapas was a rich state inhabited by a poor people; that it produced beef, electricity, gas, oil, and yet its inhabitants were malnourished and hungry; and that very few had electricity, gas, oil, or even clean drinking water. He then proclaimed the rebels' formal Declaration of War against the Mexican government, this time from a printed pamphlet. This described the PRI government as "a seventy-year dictatorship led by a clique of traitors," president Salinas as the "supreme and illegitimate federal executive," and the Federal Army as "the pillar of the Mexican dictatorship that we suffer from." Like most guerrilla declarations it claimed "this struggle [wa]s the only path" left open to them, that it was their "last hope, after having tried to utilize all legal means." Unlike other guerrilla declarations, however, it also justified the revolt by citing article 39 of the Mexican constitution: "National Sovereignty essentially and originally resides in the people. All political power emanates from the people and its purpose is to help the people. The people have, at all times, the inalienable right to alter or modify their form of government."[13] The declaration went on to state the guerrillas' intention to "advance on the capital of the country, overcoming the Mexican Federal Army, protecting in our advance the civilian population and permitting the people in the liberated area the right to freely and democratically elect their own administrative authorities." This latter point was reiterated in the final line of the declaration: "We will not stop fighting until the basic demands of our people have been met by forming a government of our country that is free and democratic."[14]

This aim is markedly different from that outlined in the FLN's statutes drawn up in 1980, but subscribed to by all those—including Marcos— present at the January 1993 meeting in Prado. Article 5 of the FLN statutes states its goal as being "to install a Socialist system . . . in order *to exercise the dictatorship of the proletariat* [and] to form a single political party based on the principles of Marxism-Leninism."[15] Interestingly, the EZLN Declaration of War made no mention whatsoever of Marxism, Leninism, Mao, Che, Yankee imperialism, the proletariat, or the bourgeoisie,[16] no doubt reflecting that it was written by Marcos, entirely independently of Germán.

Concerning Marcos's growing independence from Germán, Oppenheimer makes much of a supposed rift between Marcos and Germán, writing that the latter "was in a state of fury" at the former's "growing independence."[17] The ex-Subcommander, Daniel, also tells us that "after January 1994, Guillén disowned Germán in a communiqué."[18] However, Tello Díaz points out that Marcos's "relationship with him [Germán] was determined, as always, by the necessity of keeping open the conduits that kept him united with the rest of the organization in Mexico." He continues:

> Germán had under his responsibility the work of the secure houses of the EZLN. These were located in various states in the country besides Chiapas. . . . There, the insurgents produced the majority of the firearms destined for the EZLN. It was a very important function. Marcos needed these. . . . For him, although the EZLN did not necessarily need to fire its weapons, it at least needed to possess them.[19]

Germán, in any case, had very little to complain about. The decision to start the uprising had received his support, and its timing had been made known to him well in advance, even if he had reservations about it. More-over, Tello Díaz notes that although

> Marcos had displaced Germán in the leadership of the EZLN . . . Germán did not stop being the commander-in-chief of the EZLN, as well as also being the secretary general of the FLN. He conserved his place of honor in the hierarchy of the organization, although the true command—the control of men and arms, and above all the guerrillas' voice—was al-ready in Marcos' power.[20]

No doubt Germán reasoned that it was better to remain nominally in charge of a guerrilla force that was a highly successful wing of the FLN, while at the same time being in overall charge of the latter, than to have Marcos split from the FLN, taking the EZLN with him and leaving Germán in command of very little. In any event, Tello Díaz tells us that "communication between the two [men], despite their differences, continued more or less normally as always."[21] This is confirmed, I would argue, by various observations. First, in a communiqué dated to March 1998 in which Marcos discusses the Mexican celebration of the Day of the Dead, the Subcommander relates how "each year the Zapatistas put out an offering for Pedro (fallen in com-bat in 1974, raised up and fallen again in 1994, raised up again, struggling always)," adding that "at the dawn of each November 2, thousands of offer-ings shine for Pedro in many indigenous homes."[22] The Pedro who fell in 1974 was Germán's brother,[23] and it is surely symptomatic of a continued respect, if not closeness, between Marcos and Germán that Pedro's fall was commemorated each year. Second, and more significantly, when the EZLN made its historic march on Mexico City in 2001, the EZLN issued a commu-niqué (dated February) stating that "Yáñez the architect will be accompany-ing the Zapatista delegation . . . in the capacity of the EZLN's special guest [and] will be the person in charge of acting as an intermediary between the Zapatista delegation and the deputies, senators . . . [and] the leadership of the different Mexican political parties who wish to engage in dialogue with us."[24] The architect Fernando Yáñez Muñoz, described as "a social activist, someone who has devoted his entire life to transforming the living conditions of the Mexican poor," is none other than Comandante Germán. Third, in a more recent communiqué (29 April 2001), Marcos announced the Zapatistas's decision to break off dialogue with the government follow-ing the approval of the "COCOPA legislative proposal," stating that the EZLN "has indicated to architect Fernando Yáñez Muñoz that he completely suspend his work as liaison between the EZLN and the federal government."[25] Fourth, Marcos fondly recalls his first meeting twenty-two years earlier with Yáñez in a communiqué dated September 2002.[26] In it he calls Yáñez "big brother," and notes the architect's participation in the coming project to create a magazine called *Rebeldía* along with Javier Elorriaga (formerly Comandante Vicente). It would appear that Marcos continued to respect Germán, the man who had given him on his twenty-third birthday a figure of Che inscribed with a quotation from José Martí and who had instructed him in guerrilla ways during his early days in Chiapas. Any rift appears, like that between Marcos and Bishop Ruiz, to have been superficial and temporary.

Marcos describes the Declaration of War as "a confluence of various ideas . . . a cocktail . . . a general synthesis, a mixture of patriotic values, of the historic heritage of the clandestine Mexican left of the '70's, of elements of Indian culture, elements from Mexico's military history, of lessons from the Central American and South American guerrillas, from movements for national liberation . . . the text of minimal agreement."[27] In sum, the text, like its author, was far more than merely a product of Marxist-Leninist doctrine.

Another striking absence in the declaration is any explicit mention of the indigenous. This has been made much of by those who claim that Marcos only later played the indigenous card when he saw how effective it was in provoking the sympathy and interest of the national and international press.[28] However, closer scrutiny of the declaration reveals several implicit mentions of the indigenous. For example, it opens with the statement "we are the product of 500 years of struggle" and in its final paragraph it talks of "an undeclared genocidal war against our people." As Marcos himself observes, "There is no other social group in Mexico that is able to say this more than the indigenous; neither the workers, nor the *campesinos*, nor the intellectuals are able to say this."[29] Moreover, any hypothesis that would have Marcos emphasize the indigenous nature of the rebellion only as a last-minute, calculated, crowd-pleasing measure must ignore the fact that the Subcommander proclaimed from San Cristóbal's municipal palace balcony: "Don't forget this: This is an ethnic movement."[30] (It must also ignore the fact that even the FLN statutes, written almost a decade and one-half earlier, explicitly mention the indigenous twice in its chapter 4, "On the Goals of the Movement.")[31] Much later, Marcos explained the absence of any specific mention of the indigenous as resulting from a wish "to give a national character . . . to the movement" as opposed to merely "a regional or ethnic one," and to avoid "our war appearing as a war of Indians against *mestizos*."[32] Put simply, why risk appearing exclusionary by emphasizing the indigenous when all of Mexico's impoverished, exploited, and oppressed could be welcomed into the struggle?

Marcos arrived in the town square shortly after Comandante Felipe had finished reading out the Declaration of War with its accompanying Revolutionary Laws. Felipe had ended his speech with the cry:

> Long Live the Mexican revolution!
> Long Live the Zapatista National Liberation Army!
> Long Live the Indian people in arms![33]

Each statement was met with a "Viva!" by the Zapatistas, weapons held aloft defiantly. Felipe then descended the steps of the town hall to mingle with his troops and take charge on the ground. Marcos informs us that he had just finished distributing the arms cache from the police station when

> the Zapatista officer in charge of the seizure of the municipal palace walked towards me and told me, "There is somebody there, a gringo, asking things that nobody can understand."[34] I said, "Okay, I'll take care of him." It was a tourist who was scared that we were going to rob him, rape him, or who knows what. So I told him not to worry, that we wouldn't do anything to him, that this was a movement to achieve better living conditions for the Indians, and not against anybody, etcetera. As I was explaining this in my rudimentary English, people began to gather around us. Soon, a few journalists arrived and started asking questions, and I began to talk. That was about eight A.M.[35]

Having done this, Marcos then appears to have gone up to the balcony of the *palacio municipio* and addressed the throng below. Precisely why he did this is unclear. Certainly it was not part of the original plan. Marcos would later tell Oppenheimer, "I wasn't even supposed to show up at the central square."[36] Moreover, by doing so he was drawing undue attention to himself, since he was a good six inches taller than most of the indigenous troops and was made even more distinctive by his ski mask, walkie-talkie, and sophisticated weaponry. His mere presence on the balcony, before he ever opened his mouth, undermined Felipe and put into question just how indigenous an uprising this was. Perhaps Marcos simply could not resist standing triumphantly on the town hall's balcony watching the troops he had trained occupying the former state capital. This was, after all, the moment he had been preparing for throughout the preceding decade. Possibly, he could not help but interfere because he had never learned to stand aside and relinquish control. It was one thing to delegate the task of taking another city to one of his fellow guerrillas, but it was another thing entirely to be present at an event and to sit calmly by, contenting oneself with watching idly from the sidelines. Maybe he desperately wanted to know how the residents of San Cristóbal and, ultimately the Mexican public at large, viewed this rebellion. Having had his appetite for interactive dialogue with the crowd whetted by a series of (relatively mundane for him) questions from worried tourists pressing around him, Marcos, ever the intellectual, was now keen to answer queries of a more interesting nature. Hemmed in by a tightly packed group, with any dialogue rapidly degenerating into something of verbal free-for-all, he possibly decided to ascend to the balcony to enter into a dialogue with the 400-strong crowd below (and not just a section of the crowd). In any case, the next day's edition of *La Jornada* carried several photographs of Marcos addressing the crowd from the balcony, some taken from below and one from somebody standing behind Marcos looking down on the audience. According to journalist John Ross, Marcos did not stay long on the balcony. Apparently, "The first questions came from so deep in the crowd that Marcos had a hard time catching the drift. The Subcommander descended into the street to facilitate the interchange."[37]

A Swiss couple were among the first people to speak to him. Like many tourists they were concerned as to whether they were hostages, human shields against a government counteroffensive, or free to go. The Swiss were eager to know if they could get on with their vacation, protesting, "We have reservations to visit the ruins at Palenque." Marcos politely replied "I apologize for the inconvenience, but this is a revolution"—a response that combined apology and sarcasm. He then issued safe conducts for those wishing to cross Zapatista checkpoints set up just outside the town. The next question, from a woman within the crowd, was why he, unlike so many of his fellow guerrillas, was wearing a ski mask. He replied, "Actually, only the most handsome of us are required to wear them, for our own protection."[38] When interviewed later by reporters from Mexico City, the woman called him, "a perfect showman!"[39] Marcos was evidently thoroughly enjoying being the center of attention. He could now give vent to the playfulness, jocularity, and charm that presumably had had little outlet during his past decade in the jungle. This witty banter coupled with his image as a heroic guerrilla produced a powerful impression of charisma. As Carl Lawrence notes, "Subcommander Marcos had just become larger than life"[40]—a sentiment echoed by de la Grange and Rico, who concede: "In the moment he pronounced these words the guerrilla captured his interlocutors: tourists, onlookers, local press, who scarcely a few hours after his first public appearance converted him into a star."[41]

By 11 A.M., when Felipe reemerged to give a second press conference in the central plaza he was already eclipsed by Marcos,[42] around whom tourists, citizens and the media alike were now flocking. Marcos the superstar was now being forged; Felipe died later that day, in a bloody attack on Rancho Nuevo.[43]

Marcos, meanwhile, continued to give interviews and press conferences. He spoke to Amado Avendaño, editor of San Cristóbal's local newspaper, *El Tiempo*, in which he insisted that he was a mere subcommander, taking his orders from the indigenous comandantes such as Felipe. To Italian freelance journalist Gianni Prociettis,[44] he outlined why the Zapatistas had taken action: "This is a warning to the government that we are fed up with the lack of democracy." Robert Ovetz, who was in Chiapas on a short break from completing his doctorate at the University of Texas at Austin, also managed to obtain a taped interview, which was the first the Subcomandante was to give in English.[45] It is interesting for a number of reasons, in particular—either because it was one of the first interviews he gave, or because Marcos was speaking in a language not his own—for its remarkable candor. It contains none of the "spin" of later interviews. For example, when asked if he now considered San Cristóbal to be a liberated zone, Marcos replied, "No, no, no. It is only a call for attention," adding, "[it is] a call of attention for everybody in the country and the world that the Indians have the dignity to raise their heads." In Marcos's mind at least, if not in the minds of his cadres, the seizure of San Cristóbal was the first offensive in a media, not a guerrilla, war. Of equal interest is Marcos's reaction to the question of whether the EZLN came out of existing organizations: an emphatic, "No, God save us. God save us, no, no. It's different. This movement was born in the mountains." He went on to outline the EZLN's hopes for the overthrow of the government and its replacement by "a government of transition [which would then] call a new election," and to emphasize that "there are more kinds of struggle not only the struggle with arms . . . like demonstrations, mobilizations, but without arms, to demand the government make petitions or respond to petitions." He equated the impact of NAFTA to that made by a bomb, and asked, "If NAFTA begins on the first of January '94 and the death of these people begins on this day, why not begin the liberation of these people right this day?"[46]

Meanwhile, throughout much of the afternoon, as air force jets reconnoitered the situation, some EZLN troops, exhausted from the night's activity, sat around bonfires (made from the town hall's furniture), while others looted the local Banamex bank (just opposite the town hall) and government stores (in search of medicines, among other things), and still more marched with Felipe south along Route 190 to launch a night attack on Rancho Nuevo.

Then, as Ovetz notes, "shortly after sunset . . . the EZLN held a rally during which Marcos spoke from a second floor window, his explanations of who they were and their intentions met with cheers and applause . . . among the approximately one thousand people present." Ovetz continues:

> The question and answer period that followed would be unimaginable if I hadn't seen it myself. I never imagined people with guns would ever feel themselves compelled to be questioned by unarmed people during a rebellion. The crowd, a mixture of *mestizo*, Indian, tourists and travelers, erupted in loud applause and cheering several times. Marcos explained that they would let anyone who wished to do so leave after 6 A.M. the next morning after receiving a pass.[47]

According to Ross, Marcos added, "We have stayed too long waiting for a political response from the government," again confirming the Subcommander's assertion that the Zapatistas had rebelled so as "to know what this event will provoke."[48] The Subcommander then declared a curfew from 8 P.M. to 8 A.M., issuing it in with two shots, and telling the crowd, "Go home and don't open your doors," since the army would soon be coming to retake the city. Marcos's fear for the welfare of the civilians present was shared by those in the crowd. One British vacationer, Peter Morris, told Reuters "The rebels are fine, but I'm getting out of here before the soldiers come." Once the crowd was dispersed, and the people confined to their homes, Ovetz tells us (1994b), the Zapatistas "packed up and left only a few hours after the rally."[49]

In San Cristóbal, the Zapatistas had succeeded in making their voice heard—although later, when he returned to the city for the peace talks, the Subcommander would bewail the fact that it had been necessary "to kill and die to get anyone to pay attention to us"[50]—and Marcos, possibly unintentionally, had taken his first steps on the road to fame. Some of the Zapatista force went on to assault Rancho Nuevo, while the majority, Marcos among them, retreated back into the jungle. This is telling. The Zapatistas appear to have made no attempt to "advance on the capital"; indeed, they did not even make a serious attempt on the state capital, Tuxtla Guttiérrez, only 55 km to the west. It is possible of course that somewhere in the vicinity of San Cristóbal they awaited the result of their attack on Rancho Nuevo, ready to advance should much needed weapons fall into their hands, but retired following their failure to take the military base. Equally possibly, however, they never intended to "advance on the capital," but made the threat in order to capture the government's and the press's full attention. In support of this, Marcos himself tells us that the Zapatistas did not wait around after withdrawing from San Cristóbal, but "ran like we had never run before."[51]

In any event, as night fell, the EZLN command was left guessing as to what response they might provoke from the government—other than that of the menace of a few jet fighters. They had made their point very publicly. They had taken San Cristóbal; they had distributed their newspaper, *The Mexican Awakener*, throughout the town and had posted their message and Declaration of War on many of its buildings; they had broadcast their message all day over the radio, having seized XEOCH, the state government radio station just outside Ocosingo; they had encountered chiapanecos, fellow Mexicans, and foreign tourists, all of whom would be spreading word of their cause; and, perhaps most important, they had engaged the attention of important elements of the local, national, and foreign press and ensured that every major press organization in Mexico, North America, and Europe would be hurriedly dispatching their correspondents to Chiapas.[52]

A public relations war commenced, with the Zapatistas holding the initiative.[53] It did not take the Mexican government long before it decided to launch a military and media counterattack. Prior to examining this, however, let us consider the other theaters of the Zapatistas military offensive, since in some cases the results had a direct bearing on Marcos himself and on our assessment of his ability to train, deploy, and direct troops in the field.

Whereas the attack on San Cristóbal had gone smoothly, elsewhere things had gone less well, and even disastrously. For example, at Tzontehuitz, 12 km from San Cristóbal, the Zapatistas attempted to take a communications post located on a hill. They were beaten back by airplanes carrying rockets. A general who witnessed the event tells how "each rocket caused at least three or four victims. The bodies were thrown into the air at the moment of the explosion."[54]

So too the attack on the Rancho Nuevo military base, led by Marcos's wife Ana María was a failure. The guerrillas had pinned down the federal troops there, preventing them from coming to the relief of either San Cristóbal or other beleaguered units, but they had failed to take the compound and had to withdraw, having wasted human resources and ammunition, which was in short supply. Indeed, the guerrillas had hoped success here would yield much needed matériel. As Marcos put it in one interview, "The attack on Rancho Nuevo took place because an army hungry for weapons and ammunition has to go where there are weapons and ammunition."[55] The rebels had counted on surprise and the fact that the barracks would be greatly reduced in strength due to soldiers being granted holiday leave. They were right to do so; the troops in the barracks were, initially at least, taken by surprise and they were severely hard pressed due to being short numbered. Marcos also tells us that the guerrillas' tactics here were to feint: "We pretended to attack from the right in order to attack from both sides."[56] Unfortunately, the element of surprise did not prove decisive and the number of troops in the base was still sufficient to withstand a two-pronged assault from both flanks. This ought not to surprise us, since seldom are guerrillas able to vanquish well-armed, professional troops entrenched in a military base of their own construction. De la Grange and Rico cite an army captain present at Rancho Nuevo who says the fighting was desperate at times as the EZLN mounted a sustained assault, but that the Zapatistas failed because, badly armed and throwing themselves recklessly at the compound, they were easy targets for soldiers who possessed sophisticated night vision equipment.[57] The rebels were finally repelled in the morning, following the arrival of reinforcements from Tuxtla and sustained air support.

Worse still, at Las Margaritas, a key village en route to Comitán, 20 km away, Subcomandante Pedro was killed. As Tello Díaz relates: "Pedro left with some of his men for the central park. Everything appeared to be calm. Arriving at the center of the village however, an individual who nobody had seen because he was hiding behind a vehicle shot him in the head with a revolver. Pedro died instantly."[58] This came as a serious blow to Marcos. Tactically, it caused Marcos to recall Pedro's force and abandon the assault on Comitán, a sizable and strategically significant town on the main highway south to the Guatemalan border. As Marcos relates:

In the case of Comitán, when the column took Las Margaritas, it lost a fundamental officer charged with the advance on other positions. When he fell, another official who was charged with looking after the communities, began to advance on Comitán and I realized that the communities were going to be left unprotected. Then I gave the order by radio for them to fall back, but they were only four kilometers away and said they could see the lights [of the town] when they halted.[59]

Personally, it represented a considerable loss for Marcos who had always been very close to Pedro. Indeed, Marcos always referred to him affectionately as Pedrito, while he in turn called Marcos "Marquitos" ("dear little Marcos"), and it is said that before the uprising the two had frequently joked about how they would not stop their offensive until they were eating cheese sandwiches in Tres Marías, a village located very close to Mexico City.[60] Pedro, like Subcomandante Daniel, had been recruited to the FLN in the early 1980s while he was at Universidad Autónoma Métropolitana,[61] and one must wonder whether Marcos knew him then. If so, and it seems highly likely, Marcos would have known Pedro for around fifteen years. He, like Marcos, was jocular, and he was also one of only a tiny handful of cadres who were urban and highly educated.[62] Marcos recently wrote the following fond farewell to his comrade-in-arms:

I'm going to talk about a man, an insurgent soldier, a Zapatista. I am not going to talk much. I cannot. Not yet. His name was Pedro, and he died fighting. He held the rank of Subcomandante. . . . I am not going to say that he has not died. He is indeed dead, and I do not want him to be dead. But Pedro, like all of our dead, walks here, and every once in a while he appears and he talks and jokes and gets serious and asks for more coffee and lights his umpteenth cigarette. He's here now. It is October 26, and it's his birthday. I say to him: "Greetings, birthday boy." He lifts his little cup of coffee and says: "Greetings, Sub." . . . I tell him things, and he tells me things. We remember. We laugh. We get serious. Sometimes I tell him off. I scold him for being undisciplined, because I didn't order him to die and he died. He didn't obey. And so I tell him off. He just opens his eyes and tells me: "No way." Yes, no way. Then I show him a map. He just likes to look at maps. I point out to him how we've grown. He smiles.[63]

De la Grange and Rico note that Pedro "was, apparently, the only white person who died in the course of the Zapatista offensive."[64] The significance of this is debatable, however, since by the time of the uprising the EZLN comprised only two whites, Marcos and Pedro (Daniel having already fled the organization). Statistically, therefore, whites suffered a 50 percent mortality rate in this campaign.

But worse than the bitter personal blow of losing Pedro were the events at Ocosingo, the following day. Seizure of this town proved harder and bloodier than the capture of San Cristóbal. There the police resisted a Zapatista assault force of around four hundred troops for eight hours. They had no doubt been alerted that clandestine and illegal activity of a sort would be coming given the spate of truck and automobile thefts in the area over the past few days. However, it is also abundantly clear that even during the Zapatistas's attack the police had no idea as to what they were up against. The judicial police were attacked in their headquarters, near the school, while some twenty to thirty state police (the Public Security Forces) were penned in the town hall. The latter, when asked to surrender, responded merely with tear gas, as opposed to live ammunition.[65] The guerrillas then opened fire, the shooting lasting from around 8:30 A.M. to 2:00 P.M.

We are lucky to have two excellent eyewitness accounts of the Zapatistas's seizure of Ocosingo, one from the town's priest, Pablo Iribarren,[66] and the other from Efraín Bartolomé, winner of two national prizes for his poetry, who was born and raised in the town and who had returned there to spend Christmas with his parents. Bartolomé tells us that "there [we]re more than a thousand guerrilleros in the town," and that by 10 A.M., they had "burned down Geofísica (a Pemex property) and destroyed three airplanes."[67] By 11:15 A.M. the Zapatistas had freed prisoners from the jail and killed three Public Security police. A further four and one-half hours of sporadic shooting ensued until the state police in the City Hall surrendered at 3:41 P.M.[68] Then, in marked contrast to the mercy shown forty policemen who had surrendered in San Cristóbal, who were merely bound with their hands behind their backs shirtless on the floor, the EZLN officer in charge at Ocosingo executed the police chief. According to reliable eyewitnesses, at 4:58 P.M.: "They killed the [police] comandante. He had already surrendered, even had his hands in the air. A woman did it, right there in the doorway. Surrendered or not, they shot him in the head! And left him right there in the doorway of City Hall."[69] The perpetrator of this war crime—one of a very few incidents of human rights violations and contraventions of the Geneva Convention on the part of the EZLN[70]—was "a black, fat, female, who held the rank of captain and who managed her troops with an iron hand."[71] The Zapatistas had already proclaimed over the radio and published in their Declaration of War that they would

> initiate summary judgments against all soldiers of the Mexican Federal Army and the political police who have received training or have been paid by foreigners, accused of being traitors to our country, and against all those who have repressed and treated badly the civilian population, and robbed, or stolen from, or attempted crimes against the good of the people.[72]

However, even so, neither this forewarning, nor the fact that the judicial police in Ocosingo had themselves allegedly perpetrated serious human rights violations, including the extra-judicial murder of at least one civilian, a crippled hunchback called Martín who they beat to death,[73] excuses the Zapatista captain's action. As these occurrences, and those that were to follow, all too clearly show, something had evidently gone wrong in Ocosingo: possibly Marcos's absence from the scene resulted in his being unable to control what was a highly volatile situation there.

In short, as Efráin Bartolomé has noted, the bloodless occupation of San Cristóbal contrasted starkly with what transpired at Ocosingo.[74] Worse was still to come when the Zapatista fighters in Ocosingo did not retreat as they had done at San Cristóbal and Rancho Nuevo, but stood firm and, the following day, at around 2:30 P.M., engaged two Federal Army battalions (comprising some 1,600 men) come to retake the town. This disastrous stand cost the rebels thirty-four combatants,[75] among them Captain Hugo, a high-ranking cadre who headed the arm of the movement devoted to the organization of masses.[76] One must ask what went wrong.

In an interview he gave only a month after the event, Marcos stated:

> The plan was to withdraw the troops that took Ocosingo, and they were a big force. They began withdrawing in stages, but then we had a problem with the civilians. The compañeros in San Cristóbal realized that civilians had mixed in with our troops, out of sympathy, curiosity or what have you. And then they got caught in that mousetrap of the market. Our troops were in position, but we couldn't leave the civilians there.
>
> In order to remove the civilians, our sharpshooters had to start firing and caused Army casualties. The Army then fixed our positions and started to attack us with mortar fire. The wounded we have in our field hospital were wounded by shrapnel from rockets and mortars, not by bullets.

Our combatants were shooting from a fixed position, which is suicidal for any sharpshooter, because to protect themselves they really should keep changing their positions. A fighter has to protect the civilians, so they had to stay put in order to allow the civilians to get out.[77]

This, however, is only half the story. Marcos fails to explain why the Zapatistas did not withdraw during the night of 1 January as they had done in San Cristóbal. Admittedly, the fight to gain control of Ocosingo had lasted much longer than in San Cristóbal, but this does not explain why EZLN troops stayed in Ocosingo until 2:30 p.m. the following day: why, one wonders, had they not pulled out during the night, or at dawn?

Fortunately, Le Bot managed to draw out of Marcos more details of what exactly happened at Ocosingo in a lengthy interview with the Subcommander in 1996. There were two basic mistakes. The first was logistical; there were not enough vehicles to effect the withdrawal of the entire Zapatista force, which led to a battalion, some five hundred combatants, being left behind in the market. As Marcos relates:

> When the 1st of January had ended, at twelve at night I communicated with all the various positions and ordered them to retire at dawn on the second. At that time, one part of the garrison of Ocosingo separated in order to go north and the other part fell back to the jungle to protect the communities. This transpired in part because the retreat into the jungle had not been completed, there remained behind at battalion, the battalion of major Mario remained behind the market waiting for vehicles in order to leave. Two o'clock came, when a unit of paratroopers closed off the exit. Then, in addition, came a motorized column from the Palenque side. There were military errors; there was no defense of the periphery. But the fundamental problem was that this unit should never have been there on the second day.[78]

The second error was the failure of the guerrillas to blow up a major bridge on the route from Palenque to Ocosingo. (The Zapatistas had, it should be remembered, stolen 1,500 kg of dynamite from Pemex on 31 December, presumably for precisely this purpose.) Again, Marcos tells us:

> But in the morning of the 2nd we began to retire. The unit that went to the north, on to Tabasco, was the one in charge of obstructing the road from Palenque. But it did not demolish the bridge, they kept watch and then they went, assuming that the whole world had left Ocosingo, or that there was no one they had to protect, that the line of defense was al-

ready in the jungle. The battalion that was in the market remained alone and so the army entered without any difficulty. They should have been at the very least slowed down as they approached the bridge, but the unit that guarded it thought that already nobody remained in the town and so did not demolish it.[79]

Therefore, failure to destroy the bridge would not have proved so fatal had there not been a catastrophic failure in communication. The unit at the bridge did not know that an entire battalion of Zapatista troops remained in the market at Ocosingo, and the market unit did not know that the bridge remained intact. The comments of Ocosingo eyewitness Efráin Bartolomé are of particular interest. In his War Diary entry for 3:57 P.M. on 1 January, he notes:

> The radio from Villahermosa says that five hundred soldiers are coming from Palenque . . . Rumors: they [i.e., the Zapatistas] dynamited the bridge over La Florida (the river that comes from San Cristóbal) and the one over La Vírgen (from Palenque). I don't believe it. We would have heard the explosions. Especially the last one: it's very close.[80]

Did the Zapatista battalion in the market believe these rumors? If so, why did they not bother to check the veracity of these reports over the radio with the unit guarding the bridge? Why did they not dismiss these reports, as Efráin Bartolomé did, on the grounds that they had heard no major explosion nearby? It is, of course, possible that these rumors were based on incorrect information coming through over the radio from the bridge unit. Did, for example, the unit guarding the bridge mistakenly believe it had destroyed the bridge, when in fact they had only damaged it and it was still passable? Regrettably, these questions remain unanswered, but what does remain clear is that once again, as in the case of the army's discovery of Las Calabazas camp in the Corralchén sierra in May 1993, the Zapatistas committed a major military blunder due to a breakdown in communication during a situation where Marcos was himself absent from the scene and Major Mario was in command.

Let us now turn away from the military war and instead look to the media war waged by both sides for the "hearts and minds" of Mexican and international onlookers alike.[81]

19. "Waging a Masterful Media War"

Naturally, the government lost no time at all in launching its media counter offensive; indeed, it began this more rapidly than its military campaign, on the morning of January 1.[1] As Efráin Bartolomé noted in his diary:

> 11:40: The Mexican television presents the news. They don't say anything about the shooting, that it hasn't stopped all this time. Minimal: a group of *campesinos*, armed with sticks, has occupied the City Hall of San Cristóbal. 14:00: News on the television: "24 Hours." They totally diminish the size of the problem . . . Nothing about the Declaration of War. They talk about a group of armed Indians. 23:35: "24 Hours" hides the Declaration of War. They're passing it off as some indigenous or *campesino* demands of minor importance. The government is offering dialogue, affirming that the army will not intervene.[2]

The government's strategy was initially to play down the uprising and to portray itself as reasonable, flexible, and conciliatory. In the face of contradictory information from the U.S. media, in particular CNN, it became more hostile, claiming that the Zapatistas were rebels (law breakers); that they were committing grave atrocities (and thus were inhumane and should therefore be treated inhumanely); that they had received training and weapons from foreign powers; and that they were led by a blond-haired, blue-eyed—and therefore obviously foreign—commander (and so were not patriotic Mexicans). Within days the president, Carlos Salinas de Gortari, had singled-out Marcos, calling him "a usurper and a traitor to his country."[3] He also dubbed him "a professional of violence," to which Marcos replied that he was rather "a professional of hope."[4]

As one international human rights organization noted:

> The day that the EZLN launched its rebellion, the Eco television news program, aired by the staunchly pro-government Televisa network, in-

correctly reported that the Subcommander was, in fact, Father Pablo Romo, then the head of the Fray Bartolomé de las Casas Human Rights Center. On April 8, 1994, another Televisa news medium, the daily *Summa*, wrongly identified Subcommander *Marcos* as Father Gerónimo Hernández López, a Jesuit who had worked in Chiapas until 1992 but then had been transferred to Campeche. Around that time, the Televisa-owned daily *Ovaciones* said that *Marcos* was really Father Eugenio Maurer, a sixty-six-year-old priest who walks with a cane. Father Joel Padrón was also mistakenly identified as linked to the rebels.[5]

This was wild guesswork, but it made the government look as if it had leads and it incriminated the Church. Thus, the president hoped to kill two birds with one stone by simultaneously discrediting the EZLN and the Church, both critics of the government and agents of social reform in Chiapas. The Human Rights Watch/Americas report attests the effectiveness of the government's ploy: "News media falsely identified Subcommander Marcos of the EZLN as at least four different priests, cementing in the public a perception that the church promoted guerrilla warfare against the state," with the result that "frequent anti-church actions have taken place in an accusatory atmosphere propagated by politicians and the news media."[6] This was nothing new in Latin America. Strong, writing on Peru, notes, "Toward the end of the first year that the Shining Path took up arms, newspaper reports started to blame the terrorism on foreign priests," no doubt taking their lead from President Belaúnde and his cabinet who "ranted against false priests—especially foreign ones—who turned their flocks against the government."[7]

Marcos, for his part, decided to concentrate on imagery and rhetoric, and more specifically on appropriating the image of Zapata for the EZLN cause. Zapata's image had long since been exploited by the state. As one pair of commentators has put it:

> The most radical of the protagonists of the 1910 Revolution is given a sugar coating in an official gallery of heroes which makes it impossible to discern different political alternatives and at the same time converts heroes into the property of the State, or, to be more precise, of the victorious faction of the Revolution. Zapata is made into the co-founder and consecrator of the political regime, giving it his blessing and providing legitimacy to a project which is contrary to his own, especially since an end was declared to agrarian reform.[8]

Salinas had even gone so far as to have Zapata's image associated with himself. He named one of his sons Carlos Emiliano,[9] and his airplane was called *Emiliano Zapata*. When the president had announced the reform to article 27, he did so with a portrait of Emiliano Zapata in the background, misguidedly (but perhaps genuinely) believing that the reform was a revolution of sorts that liberated the peasants from their *ejidos*. Marcos now sought to wrest Zapata's image from the state and its president, whose grip on it had always been tenuous.[10] Here was an armed movement which called itself after Zapata; which claimed, like Zapata himself, to represent landless peasants; whose leaders dubbed themselves "poor people . . . like Zapata";[11] and whose commander-in-chief and spokesman claimed inspiration from Zapata in one of his first interviews (on 1 January)[12] and wore ammunition belts across his chest in imitation of Zapata's bandoliers. It is hardly surprising that in the minds of most Mexican people the image of Zapata rapidly became associated with Marcos and the EZLN, not with the PRI or the government. As Oppenheimer succinctly puts it: "In a country where even the president worshipped Zapata, the Zapatistas had won a public relations coup."[13] Similarly, Monsiváis notes that "an extraordinary achievement of the EZLN . . . is that it removed from the regime the monopoly on Emiliano Zapata."[14]

The government's acknowledgment of the "coup" can be seen from its speedy relinquishing of Zapata's image. For example, soon after the uprising it stopped issuing ten-peso banknotes bearing Zapata's head. Even more significantly, as has been observed by many: "After 1 January 1994 Salinas de Gortari changed the backdrop for his televised declaration, choosing instead a portrait which conveyed a precise meaning—that of Venustiano Carranza, the man who ordered Zapata's assassination."[15]

Having successfully wrestled the image of Zapata from the government, Marcos quickly set about demolishing other cherished images of the Salinas administration. For example, although in subsequent interviews Marcos would claim that the date of 1 January 1994 had been dictated by tactical considerations,[16] the Subcommander rapidly realized that by constantly attacking both the image of Mexico as a First World country and the principles of neoliberalism upon which NAFTA is predicated, he would push the Zapatistas's actions to the forefront of attention in the U.S. media and throughout the world.[17] Thus, although the effects of choosing 1 January may be described as fortuitous, from then on it was Marcos's skill, and not serendipity, that both sustained the Zapatista momentum and broadened its appeal. From this initial flirtation with the world's media, Marcos went on to court and seduce it. In short, he used his own charisma to sustain media interest in the Zapatistas in particular and Chiapas in general. (In turn, this interest, as we shall see later, rapidly evolved into a "cult of Marcos." Already, by 18 January, when the state legislature voted on a replacement for the recently deposed governor of Chiapas, the sole opposition legislator voted for Marcos, which resulted in rapturous applause—all of which was reported in the press.)[18] Being militarily weak, this was indeed the only strategy open to the Subcommander. Without outside attention the Zapatista heartland of eastern Chiapas could be isolated and systematically crushed, no doubt with gross human rights abuses.[19] (The remoteness of Acteal, in Chenalhó municipality, enabled paramilitary forces to massacre some forty-five men, women, and children on 22 December 1997.) As Marcos put it, "War will be exorcised by the pressure put on by civil society[20] throughout the country. . . . The problem will arise if civil society becomes exhausted, tired, collapses; in that case everything will be left loose and then they will jump on us through the military route."[21] Thus the battle between the government and Marcos for the "hearts and minds" of Mexico's civil society and the international community was a fight for legitimization for the former and survival for the later.

Over the next ten days Marcos responded to the Mexican government's attempts to discredit him and the Zapatista cause by writing nine communiqués. These he sent together on 10 January, with a covering letter, to *La Jornada*. In his letter Marcos joked that the erroneous description of him as blond-haired and blue-eyed would result in the army "detaining Juan del Diablo, star of the soap opera 'Savage Heart.'"[22] In his first communiqué, Marcos countered the government's initial accusations that on the 1 January the Zapatistas had attacked a Red Cross ambulance and a caravan of press vehicles and that they had held and robbed reporters from *El Tiempo* and *Excélsior*. He argued that the ambulance must have been attacked by the Federal Army, given that only it had the high-caliber weaponry necessary to inflict the kind of damage sustained by the vehicle. As for the press caravan, Marcos states that there were no Zapatista troops stationed anywhere near the scene of the attack. Marcos concedes that the reporters were detained and robbed, but alleges that they had been held for their own protection, since the position was being attacked by federal troops. The robbery, on the contrary, was "a grave and regrettable error of the unit's command . . . [for which] our EZLN asks forgiveness . . . and offers to repay as quickly as possible the amount taken."[23]

In the second communiqué, Marcos responded to the accusation made by the ministry of the interior that the EZLN was led by "violent and aggressive" foreigners, and that the uprising was "not an indigenous movement nor is it a peasant action":[24]

Our EZLN does not have foreigners in its ranks or among its leadership, nor has it ever received any support or training from revolutionary forces of other countries or from foreign governments. The reports that Guatemalans are fighting in our ranks, and that they were trained in the neighboring country are stories invented by the federal government to discredit our cause. We have not had, nor do we have now, any connection with the Salvadoran FMLN, nor with the Guatemalan URNG, nor with any other Latin American, European, African, Asiatic, or Oceanic armed movement . . . The commanders and troop elements of the EZLN are mostly Indians from Chiapas . . . The government says it is not an indigenous uprising,[25] but we believe that if thousands of indigenous people rise up in arms, then yes, it is an indigenous uprising. There are also in our movement Mexicans of other social origins and from other states of our country. They agree with us and have joined us because they do not agree with the exploitation that we suffer . . . Currently, the political leadership of our struggle is totally Indigenous: 100% of the members of the Clandestine Revolutionary Indigenous Committees in the combat zones are ethnic Tzotzil, Tzeltal, Chol, Tojolobal and others.[26]

The communiqué, after setting out the Zapatistas' conditions for a formal dialogue with the government, ended with three separate statements. The first, addressed to the national and international press, accused the Mexican army of genocide and of killing civilians and destroying public and private buildings and then attributing these actions to the Zapatistas.[27] It affirmed that the Zapatistas "are always concerned, as civilians in these cities can testify, with protecting innocent life." The second appealed to the Federal Army, calling "on officers and troops of the Army to refuse to carry out orders handed down to them by their superiors to exterminate civilians or summarily execute prisoners of war and wounded and . . . to abandon the ranks of the repressive government and to join the just cause of the people." Finally, there was a second appeal to the Mexican people, urging "workers, poor *campesinos*, teachers, students, progressive and honest intellectuals, housewives and professionals, and all independent political and economic organizations to join our struggle and to struggle with all possible means until we achieve the justice and freedom that all Mexicans desperately want."

Of the other seven communiqués, in which Marcos stipulated the requisite conditions for a cease-fire and set out the composition of a commission for mediation, the package contained one which illustrates Marcos's flair for public relations and his awareness of the importance of the proper presentation of the Zapatistas's struggle to the international community. It was addressed to "Mr. Bill Clinton, the North American Congress, [and] the people of the United States of America." Previous Latin American guerrillas had frequently—with notable exceptions[28]—adopted a vehemently anti-American stance,[29] making little or no distinction between the president, the Senate, and the American populace. Marcos cleverly drew a distinction between the president and the Congress—the two can differ widely on issues—and in particular the American ruling class (that is, president and Congress) and the American people. The communiqué reiterated the claim that the Zapatistas "do not receive aid from foreign governments, persons, or organizations," and asserted that they "have nothing to do with drug trafficking, or national and international terrorism," but instead possess a genuine "longing [for] true freedom and democracy."[30] Thus, in three short paragraphs Marcos countered Salinas's depiction of the guerrillas as the United States' nightmare—Communist-sponsored narco-terrorists. Furthermore, he went on the offensive, asking "whether the U.S. Congress and the citizens of the United States of America approved this military and economic support to combat drug trafficking or to assassinate Indigenous peoples in the Mexican Southeast?"[31] Marcos hoped to provoke the United States into scrutinizing the Mexican government's actions and possibly to take action to ensure (at least minimal) protection of human rights. That he enjoyed some success in this is reflected in a U.S. Government Accounting Office report acknowledging that

> the Mexican government has misused some U.S. provided counter-narcotic helicopters. For example, during the 1994 uprising in . . . Chiapas, several U.S.-provided helicopters were used to transport Mexican military personnel to the conflict zone, which was a violation of the transfer agreement.[32]

In the time between the writing of these communiqués—the first one dated 6 January—and their delivery and publication (on 9 and 10 January, respectively), Marcos's "fifth column," comprising the press, both national and international, was busy winning the media war for him.[33] Journalists' accounts outraged Mexicans and the international community at large with their reports and photographs of young, obviously impoverished, diminutive, poorly armed indigenous guerrillas, lying prostate on the ground, their brains blown out by the sophisticated weaponry of the Mexican Army.[34]

Of course, the majority of the press in most Western democracies would tend to feel some sympathy for impoverished indigenous people, oppressed by the military and neglected by their government. However, the media were pushed further into the Zapatista camp when, in the early days of the conflict, the Federal Army more than once opened fire on some of their colleagues. Ross documents such an incident:

> On Wednesday 5 January, a crew from the U.S.-based *Univisión* Spanish-language news was raked by air force fire as they interviewed terrified *campesinos* in Corralitos. Breathing hard, the debonair star reporter Bruno López pointed to a rocket that had smashed into the forest just meters away, and then at the *Univisión* van, a taped "T.V." marking clearly visible on its roof.[35]

As more and more journalists followed the Federal Army into the conflict zone, Mexicans from all over the country witnessed the blighted conditions endured daily by the indigenous of Chiapas. Reporters sent back increasing numbers of accounts detailing human rights abuses and escalating casualty figures resulting from the military's heavy-handedness.[36] (For example, *Reforma* reported that "the stench of death permeates Ocosingo. The buzzards smell it and circle, looking for dead meat, while helicopters circle, looking for live meat.")[37] The Mexican public began to perceive the Zapatistas more and more as poor members of the family who had stolen some bread in order to eat and not as brutal, foreign-led, Marxist guerrillas, bent on destruction of the state. As Marcos acknowledged:

> What made society change the way it looks at us was the press. Not even television; the written press, photographers and all that. . . . It's when journalists themselves say: "you see? They really are indigenous people, they aren't foreigners, and we've seen that this is the way they live," and all that. So it really was the written news media that began to waken that change, or critical distrust, that reality was totally different from what the government was saying. . . . It wasn't the government, or our weapons; nor was it Don Samuel or Camacho. It was the press that looks and looks and starts to bring out more and more information.[38]

Thus, even before Marcos's communiqués had gone to press, the European Union requested an end to the bloodshed, threatening the suspension of a recently negotiated trade pact between it and the Mexican government. Within two days of the communiqués' publication Mexican civil society, having been stung into action, was demonstrating in the streets, demanding a stop to the massacre. Salinas ordered a unilateral cease-fire. As de la Grange and Rico state: "In fact, 12 days of shooting guaranteed the Zapatista army more news coverage than 30 years of confrontations in Guatemala or in Colombia."[39] Gómez Peña notes that this coverage derived almost wholly from the Zapatistas's "self-conscious and sophisticated use of the media."[40]

20. A Cease-Fire

The sympathy evoked in the general public, repeatedly exposed to photographs in the newspapers and pictures on their televisions of slain indigenous and others dwelling in abject squalor,[1] was seen as early as the first week of the uprising when "a survey conducted on January 7, 1994, showed that 61% of the residents of Mexico City supported the Zapatistas' goals."[2] This support manifested itself in the form of a March for Peace on the afternoon of Wednesday, 12 January, comprising some 100,000 people and culminating in a mass rally in the Zócalo. The crowd held up giant placards reading "Stop the Massacre" and "Stop the Genocide," and chanted "Peace" and "First World, Ha Ha Ha!" Earlier that morning, at 10:15, Salinas had already publicly declared that he had "taken the decision to suspend all military offensives in Chiapas," having "taken into account that the Mexican army has already achieved the prime objective of its constitutional mission to guarantee security in the region, and taking into account the sentiments and opinions of the nation."[3]

Foreign and domestic pressure[4] thus combined to compel the Mexican government to enter into a dialogue with the Zapatistas instead of exterminating them, as some were urging.[5] (Porfirio Díaz offered a precedent for this: when dealing with Orozco and Villa's rebellion in Chihuahua more than eighty years earlier he "first offered the rebels a four-week truce, hoping that by its expiry the Chihuahuans would see the futility of their insurrection and lay down their arms.")[6] Perhaps, Salinas hoped that although the army would not be able to attack rebel territory openly during the truce, it would be able to conduct a clandestine low-intensity campaign. Even this course of action, however, was denied him by Marcos. When the Federal Army, having recaptured the towns seized by the Zapatistas, pushed farther into the jungle in the days following the cease-fire—ostensibly to bring aid to the communities there but also in order to obtain intelligence and intimidate the local population—Marcos promptly issued a communiqué (17 January) which was published the next day, informing the Mexican people and the international community of the army's contravention of the spirit (if not the word) of the cease-fire ordered by the president. In addition to providing the date, time, location, and nature of the incident,[7] Marcos wrote that "this case of aggression on the part of Federal troops makes the government's supposed will to seek a political solution to the conflict seem doubtful. . . . Either President Carlos Salinas de Gortari is lying or the Federal Army is not prepared to follow the orders of the Federal executive." This communiqué provoked Mexican civil society into further demonstrations in the capital throughout February and March, denouncing the army's incursions and repressive tactics and calling for peace talks.

Through these actions and Marcos's subsequent communiqués, Salinas was unable to use the early cease-fire to neutralize the EZLN and then pump millions of pesos into Chiapas, so robbing the guerrillas of their raison d'être.[8] Marcos, to his credit, was acutely aware of the importance of sustaining media and public interest in the EZLN if it was to survive, and he showed no small skill in his continuing ability to sustain the attention of such a fickle entity as the media.[9] Thus, rather than losing interest in the Zapatistas and in Chiapas, they became the focal points of discussion throughout Mexico. In particular, two communiqués from Marcos (18 January and 20 January) stimulated great debate. The first was a response to Salinas' 16 January offer of pardon to the Zapatistas, which La Jornada emblazoned across its front page the following day under the giant, one-word heading, 'Amnistía.' This communiqué is, I believe, the best that the Subcommander ever wrote. Full of righteous indignation, sarcasm, and fury, it completely turned the tables on Salinas, asking:

> Why do we need to be pardoned? What are we to be pardoned for? For not dying of hunger? For not accepting our misery in silence? For not accepting humbly the historic burden of disdain and abandonment? For having risen up in arms after we found all other paths closed? For not heeding the Chiapas penal code, one of the most absurd and repressive in history? For showing the rest of the country and the whole world that human dignity still exists even among the world's poorest peoples? For having made careful preparations before we began our uprising? For bringing guns to battle instead of bows and arrows? For being Mexicans? For being mainly indigenous? For calling on the Mexican people to fight by whatever means possible for what belongs to them? For fight-

ing for liberty, democracy and justice? For not following the example of previous guerrilla armies? For refusing to surrender? For refusing to sell ourselves out?

Who should we ask for pardon, and who can grant it? Those who for many years glutted themselves at a table of plenty while we sat with death so often, we finally stopped fearing it? Those who filled our pockets and our souls with empty promises and words?

Or should we ask pardon from the dead, our dead, who died "natural" deaths of "natural causes" like measles, whooping cough, breakbone fever, cholera, typhus, mononucleosis, tetanus, pneumonia, malaria and other lovely gastrointestinal and pulmonary diseases? Our dead, so very dead, so democratically dead from sorrow because no one did anything, because the dead, our dead, went just like that, with no one keeping count, with no one saying, "Enough!" which would at least have granted some meaning to their deaths, a meaning no one ever sought for them, the dead of all times, who are now dying once again, but now in order to live?

Should we ask pardon from those who deny us the right and capacity to govern ourselves? From those who don't respect our customs and our culture and who ask us for identification papers and obedience to a law whose existence and moral basis we don't accept? From those who oppress us, torture us, assassinate us, disappear us for the grave "crime" of wanting a piece of land, not too big and not too small, but just a simple piece of land on which we can grow something to fill our stomachs?

Who should ask for pardon, and who can grant it?[10]

This communiqué proved so powerful, so effective, that even the conservative Octavio Paz, a critic of the Zapatistas in general and of Marcos in particular, declared:

The eloquent letter that Subcommander Marcos sent to various newspapers on 18 January truly moved me, even though it was sent by someone who has taken a course of action of which I disapprove. They, the Indians of Mexico, are not the ones who should ask for pardon. Rather, we are the ones who should ask for pardon. . . . Almost all of us, to one degree or another, are guilty of the iniquitous situation in which the Indians find themselves, since our passivity and indifference have permitted the extortions and abuses of the cattlemen, coffee growers, caciques and corrupt politicians.[11]

In the second communiqué Marcos outlined his own views on the form and nature that change should take within Mexican society:

> We think that revolutionary change in Mexico is not just a question of one kind of activity only. It will come, strictly speaking, from neither an armed revolution nor an unarmed one. It will be the result of struggles on several fronts, using a lot of methods, various social forms, with different levels of commitment and participation. And the result will not be the triumph of a party, organization, or alliance of organizations with their particular social programs, but rather the creation of a democratic space for resolving the confrontations between different political proposals.[12]

This communiqué, and another issued the same day rejecting the EZLN's role as "the one, only, and true historic vanguard,"[13] is highly significant because it reveals perhaps Marcos's greatest quality, his flexibility of mind. If we look at the first twenty days of 1994 we can see the Subcommander reacting to a series of unanticipated developments in a flexible, innovative way, without recourse to mere dogma. It is quite clear, for example, that the response of the Mexican people to the uprising had come as a surprise:

> We thought the people would either not pay attention to us, or come together with us to fight. But they did not react in either of these two manners. It resulted that all of these people . . . did not want to rise up with us, but . . . neither did they want us to be annihilated. They wanted us to dialogue. This completely broke our scheme and ended up defining zapatismo, the neo-zapatismo.[14]

Thus, in less than three frenetically busy weeks, Marcos abandoned his own personal dreams of becoming a revolutionary guerrilla hero and, reacting to the general public's response to the uprising, began to explore an alternative role both for himself and the movement. He and the EZLN had been gearing themselves for a decade toward a predominantly military role. Now, almost overnight, they opted instead for a predominantly political one. Few politicians and military men have abandoned so rapidly a course of action pursued so intensely, for so long, at such a high personal cost to adapt, revise, and reject their strategies when faced with the dawning realization that they were obsolete.

These communiqués, and Salinas's promise of peace talks during his visit to Chiapas on 25 January, did much to stimulate discussion in Mexico on the role of the government, guerrillas, and civil society as well as on the course of future political reform. As one set of commentators put it, the Zapatistas had "quickly occupied more space in the media than had any other insurgent group in Mexico's if not the world's history."[15] Academics, artists, playwrights, poets, economists, and politicians clamored to put forward their own interpretation of the causes, effects, and significance of the uprising.

21. The Cult of Marcos

The general public, far from remaining a passive observer of this debate, took to the streets on several occasions throughout January and February both in the capital and in Tabasco and Chihuahua, thus displaying a continuing concern for Chiapas's predicament.[1] As Ross has observed:

> In one day in February there are 102 marches in the capital alone. Truckers park sixty huge rigs in the Zócalo . . . they pump on air horns, augmenting the aura of general insurrection. At the Metropolitan Book Fair that same weekend, young people who are pissed off because a token admission is being charged for the first time in fourteen years, push their way into the main salon, chanting, "*Marcos, Marcos!*" And just down the street, at the slowly deconstructing Palacio de Bellas Artes, where Verdi's "Nabuco"—a potent political opera—is being performed, an excited aficionado rises in the second balcony and hollers at the top of his lungs, "*Que viven los Zapatistas!*"
>
> "*Que Viven!*" the upscale, elegantly-coiffed audience on the floor of Bellas Artes responds.[2]

Nor did Marcos simply sit back and bathe in this new-found fame. He began to interact with the press,[3] explaining himself, the movement, and the predicament of the Chiapan indigenous communities. A prime example of this is his communiqué of 20 January, addressed specifically to the press,[4] in which he addresses "the anguish that is caused by the ski masks and the 'obscure' intentions of the Zapatista 'leadership.'" He treats these two issues in reverse order:

> I have the honor of having as my superiors the best women and men of the Tzeltal, Tzotzil, Chol, Tojolobal, Mam, and Zoque ethnicities. I have lived with them for more than ten years and I am proud to obey them and serve them with my arms and my life. They have taught me more than they now teach the country and the whole world. They are my

commanders and I will follow them along whatever path they choose. They are the collective and democratic leadership of the EZLN, their acceptance of dialogue is as true as is their struggling heart, and as real as is their mistrust at being tricked again.

As for the ski masks, after expressing surprise that the wearing of them has provoked so much debate, he sets about allaying fears that they are the hallmark of the terrorist. He promises that he will put an end to the intense speculation surrounding his identity by removing his mask, provided that Mexican society removes the one imposed upon it by "modernity." He predicts that Mexican society will see that he is a Mexican (and not a foreigner), and that he is just a man (and not an especially handsome one as rumor had it), far less frightening than the reality that lies underneath Mexico's own mask.

If the public had been curious about Marcos before the peace talks, his high public profile throughout those days of intense negotiations further fueled his cult. He had given numerous interviews during the talks as well as almost daily press releases and a good number of press conferences. From his humble beginnings on 1 January as a mere subcommander who was on hand and able to speak Spanish and some English, he had been transformed in the media's (and therefore the public's) perception into a star.[5] Mexico was caught up in what several authors described as "Marcos-mania."[6] When the talks were over, as McCaughan noted, "Marcos staggered out of San Cristóbal's Cathedral under the weight of 2,000 letters sent to him from every corner of Mexico, from laid-off oil workers to smitten señoritas, and even an eight-year-old girl wondering how she could become Marcos' Subcommander-ess."[7] In the following months, he did not merely restrict himself to answering this "fan mail," but was interviewed by UNAM Radio on 18 March 1994[8] and spoke to a succession of foreign journalists during May and June.

Of course, the example of Che Guevara had illustrated that Latin American revolutionaries could captivate the hearts of people throughout the world. Similarly, Mexico had provided a precedent for a masked hero whose avowed cause was to fight oppression and inequality in the form of Zorro.[9] However, filling the boots of these legendary figures would take a person of immense charisma and not inconsiderable ego. Some of Marcos's appeal no doubt derives from what one reporter has termed "guerrilla chic."[10] A certain romantic hue often attends guerrillas and bandits: those who operate outside the law, masked figures on the run, forced to live on the fringes of society, outlawed by the state. This romance was enhanced by the fact that Marcos's identity was unknown. It became a national pastime to theorize as to whose face lay behind the Subcommander's ski mask.[11] As Russell notes, "Many acres of trees were felled to print speculation as to Marcos' true identity."[12] Another writer observed:

> Though he has become the most famous Mexican celebrity of 1994, no one knows who he really is. [As a result o]bsessive discussions about Marcos' "real identity" continued to dominate conversations in homes, the workplace, in cafes, and in magazines and newspapers. Although deep inside no one wishes to unmask him, every Mexican has a colorful theory about his identity. In one of the early versions he was a foreign intellectual (he speaks fluent English, French, and a few indigenous languages), but soon his Mexico City accent spiced with *norteñismos* caused most to discard that rumor. Many detected traces of liberation theology in his communiqués and interviews, and swore he was a radical Jesuit priest. But the Catholic Church vehemently denied this hypothesis. Others perceived him as an ex-leader of the 1968 student movement. But a journalist who spent time with *el Sup* says he is only thirty-eight years old (which means that in 1968 he was a mere thirteen). Other theories have described him as a puppet of a dissident faction within the PRI, a frustrated writer enacting the book he was unable to write, a bisexual hipster, or a mystic propelled by ancient forces who is fulfilling Mayan prophecies that were written in the *Popul Vuh* and *Chilam Balam*.[13]

Even in an interview conducted in the week preceding the peace talks, journalists from *Proceso*, *El Financiero*, and the *New York Times* revealed their obsession with Marcos's true identity. Initially, they addressed the coming dialogues but then "suddenly the questions become quicker, a virtual barrage aimed at finding out a little more about Marcos' personality . . . the reporters are all speaking at the same time and the conversation is bouncing from one subject to another: 'We must get back to the Marcos of the ski mask. The one who's from Mexico City?'"[14]

However, his guerrilla status and the secrecy of his identity only partially account for Marcos's appeal; his flamboyant and witty personality must explain the rest. Marcos is a well-educated man who speaks some English and French, and he has clearly traveled abroad. He gives the impression of being sensitive and caring, with a keen sense of humor. Such attributes, when coupled with the mystery of anonymity and his status as an outlaw, apparently did much to endear the Subcommander to many women. Ann Louise Bardach, a reporter for *Vanity Fair*, wrote that "he looked the very stuff of myth," and described "his good features" and "his manner—one of palpable gentleness," all of which ensured that in her eyes "there could never be a convincing imitation of this unique creature."[15] Nor was she alone. Alma Guillermoprieto, no stranger to the guerrilla scene, was clearly very impressed with Marcos when she met him, writing that he was "more articulate, cosmopolitan, humorous, and coquetishly manipulative than any guerrilla leader of El Salvador or Nicaragua who ever locked horns with the press."[16] Likewise, *La Jornada*'s reporter, Eva Bodenstadt, was led to ask herself: "Why does this man motivate an almost irrational sexuality?"[17] When Bill Weinberg trekked into the jungle to interview Marcos he discovered he was not alone. On reaching La Realidad, he found himself in the company of adoring female groupies and commented "the *chilangas*—sophisticated young women from Mexico City—were overtly inebriated with the sheer excitement of being so near their idol."[18] When he eventually caught up with El Sup he found him "sprawling on one of the beds with his ski-mask on, puffing on his pipe, adoring women on every side, one under each arm."[19] Other women are merely content to worship him from afar. The ex-wife of the former Mexican President José López Portillo (1976–82) has written him effusive poetry (the poem appeared in *Proceso*, 28 February 1994, 14).

It would appear that in personal interviews conducted deep in rebel territory, the Subcommander, armed with wit, humor, self-deprecation, flirtatiousness, intelligence, and urbanity, consistently wielded an inescapable charm. He was aided in this by his astute sense of stage, which enabled him to construct an atmosphere conducive to him working his charm, and by his understanding of psychology. De la Grange and Rico have described Marcos's modus operandi:

> In spite of his apparent spontaneity, Marcos carefully prepared each one of his meetings with the press. . . . Daybreak was normally the moment chosen by the Zapatista leader to receive the press because, according to some, he used the daylight in order to devote himself to reading. The explanation is not so convincing for two reason: in the village [Guadalupe Tepeyac] they had electric light, and in any case, it gets dark in the jungle already at six o'clock in the evening . . . why then wake people up at three in the morning? Fidel Castro, Stalin and other personalities had previously employed this tactic in order to impress their interlocutors

who, from lack of sleep, lose some of their reflexes. Marcos appeared as fresh as a lettuce in front of a squad of journalists who presented themselves falling about like drunken idiots, with sleep in their eyes and dry mouths. It was the best means of feeding the myth of a superman who never yielded to fatigue. . . . [20] [Moreover] if the charismatic leader decided to receive them, they experienced an indescribable happiness and a profound gratitude which deletes the memory of the wait. The Stockholm syndrome, which shows itself in those hostages who end-up by identifying with their kidnappers, causes havoc in the Lacandón jungle.[21]

Similarly, Oppenheimer, himself subjected to the Subcommander's waiting game, comments:

It was vintage Marcos: Like Fidel Castro, he had a habit of letting reporters and prominent visitors wait for days at a time as a way to soften them up. After days of driving over flooded jungle roads and another long wait once they had reached their meeting place, few visitors—no matter how high their frustration—decided to turn back. Even the most hard-nosed reporters were turned into lapdogs by the time a Zapatista soldier came for them at the hospital guest house to take them to the long-sought interview.[22]

Weinberg also provides a detailed account of the seven-day ordeal he was subjected to before being granted an interview with the Subcommander.[23]

Marcos's charm worked best at the personal level, although his charisma also shines through in his communiqués. Some of these communiqués are of an intellectual nature, addressing questions of political philosophy; others are poetical and refer to writers such as Shakespeare, Neruda, and Eco; others take the form of parables or folk tales and are directed at children. As Womack puts it:

Marcos' communiqués and interviews were playful, sarcastic, poetic, arbitrary, funny, narcissistic, poignant, snide, allusive, Foucaultian, magically realistic, the perfect lingo for contemporary discourse and negotiation, not with a government or rival movements, but through the modern media with a modern public, the message being not war, or peace, or reconciliation, but endless, seductive argumentation.[24]

Marcos's knowledge of Spanish, French, and English, when coupled with his computer literacy, makes him one of the most easily accessible guerrillas of all time. Much has been rightly made of the Zapatistas being the first cyberspace guerrillas,[25] since it elevates them to a position above that of previous guerrilla groups who had confined their written propaganda mainly to localized pamphleteering.

Accessibility, however, is only of use if people identify and connect with the message being made available, and this is perhaps where the true key to Marcos's success lies. He is supremely adaptable, able to show whatever face he thinks the people viewing him want to see. Unlike other Latin American guerrilla leaders, he has been quick to realize that times have changed and that many people find certain political ideas no longer attainable or no longer desirable. Thus, unlike say Sendero Luminoso's Abimael Guzmán, he does not come across as an anachronistic extremist. Marcos is no doctrinaire Marxist or Maoist who employs jargon that (rightly or wrongly) now alienates so many people. T. Benjamin describes the Subcommander's message as transmitted through his communiqués as "a new revolutionary discourse: utopian but non-dogmatic, nationalist without being chauvinist, intellectually sophisticated but also grounded in peasant reality."[26] This absence of a doctrinaire streak is perhaps best illustrated by Marcos's assertion that

> you can't put too much emphasis on the old traditional discipline—the you're-with-us-or-you-are-dead school of thought. You can't raise the step so high that nobody can climb it; you have to make room for all the people to participate to the best of their abilities and so you are always in the process of looking for what unites people.[27]

His demands appear reasonable and attainable and, as a result, he is both the new darling of the Left and "an international darling of the anti-globalization movement."[28] He does not aim at subverting the state and taking over the state apparatus,[29] and he does not talk of the withering away of the state. Instead, he talks of creating political space and room for maneuver.[30] The role he claims for himself is that of a catalyst for social change, the leader of a pressure group—like Greenpeace—and not of the vanguard of the glorious proletarian revolution. This makes him attractive to the center Left. The Left has taken a physical and psychological beating over the last forty years. The leading examples of outright Communism and Maoism, the USSR and China, were discredited by their poor record on human rights, as demonstrated by the Russian response to the Hungarian and Prague uprisings, the utter failure of Mao's cultural revolution, and more recently the Tiananmen Square massacre. In addition, the voting out of power of the Sandinistas in Nicaragua and Cuba's human rights record make many feel uneasy about the only other examples of Western Communism. In the East, North Korea and Vietnam are hardly model societies, even if one makes allowance for the United States's wholehearted attempts to destabilize them. However, as Czeslaw Milosz puts it, 'the failure of Marx's dream has created the need for another, not the rejection of all dreams,'[31] and so many people have been crying out for a just cause. Marcos and the Zapatistas provided an acceptable alternative to global Capitalism which the consciences of liberals and those on the center Left allowed them to applaud.

Marcos was also the darling of the press.[32] He was in such demand that already by February he had received an angry letter of complaint—he called it "a scolding"—from a disgruntled Mexican newspaper, *El Sur*, accusing him of picking and choosing which newspapers he gave interviews to and objecting that it had not received its fair share of the Marcos pie.[33] *Time*, having devoted space to the Zapatistas three weeks out of four in January and February 1994, subsequently devoted a full page to the Zapatistas' peace talks with the Mexican government, complete with a glossy photograph of Marcos sitting at the table in full combat fatigues and donning his ski-mask.[34] *Newsweek* also closely followed the Zapatistas, and printed an article specifically on Marcos, "The Marcos Mystique."[35] The *Dallas Morning News* ran a story in early February under a headline that asked "Who is that masked man?" and went on to report on "the mystery surrounding the pipe-smoking Marcos' identity [that] has prompted wild speculation in the Mexican press."[36] Marcos was subsequently interviewed by. *Vanity Fair*.[37] *Esquire* sent a reporter to interview Marcos, but the Subcommander proved too elusive and the magazine had to settle with running a six-page piece, "On the Zapatista Trail."[38]

In early February, Marcos gave an hour-long videotaped interview that was shown at prime time on Mexico's leading cable network. His media profile was raised considerably in the United States when he appeared in a segment on the television show *Sixty Minutes* on 21 August, which began with the introduction: "What Robin Hood was to the people of Sherwood Forest, Subcomandante Marcos has become to the people of Mexico—a fighter for the rights of peasants who are trapped in poverty by large landowners."[39] As one viewer notes:

> Everyone got a big kick out of watching him [Marcos] handle Ed Bradley . . . Bradley, no tyro when it comes to "news maker interviews" came

across as a Zapatista groupie. They showed him only—and exactly—what they wanted him to see, they answered only those questions they wanted to answer, and they had him describing El Sub as a "hero" (which he probably is). 60 Minutes even broadcast pictures of Ed driving a military transport carrying masked and armed guerrillas—an act of war, according to the Mexican Army, for which the average campesino would be gleefully executed.[40]

Commenting on Marcos's impact on the national and international media, two *Pusmoderna* (a Mexico City magazine) editors, Mongo Sánchez Lira and Rogelio Villareal write:

> Subcomandante Marcos, the university-educated *mestizo*, spokesperson for the Zapatista National Liberation Army, is a guerrilla hero able to "inspire an insane love" in the envoy from *Vanity Fair*—well, not only in her—and to fascinate locals and foreigners alike. A charismatic and complex personality, he's been at the center of the tornado that has lashed at Mexico since the first of January. Lucid, enigmatic, serene, sensationalist, gallant, virile, romantic, sometimes almost kitschy and vain (like a hero in a gringo movie!), he is not infrequently accurate in his judgment and in his crude diagnosis of the sick body of the country. Leader of the first post-Communist revolution (in the words of accommodating Carlos Fuentes) or vulgar and loquacious in the extreme (as he was described early on by the increasingly intolerant and authoritarian Octavio Paz), the prolific, faceless writer hidden behind the ski mask of the Subcomandante shook and divided public opinion with his brilliant handling of the media.[41]

Of course, Marcos was not the first revolutionary to harness the power of the press. De la Grange and Rico, for example, are quick to draw the parallel between Marcos and Pancho Villa; the latter was certainly not camera shy, and he reenacted, and even arranged the times of, his battles for best newsreel coverage.[42] Moreover, as Gabriel Zaid has observed, the Zapatistas closely resemble the traditional Latin American university guerrilla "that resorts to arms in order to grab headlines and attention and stages scenes, uses props and symbols etc to generate visual 'takes' and to grab front page headlines."[43] As he notes, these guerrillas invite the media to carefully staged events, like military maneuvers or certain political events. Such tactics were widely employed by both the Sandinistas and the FMLN.[44] De la Grange and Rico concur, stating that Marcos's "behavior corresponds precisely to the modus operandi of the guerrillas of university origin," although they also emphasize that

> the relationship that Marcos wove with the press had no comparison either in Latin America or in the rest of the world. Despite the military and political weakness of his organization, the Zapatista leader had turned himself into an object of immeasurable attention on the part of the journalists, who responded to all his summons.[45]

The result was that Marcos and his image were now being extensively marketed nationally and internationally.[46] Marcos merchandise, including T-shirts, postcards, and posters, was readily available throughout Mexico and even North America and western Europe. So too, within months, Web sites sprang up devoted to the Subcommander, many of which contained color photographs of him as well as the text of his communiqués and interviews. Less than four years later, in 1998, de la Grange's and Rico's biography of him appeared (largely as a reaction against Marcos's immense popularity)—a privilege usually reserved for dead and martyred guerrillas, not those who have been active for only four years and who are still very much alive.

Over the next two years Marcos was to receive numerous celebrities, including the U.S. director Oliver Stone, the Mexican-American Hollywood actor Edward James Olmos, the Spanish rock-idol drummer Mikel Abrego, the French intellectual and one-time guerrilla Régis Debray, and the former French president's wife Danielle Mitterrand.

As a result, Marcos became without doubt the best-known Latin American revolutionary since Che Guevara, despite the fact that others are perhaps more deserving of fame or notoriety. One thinks, for example, of Manuel "Tirofijo" Marulanda, who has been the leader of the Revolutionary Armed Forces of Colombia (FARC in Spanish) for over thirty years; of Carlos Fonseca, who founded and then led the FSLN for sixteen years; and of Fonseca's successor, Daniel Ortega, who continued the Sandinista struggle and eventually became Nicaragua's president. Others include Harry Villegas, who fought with Guevara in Cuba, the Congo, and Bolivia, and is now brigadier general in Cuba's Revolutionary Armed Forces; Mario Payeras, who helped found Guatemala's Guerrilla Army of the Poor and later went on to write Los Dias en la Selva (Days of the Jungle), which won the Cuban Casa de las Americas prize; and Joaquín Villalobos, a member of El Salvador's FMLN guerrilla high command, who emerged after a tenacious struggle in the jungles to found the Social Democratic Party. This is not to detract from the achievements of Marcos or the Zapatistas. As the Subcommander himself points out: "How often does it happen that an armed group's declaration of war is read in public just a few feet from the National Palace, or that the government negotiates with a group that brings its weapons to the table?"[47] In a communiqué dated to 20 February 1995, he expands on the EZLN's achievements and again asks:

> What other guerrilla army . . . has carried out military actions like the EZLN did in January 1994 and again in December 1994, breaking through the military blockade. What other guerrilla force has agreed to sit down and dialogue only fifty days after having taken up arms? What other guerrilla force has appealed, not to the proletariat as the historical vanguard, but to the civic society that struggles for democracy? What other guerrilla force has stepped aside in order not to interfere in the electoral process? What other guerrilla force has convened a national democratic movement, civic and peaceful, so that armed struggle becomes useless? What other guerrilla force asks its bases of support about what it should do before doing it? What other guerrilla force has struggled to achieve a democratic space and not take power? What other guerrilla force has relied more on words than on bullets?[48]

Ordinary people, journalists, and celebrities were not the only subscribers to the cult of Marcos; even intellectuals were caught up in the Marcos mystique. Economists, political scientists, and international relations scholars have all devoted much attention to events in Chiapas over the past twelve years; botanists, archaeologists, and social anthropologists had all been researching Chiapas for decades. Economists had become increasingly interested in Mexico in general ever since talks had been initiated concerning Mexico's participation in NAFTA, but they had tended to concentrate on Northern Mexico and on issues such as illegal immigration into America and wages and conditions in the maquiladoras which line the border. The Zapatista uprising caused the beam of interest to focus on Chiapas. Books and articles covering such diverse topics as contemporary Mexican society,[49] NAFTA and neoliberal economics,[50] human rights,[51] military tactics,[52] gender and ethnicity issues in Latin America, and globalization[53] all began to devote space to discussion of Chiapas, the Zapatistas, and Subcommander Marcos.

Marcos, as ever, sought to involve himself in the debate he had started, entering into what one scholar has termed an "extended conversation with the nation."[54] His reasons were probably twofold.

The first was personal, in that his work in the jungle had been intellectually stifling, allowing him little or no scope for discussion or debate.[55] Now, after the uprising, he could indirectly sample the intellectual life he had left behind in 1984 through correspondence and by way of the press that came to interview him. Several of those who have interviewed Marcos have commented on his loquacity,[56] with Guillermoprieto going so far as to assert that the Subcommander was "in desperate need of conversation . . . he needed to talk."[57] Oppenheimer wrote that "it was clear to anybody spending some time in the Zapatista camp that he [Marcos] must have felt lonely among them [the indigenous]."[58]

The second was more political, in that Marcos, by seeking the approval of urban (especially Mexico City) intellectuals, hoped that they would form protection as "civilized opinion."[59] (This was very much in keeping with the original Zapatistas of the Mexican Revolution who also had courted the country's urban intelligentsia out of a feeling of insecurity.)[60]

Whatever his motivation, Marcos subsequently engaged a host of Mexican and international intellectuals.[61] In 1996, for example, he met the French intellectual Régis Debray, who had visited Che Guevara while Guevara was on his Bolivian campaign and who therefore was no stranger to charismatic jungle revolutionaries. And, just as Che had met and openly discussed politics with Jean-Paul Sartre and Simone de Beauvoir, Marcos courted the leading intellectual social commentators of the day, sending letters to John Berger, Eduardo Galeano, Eric Jauffret, and Mexico's leading essayist, novelist, and former ambassador to France, Carlos Fuentes. Fuentes wrote to Marcos, declaring "to you . . . is owed the reactivation of the tradition of sending letters."[62]

In addition, Marcos continued to issue communiqués, the vast majority of which were published in *La Jornada* and on the Internet, have subsequently been widely translated,[63] and have appeared in book format.[64] These communiqués rapidly won the acclaim of non-Mexican scholars as the eloquent expression of noble ideas. Womack writes of Marcos's communiqués that "the thought, the argument, and the language are clear, consecutive, articulate, cutting, powerful, aggressive, grand, vivid, commanding, mystical, arresting, heroic, and theoretically right in the swing of Mexico City's cosmopolitan discourse."[65] Consultation of these communiqués led James Petras to conclude that "Marcos is an intellectual of urban origins with a literary flair unmatched among his counterparts in Latin America."[66] Thomas Benjamin echoes this verdict, describing Marcos's communiqués as "part history lesson, part critique of Mexico's political system, and part report on indigenous Chiapas," concluding that "few insurrections in history have had such an articulate and charismatic spokesman."[67] Jim Tuck, commenting on the reception of Marcos's communiqués by academics and journalists, notes how even Alexander Cockburn, "the acerbic English Marxist who writes a column for *The Nation*, [and] rarely has anything but disdain for the intellect of other writers . . . was so impressed by a collection of Marcos communiqués reprinted in California's *Anderson Valley Advertiser* that he described them as '55,000 words of some of the most savagely eloquent prose in the history of Mexico.'"[68] Montalbán has extolled the Subcommander as "a master in the postmodern literary game of utilizing *collage*s and the intertextuality of two literary cultures, the indigenous and the Latin American."[69] I would urge that Marcos's contribution to literature lies in his promotion of *magical realism*—a literary form whereby "fact is mixed with fantasy here, truth with myth, realism with rhetoric"[70]—of which he is undoubtedly one of Latin America's leading contemporary exponents.

The strength of Marcos's writings does not lie exclusively in their style—which even his detractors seldom fault[71]—but also upon their content and the authors upon whom Marcos draws for inspiration. Inspection of Marcos's communiqués reveals his extensive reading of, for example, Brecht, Cervantes, Dante, Defoe, Lewis, Melville, Shakespeare, and Swift as well as acclaimed poets, novelists, scholars, and two Nobel Prize winners for literature.[72] Numerous interviews with the Subcommander have been conducted by eminent intellectuals and political scientists. For example, Adolfo Gilly et al. included an interview with Marcos in their *Discusion sobre la Historia*.[73] Le Bot, a member of the Centre d'Analyse et d'Intervention Sociologique de l'Ecole des Hautes Etudes en Sciences and the director of Latin American research at the Centre National de la Recherche Scientifique, also published an interview with Marcos,[74] as did the Catalan detective novelist Manuel Vázquez Montalbán.[75] The following January the social commentator Carlos Monsiváis trekked into the jungle to meet Marcos.[76] René Báez even wrote a book in which he compared Marcos's political thought with that of Che Guevara and Agustín Cueva.[77]

Regrettably, however, the Subcommander's appreciation of the need to continually engage the media's attention, when coupled with his desire to explain both himself and the movement to others, would result in an unfortunate side effect: a cult of personality. His facility with languages and his charisma, which equipped him best within the movement to interface with the media,[78] resulted in the press fixating on him to the virtual exclusion not only of other EZLN commanders, but also of the issues and demands of the movement as a whole.[79] This led some to accuse Marcos of being just another caudillo,[80] at which point the press then turned on Marcos and began to tear down the edifice they themselves had helped erect. In *Proceso* Marcos described the process whereby the press at first elevated him to great heights and was now trying to "puncture" him:

> What happens is the press itself, in its dialectic movements, turns against itself. First its *Marcos, Marcos, Marcos*. And now, goddamn *Marcos*, goddamn *Marcos*, because all we hear is *Marcos*. And the truth is that *Marcos* didn't say anything. The whole mess was made up by the press, and now they're complaining that why is *Marcos* the protagonist?[81]

Needless to say, his detractors accuse him of supreme egotism and argue that he has hijacked a noble cause for the purpose of self-aggrandizement. Some even maintain that the "star" Marcos has eclipsed the cause which he is supposed to be championing.[82] Such charges need to be addressed.

There is no doubt that Marcos is a showman, an extrovert by temperament. His education, his middle-class upbringing, his attendance at UNAM, and his brief career as a university lecturer at UAM undoubtedly led him to have a very high opinion of himself.[83] No doubt he would have shone in any milieu, but he appears to have done so first within the FLN, where we are told that even the head of the organization, Germán, was "politically very dim ('*torpe*'), so dim that in order to express his ideas in the polit-buro he had to delegate others, especially Guillén,"[84] and next in Chiapas, surrounded for almost a decade by largely unschooled peasants. Add to this the sudden and intense burst of media interest and exposure following the uprising and it is not difficult to envisage how Marcos's head may have been turned a little. (As Weinberg puts it: "It was unrealistic to expect him not to enjoy his new national popularity.")[85] To his credit, the Subcommander realized the negative effect on the Zapatista cause that his stardom was having and attempted to step back out of the limelight. In a communiqué published in *La Jornada* he declared:

> The need for a translator between the indigenous Zapatista culture and the national and international culture caused the obvious nose [that is, Marcos], in addition to sneezing, to talk and to write. All of you would be in agreement that he did it and to an excess. I talked and talked, and at times, it seemed to many that the EZLN was only this very visible nose. It was this error which we were late in seeing. . . . We did not rec-

ognize that this protagonist was, not infrequently, counter-productive to the just cause that motivates us . . . the real protagonist will now be the formal protagonists. The pronounced nose will return to more sneezing and to less speaking.[86]

Needless to say this admission appears to counter the argument that Marcos saw the indigenous as just a vehicle for his own self-promotion, or that, from the start, he exploited his new-found fame for personal gain. His readiness to come forward always had a concrete aim—to continually project a positive image of the Zapatistas. This image would prove essential for the survival of the EZLN, since the government's best hope of destroying it now lay in ensuring that the peace talks would drag on unsuccessfully, resulting in a loss of interest on the part of the media. Without media interest and the attention of Mexican society and the international community, the government would be free to repress the Zapatistas by force. Thus, Marcos's charisma served a higher cause than his own ego; it elevated the Zapatista struggle from a localized indigenous uprising to an internationally recognized symbol of resistance to neoliberalism. Marcos believes, rightly in my opinion, that his own fame and the Zapatista cause are inextricably entwined. This view is also shared by others. For example, Guillermoprieto writes:

> There was a very real sense in which, during the past thirteen months, Marcos fought the Zapatista war single-handed. It was, after all, a public relations war, and the Indian fighters—most of whom spoke little or no Spanish, and for whom the government had provided, at most, a few years of elementary schooling—were not equipped for the sophisticated exchanges with the government and the Mexican public that such a war required. It was Marcos who wrote the letters, and also the communiqués signed by something called the Clandestine Indigenous Revolutionary Command, which is supposedly the highest authority within the EZLN. (It is more likely the body, consisting of village authorities, that makes the real decisions affecting daily life in the Zapatista zone, while Marcos himself seems to have decisive influence, if not absolute power, in questions having to do with war and relations with the central government.) It was Marcos who granted the vast majority of the interviews— or, at least, the ones that got quoted. It was he who drew up the list of accredited "war correspondents" and signed our laminated mint-green credentials. It was he who stage-managed the moving EZLN events at which glamorous visitors from Mexico City and abroad watched Indian

peasants parade in homemade uniforms, carrying hunting rifles and other guns and—in the absence of real weapons—carved-wood imitations of guns. And it was his adroit manipulation of this array of symbolic weapons that mobilized public opinion in favor of the EZLN and kept the war the Zapatistas had invited at bay.[87]

SUBCOMMANDER
MARCOS AND MAJOR
MOISÉS LEADING A
ZAPATISTA PARADE INTO
LA REALIDAD (OCTOBER
1995). SCOTT SADY.

ZAPATISTAS TRAINING
IN GUADALUPE TEPEYAC
(LATE JANUARY/EARLY
FEBRUARY 1995).
SCOTT SADY.

SUBCOMMANDER
MARCOS AT A PRESS
CONFERENCE IN LA
REALIDAD (APRIL
1996). SCOTT SADY.

BISHOP SAMUEL RUIZ
AT A PEACE RALLY
IN MEXICO CITY
(SEPTEMBER 1995).
SCOTT SADY.

SUBCOMMANDER MARCOS AND COMANDANTE TACHO HOLDING
AN INFORMAL INTERVIEW WITH JOURNALISTS (1995). SCOTT SADY.

SUBCOMMANDER MARCOS, COMANDANTE TACHO (RIGHT), AND MAJOR
MOISÉS (LEFT) SAYING GOODBYE TO COMANDANTA RAMONA AS SHE LEAVES
FOR THE INDIGENOUS FORUM IN MEXICO CITY (OCTOBER 1996). SCOTT SADY.

SUBCOMMANDER
MARCOS SIGNING
AUTOGRAPHS AT THE
NATIONAL INDIGENOUS
FORUM (23–24 JULY
1996). SCOTT SADY.

SUBCOMMANDER
MARCOS GREETING
U.S. DIRECTOR OLIVER
STONE (MARCH 1995).
SCOTT SADY.

SUBCOMMANDER MARCOS PLAYING A GUITAR WHILE TAKING A
BREAK AT THE ENCUENTRO INTERCONTINENTAL (JULY/AUGUST
1996). SCOTT SADY.

SUBCOMMANDER MARCOS DISARMING BEFORE TRAVELING BY
RED CROSS VEHICLE TO SAN CRISTÓBAL DE LAS CASAS FOR
NEGOTIATIONS (OCTOBER 1996). SCOTT SADY.

22. Peace Talks

The immediate result of Marcos's high profile was that "by February 18, just as peace talks were getting under way," a survey of the residents of Mexico City conducted on 7 January, which had shown that 61 percent supported the Zapatistas's goals, now showed that "that percentage had risen to an impressive 75%."[1]

Marcos was no doubt keeping a close eye on such polls. The Zapatistas were in dire need of reassurance concerning the coming peace negotiations, since the PRI, consciously or not, was sending out messages that did little to allay EZLN fears of a government betrayal. We have already seen how Salinas de Gortari changed the backdrop for his televised declarations, swapping a portrait of Emiliano Zapata for that of Venustiano Carranza, the man who ordered Zapata to be tricked into attending peace talks in order to assassinate him. This symbolism was not lost on Mexicans,[2] least of all Marcos, who commented, "[We] are still carrying the remains of the Chinameca [where Zapata was assassinated] ghost and the haunting image of Carranza standing behind Salinas de Gortari as he announced the amnesty law."[3]

Moreover, on 9 February, General Riviello,[4] Mexico's defense minister, made a speech during the eighty-first anniversary of the March for Loyalty that rebutted charges of gross human rights abuses by the army. He stressed its loyalty and the necessity of guaranteeing internal security and of reestablishing law and order, thus legitimizing the military's presence in Chiapas.[5] The speech was subsequently published in *La Jornada*. The government of Mexico had shown that, like the governments of most Latin American countries, it was unable or unwilling to criticize its armed forces. This did not bode well should the army suddenly decide to erase its shame at having to call off its pursuit of the guerrillas in January by going on the offensive. Thus, by the time he was interviewed on 17 February, just four days before the commencement of talks, Marcos declared "Chinameca is in this whole process," adding, "our enemies know that the direction of our movement is going up there—not just some commission. They can ambush us in a minute and then bullfight with the protestors."[6]

Accordingly, Marcos issued a communiqué to nongovernmental organizations on 1 February—the same day that an Americas Watch Report accused the Mexican government of grave human rights violations in responding to the Zapatista uprising[7]—requesting them "to form a 'safety belt' or 'belt of peace' around the area in which the dialogue is to take place."[8] The precaution also had several (possibly) unintended effects. First, it highlighted to Mexican society the extent of the risk the Zapatistas were prepared to take in order to discuss peace. Second, the "safety belt" provided the Zapatistas with an immediate, permanent, and sizeable audience. Third, this audience, and the novelty of its presence, lent an element of spectacle to the proceedings. As Ross observes, "In the high-octane enthusiasm of the moment, hundreds of volunteers poured into San Cristóbal to take up the task."[9]

In the immediate run-up to the peace talks, on 16 February, the Zapatistas released the former governor of Chiapas, General Absalón Castellanos Domínguez, who they had taken from his ranch on 2 January. The general, as we have already seen, ruled the state with an iron hand from 1982 to 1987, when, according to a petition submitted to the Chamber of Deputies by the Unified Socialist Party, "he was responsible for 153 political murders, 692 arbitrary detentions, 503 cases of torture and 327 disappearances of activist campesinos."[10] Even before that, he had won a reputation for brutality when, on 15 June 1980, troops under his command opened fire on Tojolabal villagers during a protest and killed approximately fifty of them. Marcos had already issued a communiqué explaining why the general had been targeted, contrary to the Zapatista policy of not taking hostages, and listing the grievances of *campesinos* and indigenous against him. In return for releasing the general the Zapatistas had negotiated the release of thirty-eight of seventy-one alleged comrades held in Cerro Hueco, the state prison.[11] (Ross believes that the government also agreed to provide supplies for Zapatista communities in the region during the ensuing months.)[12] Even more important perhaps, the general's release enabled the Zapatistas to stage a media spectacle which they exploited to the full in order to reinforce their message.[13] At his handing over, the guerrillas read out a statement that denounced his crimes against indigenous *campesinos* during his governorship, but pardoned him for them by commuting his sentence of hard labor for life. It also detailed their remaining grievances, which took the form of the eleven demands they had previously outlined in their Declaration of War and would subsequently push for at the peace talks one week later.[14]

Thus, by the last week of February, the stage was set for the peace talks. Thanks to Marcos's skillful manipulation of the press, his volleys of communiqués, his requests for a peace cordon, and the staged event of Domínguez's release, an audience had been secured which was familiar with the EZLN's major protagonist(s) and their platform. Moreover, the peace cordon,[15] Marcos's frequent references to possible government treachery, and his refusal to state categorically whether he himself would participate,[16] charged the atmosphere with anxiety and expectation.

The peace talks opened on February 21 in the cathedral of San Cristóbal, mediated by Bishop Samuel Ruiz. Almost the whole of Mexico was gripped by the prospect of seeing what Marcos and the Zapatista delegation would do.[17] Marcos, ever the showman, capitalized on this superbly. Although he had earlier quipped that should he be chosen to serve on the Zapatistas's delegation his choice of clothing would be severely restricted, since he possessed only one item of everything,[18] in the event "his persona was a carefully crafted collage of twentieth century revolutionary symbols, costumes, and props borrowed from Zapata, Sandino, Che, and Arafat as well as from celluloid heroes such as Zorro and Mexico's movie wrestler, 'El Santo.'"[19] Moreover, Gómez Peña continues, "His serious but nonchalant demeanor, adorned with a pipe and a Zapata-style bandolera with bullets that don't match the model of his weapon, made him extremely photogenic."[20] Arriving in front of a huge throng of press photographers jostling for the perfect shot,[21] Marcos began to ascend the cathedral steps and then halted and paused in order to pull up his trouser leg and flirtatiously "show a little leg" like a starlet attending a premiere—"the cameras click[ed] in thunderous unison."[22]

The press was to get plenty of opportunities to see and hear Marcos over the next ten days of talks. He would frequently come out at the end of a day's negotiations and report on progress. Sometimes he would even field questions. The talks also gave the press (and therefore the world) their first real opportunity to meet some of the Zapatistas's other leading cadres. One of the most charismatic of these was the tiny Comandanta Ramona. Despite speaking no other language than her native Tzotzil, she managed to break through the language and cultural barrier to captivate much of her audience. Marcos's wife, Ana María, gave a press interview on the 28th, the last day of the talks. (Interestingly, one reporter noticed that she was wearing a wedding ring and asked if she was married. Little did the journalists present know who her husband was.)[23] Given the intense interest in Marcos and the other EZLN representatives fueled by the talks it is not surprising that the first Web site devoted exclusively to the Zapatistas appeared in March.[24] This did much to make the Subcommander and the Zapatistas more accessible to millions throughout the world.

Manuel Camacho Solís, the government negotiator, had been instructed to rebuff any attempts by the Zapatistas to address nationwide issues. Only points relating exclusively to the state of Chiapas were to be entertained.[25] This meant Marcos had to drop such demands as the abdication of the president and the forming of an interim government of transition which, as in Zapata's dealings with Carranza,[26] the Subcomandante had been demanding as necessary preconditions for peace.[27] This was significant, since the government clearly hoped that by localizing the discussion, the national and international press and Mexican civil society at large (especially those in the capital who had been so vociferous of late) would lose interest in the dialogue.

The Zapatista delegation agreed to limit their demands to matters affecting Chiapas[28]—possibly in return for concessions concerning the remaining points—and the talks then progressed at an unexpectedly rapid pace. Salinas had claimed even before the talks began that he had instructed Camacho to be "generous."[29] By Wednesday (23 February)—only the third day of dialogue—a quarter of the EZLN's thirty-four-point plea petition had, according to Marcos himself, been addressed.[30] Moreover, it took only another seven days for the remaining three-quarters to be addressed. The government had conceded on almost every point, two of particular significance being the repealing of the Chiapan penal code and the "promulgation of a new code designed to respect individual freedoms and rights . . . [and] to include in the new penal code the crime of expulsion of Indians from their communities."[31]

The government, having no doubt felt that it had conceded a great deal, and in any case wanting a swift resolution of the negotiations to enhance its image and to allow it to get on with preparing for the coming general elections, hailed the negotiations as an immense success. The press, national and international, always looking for a rapid, dramatic, and happy end to a story, also appeared to run away with the notion that the Zapatistas's ratification of the agreement was a foregone conclusion. *Time*, for example, featured a full-page article (complete with sizable color photograph of the EZLN delegation, Marcos in the center) under the heading "Compromise Triumphs: Zapatistas and the Government Work Out a Historic Accord

Guaranteeing Indian Rights."[32] Even Bishop Ruiz, himself undoubtedly equally eager to win credit as the broker of peace and to see life in his diocese settle down and benefit from the government's pledges, was not immune to optimism. On Wednesday 2 March, at the closing ceremony for the peace talks, he proclaimed in front of the press that the final accords could be signed "before the end of the month."[33] However, the more perceptive of those present would have noticed that Marcos, uncharacteristically, remained silent throughout. The Zapatistas's impression of the talks were given by Juan, an almost unknown member of their delegation, who contented himself with saying that the dialogue had been "a true one [with] no duplicity or lies," and that "now we must speak to the collective heart that orders us."[34]

As a foretaste of what was eventually to transpire, Marcos himself, when cornered by a reporter from *La Jornada* just prior to leaving, sounded much less upbeat than the government, the press, or the bishop, stating that the government had failed to "resolve even one percent of our problems."[35] He was not caught up in and carried away by peace euphoria as others were but drew a very clear distinction between the government's addressing pleas and resolving them. The Subcommander no doubt recalled that for the past six decades the PRI had always managed to neutralize any challenges to its hegemony—be it from other political parties, labor movements, *campesinos* groups, guerrillas, etc.—largely by co-opting them, not infrequently by appearing to acquiesce in their demands, only to renege on its promises and knife them in the back. Why should now be any different, Marcos must have mused. Moreover, closer inspection of what the government had conceded revealed very little of any real substance. Even before the peace talks, and as early as 20 January, Marcos had expressed skepticism concerning what the government was prepared to offer: "In exchange for that unconditional surrender, the government offers the usual: an audit of internal accounts, a packet of declarations, promises and more bureaucratic dependencies."[36] Now, more than a month later, with the two sides having met to negotiate a peace, the government's offers still appeared littered with vague and noncommittal promises to "evaluate," "support," and "modify," with very little commitment to actually doing anything. Indeed, the response to many of the pleas appeared unconvincingly formulaic, comprising a promise whereby "a commission would be established within ninety days to review" the situation. (As Marcos would comment a month later when explaining the Zapatistas' reasons for rejecting the peace proposal, "the government says in 30, 60 or 90 days, it will produce a plan to make a study to make a law—it's not credible.")[37] Worse still, the three most important issues— Indian autonomy, article 27, and NAFTA—had not been seriously addressed. As anthropologist Hernández Navarro observed, the prime issue of land ownership was left almost wholly unaddressed.[38] Furthermore, even where concrete solutions were proposed by the government—for example, remedying rural poverty in Chiapas or improving health services and education—these would be undertaken by preexisting PRI institutions and organizations such as ProCampo and Solidarity: precisely those bodies that had already proved at best ineffectual. They frequently misspent funds on showy but useless schemes, allowed them to be siphoned off by corrupt officials, used them to reward PRI-loyal *campesinos*, or directed them toward the cities and towns when they were most needed in the rural areas.[39] Finally, some of the Zapatistas's demands were ones that any decent government should automatically guarantee its citizens (for example, basic housing, secondary schooling, access to medical care, electricity, running water, etc.). Marcos stated on record his disgust at the fact that "Salinas continue[s] handling things like the government would fulfill our demands out of the goodness of its heart, not because it was a duty."[40]

Discussions with Camacho concerning a side issue that had recently been brought to Marcos's attention are instructive for understanding the lack of trust in the government's word. The Subcommander had been approached by representatives of those who had been expelled from their communities for not obeying their caciques—local leaders, chosen and supported by the government and, naturally, pro-PRI in their political affiliations. Marcos decided to take up their cause and demanded their "unconditional return" and the punishment of "those of the same race and blood who committed this injustice."[41] According to him, he told Camacho "that the PRI was dipping its hands in Chamula and that it protected the caciques." When Camacho told Marcos "that the government in the future would pass a law to prohibit expulsion and penalize those responsible," the Subcommander, wholly unconvinced, replied: "What had happened in the twenty past years when the rights of the expelled had been violated . . . the government is asking me to put down our arms. It would be better that I give them to the expelled to defend themselves against the caciques who are exploiting them."

Little wonder then that, as he prepared to make the arduous journey back to the jungle, Marcos is reported as saying, "Peace is still a long way off. The government's answers are just a mountain of papers, and that paper does not cure you, teach you, feed you or give you democracy."[42]

23. Courting Civil Society

On 23 March 1994, while Marcos and the other delegates from the EZLN were consulting with the Zapatista communities that comprised their support base, an incident was to take place that was to have a massive impact on the peace process as well as on Mexican society at large. Luis Donaldo Colosio, the PRI's presidential candidate in the coming general election, was assassinated. In the immediate aftermath of the killing, the Zapatistas suspended consultation with their support base and put their armed forces on full alert. As Marcos explained soon after the event: "My feeling was that this murder would be blamed on us, so I called the committee and recommended that we postpone the peace talks."[1] (Some on the right were already accusing the Zapatistas of complicity in the killing and were pushing for the military to be used against them.) Moreover, this atrocity, following so soon on those arising from the Zapatista uprising only two months earlier, caused the general public to become intolerant of any further violence. As *La Jornada* correspondent Pedro Enrique Armendares observed at the time: "The bullet that hit Colosio also knocked the gun out of Marcos' hand. It took away his option of armed response, because Mexican people can't stomach any more violence."[2] As a result, the Zapatistas felt pressured by civil society to accept the government's peace proposals.[3]

At the same time, however, the widespread belief that the assassination was arranged by a hard-line faction within the PRI to rid the party and the country of too moderate a future leader caused Marcos to doubt whether the government would ever implement any peace agreement.[4] Would, he asked, the hard-line members of the PRI party ever countenance an agreement brokered by a PRI moderate and extorted from the government by an armed group? If these hard-liners were prepared to kill one of their own party, would they not simply renege on any peace that was signed? Indeed, as Marcos himself put it:

> That [Colosio's assassination] shows the government is in crisis and can't negotiate. The bullet that killed Colosio killed the possibility of a

peace accord with the EZLN. We can't sign any pact with someone who isn't even capable of guaranteeing his heir's life. Why would he guarantee that of his enemy? Also, it reflected a political crisis that was so deep that we couldn't have reached any result.[5]

Yet the assassination of Colosio perhaps contributed only marginally to the decision by Marcos and the Zapatistas to reject the government's peace initiative. To some extent the talks had been forced upon them and the government by civil society's clamors for dialogue. The government just wanted a speedy and positive end to an embarrassing crisis. The Zapatistas, for their part, were in a difficult position. Civil society had stepped in to save the Zapatistas from annihilation at the army's hands in the first week of January and had pressured both sides to negotiate. As Patricia King and Francisco Javier Villanueva put it, "The Zapatistas were in a tight corner: they could hardly reject a cease-fire imposed on the government by civil society, when they were trying to build links with civil society; but neither could they accept negotiations whose primary purpose was to isolate them from the rest of civil society."[6] Fundamentally, however, Marcos and the Zapatistas could not accept the government's proposals for two very important reasons.

First, they needed to trust the government's promise to fulfill its end of the bargain. Given the government's past record, this was improbable. As Captain Elisa had commented even before the Zapatista rejection had been announced:

> Well, as far as I am concerned, we've seen what the government is like. We don't expect much from the talks that we had with them. We don't think they will keep their word. We have seen the way they promise things. In the past, they promised us housing, health care, land, etc. But they've never come through. That's why we took up arms, because they just talk and never do what they say they will.[7]

Marcos himself echoed this in March shortly after the peace talks. He claimed that the government's strategy is to "bet that the *compas* are going to go away with those false promises and sign a peace agreement in exchange not for highways, hospitals and schools but for the *promise* of them . . . they think that these people whom they've deceived for so long are now going to allow themselves to be deceived again."[8]

The scale of the financial aid promised and the unfeasible extravagance of the proposed programs—Philip Russell calls them "an inexhaustible cornucopia" and "seemingly endless"[9]—must have further heightened the Zapatistas's skepticism. Marcos dismissed the welfare projects as "another government ploy to build a few roads and schools, get the people to calm down, and go back to normal," adding, "unless there is a profound change, these government offers will be useless."[10]

> Take the case of that hospital, the hospital there in Guadelupe Tepeyac. It was dedicated by Salinas last year. He arrived in a helicopter, with trucks full of equipment. They unloaded the trucks, dedicated the hospital, and left. Once Salinas left, they took the equipment away, and the doctors left. The hospital never worked as it should have . . .

> If we had agreed to the government [peace] offer, the same thing would have happened to the roads, schools, and bridges. They would allow the roads to deteriorate, they would have left us with schools without teachers. They would have given us all kinds of things to calm us down, but it wouldn't be of any use to us. We know that, because the government does that all the time, because it has already done it too many times to us.[11]

Zapatista lack of faith in the government was justified in May when the PRI began pursuing its favorite tactic of using co-optation to divide and rule by "grant[ing] almost 6 million new pesos (approximately 1.8 million U.S. dollars) in credits to ARIC and other Union of Unions subsidiaries, lending credence to Marcos' accusation that the ARIC has compromised its principles for money."[12] As Russell notes, the ARIC was targeted by the government for funding precisely because it constituted "the EZLN's main rival for peasant loyalty."[13] This led Marcos to state that the peace talks had merely been "a ploy to buy time, locate the leaders, divide them, and later break them up, eliminate them, or buy them off," concluding "in short, they want to take away the movement's social base."[14] Salinas's statement made around this time to a gathering he attended in Europe that "serious problems, disputes, exist [in Chiapas], but this is not an indigenous revolt,"[15] must have made Marcos despair of the government's willingness to address the grievances of Chiapas's Indian population.

Second, given that the Zapatistas had only one card to play, namely to disarm and disband, the government would have to offer concrete solutions to all their main proposals. Since the government had not done so, the Zapatistas refused to trade in their only card for anything less than the complete satisfaction of their demands. As Marcos would put it six months later: "My opponent [Salinas] left me little maneuvering space: to dialogue he said 'surrender' . . . surrender and we'll dialogue."[16] The Subcommander was no doubt well aware of Emiliano Zapata's adage that "you must never ask, holding a hat in your hand, for justice from the government of tyrants, but only pick up a gun."[17] Indeed, he echoed its sentiment when he commented to journalists that "White people only listen to Indians if they have a gun in their hand."[18] Moreover, of course, by surrendering their arms the Zapatistas would compromise their very survival. As Marcos had put it long before the peace talks began:

> Concretely, the request to "put down arms" is the one that provokes the greatest suspicions. National and Latin American history teaches us that those who turn in their arms, trusting to the forgetfulness of those who pursue them, end their days riddled with bullet holes in any place by any death squad of any political or governing faction. What reason do we have to think that it would not happen like this in our country?[19]

So, the Zapatistas opted to reject the PRI's peace proposals[20] and await the change of government that they (and many others) believed would result from the coming general election. Given the profound and meteoric success of the EZLN in its media war[21]—if not in the military sphere—and the corresponding weakness of the PRI in the face of this onslaught, there was a widely held belief in the country that the Zapatistas could obtain more than the government had just offered. As Russell notes:

> Seven hundred delegates from 280 organizations in the State Council of Indigenous and Peasant Organizations (CEOIC) unanimously supported the EZLN decision. Similarly, the National Union of Agricultural Workers (UNTA) said the EZLN was justified in rejecting the proposed accords since PRI governments had in the past been "characterized by betrayal."[22]

Certain academics also supported the Zapatistas's decision. For example, the agrarian historian Julio Moguel pointed to signs of the government's bad faith which he believed justified the Zapatistas's choice. He drew attention to the fact that during the talks it had refused to consider any revision to articles 27 and 4 of the constitution (dealing with land reform and indigenous recognition, respectively) and that afterward it had bought considerable quantities of riot-control gear, had appointed a conservative rancher (Jorge Constantino Kanter) as a local PRI deputy candidate, and had strongly supported the EZLN's rival, ARIC, both financially and by choosing its leader (Lázaro Hernández) as another prospective local PRI deputy.[23]

The problem for Marcos was now how to maintain good relations with civil society. If the Zapatistas were not to appear ungrateful to it by rejecting the government's peace initiative, and if they were to ensure its continued support—vital for the EZLN's survival—Marcos would have to court civil society and convince it that the Zapatistas remained a good cause. The demonstrations in January and February and the security cordon around the peace talks in March had, as Harvey observes, "helped to deepen the Zapatistas' appreciation of civil society as their most effective ally in the struggle for a peaceful solution."[24]

On 11 June, therefore, the same day that they announced their rejection of the government's peace proposal, the Zapatistas also issued their *Second Declaration of the Lacandón Jungle* in which they recognized civil society's role in having previously "assumed the duty of preserving our country," and undertook to call on it in the future "to retake the protagonist's role . . . to organize itself to direct peaceful efforts towards democracy, freedom and justice." Finally, the declaration requested "all honest sectors of civil society to attend a National Dialogue for Democracy, Freedom and Justice."[25]

On 12 June, "360 'caravan of caravans' volunteers, hauling 180 tons of food and clothing in 27 vehicles, became the first civilian convoy to successfully penetrate Zapatista territory with material aid."[26] It had departed the Zócalo in Mexico City forty-eight hours previously following a ten-thousand-person strong demonstration in support of the Zapatistas, participants in which contributed some items of food, drink, and other supplies. As well as reassuring Marcos and the movement as a whole that civil society was prepared to help them, not only with words and demonstrations far away in the capital but also with practical deeds performed in Chiapas itself, the "caravan of caravans" also demonstrated the logistical viability of the coming National Democratic "Aguascalientes" Convention.

On 2–3 July the Chiapas State Democratic Convention was held in Tuxtla to discuss the Zapatistas's proposals for a state government in transition, a new constituent assembly, and a new constitution. More than sixty groups attended. Less than a week later, on 9 July, the Zapatistas and the state convention leaders convoked a National Democratic Convention to be held from 6–9 August—taking in the anniversary of the FLN's foundation, of Marcos's arrival in Chiapas (both on the 6th), and the anniversary of Zapata's birthday (8th)—in the locality of Guadalupe Tepeyac, where Salinas had officially opened a new hospital only eleven months earlier. This was the first direct meeting (as opposed to through television, over the radio, or in print) between civil society and the guerrillas. Forever with an eye to their revolutionary predecessors, the Zapatistas dubbed the National Democratic Convention "Aguascalientes," after the meeting in October 1914 convoked (but not attended) by Zapata, Villa, and other revolutionary leaders to draft a constitution in the northern town of Aguascalientes.[27]

Marcos, always the showman, took charge of assembling a stage and an audience worthy of the event. He had already had, as we have seen, previous experience in organizing reasonably large jungle spectacles,[28] but the National Democratic Convention would be by far the largest to date. At least this time, however, both the preparations for the event and its staging would not have to take place in the utmost secrecy; on the contrary, it was greatly advertised and promoted, with 711 journalists from 400 news groups in attendance.[29] Moreover, Marcos would be aided by help from a most unexpected quarter. He attributed the financing of the event to both the sacrifice of Zapatista communities who had sold livestock, produce, and other goods to fund it and to contributions from European NGOs, but much (perhaps most) of the money came from the government. In addition, the government even allowed the Zapatistas to re-route the electrical supply designated for Guadelupe Tepeyac to the Aguascalientes compound. As de la Grange and Rico observe, "In reality, those who covered the major part of the expense was . . . the government, who set aside for the revolutionary event 173,000 dollars worth of equipment and installations."[30] They argue that the government provided this funding to keep the Zapatistas busy (and quiet) during the immediate run-up to the election. They maintain, plausibly, that Marcos allowed the Zapatistas to be bought off because "he was convinced of the PRI's [coming] resounding defeat."[31] According to Oppenheimer[32]—followed by de la Grange and Rico[33]—the then governor of Chiapas, Javier López Moreno, said that the funding had received "the green light from President Salinas." However, de la Grange and Rico then quote Salinas (by then, 1996, ex-president) as denying this:

> I don't know if it was the decision of Javier López Moreno. I don't know the details and I don't recollect that Javier López Moreno ever raised this matter in our meetings in DF [Mexico City] . . . When the local level faces difficult problems, it searches out ways itself of building bridges. No, they didn't consult me, but I knew about it . . . although I am surprised, because it is much money.[34]

Salinas's assertion of ignorance is wholly unconvincing, contradicted as it is both by the governor and the president's own aides[35] as well as by common sense: it would have been a very brave state governor who allocated such massive funds to a guerrilla group behind the president's back.

The abandoning of secrecy, their newfound fame and popularity, the need to interact face-to-face with civil society, and lavish government funding allowed the Zapatistas and Marcos to create a highly impressive venue. A huge amphitheatre was erected, as Marcos put it in his opening speech, taking "600 men and women putting in 28 days of labor, 14 hours a day: a total of 235,200 hours of labor; 9,800 days of labor; 28 years of labor; 60 million old pesos . . . [with] a stage the size of the bridge on a transatlantic liner [and] wooden benches for 8,000 participants."[36] (The scale of the construction led Hermann Bellinghausen to note in *La Jornada* that those who President Salinas had dubbed "professionals of violence are also professionals of carpentry.")[37] It also had a huge awning to protect its occupants from the rain, twenty buildings to house visitors and to act as canteens, fourteen roasting pits, latrines, tanks of drinking water, and parking for 100 vehicles.[38] The compound had a powerful sound system and even a library.

The first day of the convention, held on the 6th, began in San Cristóbal and saw the delegates divide into five working groups to discuss "the transition to democracy," the "non-viability of the state-party," "non-violent ways to democracy," "elections, civil resistance, and defense of the will of the people," and the "formulation of a national project." The following day the delegates moved to Guadelupe Tepeyac.

In order to facilitate this, the state governor also made available 150 coaches to ferry the convention's 6,000 attendees from San Cristóbal to the Lacandón venue. They carried what Ross calls "Indians, and lefties, militant farmers, trade unionists, rockeros, chicanos, gachupines, and chilangos, chilangos, chilangos."[39] Heavy rains and deep mud turned a five-to-six-hour journey into a grueling daylong test of endurance. Periodic Zapatista checkpoints, checking names and searching for concealed weapons, slowed things down even more. Carlos Monsiváis, the Mexican essayist who perhaps more than any other of his countrymen had influenced Marcos with his writings,[40] suffered particularly badly. He was carrying books for Marcos and stumbled three times, spraining his ankle at one checkpoint; he was promptly carried to the "infirmary" (a medical tent) to recuperate.

Having reached Aguascalientes, civil society was further afflicted by Chiapas's typically bad weather. In the evening of the second day, just as Marcos was finishing his welcome speech, "a crowd-scattering, gully-washing, flag-ripping, toad-strangling rainstorm"[41] drenched his audience, leading them to modify the traditional chant of "Zapata lives, the struggles goes on" to "Zapata lives, the rain goes on." The 4,000 meter awning ripped, soaking all those beneath. This effectively cut the convention in half, turning what was supposed to have been a two-day event into one. It petered out the following morning as the delegates climbed aboard the coaches back to San Cristóbal and ultimately Mexico City. However, this abrupt ending damaged the Zapatista cause very little. The guerrillas had achieved their aim of an interactive encounter with civil society. Marcos had delivered an excellent speech that had met with rapturous applause from the floor, especially during the point at which he had held aloft the Mexican flag. Civil society had witnessed the harsh realities of daily life, both in Chiapas and among the guerrillas. They had also seen a military parade by the EZLN's *insurgentes* and *milicianos*, all bearing arms with white ribbons tied to them to "represent, like everything else here, a paradox: weapons that aspire to be useless."[42] They had eaten, drunk, and danced with the Zapatistas and met leading figures in the movement about whom they had previously only read, including female officers: there were chants of "Long live Ramona and Ana María" from the crowd. It may also be said that a major significance of the convention was the further development of the cult of Marcos. In a press conference he gave on the 8th, as the vast majority of visitors were returning to Mexico City, the Subcommander impressed the media as "confident like a pop star and evasive like a politician, he answered various questions ironically."[43] When one reporter asked Marcos if he would remove his ski mask, the Subcommander replied "Yes, if you want it. You tell me," which in turn was met with cries of "No!," thereby "confirm[ing] that the Marcos symbol should remain masked in order to preserve the legend and, in no way, becom[e] an ordinary, recognizable mortal."[44]

August also witnessed the EZLN embark on a project that, at the time, appeared to have comparatively little significance, but which in the months and years to come would prove even more important than the convention: the Zapatistas's launch into cyberspace.[45] It was in this month the EZLN first posted its Web page on the Internet, thereby conveying its message to the world and also incurring the epithet of "the *first informational guerrilla movement*."[46] Communiqués, interviews, and letters were from then on posted on the Internet, as were all subsequent declarations. By 2001, conservative estimates put the number of Zapatista-related Web sites at 45,000, based in twenty-six countries,[47] the most popular, http://www.ezln .org, boasted more than 4 million visits by the time it celebrated its ten-year anniversary in 2004. (Today, it carries recordings of the Zapatistas's Radio Insurgente broadcasts.)[48] Cleaver, noting the elaborate network of radio microtransmitters established in remote Zapatista communities and the existence of Melel Xojobal, an indigenous news service which collects information from isolated villages and posts it on the Internet, concludes: "Through their ability to extend their political reach via modern computer networks the Zapatistas and their supporters have woven a new electronic fabric of struggle to carry their revolution throughout Mexico and around the world."[49] As we shall see, this presence on the Internet had important repercussions in February 1995, when the government launched a fresh military offensive into Zapatista territory.

24. The Elections and Their Aftermath

Two weeks after the convention had been forcibly cut short by the elements, Mexico went to the polls (21 August). Now it would be seen whether Marcos had calculated correctly when making a secret deal with the government to remain docile during the elections in return for government sponsorship of Aguascalientes. To Marcos, and indeed many Mexicans, there could only be two outcomes of the election, both favorable to the Zapatistas: either the elections would be free and fair, in which case the PRI would lose;[1] or, more probable, the PRI would claim victory through fraud, as it had done in 1988, and Mexican civil society would vociferously demand, again as it had done in 1988, that the PRI accept defeat, but this time with their hand strengthened by the Zapatistas who had pledged to aid them in their struggle for democracy.[2] Desperate as they were to see the back of a party that had ruled the country for more than six decades[3]—during which time it had become more and more openly autocratic, self-serving, and corrupt—Marcos, the Zapatistas, and many Mexican liberals never foresaw a third electoral outcome: an apparently legitimate victory for the PRI. Indeed, they were so desirous of an opposition victory in order to break the PRI's monopoly on government, and so firm were they in their belief that the years of corruption, electoral fraud, greed, "dirty wars," massacres, disappearances, co-optations, assassinations, cover-ups, injustice, ineptitude, and so on, had discredited the party in the people's eyes,[4] that a genuine PRI victory seemed impossible. They forgot, however, two very important considerations.

The first was that Mexicans now had a high tolerance of electoral fraud. Given that the presidential election of 1988 had resulted in an outrageous travesty of democracy, anything short of an exact repeat of this would look like a fair result. In short, it would not take much for Mexicans and interested members of the international community (in particular Mexico's new fellow NAFTA partners) to be willing to suspend their disbelief and declare the elections free and fair. This is exactly what happened. The PRI's victory was anything but clean.[5] Ross states, "There is little question that fraud, as it had been in 1988, was pervasive at all levels of the August 21 elections."[6] Oppenheimer goes even further, claiming the PRI's victory "result[ed] from the most unfair electoral process in Latin America's present . . . with the exception of Cuba."[7] Castañeda echoes this, talking of "the undeniable irregularities that took place on Election Day and the scandalous unfairness which permeated the electoral process as a whole."[8] So too, after noting that "a substantial number of intellectuals and 'representatives' from civil groups had already affirmed, without blushing, that 'fraud exists in all democratic countries,' with no mention of the extraordinary magnitude of that which was perpetrated on August 21," Sánchez Lira and Villarreal list some of the more blatant ploys "that made possible for the thousandth time, the dismal perpetuation of the ruling party in power."[9] For example, there was:

> The "ratón loco" [where a voter is sent from one polling station to another on false pretexts to discourage him/her from voting] and the "merry-go-round" [the transporting en masse of PRI-voters to several polling stations at various different locations] . . . the "tacos de votos" and "operation tamale" [two methods of stuffing ballot boxes with PRI votes prior to voting] . . . the outright robbery of ballot boxes . . . the intimidation and violence directed against opposition voters, or those who were simply apathetic . . . [the] shaving thousands of voters' names from the official electoral registry . . . the magic which brought the dead back from the Great Beyond to joyously cast their votes for the Tricolor party, and finally, of course, the cyber-cosmetic makeover of results which was carried out in the offices of the government.[10]

When we add two further factors, arguably even more significant than those listed above, namely, the vast superiority in funds and financial resources[11] and access to the media[12] enjoyed by the PRI, "free" and "fair" are adjectives that hardly seem appropriate.

Many commentators argue, however, that even if one discounts the votes gained by the PRI's advantages and frauds, it still won the election[13] on account of a second and more influential consideration: the fear vote. The year 1994 had been a tumultuous one for many people.[14] It had witnessed a major guerrilla uprising in Chiapas followed by nearly two weeks of savage repression on the part of the Federal Army (January); the kidnappings of Alfredo Harp Helú and Angel Losada, two of Mexico's richest men (14 March and 25 April, respectively); the murder of Tijuana's police chief,

José Federico Benitez (28 April); and the brutal assassination of the PRI's presidential candidate, Luis Donaldo Colosio (23 March). Fear and uncertainty gripped much of the electorate, which now looked to a strong and familiar hand to steer them through these troubled waters.[15] In short, the PRI "shamelessly exploited the theme of violence in order to convince the electorate to vote for . . . Ernesto Zedillo or chaos."[16] For example, one of Zedillo's campaign slogans was "Vote Zedillo, for your family's well being." Moreover, as Ross noted, "One mass-produced PRI window sign read: 'If you don't vote for Zedillo, there may not be an afterwards.'"[17] Likewise, the media—almost exclusively pro-PRI—fed people's insecurities. As Sánchez Lira and Villarreal commented, "Television and the press offer up images of death and suffering with extraordinary abundance: from Rwanda to Bosnia, Argentina to India, from Peru to Chiapas."[18] Oppenheimer quotes a PRI adviser on how the fiercely pro-PRI television network Televisa fuelled the atmosphere of fear:

> After the Zapatista rebellion, Televisa bombarded viewers with stories about the former Yugoslavia, and about how Marshall Josip Broz Tito had built a prosperous and independent nation on the threshold of a great empire that had fallen apart within months because of political violence . . . it was part of the government's overall strategy to scare the Mexican people, telling them that something similar could happen in Mexico if the PRI was voted out of office.[19]

In the words of Castañeda, "Televisa thus had . . . one strategy: to identify the PRI with peace and stability, and the opposition with violence and chaos."[20] Oppenheimer also notes how one election campaign, ostensibly neutral but sponsored by the PRI-dominated Mexico City municipal government and the pro-PRI Association of Mexico City Radio Broadcasters, carried "a radio spot that was broadcast constantly during the five days prior to the election" which featured a worried child.[21] Asked by another child "What's wrong?" the first child replies that it is "scared"; asked why, it explains, "because my father is scared." The feature ends with a voice-over: "At no time, in no place, for any reason, should a child grow up with fear. Because we believe in the force of reason, we reject violence." This was evidently meant to contrast the PRI with the PRD, whose leader and presidential candidate, Cuauhtémoc Cárdenas, had met Marcos in the Chiapan jungle on 15 May[22] and many of whose supporters were left-wing and therefore pro-Zapatista. Chants of "Marcos, Marcos, Marcos" during Cárdenas's campaign rallies whenever he made reference to Chiapas did little to assuage the fears of the majority of Mexicans.[23] A poll conducted in June showed that of the respondents consulted, "over 50% feared post-electoral violence would soon consume Mexico."[24] In short, a vote for the PRI had been "a vote based on fear."[25] This represents one of the cruelest ironies of the Zapatista uprising: that while, as Hernández Navarro observes, "without the Zapatistas' 'armed criticism' of the government's policies, there could hardly have arisen the new 'commitment to peace, democracy and justice' that is fuelling hopes that there may actually be clean elections in Mexico,"[26] this same armed criticism, despite Marcos's best efforts,[27] encouraged frightened voters to reelect the PRI.

If Marcos's calculation that the PRI would either claim a fraudulent victory or would be democratically voted out of power proved incorrect at the national level, it was nevertheless wholly confirmed at the local level. The PRD candidate for the Chiapas governorship, Amado Avendaño Figueroa, was run off the road in a traffic incident that few believed was an accident. The details of the accident itself, when coupled with the knowledge that "more than three hundred PRD militants had been killed in confrontations with the army and the police by the end of the Salinas administration,"[28] pointed to an assassination attempt by local members of the PRI or their supporters.[29] Avendaño, who was the proprietor of San Cristóbal's independent newspaper, El Tiempo, and who had been one of the first to interview the Zapatistas at dawn on 1 January, had "practically adopted the [Zapatista's] Second Declaration [of the Lacandón Jungle] as his platform, promising if elected to form a 'transitional government' for Chiapas and convoke a constitutional convention of Chiapas' 'civil society' to write a new state constitution."[30] Clearly those in power (PRI officials) or those allied with power (large landowners) could not tolerate this and, their attempt to kill Avendaño having failed, they resorted to gross electoral fraud, subsequently declaring their candidate, Eduardo Robledo, the winner with 51.1 percent of the vote.[31] No one, least of all Marcos, believed these results.[32] La Jornada, El Financiero, and Proceso all expressed doubts as to their validity.[33] As Russell observes: "The Civic Alliance, a nonpartisan election monitoring group, noted that irregularities in Chiapas were far above the national average. They included a lack of voter secrecy at 67.82 percent of polling places, coercion at 44.54 percent, flying squads voting repeatedly at 11.33 percent, and ballot stuffing at 8.95 percent."[34] So too, the actress Ofelia Medina, who had been appointed "as a sort of peoples' electoral prosecutor," declared that "irregularities had been reported in a third of the state's 3,000 polling places, and in her final report the actress wrote that she had discovered 177 distinct ways of committing electoral fraud in the Chiapas election."[35] (For example, in the *ejido* of Morelia, Zapatista heartland, only 506 ballots were delivered to a polling station whose catchment area comprised 1,500 registered voters, most of whom were expected to vote PRD.) In short, the PRI either working on its own initiative at the local level or under orders from the national executive clearly still failed to realize that the Zapatista uprising had changed everything and thought that it was business as usual, which meant fraud and the imposition of its will on the populace.

However, the Zapatista rebellion had given many people, both inside and outside Chiapas, the confidence and the means to resist.[36] The state government had already received ample demonstration that things had changed, since its own "officials estimate that over 1,000 land invasions occurred during the 6 months following the uprising . . . [with] most invaders . . . not dislodged,"[37] while "between 1 January and 30 April 1994 31 of Chiapas' 111 mayors were forced out of office."[38] However, the authorities continued to believe they could impose their will upon the people.

Marcos immediately lambasted the PRI governor-elect, Robledo, with the backhanded statement that "speaking as one transgressor to another, I must confess that I feel you outdid your predecessor in the last election."[39] There followed massive demonstrations and widespread campaigns of civil disobedience within the state. Highways were blocked and radio stations were seized and made to broadcast pro-Avendaño messages. Marcos even made the recognition of Avendaño as the legitimate governor-elect a precondition for the resumption of peace talks.[40] Not that peace talks were really much of an option after 28 September, when, as in March, once again following a Salinas peace initiative, a hard-line faction within the PRI assassinated another of the party's leading lights, Secretary General José Francisco Ruiz Massieu.[41] In a statement that echoed the one he had made after Luis Colosio's death, Marcos told his press interviewers: "We don't know with whom we are going to speak, whether it is with the assassins of Ruiz Massieu or with the faction of the assassinated."[42] Similarly, on 8 October, a day venerated by Latin America's Left as the anniversary of Che Guevara's death, Marcos addressed a public rally on the Aguascalientes site, telling those present that "the group in power reiterated its inability to resolve internal differences. All lies about clean elections and the vote for peace are shown up by this new crime."[43] He then announced that the EZLN would no longer negotiate with the government and had mined entry points into its territory and installed anti-aircraft units.

Marcos's decision to call a halt to any further negotiations with the government requires explanation. Massieu's assassination was a contributing factor. As Marcos explained to one journalist: "How can we convince our people that the government will respect our lives when it doesn't even respect the lives of its own?"[44] The PRI's imposition of its own candidate on Chiapas and the composition of the president-elect's cabinet, stacked with the same men that Salinas used,[45] must have made Marcos despair of any change in the government's stance. The personal histories of some of the protagonists perhaps also played a part. Marcos had already expressed uneasiness about Zedillo in late July and early August: "Zedillo is backed by the hard-line of the party, which is gaining ground. . . . Zedillo arrived at his candidacy without a political personality and was given one by the hard-liners. They created his personality of toughness and intolerance. We think that's not the real Zedillo, but that he is being controlled by the hard-liners."[46]

Zedillo, Marcos thought (and others agreed),[47] had already revealed his nature two years earlier, in 1992, when, as secretary for education, he had commissioned new history textbooks that had downplayed the role of the Niños Héroes (Heroic Children of Chapultepec) in Mexico's war with the United States (1848) and had attempted to lessen the significance of Zapata himself. These had proved so unpopular that "the 6.8 million books, which had cost $4.05 million, ended up gathering dust in a government warehouse."[48] Marcos had taunted him over this issue months earlier. Asked by a reporter, "Is it true that you want to speak with Zedillo?," the Subcommander replied, "No, I have never said that [but] I can give him some suggestions on how to write textbooks."[49] Now, in October, Zedillo was dragging his feet in recognizing the legitimacy of Bishop Samuel Ruiz's newly formed Comisión Nacional de Intermediación (CONAI, National Commission of Intermediation) to mediate between the incoming administration and the EZLN—this despite (or perhaps because) the Zapatistas had been quick to do so. Instead, the president-elect preferred to attempt to engage Marcos in clandestine talks, much to the Subcommander's disdain.[50] The government's replacement of Camacho with Jorge Madrazo Cuellar as its peace and reconciliation officer acted as a further impediment to progress. Madrazo had pointedly not criticized army abuses at Ocosingo or Morelia in January.

But possibly the most important factor in the decision to withdraw from peaceful dialogue was the Federal Army's presence in the region. Its brutal repression in January had been terrible enough, although not wholly unexpected. However, since then, it had become an army of occupation in Chiapas, the results of which historian García de León describes:

> Dispirited, bored, far from their families, they [the soldiers] channel their frustration toward the defenseless peasants who must cross their military checkpoints. The rape of two Tzeltal women at the Altamirano checkpoint—and the soldiers seeing Zapatistas in every peasant that dares look them in the eye—contributed to this increasing tension.[51]

Now, with the PRI having secured the reins of power for a further six years, "the military was on the prowl in the jungle . . . occup[ying] Toniná, the Mayan ruins outside of Ocosingo, where a new military zone would soon be under construction."[52] Marcos soon decried the fact that "the amount of troops have increased and the reinforcement of a clear disposition to annihilation is evident," adding, "from the 14th day of November there are obvious and continuous intrusions of airplanes, of 'Hercules' transports which move men and military supplies to the units used against insurgents on the Guatemalan border."[53] Just over three years later, *Proceso* published a document written in October 1994 by the general commanding the Seventh Military Region (headquarters in Tuxtla Gutiérrez) in which he stated: "In order to break the support relationship that exists between the population and the transgressors of the law," the military intelligence services should "secretly organize certain sectors of the civilian population, including ranchers, small business owners and individuals characterized by a high sense of patriotic duty, who will be employed in support of our operations."[54] The military was beginning to utilize paramilitary groups to undermine the Zapatistas's support bases. This tactic had worrying repercussions for Marcos himself, since, as Debray notes, it placed the Subcommander "in the unpleasant dilemma of either being . . . turned into the diabolical figure of a murderer if he responds to military pressure closing in [or] ridiculed as a bluffer if he reacts by withdrawing."[55]

So talks were abandoned, tensions mounted, and Marcos's calls for Avendaño's recognition grew even stronger. On Columbus Day (12 October), between 15,000 and 25,000 indigenous demonstrators swamped San Cristóbal in support of Avendaño. A message from Marcos was read out claiming Robledo was "a governor who is not ours," and stating: "We prefer to die rather than living with the shame of having a tyrant dictating our actions and words."[56] At the same rally, the Consejo Estatal de Organizaciones Indígenas y Campesinas (CEOIC, Chiapas State Indigenous Peasant Council), established in the immediate aftermath of the uprising in January bringing together 280 indigenous and *campesino* organizations, declared nine areas in the state to be multiethnic zones and their towns "autonomous."[57] (The same decree also recognized only Avendaño as governor and refused to pay taxes or utility bills to Robledo's state government.) From now on, obtaining official recognition of this autonomy would be center stage in the Chiapan political arena.

In the week following the rally, Marcos went one step further and claimed: "Things will blow up because of the problems faced by imposing Robledo. He faces not only an armed movement, but an uncontrollable, peaceful civilian movement."[58] Two days later he declared: "If Robledo is imposed as governor, there is going to be war here. And here means Mexico, not just Chiapas."[59]

The rally provoked an immediate aggressive response from the military. The following day, troops marched through the Zapatista *ejido* of Morelia, in what Ross notes was "an unprecedented violation of the neutrality of the free zones."[60] The Zapatistas responded to this on 14 October by gathering in huge numbers at Aguascalientes and firing a single volley into the sky in a mark of defiance.

In this air of increasing tension Marcos convened a Second Aguascalientes from 2 to 4 November in a renewed attempt to galvanize civil society. During this, the National Convention for Democracy was established as a civilian affiliate to the EZLN. However, as Collier and Quaratiello note, the Second Aguascalientes "drew a disappointing turn out."[61] This, plus the fact that those who did attend proved unable to agree on anything, led the Zapatistas to turn from trying to organize and direct Mexican civil society at large[62] to pursuing the demands of local indigenous and *campesino* groups such as those that made up the CEOIC. This entailed taking up the banner of more specifically Indian demands, most notably "autonomy," a concept which was to grow and develop over the next eighteen months. Meanwhile, on the final day of the Second Aguascalientes (6 November), far away in the state capital Tuxtla, Avendaño addressed a PRD rally calling on those present to occupy the city on 8 December, when Robledo was due to be inaugurated there.

On 17 November of every year the EZLN celebrated the foundation of its first Zapatista camp. Oppenheimer describes the scene:

Deep in the Lacandón jungle, near the border with Guatemala, more than a thousand Indian rebels clad in military uniforms were standing firm, their left hands raised in a military salute,[63] their eyes fixed on the distance. At a sign from one of their commanders, they began to sing the Zapatista anthem, "The Horizon." "*Ya se mira el horizonte, combatiente Zapatista!*" ("One can see the horizon, Zapatista combatant!"), the rebel troops intoned with devotion. Then, about a dozen Mayan leaders clad in their respective costumes—the Tzeltales in their white shirts and black ponchos, the Tzotziles with their distinctive red ponchos, the Chols with their black slacks, and the Tojolabales in their all-white clothing—stepped forward and handed over the staff of command, a scepter made out of an ocote tree branch, to a white man standing in front of them. It was Subcommander Marcos . . . He wore a black poncho, black slacks, munition-filled bandoliers, and a revolver and an Ingram submachine gun tucked into his belt, a Rambo-style outfit that stood out immediately amid the assortment of red and white clothes worn by the Mayan leaders standing in front of him. He humbly lowered his head and took the ocote branch with both hands, stressing the significance he attached to the moment. The Mayan leaders were formally commissioning him to lead them in a revolution against the Mexican government.

With the scepter in his hand, Marcos sat down on a bench and received, one by one, seven war symbols from as many tribes: A Mexican flag, a red-and-black Zapatista flag, a rifle, a bullet, a container with human blood, a piece of corn, and a handful of clay. The first four were emblems of combat, the other three reminders of life. One of the Indian chiefs closed the ceremony with a prayer in Tzeltal: "Seven words, seven forces, seven roads. Life, truth, men, peace, democracy, freedom, and justice. Seven forces that empower the staff of command. Take the scepter of the seven forces and hold it with honor." [64]

The ceremony, Oppenheimer notes, "was partly Indian tradition, partly Mexicans' age-old fondness for ritual, and partly Marcos's own penchant for theatrics . . . Marcos had borrowed from ancient Mayan rites to help give the new Zapatista army a fervent sense of mission." [65]

At the ceremony, cadres and in particular their leaders, were encouraged to reflect on the successes and failures of the past year. Marcos had always conscientiously followed this traditional guerrilla act of introspection and self-assessment, which had been favored greatly by Che Guevara, publishing his evaluation in *Neplanta*. The 1994 anniversary—the EZLN's eleventh—was no different. Three thousand Zapatista *insurgentes* and *milicianos* turned out to hear Marcos deliver a speech in which he assessed the developments of the last twelve months. He talked candidly about the movement's achievements and of "the many errors committed on the part of the EZLN: some of them the product of our political stupidity, our ignorance."[66] He did not spare himself from criticism, stating that there had been "other errors, the product of the protagonistic excesses of he who is the voice of the EZLN . . . [who] has been mistaken on not a few occasions in his words and with whom he chose to speak." These included "having provoked more often than not, in place of the promotion of unity and clarity, the encouragement of confusion and quarrels and resentment"; the nonfulfillment of "the respect for human rights of civilians, to which we are bound by our commitment to the military laws approved by the Geneva Convention," whereby "on occasions the EZLN has forced villages that do not share our way of struggling into joining it"; and the harassment of certain small landowners because of the deliberate or mistaken interpretation and application of the revolutionary agrarian laws. Marcos then went on to outline the ways in which he and the CCRI's General Command were seeking to address these errors, in particular "to solicit respectfully from human rights NGOs that they watch over the fundamental rights of all human beings within the conflict zones, irrespective of their political affiliation, religious creed, race or social class," and to initiate "a process of adjustment to guarantee . . . that genuine small property owners will not be affected."

This process of introspection, stimulated by the anniversary event, perhaps led Marcos to reflect on how the year had impacted on him personally. He no doubt had very mixed feelings: military and political success had been at the cost of many lives, some of those of people very close to him, for example Subcomandante Pedro and Capitán Hugo.[67] (He was finally learning the painful lesson that Germán and Elisa already knew from bitter experience, that being a guerrilla involved sacrifice, and not just self-sacrifice in the form of enduring physical hardships and privations, but that of losing dear ones from violent deaths.) In the spring, Marcos had become the focus of tremendous media interest, with members of the national and international press seeking him out for interviews, frequently bringing with them publications from their own countries bearing his face blazoned across the front pages with captions heralding him as the new Che Guevara or the first postmodern guerrilla, but again this excitement must have been tempered by sorrow, as Marcos received news of the death of his long-standing friend and mentor, Old Antonio, in May or June,[68] and of his beloved brother, Carlos, in July.[69] It is perhaps remarkable that in the face of these deaths Marcos, unlike so many other guerrillas, did not become increasingly hard line, uncompromising, embittered, and brutal.

After Marcos had concluded his speech, Comandante Tacho initiated the ceremonial handing over of the Staff of Command. As noted above, Marcos had first received this at the same ceremony one year before, the difference now being that whereas the 1993 ceremony had taken place in secrecy, the 1994 one took place in the full glare of the press. Cameras clicked as Marcos was given the Seven Staffs of Military Command, one from each major ethnic group of the EZLN (Tojolabals, Tzeltals, Tzotzils, Chols, Mams, Zoques, and mestizos), and other highly symbolic items (such as the Mexican and Zapatista flags, the Staff of Dignity, the Arms of Peace, the Bullet of Justice, the Blood of Truth, the Corn of Obeying the Will of the People, and the Soil of the Living Dead).[70] The ceremony symbolized the placing of all military personnel and materiel at Marcos's disposal. However, given that the last time this had happened, there followed an aggressive guerrilla offensive, the 1994 ceremony could also be taken to symbolize the threat of renewed hostilities. It was, perhaps, the only peaceful means Marcos had left to convince the government to install Avedaño as Chiapas's governor. The media lapped up yet another wonderfully staged display of guerrilla posturing. The government, however, remained implacable.

On 1 December, Zedillo delivered his inauguration speech. Marcos evidently listened to it over the radio since he promptly dispatched a communiqué in response. In his letter, he pointed out that Zedillo's cabinet was largely identical to that of Salinas's, and he generally deplored the new president's failure to break with the approach adopted by the previous administration.[71] He then launched into a damning indictment of "the crimes of the State," which "began with the assassination of the one from whom you inherited your candidacy [that is, Colosio] . . . continued in the mockery of the electoral campaigns . . . passed a self-test on the 21st of August and . . . culminates in this fateful December 1st." He added, "The first of December completes the burial of what began before the 21st of August; burial of a hope for the peaceful transition to democracy, liberty, and justice."

When it came to the swearing-in of the governor of Chiapas on 8 December, Avendaño refused to acknowledge defeat. Zedillo, himself having been inaugurated as president only seven days earlier, was forced to make "an odd agreement," whereby Avendaño "would be permitted to hold an outdoor swearing-in ceremony in the center of Tuxtla Gutiérrez on the same day as Robledo took the oath in a nearby theatre—but Avendaño must vacate the state capital immediately thereafter for San Cristóbal, where the interior secretary even offered his government-in-rebellion rent-free offices."[72] Samuel Ruiz, in one of his December homilies, described the situation as "grave," adding, "at this moment there are two states of Chiapas, two governors, two governments and two armies: this is the beginning of civil war."[73] Robledo stated that he would step down as governor if the Zapatistas agreed to lay down their arms. Not surprisingly, Marcos rejected this proposal outright: "It's a really bad joke, to be playing with fire by supposing that you can exchange an imposed government for an entire movement which has risen up with dignity and justice. Positions of this kind assure that there will be war. There is no doubt, they are mocking us."[74] To make matters worse, in an attempt to bolster an unpopular (and in many people's eyes illegitimate) new PRI governor, Zedillo decided to attend Robledo's inauguration. Marcos interpreted this as the new president firmly nailing his colors to the mast and revealing himself to be equally as undemocratic and authoritarian as his predecessor. In short, it confirmed the Subcommander in his belief that Zedillo was cast very much in the same mold as Salinas and that therefore further negotiation would prove futile.[75] He declared that the event "formalizes the end of the cease-fire, we are saying it has been . . . broken by the government."[76] No doubt bolstered by a poll conducted in Mexico City on 8 and 9 December showing that 59 percent of residents retained a "good opinion" of the Zapatistas, and 78 percent thought their demands were justified,[77] the Subcommander decided that something needed to be done if the EZLN was to break the cycle of governmental complacency, indifference, and repression practiced over the preceding twelve months.[78] Part of his strategy involved the Subcommander secretly meeting with the PRD candidate Cárdenas, Rosario Ibarra (the leading activist for those "disappeared" by the government), and Andrés Manuel López Obrador (the PRD candidate for the governorship of Tabasco who, like Chiapas's Avandaño, was widely believed to have been the victim of electoral fraud) in his jungle retreat on 13 December. The forging of links with these important figures outside Chiapas broke the government's quarantine of the Zapatistas and allowed the planning of some degree of concerted action (or at least the identification of common aims). Marcos also stated that another solution to the current impasse may well take the form of a "return to combat" or "some military action," although he acknowledged that "in military terms, the situation is balanced against us."[79]

Consequently, in the fortnight prior to Christmas, the Federal Army readied itself for a resumption of hostilities, while Chiapas in general braced itself for a return to war. Would the Zapatistas commit military suicide by confronting an alert, infinitely better equipped, and more numerous foe that had already surrounded them, or would they back down and endure the imposition of Robledo as governor?

What happened next revealed both Marcos's tactical genius and the EZLN's capacity for coordinated, clandestine military maneuvers on a sizeable scale. As Tangeman describes it:

> On December 19, after eleven ominous days of silence from the jungle following Robledo's inauguration, journalists in San Cristóbal were summoned to an early morning press conference in rebel-held territory near the town of Guadalupe Tepeyac, during which the rebel's Sub-commander Marcos claimed that Zapatista columns had filtered past the army back into the Chiapas highlands and were staging highway and town hall takeovers in thirty-eight municipalities statewide.[80]

Without firing a shot, and therefore without breaking the cease-fire, the Zapatistas had managed to refocus the nation's attention on Chiapas, break the military stranglehold of the Federal Army, and demonstrate their continued capacity to go on the offensive. The Zapatistas called this bold stroke the Campaign for Peace with Justice and Dignity for the Indian Peoples which, as one noted anthropologist has observed, "marked the beginning of the demand for autonomy in the Zapatista territories."[81]

Of course, such a move was risky. The government or the local military could have interpreted it as a resumption of outright war and responded with overwhelming force. However, a number of factors militated against this. First, many of those seizing highways and municipal buildings in the name of the Zapatistas were unarmed. Local eyewitnesses, while noting that the perpetrators wore Zapatista-style ski masks, nonetheless claimed that they could not be sure if they were Zapatista troops or just civilian supporters.[82] In all probability they were members of the EZLN's *milicianos* who were always more numerous than the number of actual *insurgentes*. Second, "They were protected by their relentless media connection, and by their Internet-based worldwide alliances, from outright repression."[83] Marcos's efforts at forging strong bonds with the press and Mexican civil society, though a long and frequently frustrating process, were paying off. Third, the Zapatistas were also protected to some extent by Bishop Samuel Ruiz who, immediately on hearing the news, proclaimed himself to be on a "fast for peace," in an attempt to head off any violent retaliation on the part of the Federal Army. He was rapidly followed in this by twenty-three other prominent Mexicans, among them Ofelia Medina.

The government and the army appear to have been caught completely off guard. It would appear that they had believed that the Zapatistas had only two courses of action left open to them: impotent rhetorical denunciation of the PRI or military confrontation. To be fair, during the preceding weeks, President Zedillo had been preoccupied with financial matters. Given his training as an economist and given the grave state of the country's economy as left him by Salinas, he had, not unnaturally, been focusing on the nation's finances. On most analyses,[84] Salinas, as outgoing president, should have devalued the peso.[85] Now this fell to Zedillo, despite earlier assurances that he would do no such thing. In order to save face, therefore, he decided to link the devaluation to the Zapatista's new offensive, hoping that their highly successful campaign would be perceived by the public as a selfish and reckless publicity stunt that had endangered the nation's economic well-being.[86] He announced the peso's devaluation early on the morning of December 20.

The results were catastrophic. As Tangeman notes:

> Finance Secretary Jaime Serra announced the decision to let the peso move to the edge of the fixed exchange band against the U.S. Dollar, effectively devaluating the currency by 15 percent. What followed, however, was a financial disaster for Mexico. The Mexico City stock exchange plummeted, interest rates rose by more than 50 percent and there was a major run on the peso. Late on December 21, Serra announced the peso would be allowed to float freely against the dollar and within twenty-four hours the Mexican currency had lost 30 percent of its value—and was still falling. . . . Mexico once again was on the advent of a foreign debt crisis—with the debt denominated in dollars, the devaluation shrunk Mexico's gross domestic product (GDP) in dollar terms by more than 30 percent, thereby increasing Mexico's foreign debt from 23.5 percent of GDP prior to the devaluation, to 41.3 percent of GDP at the year's end.[87]

The crisis had the effect of bringing about "a decline of real wages of over 50 per cent."[88] As Barkin et al. note:

> The economic crisis saw the collapse of the country's internal market, the virtual disappearance of credit for small and medium-sized businesses, a dramatic contraction of formal employment and an alarming growth of poverty. Twelve months after the peso debacle, an estimated

75% of Mexican families could not afford the "basic basket" of goods and services considered necessary to bring a family above the official poverty line.[89]

Moreover, the end of the crisis proved even more damaging to the average Mexican worker. On 29 December, Serra was forced to resign and on 3 January 1995 the IMF sent a delegation to Mexico. The latter recommended its usual antidote, a cocktail of austerity measures, including a drastic cutting of government expenditure, which generally has an especially harsh impact on the poor since it entails the capping of public-sector workers' wages and the government cutting back on the social services it provides. As MacEoin notes, "As a result of decreased spending on social services, Mexico fell from forty-fifth to fifty-third place on the Human Development Index of the United Nations."[90] All this confirmed Marcos's frequent assertions during the preceding twelve months that the rosy picture of a First World Mexico painted by Salinas over the past six years was false, designed to lull the country into ignoring the unpalatable reality that a considerable number of Mexicans were living in poverty and that the seemingly ebullient economy was a house of cards that at any moment could rapidly come tumbling down.[91] Also justified were Marcos's accusations that Salinas had, through large-scale privatizations, impoverished ordinary Mexicans while enriching his or the PRI's cronies, as were his assertions that the president's economic policy in general was ruinous to the average Mexican.[92] Finally, part of the financial rescue package involved $20 billion pledged, not without debate and reservation,[93] by U.S. President Bill Clinton, on condition that "Mexico's oil revenue would serve as collateral and be paid directly into the Federal Reserve Bank in New York."[94] This was an intolerable indignity to patriotic Mexicans, who are always acutely sensitive to Yanqui interference, since, as Carlos Fuentes observes, "Sovereignty was severely affected: the agreement gave the U.S. the right to monitor Mexico's economic policies."[95] Indeed, Marcos himself described the financial rescue package as "the most ignominious loan in world history."[96] He also wondered whether "the secret conditions agreed to by Mr. Zedillo for the U.S. loan is the condition to annihilate us."[97] Lest anyone suspect the Subcommander of paranoia, it should be remembered that a recent newsletter circulated by the Chase Manhattan Bank had stated that in order to restore foreign investor confidence in Mexico, "the government will need to eliminate the Zapatistas to demonstrate their effective control of the national territory and of security policy."[98] Nor was Chase Manhattan a voice crying out in the desert; Joyce Chang of Saloman Brothers argued that "the success of the government in quelling unrest there will be critical to solving the economic crisis."[99]

Given that some sort of temporary solution to the crisis in Chiapas was required, if only to restore investor confidence in the country, on 23 December, the president dispatched the undersecretary of the interior, Beatriz Paredes, to Chiapas to make contact with the Zapatistas through Bishop Ruiz's mediation body, CONAI, which Zedillo now agreed to recognize. By the 28th, both the Federal Army and the EZLN were pulling back from their advanced positions, and a week later Bishop Ruiz ended his fast. Zedillo, meanwhile, had been forced, in the space of less than three weeks, to effect a complete volte-face toward the situation in Chiapas.

25. Marcos Unmasked and Rafael Revealed

On New Year's Day 1995 the Zapatistas commemorated the first anniversary of their uprising. At Guadalupe Tepeyac, three hundred masked and armed rebels danced the marimba with local peasants, listened to a tape-recorded speech by Subcommander Marcos, and conducted a military parade.[1] The EZLN leadership then announced a unilateral six-day cease-fire, which they subsequently extended on 12 January and finally declared to be indefinite on 16 January. Also on 1 January, the Zapatistas broadcast their *Third Declaration of the Lacandón Jungle*. This represents yet another attempt by Marcos to harness the power of civil society. The preceding twelve months had shown him just how powerful this could prove if channeled correctly, but also, especially recently, just how difficult it was to coordinate. Marcos's new proposal was for the forming of a broad opposition front, to be called the Movimiento de Liberación Nacional (MLN, National Liberation Movement) and to be led by Cárdenas—thus revealing what the Subcommander and the PRD leader had discussed in private on 13 December. The main aims of the MLN were indigenous autonomy, electoral reform, the ousting of the PRI and establishment of a government of transition, and a revised constitution. After the failure of the Second Aguascalientes in November, Marcos no doubt continued to harbor concerns about the viability of consolidating the MLN, but he must have been encouraged by the recent economic crisis, which might prove to have been enough of a catastrophe to drive together the disparate groups which formed civil society. At the very least, Marcos perhaps calculated, many of Mexico's middle class, whose position had in any case always been precarious and had been further compromised by a botched devaluation which had caused savings to plummet 50 percent, would hasten to join in any attempt to dismiss a government they felt responsible for their recent plight and might even empathize more closely with impoverished Indians.

On 15 January the secretary of the interior, Esteban Moctezuma, met the Zapatistas. On the 17th, in an action that could hardly have been coincidental, Zedillo chaired a national political agreement involving all the major parties (the PRI, the PAN, and the PRD) and the new Labor Party that was designed to resolve post-election conflicts throughout the country. The resultant accord was called the Los Pinos Pact. Things were beginning to look up for the beleaguered president until, on the 19th, the local branch of the PRI in Villahermosa, Tabasco, decided to flex its muscles. The reason why the Zapatistas had been prepared to extend their cease-fire indefinitely, and why the PRD had agreed to sign the Los Pinos Pact, was in large part based on Zedillo's concession that in Chiapas Robledo would take a nine-month leave of absence, leaving Avendaño to govern the state from San Cristóbal,[2] while in Tabasco the PRI governor, Roberto Madrazo, would resign in favor of the PRD candidate who many believed had won the election. The local PRI in Tabasco got wind of this agreement, deemed it an intolerable concession to guerrillas and their PRD allies, not to mention a betrayal of the local candidate, party, and voters, and decided to reinstate Madrazo. Ross describes the scene:

> A riot was quickly organized. For hours, drunken PRIistas rampaged through that tropical city [Villahermosa] . . . looting stores, tossing Molotov cocktails, torching cars and beating PRD militants to a pulp while the police stood by, occasionally tear-gassing the press. Madrazo was carried into the government palace on the shoulders of the loutish mob. There would be no deal for his resignation.[3]

Both the Zapatistas and the PRD considered this to be yet another example of the PRI reneging or the weakness of the president in the face of hardliners within his party. It was quite clear to both Marcos and Cárdenas that it was as futile negotiating with the new PRI president as it had been with the old one.

If January had witnessed the dashing of Marcos's hopes of an agreement with the Zedillo administration, then February saw the shattering of his illusions as to the harnessing of civil society for Zapatista ends. From 3 to 5 February the Subcommander coordinated a third convention, held in the city of Querétaro (in the Bajío region of central Mexico), in which he hoped to forge some sort of united opposition front to press home Zapatista demands and unseat the government. As was usual with Marcos, both the timing and the venue were chosen for their historical and symbolic significance. Querétaro had been where the Mexican constitution that had emerged from the Revolution had been signed exactly seventy-eight years before (in 1917). Given this, Zedillo's presence in the city was assured; no doubt, El Sup had planned to upstage the president, rob the PRI of its claim to revolutionary heritage, and force Zedillo to respond (or at least react) to this new coalition. But things did not turn out as planned. The 4,000 participants—different in class, ethnicity, political persuasion, religion, age, occupation, and life experience—proved again so divided that even their hatred of the PRI and the recent financial harm done to them by it could not unite them. Again Ross describes the scene:

> Ideological cat fights broke out in the *mesas*. When the "Plan of Querétaro," which would have officialized the birth of the MLN, was brought to a vote, it was greeted by whistles and rhythmic foot-stomping and the mindless chanting of "*Frente de Masas!*" ("Front of the Masses!").
>
> Just then, Cárdenas and a pride of party cronies strode into the auditorium. Had the CND franchise been sold to the PRD? The jeers (and not a few tossed paper cups) drove Cuauhtémoc from the stage before he could even assume command of the MLN. And thus the Zapatistas' latest scheme for mobilizing civil society died stillborn in a single afternoon of leftist hectoring. With it collapsed the CND, which divided into separate conventions and would never meet again as a single body.[4]

Marcos learned two very important lessons from this. The first was that there were limits to what his charisma could achieve: even he could not unite such disparate factions as had come together at the two Aguascalientes and at Querétaro. The second was that there were also limits to what civil society could accomplish. When stung into action by gross acts of government repression, it could be counted on to mobilize and demonstrate with enough force to halt the government in its tracks. However, in the absence of any direct and immediate threat, it could not agree on a plan of action, let alone be steered toward any fixed goal.

Zedillo's speech, delivered only a few hundred meters away, appeared far more uncompromising toward the Zapatistas than those he had made in January. Indeed, it sounded more like an ultimatum as the president declared that he would turn over future dialogue with the Zapatistas to Congress (PRI dominated and harboring some vehement hard-liners), if the Zapatistas did not agree to immediate negotiation. Zedillo no doubt drew strength from news that the Marcos-inspired third convention had degenerated into a free-for-all. However, more than this, his newfound implacability undoubtedly derived from other new information.

Having been thwarted and humiliated by Marcos throughout the previous year, the Mexican government was given the means to go on the offensive in February 1995 thanks to information provided by a Zapatista defector, himself a former Subcommander who agreed to reveal everything he knew—including Marcos's true identity—about the FLN and EZLN. This defector, who was now calling himself "Javier," turned out to be Salvador Morales Garibay (alias Daniel), who had left the EZLN in 1993 and had fled to the United States, from where he had contacted Mexican army intelligence offering information.[5] A great opportunity presented itself to the government of reversing the losses it had hitherto suffered in the media war.[6]

This is not to say that President Zedillo was motivated only by the desire to reverse these losses. In the complex world of Mexico politics myriad forces were pushing Zedillo toward a swift military solution to the Zapatista problem. First, as Oppenheimer observes, a military offensive would act as a sop to the PRI's hard-liners, who were none too pleased with what they perceived as Salinas's and Zedillo's weakness in dealing with the rebels, and who needed to be appeased in the face of an almost certain victory for the PAN candidate in the forthcoming (12 February) elections in Jalisco.[7] Second, a show of military strength would also help keep the army compliant. This was necessary given that its image as an effective fighting force had been tarnished by Salinas's decision twice to withdraw it from action (after the battle at Corralchén in May 1993 and again in January 1994) and Zedillo's failure to allow it to respond to the recent Zapatista breaking of its military cordon. If Zedillo's new offensive, scheduled for 8 February, worked, news of its success, and in particular the capture of the EZLN leadership, would be announced just after the 82nd Anniversary of the March for Loyalty—Mexico's Army Day parade, where typically the minister of defense gives a speech praising the loyalty of the army—the following day.[8] Finally, and arguably most important, at least to a president whose background was in economics, decisive and conclusive action against the Zapatistas would benefit the flagging Mexican economy. On Wednesday, 8 February, the Mexican stock market index had closed at its lowest level for almost eighteen months. If this desperate economic situation was to be reversed, investors' confidence in Mexico would have to be restored: the country could only attract foreign capital, upon which it had become dependent, if it could successfully promote an image of itself as a stable, burgeoning market. As Oppenheimer notes, "The planned military invasion was also likely to please Wall Street bankers, many of whom were pressing for a decisive action against the Zapatistas as a way to help reverse Mexico's new image of instability."[9] (Here was a classic case of Mexican history repeating itself. Over eighty years previously, another Mexican president, Porfirio Díaz, had attacked Pancho Villa and Pascual Orozco in an attempt to reassure the national and international business community.)[10] However, the military invasion and its failure to capture the EZLN leadership resulted in the opposite effect: "The Mexican stock market fell to its lowest point, along with the value of the peso."[11]

Zedillo's plan was as follows.[12] Salvador Morales would be brought before a judge early on the morning of Wednesday, 8 February.[13] There he would tell the magistrate what he had already told Mexican army intelligence and, based on his testimony, the judge would issue search warrants for FLN safe houses in Mexico City, Cacalomacán (100 km to the east of the capital), and Veracruz. Simultaneously, the Federal Army would advance on EZLN camps in Chiapas in what they called Operation Rainbow. On 9 February, the president would go on national television to announce the discovery of sizable arms caches in the Zapatista safe houses, to disclose Marcos's identity to the Mexican public, and to issue warrants for the arrest of the FLN and EZLN's leadership. With any luck, the Zapatistas would be caught napping and the arrests executed almost before the president had finished his broadcast.

Things, however, did not go according to plan. Although the safe houses were raided and twenty individuals were apprehended, including Elisa in Mexico City and Vicente in *ejido* Gabino Vásquez (Chiapas), Germán managed to escape, evading capture until October 1995, and there were no significant caches of weapons. Thus, when, the president went on television before the nation to justify the new offensive—which was in direct violation of the 1994 cease-fire—claiming to possess evidence showing that "the EZLN were preparing bigger acts of violence, not only in Chiapas but throughout the country . . . [and] were about to start new actions of violence," and emphasizing his commitment "not to remain indifferent to violations of the Constitution, which in this case clearly imply a threat against the people of Mexico and public order,"[14] his claims rang hollow. (Equally unconvincing was Zedillo's assertion that the Federal Army troops dispatched into the Chiapan jungle were only meant to aid the Procuraduría General de la República in arresting five top EZLN commanders.)

In Chiapas, Operation Rainbow proved even less successful—Oppenheimer calls it "a miserable failure."[15] First, although Vicente was arrested, and in less than five days the Federal Army had retaken all the land recently occupied by the EZLN, Marcos managed to escape into the vast Chiapan hinterland. The army had to content itself with venting its frustration on

Aguascalientes, or at least on its structures, in the form of the convention center and library[16] erected there the previous year. As Marcos relates, "when the government troops entered the 'Aguascalientes,' the first things they did were to destroy the little library and the safe house . . . then they destroyed the rest."[17] In a subsequent communiqué he concluded: "The federal forces had no other victory than the destruction of a library, an auditorium for cultural events, a dance floor and the pillaging of the few belongings of the indigenous people of the Lacandón jungle."[18] In response, the Zapatistas turned Augascalientes into a concept, moving it to various other locations in the years that followed (for example, in Oventic, La Realidad, La Garrucha, Morelia, Roberto Barrios, and even in the San Francisco Bay area), leading Collier and Quaratiello to conclude: "Aguascalientes has become a symbolic location that can move from place to place as a forum for meeting with civilians, much as with 'town hall' meetings in the U.S."[19]

Second, and more important in the long run, as Hernández Navarro comments, "The 1995 military offensive against the EZLN . . . did nothing to stop the spread of the autonomous local governments. Within the official geopolitical logic, these municipalities had taken on the same meaning as the liberated Zapatista areas prior to the government offensive."[20]

The official explanation given for the military's failure to seize the Subcommander, despite knowing the precise location of his headquarters and supposedly possessing the element of surprise, was that "a local judge in Chiapas had delayed for several hours the paperwork to carry out the president's order to arrest Marcos,"[21] with the result that, in the words of one of Zedillo's closest aides, "The operation started about twelve hours late."[22] However, this explanation is suspect on several counts. First, given the fact that in 1995 the Chiapan judiciary was PRI dominated, and given the obvious importance of this warrant being issued for the apprehension of Subcommander Marcos, it seems highly unlikely that any Chiapan magistrate would have delayed in this matter. Second, as is abundantly evident from Oppenheimer[23] and several human rights reports,[24] in Mexico City, Cacalomacán, and Veracruz, the police had failed to act in accordance with proper judicial process. Is it really plausible that the Mexican Army would have patiently waited for the proper documents at the risk of missing the opportunity to seize Marcos, while security forces in the capital and elsewhere were showing total disregard for due process? A more realistic explanation is that afforded by Oppenheimer: "Marcos had been tipped off a day earlier . . . [by] Zapatista sympathizers who had heard about the capture of their comrades in Veracruz and Mexico City [and] had telephoned their contacts in San Cristóbal de las Casas, who in turn had radioed Marcos in the jungle."[25] The Subcommander had an escape plan for just such an eventuality, having foreseen the possibility of a surprise government offensive almost a year before. In an interview given in spring 1994 Marcos had observed: "There is a kind of attack the Americans call a surgical strike. This is what we believe the army wants to do: A surgical strike to eliminate me and the committee. It would have low political cost, because they would not be invading and killing many people."[26] This contingency plan now involved an elaborate radio advanced warning system and the dissemination on the Internet—in particular on the EZLN's home page—of rumors of army atrocities, including the bombing of San Cristóbal's suburbs (which had actually occurred in January 1994), mass killings, and systematic rape. Although these reports proved false,[27] because of the speed and the absence of any system of verification of the Internet they had already reached millions and had been presented as fact. In this way, great national and international pressure was put on the government to halt the offensive before it could achieve its aim. As MacEoin observes, "Protest letters published in *La Jornada*, one of the few Mexico City newspapers not controlled by the PRI, came from Nobel Laureates, U.S. film makers, Italian artists, and members of Australia's parliament."[28] Ross provides more specific information concerning the identity of these correspondents, telling us they included such notables as Umberto Eco, Noam Chomsky, Rigoberta Menchú, Willie Nelson, and Adolfo Esquivel Pérez.[29] The media in turn published numerous articles emphasizing the innovative and astute use of cyberspace by the EZLN, thereby focusing yet more attention on Marcos and the Zapatistas.[30] All of this led Mexico's foreign minister, José Angel Gurría, in an April gathering of businessmen and women at the World Trade Center, to dismiss the Zapatista conflict as merely "a war of ink, of the written word and a war of the internet."[31]

In terms of public relations the military offensive proved an unmitigated disaster. Mexican civil society evidently felt it wholly unjustified, and so took to the streets. Three mass demonstrations took place in the capital in a single week. On 11 February, an estimated 100,000 predominantly pro-PRD citizens marched into the central square in Mexico City demanding a halt to the offensive. Moreover, whereas in 1994 their shouts had been neutral—in favor of peace and dialogue between both sides—they now chanted "*todos somos Marcos*" ("We are all Marcos") and "Zapata lives, the struggle continues." On the international scene, as Womack has observed, the offensive "provoked notable pro-Zapatista demonstrations in the United States and across Europe (two in Paris), making Marcos an international pop idol and the Indians of Chiapas famous and fantastically attractive.[32] This led Marcos to date the internationalization of the Zapatista cause to this time, telling one interviewer, "It's after the betrayal of '95 that people remember us: Then the movement took off."[33]

The Mexican government was to receive yet more negative press in succeeding months when a host of human rights organizations, both national and international, published (and posted on the Internet) reports of flagrant abuses committed by the security forces.[34] In America, as Reuters observed, there was a highly publicized campaign conducted by a group of U.S. House members (including Senator Robert Torricelli) and Amnesty International USA to pressure the Mexican government into abandoning its offensive.[35]

President Zedillo identified Marcos as Rafael Sebastián Guillén Vicente live on national television at 6 P.M. on Thursday, 9 February, holding an old photograph[36] of the thirty-seven-year-old, five-feet seven-inch philosophy graduate.[37] Zedillo no doubt hoped that by doing so he would somehow demystify the Subcommander and rob him of his appeal.[38] This was to prove wholly misplaced however. Although the intense, yearlong speculation as to Marcos's identity on the part of Mexican people was now at an end, he appeared to have lost none of his appeal, especially among women. (As de la Grange and Rico observe: "The uncovering of Marcos did not cause dejection among his numerous [female] admirers who had allowed their imaginations to gallop away with them during these months and who, at any rate, were not disposed to break the spell."[39] Marcos himself would quip in his first communiqué after Zedillo had unmasked him: "This new Subcomandante Marcos, is he handsome? Because lately they have thrown at me only ugly ones and it ruins all the correspondence from females.")[40] In the weeks that followed, a public opinion poll on the issue of Marcos's unmasking was undertaken. Ross observes, "*Reforma* reported that 50% of those polled did not buy Zedillo's identification, and of the half that did, 22% didn't think the *Sup* had done anything wrong anyway."[41]

In short, Marcos's mystery identity proved only partially responsible for his popularity;[42] his personality, lifestyle, and cause were all far more significant. Quite why the government believed that "the revelation of the Zapatista leaders' identities would help undo Subcommander Marcos' larger-than-life image and reduce him to an ordinary terrorist,"[43] remains a puzzle. After all, Che Guevara, arguably the world's greatest revolutionary icon, had not suffered because everyone knew that he was a middle-class, Argentine doctor named Ernesto. When interviewed almost exactly six years later, in March 2001, by Gabriel García Márquez and Roberto Pombo, Marcos responded to the question "If everyone knows who you are, why the mask?" with "A touch of coquetry. They don't know who I am, but it doesn't matter to them anyway. At stake is what Subcomandante Marcos is, not who he was."[44]

Worse still, from the government's point of view, the public's predominantly favorable perception of the Zapatistas continued undiminished, despite their flight into the jungle and the exposure of their Subcommander. As MacEoin observes, "An opinion poll taken in Mexico City in April showed that 75 percent of the capital sympathized with them."[45] In other words, Salinas's claims of an imminent Zapatista campaign of terror had had almost no effect on the Zapatistas's popularity, public support for the latter having dropped a mere 3 percent since 9 December.[46]

In one way, and in one way only, was the government's offensive a success. As Thomas Benjamin observes, "Although Marcos and most other leaders escaped arrest, any remaining mystique of the EZLN as a military force was now thoroughly shattered."[47] The *Dallas Morning News* ran a story which opened: "Subcomandante Marcos threatened war for more than a year; but when Mexican troops finally closed in, the rebel leader had only one choice: he ran for his life."[48] Much of the Zapatistas's bargaining power had come from its threat of arms,[49] but it could no longer pass itself off as an effective armed reformist group or an armed pressure group if no one believed it had the military capability to carry out its threats.[50] From now on Marcos would have to play down the EZLN's threat of military action and emphasize its ability to mobilize civil society and harness the power of the media. Of course, some observers saw a more noble reason behind the Zapatistas's refusal to fight. They pointed to the Zapatistas desire to protect the villages that acted as their support base and a general, laudable, pacifistic desire not to kill. As Ross would put it: "The EZLN's decision to retreat without firing a single shot revealed a soft-heartedness that betrayed the Zapatistas' military pretensions."[51] Much of Mexican society, sickened by the violence of 1994, would see heroism in such soft-heartedness.

In the aftermath of the failed offensive, the government attempted to gain at least some advantage from having mobilized against the Zapatistas by intimidating and investigating any groups it felt had either sympathized with or aided the Zapatistas at any time. The security forces listed 2,275 individuals involved with the EZLN, which "included 134 members of religious orders (some Mexican and others foreign), as well as three bishops, Samuel Ruiz, Arturo Loma Reyes (Tehuantepec), and José Luis Dibildo Martínez (Tarahumara)."[52] As a result, the "houses of the Jesuits and Dominicans and of other religious orders were searched from top to bottom, as were the San Cristóbal offices of CONPAZ, the coalition of Mexican non-governmental organizations (NGOS) committed to the defense of human rights."[53] As a Human Rights Watch Americas report put it:

> When the Mexican government began a crackdown on the EZLN in February 1995, the Catholic Church in Chiapas was among the targets. The crackdown was initiated when an alleged government informant said that Bishop Ruiz provided arms to the EZLN. Police arrested lay Catholic workers and attempted to arrest Father Javier Ruiz Velasco of Teopisca on February 12. On February 15, police with a warrant searched the San Jacinto de Polonia church and rectory for arms, finding nothing.[54]

The pronouncements of the Episcopal Conference of Latin American Bishops, which also met in February, did little to dissuade Ernest Zedillo's pro-neoliberal, free-market government from believing that the Catholic Church was diametrically opposed to it. The bishops denounced the current continent-wide economic conditions, defined as "the many signs of death which appear everywhere: extreme poverty, growing unemployment, uncontainable violence and so many forms of corruption and impunity which submerge millions of families in anguish and pain."[55] There followed a spate of expulsions of foreign priests, including (in May alone) those of Rodolfo Izal Elorz (from Spain), Loren Riebe (from the United States), and Jorge Alberto Barón Guitein (from Argentina), all without even lip service being paid to due process. Then, on 15 September, father Paul John Nadolny was refused reentry into Mexico on an alleged minor technicality. (It is surely not coincidental that this priest had acted as a witness on behalf of PRD victims of an attack by PRI supporters that had led to the shooting of two men in the hamlet of Lote Ocho in Salto de Agua municipality on 15 March.)[56]

Meanwhile, the Subcommander was on the run. He had fled his jungle hideout near Guadalupe Tepeyac just in time. Federal Army troops, descending by helicopter, found it had been hastily abandoned. In his hurry,

Marcos left behind some personal effects, among them "*History Will Absolve Me*, by Fidel Castro, and *Revolutionary Works*, by Che Guevara, next to Microsoft Windows manuals and a pipe."[57] He headed for the interior of the Lacandón jungle, to the Montes Azules, a place he knew well from his early days in Chiapas. This was now a United Nations biosphere, making a full-scale Federal Army assault on it a dubious proposition for the Mexican government in terms of its international image. Here, the EZLN comandancia eventually re-grouped, having split up in order to lessen the chance of complete capture, and planned its next course of action.

Marcos himself has left an account of his escape from the Federal Army in the form of a communiqué dispatched to the Mexican and international press (dated 20 February). It is an important document which demands analysis, not because it provides an accurate factual account of Marcos's escape — it almost certainly does not — but because it reveals much about both the image he is attempting to construct of himself and the influences that underpin this image.

> At dawn on the fifteenth we were going to drink our own urine. I say, "We were going to," because we didn't do it; we all began to vomit after the first swallow. Previously there had been a discussion. Although we all agreed that each person should drink his or her own urine, Camilo suggested we wait until dawn and let the night cool the urine in the canteens so we could drink it imagining it to be soda. In defense of his suggestion, Camilo argued that he had heard on the radio that imagination made anything possible. I opposed the idea, suggesting that time would only make the odor stronger, and that the radio had not been too objective lately. . . . Finally, we decided to take a sip, all at the same time, to see what would happen.
>
> I don't know who began the "concert," but almost immediately we all began to vomit what we had ingested, and also what we hadn't. We were left even more dehydrated, prostrate on the ground, like dunces, stinking of urine. I think that our image was hardly soldier-like. Hours before sun up, a sudden rain washed over us, alleviating our thirst and our spirits. With the first light of the sixth day we continued walking. In the afternoon, we reached the outskirts of a small village. Camilo went to ask for something to eat.
>
> He returned with a little fried pork, hard and cold. We ate it right there without any modesty. In a few minutes the cramps had began. The diarrhea was memorable. We were strewn at the foot of a small wooded

hill. A federal troops patrol passed us by a mere 500 meters away. They didn't find us because God is grand. The smell of shit and urine could be smelled kilometers away.[58]

De la Grange and Rico dismiss this as an "anecdote, which like many others, was invented from start to finish with the aim of sensitizing the EZLN's urban supporters and mobilizing them against the military offensive unleashed by the government,"[59] citing as proof of the tale's fallacy the observation that water is not in short supply in Chiapas, where it rains for eight months of the year. However, this is to miss the point. Marcos here is not aiming at faithfully recounting the days following the Federal Army's offensive; he is crafting an image, the image of the mock-heroic guerrilla.[60]

The story of drinking urine Marcos evidently borrowed from Che's *Bolivian Diary* where, under the heading for 30 August 1967, Guevara wrote: "The situation was becoming distressing. The machete users were suffering fainting spells. Miguel and Darío drank their own urine, as did Chino, with the unfortunate result of diarrhea and cramps."[61] (Pancho Villa's troops are also said to have drank their horses' urine when crossing Coahuila desert in July 1920, an anecdote with which Marcos must have been equally acquainted.)[62] So too, the "concert" effects of drinking urine described by Marcos bear a striking likeness to the "veritable organ concert" of "a day of belching, farting, vomiting, and diarrhea" described by Che in the same diary.[63] Similarly, Che recounts a case of dysentery he contracted which caused him to soil himself while being stretchered around. He claims that his comrades "loaned me a pair of pants, but without water my stench could be smelled a league away."[64] This was perhaps the source of inspiration for Marcos's final sentence.

It is clear from another communiqué dated the same day that Marcos was writing very much with his hero, Che Guevara, in mind. He asks those in charge of capturing him, "What is your next move? Go to Yeso in Jatate? Or the Break in Yuro in Montes Azules?"[65] As Castañeda observes, "The rearguard of Che's guerrilla column in Bolivia was annihilated in Vado del Yeso," while "Che himself was taken prisoner at la Quebrada de Yuro, on the outskirts of a town called La Higuera."[66]

Moreover, in another communiqué written soon after, in which Marcos again details his escape, the Subcommander's writing appears very much in keeping with Che's frequently self-mocking syle.[67] Marcos discusses his current flight with his alter ego, defending himself against the accusation that he "ran" by repeatedly calling his action (unconvincingly even to himself) a "strategic withdrawal" and a "tactical retreat." Che did much the same sort of thing in his *Diary of the Cuban Revolutionary War*: "I must confess that my rifle caused neither death nor wounds, for I did nothing more than beat a speedy 'strategic retreat.'"[68] Che repeats this phrase again in his entry for March–April 1957: "There I found a piece of my blanket, tangled in the brambles as a reminder of my speedy 'strategic retreat.'"[69]

In several subsequent communiqués, issued in February and March, Marcos taunted the government for its failure to catch him, berated Zedillo's duplicity, decried the army's destruction of peasants' property; mocked the pompous tone of the attorney general's office's arrest warrant for him; and even engaged in some defiant guerrilla posturing.[70] In short, the government offensive had given the Subcommander plenty of ammunition for the continuance of his war of words.

On Valentine's Day, only five days after the offensive was launched, Zedillo called a halt to the military operation. He then offered the Zapatistas amnesty—an offer that had already been made by Salinas in January 1994 and had been brutally rebuffed by Marcos in his communiqué asking "Who should ask for forgiveness and who can grant it?" Without waiting for another possible refusal from the Zapatista leadership—and in particular another savage rebuttal from the Subcommander—Zedillo drafted the offer as a law and sent it to Congress for ratification. This became the Law for Dialogue, Reconciliation, and a Dignified Peace in Chiapas passed on 11 March. It established basic rules concerning the dialogue, the mediators, and the location at which any future talks would take place, while forbidding further troop deployment in Chiapas during the negotiation process. In line with this law, Congress created the cross-party Comisión de Concordia y Pacificación (COCOPA, Mediation and Pacification Commission), consisting of members from five different political parties with a rotating chair.[71] Zedillo also temporarily suspended the arrest warrants for Marcos, Germán, and other leading EZLN and FLN cadres and arranged for the resignation of Chiapas's PRI governor. In case the EZLN (or the PRI party hardliners and the military) was tempted to view this as a sign of weakness, the president also issued the ultimatum that unless negotiations began within 30 days he would order the reinstatement of the arrest warrants.

The offensive had of course laid bare the vulnerability of the Zapatistas's support communities to army incursions. There had been numerous reports, both during and immediately after the offensive, of soldiers destroying and stealing property, money, livestock, and tools and indulging in wanton acts of vandalism and desecration.[72] To deter any further hostile action on the part of the Federal Army, peace camps were established predominantly in Zapatista-held territory. These were generally staffed by foreigners who had been invited by the diocese or by NGOs affiliated with Bishop Ruiz's Fray Bartolomé Human Rights Center, and their presence was greatly welcomed by the Subcommander, who, in a communiqué dated 17 March (St. Patrick's Day), lauded them as modern-day San Patricios—the famous Irish volunteer force that fought against American imperialism in the 1846–48 war.[73]

Having no other option, the Zapatistas agreed to come to the peace table. However, in the weeks during the run-up to the talks Marcos tried to make the best of a bad hand by proposing a venue in Mexico City. Having failed almost exactly a year before to get the Zapatistas's national demands even discussed, the Subcommander again decided to try to nationalize the EZLN's struggle by having the talks take place in the capital. He proposed four sites in the heart of Mexico City as possible locations. (Marcos possibly reasoned that the EZLN had now become a national force, given that several thousand Mexico City denizens had flocked to the National Democratic Convention [CND] at Aguascalientes only six months previously.) Unsurprisingly, Zedillo would hear none of it.[74] Nor would he brook the Zapatistas's next choice of venue, neighboring Belize—for if the president was reluctant to nationalize the Chiapas uprising he was even less enthusiastic about its internationalization. Indeed, Zedillo pushed hard for the venue to be within Zapatista-held territory, so as to limit the talks' scope as much as possible. In the end, on 8 April, just as the thirty-day deadline was about to expire, the government and the Zapatistas met in the Zapatista village of San Miguel. Also present were representatives from COCOPA and Bishop Ruiz's peace-brokering committee, CONAI. Outside, members of civil society again formed a peace cordon around the Zapatistas, as they had done during the peace talks in the cathedral. They were joined by many locals, who chanted their praise for Marcos and their condemnation of the government—the price Zedillo had to pay for talks within Zapatista territory. In short, the EZLN negotiators would have all the benefits of a team that plays on home turf.

In this first session, which Marcos did not participate in personally, the government and the Zapatistas merely agreed on a set of preconditions necessary for further negotiation, known as the San Miguel Accord. The meeting date was set for 20 April, at San Andrés Larraínzar, also located within an autonomous municipality deep in Zapatista heartland. Again, the government's insistence on a venue within the conflict zone—and specifically in an area that comprised 20,000 indigenous people distributed throughout 46 pro-Zapatista communities—would have uncomfortable repercussions for its negotiators. Not the least of these was the appearance at the talks of 7,000 indigenous supporters wearing traditional garb and chanting *vivas* for Marcos and chants hostile toward the government. (What the government gained—given that San Andrés Larráinzar is located in the highlands—was a venue far less accessible than San Cristóbal had been in 1994.) The buildings in which the talks took place were little more than hastily erected temporary shelters constructed on a basketball court—a far cry from the picturesque yet imposing cathedral of San Cristóbal.

The main point for discussion was now control of territory. The Zapatistas wanted the Federal Army to retreat to the positions it held prior to the February offensive, while the government proposed a bizarre "corralling" scheme, whereby the Zapatistas would be assigned three enclaves in which they would remain until negotiations had been successfully concluded. Unsurprisingly, given the disparity between the two sides' demands, no agreement could be reached. This round of the talks ended, but both the EZLN and the government agreed to meet again on 12 May.

When talks were renewed the Zapatistas made a new proposal: that if the army withdrew to its pre-February positions, the Zapatistas would undertake not to fill the vacuum. The government flatly rejected the idea, unwilling to give up territory it had so recently recovered. Instead, the government negotiators proposed that the Zapatistas could retain their authority in the zones they occupied, provided that the Federal Army was free to patrol eight routes that ran through this territory. Two days later, on 14 May, the government and the Zapatistas signed a "minimum accord" by which they agreed to meet again on 7 June, after the EZLN had consulted its support base communities on whether to accept the new proposal.

This time, unlike the previous year, the Zapatistas invited along observers—including members of the government's negotiating team (who declined the invitation)—to witness the consultation process. They were no doubt sensitive to accusations made previously that the decision to reject the government's peace initiative in 1994 had been taken by Marcos and other leading cadres, not by the people.[75] As Weinberg puts it: "The EZLN scored a media coup by inviting federal negotiators to observe *consultas*, undermining the government's claim that the *consultas* were a myth and all decisions were really made by Marcos and his cabal of violent extremists."[76] They would do the same again in spring 1996, when the EZLN consulted its base communities as to accepting the San Andrés Accords on Indian rights and culture.

On 7 June the two sides reconvened as arranged. The first two days saw fruitless discussion over control of territory, and in particular the extent and nature of troop movement and deployment along the eight proposed patrol routes. With no headway made (and none imminent), the CONAI team proposed turning the discussion toward meeting the Zapatistas's demands. In marked contrast to the previous year's negotiations, the EZLN did not lump all its demands together—to be rejected or accepted in their entirety—but proposed a series of *mesas* (tables), each of which would discuss certain issues, democracy and justice, Indian rights and culture, women's rights, agrarian rights and economic welfare, and so on. The Zapatista leadership had clearly learned from its mistakes and was now attempting to apply the techniques it had developed during the National Democratic Convention the preceding August to its discussions with the government. Once again, however, as in 1994, the government negotiating team flatly refused to discuss national issues, and talks broke off once more on 12 June. The next session was scheduled for 4 July.

At the fourth San Andrés meeting, the government opened by reiterating its rejection of the Zapatistas's rights to discuss national issues. The Zapatistas, for their part, had been busy during the intervening three weeks formulating their ideas on the precise form and structure of the *mesas*. These proved complex and confounded the government side, which had given very little thought to the actual working of the *mesas*. They requested a recess of almost three weeks to examine and react to these proposals.

The fifth San Andrés meeting began on 24 July. The government team was by now becoming exasperated with the length of the talks. They had no doubt calculated on swift progress, given that the 1994 talks, though ultimately a failure, had at least moved at a fairly rapid pace. Moreover, the government team evidently believed that this time the Zapatistas would surely be even more disposed to peaceful overtures given their military vulnerability. In order to speed things along, it threatened to do what Salinas had done in the spring and early summer of 1994—namely to pump massive sums of money into Chiapas in order to buy off the Zapatistas's support bases. Refusing to submit to such pressure, the Zapatistas again pressed their rights to discuss national matters. With no progress likely, both sides again agreed to postpone discussions until 5 September—significantly, after the Zapatistas's August 27 Consulta for Democracy and

Peace in Chiapas. However, both sides agreed to exchange their respective proposals for the themes and procedures of the *mesas* by 20 August.

The Consulta, which had been proposed by the CCRI in a communiqué in June, was conducted on behalf of the Zapatistas in all 2,438 Mexican municipalities and in both the United States and Europe by the independent electoral supervisory body, Alianza Cívica (Civic Alliance). It asked respondents to answer yes or no to five questions: (1) Did they agree with the Zapatistas' eleven basic demands from 1994? (2) Should democratic forces unite to realize these demands? (3) Would profound reform be required in order to transform Mexico into a true democracy? (4) Should the EZLN transform itself into a political force? (5) Should the EZLN join democratic organizations to create a new oppositional alliance? The CND added a sixth: Should women be given an equal role in a newly democratized Mexico?

To issue in the Consulta, the CND convened in Mexico City on the anniversary of Aguascalientes. To be more precise, two convocations were held, one for the ultras and one for the moderates—the CND, always a loose and fragile confederation of disparate groups, had already fractured. The moderate convocation was presided over by Rosario Ibarra, veteran leader of the Mothers of the Disappeared movement and—coincidentally or not—former neighbor and friend of the family of Germán. At this event a ninety-minute video address by Marcos was shown on a giant television screen. This was the first major public appearance by the Subcommander in months (and even this was not in person): Marcos had taken a backseat during all the San Andrés discussions, allowing Comandantes Tacho and David to come to the fore.

The Consulta itself involved 10,000 polling stations located in twenty-four of the nation's thirty-two states. There was even a special children's Consulta in which 200,000 juveniles cast their vote. In the capital, voting booths were placed in very accessible and high-profile locations such as major public plazas and entrances to subway stations. In Chiapas, 1,307 communal assemblies were called and the six questions debated in traditional indigenous communal assemblies. Internationally, the Consulta was a massive public relations success. In North America, Hollywood stars such as Antonio Banderas, his partner Melanie Griffith, Salma Hayek, and Susan Sarandon took part, as did the directors Quentin Tarantino and Oliver Stone. Meanwhile, in Europe, and in particular in Italy—in Milan alone 50,000 cast their votes at a massive rally—participation in and support for the Consulta was tremendous: 1.3 million votes were cast. Interestingly, as Ross observes, "The most votes previously tallied in such a citizens' plebiscite, a call for the indictment of the universally reviled Carlos Salinas, was 600,000 votes."[77] Questions one, two, and three, not unsurprisingly, received a 90-plus percent affirmative. Questions four and five drew responses of just over 50 percent affirmative in the former and a little under that in the latter.

On the last day of August, the eve of Zedillo's first State of the Nation address, and less than a week before the next scheduled San Andrés negotiations were about to begin, Marcos issued a statement that the dialogues had become *agotado*. The word is generally used to mean "exhausted," "used up," "depleted," or "flat," carrying with it a connotation similar to the English "spent." However, like "spent," *agotado* can also be taken to mean "finished," and this was the interpretation the press placed on it. Once again, as in 1994, Marcos had been misunderstood in his terminology concerning the peace talks underway. A year before, the press had interpreted Marcos's statement that the government had "addressed" most of the Zapatistas's demands as the government having "resolved" them—such was the air of optimism for those wishing peace in a troubled Mexico that spring. Now, the atmosphere was much more pessimistic, with *agotado* being interpreted widely as "exhausted" or "broken off."

Despite this misunderstanding, the 5 September talks began. Moreover, not inconsiderable progress was made, at least when compared with some of the earlier sessions.[78] CONAI had distilled the Zapatistas's sixteen proposed *mesas* into just four: Indian rights and culture; democracy and justice; development and welfare; and women's rights. For its part, the government agreed to form special "forums" for discussion of national issues, the proposals of which would then go before Congress for ratification or rejection. The order in which these *mesas* would take place was, however, controversial. The Zapatistas, aware that talks were being conducted in Mexico City between the government and the opposition parties on precisely the issue of electoral reform, pushed for Democracy and Justice to be the first subject of debate, so that they could contribute to the current discussions in the capital. The government opposed this, not wishing to give the Zapatistas the opportunity to involve themselves in any national issue. Instead, it pushed for Indian Rights and Culture, hoping that this would be perceived by the press and the public as a local (or at least a minority) issue and so be overshadowed by the national debate over electoral reform. After much discussion, the government had its way, with Indian Rights and Culture being scheduled for discussion at the seventh San Andrés meeting on 1 October. Both sides would be permitted to bring their own hand-picked team of advisors to the talks.

Before this took place, at the end of September, and over six months since his last public appearance in person, Marcos rode out of the jungle and into La Realidad to be met by members of COCOPA, Bishop Ruiz, and various elements of civil society. Ross describes the Subcommander's grand entrance:

> A gaunt horseman, flanked by a hundred armed troops, thundered in from the dark mountain under a hangnail moon and entered the hamlet of La Realidad, 15 kilometers east of Guadalupe Tepeyac, where the locals were building a new Aguascalientes to welcome their leaders in from the cold.
>
> The Sup's familiar figure, equipped with trademark bandoliers and Sherlock Homes [sic] pipe, seemed so thin and pale that he had to convince the onlookers that he really was who he said he was. "Pardon my sad physique—the months have been difficult ones—but I really am Marcos," he told the crowd that had turned out to greet him.[79]

Quite what had happened to Marcos since the military offensive is unknown. As we have seen, his own communiqués relate that he had had to flee at a moment's notice and make the arduous—though probably not as arduous as he claimed—trek into the interior with the Federal Army hot on his heels. However, he had released details of his adventures shortly afterward, so we must assume that no serious calamity had befallen him that spring. Likewise, his decision to make Comandantes Tacho and David head the San Andrés Accords need not be taken to suggest anything other than that Marcos was attempting to remedy what he (and many others) perceived to be the failings of the previous year, when the Subcommander had stolen all the limelight and had overshadowed the peace talks in the Cathedral. However, Marcos's pitiful appearance in late September is perplexing: what had happened to make Marcos lose the "incipient pot-belly" Oppenheimer had described in late July 1994 and become so gaunt?[80] Ross notes how August is an especially terrible month in Chiapas, being at the height of the rainy season, and that "jungle living" during that month entails "incessant assault from zancudos, chaquistes, garrapatas [mosquitoes, sand fleas, and ticks], and other household pests, and . . . only thin pozol (corn gruel) for dinner."[81] Marcos had lived in the jungle before, when he first came to Chiapas, but this was now almost a decade away. Was it ten years of camp life that had made jungle living hard, especially for a man in his late thirties? Or was there some other explanation, possibly a subsequent jungle illness? (The Subcommander had previously contracted acute gastritis in March 1992 and went to Mexico City for treatment—an option that was no longer open to him.) It is interesting to note that there have been several occasions during the period from 1994 onward when the Subcommander has remained silent, simply disappearing for months and months at a time.

In any event, despite Marcos's condition, the meeting in La Realidad was a great success. It did much to cement a bond of goodwill between the COCOPA members and the Subcommander (neither of whom had previously met). As Ross put it, "The get-together, on the eve of the initial October round of talks in San Andrés, would smooth the way for substantive talks on Indian Rights and Culture and reaffirm EZLN participation in the 'national dialogue.'"[82] It would seem that the eating, drinking, singing, and dancing indulged in by the Zapatista leadership and COCOPA members that evening formed a bond of respect and liking that even the formal and often tense atmosphere of subsequent negotiations could not easily erase.

The following day, the eighth session of the San Andrés talks commenced. The Zapatistas now turned to discussion of indigenous autonomy, for which they had pressed as early as the February/March 1994 peace talks.[83] The issue had been given special topicality by events in neighboring Guatemala—on 31 March that country's government and the Guatemalan National Revolutionary Union had signed an accord on Identity and the Rights of Indigenous Peoples[84]—and by the fact that 1995 marked the start of the Decade of the World's Indigenous People (1995–2004), declared by the United Nations.[85] This session was brief, simply establishing the ground rules for the coming debate on Indian rights and culture. There would be six *mesas*—five held in San Cristóbal and the main one in San Andrés—to which both sides would bring their advisors. The government team would comprise 215 members, mainly officials from the National Indigenous Institute, the CNC (precisely those pro-PRI indigenous *campesinos* accused by the Zapatistas of selling out to the government by accepting funds in return for their support), and Tzotzil scholar Jacinto Arias (head of the state Indian Affairs organization). The Zapatistas invited 358 guests. Among these were eminent members of civil society; scholars (predominantly anthropologists and agrarian historians); the Chiapas governor-in-rebellion, Amado Avendaño; representatives of the numerous indigenous groups in Chiapas; the *Abejas* (Bees), a pacifist organization of coffee and honey producers from the central highlands of Chiapas; and, cleverly, three deported foreign priests who had recently been expelled by the Mexican government and seventeen alleged Zapatistas who had been arrested during the February offensive. The eighth San Andrés talks would begin discussing Indian Rights and Culture on 18 October.

In the intervening few days, on 15 October, Chiapas state elections took place in which local presidents for the 112 municipalities comprising Chiapas were to be elected. The elections were marked by massive voter abstention (67 percent), which led to the PRI sweeping the board. In some areas, especially in the north of Chiapas, abstention resulted from fear—in Tila, pro-PRI White Guards ensured at gunpoint that all voters chose PRI candidates. Elsewhere, in EZLN-controlled spheres, the Zapatistas themselves counseled abstention as a means of signaling to the world the extent and power of the Zapatista movement.[86] This it did, but at a considerable cost: the PRI took 84 of 109 municipalities and every one of the 21 local congressional districts. The only significant gain for the opposition was the PAN's surprise taking of the state capital, Tuxtla.

Three days later the next round of the San Andrés talks commenced. Nearly five hundred invitees were present, as were twenty Zapatista Comandantes. The talks lasted six days. Much of the debate was conducted in various indigenous languages, much to the chagrin of the predominantly white, monoglot Spanish-speaking government negotiators—the same people who, at previous San Andrés sessions, had complained that progress was too slow because they could not understand the Zapatista delegates' halting Spanish. The government side could not readily follow discussion in these languages and, worse still, the common bond of language between both sides' indigenous delegates appeared to be uniting them.[87] One government advisor, Magda Gómez from the Instituto Nacional Indigenista (National Indigenous Institute), even defected to the Zapatista side and was not alone in doing so. Finally, almost all delegates agreed that discussion on Indian Rights and Culture could not be restricted to Chiapas, but was of national importance. From this point on, autonomy would become "a kind of umbrella demand, encompassing a host of cultural, political, economic and social grievances . . . some . . . unique to Indian communities—such as the exercise of Indian law—others overlap[ping] quite extensively with demands articulated from within civil society."[88] After six days, COCOPA and CONAI proposed a brief recess, until 13 November, for both sides to take stock. All appeared relatively happy with how things had proceeded so far.

As the two sides went their separate ways, pledging to return to the table in November, an event took place in Mexico City that threatened to jeopardize the entire peace process. Federal police stopped Comandante Germán on his way back from visiting friends and arrested him for allegedly having two firearms and 1.4 grams of cocaine in his possession.[89] The current suspension of his arrest warrant did not allow exemption from any new, post-February, infractions. Germán was held briefly in Military Camp Number One before being arraigned for the possession of firearms (the drug charge was dropped). News of the arrest had a dramatic impact on the EZLN comandancia, who began withdrawing into the jungle. If Germán could be arrested at the drop of a hat, so could Marcos and at least ten other EZLN/FLN members who had outstanding warrants against them. They must also have reasoned that if the government was capable of such a volte-face at a crucial time, how could it be trusted to abide by any agreement reached at San Andrés? Interestingly, Germán had been picked up by police while Zedillo was out of the country, raising the question of whether this was done behind his back, either (at the low level) by overzealous police officers or (at the high level) by hard-liners determined to wreck the San Andrés Accords.

The government was under pressure, not only from the withdrawal of the EZLN negotiating team, but also from the head of the COCOPA, who threatened to resign if Germán was found guilty and sentenced. The charges were dropped, on the unconvincing technicality that Germán had misinterpreted the conditions of his legal immunity.

The next round of the San Andrés Accords could therefore open, as scheduled, on 13 November 1995, with very little sign of the stress of the past few days. One thing that had changed, however, was the government's negotiation team: gone were the indigenous advisors, replaced by white state bureaucrats.[90] Moreover, the government team now repeatedly referred to the indigenous as *comunidades indígenas* (Indian communities), in contrast with the Zapatistas's *Pueblos Indios* (Indian peoples). There was a world of difference between establishing rights for an Indian nation or Indian peoples on one hand and Indian communities on the other—the former were clearly national in scope, the latter regional. Despite these problems, the ninth San Andrés talks succeeded in arriving at fifty-seven points of consensus. A shared commitment to some level of Indian autonomy was agreed, as was the right of indigenous people to establish their own forms of organization—both of which had to some extent already been granted to indigenous people by the governments of Panama

(1925–38), Nicaragua (1984–87), Colombia (1991), and Bolivia (1993),[91] and would soon be granted by their Ecuadorian (1998) and Venezuelan (1999) counterparts. Key points, however, still eluded agreement, in particular revision to article 27, one of the main reasons behind the indigenous *campesinos* having taken up arms in the first place. The ninth session ended on 19 November, with a Zapatista proposed Magna Forum on Indian Rights and Culture sponsored by COCOPA being set for 3–8 January 1996 in San Cristóbal. The tenth session of the San Andrés talks would follow on 10 January.

While December saw no negotiations between the two sides, this did not mean that the government remained inactive in Chiapas; rather, it stepped up its military activity. Army patrols and flyovers were all increased in the run-up to Christmas. These were so intense that the EZLN comandancia had to cancel a proposed further meeting with COCOPA on 4 December. They also created a general atmosphere of tension and fear. This was, no doubt, intended: the government hoped such activity would sap the will of the Zapatistas and their base communities to prolong negotiations.

Outside the now severely curtailed Zapatista territory, however, the Chiapan peasantry had been on the move, accelerating the rate and number of land takeovers. In 1994 there had been over a thousand of these operations; 1995 witnessed more than two thousand.[92] Although hemmed in themselves, the Zapatista example had unleashed what appeared to be a growing tide of land seizures.

26. Nationalizing and Internationalizing the Struggle

The year 1996 was perhaps the EZLN's zenith in the period after the uprising, for it witnessed the establishing of the Frente Zapatista de Liberación (FZLN, Zapatista National Liberation Front), the negotiation of the San Andrés Accord, the convocation of La Realidad, and the Intercontinental Encuentro. Marcos, as always, was the star around which all these orbited.

On 1 January 1996 the EZLN issued *The Fourth Declaration of the Lacandón Jungle*, written, as usual, by Marcos, although signed by the CCRI-CG (general command). Ana María read it out to a crowd of hundreds, including some highly dedicated Europeans (most notably a large contingent of Italians), at La Realidad, filmed by camera crews from Europe, Asia, and South America. It differed from the first three Declarations in that its main emphasis was on the indigenous aspect of the Zapatista cause. True, indigenous peoples' rights had featured to varying degrees in the Second and Third Declarations (although, significantly, not explicitly in the First), but had not been their main focus. Now, in the midst of discussion between the EZLN and the government on indigenous autonomy, this document had the effect of ensuring that this issue would engage the attention of the western European and North American presses.

The Fourth Declaration also called for the establishment of the FZLN in order to cement the connection between the jungle based Zapatistas and Mexican civil society—the first step toward becoming the political force called for in the August Consulta. Thus far, the link had proved effective but erratic and therefore ultimately unpredictable.[1] *Tiempo* and *La Jornada* both regularly published Marcos's communiqués, and the EZLN's civil cells in Mexico City had been active on their behalf, while the CND and the MLN had enjoyed some degree of success. However, the formation of the FZLN strengthened this bond, enabling Marcos to reach out to Mexican society and the world at large. As he subsequently explained, "We need new forms, because as it stands now, the people can only sympathize with us and not participate in our work."[2] Money could now easily be raised, propaganda readily distributed, demonstrations better orchestrated, and the international media kept abreast of events in remote Chiapas. So as not to appear acting as civil society's vanguard—with all the unpalatable connotations that had traditionally accompanied Leftist vanguards—Marcos declared that he and the Clandestine Committee would not be joining it.

On 3 January began the Special Forum on Indian Rights and Culture proposed by the Zapatistas and by COCOPA in San Cristóbal. A total of 359 indigenous representatives—not just from Mexico but from throughout the continent—flocked to the city. One scholar has persuasively viewed the forum as "One of the strategies the EZLN employed to keep pressure on the government during the dialogue process . . . us[ing] popular mobilization—congresses, marches, and peaceful demonstrations—to demonstrate the support that it had from 'civil society.'"[3] This strategy bears Marcos's hallmark; it is the one he perfected and pursued persistently from 1 January 1994. As in the San Andrés series of discussions, Comandantes David and Tacho led the Zapatista delegation of twenty-four EZLN members, with Marcos arriving four days later to close the event.[4] As in the case of the MLN, the forum had been marked by heated debate. Nonetheless, a concluding document representing a general consensus was agreed upon and publicized. The San Andrés Accords signed the following month would largely reflect its proposals.[5]

The tenth San Andrés talks began on 10 January. The government made a new offer. Conceding that discussions over Indian Rights and Culture were indeed national in scope, it was prepared to grant a limited indigenous system of justice and the authority to appoint local authorities. However, Zedillo's team flatly rejected any notion of indigenous autonomy at the municipal or regional level. Faced with what appeared to be a conciliation and (relative) flexibility on the government's part, some of the Zapatistas's advisors counseled acceptance, if only because they felt that this was the best offer they could reasonably expect from Zedillo. Thus, on 18 January, the Zapatista delegation, under pressure from their own advisors, agreed to refer the government's proposals to their communities. History was in danger of repeating itself. Would the base communities reject the offer as they had done almost two years previously? Sensing the potential for repetition, and wishing to avoid it, Marcos cynically quipped, "tell the PRI not to kill any more of its leaders until we have finished with the Consulta"[6]—a reference to Colosio's assassination. Again the Zapatistas invited witnesses to observe their consultation with their support bases.

Six weeks later, on St. Valentine's Day, the Zapatistas revealed the results of their consultation. In stark contrast to the results of the 1994 Consulta, 97 percent of respondents voted in favor of accepting the government's offer. (However, 100 percent also expressed their dismay at the government's refusal to revise article 27 and its insistence that indigenous autonomy be restricted to the community level.) On 16 February the San Andrés Accord was signed by Comandantes Tacho, David, and Zebedeo.[7] The Zapatistas, sensing Zedillo's desire for a photo opportunity,[8] insisted that the signing take place without photographers present.[9]

Harvey analyzes the accord, pointing out that

> the accord recommended reforms to several articles of the Constitution (including Article 4) that would allow for the redrawing of municipal boundaries and the recognition of the right of indigenous people to compete for public office independently of national political parties. At the state level, similar reforms would be implemented with the goal of increasing political representation of indigenous people in the local congress. In addition, a state-level Law of Justice and Agrarian Development would be drawn up and a special committee would be created to discuss the agrarian problems in Chiapas, with the participation of representatives of the EZLN, other indigenous and peasant organizations, and government ministries. This body would also be responsible for drawing up a census of landholding in the state.[10]

There were, however, important guarantees that the agreement did not provide. For example, indigenous people would still not have "control over the use of land and natural resources in their traditional territories," nor would there be established "pluriethnic autonomous regions as a 'fourth level' of government alongside the current federal, state and municipal levels."[11] The Accord fell far short of what Nicaragua's indigenous people had managed to obtain from the Sandinistas—which may or may not have been Marcos's benchmark.[12] As Womack observes:

> The Sandinistas sponsored hot debates (including sympathetic Mexican anthropologists) on Nicaragua's "national-ethnic question," in 1984 created a National Commission for autonomy to negotiate with the indigenous, in 1985 surveyed indigenous opinion in the contested region, in 1986 hosted an international symposium on "the State, Autonomy, and Indigenous Rights," wrote such rights and a mandate for indigenous "autonomous governments" into Nicaragua's new Constitution, and

in 1987 passed an indigenous bill for these governments into national law.[13]

What the Mexican government was offering was a far cry from this. Ross scathingly reduced the accords to "really nothing more than a shopping list of good intentions, a symbol of a new relationship whose transformation into the law of the land was a dubious proposition."[14] As it turned out, it did not matter what the accords stated, since Zedillo would refuse to sign them. Even now, the government refused to allow Zapatistas to sit on the commission in charge of overseeing the implementation of the Indian Rights Accord. This was supposed to comprise members of all four groups which had participated in the negotiations—the government, CONAI, COCOPA, and the EZLN—but Zedillo wanted to bar the Zapatistas from serving on the commission to prevent them from traveling unimpeded throughout Mexico in their supervisory role.

Nonetheless, their misgivings not withstanding, the Zapatistas and the government turned to the next issue on the list, democracy and justice. The twelfth San Andrés meeting was set for 19 March. The EZLN proposed sixteen sub-*mesas* and sixty-one discussion points, which the government reduced to five sub-*mesas* and fourteen discussion points. Again the Zapatistas invited several hundred advisors, including historians, economists, activists, and politicians (among them Cárdenas from the PRD, and Vicente Fox from the PAN—as it happened, Fox became the next president of Mexico).

This was a dangerous time for the EZLN. For although the accord merely established a minimum agreement by which the government and the Zapatistas could work together, the media were already declaring "Peace" and "An Agreement." The general public was likely to assume that everything had been settled, and thus its attention was in danger of being diverted away from Chiapas and the low-intensity war that was developing there—a war that could be used to provoke the Zapatistas into breaking the cease-fire and give the government the moral authority to crush them. Given that Zedillo was now in the uncomfortable position of having to negotiate further with the EZLN, which hard-liners in the PRI vehemently opposed, a resumption of hostilities could provide the president with a pretext for withdrawal from future negotiation.

To prevent this, Marcos devised a series of projects designed to keep national and international attention firmly focused on Chiapas.

The first was the Continental Encounter for Humanity Against Neo-

Liberalism, convened in the remote Chiapan community of La Realidad on 3–8 April. At the same time, similar Encounters in Asia (Tokyo), Europe (Berlin), and Oceania (Sydney)—details of an African Encounter were promised—were announced as forthcoming. The idea was that each continental Encounter would then announce its findings at an Intercontinental Encuentro to be held in Chiapas in the summer. A host of Latin American and North American celebrities was invited to attend. Among those who made it through the jungle were U.S. film director Oliver Stone (25 March) and the former French president's wife, Danielle Mitterrand (18 April).[15] *Newsweek* devoted a whole page to the event, complete with a photograph of Stone riding alongside the Subcommander, and another with Madame Mitterrand standing among a group of Zapatista women.[16]

Another influential French visitor to El Sup during this time was the socialist intellectual and veteran of Che Guevara's Bolivian campaign, Régis Debray. The two apparently got on very well with one another. Marcos was no doubt gratified to chat in the remote village of La Realidad—which Debray would later claim reminded him of Che's Bolivian base camp, Ñancahuazú—with a man who had been at his childhood hero's side just before his capture and execution. Debray's interview resulted in a lengthy and favorable essay on the Zapatistas in *Le Monde*, in which he wrote of the Subcommander that "while still alive, he has acquired a little of the kind of legend that posthumously hung around Che"; he had already written a piece in which he had called Marcos "the best Latin American writer today."[17] Marcos's courting of Debray is of particular significance, since the Subcommander had recently been experiencing difficulties with the French newspaper's Chiapas correspondent, Bertrand de la Grange, who had been depicting him in a less than favorable light.

Ross claims that Marcos is a true "Francophile," "more fluent in French than he is in English," who grants Parisian reporters interviews in preference to English-speaking ones. He adds, "One explanation for the Subcomandante's galloping Francophilia: Alfonso Guillén, Rafael's father, brags that his son studied at the Sorbonne and even fathered a child there."[18] In actuality, Rafael appears never to have studied at the Sorbonne, telling his parents that he had done so only in order to conceal from them the fact that at that time (the early 1980s) he was already embarking on clandestine guerrilla activity in the safe houses around Mexico City and in the jungles of Chiapas. However, we do know from Rafael's father that prior to his going to study at UNAM, the family "sent him on a two-month trip [to Paris] in order to learn French."[19] We also know from Rafael himself that he studied French at university, that the political-philosophers who influenced him most at that stage were all French (Althusser, Derrida, and Foucault), and that he regularly listened to Radio France International while in the jungles of Chiapas. However, as noted in chapter 4, Marcos's proficiency in spoken French is far from certain.

Not surprisingly, the Americas Encounter concluded with a resounding condemnation of neoliberalism, which would be reiterated and amplified at the forthcoming summer Intercontinental Encounter. The latter was now being dubbed, by the Subcommander-of-hype, the Intergáluctica.

Meanwhile the government stepped up its low-intensity war in Chiapas, filling communities with troops and intimidating the peasantry with constant surveillance and displays of military hardware.[20] One indication of the extent of the militarization that accompanied this activity is, as Weinberg notes, that "U.S. Foreign military sales to Mexico jumped from $4.8 million in 1996 to $28 million in 1997—this on top of outright Pentagon donations, and at least $12 million in sales from private U.S. arms companies," and also that "between 1996 and 1997, the number of Mexican military officers receiving Pentagon training jumped from 300 to 1,500."[21] As Harvey points out, the government had begun moving in this direction since November 1995, when the second rounds of talks had commenced:

> We must also bear in mind that the political context shifted significantly in the period between November 1995 and January 1996. During the first round of talks the government negotiators were more open to the idea of indigenous peoples' regional autonomy. This position changed radically when the team of reformist advisors from the INI was replaced for the second round by hard-liners from the Chiapas state government. Military maneuvers close to Zapatista bases in late December were another ominous sign of a shift in the government's position prior to the final round of talks. During 1996 many observers feared that the continued militarization of Chiapas and the hardening of the government's position on each of the issues to be negotiated at San Andrés would lead to a break down of the entire peace process.[22]

The result, Nash observes, was that whereas "before the February 9, 1995, invasion, there were 13 military encampments in Chiapas; by June 1996, there were 44 in operation."[23]

San Andrés thirteen opened on 18 April to push forward negotiations on democracy and justice. The following day, Danielle Mitterrand, returning from her meeting with the Subcommander, attended the *mesa*, at Marcos's request,[24] to deliver the message that Europe was paying close attention to the situation in Chiapas. Tellingly, in the event, the government called upon no outside advisors to put forward its case.

More alarming still, on 2 May, Javier Elorriaga Berdegué[25] and Sebastián Entzin, who had been arrested in the February 1995 government offensive and charged with terrorism, were tried and sentenced to thirteen and six years, respectively, for their alleged part in the Zapatista uprising. The EZLN viewed this as further evidence of the government adopting a more hard-line stance and, more importantly, as a direct contravention of the Dialogue Law of March 1995. They immediately declared a red alert and broke off negotiations. Even to non-EZLN members, the sentencing had appeared farcical, doing much to confirm people in their belief in the lack of justice in Mexico—one of two main topics being discussed at the current *mesa*. The evidence against Elorriaga was minimal, consisting mainly of the testimony of Salvador Morales Garibay (former Subcommander Daniel), who had now been summoned to testify eight times and had failed to appear on every occasion, and on that of Elorriaga's wife (Comandanta Elisa), which another judge had previously ruled inadmissible on the grounds that it had clearly been obtained through torture. Based on such scant evidence a charge of terrorism, carrying with it a penalty of thirteen years, seemed the very embodiment of injustice.[26] Even leading members of COCOPA, such as PRD senator Heberto Castillo, declared publicly against the sentences, arguing that they hardly created an atmosphere conducive to the negotiation of peace and reconciliation. The Zapatista leadership worked furiously in the following weeks to highlight Elorriaga's plight in the national and international media, hoping to influence the appeal scheduled for 6 June.[27]

In response to the EZLN breaking off negotiations, the government became even more hard-line. First, it issued an ultimatum: "If the Zapatistas don't show up on 5 June [the scheduled date for the next round of talks], then we will carry out arrest warrants against them and everything will be ruined."[28] Then, under the guise of conducting a war against drugs, it sent thousands of troops and military hardware into Zapatista-controlled territory. Near the EZLN stronghold of Oventic, for example, 153 soldiers employing the (sinister) code words "Bosnia, Bosnia, Bosnia" scoured the land in search of drug cultivation, before setting up camp in the community of Jolbash just two kilometers away. Moreover, every day, at dawn and dusk, flyovers by military helicopters added to the intimidation of this Zapatista support base. In Altamirano, a convoy comprising eight trucks and three tanks, again ostensibly searching for narcotics cultivation, rumbled through the *ejido*; while at San Quintín, just a few kilometers from La Realidad, the army established a Special Training Camp for Jungle Operations.

On 6 June, Elorriaga was released from jail after having been held in detention for sixteen months. An appeal judge had overturned the original (May) verdict.[29] Elorriaga immediately assumed the role of head of FZLN — a highly experienced propagandist for the EZLN, he had been editing the organization's monthly publication, *Espejo* (*Mirror*), during his time behind bars. He later visited Paris in November 1996 with his wife (Comandanta Elisa) to promote the Zapatista cause in Europe, and subsequently appeared in two English-language documentary videos, *Zapatista* and Nettie Wild's *A Place Called Chiapas*, explaining the movement's aims to an English-speaking audience. Zapatista public and international relations went from strength to strength in 1996.

In waiting until 6 June for news of Elorriaga's appeal result, the Zapatistas had failed to turn up for the next scheduled round of the San Andrés dialogues, thereby breaking the agreement they had signed in March 1995. However, the talks were already in crisis since the government had failed both to send the Indian Rights Accord to Congress for ratification (which it was supposed to have done by March 15) and to appoint a commission to oversee the implementation of the Accord at grass-roots level.

As if this illustration of the government's bad faith was not worrying enough, the Zapatistas still had sixteen members in prison and, during the week of 14–21 June, paramilitary activity in the north of Chiapas left eleven dead.

On 6 July COCOPA succeeded in getting the EZLN and the government to return to the negotiating table. This meeting was intended only to draw up the rules for future negotiations. Significantly, it also brokered a solution to the problem of the composition of the overseeing commission for the Indigenous Rights Accords, with the government backing down, allowing Zapatistas to supervise and assess these implementations. This round of discussion ended on the 12th, with a three-day interval before San Andrés fifteen (*Mesa* II, second meeting on democracy and justice). At these talks, both sides made their recommendations for enhancing democracy and justice. Tellingly, the government's proposal was just eight pages long— indicating that they believed the existing system merely required minor readjustments—whereas the Zapatistas's ran to thirty-seven pages. The Zapatistas dismissed the government's proposal as woefully insufficient, while the government representatives refused to discuss issues such as the writing of a new constitution or the re-writing of NAFTA's terms. Thus, although the next round of talks was scheduled for 6 August, the prospect of any sort of agreement appeared poor.

In July the EZLN held another meeting of the National Indigenous Forum (23–24 July), which was swiftly followed (27 July–3 August) by Marcos's project, the Encuentro Intercontinental Por la Humanidad y Contra el Neoliberalismo. It is clear from Marcos's own words that even the preliminary organization for this event helped strengthen the EZLN. He told one interviewer, "The movement really . . . took form with the preparation for the Intercontinental encounter."[30] For the second time that year, celebrities and the press flocked to the Lacandón jungle.[31] The gathering was truly international, with representatives from fifty-five nations. Those present included "ideologues from the European left parties—the Italian 'Communist Refoundation,' the Spanish trade unionists, Basque independence fighters, Greens, German anarchist posses—intermeshed with the Brazilian Party of Labor, retired guerrilla leaders like Douglas Bravo (Venezuela) and Hugo Blanco (Peru), the Sem Terras (sometimes called Brazil's Zapatistas), [and] even a very formal Cuban delegation."[32] To some extent this diversity was encouraged by Marcos's charisma, which buoyed up certain groups temporarily to ignore their differences, but for the most part it probably resulted from the lack of definition of the Zapatista cause.[33] (As soon as the Zapatista uprising began, myriad special interest groups laid claim to the movement. In an interview with Marcos for an anarchist publication [11 May 1994], a journalist had commented: "There are many who are trying to claim your struggle as their own. The Maoists say you are Maoists, the Trotskyists say you are Trotskyists, and the list goes on.")[34] Marcos reflected on the issue of ambiguity and its effect on the Intercontinental thus:

> Zapatismo is the common point, or the pretext for converging. Each one has his own logic, but recognizes himself in certain very general propositions of Zapatismo. I see no resemblance at all among the Basque, Catalán, Greek, Kurdish, Swedish, Japanese Zapatistas, except that they all come here and each has its idea of Zapatismo or what it should be. . . . [Zapatismo] aims more to retrieve a series of universal values that can serve well for Australians, Japanese, Greeks, Kurds, Cataláns, Chicanos, Indians from Ecuador, for example, or the Mapuche. . . . Especially, I believe that the generality, the lack of definition of Zapatismo, is particularly important in this case, that we have to maintain it.[35]

Newspaper reporters described to their readers either the Left's last stand or the first rallying of those opposing neoliberalism (depending on their political leanings). Meanwhile, the attendees returned to their own countries, many eagerly awaiting the proposed Second Intergalactic Encuentro to be held a year hence, this time in Europe.

As well as being a public relations success, the Encuentro was also a financial one. In excess of 3,000 people attended, each paying $100, thereby swelling the EZLN's coffers by over a quarter of a million dollars.[36] These funds went not on improving the EZLN's outdated weaponry, but on buying corn and seed for the Zapatista base communities.[37] Nor was money the only benefit. Representatives from Radio Free Berkeley donated a 10-watt pirate radio system for the Zapatistas to broadcast their Radio Insurgente.

Marcos also used the International Encuentro to further enhance his media profile. In addition to acting as the host and impresario, he granted several interviews. Most notable among these was the one he gave to Le Bot, which was subsequently incorporated into his *El sueño zapatista* (1997). The Canadian documentary maker, Nettie Wild, filmed proceedings, and Marcos posed for photographers from *Marie Clare* and a host of other publications.

Marcos had entered the Encuentro on horseback, adding to his heroic guerrilla image. As Enrique Rajchenberg and Catherine Héau-Lambert observe:

In Mexico the sign of a hero is not a gun but a horse, and the Mexican popular imagination has woven a series of representations around the horse, which have changed according to historical circumstance. . . . The horse has been appropriated as a symbol of victorious strength at the service of the popular hero. . . . The horse in its warrior role is part of the myth of the hero. . . . Mexican heroes prance their bronze horses in city parks, silent witnesses of a historical epoch. Siqueiros painted fiery horses as a symbol of popular strength: the horse as a symbol of a heroic people and not just of one hero. In his mural at the Palace of Cortés in Cuernavaca, Diego Rivera painted a white horse as the stand-in for Emiliano Zapata; the mythical white horse of all great generals. Furthermore, there is not a single film about the Mexican Revolution which does not include spectacular cavalry charges. Villistas and Zapatistas were exceptional horsemen.[38]

On 6 August 1996 San Andrés sixteen was convened. Unsurprisingly, given the diametrically opposed viewpoints of the government and the

EZLN, this session went nowhere. The EZLN promised to undertake another Consulta to see whether their support communities would accept the government's eight-page proposal, but given that the Zapatistas's leadership had dismissed it outright, and that this same leadership was comprised of influential and respected community leaders, its rejection was a foregone conclusion. Moreover, the government's attitude toward the EZLN had by now radically changed. The Intergalactic Encuentro had greatly upset a government hopeful of restricting the EZLN's influence to a local level. Its anger is perhaps reflected in the sentencing of the "Yanga Seven"[39] to up to six years in prison for possessing firearms and making explosives and other more minor offenses. The Mexican judiciary, at that time, was generally sensitive to the government's wishes when it came to ruling on important cases. Furthermore, as if to highlight the importance of the subject under discussion at San Andrés—justice—according to Human Rights Watch, in the Yanga case "the judge argued that even if it had been proven that the detainees' statements were forced through torture, he would accept them, citing the Mexican legal precedent that holds that the first statement made by a detainee has more legal validity than later statements, including retractions."[40] This was despite the fact that as Human Rights Watch observes, "Mexican legislation expressly prohibits and penalizes the use of torture and renders invalid legal statements made under torture."[41]

In addition, the government's interest in the San Andrés Accords had been diverted by the dramatic appearance of another guerrilla group, this time operating in neighboring Guerrero. This group, which called itself the Ejército Popular Revolucionario (EPR, Popular Revolutionary Army), had made its debut on 28 June, when its masked and armed members made an impromptu appearance at a ceremony commemorating the deaths of seventeen unarmed farmers, shot by government troops the previous year while demonstrating. The EPR had then engaged in a series of attacks on government, police, and military targets, killing perhaps as many as fifty or sixty people. The EPR, unlike the EZLN, belonged to the old, political-military, hard-left guerrillas of the 1960s and 1970s. Its rhetoric was, for example, very much centered on the Marxist discourse of earlier guerrilla groups and was certainly not ethnic. Its leader, Comandante José Arturo, evidently took pride in the movement's weaponry—purchased with money obtained through kidnapping—and in its ability and willingness to kill, contrasting this with what he perceived as the weakness of the EZLN and, in particular, of its leader. Marcos, Arturo commented disparagingly, appeared to confuse poetry for politics.[42] (Marcos later responded to this by comparing the EPR to those doctrinaire hard-liners within El Salvador's revolutionary movement who had murdered the poet Roque Dalton over ideological differences. He also rejected the EPR's claim to be a vanguard of the people and its intention to seize state power, stating, "You fight to take power. We fight for democracy, liberty and justice. It is not the same thing.")[43] Like the Zapatistas, however, the EPR was also interested in capturing media attention, and it gave a press conference at Huesteca in which it outlined its aims and the similarities and differences between it and the EZLN. The result was that the EPR temporarily eclipsed the EZLN in the media, both national and foreign,[44] and appeared for a time to be the government's most pressing problem. (On 28 August, the EPR launched a single coordinated offensive across eight states, which resulted in the deaths of fifteen people and the wounding of twenty-three others.) In the long run, however, both the EPR, and its more moderate, less doctrinaire offshoot, the ERPI (Revolutionary Army of the Insurgent Poor), faltered and eventually disappeared.[45] The EZLN would prove a far more enduring problem for the Zedillo regime despite its recent, temporary eclipse.

On 3 September, just after the president had given his state of the nation address (1 September), in which he had tellingly failed even to mention the San Andrés Accords, the EZLN announced the results of its Consulta on the government's proposal on democracy and justice—overwhelming rejection by the base communities. The comandancia announced that it was withdrawing from the San Andrés dialogues and would rejoin only after the government had implemented the Indian Accords and established a supervisory body, released any remaining alleged Zapatista prisoners, put forward a more comprehensive proposal addressing democracy and justice, ended the intimidation of Zapatista communities using the Federal Army, and replaced its inflexible negotiator, Marco Antonio Bernal. As Kampwirth notes, it was not only the Zapatistas who felt the government was doing far less than it could to achieve peace: an August poll showed that "while almost 76 percent thought that the EZLN was doing the best it could to achieve peace through dialogue, only 22 percent thought that the government was doing the best it could."[46]

The following month saw a dramatic rise in tension between the government and the EZLN, when the latter announced that it would attend the Indigenous Forum to be held from 8–12 October in Mexico City. (The Forum had come into being as a result of the Special Forum on Indian Rights held in January 1996 which had triggered a subsequent Indigenous Forum at Oventic on 10 April 1996.) Zapatistas attending a high-profile event in the capital would strengthen the EZLN's claims to be a national entity and would further refocus attention on Chiapas. It would also mean that the Zapatistas had successfully broken the government's military, political, economic, and press cordon. The government's response was to threaten to arrest any Zapatistas found outside the state of Chiapas. Some eminent Mexicans, however, pointed out that the Dialogue Law of February 1995 made no mention of restricting the movements of Zapatistas. The government was forced to back down, but only slightly. It would now allow ten unarmed Zapatista delegates to attend, but only if the individuals concerned did not have outstanding (that is, temporarily suspended) arrest warrants. The intention was clear: to bar Marcos, who had cried foul at the government's announcement of the initial ban, and who kept insisting to reporters that the Zapatistas would attend the forum. The last thing the government was going to permit was an already immensely popular Marcos working his rhetorical magic on the capital's citizens. In the run-up to the event, the government propaganda machine went into overdrive attempting to portray the ten permitted Zapatista delegates as hardened, bloody guerrillas. But it met its match in Marcos. At the last moment, and after several days of talking-up the EZLN delegation as comprising the movement's "most aggressive side, our most belligerent and intransigent part, and our greatest symbol of war,"[47] the Subcommander revealed that it was to be made up of only one person, the diminutive and critically ill (and therefore not in the least bit threatening) Comandanta Ramona. This ploy had the double advantage of making the government look ridiculous and allowing Ramona to gain access to much needed medical treatment unavailable in Chiapas. It is doubtful whether the Subcommander ever entertained a notion of attending the forum himself. It was, after all, an indigenous forum and he, as his many detractors repeatedly pointed out, is not indigenous. Six hundred delegates representing thirty different indigenous peoples and fifty thousand Mexico City residents flocked to the Zócalo to hear Ramona.

Shortly after, on 15 October, thanks to the commitment of COCOPA, there was a new attempt at bringing the EZLN back to the negotiating table, in what came to be known as the Tripartite talks. The suggested procedure was that, instead of the EZLN, CONAI, COCOPA, and the government trying to negotiate an accord together, the first three would hammer out a proposal for submission to the government for rejection or acceptance (but not, it should be noted, for amendment). First, however, the government would have to fulfill the five conditions set out by the Zapatistas in

September. In line with this, certain high-profile prisoners, such as the Cacalomacán Eight (and in January the Yanga Seven), were released. Moreover, COSEVER, the body overseeing the implementation of the Indigenous Rights Accords, was established. The government later reneged on its commitment to implement the accords, but at the time it appeared to be acting in earnest, and the Zapatistas matched it by having Marcos attend the talks. On 29 November, COCOPA submitted a nonnegotiable proposal to the government and the EZLN on the form and content of the implementation of the Indian Rights Accords.[48] The following day, the EZLN gave its response: despite considerable misgivings it was prepared to accept the package. The government, however, was still contemplating the matter several days later. It then announced that it had misgivings concerning thirty-three points in the proposal's text—an irrelevance since this was not subject to amendment. The president further requested an additional fifteen days to consult on the matter with top legislators. As the EZLN and many others saw it, "After 22 months of negotiating an agreement his own representatives had long ago signed, the President wanted two more weeks to make up his mind about honoring it."[49] On 19 December Zedillo made a counterproposal to the EZLN: not exactly the Christmas present the Zapatistas had been hoping for.

27. A March and a Massacre

Christmas came and went, as did an unusually quiet and uneventful third anniversary of the uprising on New Year's Day: there was no *Declaration of the Lacandón Jungle* as there had been in 1994, 1995, and 1996. This eerie silence typified the first six months of the year. On 11 January, Marcos mounted his horse Lucerito and rode to La Realidad to meet the COCOPA and CONAI representatives and deliver the EZLN's response to Zedillo's counterproposal: a resounding No! Marcos delivered two communiqués that dismissed the proposal as "based upon an ethnocentric, discriminatory and racist conception,"[1] and "an infamous and bald-faced mockery of the struggle of the Indian people of Mexico, of the EZLN's will for dialogue, of the efforts of the Cocopa."[2] Indeed, most non-Mexican observers concur that Zedillo's "counterproposal . . . bore little relation to the existing accords."[3] Weinberg details these discrepancies at length:

> The EZLN-COCOPA version called for the Constitution to "recognize" indigenous rights; the federal executive version would "grant" rights. The EZLN-COCOPA version established the right of indigenous peoples to "the sustainable use" and a share of "all benefits derived from the use and development of natural resources in the territories they occupy." The executive version deleted the reference to indigenous "territories" and restricted use of natural resources to "the forms and modalities of property delineated in Article 27 of this Constitution" (private, state, *ejidal* and communal). The EZLN-COCOPA version recognized the right of indigenous peoples to determine the forms of development in their territories; the executive version obliged the government to "take account of" indigenous peoples in development programs. Finally, the executive version rejected the remunicipalization proposal, instead restricting the powers of indigenous communities to economic and social spheres, excluding the juridical and political.[4]

The Subcommander then climbed back on his horse and, as Ross puts it, "rode off into the mountain without ever looking back."[5] During the subsequent six months scarcely anything was heard from him—a silence made all the more foreboding by the fact that it ran so contrary to his usual loquacity.

Throughout the winter, spring, and early summer Marcos was unavailable for interview and had not shown his face, or rather his balaclava, in La Realidad. In the period from the Zapatistas's rejection of Zedillo's counterproposal (11 January) to July "only seven communiqués signed by either Subcomandante Marcos or the CCRI, one every 27 days, radiated from the jungles of Chiapas."[6] Marcos briefly broke his silence when the government responded to the Zapatistas's rejection by dismissing the original draft (drawn up, it will be remembered, by a government team) as "separatist" and claiming that it would result in the "Balkanization" of Mexico.[7] In a communiqué dated 7 March Marcos countered: "If the government is afraid of being fragmented, it should look at the example of other countries that have organized and legislated their (various) autonomies and not fallen apart, while countries that have not done so have been splitting into many parts."[8] The Subcommander, however, made no further response to the ensuing, sustained government and right-wing campaign to undermine the original accords. The pro-government press immediately went to work trying to turn the public against the notion of indigenous autonomy, claiming that it would lead to the disintegration of Mexico, with indigenous communities seceding from the nation-state. Some commentators, such as Ignacio Burgoa Orihuela, a legal expert who acted as an advisor to Zedillo on the issue of autonomy and ratification of the San Andrés Accords, fell back on sensationalizing racial stereotypes, claiming that if granted autonomy, these primitive, violent, antidemocratic indigenous peoples might even revert to "human sacrifice."[9] Even the escalation in state repression and paramilitary violence in these months did not provoke Marcos into putting pen to paper.[10]

Myriad rumors, all attesting to a continued fascination with Marcos on the part of the press and the public, now circulated as to what lay behind El Sup's silence. Some thought that he had taken a well-deserved vacation, slipping out of the country and touring France, Spain, and Italy, or had even retired, turning his back on the hardships of guerrilla life. Others speculated that the Subcommander was ill, perhaps having contracted malaria or having been bitten by a poisonous snake.

In hindsight, the reality was far less titillating, although, in the long run, far more significant. For it would appear that Marcos and the EZLN comandancia had been silent but far from idle. During these long months they had been busy shaping and strengthening autonomous municipalities in the region. These municipalities united to constitute regional governments that functioned outside the control of and frequently in opposition to the government-sanctioned municipal governments. Of the thirty-eight proclaimed in December 1995, thirty-two still existed in 1997, in varying stages of development. A tradition of alternative, indigenous government in the Tojolabal region went back to 1988 if not earlier.[11] The Zapatistas, whose heartland was in this territory, were able to build on this preexisting tradition, expanding it far beyond its original conception. As Héctor Díaz-Polanco, an anthropologist who had advised the Sandinista government on autonomy, observes, "It was not as if the demand for autonomy was completely absent before the Zapatista uprising . . . but with the Zapatista uprising, the theme of autonomy acquired a national relevance, democratic vigor and a more defined profile."[12] The EZLN quickly set to work promoting the establishment of new authorities in these communities. Communal assemblies were brokered or strengthened to establish indigenous customs and usages and to set up commissions covering issues such as health, education, and justice. The Zapatistas and their support communities had evidently come to the conclusion that there was no point in negotiating with a dishonest government for its approval of concepts that they had already begun to put into effect and which, even if recognized by the federal government, would still in all likelihood be deeply opposed by the Chiapan state government.[13] Thus, while the government was refusing to ratify the accords on indigenous rights, the EZLN was implementing them at the grassroots level. One lamentable result of the strengthening of these autonomous communities was, however, the increased paramilitary response they drew from right-wingers, fearing this new expression of indigenous, antigovernment, pro-Zapatista sentiment.

Media attention on the Zapatistas continued to wane throughout the summer. By being silent for so long, the Subcommander had lost his grip on public interest, and this would be difficult to regain. The Second International Encuentro for Humanity and Against Neo-Liberalism, held in Madrid, attracted little coverage from the Mexican and U.S. media, predominantly because it did not take place in the "exotic" and "romantic" Chiapas jungle and was not presided over by the charismatic Marcos. The

Encuentro did, however, provide a stage for western European supporters of the Zapatistas and engaged the local liberal press, which covered the event in great detail.

Furthermore, the Mexican mid-term elections (6 July), viewed (probably correctly) as (generally) fair, tended to overshadow all other news. This is perhaps not surprising given that the elections resulted for the first time in the PRI losing its absolute majority in the Chamber of Deputies,[14] in the election of the PRD candidate, Cuauhtémoc Cárdenas, as mayor of Mexico City, in the ruling party's loss of twenty-nine of the capital's thirty federal congressional districts, in the number of opposition legislators in the Senate rising from 26 percent to 40 percent, and in opposition parties taking power in six states and fifteen state capitals.

The election results had, however, the side effect of weakening the EZLN's position, since many in Mexico began to regain (or acquire for the first time) faith in the political system and in peaceful, democratic forms of bringing about desired changes. As Oppenheimer puts it, "after nearly seven decades of monolithic rule by the governing party, the 1997 elections unleashed a wave of optimism."[15] Despite the fact that, as Oppenheimer goes on to emphasize, the PRI still "controlled the powerful presidency and retained an absolute majority in the Senate, which could give it effective veto on bills emerging from the Chamber of Deputies,"[16] many Mexicans nonetheless began to wonder whether the country still needed masked gunmen to extort change from the government. (The fact that in Chiapas Zapatista communities had by and large refused to vote, thus ceding ten of the state's twelve congressional seats to the PRI, did much to foster the view that the EZLN was inflexible and to some extent counterproductive if its main aim was to dislodge the PRI from government.)

The Subcommander desperately needed to recapture the political initiative, and so, on 8 August, six days after the return of the Zapatista delegates from Spain, Marcos announced a forthcoming march to Mexico City of 1,111 Zapatistas—one for each of the indigenous communities supporting the EZLN. On 8 September, the 1,111 indigenous men, women, and children gathered in the central plaza in San Cristóbal and set off, in thirty-eight coaches, for the capital, waved off by 15,000 onlookers. Over the next few days, as this caravan slowly made its way north, it was swollen by a further 120 vehicles accompanying them in solidarity. On the approach to the capital, the caravan symbolically followed exactly the same route that Emiliano Zapata had traveled in 1914, as he joined Pancho Villa and his Army of the North. By the time they reached Mexico City's Zócalo, on 12 September, a

crowd numbering 25,000 to 80,000 (depending on the sources) was waiting to greet them. Once again, Marcos had nudged the ribs of Mexican civil
society, and it had responded well.[17]

The Zapatista delegation did not content itself with reclaiming the spotlight for the EZLN; it also set about forging links with other indigenous
groups by attending an assembly of the National Indigenous Congress, and
it oversaw the establishment of the FZLN as a grassroots social movement.
Although this had been called for in the *Fourth Declaration of the Lacandón
Jungle* (1 January 1996), only now did it take form, with two thousand delegates present to witness its inauguration. In the long run the FZLN would
actually achieve very little—hamstrung as it was from the beginning by its
own stipulation that all members must renounce existing membership of
any political party, by its exclusion of any professional politicians, and by
its insistence that none of its members could hold political office. But now,
however, was an exciting time, pregnant with hope for the purely political
(as opposed to the politico-military) wing of the Zapatista movement, and
one of a good deal of public and media interest.

Then, in late December, an event took place that further focused attention on Chiapas and led many Mexicans to question how effective
democratic methods were in transforming the Mexican government into a
liberal, progressive entity. This was the massacre, three days before Christmas, of forty-five members—forty-six if one includes an unborn infant
ripped from its mother's body—of the Chenalhó highland community of
Acteal. The general human rights situation in Chiapas had continued to
be abominable even after the January 1994 cease-fire, as a Human Rights
Watch publication made abundantly clear.[18] On 30 January 1997, *La Jornada* had noted that since the 12 January 1994 cease-fire there had been
more than three hundred deaths stemming from political violence in the
state of Chiapas—it subsequently catalogued thirty killings in the period
from May 24 to the massacre.[19] Even more recently, the area in and around
Acteal had witnessed a spate of killings, arson, kidnapping, and other acts
of violence.[20] However, the massacre at Acteal represented undoubtedly the
grossest abuse of human rights in the state in recent years. Although the
massacre was not conducted by the Federal Army, the culprits were pro-
PRI paramilitaries with strong ties to the party and the Mexican security
forces. To make matters worse, the killers were armed with government
weapons, allegedly supplied by local security forces. Moreover, the government had ignored several warnings that the massacre would happen,
failed to respond to reports that it was taking place, and finally bungled the

clear-up (and cover-up) operation.[21] As Oppenheimer notes, "The Acteal massacre . . . had underscored the fact that Zedillo's strategy of militarizing Chiapas had failed to stem the violence in that state."[22]

The following day, 23 December, Marcos wrote a communiqué roundly condemning the government for the massacre by stating bluntly that "those who are investigating Acteal are the very ones who planned it."[23] This was published by La Jornada and simultaneously posted on the Internet. As Bonner observes:

> Less than a decade earlier, events in the mountains of Chiapas would hardly have rated more than a few paragraphs in the most international of newspapers. Now, with cyberspace, a call went out after the Acteal massacre for support of the Zapatistas. . . . In just twenty days, according to a compilation prepared by Stefan Wray, of the department of Culture and Communication of New York University, there were more than 122 actions involving "tens of thousands" of people in 61 cities and towns in 15 countries on four continents.[24]

Ross describes just some of these actions:

> On Christmas night a hundred protesters circled in front of the White House. . . . But the real fury was in the street outside the Mexican embassies and consulates, from Tokyo to Togo (where the Organization of African Unity was meeting) to Oslo (blood-red paint on the embassy wall) to Vermont (Ben and Jerry would buy Abeja coffee for their gourmet ice cream). 60,000 marched in Rome, hundreds more in Prague and Portugal. In Hamburg, Zap-symps danced cumbias on the desktops at the Mexican consulate. Paris protests were so effective that Le Monde suspended Bertrand de la Grange after he penned a particularly poisonous piece blaming the EZLN for Acteal. . . . When Zedillo flew into Davos for the annual World Economic Summit, he was met with spray paint and loud demonstrations. Latin protestors gathered from the Plaza de Mayo in Argentina to Nicaragua's Plaza Sandino.[25]

The year had ended on a bitter note—perhaps the most bitter since the uprising began—but once again the eyes of Mexican civil society,[26] the international community, and over two hundred NGOs were firmly fixed on southeast Mexico.[27]

28. Speedy Gonzalez Breaks the Silence

The fourth anniversary of the Zapatistas's uprising passed as quietly as their third. Once again, no *Declaration of the Lacandón Jungle* was issued. Few in Chiapas were in the mood for celebration so soon after the Acteal massacre. As in 1997, the first half of 1998 was one of relative public relations inactivity on Marcos's part. Possibly, he had decided to keep a low profile in order not to steal Elorriaga's limelight and eclipse the activities of the newly established FZLN. (In a speech written by Marcos, but delivered by one of the Zapatista delegates who attended the FZLN's inauguration the previous September, the Subcommander had commented: "We [the EZLN] stand aside so that you [the FZLN] can find your own face.")[1] In any event, Marcos remained silent, granting no interviews and issuing no communiqués between the end of February and the start of July, despite ever-increasing provocation by the government.

On 3 January Zedillo appointed a new interior minister, Francisco Labastida, who, in his first press conference, laid the blame for Acteal squarely on the Zapatistas and their autonomous communities. In addition, he also repeatedly referred to Marcos as Rafael Sebastián Guillén Vicente, even when offering to meet and negotiate with the Subcommander—something that was guaranteed to annoy El Sup since he has always denied this identification. Labastida also proclaimed his intention to disarm all armed groups in Chiapas, including the EZLN—a process that would require entering and searching Zapatista territory and confiscating weapons, acts prohibited by the 1995 Dialogue Law. Furthermore, he appointed as his chief advisor a former Maoist leader, Adolfo Orive, who was known to be hated by both Subcommander Marcos and Bishop Samuel Ruiz, and he began a hostile campaign against foreign NGOs—many of which had worked ceaselessly in providing aid to Zapatista autonomous communities.

As if all this was not sufficient to sour permanently relations between the Zapatistas and the government, on 3 January the Federal Army made a sweep through La Realidad questioning inhabitants as to the Sub-commander's location. They beat a hasty retreat seven hours later after both CONAI and the press had been notified of this fresh act of provocation, with the minister of defense vehemently denying that any incursion had taken place. Furthermore, nine days later the state's blatant disregard for the lives of its indigenous citizens was again demonstrated when security forces opened fire on a demonstration protesting against the Acteal massacre in Ocosingo, killing a young indigenous mother and injuring her baby, an act caught on national television. At her funeral three days later, Marcos broadcast his condolences over Radio Insurgente.

This latest killing did nothing for the Mexican government's public relations image, either at home or abroad. Indeed, the international community was exhibiting increasing concern in, and with it an increased scrutiny of, its policy toward Chiapas. For example, in mid-February a delegation of 170 European politicians, intellectuals, and human rights observers traveled to Chiapas to see for themselves what was going on there and to report back to the European Parliament.

In an attempt to offset this negative image, on 15 March, Zedillo "sent a diluted version of the [San Andrés] agreement to Congress as a bill on 'Indigenous Rights and Culture.'"[2] (As Mattiace observes, "Countries that recognized indigenous rights were viewed as more modern and, thus, more legitimate in the eyes of the international community than countries that did not"[3]—and at this point in time the Zedillo regime was in much need of both legitimacy and a positive image abroad.) So diluted was Zedillo's version that Ross likened the difference between it and what had been negotiated at San Andrés to that between a fully grown tree and a bonsai. Luis Hernández, the EZLN's advisor at San Andrés, went one step further, comparing the differences to those between "an abortion and a live birth."[4] Aubry contrasts the document sent to Congress by Zedillo with the one negotiated between the EZLN and COCOPA thus:

> It [Zedillo's draft] reduces the concept of "original peoples" to that of "community," generously "grants" autonomy instead of "recognizing" it as a right, obliterates the collective right to be different, silences its repercussions in the collective management of natural resources, denies autonomy any territorial dimension, and rejects the juridical logic of its "normative systems"; in other words it is very selective with regard to the accords, depriving them of their spirit and coherence.[5]

However, throughout the submission process Zedillo trumpeted the fact that "this government will comply with the San Andrés Accords"[6] in the government-owned newspapers and television stations.

Surprisingly, all this elicited no savage response from Marcos's usually prolific and acerbic pen. Nor did the Subcommander break his silence during the following months when, reacting to the flood of foreigners into Chiapas—human rights workers, members of NGOs, and "Zapatista tourists" on trips organized by Global Exchange—the government initiated a wave of expulsions. In the first six months of 1998, seventy-six foreigners were expelled, including members of NGOs, human rights activists, tourists, and clergy.[7] By the time Ronfeldt et al. had published their book, *The Zapatista Social Netwar in Mexico*, the number of expulsions since Acteal had risen to "over 200."[8] At one point, overzealous prosecution of these expulsions threatened to cause an international diplomatic incident. In May, Mexican authorities deported 141 Italian "peace observers," some of whom were left-wing parliamentarians, and banned them from reentering the country for life[9] (in what appears to have been a fit of petty vindictiveness in response to the city of Venice having granted the EZLN the Gold Lion, its highest honor).[10] Italy made its displeasure felt the following year when it (alone of the fifteen states in the European Union) voted against signing a free trade pact with Mexico.

The Subcommander even refused to break his silence when the government took military action against the autonomous municipalities. On 10 April, a 900-strong combined force of soldiers and police dismantled the autonomous municipality of Flores Magón. Burguete Cal y Mayor describes the scene:

> After destroying the Rebel Council's pavilion and auditorium, the military forces occupied and encircled almost one hectare of land with barbed wire, virtually kidnapping the Zapatista population within its perimeter. As they established their camp, thirty members of the Public Safety Police were in charge of digging barricades and posting stakes to prevent a subsequent response by Zapatista sympathizers.[11]

Then, on 1 May, the autonomous municipality of Tierra y Libertad, which incorporated more than one hundred hamlets and villages, had its own commissions for education and health, and had been described by one leading anthropologist as "the most consolidated autonomous municipality in Chiapas,"[12] received the same treatment as Flores Magón. The state security forces entered the community and arrested and imprisoned fifty-six of its citizens. On 3 June action was taken against yet another autonomous community, that of Nicolás Ruiz—this time 161 of its residents were imprisoned in the raid. Zedillo attempted to justify this in the same way he had attempted to justify the February 1995 offensive—by appealing to the rule of law: "Violation of the law is not a form of peace. The law must be enforced to avoid more violence, more pain, more insecurity."[13] (Zedillo asserted that these autonomous communities were illegal, which was true, but it must be remembered that they were only so because the government had reneged on its promise to legalize autonomy by having the accords that it itself had signed ratified by Congress.) Reverend Pablo Romo, working for the Fray Bartolomé de las Casas Human Rights Center noted how the new government policy actually increased violence, pain, and insecurity: "The army is directly attacking communities, and we haven't seen that in a long time. . . . [there is] no mediation, and we have no conditions to reestablish a dialogue. The situation is much worse."[14] The late evening of 10 June witnessed another attack on an autonomous community, and the jailing of a further fifty-three citizens. Weinberg relates how

> a thousand soldiers and police entered Autonomous municipality San Juan la Libertad . . . in the official *municipio* of El Bosque. When the Tzotzil residents tried to block their way, the troops responded with tear gas and machine guns. When the shooting was over, eight *campesinos* and one police agent were dead. Residents fled into the mountains. Gov. Albores claimed his troops had been fired on first by ski-masked men. Residents said the government troops had forced local youths at gunpoint to put on ski-masks, hold rifles and pose for police cameras.[15]

Regardless of what exactly happened, one thing is clear: now, for the first time during the government's suppression of the autonomous municipalities, the Zapatistas had met force with force. Ross, noting that this attack represented the final one conducted that year, argued, "If anything derailed the government's enthusiasm to extinguish the rebels, it was the fact that, for once, the EZLN had fired back."[16]

As Weinberg notes, in a new, low-profile strategy adopted by the government, "The authorities were knocking over the autonomous municipalities one by one, with piecemeal bloodshed rather than the wholesale type exhibited at Acteal, so as to avoid unseemly international attention."[17] The government's ploy was not, however, entirely successful, since in June the U.N. High Commissioner for Human Rights, Mary Robinson, expressed her concern over Chiapas. Her comments were met by the Mexican government with "swift and unequivocal dismissal."[18]

Even before the attack on San Juan la Libertad, on 7 June, Bishop Samuel Ruiz had, in the current circumstances of renewed aggression by the government, already announced the dissolution of CONAI, charging the Zedillo administration with having turned its back on the means of achieving a negotiated settlement to the Chiapan conflict. Yet even this elicited no response from Marcos.

It is surely a sign of Marcos's celebrity that this silence led to intense speculation, not just in Mexico but throughout North America and western Europe. Such was the media's infatuation with Marcos that several publications ran "nonstories" entirely devoted to his silence.[19] *Semana* lists just some of the rumors circulating: he had died in a clash with the Federal Army or with right-wing paramilitaries in the jungle; he had been assassinated by the CIA, rival guerrillas, or hard-liners within the EZLN; he lay ill in bed with malaria; he was resting in Mexico City; he was touring Saudi Arabia; he had gone to Italy to see his wife; he had gone to France to visit his daughter; he had traveled incognito to France to watch the World Cup; he had asked for asylum in the European Union; he had been given a house in McAllen, Texas; he had been seen in various shopping malls; and even that he had been kidnapped by UFOS.[20] Given Zedillo's phony Indian rights and culture bill, the widespread expulsion of foreigners, the attacks on the autonomous communities, and the dissolution of CONAI, most people guessed that something very serious must have been at work to keep the Subcommander from issuing communiqués for the past 120 days. Ross, commenting on how "the silence itself had by now become the subject of many words," observes how sympathizers and critics alike read into it what they willed:

> "A Funereal Silence," *Proceso* front-covered in somber black letters. "An insulting silence," rightist bishop Genaro Alamilla called it. "An eloquent silence, an active silence," responded his ecclesiastical rival Mario López, Mexican provincial of the Jesuits. "Who remains in silence is ungovernable," Luis Hernández quoted the liberation educator Ivan Illich.[21]

Later, in November 1998, Marcos would justify his reticence by stating that the Zapatistas "had said all we needed to say: we decided to let Zedillo do the talking and make a fool of himself, figuring that the people would soon get tired of it."[22]

Marcos broke cover on 15 July, in two communiqués. In the first he simply repeated the exuberant cry of Speedy Gonzalez ("Yepa, yepa, yepa! Andale, andale! Arriba, arriba! Yepa, yepa!"), signing it "Subcomandante Marcos, alias El Sup Speedy Gonzalez, or, what amounts to the same thing, 'the stone in the shoe.'"[23] In the second, written in Nahuatl, the indigenous language spoken by Emiliano Zapata (but not by Chiapas's indigenous), he proclaimed "Zapata Lives." Both communiqués were clearly intended to herald the return of Marcos to the public scene, to allay fears concerning his demise, and to taunt the Mexican government. Two days later, Marcos issued a third communiqué in which he denounced the Mexican president for his duplicity and deplored the increased militarization of the region. *La Jornada* published all twenty-four pages of it on 17 July. This was one of Marcos's most vitriolic and most erudite pieces of prose. It was also one of his most literary and philosophical works, containing quotations from Shakespeare (*Hamlet*) and Manuel Vázquez Montalbán, and embodying a searing indictment of modernity and globalization. In it the Subcommander returned to his leitmotif, the theme of masks, identifying several that were currently concealing the true face of Mexico, including the masks of modernity, of a successful economic program, of a war on drugs, of the end of Mexico as a populist state, and so on. El Sup also identified the wider casualties arising from the government's recent offensive: peace, dialogue, the indigenous, civil society, democracy, national sovereignty, CONAI, and COCOPA. Concerning the last, Marcos expressed his dismay that Zedillo had treated COCOPA so cynically and affirmed the EZLN's commitment to the body—an expression that did much to convince COCOPA that its relationship with the EZLN had been largely restored.

The communiqué also contained two parables by Marcos. The first was a tale of how Old Antonio had killed a lion by feeding it the heart of a calf studded with shards from a broken mirror. Unable to differentiate between the blood from the calf's heart and its own lacerated mouth, the lion devoured itself. Although never made explicit, it is not unreasonable to suppose that this bestial act of self-destruction was meant to mirror that of the Mexican government's: by devouring the indigenous people, Zedillo's regime was also, like the lion, destroying itself by its failure to distinguish between its own life-blood and that of its victim. Such a reading fits well with Marcos's accusation elsewhere that "the government is drunk on Indian blood."[24] The second parable was less subtle, and was meant to ridicule a strategy commonly recommended in counterinsurgency manuals for destroying guerrillas—who, Mao had declared, must move like a fish in water—by draining their "water." The Subcommander related how a lion who wishes to devour a large river fish is told that he must first drink up all the water, leaving the fish high and dry and therefore easy to devour. When he follows this advice the lion dies, bloated with water. The implication is clear: if the government attempted to destroy the EZLN by "draining" the people, it would have to try to eradicate everyone, and by doing so perish.

Less than a week later, on 21 July, just as Kofi Annan, the secretary general of the UN, landed in Mexico, the EZLN issued its *Fifth Declaration of the Lacandón Jungle*, calling for the recognition of Indian rights and a national Consulta in support of Indian rights and culture. The government's response was to increase the military presence in the region, bringing in an additional five regiments from neighboring Tabasco, and to increase the harassment of La Realidad's citizens by upping the number of local ground patrols and aerial passes. Moreover, the minister of the interior rejected the idea of a national Consulta on the grounds that one had already been undertaken in 1995. He even went so far as to dismiss "Guillén," as he persistently referred to Marcos, as an irrelevance, who could stay in the Chiapan jungle for another two, or even five, years without affecting the government. In his 1 September annual state of the nation address, Zedillo made no reference to Chiapas.

In early November, Marcos gave a lengthy interview to *La Jornada*, the first in nine months. In line with the date (almost the fifteenth anniversary of the EZLN's inception) and the guerrilla tendency for self-evaluation (inherited from Mao and advocated by Che Guevara), Marcos devoted some time to outlining the errors he believed he had committed as the Zapatistas's spokesman. Chief among these, he said, was his tendency to pass judgment on others (for example, the PRD, the PAN, the Church) and to tar the entire PRI with the same brush—a trait that had led to the alienation of potential supporters and exacerbated the Zapatistas's isolation.

After some tentative approaches, the EZLN and members of COCOPA agreed to meet in November. Initially, the plan was that the two would meet at La Realidad, but when the COCOPA arrived in San Cristóbal Marcos announced that the recent increase in military patrols had made it too dangerous for the comandancia to leave its jungle hideouts. (The vulnerability of La Realidad had been shown by a recent impromptu military search and sweep of the community.) Instead, the Subcommander proposed that the COCOPA arrange for the safe passage of the comandancia to San Cristóbal and meet there from 20–22 November to discuss future negotiations. These dates, however, coincided with another proposed meeting, between the CCRI and civil society, and it began to look to some as if Marcos had calculatingly used the proposed COCOPA meeting as a means of ensuring security for the CCRI's trip. As Ross comments, "The EZLN's cleverness was transparent . . . the COCOPAS wondered if they had been sandbagged by the Sup."[25]

Nonetheless, the arrangements were made and the CCRI went to San Cristóbal, escorted by the International Red Cross, to meet the COCOPA. Unfortunately, this meeting started off on a very bad footing. The El Carmen convent, which the COCOPA had arranged for the Zapatista delegation to be housed in, appeared woefully substandard to the comandantes. On meeting at 6 P.M. on 20 November (the anniversary of the start of the Mexican Revolution) the Zapatista delegation, furious at the lack of telephones, faxes, blankets, hot water, mattresses, and flushing toilets, harangued the twelve-person COCOPA delegation. Indeed, Comandante Tacho accused the COCOPA of racism and claimed that the Zapatista delegation had been deliberately humiliated. This verbal attack, coupled with the CO-COPA's suspicions that they had already been manipulated by the EZLN, created an atmosphere of mutual ill will. The two sides parted having achieved nothing.

If the COCOPA meeting proved fruitless, the meeting with civil society was far more productive. Twenty-nine comandantes met with 3,000 members of civil society, during which the plans for another Consulta were drawn up. This Consulta was set for 21 March 1999 and was conceived as a huge undertaking: 5,000 Zapatistas, comprising an equal number of men and women, would be sent out into as many as possible of Mexico's 2,438 municipalities to put five questions to as many people as possible over the age of twelve. (Unlike the 1995 Consulta, this one, although international in that it consulted Mexicans living abroad, excluded non-Mexicans.) The first four questions would be difficult for any rational human being to answer "no" to. (1) Should Mexico's indigenous be allowed to take an active part in Mexico's future? (2) Should peace be sought through dialogue and the Federal Army returned to barracks? (3) Should the government abide by the result of the Consulta? (4) Should the San Andrés Accords, signed by the government's own negotiation team be incorporated into the Mexican constitution? The fifth question, however, was much more controversial and reflected a debate that had developed in Mexico in recent years: should Mexicans residing in foreign countries be allowed to vote in national elections? Its inclusion was shrewd, since it raised a contentious issue that all Mexicans would have an opinion on, even if they cared little for what was happening far away in Chiapas.[26] The fact that some 3 million Mexicans were residing in the United States meant that the Zapatista struggle would again be internationalized, with the U.S. media focusing on the issue, especially in states containing a high concentration of Mexicans. The remaining weeks of the year, and the first two months of 1999, were taken up in orchestrating this massive endeavor.

29. A Consulta, a Story, and a Strike

The first of January 1999 followed the pattern of the preceding two years, that is, one of silence on the part of the Zapatistas. Once again there were no high-profile celebrations to commemorate the uprising, and no *Declaration of the Lacandón Jungle* issued forth from the mountains of southeast Mexico. However, the Zapatistas were far from idle: they were pouring all their energies into the coming Consulta.

Zapatista representatives fanned out across the country visiting 1,299 municipalities and making contact with 64,598,409 Mexicans.[1] Of course, the Zapatista cause had always been strong in Chiapas, neighboring Oaxaca, and among the more progressive elements of large cities such as Mexico City and Guadalajara, which had a considerable student population. The Consulta, however, forced Mexicans in many other places, very much removed ethnically, socially, and geopolitically from Chiapas, to think about indigenous rights. Suddenly, northern cities such as Tijuana and Ciudad Juárez, whose indigenous population is comparatively miniscule (both in absolute terms and as a percentage of their populations), and whose attentions tend to be focused on issues such as drugs and their relationship with the United States, were now invited to turn their gaze southward, to an area as distant from them as Canada but inextricably linked to them by ties of national and cultural identity. The Consulta also provided many Mexicans with their first opportunity of seeing and meeting a Zapatista. As Marcos put it, "The people are going to get to know the Zapatistas, not just through the television or newspapers, but in the flesh."[2] In certain suburbs of certain cities, few had ever met and talked with an indigenous person. Now, people were forced to form an opinion based on fact and in some instances to come to terms with their own prejudices.

Meanwhile, question five had ensured that the international response was huge, with Mexicans throughout the world registering their views through the Consulta. Local Zapatista support groups in twenty-nine regions as far afield as Southeast Asia, northern Europe, the Middle East, the Far East, and Africa, made aware of the Consulta through Marcos's communiqués posted on the Internet, worked hard to ensure that Mexican expatriates everywhere could express their views on the Indian issue.

The results of the Consulta were counted on 21 March. There had been an impressive turnout. As Ross emphasized:

> The EZLN had to weigh in considerably stronger than the 1.3 million votes it garnered in 1995 and also equal or better the 3.1 million votes accumulated by the PRD in its August FOBAPROA plebiscite. The totals came close to the mark: 2,830,000 votes were tallied in country and 65,000 in the Diaspora, about 2.9 million in all, which more than doubled '95 and came in just a shade under the PRD's referendum.[3]

The Consulta's results were published as far away as Britain, with the *Guardian* publishing an article, "Millions Back Mexican Rebels in Referendum."[4]

The Zedillo administration ignored all this. It had long since shown its imperviousness to public opinion, especially concerning Chiapas, while the issue of expatriates voting in the coming 2000 general election would be rejected since the PRI knew only too well that, as Ross puts it, "Having already voted with their feet against the economic and political travesty in their homeland, most of the voters would go to the opposition."[5] Thus, although the opposition-dominated lower house of Congress passed a bill encapsulating the people's responses to the Consulta, this was defeated in the predominantly PRI Senate.

Eight days after the Consulta results were made public, the PRI governor of Chiapas, in a transparent attempt to regain the public relations initiative, orchestrated what one recent author has dubbed a "jungle Vaudeville"[6] in which sixteen supposed Zapatistas spontaneously "deserted" and surrendered their weapons—taking advantage of the governor's amnesty, issued exactly one year after the massacre at Acteal—in front of media representatives who just happened to be on hand to witness it. The incident was given extensive coverage on national television, although many doubted its authenticity and even those who believed it wondered how significant the desertion of sixteen would be from an army that was estimated in thousands. Worse still for the government, when Chiapas's governor and the interior minister attempted to counter such doubts by stating that between fifteen and twenty thousand Zapatistas either had defected or were in the process of doing so, Marcos hoisted them by their own petards. Had not, the Subcommander coyly asked, the government always hitherto claimed that the

EZLN numbered only between three hundred and five hundred located in only four municipios? If so, how could thirty times that number have defected in ten municipios as the government was now claiming? Was he the only Zapatista remaining, Marcos mused? What was to be made of the fact that more than 460,000 chiapanecos had supported Zapatista proposals in the recent Consulta? Were not these then Zapatistas of sorts, and if so, at the present rate of defections claimed by the authorities (i.e., 3,062 each year), would it not take 150 years before all "Zapatistas" had abandoned the movement?[7] The government, by opportunistically changing its version of the truth to suit its immediate needs, had allowed Marcos once again to expose its inconsistency, its stupidity, and its lies.

Spring 1999 also witnessed the publication of Marcos's book, *La Historia de los Colores/The Story of Colors*. This is a bilingual (Spanish and English) work, lavishly illustrated with indigenous artwork, that originated as a communiqué Marcos wrote in 1994. The book, hardback and a mere forty pages long, created a storm of controversy even before it went to press. Funding for its publication had initially been sought by a U.S. publisher from the National Endowment for the Arts (NEA). Discussions appeared to be going well, and the NEA was on the verge of agreeing a $7,500 grant, when it suddenly performed a volte-face. This was on the strength of a phone call from Julia Preston (of the *New York Times*), who pointed out to the NEA's chairman, William J. Ivey, the controversy that could possibly arise from U.S. taxpayers indirectly sponsoring a work by a Mexican guerrilla leader. Ivey rapidly countermanded the NEA's grant-approval body.[8] The book was nevertheless subsequently published without NEA funding and has indeed aroused considerable controversy, which in turn led to considerable sales—6,000 copies in the first forty-eight hours. Generally, however, those reviewers who have confined their comments to the work itself, and not its author, have praised its eloquence, artwork, and educational value.

Spring 1999 also saw, after a break of more than six months, another government attack on an autonomous community. On 7 April 1999, Roberto Armando Albores Guillén, the interim state governor of Chiapas, attempted to dismantle the autonomous center at San Andrés Sakamchem, the site of the San Andrés Accords negotiations. The building where the negotiations had been conducted was seized and a PRI municipal president installed. The Zapatistas's response was not long in coming. At noon on the following day, 3,000 Zapatistas and their sympathizers reclaimed the community, running the PRI president and his small security force out of town. Two days later, 10,000 gathered in the community's main square to celebrate victory over the "bad government" and to commemorate the anniversary of Emiliano Zapata's assassination. In a communiqué released soon after, Marcos ridiculed the state governor for being "so stupid that he thinks ten thousand Zapatistas have come to Sakamchem to defect!"[9] However, although Marcos and the Zapatistas had achieved a victory at San Andrés Sakamchem, the situation in the rest of Chiapas was looking far less promising as the government continued to increase its policy of militarization. Indeed, according to one reporter who lived alongside Zapatista communities for seven years (including 1999), in this year "The Mexican army amplified its sphere of influence into 66 of Chiapas' 111 municipalites."[10] She adds that "37,000 soldiers were stationed in the five municipalities of Ocosingo, Altamirano, Las Margaritas, La Independencia and La Trinitaria, which together had a population of less than 300,000, so that there was one soldier for every nine inhabitants."[11]

Two weeks later, on 20 April, a general strike broke out at UNAM over a proposed substantial increase in tuition fees. Naturally, this proposal attracted adverse comment from every leftist group in Mexico, but the Zapatistas, and Marcos in particular, enjoyed even closer links with the students because of the support given to the EZLN by them over the preceding five years and because UNAM was Marcos's alma mater. Marcos therefore embroiled himself and the EZLN in the strike, again ensuring that the media spotlight would fall on the Zapatistas, even if this time they were not center stage.

On 10 May, striking students were invited to La Realidad for another meeting with civil society—nearly two thousand people turned up—along the lines of the one held in San Cristóbal the previous November that had organized the Consulta. Media representatives flocked to the jungle rendezvous to capture the moment when students met their idol. Many had devotedly followed Marcos's career, reading his communiqués and every interview with him, attending pro-Zapatista rallies in the Zócalo, buying Marcos merchandise, and so on. Some felt that they had practically grown up with El Sup—he had blazed across their television screens as they had entered their teens and had been with them ever since, part of a popular culture of resistance. The press, too, many of whom who had not glimpsed Marcos since his last major appearance in January 1997, eagerly awaited the Subcommander's grand entrance. Thus, as Ross notes, when the Subcommander rode into La Realidad on 11 May, "strong women and grown men swooned . . . absence had not dimmed the Subcomandante's charisma."[12]

In the summer, as the UNAM strike crystallized and then fractured into "moderates," "ultras," and "mega-ultras," five Zapatista representatives were dispatched from Chiapas to the campus in solidarity. Over the months Marcos issued no fewer than ten communiqués in support of the strike and even diverted funds amounting to 21,900 pesos, raised by the Independent Union of Workers of the Autonomous Metropolitan University "for the purchase of maize for the communities in resistance," to help the striking students at UNAM.[13] In June, Marcos was joined at La Realidad by a large group of student strikers. No doubt the Subcommander felt twinges of nostalgia when talking to these young UNAM students, reflecting on his own days, two decades earlier, as a student activist supporting a strike by the University Union over contracts for administrative and academic staff.

Marcos, however, did not confine his comments on the strike to students. He openly challenged certain academics at the university and those intellectual commentators who advocated compromise with the government on this issue. He publicly rebuked both Adolfo Gilly and Carlos Monsiváis for their collaboratist tendencies, an action that caused great media interest—the Mexican press, after all, enjoys left-wing intellectuals accusing one another of selling out, the more so when they had formerly been allies. This dispute has, however, perhaps been overplayed by some.[14] All publicity is good publicity, and Carlos Monsiváis was clearly not excessively aggrieved, since only six months later, in January 2001, he made the arduous trek into the jungle to interview Marcos.

The summer also witnessed Marcos seeking to capture the attention of the international community. In June, he wrote the communiqué,[15] "'No!' to the War in the Balkans," which he addressed to "the peoples in the struggle against the war, to civil Europe, to the men and women who are saying 'No!'" Marcos no doubt felt strongly about this issue, but by electing to express his views so publicly he was again internationalizing the Zapatista struggle.

Also in June, Marcos took the curious decision to write to Asma Jahangir, the UN special reporter for extrajudicial, summary, and arbitrary executions, asking her not to meet the Zapatistas in her forthcoming visit to Mexico. It is not certain whether this decision was due to Marcos's expressed belief that the United Nations "no longer represents anything"[16] and had tainted itself with its involvement in Kosovo, or whether it was calculated to gain even more attention. (As Ross observes, it "set an international precedent: in a post-Kosovo world, a group victimized by governmental persecution had refused to talk with the U.N. on ethical grounds. . . . During the U.N.'s half century of assuaging world conflict, most beleaguered national liberation movements had always cried out for an audience with the United Nations.")[17]

Once again, in what by now was becoming Zedillo's standard policy, the president omitted any mention of Chiapas in his state of the nation address on 1 September. This was the third year in a row now that he had failed to invoke the name of the nation's most troubled state, having done so only once, in his very first address in 1995.

Marcos had perhaps calculated that he could afford to take a cool stance toward Asma Jahangir in June, since he knew that her visit would be followed in November by that of the more eminent Mary Robinson, the UN High Commissioner for Human Rights. Although Marcos did not meet Robinson either, her visit attracted much more international attention and sparked a series of civil actions within Mexico. Robinson concluded her visit by condemning the widespread human rights abuses in Mexico, by insisting that all claims of such abuses should be investigated thoroughly and by stating her belief that the Federal Army should pull back from its front-line positions in Chiapas so as to end its disruption of the daily lives of the chiapanecos. To some extent Marcos could sit back and watch his work being done for him.

So in Chiapas, 1999 (and indeed the twentieth century) ended not so much with a bang as a whimper. The Zapatistas continued their work developing the autonomous communities while ignoring, and being ignored by, the government.

30. A Change of Government

As had become the norm, there were no celebrations at La Realidad on 1 January 2000, even though this was the sixth anniversary of the rebellion and much of the world was (erroneously[1]) celebrating the dawn of a new millennium. What was there for an average chiapaneco residing deep in the Zapatista zone to celebrate? True, as Kampwirth observes, by now "80 percent of the predominantly indigenous municipalities of Chiapas had declared their autonomy."[2] However, the government continued to ignore their demands, the Federal Army continued to harass them, and paramilitaries continued to murder them. A 1999 Human Rights Watch report, "Systematic Injustice: Torture, 'Disappearance,' and Extrajudicial Execution in Mexico," had concluded that "the obstacles to justice in human rights cases are immense in Mexico," having already commented on its opening page that "torture, 'disappearance,' and extrajudicial executions remain widespread in Mexico . . . because political leaders have been unwilling to ensure that existing human rights–related laws are applied vigorously . . . [and] authorities are more likely to close ranks and deny that even well-documented abuses ever took place than they are to insist that those responsible be brought to justice."[3] Although such abuses were not restricted to autonomous communities, they certainly bore the brunt of them, and the price to be paid for autonomy was high.

Almost from the outset 2000 was dominated by the forthcoming general election to be held on 2 July. The attention of the Mexican people, and of the international media, whenever it chose to look at Mexico, was focused on the election campaign to the virtual exclusion of all other issues. For example, little space was devoted in either the national or international media to a report presented in February by Asma Jahangir, the UN special commissioner for extrajudicial, arbitrary, and summary executions, which concluded that these were widespread in Mexico and that both federal and local governments were not infrequently involved in them. Little, too, was made by the press of a report drawn up in April by Mexican legislators who had visited Chiapas, in which it was stated that military and paramilitary activity were both on the increase in that state, despite government claims to the contrary. Even a story by award-winning journalist, Hermann Bellinghausen, which noted that Chiapas now contained "more than seven hundred different military installations," was relegated to page five of *La Jornada* and in any case failed to create a stir.[4] So too, the government's repression of the UNAM strike in early February, using riot police who arrested a thousand students in three days, only briefly distracted the nation.

This is not to say, however, that the nation's fixation on the coming elections was entirely misplaced. The prospect, now very real,[5] of the PRI being dismissed from office after seventy years in power was a natural preoccupation. Unfortunately for the Zapatistas, the coming election not only stole their limelight for the first six months of the year, it also threatened the movement's destruction whatever the result. If the PRI won again, it was feared that Zedillo would order a massive military offensive against the Zapatistas, partly in revenge, but also to clear the way for his successor. If the PRD or PAN won, then the military might well spontaneously seize the initiative in order to make good their past humiliations at the EZLN's hands and to demonstrate their power to the new civilian government. Either way, the future was not looking good for the Zapatistas and Marcos knew it. On 9 June, the Zapatistas organized a demonstration in the Zócalo by civil society to express their fears for the future and to capture a little of the spotlight that had so far eluded them that year. Regrettably, the pull of the election, only three weeks away, resulted in only a few hundred supporters turning out, the lowest since the uprising began. All that was left for Marcos to do was to write a communiqué despairing at the superficial and circus-like manner in which the election was being conducted and warning about the dangers posed to democracy by the media's concentration on the personalities of the presidential candidates as opposed to the policies of the parties which they represented.

In the event, the PRI lost to the PAN, stunning Mexicans and the international community. In Chiapas there was less cause for celebration than elsewhere in the country since, as Kampwirth notes:

> Even when the PRI's grip on national power was at its weakest, it remained fairly strong in the state of Chiapas. In the July election, the ruling party took eleven of the twelve congressional seats from the state

. . . though a month later, in August, the PRI lost its hold on the governorship to Pablo Salazar, representative of the opposition coalition, *Alianza por Chiapas*.[6]

Nonetheless, the election result still represented a massive psychological break with the past and for four months everybody—including even Marcos, who issued no communiqués—pondered the possibilities that a change of government entailed.

On the very few occasions in which the election result was mentioned in connection with the EZLN, it was said that perhaps there was no longer a place for the Zapatistas in Mexican politics, since one of their major aims, the removal of the PRI, had been achieved.[7] Indeed, George Collier commented that since one of the Zapatistas's overriding agendas was "to end the PRI's domination of Mexican politics . . . the fact that there has been an election where the PAN won undercuts a lot of support within Mexican society that might otherwise have continued."[8] Others put it even more starkly, declaring that a PAN electoral victory had destroyed the Zapatistas's entire raison d'être. In November, a correspondent from the *Financial Times* lamented the fading away of Marcos in an article headlined "Adiós Zapatistas."[9]

This, however, was not only to underestimate the Zapatistas, and in particular Marcos, but also to misunderstand the aims and views of the EZLN. An irate Subcommander had already had to point out to a reporter who had asked him who he favored in the coming elections, "We didn't make this revolution to vote for a political party."[10] Indeed, the Subcommander's faith in all of Mexico's political parties had perhaps completely evaporated because of what had happened during the six years of the rebellion. Why the PAN should be especially repugnant to Marcos is not difficult to see. To think that the PAN represents any sort of victory for the Left or even the liberal center is misguided. In 1994, two Mexico City magazine (*Pusmoderna*) editors, Mongo Sánchez Lira and Rogelio Villarreal, described the PAN as "rightist," "intolerant and reactionary."[11] So too, Ross echoes this verdict. After outlining the origins of the party ("the right-of-center National Action Party [is] the 54-year-old, pro-Catholic, pro-Capitalist PAN, founded in 1939 by conservative banker Manuel Gómez Morín in 1939 to hex the red despotism with which President Lazaro Cárdenas menaced the land"), he concludes that "Chiapas was a distant republic to the PAN whose upwardly-mobile, middle-class base had little contact with indigenous issues other than how much to pay their maids each week." He also

observes that the party's "economic outlook and offer of limited and negotiated democratic reform coincided quite comfortably with that of the PRI."[12]
Fuentes, when writing about PAN, likewise emphasized "the reactionary
nature of its antigay, antiabortion, proclerical social agenda."[13]

Marcos had already made his views on the PAN known. When talking
of the "fascist right," he had included as an example, "the most organized
expression of that right, the PAN."[14] Furthermore, the Subcommander had
already had a glimpse of the PAN's vision for the future and had not liked
what he had seen. In mid-August 1999, Marcos had held a meeting deep
in the Lacandón with four hundred scholars (predominantly anthropologists), students, and indigenous people to discuss ways of opposing a constitutional amendment proposed by the PAN that would privatize national
heritage sites and monuments such as Palenque and Toniná in Chiapas
(and Teotihuacán near Mexico City).

In this respect, an interesting exchange had taken place between the
Subcommander and Medea Benjamin, co-director of Global Exchange and
part of the first human rights delegation to go to Chiapas, during a 1994
interview. Marcos had just explained the reasons for the uprising: "The
war should only be to open up space in the political arena so that people
can really have a choice. . . . It doesn't matter who wins, it doesn't matter if it's the extreme Right or the extreme Left, as long as they earn the
confidence of the people." This prompted Benjamin to ask the prescient
question: "Would you really be happy to make these incredible sacrifices
so that an ultraright party could come to power?" Marcos replied: "We want
to create the political space, and we want the people to have the education
and the political maturity to make good choices."[15] The Subcommander's
clear side-stepping of this question perhaps reveals his true thoughts on a
reality that in 2000 he was now forced to face.[16]

Perhaps in answer to suggestions concerning the redundancy of the Zapatistas, Marcos broke his silence in late November, issuing a communiqué to the outgoing President Zedillo which reads as a damning indictment not just of his dealings with the Zapatistas[17] but also of his policies
in general.[18] He then called a press conference for 2 December, in which
he promised to outline the Zapatistas's stance toward the new government.
At the conference, Marcos sensibly warned against euphoria, emphasizing
that although the requisite conditions for democracy were now in place,
democracy would not automatically ensue—it would have to be worked at
long and hard, and the pitfall of "presidentialism" would have to be avoided.

Footage of this conference and, in particular, Marcos's response to the new PAN government, was beamed across the world. The BBC's *News 24* took up the story, while the following day even Japan's rather conservative NHK showed the same footage on its 10 P.M. news.[19]

The Zapatistas were center stage again, with reports of their and Marcos's demise having proved somewhat exaggerated.[20] Indeed, 2000 saw the publication of several books[21] on Marcos or dealing with the Zapatistas in general, with others following in 2001 and 2002.[22]

To capitalize on their return to the limelight, and to ensure that attention remained firmly fixed upon the Zapatistas' cause, shortly afterward Marcos announced the sending of a delegation comprising twenty-three comandantes to the capital early in the coming year, in the form of a march.[23] The director of *Le Monde Diplomatique*, Ignacio Ramonet, calls the announcement a "bombshell," which caught "politicians across the board . . . off guard," adding "It was a bold move at a delicate moment."[24] He is surely correct. Marcos was no doubt gambling that Vicente Fox would be thrown off balance by the march and would accept talks with the delegation as a means of commencing his presidency with a positive move that addressed the nation's most serious problem of the last six years. (The recent announcement by Colombia's president Andrés Pastrana that he would meet the FARC guerrillas' leader, Manuel "Sure-shot" Marulanda, provided a perfect backdrop for Marcos's move. How could Mexico's president oppose the Zapatista delegation's march on the capital when Colombia's president was prepared to venture into the heart of rebel territory in his search for reconciliation?) Marcos may also have wanted to test the new president's resolve to remedy the Chiapas situation, since during his election campaign Fox had boasted that he would solve the crisis politically and without violence "in fifteen minutes"—the Subcommander's timing, on the eve of Fox's inauguration, perhaps served to remind both the president and the public of this pledge, and to gently rebuke him for making such a rash promise.[25] In any event, as Carlos Monsiváis observed:

> The march was a stroke of genius. The government will have to work to a timetable set by Marcos. That gives him the initiative. And Fox has to accept it—partly because he's being pushed by national and international pressure, and partly because, by coming to talk to the new government in Mexico City, Marcos is giving it a legitimacy that he never gave the Salinas and Zedillo regimes—which the Zapatistas and many other Mexicans saw as frauds and cheats.[26]

The newly inaugurated president sent COCOPA's proposal for constitutional reform to the Senate only days later on 5 December. The stage was set for 2001 to be a landmark year for Mexico.

31. The Zapatour

Early in 2001, Marcos issued a communiqué announcing the details of the Zapatistas's embassy to the capital, outlining how a Zapatista caravan would leave San Cristóbal de las Casas in Chiapas on 24 February, wind its way through thirteen states for fifteen days, and finally arrive in Mexico City on 11 March. This would be the Zapatistas's biggest public relations exercise so far and something of a gamble since Marcos could not be sure of the strength of support for the Zapatistas in urban areas.[1] (He need not have worried; a poll taken shortly before the caravan set off showed that "57 percent of Mexicans thought the march 'was positive for the political life of the country.'"[2] Marcos himself, realizing the positive and eager anticipation of Mexican society toward the caravan, reflected a few days later that "we had not expected such a response and it has outstripped all our expectations.")[3] The March for Indian Dignity (as Marcos called it) or the Zapatour (as the media soon dubbed it) comprised twenty-three Zapatista comandantes, together with Marcos himself—the first time the Subcommander had been seen outside Chiapas—and an entourage of press and supporters. (Fernando Yáñez Muñoz [alias Comandante Germán] would also be joining the delegation, as an EZLN communiqué stated, being "the person in charge of acting as an intermediary between the zapatista delegation and the deputies and senators [as well as] the leadership of the different Mexican political parties who wish to engage in dialogue with us.")[4] The caravan would snake its way northward for 3,000 km, stopping at thirty-three communities to spread their word and eventually arriving in Mexico City to petition the 628 deputies and senators comprising the Mexican Congress of Union to implement the San Andrés Accords.

Throughout January and February President Fox was in private busy allaying the worries of the business community and international investors, while in public lauding the Zapatista march as a golden opportunity for peace to be brought to Chiapas after six long years. He had appeared indifferent, if not blasé, when first informed of the march, merely com-

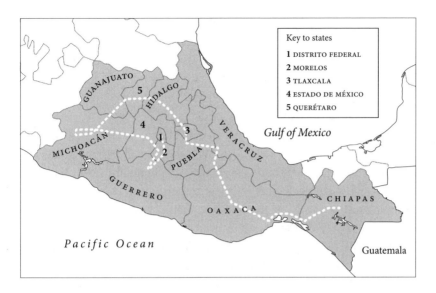

MAP 3: ROUTE OF THE ZAPATOUR (COURTESY OF THE IRISH
MEXICO GROUP).

menting that "the country is more than just Chiapas . . . if they march, they
march. If they don't want to march, they won't march; as they like."[5] As the
time approached, however, Fox became far more enthusiastic, stating that,
"My priority, these days, is that the march of the EZLN goes well."[6] So effusive was Fox in his support of the march that Marcos's suspicions became
aroused with him claiming that "the president is trying to appropriate the
Zapatista march, virtually presenting it as a Foxist march."[7] Marcos outlined what he believed were the true motives behind Fox's overtures: "His
[Fox's] strategy is to pressure the EZLN by telling the world that peace has
already been achieved, and if it's not signed, it's the Zapatistas' fault. This
is a kind of blackmail. He wants the EZLN to surrender unconditionally."[8]
In order to guard against this, and as a test of Fox's genuine commitment
to negotiate a fair peace and his ability to rein in hard-liners and the military, the Subcommander asked "for three small signs of goodwill on his
part: the release of all Zapatista prisoners, a withdrawal of the army from
seven military positions, and the ratification of the San Andrés Accords
on the rights of indigenous people, signed by the government in 1996 but
never implemented."[9] By the time the march commenced on 24 February Fox had released sixty (out of one hundred) Zapatista prisoners and
had pulled the army back from four of the seven positions identified by
Marcos. Compared with the previous actions of the Salinas and Zedillo

regimes, this was a promising start—Fox's government had done more in two months to address the Zapatistas's demands than his PRI predecessors had in six years—but, it was just a start. Much would depend on whether and how rapidly the other forty prisoners would be released, the remaining three army positions would be vacated and, perhaps most difficult of all, what fate awaited the San Andrés Accords.

From the very beginning of the march Marcos was the centerpiece. On leaving La Realidad for San Cristóbal, the formal starting point, the press focused on the Subcommander, photographing him slowly and self-consciously disarming for his journey to the capital. These pictures appeared almost instantly on the Internet, thanks to Associated Press and Reuters. He also took the opportunity to give an interview to the Mexico City newspaper, *Reforma*, in which, for the first time, he discussed personal relationships in some detail. He revealed that the "La Mar" he had made reference to in several communiqués[10] was short for "Mariana," and that "We are married according to our laws," adding "and we have no reason to hide it because it's something that goes back a while." As if to illustrate this, on the march Marcos could be seen clearly wearing a wedding ring.[11]

Interestingly, however, Marcos had not advertised this fact previously. For example, he wore no wedding ring; he flirted outrageously with female reporters, special guests (such as Danielle Mitterrand, whose hand he kissed, to whom he presented a paper rose, and with whom he walked arm in arm),[12] and young admirers who had trekked into the jungle to meet him; and he had written some fairly florid poetry and prose to admiring female correspondents. Moreover, in at least one interview he had explicitly claimed not to have a partner.[13] The reasons for his past deception are perhaps easier to understand than the motive behind this new revelation. There had always been the question of personal security. His enemies could have used this knowledge to get at Marcos or his partner. In addition, his "single" status was good for public relations—a large part of his fan base was women, for whom his mystique and romance would be diminished by the knowledge that he was already married—a vital aspect of the Zapatista cause. As far as the revelation is concerned, since this was the first time in at least six years that he was leaving Chiapas, he may have felt that this was the appropriate moment to tell the world about his love.

In fact Marcos revealed very little about the relationship other than that Mariana was "a political animal and a voracious reader" whose function within the movement was now to monitor the press coverage of the Zapatistas.[14] He then went on to give his opinion on relationships in general: "In every part of the world, in the Lacandón Jungle, love is a very difficult feeling, because a relationship is a shared thing." He added, "Separate from the affection that one gives the other, it has a lot to do with sharing, and in the final analysis 'sharing' means respecting the other person." Finally, Marcos said he would like to have children, when conditions were right.[15] Given that conditions in Chiapas have not substantially improved since 2001 it seems likely that the couple remain childless, although it is possible that they have had a child in secret.[16]

In his desire for children, Marcos is conforming very much to the general pattern of guerrillas. As Anderson, in his study of guerrillas, notes:

In the end, whatever the cultures they are from, however committed they are to their struggles, and even after many years of warfare, no guerrillas are quite capable of sacrificing all personal desires. In all of them, there is at least the private hope for a family of their own. It is as if men and women finally become aware that ideals are fragile things, and as the only certain legacy for a guerrilla's life is the quest for their fulfillment, they seek something more tangible to mold, even as they pursue the course of death.[17]

Between fifteen and twenty thousand people, for the most part probably from the Zapatistas's support base communities, turned out in San Cristóbal to see off the Zapatour. As one indigenous onlooker explained, he had waited seven years to see with his own eyes "this man [i.e., Marcos] who has come to us with so many ideas," adding, "to see so many different people here coming to support us is wonderful."[18] After singing the national anthem and the Zapatista anthem the predominantly indigenous crowd chanted "Marcos! Marcos! Marcos!" punctuated by individual shouts of "Viva, viva el Subcomandante Marcos!" as the Subcommander took the platform at 10 P.M. to deliver his speech. What he said that day (24 February) has been described by Carlos Monsiváis, no stranger to the power of eloquence, as "a classic" and a "message wrapped in rhetoric, yearning to communicate through the breath of poetry."[19]

We Mexican Indians are Indians and we are Mexicans. We want to be Indians and we want to be Mexicans. But the lord with a lot of tongue and not much ear, the one who governs us, offers us lies instead of a flag. Ours is the march of Indian dignity. The march of those of us who are the color of the earth and the march of all who are all the colors of the earth.

Compañeros and *compañeras* of the EZLN: For seven years we have resisted all sorts of attacks. They've attacked us with bombs and bullets, with torture and jailings, with lies and calumny, with scorn and neglect. But we have survived. We are the rebels of dignity. We are the forgotten heart of our country. We are the very first memory. We are the brown blood in the mountains that illuminates our history. We are those who struggle and live and die. We are those who say, "For everyone, everything; nothing for ourselves." We are the Zapatistas, the smallest of these lands. We salute the communities who lead us and care for us.

The march begins on Flag Day. Patriotism is reborn in those called unpatriotic by the governor of Querétaro, Ignacio Loyola.[20]

In playing the Mexican and Zapatista anthems, emphasizing that the rally was taking place on Flag Day, and in showing patriotism, Marcos succeeded in countering all the major criticisms leveled at the Zapatistas— that they were traitors who were using the indigenous to destroy Mexico through secession. Indeed, concerning this last point, which hard-liners and the right-wing press were stressing, Marcos had already told reporters for *Le Monde Diplomatique*, when they visited him in La Realidad on the eve of the commencement of the march:

We are not calling for an autonomy that will exclude others . . . we are not calling for independence. We don't want to proclaim the birth of the Maya nation, or fragment the country into lots of small indigenous countries. We are just asking for the recognition of the rights of an important part of Mexican society which has its own forms of organization that it wants to be legally recognized.[21]

(Later, during a speech he gave while on the tour, Marcos reiterated his reassurances concerning the Zapatistas's desire for an inclusive autonomy employing the slogan: "Don't let there be another dawn without the flag having a place for us.")[22]

The caravan, consisting of the Zapatistas themselves and a further "3,000 people of diverse organizations and nationalities,"[23] then set out from San Cristóbal on their long haul across the country. The Red Cross had refused to provide security for the caravan, so the task of protecting the delegation fell to a group of Italian anarchists, called Ya Basta! (Enough is enough!) after the Zapatistas's slogan, many of whom dressed in bright white boiler suits to ensure they stood out. The convoy arrived first in Oaxaca, the state which contains more indigenous people than any other in Mexico. Again,

Monsiváis describes the scene: "In Oaxaca, the spirit is more festive than in San Cristóbal, or more festive according to my traditional understanding of community jubilation. The frenzy, repeated a thousand times, comes from wanting to see, to hear, to witness Marcos, who is probably turning into a media-made myth."[24] A few days later, the Zapatour arrived at Ixmiquilpan. Here the Subcommander excelled himself in his showmanship, turning a sudden and torrential downpour to his advantage. After quipping that "Ixmiquilpan means place of sterile clouds: Seems like that's no longer the case," Marcos rebuffed an attempt to shelter him from the rain by pointing to the audience and declaring "No, if they get wet, so will I."[25] Thunderous applause ensued. He then continued with his speech. Once again, we must turn to Monsiváis for what followed.

> Marcos persists . . . "Is the EZLN the vanguard of the Mexican Indian movement?"
>
> "Yessss," shouts the crowd.
>
> I'm floored. The terrible history of "vanguardism" flashes through my mind, the arrogance of showing the people (civil society) the way. Seconds later, Marcos dispels my foreboding.
>
> "No way. The vanguard of the national Indian movement is made up of the Indian peoples of all Mexico."
>
> This line of questioning is risky, but for once it came out right.
>
> "The second question: Are you happy here with the EZLN?"
>
> "Yesss!"
>
> "Are we wet? No, not that one. Are we happy to have met?"
>
> Who could doubt the response.
>
> "Should the EZLN surrender?"
>
> "Noooo."
>
> "Will the EZLN sell out?"
>
> "Nooo."
>
> Marcos, wet, happy, humidly charismatic, caps it off: "We in the EZLN know we are not alone. Yes, we know we are not alone."[26]

Monsiváis concluded: "As much as I would like to wait a few years before using it, the adjective "historical" keeps circling me. What I've seen—the crowd in the rain—is a show, but what lies beneath it, each person's decision, is the greatest show of all."[27]

Throughout its journey the international media covered the caravan's progress on a daily basis. The Associated Press, Reuters, the BBC, a host of international magazines, and many national newspapers broadcast and published articles and an unprecedented number of photographs of the Zapatistas.[28]

Symbolically, just as with the 1997 march on Mexico City by 1,111 Zapatistas, Marcos and the other comandantes made their way along precisely the same route taken by Emiliano Zapata in 1914, when he conquered Mexico City. As they reached their final destination, the Zócalo, between 100,000 and 160,000 people turned out to meet them for what the international press variously described as their grand or triumphal entry.[29] A good many international figures attended as the Zapatistas's guests, including celebrities such as Oliver Stone, Nobel prize-winning author José Saramago, novelist Manuel Vázquez Montalbán, actor Robert Redford, and politicians such as Danielle Mitterrand, Euro MP Sami Naïr, and trade unionist José Bové. Once again the Subcommander had managed to maneuver himself into a position from which he could capitalize on his flair for theatrics and symbolism. As poet and former ambassador Homero Aridjis observed:

> The act staged by Marcos in the Zócalo on Sunday, 11 March was full of political symbolism: the Cathedral on the right, city hall on the left, the Mexican flag in the middle of the plaza, the Zapatista high command with their backs turned to the balcony of the National Palace (the most important political space in the country). This is where the President of the Republic gives the traditional "shout of independence." Marcos' own lyrical shout evoked indigenous poetry in its rhetoric. The Zapatistas' arrival in the Zócalo was by way of the *Avenue 20 de Noviembre*, which commemorates the Mexican Revolution. In fact, the event in the Zócalo was a symbolic political overthrow. Of course, if someone (Marcos) gains political space, someone else (Fox) loses it.[30]

The Subcommander's timing was, as ever, impeccable: he delivered his speech on the same day that Vicente Fox celebrated his hundredth day as president.

Once the Zócalo rally had finished, the comandantes moved to the nearby School of National Anthropology to learn if they would be heard by Congress. The invitation was not long in coming, but turned out to be a pale shadow of what the Zapatistas had been hoping for. The comandantes were to meet behind closed doors with only a select group (twenty members) of deputies, whose task it was to introduce the Indigenous Rights Bill to both houses of Congress. The argument was that there was no legislative precedent for the Chamber to be addressed by masked speakers.[31] This was a far cry from the Zapatistas's dreams of standing at the podium before a packed Congress. In addition, the invitation came in the form of an unsigned statement on plain—not headed—paper. Incensed at what they perceived as a deliberate slight, the Zapatistas immediately rejected it as "humiliating." Marcos lambasted the Congress's treatment of the Zapatista delegation: "We didn't come all this way to knock on doors and beg for an audience. Indian rights are a national clamor. We will not be treated like second-class bureaucrats assigned to some subcommittee."[32] The comandantes then sat back to await the Congress's next move. Marcos was probably in no hurry, for once the Zapatista delegation had addressed the Congress its reason for remaining in the capital would evaporate and it would have to return to Chiapas. Instead, he worked feverishly to influence as many people as possible. After all, this could prove the only occasion when ordinary Mexico City citizens, who had been so avidly reading about the Zapatistas in their newspapers, would be able to have direct access to the EZLN. Moreover, his presence in the capital ensured the attention of the international press, which would also gain access to Marcos far more easily there than in Chiapas. Thus he set about touring the Indian suburbs of the city (which together hold more than a million indigenous people), holding an enormous (40,000 strong) rally at UNAM, and delivering a feisty speech at the National Polytechnic Institute. The Subcommander later claimed that during the "Zapatour" he and the comandancia "held seventy-seven public events."[33] Marcos made a special effort to meet foreign intellectuals as well as Mexico's literary elite. He gave an interview with García Márquez and Pombo in which he explained the Zapatista's platform and answered some of the questions that Mexicans (and many throughout the world) had wanted to put to him over the last few years. In particular, the Subcommander was to use this opportunity to reiterate his (and the Zapatistas') rejection of vanguardism:

> You cannot reconstruct the world or society, nor rebuild national states now in ruins, on the basis of a quarrel over who will impose their hegemony on society. The world in general, and Mexican society in particular, is composed of different kinds of people, and the relationships between them have to be founded on respect and tolerance, things that appear in none of the discourses of the politico-military organizations of the sixties and seventies.[34]

After a week of doing the rounds, pressing the flesh, and making speeches, Marcos announced at a press conference that the delegation would now return to Chiapas. This was a masterful piece of political brinksmanship; the threat was thought serious enough to prompt the headline "Zapatistas Head Back to Jungle" on the BBC's World Service home page on Tuesday, 20 March 2001. Certainly, as Ross observed, "The Zapatistas' threatened leave-taking doused President Fox like a pail of coldwater."[35] Fox now saw his chance to settle the Chiapas crisis "in fifteen minutes" slipping through his fingers. He had staked much of his reputation as a politician and as a president who was cast in a different mold from his two PRI predecessors on his ability to resolve (or at least address) the Zapatista problem. Moreover, this was the first difficult test for his administration. How would it look if the Zapatistas returned to their jungle retreats harboring an even greater resentment toward the nation's ruling elite? It is in this context that Fox hastily agreed to release the remaining forty or so Zapatista prisoners and pull the army out of the remaining three bases that were in contention with the EZLN. Now there remained only the question of the Congress's approval of the San Andrés Accords—which could be solved only by a body that was currently refusing even to allow the Zapatistas to address it.

No doubt hoping that he could appease the Zapatistas by circumventing Congress and by appealing to what he perceived as the vanity of Marcos, Fox offered to meet the Subcommander face-to-face either in the Presidential Palace or anywhere that Marcos wanted, to discuss the situation in Chiapas. Marcos rejected Fox's initiative. He told interviewers Gabriel García Márquez and Roberto Pombo: "What Fox is saying is that he wants a slice of the media cake, in what has become a popularity contest, rather than a dialogue or negotiation. Fox is looking for a photo opportunity, to maintain his grip on the media."[36]

Instead, Marcos prepared for the leaving speech he would make on 22 March in the Zapatistas's much publicized departure from the capital. The Zapatistas chose as the venue for their farewell rally the pavement in front of the Chamber of Deputies (the lower house of Congress). (Never failing to miss an opportunity for symbolism, Marcos had the Zapatista caravan parked only meters away on, Emiliano Zapata Street.) At the same time, inside the building, a vote was being taken as to whether to allow the Zapatistas to address the house. As Ross puts it, "The pieces were in place for the showdown."[37] The announcement by the upper house (the Senate) that they had decided by only five votes not to permit the Zapatistas to address them added to the atmosphere of tension. Minutes later, the lower house voted by almost as narrow a margin (ten votes) in favor of allowing the Zapatistas entry.[38] Although the latter was a victory of sorts, voting by both houses of the Congress had done nothing to inspire hope for the passing of the Indigenous Rights Bill. For this to happen, there had to be a two-thirds majority in both houses. To make matters worse, as Ross observes, some of those deputies voting in favor of permitting the Zapatistas to take the podium were not motivated to do so by a genuine desire to see justice done: "The decisive margin was cast by the PRI, longtime foe of the Zapatista Army of National Liberation, which voted the insurgents' cause up March 22 just to *"chingar el PAN"* (fuck the PAN)."[39]

In a shrewd move Marcos absented himself from the delegation to the Chamber so as to confirm the Zapatistas's indigenous credentials and the movement's commitment to peaceful means. He had, after all, secured his aim of a hearing for the Zapatistas, against the wishes of many of the Chamber's members.

Having thus "captured" the capital more than seven years after they had set out to do so, the Zapatistas returned to the jungle to await the results of the Senate's verdict on the San Andrés Indigenous Rights Bill. In the event, the Senate considerably modified the bill, in particular (but not exclusively) by restricting indigenous autonomy to the municipal (and not regional) level—a limitation not envisaged in the original COCOPA-brokered proposal. Indeed, COCOPA immediately repudiated the Senate's modified bill, as of course did the EZLN. Nonetheless, despite opposition from the senators who had comprised COCOPA, it was passed by the Senate on 25 April. Three days later, it was passed in the lower house, with 360 voting for and only 60 against. A majority of state congresses also passed the new bill, although the margin of success here was far less impressive than in Congress: out of thirty-two states, nineteen voted to adopt it, nine voted against it, two did not vote at all, and one had the vote suspended.[40] On 14 August the constitutional reforms relating to Indian rights and culture became law. However, in effect, this merely allowed those indigenous communities who opposed them to begin the next stage of their opposition, namely, to submit "constitutional controversies" to the Supreme Court stating their belief that a violation or infringement of their constitutional rights had taken place as a result of the passing of this law. As Mattiace has observed: "By June 2002, indigenous municipalities in twenty-one states (for example, Puebla, Veracruz, Oaxaca, Chiapas, Tabasco, and Guerrero, among others) had submitted more than three hundred such controversies," adding that "these controversies address the content of the constitutional reforms on Indian rights and culture as well as the procedure followed in ratifying them."[41] (Chief among the latter objections was the widely held belief that ILO Convention 169, which Mexico had ratified in 1990, dictated that the indigenous people should have been consulted on the drafting of a reform such as this.) In these "controversies" the frequent demand was for the Supreme Court to rule the law invalid and for the original COCOPA bill instead to be submitted to Congress for a vote.

32. Marcos Today

Between his return to the jungle in 2001 and the start of 2005, Marcos kept a comparatively low profile, although the Zapatistas who follow him did not always do the same.[1] True, he continued to issue communiqués and make frequent contributions to the FZLN's *Rebeldía* magazine which has, as its three advisory editors, Fernando Yáñez Muñoz (formerly Comandante Germán), Gloria Muñoz Ramírez (see below), and Javier Elorriaga (formerly Comandante Vicente).[2] In his communiqués, in addition to roundly condemning the wars in Kosovo and Iraq,[3] and getting embroiled in a heated exchange with members of the Basque separatist group ETA (Euskadi Ta Askatasuna) following an offer by the Subcommander to mediate between them and the Spanish government,[4] Marcos catalogued cases of corruption, poverty, repression, disappearances, and proposed privatizations of historical national heritage sites in Mexico, and detailed indigenous (and other) opposition to such scandals and abuses.[5] However, in that period there were none of the high-profile public relations events that characterized the years 1994–2001, with the Subcommander's apparent lack of activity occasioning little comment in the international press, distracted as it was by the fallout from George W. Bush's "war on terror." The few people who did comment on Marcos's retreat into relative obscurity put this down to his having been "foxed" (pun intended) by Mexico's move from a one-party dictatorship toward democracy. Gillespie, an expert on guerrillas, noted: "Unfortunately, although Guevara warned against initiating guerrilla warfare against democratically elected governments, he had left behind no advice on how to respond to democratization once the guerrilla struggle was underway."[6] With the PAN having been voted into power, Marcos found himself opposing a comparatively more democratic regime with Che affording no advice on what to do.

However, there exists a more plausible explanation for Marcos's ostensible "inertia." This hitherto private stage of the Zapatistas's struggle during the period from April 2001 to the summer of 2005 has recently been illuminated in *The Sixth Declaration of the Lacandón Jungle* (June 2005).[7] The document's lengthy peroration begins with a brief overview of the history of the Zapatista movement from its inception in 1983. Significantly, however, it emphasizes the EZLN's total disillusionment with Mexico's politicians following the ratification of the law on Indian rights and culture:

> In April of 2001 . . . the politicians demonstrated quite clearly there that they had no decency whatsoever, and they were swine who thought only about making their good money as the bad politicians they were. . . . On that day, when the politicians from the PRI, PAN and PRD approved a law that was no good, they killed dialogue once and for all, and they clearly stated that it did not matter what they had agreed to and signed, because they did not keep their word . . . that dialogue and negotiation had failed as a result of those political parties. We saw that blood did not matter to them, nor did death, suffering, mobilizations, consultas, efforts, national and international statements, encuentros, accords, signatures, commitments. And then we saw all of that, and we wondered in our hearts what we were going to do.

And so, the Declaration tells us:

> For four years, since the middle of 2001 until the middle of 2005, we have devoted ourselves to . . . continue on ahead in the struggle, in spite of those lazy parasites of politicians . . . to carry out, alone . . . the San Andrés Accords regarding indigenous rights and culture . . . encouraging the autonomous rebel Zapatista municipalities . . . in order to make themselves stronger.

In short, the Zapatista leadership was busy with the daily business of helping to organize and run the indigenous autonomous communities. The difficulties involved in such a task ought not to be underestimated, as the EZLN itself makes clear:

> We saw that the Autonomous Municipalities were not level. There were some that were more advanced and which had more support from civil society, and others were more neglected. The organization was lacking to make them more on a par with each other. And we also saw that the EZLN, with its political-military component, was involving itself in decisions which belonged to the democratic authorities . . . what we then did about this problem was to begin separating the political-military from the autonomous and democratic aspects of organization in the Zapa-

tista communities. And so, actions and decisions which had previously been made and taken by the EZLN were being passed, little by little, to the democratically elected authorities in the villages. It is easy to say, of course, but it was very difficult in practice, because many years have passed—first in the preparation for the war and then the war itself—and the political-military aspects have become customary. . . . That was how the Good Government Juntas were born, in August of 2003. . . . From that time and until the middle of 2005, the EZLN leadership has no longer involved itself in giving orders in civil matters, but it has accompanied and helped the authorities who are democratically elected by the peoples. It has also kept watch that the peoples and national and international civil society are kept well informed concerning the aid that is received and how it is used. And now we are passing the work of safeguarding good government to the Zapatista support bases, with temporary positions which are rotated, so that everyone learns and carries out this work.

Throughout this period, the Declaration notes, the EZLN "also handed over to the Good Government Juntas and the Autonomous Municipalities the aid and contacts which they had attained throughout Mexico and the world during these years of war and resistance," with the result that "there has also been much improvement in the projects in the communities[8] . . . the distribution of projects and aid given by civil society from all over the world has become more level."

As 2005 approached, Marcos began to initiate a number of projects designed to rekindle his media profile. In winter 2004 Marcos approached Mexican writer Paco Ignacio Taibo II about working on a joint literary project: a detective novel. The two men, without meeting one another, would take it in turn to write a chapter, each starting from where the other had left off. This would then be published each Sunday in *La Jornada*. Marcos wrote the first chapter, which appeared on 5 December. Entitled *Muertos incómodos* (The Uncomfortable Dead), the novel pits two detectives, one a Zapatista investigator named Elías Contreras from Chiapas, and the other Héctor Belascoarán Shayne, the urban investigator who features in many of Taibo's novels, against a villain named Morales who personifies the "evil system." Contreras goes to Mexico City to investigate the disappearance of a Zapatista, while Belascoarán investigates a series of mysterious telephone messages left by a student who had supposedly died in Mexico's "dirty war" in the 1970s. Needless to say, given the popularity of Marcos and Taibo, the serialization of this story was an immense success. *La Jornada*'s editor claims the newspaper's Web page on Sundays drew in more than 50,000 visitors, and that the paper's Sunday sales rose 20 percent during the serialization. The stories were subsequently published in book form, with an English translation forthcoming. The co-authors agreed to channel any profits to Zapatista communities through the Chiapas-based, nonprofit group Enlace Civil. Needless to say, this joint venture did much to bring Marcos back into the media's focus, with news agencies worldwide publicizing the project.

In May 2005, Marcos sent an invitation to Inter Milan's president, Massimo Moratti, challenging the soccer team to a match against the Zapatistas. (The Italian team already had links with the EZLN, having funded sports, water, and health projects in Zapatista communities; the team's manager, Bruno Bartolozzi, had paid a visit to Chiapas the previous June bearing donations from the club and its president.) The challenge was immediately accepted by the Inter Milan's captain, the Argentine Javier Zanetti. (Zanetti had previously published a letter in which he expressed his admiration for the Zapatistas and their idealistic struggle.) Marcos proposed two games: one at UAM's stadium in Mexico City and the other in Milan, with Argentine legend Diego Maradona officiating. As of this writing, no match has been played, but the mere rumor of it raised the Zapatistas's media profile greatly during spring 2005.

In May, Marcos made his first appearance in the flesh in four years sporting a potbelly. A decade earlier, he had stated in an interview that: "Marcos can abandon the struggle, or can die, or can even turn himself into a politician with a paunch."[9] Having clearly recoiled from becoming a politician, he had instead embraced a paunch. The press, true to form, naturally picked up on such a "weighty" issue and promptly set about poking fun at the forty-eight-year-old Zapatista leader. Marcos, with his usual mixture of self-deprecation and humor, confessed that his days as a sex-symbol may be limited, quipping that "I tell you, now I don't even heat up the coffee," and adding that things could have been much worse, since if he had removed his ammunition belt, "There would be a paunch like a six-month pregnancy." He also jokingly accused the photographers who took shots of his paunch of abetting his right-wing foes: "If not, well, they would have warned me and I could pull in my belly at the moment of the shot."[10]

In June, the EZLN published its *Sixth Declaration of the Lacandón Jungle*, from which it is clear that, having come so far, the movement now felt it had arrived at a critical juncture:

We have reached a point where we cannot go any further, and, in addition, it is possible that we could lose everything we have if we remain as we are and do nothing more in order to move forward. The hour has come to take a risk once again and to take a step which is dangerous but which is worthwhile. Because, perhaps united with other social sectors who suffer from the same wants as we do, it will be possible to achieve what we need and what we deserve.

It is obvious from the Declaration, which savagely lambastes Mexico's political class,[11] that the EZLN does not see the way forward involving, as some have conjectured, Marcos's or the Zapatistas's entry into mainstream politics:

Are we saying that politics serves no purpose? No, what we mean is that THAT politics serves no purpose. . . . It is useless because it does not take the people into account. It does not listen to them, it does not pay any attention to them, it just approaches them when there are elections. . . . And then just promises about what this one [politician] is going to do and what the other one is going to do, then it's bye, I'll see you, but you don't see them again, except when they appear in the news when they've just stolen a lot of money and nothing is going to be done to them because the law—which those same politicians made—protects them.

Rather, the EZLN advocates an alternative:

What we are going to do is to take heed of the thoughts of the simple and humble people, and perhaps we will . . . find something like a program that has what we all want, and a plan for how we are going to achieve the realization of that program, which is called the "national program of struggle." We are going to try to build, or rebuild, another way of doing politics, one which once again has the spirit of serving others, without material interests, with sacrifice, with dedication, with honesty, which keeps its word. . . . We are also going to go about raising a struggle in order to demand that we make a new Constitution, new laws which take into account the demands of the Mexican people.

And so:

The EZLN will send a delegation of its leadership in order to do this work throughout the national territory and for an indefinite period of time . . . go[ing] to those places where they are expressly invited. We are also letting you know that the EZLN will establish a policy of alliances with non-electoral organizations and movements which define themselves, in theory and practice, as being of the left . . . inviting the[m] to meet with us, at the time, place and manner in which we shall propose at the proper time, to organize a national campaign, visiting all possible corners of our Patria, in order to listen to and organize the word of our people. It is like a campaign, then, but very otherly, because it is not electoral . . . [but rather a] NATIONAL CAMPAIGN for building another way of doing politics, for a program of national struggle of the left, and for a new Constitution.

On 19 June, Marcos released a statement declaring a red alert whereby the EZLN was sending its leadership into hiding as a "precautionary defensive measure" while members discuss the future of their fight against Mexico's government. Marcos claimed the actions allowed the rebels to discuss their next move. Some speculated that the red alert was in response to the Mexican army having recently raided several acres of marijuana plantations in proximity to Zapatista territory. However, it is more likely that it was issued as a trumpet call to draw attention to the coming statement by the Zapatistas concerning their next plan of action. It certainly worked, since the world's media strained its ears to hear what Marcos would announce. Four weeks later, on July 15, Marcos declared the red alert over and issued a series of four communiqués detailing the Zapatistas's future plans. In August and September the Zapatistas would convene six meetings in as many weeks with almost 300 friendly organizations and representatives of civil society. In the event, each of the meetings lasted two days and saw presentations lasting more than twenty hours.[12] The aim was to garner support among the participants for the *Sixth Declaration*, and, in line with its stated objective, to "find something like a program that has what we all want, and a plan for how we are going to achieve the realization of . . . the 'national program of struggle.'"

On 16 September, the media's focus on the Zapatistas's trajectory was temporarily distracted when a Mexican monthly celebrity magazine, *Quien*, published an article rumoring details of an alleged relationship between Marcos and the thirty-seven-year-old Mexican journalist Gloria Muñoz Ramírez, a former reporter for *La Jornada*.[13] The two had first met more than ten years previously, in the first years of the Zapatista uprising. The magazine even alleges that the two have a child. Unfortunately, no concrete proof is offered to support these intriguing allegations, and so the story's reliability cannot be ascertained. Interestingly, however, *The Christian Sci-*

ence Monitor published an article which refers to Commander Ana María as "Marcos's former wife" and claims that a power struggle is taking place between her, representing a radical approach, and the more moderate Subcommander.[14] For now, however, all this must remain pure speculation.

On Friday, 16 September, at La Garrucha, rumor took a back seat to serious political substance in media reports as Marcos announced to twenty-two comandantes and the press a six-month tour of Mexico by him beginning 1 January 2006. The tour would be unarmed and would include stops of a week or more in each of the country's thirty-two states, as part of the Zapatistas's Other Campaign. As this book goes into production, Marcos has produced a detailed itinerary of the tour[15] and vowed that "What we're going to do is shake this country up from below . . . [to] Pick it up and turn it on its head."[16] He has also announced that throughout the trip (and perhaps beyond) Subcommander Marcos will be known as Sub-Delegate Zero, thus reinventing himself once again.

Regardless of what happens on this tour, or what the long-term future may hold for Marcos, his place in history is already assured. His contribution to Mexican society and politics, Latin American literature, the tradition of the armed Left and the antineoliberal cause is indisputable. The distinguished Mexican author Carlos Fuentes insists:

> You must never forget that the Mexican political process owes a great deal to Subcomandante Marcos and the Zapatistas. Without the political earthquake of January 1994—which demonstrated that unless quick progress was made to solve the country's political problems there would be outbursts of insurgency—it would have been impossible to begin a new political era. That was the warning from Subcomandante Marcos, and president Carlos Salinas de Gortari understood it. Thanks to the Chiapas insurrection and the political response of Salinas, that new era has begun.[17]

Elsewhere he asserts that the Subcommander "is a fine man, period," continuing, "he has changed the history of this country."[18] Similarly, the scholar, writer, and filmmaker Saul Landau has declared: "Marcos not only challenged the establishment, provoked the complacent, and lit a spark to the passive, he forced the entire thinking world to begin to deal with issues that surround indigenous people in the age of corporate globalization."[19] So too, Oppenheimer, certainly no stargazer when it comes to Leftist guerrillas in general or Marcos in particular, has written: "To be sure, Subcommander Marcos deserves praise for drawing world attention to the dismal conditions of the Chiapas Indians and the rampant government corruption in that state (and most of Mexico, for that matter)."[20]

Even de la Grange and Rico, Marcos's fiercest critics, begrudgingly concede that "one of the merits of Marcos—his only real success—has been to open the Pandora's box by unmasking the official discourse that had invented a prosperous and democratic country respectful of its native people."[21] Finally, the eminent French sociologist Alain Touraine expresses his belief that

> history will recall the physical, political, and intellectual courage of Subcomandante Marcos, a sociologist on horseback, a mixed-blood among Indians, a Mexican patriot and a militant global revolutionary, who risks his life in order to once again unite, in Latin America and elsewhere, revolutionary struggle and political liberty.[22]

CONCLUSION

In the preceding pages we have witnessed the birth, upbringing, and education of Rafael Sebastián Guillén Vicente and his transformation from clandestine, would-be Marxist revolutionary into Subcommander Marcos, a high-profile guerrilla spokesman and arguably the most famous left-wing icon and revolutionary figure since Che Guevara.[1]

Throughout this work, rather than directly passing judgment on the Subcommander, I have emphasized certain aspects of his persona. I hope to have illustrated that whereas a large part of Marcos's fame has derived from his talent for media relations (which many observers have recognized), most of his success should be credited to his great flexibility of mind (which has largely been overlooked). Both strengths, though present in other guerrilla leaders, Marcos combined and developed to the highest level, leading Adolfo Gilly to comment that

> in this singular combination of ancient myths, mobilized communities, clandestine army, *golpes de escena*, literary resources, and political initiatives, the figure of the military chief of the rebellion, Subcomandante Marcos, is immensely important. . . . The chief merit of Marcos, if it were necessary to assign one, would thus be that he knew enough, first to comprehend and assimilate that substance and, then, how to be the mediator or the guide through which its image was transmitted to urban society.[2]

True, the Subcommander benefited from factors outside his control. For example, the sudden and rapid development of the Internet greatly facilitated his ability to wage a media war—but it should be noted that other guerrilla leaders have proved much slower in utilizing this medium.[3] And true, Marcos's flexibility of mind derived in part at least from the culture clash he experienced with indigenous chiapanecos and from the general rethinking of doctrines that followed the demise of Soviet Communism—but, once again, other guerrillas had previously ignored or crushed any opposition by indigenous people to the continued imposition of Marxist or Maoist doctrines.

If anyone doubts how vital publicity and flexibility have become in recent times, they should observe the fate of the EPR (Popular Revolutionary Army). On paper at least, the EPR and the EZLN share many similarities. The EPR was contemporaneous with the EZLN (it appeared in 1996). It operated in the nearby state of Guerrero, ranked only below Chiapas and Oaxaca in impoverishment. It was well armed and well organized. It issued communiqués and manifestos. It called press conferences. And it even had a comandante spokesman, José Arturo. The difference between them and the EZLN proved, however, more significant than the similarities. As Ross observes:

> Despite its classic guerrilla pose, exemplary weaponry, headline-grabbing attacks, hundreds of political prisoners (300 alone from the Loxichas in Oaxaca), and detailed reports of human rights atrocities committed against Indian villages, the EPR never galvanized much popular support. The new guerrilla movement had no Marcos to speak for it, and its rhetoric was clunky and lacked poetry to reach the national heart. Although the EPR dispatched dozens of communiqués to the Mexican press, unlike those of the silver-tongued Zapatistas, they were never published.[4]

It must also be remembered, however, that the Subcommander had precursors in the form of a long line of notable guerrillas and revolutionaries who formed the Latin American tradition of armed, left-wing struggle.[5] If we wish to fully appreciate Marcos, we must set him firmly within this tradition.

Of course, Marcos's most obvious precursor is the Mexican revolutionary Emiliano Zapata, from whom the Zapatistas took their name and the Subcommander his penchant for wearing two crossed bandoliers and riding a horse. When asked on the first day of the uprising "Who do you take inspiration from?" Marcos replied not with Che Guevara but "Zapata."[6] Indeed, the figure of Zapata acts as the reference point for the entire movement. Like their predecessors and namesakes, the modern Zapatistas are an indigenous southern *campesino* movement which has struggled repeatedly and unsuccessfully to obtain land reform from successive regimes in Mexico City. They too have boosted indigenous pride and refused to compromise or sell out despite considerable pressure to do so. They too have sought to attract academics and the intelligentsia to their banner, in much the same way as the original Zapatistas.[7]

Emiliano Zapata was, however, but one of many in the revolutionary tradition to which Marcos belongs. For example, in terms of mastery of the media, it should be remembered that Pancho Villa actively courted the U.S. press and even staged battles as part of his public relations campaign. Fidel Castro's keen appreciation of the importance of the media was evidenced by his giving an interview with *New York Times* journalist Herbert Matthews, deep in the Sierra Maestra of Cuba, on 7 February 1957, and again with Homer Bigart, also of the *New York Times*, on 25 February 1958.[8] More recently, El Salvador's FMLN guerrillas skillfully exploited the national and international press, and their use of Radio Venceremos to disseminate their message was as an early precursor to Marcos's use of the Internet.

The Subcommander's more enlightened conception of the indigenous and their revolutionary potential was anticipated by the leaders of Guatemala's EGP guerrillas. Rolando Morán, the leader of the EGP, was interviewed by Jorge Castañeda on 21 December 1991 and is quoted as saying:

> One of our main differences with the past was something that would have unsuspected historical importance in the future, the indispensable relationship established by the EGP with the indigenous peoples of Guatemala from the outset. The EGP asserts for the first time that the revolution in Guatemala must have two facets: the class struggle and the ethnic-national struggle. It postulates that the two aspects are inseparably bound, one cannot triumph without the other.[9]

Mario Payeras, second-in-command of the EGP, can indeed be viewed very much as a precursor to Subcommander Marcos. In the late 1960s, Payeras and his guerrilla *foco* chose Chiapas for their training base and springboard from which to launch their guerrilla insurgence in Guatemala. He, like Marcos, spent many years clandestinely building up a people's army largely comprised of indigenous cadres whose potential he was one of the first to recognize,[10] creating over a period of years a popular army and support base that emerged later to wage both a local guerrilla war and a more widespread public relations war aimed at gaining international support and recognition. Payeras was also a prolific and able writer: Castañeda calls him "one of the best writers to emerge from the ranks of the Latin American revolutionary left."[11] During the 1980s he wrote several books on Guatemala in general and more specifically on his own experiences as a guerrilla. The most famous of these, *Los Dias en la Selva* (*Days of the Jungle*), won the Cuban Casa de las Americas prize. He went on to write poetry and children's stories, both of which, like Marcos's subsequent writings, were strongly subject to Mayan influences.[12]

Nor is Payeras alone in his resemblance to the future Subcommander. In more minor ways others had foreshadowed Marcos. Joaquín Villalobos of El Salvador's FMLN had written an article published by the journal *Foreign Policy* in which he repeatedly rejected Marxist dogmatism, arguing instead "for more flexibility" and for an all inclusive democracy "forged from above and below" in which every section of society would participate.[13] Miguel Angel Asturias had created the Revolutionary Organization of the Armed People in Mexico in 1972, which he then deployed in his native Guatemala. It placed great emphasis on the region's indigenous Maya population and, like the Zapatistas, sought "a strategy of making broad alliances with progressive middle-class intellectuals and professionals."[14] It too rejected dogmatism, to the extent that Castañeda dubbed it "perhaps the least ideological, the most pragmatic, and the most 'un-Marxist' of Latin American political military organizations."[15] Similarly lacking in excessive dogmatism was Jaime Wheelock, of Nicaragua's FSLN. In an interview given in 1983, he observed how "far from having a narrowly dogmatic mentality, we Latin Americans have a strong tradition of humanism, and a deep interest in culture."[16] Marcos was very much part of this tradition.

Carlos Fonseca of Nicaragua's Sandinistas may also be seen as a forerunner of Marcos in that, like Rafael, he appears to have been academically gifted. In 1955, Fonseca won a gold star at his High School College, the Matagalpa Instituto Nacional de Norte, for being the best student in his class for five consecutive years, and had then gone on to rank "near the top of his class at the end of his first year at the Universidad Nacional Autónomia de Nicaragua";[17] twenty-five years later, in 1980, Rafael Guillén won UNAM's Gabino Barreda Award for the most distinguished university student of his generation. So too, both men show signs of having been intellectually precocious, founding and co-editing high school magazines. More importantly, both men shared a common hero in Che Guevara, while at the same time promoting one of their own countrymen as a national, revolutionary hero. Whereas "Carlos Fonseca followed in the footsteps of two individuals above all others, Che Guevara and Augusto César Sandino," Marcos followed in the footsteps of Che and Emiliano Zapata; whereas Fonseca brought about "the resurrection and reinterpretation of Augusto César Sandino," Marcos did likewise for Emiliano Zapata; and whereas "Fonseca's political philosophy . . . [was] symbolized by his constant pairing of Che Guevara and Augusto César Sandino," Marcos's couples Che with

Zapata.[18] Finally, though less significant, Fonseca and Marcos had both conducted revolutionary marriage ceremonies for cadres under them.

Marcos even shares certain similarities with Abimael Guzmán, leader of Peru's Sendero Luminoso.[19] Although in terms of their ages and methods the two men are completely different, their social background and even certain of their habits are far from dissimilar. For example, both are sons of middle-class merchants (not such a large class in Latin America), who attended Jesuit high schools, wrote pieces for their school magazines, and subsequently majored in philosophy before going on to become university professors. Both men wrote theses that presented emotional (not rational) *apologiae* for revolutions, spoke more than one language, and shared a love of Pablo Neruda's poetry. Both of these white, bearded intellectuals disappeared from their respective university posts, entering the clandestine world of guerrillas, and both eventually succeeded, by learning Indian languages and harnessing indigenous cultural icons, in attracting a large indigenous support base in indigenous areas typified by their poverty, discrimination, and repression. Finally, both men's smoking habits were eccentric enough to serve to identify them personally.[20]

However, undoubtedly of all the Latin American revolutionaries who foreshadowed Marcos, Che Guevara deserves preeminence, both as a revolutionary icon and as Marcos' self-declared model.[21] Indeed, Marcos is so indebted to the Guevaran tradition[22] that Jon Lee Anderson, the author of the definitive biography of Che, has written, "It is hard not to see Marcos as a reborn Che Guevara, adapted to modern times—less utopian still idealistic, but still willing to fight for his beliefs—perhaps having learned from his predecessor's mistakes but modeled on him nonetheless."[23] True, for almost half a century revolutionary groups the world over have taken their inspiration from Che. However, few have modeled themselves on him so completely as Marcos, imitating the man as well as the revolutionary icon. Marcos appears to have adopted Che's pipe,[24] his beard, his cap, his tendency toward harsh self-evaluation, his mock-heroic writing style (largely influenced by *Don Quixote*), his two watches,[25] perhaps his appreciation of Pablo Neruda's poetry, and possibly even more besides.[26] Marcos talked at length about Che and the influence Guevara had on him in his most extensive interview to date, that with Le Bot.[27] However, if we look closely at what he has to say about his hero, we can see that the Subcommander is not blind in his imitation. He shows care in choosing which aspects of Guevara to emulate and which to reject. For example, Marcos rejects Che's "political proposal or his manual for taking power . . . [and his] guerrilla methods, the Guevarist foco," electing to concentrate on "the more human side, the side of resistance, of rebelliousness . . . the sense of sacrifice, the devotion to a cause, and above all importance, the conviction."[28]

More than in his direct imitation of Che's appearance and behavior, Marcos resembles his precursor most in the fact that they both belong to the same "robust tradition of revolutionaries, overpopulated by . . . disenfranchised middle-class intellectuals"[29]—what Castañeda describes as "an intellectual middle class'outraged by an intolerable estrangement from the society it lives in and the abyss separating that class from the vast, undifferentiated universe of the poor . . . who rose up in the best way they could find, against a status quo they eventually discovered to be unlivable."[30] That Marcos is very much part of this Latin American tradition is seen in his assertion that "the Man, woman, homosexual, lesbian, child, youth, old one, that is, the true human being, does not look at which side lives better, but on which side duty lies." This updated adaptation of a José Martí quotation, Marcos believes, represents "better than anything else what the rebel's vocation is, and . . . surpass[es] anything I could say to you or to anyone on the subject."[31] Marcos, of course, was not the only Latin American of his generation to belong to this tradition, which dated back to at least José Martí and incorporated Che, the world's most famous revolutionary. For example, Sandinista Jaime Wheelock, stated in an interview: "I recall feeling increasingly indignant and ashamed of the society I was born into—the reality of poverty, injustice and abuse . . . for a decent person, raised with humanistic, Christian ideas, it was utterly impossible to live in that society under those conditions, and devote oneself quietly to a middle class profession."[32] Even in Mexico Marcos was certainly not unique among his generation in this respect—a fact which perhaps goes a long way to explain his immense popularity among certain sectors of Mexican society which share his antipathy toward an iniquitous status quo. Although perhaps exceptional in the results he achieved, he was just one of many university-educated, middle-class, mestizo Mexicans growing up in the 1960s and 1970s who, like Che, felt the same "anguish . . . at being affluent and comfortable islands in a sea of destitution"[33] and who tried, each in their own way, to reconcile themselves with this feeling.[34] In this sense, he was very much a product of his nationality, class, and the time into which he was born.

Of course, recognition of these precursors and of their contributions does not in any way detract from the image of Marcos as a highly innovative figure. It simply reminds us that, like all great historical figures, he can be seen as part of much wider developments. Although Marcos's political philosophy, character, strategy, and tactics may not be as original as some have suggested,[35] his genius can be said to lie in his very interpretation of his antecedents, and in his extension, modification, and execution of their strategies. In this respect, Castañeda offers perhaps one of the most astute appraisals of Marcos:

> The Zapatistas forged their own coherent interpretation of the armed struggle in El Salvador. In their view, the FMLN —thanks precisely to the armed struggle—achieved precisely what nobody else had in decades: not the conquest of power, nor the Socialist revolution, but in-depth political reforms, clean elections, the rule of law, an end to violence and the repression of the poor, and various social and economic reforms, including the beginnings of land redistribution and a purge of the military and security forces. . . . Indeed, Marcos' reasoning was novel precisely because it was so reformist: the EZLN did not seek to take power or overthrow Mexico's one-party system by the strength of its arms; rather, it would use them to help those without arms achieve something like democracy in Mexico.[36]

Finally, I would argue that Subcommander Marcos represents the most advanced stage so far in the evolution of the revolutionary—a Homo sapiens in a world of Neanderthals.[37] The key question in the considerable debate concerning the future of revolutions, and therefore the role of revolutionaries and guerrillas,[38] is whether Marcos is the last of a dying breed or the next link in the evolutionary chain. If the latter, which is perhaps the more probable given the perpetual nature of evolution and the persistence of the political, economic, and social conditions that spawn revolutions, Marcos's fate is to be emulated and, in time, surpassed by the next guerrilla who has the wit to adopt and perfect the talents of his or her predecessors. Of course, a third possibility—rare in the natural world, but not unknown—is that Marcos represents a deviation in the evolution of the revolutionary. If this is the case, it will again be interesting to see whether this evolutionary experiment succeeds in surviving, thereby taking its place alongside the main branch of Latin American armed revolutionaries, or whether the experiment ultimately proves a failure, whereby this anomalous side branch withers and dies.

NOTES

INTRODUCTION

1. See chapter 19 for media coverage of Marcos and chapter 21 for his publications.
2. This often affectionate tag is an abbreviation and slight corruption of *Subcomandante*.
3. Romero 1994.
4. Lawrence argues that Marcos "played the press like a musical instrument, and much of the world sang along" (1999, 113). Similarly, Oppenheimer observes that Marcos "played the media masterfully" (1996/1998, 66).
5. Romero 1994, 103; quoted and translated in Russell 1995, 56.
6. De la Grange and Rico 1998.
7. Ross calls it "a snide send-up of Marcos" (2000, 170). De la Grange and Rico deny that the book is hostile, stating (in de la Vega, 1998, 14): "We never had the idea of producing a negative profile because he is not a negative person, but rather a very complex person whose facets we reflect in the book." Tellingly, however, they go on to add, "Marcos has his very attractive sides, although he also has his darker sides, which have been getting worse these last years and in particular in the last few months."
8. Ross 2000, 254: "*Le Monde* suspended Bertrand de la Grange after he penned a particularly poisonous piece blaming the EZLN for Acteal. De la Grange's masterwork on *Subcomandante Marcos, la genial impostura* (*Marcos, the Brilliant Myth*), was distributed by the Mexican government as a tool in its post-Acteal counterattack against the Zapatistas."
9. See Ross 2000, 76: "*Le Monde's* Bertrand de la Grange was so traumatized by the veto that he has carried on an obsessive vendetta against Marcos ever since." So too Womack: "For months it [the EZLN] had had trouble with *Le Monde's* correspondent in Mexico [i.e., de la Grange], who had reported its defects and whom someone speaking for the EZLN (fingers pointed in various directions) had barred from the 'encounter' at La Realidad" (1999, 319). De la Grange (in de la Vega 1998, 14) has vehemently denied that his book was written as a result of "rancor" at Marcos's veto, arguing that he does not believe that it was the Subcommander who was responsible for his being barred, but rather the decision of others around him.

10. See Correa 1996, 32. Even before this, however, de la Grange's frequently hostile coverage of the Sandinistas in Nicaragua and of the Castro regime in Cuba had no doubt done little to endear him to the EZLN leadership.

11. De la Grange is not alone in this. De Mora makes much of the fact that "el 'subcomandante Marcos' no es indio, es completamente blanco" (1995, 161, 183).

12. Gossen 1996, 116. Similarly, Hernández Castillo: "To present indigenous . . . Zapatista supporters as manipulated by *mestizo* leaders denies them their capacity for human agency and reproduces racist stereotypes of Indians as passive peoples somehow suspended in time" (2003, 83).

13. Gossen 1996, 116; reiterated almost verbatim in Gossen 1999, 259.

14. Gossen 1996, 117; again reiterated almost verbatim in Gossen 1999, 260.

15. Carlos Salinas de Gortari, the Mexican president during whose term of office (1988–1994) the Zapatistas rose up, and his infamous brother Raúl had both belonged to a militant Maoist group in their youth. Ironically, this group had operated in Rafael/Marcos's home state of Tamaulipas. Raúl, as journalist Andres Oppenheimer observes, had even "unsuccessfully attempted to ignite a social uprising in Chiapas in the early seventies" (1996/1998, 12, similarly at 45).

16. Monsiváis 2002, 130.

17. Subcomandante Marcos 1995c, 131 ff.; Le Bot 1997, 109–13. For similarly frank interviews, see chap. 7, n. 15.

18. See Subcomandante Marcos 1995b, 22: "Our conception of the world and of revolution was badly dented in the confrontation with the indigenous realities of Chiapas. Out of those blows, something new (which does not necessarily mean 'good') emerged, that which today is known as 'neo-Zapatismo.'"

19. Lorenzano 1998, 128.

20. Tello Díaz 1995/2001; Oppenheimer 2002, 54. Harvey writes of *La rebelión de las Cañadas* that "for Tello, the Socialist origins of Marcos and other Zapatista leaders overshadow their current political discourse of democracy and freedom. The shift from revolution to democracy is portrayed by Tello as nothing more than an opportunistic reaction to the collapse of socialism in the East and the demise of guerrilla movements (and the Sandinista government) in Central America" (1998, 9).

21. Lorenzano 1998, 154.

22. Reprinted and translated in Fuentes 1994/1997, 126.

23. One quotation here will suffice to illustrate how de la Grange himself patronizes the Indians and fails to account for the success of Marcos in winning them over: "The Indian cause was never a priority of Marcos nor of the rest of the FLN and their Zapatista branch. . . . They are simply guinea pigs, instruments at the service of certain political and religious organizations" (de la Grange and Rico, 1998, 432). For similar insistences that the indige-

nous of Chiapas had been duped and manipulated by unscrupulous outsiders for their own self-serving aims, see Paz 1994, 14: "Las comunidades
indígenas han sido engañadas por un grupo de irresponsables demagogos";
Krauze (1994, 9); Pazos (1994, 1–15); and de Mora (1995), whose front cover
reads: "¡Yo Acuso! A los gobiernos de México de haber robado, explotado,
asesinado y manipulado a nuestros indios y al EZLN de ser otra manipula-
ción de indios y un instrumento para desestabilizar al país a costa de vidas
indígenas."

24. I am not alone in this view; see anthropologist Hernández Navarro: "Clearly,
they [the indigenous] are not rebelling because they have been duped by
anyone, but rather because they have chosen a path—a questionable one
perhaps—in response to their perception of their dwindling prospects"
(1994a, 51).

25. Certainly the number of humble and self-effacing individuals who have gone
on to lead thousands of others is very small indeed—it becomes minute if
we concentrate purely on politico-military leaders.

26. Debray 2002, 350. Earlier in the same article Debray, while acknowledging Marcos's "self-confidence," nonetheless states that the Subcommander
"does not give the impression of being full of himself" (347). For Marcos's
love of chocolate, see Oppenheimer (1996/1998, 71).

27. De Mora 1995, 169, 188; quoted and translated in Bonner 1999, 153. Aceituno entitles his article for *Siempre!*: "Marcos: autoafirmación narcisista"
(1998, 28). *Siempre!* (2001, 6) goes even further in its accusations of narcis-
sicism, bearing the heading "Marcos se cree Jesucristo."

28. Krauze 1997, 793. In a letter he sent to *La Jornada* (18 November 2002),
Marcos wrote: "There is, for example, the cultural myth which chants:
'Enrique Krauze is an intellectual,' when we all know that he's nothing but
a mediocre businessman," translated and published in Vodovnik 2004,
555.

29. Poniatowska 2002b, 378.

30. Quoted in Debray 2002, 348.

31. Collier and Quaratiello 1994/1999, 194.

32. Montalbán 2000, 48, 83–87.

33. Ibid., 152.

34. Ross 1995a, 297, 301. Of course, in this case, unlike in statements concerning Marcos's identity, it should be noted that none of these explanations are
mutually exclusive.

35. Simon 2002, 46.

36. Oppenheimer 1996/1998, 74.

37. See his interview in Autonomedia 1994, 201. See also Stavans 2002, 391:
"El Sup said his idols were the nationally known 'new journalists' Carlos
Monsiváis and Elena Poniatowska."

38. Monsiváis 2001.

39. Autonomedia 1994, 201.
40. García Márquez and Pombo 2001, 74, 79.
41. Oppenheimer 1996/1998, 75.
42. Landau 1996, 29.
43. A term coined by Tim Golden (1994).
44. This was what then President of Mexico Carlos Salinas di Gortari dubbed Marcos during the early days of the uprising. Romero 1994, 27.
45. A term coined by journalists. Ross 1995a, 370.
46. Debray 2002, 348.
47. Castañeda 1994a, 80.
48. Hayden 2002, 318.
49. "The retreat is making us almost scratch the sky" (20 February 1995); published in Ponce de León 2001, 230.
50. McCaughan 1995, 36.
51. Published in Autonomedia 1994, 146–47.
52. To provide but a few recent examples of those debating this question: Katz 1999; Snyder 1999; Nodia 2001; Goodwin 2001; Selbin 2001; Foran 2003a.

1 BIRTH AND FAMILY

1. Le Bot 1997, 16.
2. It is interesting (and a little ironic) that, as Guillermoprieto points out, Tamaulipas was the state where "a small but influential group of once-radical—Maoist—politicians close to Raúl Salinas and his powerful brother" had operated (1995b, 251).
3. See Grahame Greene 1939/1981, 184: "The reservoir, half finished, standing there to crack into ruin in the winter because there was no more money: all money was diverted to Tampico and the oilfields."
4. See Kampwirth 2002, 12. When discussing the decision to rebel made by the guerrillas in her case study, she states that "year of birth may have been the single most important personal factor."
5. It is perhaps worth noting that Jon Lee Anderson, author of the definitive biography of Che Guevara, was, like Rafael, aged ten when Che was shot dead. In the introduction to his book *Guerrillas*, he writes of the impact this had on him: "In 1967, as a ten-year-old boy, I saw the gritty front-page photograph of Che Guevara on his deathbed. The image is now a classic. . . . Before this I had never heard of Che Guevara or his plan to liberate the Americas with guerrilla warfare. His death was my first awareness that people like him existed, but from that moment on, I was fascinated by the image of the rebel, the guerrilla" (1992/1993, xi). One wonders whether Rafael was similarly influenced by this event.
6. García Márquez and Pombo 2001, 77.

7. Quoted in Krauze 1997, 736, my emphasis. The emphasized statement is again quoted on page 784. Originally cited in Poniatowska 1971/1994, 91.

8. Ponce de León 2001, 151–54.

9. Autonomedia 1994, 147.

10. V. I. Lenin was the fourth of eight children, but two of these died in infancy, making him the third of six by the time he was ten.

11. Sulloway 1996/1997.

12. Ibid., xiii.

13. Ibid., xv

14. Ibid., 21, and similarly xiv.

15. Ibid., 146.

16. Ibid., 356, 364.

17. Ibid., 70, 297. See also 74, "Laterborns are more nonconforming, adventurous, and unconventional," and 287, "Laterborns . . . tend to exhibit compassion for people who are less fortunate than themselves."

18. Ibid., 361. Earlier he states: "Professional revolutionaries are eighteen times more likely to be laterborns than firstborns" (297).

19. Ibid., xiv. See also 21, 54, and 356.

20. Castro was the third of six children.

21. Ibid., 303.

22. Rejai and Phillips 1983, 152, 156–57.

23. De la Grange and Rico 1998, 68. Years later, as Subcommander Marcos, Rafael would defend utopianism: "As for utopia, what social change in the history of the world was not brought into being by utopianism? None." Quoted in Montalbán 2002, 480.

24. De la Grange 1998, 68. See also *Proceso* 1995a.

25. Rejai and Phillips 1983, 50, 51, 58, 59, 120, 152, 153, summarized on 162–63.

26. Salmon and Daly 1998, 305. In one study, when asked, "Whom, of all the people you know, are you closest to?," 64 percent of firstborns named a parent, compared to 39 percent of lastborns and just 10 percent of middleborns (303); in another study asking the same question, 36 percent of firstborns, 29 percent of lastborns, and a mere 7 percent of middleborns named a parent (306).

27. Ibid., 306. When asked "To whom would you turn for emotional support," 42 percent of firstborns named a parent, compared to 44 percent of lastborns and just 21 percent of middleborns.

28. Bardach 1994, 67–68.

29. De la Grange and Rico 1998, 70, my emphasis.

30. Ibid.

31. García Márquez and Pombo 2001, 77.

32. Ibid., 77–78.

33. Ibid., 78.

34. Benjamin 1995, 60.
35. In Bardach 1994, 67.

2 SCHOOL YEARS

1. Pizarro 1995, 18.
2. Ibid.
3. Ibid.
4. Autonomedia 1994, 197.
5. Bardach 1994, 67.
6. García Márquez and Pombo 2001, 78.
7. Marcos quoted in Durán 1994, 21, and Rovira 1994, 52.
8. García Márquez and Pombo 2001, 79.
9. Rocinante was Don Quixote's horse.
10. Guevara 1994/1996, 316.
11. On Che's fondness for Neruda, see Anderson 1997, 38, 115, 306, 569, 634.
12. Interestingly, in the Sierra Maestra Che gave a captured army officer his copy of Neruda's *Canto General*.
13. Romero 1994, 35.
14. Entitled "Democratic Teachers and the Zapatista Dream" (31 July 1999).
15. De la Grange and Rico 1998, 68.
16. Bardach 1994, 68.
17. García Márquez and Pombo 2001, 78.

3 HIGH SCHOOL COLLEGE

1. Pizarro 1995, 21.
2. Ibid. When asked what he thought of Rafael turning out to be Subcomandante Marcos, the monk replied: "I am happy with my former pupil, I admire his heroic valor, his aims are noble and I respect and admire them. It is great that he cares about the indigenous. In Mexico today there is no one like him. The government is not only bad to the indigenous, it is bad to all citizens, but we do not have the courage that Rafael has. The only thing I disagree with is his methods, the war, but perhaps the circumstances dictate this. If they have spoken and no-one listens . . . only God is able to judge him" (ibid., 19).
3. McCaughan 1995, 36.
4. Pizarro 1995, 21.
5. Ibid.
6. Fuentes's synopsis from the back cover of *El tuerto es rey* (1970).
7. Pizarro 1995, 19.
8. Ibid.
9. Gómez Peña 1995, 89. See also Haas's article entitled "Marcos: Maestro

de la teatralidad" (2001a, 37) and Míguez (2001, 53), who calls Marcos a "maestro del espectáculo."

10. Pizarro 1995, 19.

11. De la Grange and Rico 1998, 73.

12. Ibid. Heredia Niño told *Proceso* reporters (Pizarro 1995, 21) that Sub-commander Marcos's "principal merit is that he has awakened consciences and has made Mexico think. He questions things that are taken for granted. There are people who say that he is responsible for paralyzing the country. On the contrary, his intention has been to defend the needy, to obtain respect for the indigenous and to question the government."

13. Pizarro 1995, 21.

14. De la Grange and Rico 1998, 72–73.

15. Ibid., 73.

16. Pizarro 1995, 21.

17. De la Grange and Rico 1998, 72.

18. Pizarro 1995, 21.

19. Marcos quoted in Rovira 1994, 51.

20. For example, in the communiqués dated 22 September 1994 and 14 March 1995, printed in EZLN 1995, 49–80, at 79; and 269–74, at 273, respectively.

21. Borge 1992, 259.

22. See Zimmermann 2000/2004, 33ff. Carlos Fonseca, founder of Nicaragua's FSLN, had founded and co-edited the magazine *Segovia* while he was studying at the Matagalpa Instituto Nacional de Norte in 1955; Rafael and Fonseca were both eighteen when they started their magazines.

23. De la Grange and Rico 1998, 73–74.

24. Ibid., 74.

25. Pizarro 1995, 19.

26. J. Ramírez 1997.

27. Translated in Ponce de León 2001, 102.

28. Le Bot 1997, 266; translated in Weinberg 2000, 189. However Marcos carefully distances himself and the EZLN from Che's "guerrilla method, the Guevarist *foco*."

29. Pizarro 1995, 21.

30. Ibid.

31. See Castañeda 1997, 192, who notes that Che extolled to revolutionaries the benefits of smoking a pipe, adding, "nor could Che have foreseen that one of his later disciples, the Mexican rebel *Subcomandante Marcos*, would take the precept of the pipe to levels of international media fame that Guevara would never have imagined."

32. De la Grange and Rico 1998, 73.

33. See de la Grange and Rico 1998, 74.

1. Bardach 1994, 67.
2. García Márquez and Pombo 2001, 77.
3. Ibid.
4. Rius was the pen name of Eduardo Del Rio. He wrote *Los Agachados* and *Los Supermachos*, two of Marcos's favorites, and also *Cuba for Beginners*. Ross (1995a, 298) writes that Rius's "distribution came mainly through street sales by itinerant Mexico City hippies," adding that these works were "a key relay station in spreading the culture of the Revolution throughout the country in the 1960s."
5. Autonomedia 1994, 201.
6. De la Grange and Rico 1998, 75.
7. Ibid., 85–86.
8. Ibid., 103.
9. See de la Grange and Rico 1999, 77.
10. For example: "We Do Indeed Support the UNAM Strike Movement" (June 1999); "On the UNAM Strikers Visit" (September 1999); "Protest Over the Paramilitary Occupation of the UNAM" (February 2000); "A University Filled with Soldiers and a Jail Filled with Students" (February 2000).
11. See chapter 29.
12. The Procuraduría General de la Repúblic, is an office like that of the U.S. Justice Department, which was put in charge of ascertaining the true identity of Marcos.
13. Subcomandante Marcos 1995a, 115; also translated in Autonomedia 1994, 171. Snowball (*bola de nieve* in Spanish) was the nickname of the Cuban-born, pro-revolutionary musician Ignacio Villa, who lived in Mexico for several years. He died in Mexico City on 2 October 1971, six years prior to Rafael attending UNAM.
14. This interview appears as a bonus feature in the DVD edition of *Zapatista* (Big Noise Films, 1998).
15. Corro 1995, 25–26.
16. Mancillas 2002, 156.
17. See de la Grange and Rico 1998, 76.
18. This nom de guerre may have been chosen in honor of Rafael's only sister, Mercedes. Another possible candidate is a young female UNAM professor, Mercedes Garzón, who was on the adjudicating panel that assessed Rafael's thesis. In any case, Rocío evidently felt a strong affinity with the appellation (and/or its original owner) since she subsequently named her daughter Mercedes.
19. De la Grange and Rico 1998, 88.
20. Pizarro 1995, 21.
21. Cited and translated in Oppenheimer 1996/1998, 250.

22. Corro 1995, 26.

23. Cited and translated in Oppenheimer 1996/1998, 250.

24. De la Grange and Rico 1998, 83.

25. This interview appears as a bonus feature in the DVD edition of *Zapatista*.

26. For more on Orive, see Ross (1995a, 274–76), Womack (1999, 175–81), and Harvey (1998, 85–90).

27. De la Grange and Rico 1998, 87.

28. Majumdar 1995, 109.

29. Gane 1983, 435–36.

30. The source is Castañeda 1994a, 70.

31. See Bonner (1999, 142), drawing on *La Repubblica*, 10 February 1995: "In May 1978, he presented seminar papers titled *Elements for an Analysis of Political Discourse* and *The Dominant Ideology* and presented a report, *Philosophy and the Production of Knowledge*, at a series of seminars titled *Critique of the Popular Movements in Mexico for the Last Decade*. In early 1979, at the Second Meeting of Historians at UNAM, he gave an address, *The Struggle of the Masses and Ideological Struggle*."

32. The full title was *Filosofía y Educación: Prácticas discursivas y prácticas ideológicas. Sujeto y cambio históricos en libros de texto oficiales para la educación primaria en México*. For a reproduction of the thesis's title page and a more detailed discussion of the work, complete with a summary and quotations from it, see *Proceso*, no. 954, 13 February 1995, 24–25.

33. Quoted and translated in Oppenheimer 1996/1998, 252.

34. Ibid.

35. Ibid.

36. In his *Theses on Feuerbach*, Marx (1845, 145) wrote: "Philosophers have only interpreted the world, in various ways; the point is to change it."

37. Quoted and translated in Oppenheimer 1996/1998, 252.

38. Ibid., 251.

39. Communiqué dated 11 February 1994, translated in Subcomandante Marcos 1995a, 130–31, and in Autonomedia 1994, 180.

40. Morales states: "There was nothing either in his activities, or in his thesis, or in his profile that pointed towards [Rafael belonging to] an armed movement." Híjar states: "*Subcommander Marcos* has nothing to do with the Althusserian Rafael Guillén." Both quoted in de la Grange and Rico 1998, 93.

41. See Borge 1996, 89. On 8 October, just one month before he was killed in a shootout with the National Guard, Fonseca issued his "Notas sobre la Montaña y algunos Otros Temas" from "somewhere in the Segovian Mountains."

42. See de la Grange and Rico 1998, 90. The communiqué mentioned in the text is that of 5 January 1994 to the Red Cross and the press.

43. Foucault 1984, 10.

44. The award is named after the Mexican positivist Gabino Barreda and is awarded for outstanding academic work conducted by students.
45. Corro 1995, 26.
46. For the date the thesis was submitted, see Oppenheimer 1996/1998, 355. The article written by Gane (1983, 439) contains the subheading "Withdrawal of the I.S.A.s"; Gane states that in 1979, "the concept of the ISAS is not dissolved but simply abandoned [by Althusser]."
47. Oppenheimer 1996/1998, 72.
48. See Mitterand 1996, 29, and Lang 1996, 17.
49. See Mitterand 1996, 44–45: "His sentences are regularly cut by Anita, who's translating in French. . . . His look expresses all the emotions that he cannot say because of the language barrier."
50. Lang 1996, 17.
51. This interview appears as a bonus feature in the DVD edition of *Zapatista*.
52. For Elorriaga's personal details, see Tello Díaz (1995/2001, 127, 133–34) and Elorriaga's short biography following his essay, "An Analysis of Evolving Zapatismo," at http://www.inmotionmagazine.com/chiapas1.html#anchor695207.
53. See Ronfeldt et al. (1998, 31, n. 10): "Some activists we interviewed criticized Tello for reputedly relying partly on Mexican intelligence materials." Similarly, Collier and Quaratiello (1994/1999, 193–94): "Zapatista sympathizers . . . claimed that Tello must have used government intelligence sources." Marcos himself makes this claim in Le Bot (1997, 161): "A Tello le dan la historia en el CISEN [Centro de Investigacíon y Seguridad Nacional: servicio de inteligencia de la Secretaría de Gobernación]."
54. See de la Grange and Rico 1999, 77.
55. Communiqué entitled "We Are in Silence—And the Silence Is Not Being Broken,"http://flag.blackened.net/revolt/mexico/ezln/2002/marcos/silence SEPT.html.
56. Quoted in Pinchetti 1995, 50.
57. Ibid.
58. De la Grange and Rico 1998, 87–88, for the month and year, and again at 95 and 101 for the year only.
59. Ibid., 101.
60. *Proceso* 1995b.
61. See de la Grange and Rico 1998, 96–97, for more details about this process.
62. Ibid.
63. See Pinchetti 1995, 50–54, for these details and others, namely, that he played with the local children, always carried a white shoulder bag, never wasted food, talked gently, joked, was rather solitary, and conducted vaccination campaigns.
64. Ibid. and de la Grange and Rico 1998, 101.

65. Idem.

66. De la Grange and Rico 1998, 101.

67. Ibid.

68. Pinchetti 1995, 52.

69. De la Grange and Rico 1998, 101.

70. Pinchetti 1995, 51. Marina is said to have exclaimed on seeing the photograph that "it is him, it is unmistakable," adding, "only that he was thinner then."

71. Le Bot 1997, 123.

72. Le Bot: "It is said that you [i.e., the Zapatistas—he uses the plural form of 'you,' *ustedes*] have been in El Salvador and Nicaragua, is it true?" Marcos: "No . . . We never received training either in Cuba, Nicaragua, El Salvador, Guatemala, Moscow or Korea."

73. Le Bot: "You [i.e., Marcos—he uses the singular form of 'you,' *usted*] weren't in the Sandinista literacy campaign in 1980 either?"

74. Tello Díaz 1995/2001, 113. Similarly, de la Grange and Rico (1998, 95) describe the purpose as "to give a brief course of graphic design to unions and social organizations linked to the Sandinista Front of National Liberation."

75. De la Grange and Rico 1998, 101: "Nadie en Nicaragua recuerda haberlo visito en el frente militar." For these rejections see ibid., 98f, and Pinchetti 1995, 50–51.

76. De la Grange and Rico 1998, 87, 96. They imply a second trip by referring to the late 1979/early 1980 visit as "the first time"; the six-month period of unpaid leave is noted on 28 and 95.

77. Pinchetti 1995, 51. For discussion of the later date, see chapter 11.

78. Tello Díaz 1995/2001, 291–92, n. 17.

5 THE GRADUATE

1. During the period 1974–80, Velasco Ugalde headed the Centre of Educational Investigations and played a significant part in forming UAM's Union of Independent Workers (SITUAM in Spanish).

2. Mergier 1995, 14.

3. Stavans 2002, 393.

4. Delgado 1995, 13.

5. Mergier 1995, 15.

6. Delgado 1995, 19.

7. Quoted in Guillermoprieto 1995a, 210.

8. Mergier 1995, 14.

9. Quoted in Guillermoprieto 1995a, 210.

10. Quoted in ibid., 210–11.

11. For example, *La verdad del proletariat* ("Proletarian Truth") for the workers; *El despertar del pueblo* ("The People's Awakener") for the peasants; *El estrella*

roja ("The Red Star") for the militia members; and *Neplanta* and *Nupi* for the FLN's high-ranking cadres and the insurgents they commanded.

12. See de la Grange and Rico 1998, 95, and 1999, 77.
13. De la Grange and Rico 1999, 77.
14. Oppenheimer 1996/1998, 237.
15. For example, Rafael, Rocío, Daniel, and Javier Elorriaga (also known as Vicente) had undertaken studies in UNAM's faculty of philosophy and arts.
16. Le Bot 1997, 110.
17. McClintock 1998, 260.
18. Rafael/Marcos taught at UAM and Daniel was a teaching assistant there. Although Elisa had no formal connection with UAM, she did participate in a UAM trip to Nicaragua in the early eighties, no doubt through her connection with Silvia. Elisa had been recruited to the FLN during her student days at Nuevo León University.
19. Stavans 2002, 394.
20. Delgado 1995, 17.
21. Ibid.
22. Ibid., 13.
23. Stavans 2002, 393.
24. Delgado 1995, 13.
25. Ibid.
26. In de la Grange and Rico 1999, 77.
27. Delgado 1995, 13.
28. "Those of us who are more handsome always have to protect ourselves"; interview from 1 January 1994, http://www.hist.umn.edu/~rmccaa/la20c/ezlnday1.htm. See also Bardach 1994, 67: "If I took the mask off it [i.e., his sex-symbol status] would be much worse, because I am so good looking."
29. Oppenheimer 1996/1998, 74: "They [his indigenous comrades] say women in Mexico City say I'm handsome because they haven't seen me without my ski mask."
30. Delgado 1995, 18.
31. Ibid., 13.
32. Ibid.
33. Ibid., 18.
34. Ibid.
35. Ibid., 13.
36. Ibid., 18.
37. De la Grange and Rico 1998, 88.
38. See de la Grange and Rico 1999, 77.
39. Durán de Huerta 1994, 14–15.
40. Delgado 1995, 19.
41. Ibid., 18.
42. In de la Grange and Rico 1999, 78.

43. Stavans 2002, 393–94.
44. Quoted in Barkin et al. 1997a, 18–19.
45. Mergier 1995, 15.
46. Stavans 2002, 391.
47. For example, he traveled with "Marcos" from whom he later took his nom de guerre when the latter had died; see chapter 7.
48. Tello Díaz 1995/2001, 114, 292, n. 17. I have been unable to locate this assertion of Daniel's in any published medium, and so we must perhaps assume that this testimony was given to Tello Díaz by the Mexican Security forces.
49. Oppenheimer 1996/1998, 237–38.
50. Ibid.
51. See ibid., 253, 257, and 355. That the FLN had at least some connection with the Route 100 company is argued strongly for by Oppenheimer (257–59). Nothing concrete, however, links specifically Rafael to the Route 100 union.
52. De la Grange and Rico (1998, 187). Earlier, on page 76, Rafael's father recalls that his son had told him that he had visited the United States to give a conference paper and while there had supported the Chicano cause.
53. One oft-cited supposed proof of Marcos having visited the United States is the fact that he recognized a *Vanity Fair* reporter's cheap tape recorder as coming from Radio Shack, despite the fact that it only bore the brand name on it, and joked about its poor quality. See Bardach 1994, 67; cited again as proof of the Subcommander having visited the United States by Ross 1995a, 297. In fact, this proves nothing. Certain U.S. stores are famous all over the world. Many non-Americans who have never even visited the country are acquainted with Wal-Mart and its reputation, for example. Moreover, given that Rafael worked in the family business, a large part of which involved selling imported electrical appliances (de la Grange and Rico 1998, 65), a basic knowledge of U.S. electrical stores need not be taken as proof of his having visited the United States. Whereas Bardach believes Marcos accidentally "had betrayed himself" by mentioning Radio Shack, I would argue that the Subcommander deliberately name-dropped in order to give the impression (possibly false) that he was well acquainted with the United States. To my mind this "slip" represents yet another example of El Sup playing the press.
54. De la Grange and Rico 1998, 127–28, 137–38.
55. Although Daniel Alarcón, head of the Cuban "Special Schools of the Revolution" which gave training to foreign would-be revolutionaries, claims to have met Marcos during the 1980s, he stipulates that this was in Mexico and not Cuba. See Tello Díaz 1995/2001, 91–92, n. 17), drawing to some extent on *Proceso* 1996.
56. Tello Díaz 1995/2001, 291–92, n. 17.

57. Ibid., 144, 291–92, n. 17.
58. Vodovnik 2004, 630.

6 CHIAPAS

1. For detailed background information on Chiapas prior to 1984, see, in particular, T. Benjamin 1989/1996, and also Collier and Quaratiello 1994/1999, Ross 1995a, Russell 1995, Harvey 1998, and Womack 1999.
2. Guatemala's sensitivity to Mexican military action in the area stemmed from the quite natural fear small countries have of large, powerful neighbors and was heightened by a traditional feeling of insecurity concerning Chiapas's status based on the fact that it had belonged to Guatemala until its secession in 1823.
3. See de la Grange and Rico 1999, 78. Marcos himself confirms this (Le Bot 1997, 118), telling us that the FLN high command selected Chiapas, saying "there is the Lacandón Jungle, there are places where the government has not come, where the White Guards have not come, where the large landowners have not come, where roads have not come . . . because these zones are very remote."
4. McCaughan 1995, 35.
5. Sereseres (1985, 110) sums up the EGP's strategy as being to "reject *foquismo* and plan for a *guerra prolongada* . . . [and] involve the Indian population; pursue a second, equally important front in the international community."
6. The Mexican president Miguel de la Madrid (1982–88) had recognized in early 1983 that "the Mexican Revolution has not yet fulfilled its mission in Chiapas and there are places where the Revolution is unknown"; quoted and translated in T. Benjamin 1989/1996, 247. Marcos himself would later talk of the Zapatistas trying "to do what the Mexican Revolution never did in the Southeast"; http://flag.blackened.net/revolt/mexico/ezln/inter_marcos_dec94.html. See also Hernández Navarro (1994a, 51): "Chiapas, as it is well known, did not fully experience the Revolution of 1910–17."
7. Greene 1939/1981, 155, 177.
8. See Kampwirth 2002, 87: "In Chiapas, 22.3 people per 100,000 die each year as a result of nutritional deficiencies." Note that the national average is 10.5 people per year.
9. McClintock 1998, 11.
10. "I identify political exclusion as the sine qua non for the Salvadoran revolutionary equation and economic crisis as the sine qua non for the Peruvian equation" (ibid., 281). Although McClintock here cites "political exclusion" for the Salvadoran revolution, elsewhere she substitutes this for "repression"—e.g., "as the FMLN militants emphasize in their statements, the drastic change for Salvadoran peasants was the severity of the govern-

ment's repression of their originally nonviolent organizational efforts . . . in the absence of state repression, they would not have taken up arms" (ibid., 284)—leaving the reader unsure as to which of these two she thinks was a more important factor.

11. Barkin et al. 1997a, 20.

12. Petras 1997, 38.

13. Gonzalez 2002, 436.

14. Stephenson 1995, 9.

15. Typically, given the high-level corruption in Chiapas, "most of the 2.5 million pesos allocated to assist the Zoques disappeared when Governor Sabines Gutiérrez left office"; quoted in T. Benjamin 1989/1996, 246.

16. Coote 1995, 3: "The *status quo* is maintained by the region's corrupt political and judicial systems, which are fashioned to protect the interests of the landowners. As a result, the peasants have no recourse to social or economic justice through democratic means."

17. See Russell 1995, 9.

18. See Human Rights Watch 1991 on abuses in Chiapas.

19. See the introduction to Jan Rus et al. 2003, 24, n. 12: "In Chiapas's indigenous regions, 165 members of independent organizations were murdered between 1974 and mid-1987—an average of one a month for almost thirteen years."

20. Ominously, in 1980, two years prior to being made governor, the general had been commander of the 31st Military Zone in Chiapas when Federal Army soldiers there had massacred Indians at Golonchán. In July 1980, troops under the general's control wiped the community of Wolochán off the face of the map, killing twelve Tzeltals and burning their bodies.

21. See Oppenheimer 1996/1998, 50: "Article 225 of Chiapas' Criminal Code called for sentences of up to four years in prison for those seizing land, buildings, public squares, 'or obstructing communication arteries,' which meant that Mayans risked long terms in jail just for taking their protests to the street." For the code in general, see Minnesota Advocates for Human Rights 1994. For a partial translation and commentary on the code, see Womack 1999, 227–33.

22. Quoted in Russell 1995, 10. See also, Oppenheimer 1996/1998, 59, who notes that after the 1991 legislative elections both Chiapas's governor and its city mayor were from the PRI; that "the PRI ruled all but one of the 110 Chiapas municipalities and controlled the state congress at will"; and that "all judges were from the PRI, and so were the police and military authorities."

23. Hayden 2002, 10.

24. Tangeman 1995, 73.

25. Burbach 2001, 127. He continues: "During 1990 a protest of small-scale

sugar producers was fired upon, leaving six people injured, and several months later peaceful protesters marching on the state capital of Tuxtla Gutiérrez were fired upon. During the same period, several land settlements that even had presidential decrees in their favor were violently uprooted by state police and landowners."

26. See Russell 1995, 56.
27. Burbach 2001, 121.
28. The average number issued by the general's eight predecessors were 30.2 each.
29. Harvey 1998, 155.
30. Russell 1995, 6. He continues: "Some 85,000 Chiapan peasants have 2,847 of such outstanding claims." Harvey (1994, 40) notes that in 1992 Chiapas's unresolved land petitions "represented 27 per cent of the total backlog of the country."
31. Burbach 2001, 124.
32. As Marcos himself put it in 1994: "The problem of the land is one of productivity. It will be necessary not only to subdivide estates and regularize land titles, but to make massive investment in infrastructure, which will increase yield per hectare. In the Lacandón jungle the average yield is half a ton of corn per hectare, while in the rest of the country it is eight tons per hectare"; quoted in Romero 1994, 93, and subsequently translated in Russell 1995, 105.
33. On the militarization of Chiapas from 1981 to 1983, see Harvey 1998, 148–52.
34. Benjamin 1989/1996, 245.
35. Quoted and translated in T. Benjamin 1989/1996, 245. Harvey (1998, 254, n. 39) notes instances of the military intimidating members of Chiapan peasant organizations.
36. Ignacio Ramírez, "Tropas y policías con mandos castrenses se extienden por el país," *Proceso*, no. 543, 30 March 1987, 21, translated in T. Benjamin 1989/1996, 332, n. 84.
37. See Ross 2000, 41–44.
38. See McClintock (1998, 284) on El Salvador: "There were economic grievances among the Salvadoran peasantry, and if there had not been, neither peasants, nor university students, nor church people would have sought agrarian reform; but, in the absence of repression, they would not have taken up arms." Kincaid (1993, 140) concurs: "The radicalization of the movement . . . appears much more the consequence of the repression unleashed against it at a time when it sought much more limited objectives."
39. Guevara 1996, 256–57.
40. On the Catholic Church in Chiapas, see Tangeman 1995; Legorreta Díaz 1998, 41ff; Bonner 1999; Lawrence 1999; and MacEoin 1996/2000. On

the Maoists, see Ross 1995a, 276–77; de la Grange and Rico 1998, 147–51; Harvey 1998, 79–90; Legorreta Díaz 1998, 97; Collier and Quaratiello 1994/1999, 71–76; Womack 1999, 173–81; and Tello Díaz 1995/2001, 80–98.

41. De la Grange and Rico 1999, 78.

42. *Tiempo* 9 February 1994, 3; translated in Collier and Quaratiello 1994/1999, 83.

43. M. Benjamin 1995, 64–65.

44. *Tiempo* 11 February 1994, 3—a printing error means that this issue is dated 10 February; translated in Collier and Quaratiello 1994/1999, 87.

45. T. Benjamin 1989/1996, 234.

46. Communiqué entitled "Chiapas: The Thirteenth Stele, Part Two: A Death," 25 July 2003, http://flag.blackened.net/revolt/mexico/ezlnco.html.

47. See T. Benjamin 1989/1996, xiv, 249.

48. Burbach 2001, 124.

49. See T. Benjamin 1989/1996, xiv and 247.

50. Quoted and translated in ibid., 250.

7   GUERRILLA INCEPTION

1. In de la Grange and Rico 1999, 78.

2. In Vodovnik 2004, 630.

3. A small local minivan with about a ten-person capacity predominantly used by indigenous villagers to traverse those areas not covered by major bus companies.

4. Quoted and translated in Ponce de León 2001, 27.

5. FLN, Fuerzas de Liberación Nacional (Forces of National Liberation); EZLN, Ejército Zapatista de Liberación Nacional (Zapatista Army of National Liberation).

6. The FLN at that time called itself the Armed Forces of National Liberation (FALN).

7. See de la Grange and Rico 1999, 78.

8. Tello Díaz 1995/2001, 93, 134, 286–87, n. 57.

9. Concerning the term *foco*, Marcos himself tells us that even when he arrived the following year, this group still saw themselves "as a traditional guerrilla, very similar to a 'Guevarist foco'"; interview with Jaime Avilés and Gianni Minà 1998, 155. See also his interview with Le Bot 1997, 109: "Y en ese sentido se planteaba una guerrilla en términos muy cercanos al foco guerrillerro."

10. Debray (1967, 32) had noted that typically "the initial group [of guerrillas] experiences at the outset a period of absolute nomadism."

11. De la Grange and Rico 1998, 175. Similarly, see Marcos (in Vodovnik 2004,

630): "With the aid of lanterns these men and women were putting up a plastic roof, using a cord as crossbar, hanging up their hammocks, looking for dry firewood and, setting fire to a plastic bag, lighting the bonfire."

12. Similarly, in Le Bot 1997, 118: "The camp was paradoxically called 'The Nightmare' (La Pesadilla)," explaining: "We asked him [the scout] what this place was like: 'It is very pretty, very pleasant, it has a river and trees, there is food, one can hunt'—it was because of this that we survived—'it is a dream!,' he said. When we came and we saw it, we said 'is it a dream? No, it's a nightmare!' and the name 'The nightmare' remained."

13. In Vodovnik 2004, 631. Pedro, who later rose to the ranks of Subcommander, was Héctor Ochoa, a native of the Federal District.

14. See de la Grange and Rico 1999, 78.

15. Interview between Marcos and anarchist journalists (11 May 1994); translated in Autonomedia 1994, 290. Similarly, see Zack de la Rocha's interview with Marcos (June 1996): "Let me remind you that the EZLN was born as a political-military organization, similar to the political-military organizations of the sixties and seventies"; http://www.musicfanclubs.org/rage/articles/marcos.htm. Elsewhere, in Montalbán (2002, 105), Marcos has described the situation even more bluntly, stating: "We came to the forest as a classic revolutionary elite in search of . . . the proletariat in the classic Marxist-Leninist sense." Similarly, see Le Bot's interview with Marcos (1997, 109–10).

16. Published and circulated internally within the organization in 1985; quoted in Tello Díaz 1995/2001, 292, n. 18.

17. Le Bot 1997, 143, 147.

18. Collier and Quaratiello 1994/1999, 83.

19. Vodovnik 2004, 631.

20. De la Grange and Rico 1999, 78.

21. De la Grange and Rico 1998, 175.

22. De la Grange and Rico 1999, 83.

23. See Womack 1999, 191.

24. For example, Germán took his nom de guerre from his dead brother César Germán Yáñez (alias Pedro), while Elisa took hers from a fallen comrade, Elisa Sáenez. The future Subcomandante Pedro took his from the nom de guerre of Germán's dead brother. More generally, Zimmermann (2000/2004, 113) notes that in Nicaragua "FSLN members often took the names of comrades killed in action."

25. De la Grange and Rico (1998, 131) states that Marcos took his nom de guerre from Alfredo Zárate who used the alias "Marcos" and who had been the FLN's second-in-command before his death at the Neplanta safe house in 1974. However, this is contradicted both by Marcos himself and by Tello Díaz 1995/2001, 291, n. 16.

26. Le Bot 1997, 141. See also Tello Díaz 1995/2001, 114, esp. 290–91, n. 16.

27. Communiqué entitled "Account of the Events" (July 2002); http://flag
.blackened.net/revolt/mexico/ezln/2002/marcos/eventsJULY.html. Marcos
introduces his verses as "this rudimentary attempt at a poem, entitled 'Account of the Events'—which I wrote 18 years ago, at the dawn of the EZLN."

28. Quoted in Durán de Huerta 1994, 21. Similarly, see Marcos as quoted in
Rovira 1994, 51–52.

29. Interview with reporters from *Proceso, El Financiero*, and the *New York
Times*, published in *Proceso* 21 February 1994; translated in Autonomedia
1994, 201. Similarly, Marcos is quoted in Rovira (1994, 52) and McCaughan
(2002, 72) as saying: "I was carrying some 15 books, some five or ten kilos
. . . There is a logic among guerrillas that states: One kilo weighs two after
an hour. After two hours, it weighs four and you just want to dump the
whole fucking lot."

30. Quoted in McCaughan 2002, 72.

31. "He arrived in the Lacandón jungle in May 1984" (Tello Díaz 1995/2001,
114); "That day—the 20 May—Marcos celebrated the anniversary of his arrival . . . in the Lacandón jungle" (ibid., 185).

32. "In October 1984, five months after his arrival in the jungle" (de la Grange
and Rico, 1998, 177).

33. See Harvey (1998, 247, n. 2) for a critique of Tello Díaz's methodology:
"[Tello Díaz] made no mention to the sources of his information [and that]
the story has no gaps or contradictions, no competing evidence, and no
citations at critical points in the text." Much the same, I feel, can be said
of de la Grange's and Rico's book, which relies on a very limited number of
sources—most notably Antonio—and seldom, if ever, cites conflicting or
contradictory evidence even where it is known to exist.

34. Quoted and translated in Ponce de León 2001, 229. In a more recent piece
Marcos (in Vodovnik 2004, 631) tells us: "I arrived in the Lacandon jungle
. . . in 1984, around August-September of that year, some nine months after
the first group had gotten there."

35. Ponce de León 2001, 210.

36. Ibid., 212.

37. On the founding of the FLN, see Tello Díaz 1995/2001, 67: "There, on the
6 August 1969, a Wednesday, in a very humble house in Monterrey, located
in the 5th of May Street, they founded with other comrades the Forces of
National Liberation"; and de la Grange and Rico (1998, 117): "From Monterrey there also proceeded a group of university students which in August
1969, a year after the Tlatelolco massacre, founded the Forces of National
Liberation (FLN)."

38. Ponce de León 2001, 212. Similarly, see Marcos's closing speech at the National Encuentro in Defense of Cultural Heritage (14 August 1999): "It was
fifteen years ago that I first came to these mountains. It was then, in one of
the guerrilla camps, that I was told a story at dawn—as was mandated—of

fifteen years before. In this August that soaks us, thirty years will have gone by"; ibid., 280.

39. Similarly, see Payeras (1983, 25) who, describing the hardships he and his guerrilla comrades endured, tells us: "If anyone, at those moments, had talked to us about taking power and building a Socialist society, we would probably have told him to drop dead."

40. Elsewhere Marcos tells us that he came to Chiapas "with two other compañeros: a Chol indigenous compañera and a Tzotzil indigenous compañero" (Vodovnik 2004, 631).

41. The Milky Way exerts some influence over Marcos, as is shown by his communiqué entitled "The Story of the Milky Way" (dated 24 June 1999).

42. Translated in Ponce de León 2001, 210–12. Similarly, see also his communiqué from March 1995; http://flag.blackened.net/revolt/mexico/ezln/marcos_ecuador_peru_mar95.html.

43. Captain Maribel describes her first guerrilla training exercise, perhaps climbing the same mountain as Marcos, which possibly all new recruits were subjected to: "The toughest moment in those nine years was when I had to climb the first hill, called 'the hill from hell'"; translated in Ponce de León 2001, 8.

44. The FLN's statutes (6 August 1980) state in articles 12 (r) and 14 (i) that cadres should "stay in excellent physical condition . . . by means of physical exercise."

45. See Tello Díaz 1995/2001, 295, n. 32.

46. On Marcos emulating Che's mock heroic guerrilla writings, see chapter 25.

47. De la Grange and Rico, 1999, 78. Similarly, Marcos (in Vodovnik 2004, 630): "Practices were organized for one or two months in the selva, during which the performance of those in attendance was evaluated in order to see who would 'make the cut.'"

48. See de la Grange and Rico 1999, 78. See Tello Díaz 1995/2001, 305, n. 34, drawing to some extent on Proceso 1996. Gérman, it would appear, perhaps learned his military training in Cuba during the early 1970s.

49. La Jornada 8 February 1994, translated in Autonomedia 1994, 147.

50. A Place Called Chiapas (1998).

51. See de la Grange and Rico 1999, 82.

52. Guevara (1996, 325) writes of the difficulties encountered on his final push towards Santa Clara: "We walked through difficult flooded terrain, suffering attacks by swarms of mosquitoes that made the hours of rest unbearable, eating little and poorly, drinking water from swampy rivers or simply from swamps."

53. In Days of the Jungle (1983) Payeras tells of "the plague of mosquitoes and gnats . . . the deadly coral snake . . . and the colmovote, the worm that a mosquito buries under the skin" (23); "clothes torn to shreds as we pushed our way through the dense vegetation" (25); "the paleness peculiar to those who

have lived for a long time without sunlight and . . . severe stomach cramps and constant diarrhea" (31); "malaria and . . . mosquitoes in our mouths" (46); and "great equatorial heat and swarms of ticks" (47).

54. Sandinista Borge wrote in his *The Patient Impatience* (1992, 152, 157) of the "mountain leprosy . . . caused by a parasite called leishmania . . . the ulcer [from which] grows and resembles a festering puddle, a little sewer," and "feet tortured by stones and blisters, scratches and bruises on our half-naked ribs . . . hands torn by thorns."

55. For Marcos's accounts of the rodents, diarrhea, vipers, torrential downpours, mud, hunger, thirst, fatigue, darkness, solitude, food cravings, etc., that accompany guerrilla life see, Durán de Huerta's chapter entitled "La montaña" (1994, 83–98).

56. Ibid., 34.

8 THE WILDERNESS YEARS

1. Quoted in Subcomandante Marcos 1995c, 132.
2. Le Bot 1997, 121.
3. Subcomandante Marcos 1995c, 133.
4. "Esos primeros años, 83–85, son muy solitarios para estos grupos" (Le Bot 1997, 122); and "Pero fue una época muy solitaria . . . eramos una guerrilla muy aislada. . . . Eramos el máximo ejemplo de la soledad, del aislamiento en todos sentidos" (124–25).
5. Avilés and Minà 1998, 161.
6. Landau 2002, 148.
7. Ibid., 147.
8. Durán de Huerta 1994, 83–98.
9. Subcomandante Marcos 1995c, 133. See also Le Bot 1997, 123: "Then we lived off wild fruit, from hunting wild animals, recognizing routes and pathways, we permeated the terrain, we had a network of roads that we used."
10. Durán de Huerta 1994, 86, reprinted in Montalbán 2000, 21.
11. See the testimony of an El Salvadoran guerrilla in López Vigil 1991, 159: "You've got to see how we live and sleep and roll around in the mud in a guerrilla camp. Yearning for adventure or just plain stubbornness won't get you through nine or ten years under those conditions."
12. Quoted in Durán de Huerta 1994, 97.
13. Ibid., 87–88.
14. Ibid., 94, where Marcos calls rodents "the principal enemy of the guerrilla because they eat your food while you are sleeping."
15. Ibid., 91.
16. Subcomandante Marcos 1995c, 135.
17. The same situation prevailed with the El Salvadoran guerrillas at this time.

As one put it: "The combatants lived in what was perhaps a very small world, very local, with some national vision and not much awareness beyond that"; in López Vigil 1991, 141.

18. Subcomandante Marcos (1995c, 135). Similarly, Marcos's interview with Oppenheimer 1996/1998, 72.

19. Marcos informs us that "the solitude was not only physical, but also political, because the news we were receiving that reached us from the outside world was that from short-wave radio stations: The *Voice of America*, *Radio France International*, London's BBC, *Radio Exterior* from Spain, *Radio Havana* from Cuba, and *La Voz de los Andes*" (Le Bot 1997, 124); he tells us that he listened to news of the FMLN's 1989 offensive on Radio Venceremos and the URNG's Radio Voz Popular (121).

20. Tello Díaz 1995/2001, 111.

21. Vodovnik 2004, 361.

22. Le Bot 1997, 123.

23. See de la Grange and Rico 1999, 79.

24. Quoted in Durán de Huerta 1994, 96.

25. *Tiempo* 9 February 1994, 2; quoted and translated in Collier and Quaratiello 1994/1999, 84–85. See also an interview Marcos gave with anarchist reporters (11 May 1994), reprinted and translated in Autonomedia 1994, 291: "When the first group of the EZLN arrived here . . . it began to adapt itself to the surroundings, to try to survive—that is to say, to permeate the territory, to make it survivable. . . . This first stage was, in effect, about two things: surviving and beginning our political work."

26. Subcomandante Marcos 1995c, 132. Similarly, see the video interview with Marcos entitled *Marcos: palabras y historia / Words and History* (1995), where he says that they "didn't do any political labor either within or without of the communities."

27. Landau 2002, 147–48.

28. Interview with anarchist reporters, 11 May 1994; reported and translated in Autonomedia 1994, 293. See earlier in the interview also, where Marcos tells us that this experience "began to forge . . . in that initial group of combatants, the physical and ideological strength needed for the guerrilla process. By this I mean that the mountains served as a school for cadres, inflexible and constant, day and night" (290).

29. Vodovnik 2004, 632. Marcos tells us this celebration occurred in the "Margaret Thatcher" camp, so called because outside it they had hung a huge hog resembling the then British prime minister.

30. "I began to move up through the ranks: sub-lieutenant, lieutenant, first captain, second captain, subcommander" (interview between Marcos and journalists from *La Jornada*, published in that newspaper on 8 February 1994; translated in Autonomedia 1994, 147). See also Marcos's communiqué entitled "The Story of Looking" (August 1999), in which he tells us "that at

the time when I met 'Old Antonio' [December 1984], I had the rank of Insurgent Second Captain of Infantry"; translated in Subcomandante Marcos 2001b, 138.

31. See Le Bot 1997, 150, where Major Moisés tells us that he had encountered the guerrillas, who he describes as "a group of men who said that they were tourists."

32. On this meeting, see de la Grange and Rico 1998, 265f, and Tello Díaz 1995/2001, 114f.

33. See T. Benjamin 1989/1996, 237, 239. On the power of the Unión de Uniones, see Leyva Solano 2003, 163–64, 173–75.

34. For his role both within Asociación Rural de Interés Colectivo (ARIC, Rural Association of Collective Interests) and the EZLN, and his subsequent career after the 1994 uprising, see chapter 15.

35. Here Marcos describes his rank as "infantry lieutenant," but see above, n. 30, where he tells us he was a "Second Captain of Infantry" when he first met "Old Antonio."

36. "The Story of Questions" (13 December 1994); translated in Ponce de León 2001, 413.

37. Communiqué entitled "Twelve Women in the Twelfth Year" (dated 11 March 1996); translated in Ponce de León 2001, 5.

38. In de la Grange and Rico 1999, 82.

39. "The Story of Questions" (13 December 1994); translated in Ponce de León 2001, 413. This translation is that of Dinah Livingstone in Subcomandante Marcos 2001b, 91.

9 FIRST CONTACT

1. Le Bot 1997, 123. Concerning the *foco*'s composition, Yolanda and Mario had arrived in December 1984 to increase the nine to eleven. However, around this time Benjamín had been summarily executed (see chapter 10), and Rodolfo was relocated to his home state of Chihuahua where he took command of the newly implanted Villa Front. We also know from Major Moisés (quoted in G. Ramírez 2003, 42) that Pedro left Chiapas for a few months during his early days in the jungle in order to receive medical treatment and that he returned there before Moisés went back to the jungle in 1985. If, and certainty is impossible here, Pedro's treatment was during winter 1984–85, this left eight remaining in Chiapas in January 1985.

2. Subcomandante Marcos 1995c, 135, adding: "And in us was the ghost of Che, of Bolivia, more precisely, of the lack of campesino support for an artificially implanted guerrilla . . . We thought that what had happened to Che could possibly happen to us."

3. Stephenson 1995, 13.

4. Montalbán 2000, 139.

5. Quoted in de la Grange and Rico 1998, 177.

6. Le Bot 1997, 128. For more on recruitment along kinship lines, see chapter 15.

7. Ibid.

8. In de la Grange and Rico 1998, 176.

9. Le Bot 1997, 127–28. Similarly, though more succinctly, see the interview between Marcos and anarchist journalists (11 May 1994); translated and published in Autonomedia 1994, 291–92: "In this common point of necessity of armed struggle a relationship began to develop. They needed military instruction, and we needed the support of a social base."

10. Interview between Marcos and Anarchist journalists (11 May 1994); translated and published in Autonomedia 1994, 291–92.

11. Similarly, Comandanta Elisa: "The communities saw the armed struggle as self defense: for us it was a means of accessing a political transformation"; quoted in de la Grange and Rico 1998, 178.

12. Harvey 1994, 21, and again at 31.

13. Urgent Action Bulletin AMR 41/14/85 and "Reported Killings, Detentions and Torture in the State of Chiapas," Urgent Action Bulletin (9 July 1986), respectively.

14. For Marcos witnessing the deaths of children from disease, and in particular the death of a girl named Patricia, see his interview with UNAM Radio (18 March 1994), published in EZLN (1994a, vol. 2, 69–70) and partially quoted and translated in Holloway (1998, 163). See also Durán de Huerta 1994, 28–29, for excerpts from the same interview specifically on the death of Chiapan children from disease. This was to become a recurrent theme in Marcos's communiqués, for example, in "Olivio Plays Football" (July 1996) and most recently in the "Devils of the New Century: Zapatista Children in the Year 2001, the Seventh Year of the War against Oblivion" (February 2001), both published and translated in Subcomandante Marcos 2001b, 153, 166. See also his communiqué entitled "A Death Has Been Decided" (July 2003), http://flag.blackened.net/revolt/mexico/ezln/2003/marcos/deathJULY.html: "There wasn't a day when someone didn't report the death of a little boy, of a little girl, of a mother."

15. *Proceso*, 21 February 1994, 9–10; translated in Autonomedia 1994, 199.

16. Quoted in de la Grange and Rico 1998, 177.

17. See de la Grange and Rico 1999, 78, where Daniel himself tells us he arrived in 1985.

18. In de la Grange and Rico 1999, 77.

19. Ibid., 78.

20. See Tello Díaz 1995/2001, 190.

21. Marcos 1995a, 241.

22. Cf. Subcomandante Marcos (1995c, 137), where he claims that Old Antonio invited the guerrillas into his village in 1986: "Ahí es donde nosotros entra-

mos por primera vez, armadas, de día, a un poblado, es el primer poblado del viejo Antonio, a invitación de él."

23. Ibid.

24. On 31 July 1994 Marcos sent several pages of his logbook to the editor of *Proceso* for publication. They appeared in *Proceso* 1994b.

25. Quoted in Tello Díaz 1995/2001, 124.

26. In Vodovnik 2004, 632.

27. Ibid.

28. Barkin et al. 1997a, 19. See also Castañeda 1994a, 224: "For days students, housewives, bureaucrats, and workers helped pull babies and bodies from out of the rubble. The rescue operations lasted for up to a month, and their sequel took over where they left off: organizing the homeless, the jobless, the maimed and sick. These efforts continued for nearly two years, and the urban groups survived into the 1990s."

29. *Entrada libre: crónicas de una sociedad que se organiza* (Mexico City: Ediciones Era, 1988), 239; cited and translated in Castañeda (1994a, 224).

30. Translated in Ponce de León 2001, 128–29.

31. In July, another peasant organization, the Central Independiente de Obreros y Agrícolas y Campesinos (CIOAC), also had their demonstration in Tuxtla forcibly broken up by police. For these events, see Harvey 1998, 157, 159.

32. Again, see Harvey 1998, 159. Comandante Tacho makes it clear that Andulio Gálvez's death was a turning point for him and others in the decision to turn away from peaceful protest to the armed struggle. See "*Paz con justicia y dignidad para los pueblos Indios*" 1995. Stephen (2002, 129) translates part of Tacho's statement into English.

33. Volman 1985. He continued, prophetically as it would turn out: "Politically moderate US experts on rural development who have worked with Indian communities in Mexico for many years say that stationing large numbers of troops in the province would likely lead to a wave of repression against the Indian population. The local Indian population would revolt leading to further violence."

10 PROMOTION AND EXPANSION

1. Tello Díaz 1995/2001, 126.

2. Oppenheimer 1996/1998, 257.

3. Ibid., 258.

4. See chapter 19 for this communiqué of Marcos.

5. "The Story of the Seven Rainbows" (7 January 1996); translated in Ponce de León 2001, 383.

6. *Proceso*, no. 904, 21 February 1994, 9–10; translated in Russell 1995, 33.

7. Subcomandante Marcos 1995c, 136.

8. Interview with reporters from *Proceso*, *El Financiero*, and the *New York Times*,

published in *Proceso*, 21 February 1994; translated in Autonomedia 1994, 202. Even this erosion rate was better than that of Che Guevara's during his doomed Bolivian adventure. Guevara (1994/1996, 249) noted in his diary entry for 7 August 1967: "Of the initial six, two are dead, one is missing, and two are wounded; then there is me with asthma, which I don't know how to stop."

9. The interview published in Subcomandante Marcos 1995c dates to 24 October 1994.

10. Subcomandante Marcos 1995c, 136.

11. Tello Díaz (1995/2001, 293, n. 22) notes that during the Mexico City earthquake, for example: "The highest leaders of the EZLN in the jungle: Germán, Marcos, Pedro, Daniel and Rodolfo were in their River Negro camp, near La Candelaria, awaiting the arrival of Elisa, who had just spent some days in San Cristóbal de las Casas."

12. Tello Díaz 1995/2001, 21; see also 261: "Pedro, the most important of the rebels' cadres after Marcos."

13. Ibid., 189.

14. Moisés is quoted in G. Ramírez 2003, 42.

15. Subcomandante Marcos 1995c, 136: "It then occurred that these indigenous compañeros were allowed to visit their families and to do political work there."

16. Ibid. Vodovnik (2004, 633) quotes Marcos as saying: "First we would talk with one person, and then he would talk with his family. From the family it went to the village."

17. Quoted in Stephen 2002, 190.

18. Montalbán (2000, 139) quotes him as saying: "The indigenous with whom we first came into contact were very politicized, very conscious and today many of them are leaders in the guerrilla movement." Marcos talks of "what we should call an elite, politicized indigenous, with a great organizational capacity and with a very rich experience of political struggle . . . a people with a political culture and a surprising national consciousness" in Le Bot 1997, 117; see also 118, 119, 121, 127.

19. De la Grange and Rico 1998, 182.

20. The same source claims to have received instruction from Lucía at Tuxtla Gutiérrez (ibid., 180–81).

21. Ibid.

22. Ibid., 181.

23. See chapter 23 for the significance of this name in Mexican history.

24. Communiqué entitled "The Spiral from the End and the Beginning" (dated 23 October 1996); translated in Ponce de León 2001, 136.

25. Subcomandante Marcos 1995c, 136. See also Le Bot 1997, 122: "At times they hassled us because they said that we were cattle rustlers or bandits or sorcerers."

26. Quoted in De la Grange and Rico 1998, 177.

27. Interview with Le Bot 1997, 164–65; partially quoted and translated into English in Stephen 2002, 135.

28. Subcomandante Marcos 1995c, 137.

29. Ibid.

30. De la Grange and Rico 1998, 175.

31. Ibid.

32. In Nettie Wild's documentary, *A Place Called Chiapas* (1998).

33. Quoted in de la Grange and Rico 1998, 177.

34. Le Bot 1997, 128: "El choque, para nosotros, es que teníamos que hablar la lengua."

35. Quoted and translated in Subcomandante Marcos 2001a, 112.

36. Ibid.

37. De la Grange and Rico 1999, 82.

38. Weinberg (2000, 127) describes Marcos's English as "halting but correct." Ross (1995a, 301) calls it "middling," while Simon (2002, 46) calls it "fluent, accented English." Bardach (1994, 67) calls it "the phonetic English of someone who has heard the language a lot, not, as he [Marcos] has said, English learned solely from reading CIA manuals." The U.S. scriptwriter Anne Moore comments that Marcos spoke English "with an accent, but not very marked" (*Proceso*, no. 980, 14 August 1995, 24).

39. Subcomandante Marcos 1995c, 137–38.

40. Montalbán 2000, 139.

41. In a recent communiqué (25 July 2003) from Marcos entitled "Chiapas: The Thirteenth Stele. Part Two: A Death," http://www.ezln.org/documentos/ 2003/index.html.

42. Montalbán 2000, 139.

43. Quoted in Le Bot 1997, 145; the translation here is that of Nash 2001, 226.

44. Quoted in Montalbán 2002, 476.

45. Communiqué entitled "A Death Has Been Decided" (July 2003), http://flag .blackened.net/revolt/mexico/ezln/2003/marcos/deathJULY.html.

46. Amnesty International (1986, 65) talks of "a pattern of apparently deliberate political killings."

47. "The Story of the Seven Rainbows" (dated 7 January 1996); translated in Ponce de León 2001, 383.

48. De la Grange and Rico 1998, 186.

49. Vodovnik 2004, 632.

50. Both are quoted in G. Ramírez 2003, 28, 30, 32, respectively.

51. See Tello Díaz 1995/2001, 128.

52. *Marcos: palabras y historia/Words and History* 1995.

53. De la Grange and Rico 1998, 198: "When the military discovered [Daniel's] camp in the Sierra Corralchén in May 1993, they found, to their great surprise, that the insurgents had generators and regularly watched television."

He goes on to quote Antonio as saying, "We were able to pick-up three television channels and watch the news."

54. See de la Grange and Rico 1998, 192.

55. In Vodovnik 2004, 632. Marcos is confused here. Papa Doc had died more than a decade earlier, in 1971. Baby Doc then took over until he was overthrown in 1986.

56. See De la Grange and Rico 1998, 111. Official government figures place the number of people "disappeared" in Mexico between 1965 and 1975 at 600; one NGO (the Centro de Investigaciones Históricas de los Movimientos Armados [CIHMA]) claims "three thousand Mexicans died in combat or were assassinated between 1965 and 1975."

57. Ibid., 191.

58. See Tello Díaz 1995/2001, 203, for both of these quotations. See, too, *Proceso*, no. 1270, 4 March 2001, the cover of which reads, "Germán, el Comandante duro." Cf., however, *Proceso*, no. 1271, 11 March 2001, 36, where members of COCOPA affirm that "Germán no es duro."

59. For the execution of Benjamín at Germán's hands, see Tello Díaz 1995/2001, 221, 316, n. 25; and De la Grange and Rico 1998, 409.

60. See Tello Díaz (1995/2001, 296, n. 40), where he quotes Germán as stating as late as 1987 that "the armed revolutionary struggle should be lead by the working class"; and Rodrigo in the same year as saying "the working class should play the principal role in the Socialist revolution." De la Grange and Rico (1998, 190–91) cite a former Zapatista who attests that "Rodrigo's language was very tough" adding that "he was full of fight. . . . He spoke all the time about having to fight against imperialism and for socialism."

61. See Tello Díaz 1995/2001, 203.

62. Ibid., 295, n. 30.

63. Quoted in de la Grange and Rico 1998, 170.

64. Marcos 1995a, 22–23.

65. On this theme, see most recently Kampwirth 2002.

66. From the video documentary *Marcos: palabras y historia /Words and History* (1995).

67. Millán 1998, 65. She also tells how if there is not enough food to go around the man eats first, the children next, and often the women have nothing. If they only have enough money for one pair of shoes, the man has them, and the women walk barefoot.

68. Ibid., 69.

69. In Castro 1995, 112.

70. In Poniatowska 1995, 106–7.

71. Idem, 72.

72. Quoted in Hermosilla et al. 1995, 37. Similarly, Captain Elisa (Millán 1998, 73) claims, "When I lived at home with my family, I didn't know anything. I didn't know how to read. I didn't go to school. But, when I joined the EZLN, I

learned to read. I learned all the Spanish I know. I learned to read and write, and I trained for combat."

73. *Tiempo* 11 February 1994, 3 — a printing error dates this issue is to 10 February.

74. See de la Grange and Rico 1999, 80. Marcos instead emphasizes the lack of access to major arms dealers over a lack of finances. As he would later half-jokingly boast to one group of journalists in February 1994: "What we never found was an arms trafficker. If we'd found one, now we'd be talking in Cerro del Ajusco [above Mexico City]." Translated in Autonomedia 1994, 204, and also in Ross 1995, 285.

75. As former Subcommander-turned-informer Daniel tells us (de la Grange and Rico 1999, 80): "The weapons were bought in the United States, it was part of Germán's task."

76. De la Grange and Rico 1999, 81.

77. Subcomandante Marcos 1995c, 139.

78. Ibid., 136.

79. Quoted in Anderson 1997, 600.

80. See Tello Díaz 1995/2001, 297, n. 50.

81. De la Grange and Rico 1998, 187–88)

82. Ibid., 179.

83. Ibid., 198. For discussion of this alleged trip to Nicaragua, see chapter 11, where another source dates such a visit to August of the following year (1987).

84. Le Bot 1997, 123.

85. *Tiempo* 6 February 1994, 2. Similarly, Comandanta Elisa claims: "We organized . . . from 'Gringo' military manuals and Mexican Army ones, which we had previously got in bookshops in Mexico City"; quoted in de la Grange and Rico 1998, 178.

86. De la Grange and Rico 1999, 81.

87. Tello Díaz (1995/2001, 189) notes that Subcomandante Pedro had worked as a driver for Pemex in Macuspana, Tabasco, during the early 1980s. It is therefore not implausible that the company's uniforms were acquired either through him or through contacts he had made while working there.

88. Quoted in De la Grange and Rico 1998, 188–89.

89. Durán de Huerta 1994, 89.

90. Camín and Meyer 1993, 229–30.

11 A JUNGLE WEDDING

1. Her true identity is not known. Equally, the reason behind the choice of the nom de guerre Yolanda is a mystery. We can, however, posit two possible explanations for the choice of Ana María: it could have been chosen in honor of Zapata's daughter of that same name or in honor of Mélida

Anaya Montes, one of the FMLN's leading cadres until she was assassinated in spring 1984 (about nine months prior to Yolanda's/Ana María's joining the EZLN) whose nom de guerre was also Ana María.

2. Translated in Clarke and Ross 1994/2000, 81; partially reprinted in Millán 1998, 64–80.

3. Clarke and Ross 1994/2000, 82: "I entered [the EZLN] when I was very young. I was fourteen years old when I entered the struggle."

4. This communiqué (11 March 1996) is devoted exclusively to the women who make up the Zapatistas and was written in reaction to the Conference of Women in Beijing.

5. Translated in Ponce de León 2001, 5.

6. Carlos Tello Díaz 1995/2001: 93, 157, 286–87, n. 57. Tello Díaz tells us that Frank was Yolanda's nephew—Paco was thus Yolanda's relation also (164).

7. Ibid., 106–7. So too, Womack 1999, 191: "Using old relations in another direction, in Sabanilla, he [Jacobo] carefully recruited a Tzotzil leader of land invasions in the north, who in turn carefully recruited other militants there with kinfolk in the canyons." Possibly Ana María/Yolanda, or one of her family members, was one such recruit.

8. See Tello Díaz 1995/2001, 138.

9. In the same interview she adds, "We joined this struggle more than ten years ago. First they were peaceful struggles in which I participated with my sisters and brothers."

10. One probable such organization was the Central Committee, which was established in the immediate aftermath of the Indigenous Council of 1974. Initially at least it pursued purely legal means in order to petition for agricultural reform and social justice. By 1977, it represented twenty-seven *ejidos* in northern Chiapas, including Sabanilla. Frustrated at the poor results yielded by legitimate actions, the Central Committee subsequently adopted a strategy of direct action—predominantly, though not exclusively, land invasions—in 1976. See T. Benjamin 1989/1996, 239f on the Central Committee.

11. Clarke and Ross 1994/2000, 82.

12. Kampwirth 2002, 11, n. 14. As Kampwirth notes, however, "they [families] are also almost always ignored by revolutionary theorists."

13. Womack (1999, 191) notes that San Andrés Larráinzar was "perhaps the poorest and probably the most rebellious of the Tzotzil municipalities, from which many angry young Indians went to the canyons."

14. Quoted, translated, and reprinted in Millán 1998, 73.

15. See de la Grange and Rico 1998, 195.

16. See Captain Maribel quoted in Rovira (2002, 459): "When the compañeros sign the [marriage] agreement, the commanding officers present stand to attention with those of us at the celebration, we cross our rifles and they walk underneath. This also means that we defend their marriage and we are

happy fighting along with them and we have a party and—bingo!—they are married."

17. Borge 1992, 441.

18. Zimmermann (2000/2004, 199) quotes Rivera as saying that "Fonseca, holding the bride and groom by the hands, 'declared us man and wife by the laws of the revolution.'"

19. Communiqué entitled "We Know What We're Doing; It Is Worth It" (dated December 1994); translated in Ponce de León 2001, 218. According to *Proceso*, no. 1008, 26 February 1996, 14, Eva and Beto are Comandante Tacho's children. For a similarly domestic scene involving Ana María, Marcos, and Heriberto, see the communiqué entitled "The Story of Colors," posted on the Internet at http://www.ezln.org/documentos/1994/199410xx.en.htm.

20. His reports appeared in the Nicaraguan newspaper *La Tribuna* (17 and 18 February 1995). For a more accessible account and a good summary of the content of these reports, see de la Grange and Rico 1998, 98; and also Pinchetti 1995, 51.

21. These denials are quoted in de la Grange and Rico (1998, 98f); and also Pinchetti (1995, 51).

22. On Doctor Carlos, see de la Grange and Rico (1998, 88, 101) and Tello Díaz (1995/2001, 177ff, 233). However, since I have been unable to discover even an approximate physical description of Gabriel Ramírez (alias Doctor Carlos), this proposal must remain pure speculation.

23. Mattiace 2003b, 143.

24. Castañeda 1994a, 257.

25. Camín and Meyer 1993, 228.

26. Cited in Harvey 1998, 160.

27. Harvey 1994, 22.

12 AN ELECTION, EXPONENTIAL GROWTH, AND A RIFT

1. The site was used by Marcos to stage mock battles with the army. See Tello Díaz 1995/2001, 266: "He [Marcos] had recreated with his troops a military confrontation on land of the San Francisco ejido."

2. De la Grange and Rico 1998, 161.

3. Ibid., 161–62.

4. See Tello Díaz 1995/2001, 297, n. 48.

5. Russell (1995, 8). He continues: "The 88.8 % vote reported for the PRI [in Chiapas] was certainly not grateful citizens rewarding the incumbents for serving their interests."

6. Interview between Marcos and journalists from *La Jornada*, published in that newspaper on 8 February 1994; translated in Autonomedia (1994, 151).

7. This figure must be wrong. It is possibly a typographical error (i.e., "50 mil"

instead of "5 mil") or perhaps Marcos is exaggerating—although nowhere else does he make such an exaggerated claim. Elsewhere (see chapter 15) he tells us that the EZLN mustered 5,000 troops in 1992 at La Sultana to mark the 500-year anniversary of indigenous resistance.

8. Avilés and Gianni Minà 1998, 161–62.

9. Subcomandante Marcos 1995c, 139.

10. Le Bot 1997, 155–6.

11. See the video entitled *Viaje al centro de la selva* (1994).

12. For further details see de la Grange and Rico (1998, 160–65) and Tello Díaz (1995/2001, 135, 297–98, nn. 49, 50, 51).

13. See de la Grange and Rico 1999, 78.

14. Ibid., 83.

15. See Womack (1999, 37) for a different date and interpretation. He writes: "That same month [March] the FLN national executive withdrew its zone commander from Chiapas and made Subcomandante Marcos head of the EZLN's Southeastern Combat Front." However, Womack fails to cite his source for this information, and no testimony I have read corroborates this date or directly confirms Marcos's superior authority over the two other Subcommanders, Pedro and Daniel, in Chiapas.

16. Marcos commanded the Ocosingo region, Daniel the Altamirano region, and Pedro the Las Margaritas region.

17. Subcommander Daniel tells us that Elorriaga and Elisa "met in 1985 and it was love at first sight"; in de la Grange and Rico 1999, 83.

18. Tello Díaz (1995/2001, 133) followed by Womack (1999, 192).

19. Oppenheimer (1996/1998, 26) tells us that Elisa lost "her baby daughter in Chiapas, where bad medical attention in a rebel camp caused the child's death." However, although Oppenheimer is generally very reliable, having access to excellent sources both in the guerrilla movement and the Mexican security forces, he is the only author to assert this and his chronology is very loose indeed here—he provides no indication of dates but appears to suggest this must have taken place during the late seventies or early eighties. In any event, he states that it was only later, after the death of her daughter, that Elisa had begun her relationship with Vicente and that they subsequently had to try for several years to have a baby.

20. Gilly 2002, 339.

21. De la Grange and Rico 1998, 268.

22. The diocese began describing the EZLN's relationship with the Church as being akin to that of the parasitic Majanté plant (strangler fig) which kills the host tree it feeds off of.

23. De la Grange and Rico 1998, 259.

24. For this quotation and its explanation, see Krauze 2002, 414.

25. Kampwirth 2002, 96. Elsewhere (2003, 234) she states: "The church did not create the EZLN . . . but it helped set the stage."

26. In the magazine *Época*, June 1992 (reproduced in its 25 December 1995 edition, 83), and quoted in de la Grange and Rico 1998, 276.

27. De la Grange and Rico 1999, 79.

28. Legorreta Díaz (1998, 225) quotes an anonymous ex-insurgent from the San Antonio *ejido* as saying, "I left the EZLN in 1989, because at that time Marcos began to say to us that 'I don't give a shit about the Word of God' . . . Marcos began to speak badly about the Word of God, that God did not exist, and so on."

29. See Martin 1987, 17: "In other Central American countries [than Nicaragua], meanwhile, Jesuits not only participated in guerrilla training of Marxist cadres, but became guerrilla fighters themselves."

30. *Tiempo*, 19 January 1994, 3, translated and published in Collier and Quaratiello 1994/1999, 66.

31. Comandante Tacho had, in the seventies, been sent to the Marists in San Cristóbal to attend three-month-long Bible study workshops in which he was also instructed in arithmetic, first aid, Mexican history, agrarian rights, and the establishment of cooperatives.

32. As de la Grange and Rico (1998, 282) put it, "Since 1960 the bishop had patiently traversed his immense territory in order to spread the word of God, and now, suddenly, this upstart, who had disembarked here just a short time ago and who did not even speak any indigenous languages, had gone, in a single leap, to the top of the tree that had been carefully planted by the church."

33. See de la Grange and Rico 1998, 272–23, and Tello Díaz 1995/2001, 139–41.

34. Nor were desertions limited purely to the lower ranks of the EZLN; it lost at least two captains, Cristina and Ramón.

35. See de la Grange and Rico 1999, 80.

36. Ibid.

37. See Tello Díaz 1995/2001, 141.

38. See de la Grange and Rico 1999, 80.

39. Ibid.

40. De la Grange and Rico 1998, 266.

41. *Tiempo*, 19 January 1994, 3, translated and published in Collier and Quaratiello 1994/1999, 66.

42. See, for example, his interview with the documentary film director Nettie Wild in *A Place Called Chiapas* (1998): "I'm not justifying what they [the EZLN] did, just explaining. Many other indigenous people didn't take up arms. There are other ways to fight for justice. But we realize that this war wasn't about spilling blood and taking power; it was about being heard. When they were heard, their guns were silenced and now they're on the path to dialogue." See also the curate Gonzalo Ituarte's comments to Régis Debray: "We are not in agreement with the armed struggle, but we under-

stand its motives. The Zapatistas struggle for the same thing we do. If you argue from a theological standpoint it is a just war. The social situation is already intolerable" (*Le Monde*, 14 May 1996—also printed in Spanish in *Proceso*, no. 1019, 13 May 1996).

43. Krauze 2002, 314.

44. Indeed, in a communiqué issued as early as 20 January the Zapatistas stated: "We will only consider as valid those communications which we receive through bishop Samuel Ruiz." This was reiterated in another communiqué issued on the same day. Both communiqués are translated in Autonomedia 1994, 109, 112.

45. Le Bot 1997, 160.

46. Bishop Samuel Ruiz, "In This Hour of Grace," in the Catholic News Service's weekly publication, *Origins*, 10 February 1994, 587–602; reprinted in Womack 1999, 241.

47. The testimony is that of María Patricia, an activist for women's rights in Chiapas; quoted in Kampwirth 2002, 100.

48. Minnesota Advocates for Human Rights 1993, ix.

49. Hernández Navarro 1994a, 59.

50. Minnesota Advocates for Human Rights 1993, 48. See also Van Cott 1996: "In addition, upon taking office in December of 1988, the PRI governor signed a decree altering the penal code to broaden his powers to stifle dissent and criminalizing the common modes of political protest of the campesino and indigenous movement: land invasions, organized demonstrations, and mass protest aimed at government authorities."

51. The testimony is that of María Patricia, an activist for women's rights in Chiapas; quoted in Kampwirth 2002, 100.

52. Harvey 1994, 22.

53. In Le Bot 1997, 155–56.

54. Castañeda 1994a, 233–34.

55. MacEoin 1996/2000, 41.

56. Castañeda 1994a, 257, n. 28.

57. Harvey 1994, 11.

13 BUST AND BOOM

1. Le Bot 1997, 159. Marcos was perhaps absent from this opening ceremony, since we know that the same month saw him attend the FLN's fifteenth anniversary of Neplanta in Chihuahua. (There, on 14 February 1974, in Monterrey, an FLN safe house had been discovered by Mexican security forces and a shootout ensued, resulting in the capture of Gloria Benavides (later Comandanta Elisa) and the death of several cadres.) Germán was also present at this anniversary in Chihuahua and would no doubt have used the

opportunity to impress on Marcos the importance of continued good relations with Bishop Ruiz.

2. Quoted in G. Ramírez 2003, 56.
3. Stephenson 1995, 15.
4. Le Bot 1997, 121.
5. Ibid., where Marcos says of the FMLN that "eran más nuestro referente y concitaban nuestra admiración. Lo que admirábamos mucho era la ofensiva sobre San Salvador, en el 89."
6. Ibid., 154.
7. Ibid. 10 April marks the anniversary of Emiliano Zapata's death in 1919; 17 November marks the anniversary of the EZLN's foundation in Chiapas in 1983; and 16 September marks the anniversary of el Grito de Dolores, which opened the War of Independence in 1810.
8. *Proceso*, no. 903, 14 February 1994, 29. Quoted and translated in Russell 1995, 11.
9. Newdick 1995, 134.
10. Indeed, see Subcomandante Marcos (1992): "In spite of the current trend towards ecological awareness, the plunder of wood continues in Chiapas's forests. Between 1981 and 1989, 2,444,777 cubic meters of precious woods, conifers, and tropical trees were taken from Chiapas. . . . In 1988 wood exports brought a revenue of 23,900,000,000 pesos, 6000% more than in 1980"; the translation is that of Autonomedia 1994, 28.
11. Russell 1995, 7.
12. Montiel 1995b, 131. See also Russell 1995, 14: "Small [coffee] producers suffered an estimated 70 percent drop in income between 1989 and 1993."
13. Hernández Castillo 2001, 191.
14. Cf. Rus and Collier 2003, 44: "The jobs . . . in large-scale coffee production alone had declined from some eighty thousand in 1980 to barely fifteen thousand by 1988, and even fewer after 1989."
15. Subcomandante Marcos 1992. This translation is from Autonomedia 1994, 26. See also Ouweneel 1996, 87: "Some seventy thousand of the 190 thousand coffee growers in the country live in Chiapas, and seventeen thousand alone in the Lacandón Jungle."
16. See Harvey 1994, 12: "By the end of 1989 it was clear that the future agricultural sector would be subordinated to the economic goals of the Salinas administration."
17. The year 1989 saw the removal of a major mechanism that helped to soften such blows: the National Bank of Rural Credit (Banrural) suddenly refused to continue lending to producers who were in default of preexisting loans.
18. Van Cott 1996.
19. Le Bot 1997, 155–56.
20. Van Cott 1996.

21. Castañeda 1994a, 6.
22. Quoted in Castañeda 1994a, 254.
23. See Tello Díaz 1995/2001, 266.
24. Le Bot 1997, 158.

14 FALLOUT

1. Tello Díaz 1995/2001, 270.
2. Oppenheimer 1996/1998, 49.
3. The following month saw Quito hold the First Continental Meeting of Indigenous People, which formulated the Declaration of Quito (July) detailing indigenous rights.
4. Weinberg 2000, 63–64.
5. Montiel 1995a, 33–34.
6. Ibid.
7. Montiel 1995b, 131–32. Harvey (1994, 27) puts the demographic growth rate for Chiapas at 4.4 percent, but notes that for Ocosingo the rate was 5.6 percent and for Las Margaritas 7.4 percent.
8. Huerta 1995, 30. Cf. T. Benjamin (1989/1996, 242), who states that this organization had been created from the union of several other organizations—for example, the Casa del Pueblo—which together formed the Coordinadora Provisional de Chiapas. The latter was renamed the Organización Campesina Emiliano Zapata (OCEZ, Emiliano Zapata Peasant Organization) in July 1982. Benjamin goes on to quote a Jesuit priest with over thirty years of experience in Chiapas as saying: "It appears that the OCEZ and the ANCIEZ are the same but with different names and fronts" (ibid., 253).
9. Russell 1995, 11.
10. Harvey 1994, 32.
11. Human Rights Watch 1990, 1991; Amnesty International 1991; Minnesota Advocates for Human Rights 1992.
12. See del Muro 1994, 16.

15 PEOPLE'S GUERRILLA TO GUERRILLA PEOPLE

1. See Harvey 1998, 197.
2. Interview with reporters from *Proceso*, *El Financiero*, and the *New York Times*, translated in Autonomedia 1994, 196–97, and partially quoted in Ross 1995a, 281.
3. Quoted and translated in Harvey 1998, 197.
4. As Marcos conceded to one interviewer (Landau, 2002, 148), "The whole world was telling us the same thing. The Socialist camp was collapsing, the armed struggle was being completely abandoned, and we were like some nuts clinging to a dream: dreaming, yes, that was the truth."

5. Quoted in Le Bot 1997, 131.

6. Interview between Marcos and Guillermoprieto (1995c, 39).

7. From Marcos's videotaped interview, *Marcos: palabras y historia/Words and History*. Similarly, see Marcos in Le Bot 1997, 132: "Yo pienso que lo que le permitío al EZLN sobrevivir y crecer fue aceptar esa derrota."

8. See his communiqué entitled "A Death Has Been Decided" (July 2003), http://flag.blackened.net/revolt/mexico/ezln/2003/marcos/deathJULY .html, where he states: "That had been the EZLN's fundamental origin: a group of 'illuminati' who came from the city in order to 'liberate' the exploited and who looked, when confronted with the reality of the indigenous communities, more like burnt out light bulbs than 'illuminati.'"

9. Kampwirth 2002, 108–9.

10. "A Death Has Been Decided" (July 2003), http://flag.blackened.net/revolt/ mexico/ezln/2003/marcos/deathJULY.html.

11. From *Marcos: palabras y historia/Words and History*.

12. Lorenzano 1998, 143.

13. Guillermoprieto 1994, 202.

14. Le Bot 1997, 158.

15. Ibid., 122. Here Marcos tells us that the EZLN's formal structure as a regular army divided into platoons, sections, companies, divisions, etc., came from studying "the war of Independence, we learned from the army of Morelos, and of the revolution, above all Villa's Division of the North and Zapata's Liberation Army of the South . . . our scheme was very close to the scheme of the armies of Villa and Zapata."

16. These three regiments were called El Machete (the machete), La Hacha (the ax), and El Martillo (the hammer).

17. Information on military structure of the EZLN comes from de la Grange and Rico 1998, 212.

18. Le Bot 1997, 159.

19. As Harvey (1998, 84) observes, the Unión de Uniones alone represented "12,000 mainly indigenous families from 180 communities in eleven municipalities."

20. Leyva Solano 2003, 182, n. 19.

21. Such is the hypocrisy of the U.S. government that in the 1980s it backed viciously oppressive regimes in El Salvador and Guatemala and fueled a civil war in Nicaragua, only to spend much of the 1990s attempting to shore up its borders against the tide of immigrants who were attempting to escape these appalling conditions.

22. De la Grange and Rico 1998, 208.

23. Weller 2000, 74.

24. Collier and Quaratiello 1994/1999, 166.

25. *New York Times*, 26 August 1991, 18.

26. MacEoin 2000, 47.

27. Oppenheimer 1996/1998, 59.

28. Russell 1995, 9. In early 1993 Garrido was to be rewarded for his services in keeping Chiapas firmly under the PRI's control, using a combination of electoral fraud and the newly revised penal code, by being promoted to minister of the interior. He was subsequently stripped of this position by President Salinas on 10 January 1994 shortly after the Zapatista rebellion.

29. This organization was originally called simply ACIEZ, but the "N" for "Nacional" was added in early 1992; see Harvey 1998, 195.

30. For this incident and Ruiz's reaction to it, see MacEoin 1996/2000, 42.

31. *La Jornada*, 23 September 1991.

32. *The South East in Two Winds* (1992), translated in Autonomedia 1994, 37.

33. The report is quoted in Oppenheimer 1996/1998, 31–32.

34. MacEoin (1996/2000, 49) notes that the police were "applying a clause introduced into the state penal code in 1989 that classified unarmed mass protests 'by the mentally weak, minors, or illiterate people who do not speak Spanish' as a threat to public order punishable with up to four years' imprisonment."

16 INDIGENOUS INDIGNATION

1. The following year (1993) saw the United Nations–appointed Working Group on Indigenous Populations finish drafting a Declaration on the Rights of Indigenous People, which it had been working on since 1982, and also establish a forum to aid indigenous representation within the United Nations.

2. Collier and Quaratiello 1994/1999, 160. Interestingly, Mexico was the second country in the world (after Norway) to ratify Convention 169. The text of Convention 169 is posted at http://www.unhchr.ch/html/menu3/b/62.htm.

3. Mattiace 2003b, 95.

4. Similarly, ibid., 28.

5. Van Cott 1996, 69–70.

6. M. Benjamin 1995, 64–65.

7. This it singularly failed to do. See Harvey 1994, 15: "In 1993 less than 1 percent of foreign investment in Mexico went into agriculture."

8. As anthropologist Antonio García de León (1995, 214) puts it: "Ostensibly, the reform gives ejido-members the right to choose between selling their land or maintaining it as communal property. To say this much does not recognize the context of crisis and economic pressure which makes this so-called 'option' obsolete."

9. Mattiace 2003b, 43. See also a recent communiqué from Marcos entitled

"Chiapas: The Thirteenth Stele, Part two: A Death" (25 July 2003): "The land is not merchandise, but it has cultural, religious and historic connotations"; http://flag.blackened.net/revolt/mexico/ezlnco.html. In one interview Marcos states that for an indigenous person to lose his land does not only mean that "he loses his means of production, but he also loses his history"; http://flag.blackened.net/revolt/mexico/ezln/inter_marcos_aut95.html.

10. García de León 1995, 211.
11. As Stephenson (1995, 3) has observed, "The rebels drew their greatest strength from the Salinas Administration's abandonment of major tenets of the 1910 Revolution which have given every government since 1924 its legitimacy—land reform, control of foreign investment and social welfare measures."
12. See Harvey 1994, 34.
13. García de León 1995, 214–15.
14. *Tiempo*, 20 January 1994, 3. A month later—on 11 February 1994, 3 (a printing error dates this issue to 10 February)—in the same newspaper, he described the reform of article 27 as "an important catalyst," adding, "the reforms negated any legal possibility of obtaining land, and it was land that was at the basis of peasants' self-defense."
15. *La Jornada*, 7 February 1994; quoted and translated in Harvey 1998, 258, n. 13.
16. Lorenzano 1998, 136. He also states: "The great wave of affiliations occurred in 1992–3, following the reforms to Article 27 of the Constitution and the agrarian legislation, and on the eve of the implementation of the North American Free Trade Agreement (NAFTA)."
17. Markoff 1997, 62.
18. De la Grange and Rico 1998, 198–99.
19. Guillén Vicente 1992.
20. For this quotation, and indeed the majority of the information concerning Marcos's brief home visit, see de la Grange and Rico 1998, 77–80.
21. As Mattiace (2003b, 60) observes, quoting and translating from the INI's own rubric, the INI was created in 1948 by President Alemán (1946–52) "as a public, decentralized organism of the federal government in charge of designing and instituting government policy toward the indigenous peoples of Mexico."
22. Translated in Autonomedia 1994, 45–46.
23. Harvey 1998, 195.
24. Durán de Huerta 1994, 70, and Tello Díaz 1995/2001, 184–85, n. 54, 307–8. See also Le Bot 1997, 159, where Marcos claims that "in 1992, in La Sultana a march of 5000 men came together in order to celebrate the 500 years of resistance."

25. De la Grange and Rico 1999, 81.
26. Ibid.
27. Tello Díaz 1995/2001, 261.
28. Interview with Le Bot 1997, 190; translated into English by Stephen 2002, 139.
29. It remained unpublished until 27 January 1994.
30. Le Bot 1997, 90–92; translated into English by Stephen 2002, 139–41.
31. Cited in Tello Díaz 1995/2001, 188.
32. De la Grange and Rico 1998, 205. "De hecho, el proceso no había sido demasiado democrático."
33. Womack 1999, 43.
34. Stephen 2002, 348, n. 8.
35. Subcomandante Marcos 1995a, 211–12.
36. M. Benjamin 1995, 64–65. Similarly, see the interview with Marcos quoted and translated in Harvey 1998, 198.
37. Le Bot 1997, 190–92. Quoted and translated into English by Stephen 2002, 139–41.
38. De la Grange and Rico 1999, 81.
39. Ibid. See also 82: "Guillén has the capacity to convince people of what he wants to."
40. Ibid., 82: "Guillén sí manejaba mucho el figura del Che," and "Del Che habla mucho."
41. Indeed, Legorreta Díaz (1998, 231) notes that according to an ex-insurgent from the Avellanal region Marcos would tell the peasants that their problems "would never be resolved by the bourgeois government of the PRI, but only by a total change in the social system." See, too, 237, where Legorreta Díaz claims that the EZLN leadership would constantly reiterate the argument that "Socialism was still possible . . . [and] that everything else was a means whereby the bad government tricked the people."
42. Petrich 1995, 53.
43. Gilly 2002, 338.
44. Oppenheimer 1996/1998, 27.
45. Orwell 1968/1994, 22.
46. Ibid.
47. See Tello Díaz 1995/2001, 199–201, and de la Grange and Rico 1999, 81.
48. See the comments of three senior FMLN leaders: Shafik Handel: "[In 1980] tens of thousands of persons went defiantly to demonstrations knowing that they would be massacred . . . they were ready to give their lives for the revolution. But we [guerrillas] were only in the conditions to launch a great offensive by January 1981 . . . when . . . the insurrectional situation had declined"; Joaquín Villalobos: "1980 was the moment for popular insurrection, but the FMLN wasn't even formed yet"; and Gerson Martínez: "There

was a great popular surge. If we had been able to rise on that wave, things would have been more successful. But we weren't ready, and we were ready when that wave had already passed." Quoted in McClintock 1998, 54, 334, n. 29, 55.

49. Debray 1967, 120.

50. De la Grange and Rico 1998, 209.

51. Guevara 1994/1996, 212. See also Guevara 1961/1998, 44: "Generally the maximum age of combatants in the completely nomadic stage of the guerrilla struggle ought not to exceed forty years." This advice appears to have had an impact on other Latin American guerrillas, too. Sandinista Tomás Borge (1992, 259) makes reference to it in his memoir: "I have reached the age of 39, Che, and I am inexorably approaching the stage where it is difficult to be a guerrilla."

52. It was the last house on left (no. 63) on the road to Tenejapa, opposite a scrap yard and a big pine tree, and it had a green façade and tiled roof.

53. De la Grange and Rico 1998, 221. Marcos is quoted as saying of Rodrigo, "It is he who blocks everything . . . he does not realize what the people here are impatient for."

54. Ibid.

55. These are posted at http://flag.blackened.net/revolt/mexico/revlaw.html.

56. The Women's Revolutionary Law was later added in March 1993; see chapter 17.

57. De la Grange and Rico (1998, 224) dismiss the Revolutionary Agrarian Law as follows: "The leaders of the Zapatistas ignored the basic economic rule which governed them [and instead] produced a catalogue of good intentions that had nothing to do with reality." They pointedly attack the Zapatista clause on making foreign companies pay wages equal to those in their own country, saying that this would frighten away foreign investors.

58. Ibid., 225.

59. "Human Rights," in Katzenberger 1995, 55.

60. Harvey 1994, 33.

61. This was caught on camera and subsequently published by the Chiapas-based photographer Antonio Turok (1998, 125), who also posted it at http://www.historycoop.org/journals/ahr/105.2/images/benjamin_f1.jpg.

62. Marcos's love of filming movies, as exhibited in his youth, persisted: he videoed several EZLN training exercises, tapes of which were found when the army discovered Daniel's camp in May 1993.

63. De la Grange and Rico 1998, 199.

64. Marcos declares, "I don't drink alcoholic beverages" in a communiqué dated 2 February 1994, translated in Autonomedia 1994, 131. He is not the first Latin American (or even Mexican) revolutionary to have abstained from alcohol. McLynn (2000, 275) notes that Pancho Villa did not drink, and

Zimmermann (2000/2004, 153) observes that Sandinista leader "Carlos Fonseca almost never drank alcohol, and, according to him, neither did Sandino."

65. Weinberg (2000, 158), noting that "alcohol had always been banned in Zapatista territory," talks of "the EZLN's own puritanical instincts." However, Eber (2003, 142) notes that although certain religious groups in Chiapas "favored prohibiting alcohol, their reasons were not narrowly moralistic. Their concern for conserving precious cash, as well as personal respect, was a primary consideration."

66. See, for example, López Vigil (1991, 240), where James Painter contrasts El Salvador's guerrilla days with the present: "[Now] you can even buy a beer, previously banned after one over-spirited compa gave away a military secret."

67. Bonner 1999, 31–34, 100, 124. See also Eber 2000 and 2003.

68. Bonner 1999.

69. In Bonner 1999, 33. Womack (1999, 57) cites Tzeltal grievances concerning the sale of liquor at the Indigenous Council (1974).

70. Eber (2003, 142) notes: "By 1988 and 1989 many hamlets in Chenalhó had agreed on stricter controls for alcohol sales and uses, partly in response to the strength of women's testimonies and analyses."

71. The translation here is my own; Ponce de León (2001, 241ff) gives an alternative one.

17 AN INTERNAL COUP AND THE ROAD TO WAR

1. De la Grange and Rico 1998, 227.

2. Oppenheimer 1996/1998, 49; 2002, 54.

3. Interestingly, a precedent of sorts existed for this body in the establishment fourteen years earlier of the Clandestine Committee Area Commands and Clandestine Committee Local Comands as outlined in article 32 of the Statutes of the FLN (6 August 1980).

4. Interview with Marcos for the video documentary *Marcos: palabras y historia/Words and History*.

5. De la Grange and Rico 1999, 82. Articles 32 and 52 of the Statutes of the FLN (6 August 1980) make it clear that initially at least the forerunners to the CCRI (the Clandestine Committee Area Commands and Clandestine Committee Local Comands) were very much under the direction of the local commander and ultimately the National Directive.

6. Ross 1995a, 287.

7. De la Grange and Rico 1998, 234.

8. Ibid.

9. Interview with Marcos quoted in *El Tiempo*, 6 February 1994, 3.

10. M. Benjamin 1995, 65.

11. De la Grange and Rico 1999, 82.
12. Ibid.
13. De la Grange and Rico 1998, 236.
14. De la Grange and Rico 1999, 81.
15. Quoted in de la Grange and Rico 1998, 236.
16. Ibid.
17. Daniel's own words, quoted in Tello Díaz 1995/2001, 233.
18. De la Grange and Rico 1999, 81.
19. Ibid; see also 83.
20. See Oppenheimer 1996/1998, 240, on this matter. Oppenheimer has sources deep within the Mexican Security Forces who had interviewed and taken statements from Daniel several times after he turned informer and who provided the journalist with transcripts of Daniel's testimonies. It is not certain precisely what these electronic gadgets were, but if they were radio communications they were to prove invaluable during the February 1995 offensive; if they were computer equipment this too proved equally vital during the EZLN's media war from 1994 onward.
21. See de la Grange and Rico 1999, 83: "Personally speaking, my brushes with Marcos multiplied."
22. Ibid. "The lies angered me. I never saw the military as an enemy. I wasn't able to. The image of them that I had was of them rescuing me from the floods in my village."
23. Ibid.
24. Ibid. López y Rivas 2000, drawing on a source linked to the Mexican intelligence services, claims that "*Daniel* separated from the EZLN in October 1993, when he left the jungle on the pretext of making contact with an arms cargo coming from Central America. He never returned."
25. See Oppenheimer 1996/1998, 240, and de la Grange and Rico 1999, 81.
26. Certainly one cannot imagine Peru's Sendero Luminoso, El Salvador's FMLN, or Colombia's FARC tolerating such loose cannon.
27. Harvey 1998, 198.
28. The same phenomenon had also helped the Guatemalan guerrillas. As one of their leaders, Mario Payeras (1983, 70), writes: "And despite the fact that the 'secret' of our existence was known throughout the region, the enemy never found out. Ethnic barriers helped us keep our secret, and no information leaked out."
29. See also a recent communiqué from Marcos entitled "Chiapas: The Thirteenth Stele, Part Two: A Death" (25 July 2003), "As part of my responsibilities, it was up to me at that time to check in with the now hundreds of villages by radio"; http://flag.blackened.net/revolt/mexico/ezlnco.html.
30. EZLN combatants from this village seized San Cristóbal on 1 January 1994.
31. For Marcos's account of this meeting, see his communiqué dated 26 January 1994; translated in Autonomedia, 1994, 117–19.

32. M. Benjamin 1995, 63.

33. The EZLN claims that a further twelve soldiers were killed a few days later when two army patrols clashed, each mistakenly believing the other were guerrillas. The Federal Army has never commented on this claim.

34. California-based Mexican oil consultant George Baker gave a paper at UNAM's School of Engineering (4 September 1991) entitled "Oil Deposits in the South-east of Mexico" in which he identified the "Ocosingo oilfield." Three months previously (1 June) the *Oil and Gas Journal* had identified a major deposit in the Petén Basin, a considerable part of which was located in the basin of the Chiapas mountains.

35. Again, George Baker notes, "Mexico needs natural gas more than it needs oil right now," adding "Ocosingo could be that new field"; quoted in Ross 1996.

36. The previous year (1992) Marcos had written in his *The South East in Two Winds* that "the beast is still not satisfied and has extended its tentacles to the Lacandón jungle: eight petroleum deposits are under exploration"; translated in Autonomedia 1994, 26.

37. Ceceña and Barreda 1998, 48.

38. Marcos no doubt felt vindicated in his assertions that Las Calabazas should have been dismantled when, less than four months later, the army discovered the camp.

39. For the video's background music, Marcos chose one of his favorites, the Catalan singer Joan Manuel Serrat. Part of the video appears in the documentary *Viaje al centro de la selva: memorial Zapatista* (1994).

40. See Zimmermann 2000/2004, 119, who notes that in 1973, following the discovery of a Sandinista safe house and a subsequent shoot-out with the National Guard which resulted in the death of two cadres, "Carlos Fonseca wrote a twenty-three page document spelling out the security transgressions that had led to this disaster."

41. Article 12 (h) and (i) state that "the militant's duties [are] to report with objectivity . . . without hiding flaws, mistakes or omissions . . . making use of revolutionary criticism and self-criticism."

42. De la Grange and Rico 1999, 81.

43. For these details and those that follow, see Tello Díaz 1995/2001, 313.

44. Ibid.

45. Cited in de la Grange and Rico 1998, 253.

46. He wrote in the introduction to his report, entitled "The Errors Committed in the Battle of La Corralchén": "Dear Comrades, the purpose of revolutionary criticism and self-criticism is to recognize and accept those errors committed so as not to repeat them, and this constitutes in part the apprenticeship of our people and their revolutionary forces on the difficult road towards the liberation of our country"; quoted in Tello Díaz 1995/2001, 317, n. 31.

47. Cited in de la Grange and Rico 1998, 252.

48. De la Grange and Rico 1999, 81.

49. Ibid.

50. De la Grange and Rico 1998, 256.

51. Ibid.

52. Quoted in Oppenheimer 1996/1998, 74. See also Major Mario, who is quoted in Rovira (1994, 70) as saying: "In the mountains Subcomandante Marcos was my military and political jefe. He taught me the use of arms and the way of the mountains, how to hunt, how to survive, how to be a guerrilla."

53. De la Grange and Rico 1998, 244.

54. Quoted and translated in Oppenheimer 1996/1998, 33.

55. Ibid., 33–34.

56. The report, quoted in *Proceso*, no. 903, 14 February 1994, 15, stated that state security forces numbering 1,000 and aided by local landowners attacked the communities of Chalán del Carmen, Río Florido, Nuevo Sacrificio, Edén del Carmen, and El Carrizal.

57. In Autonomedia 1994, 196. Similarly, Marcos's interview with Oppenheimer 1996/1998, 34–35: "The army . . . started to deploy their troops, to position themselves to finish with the guerrillas. But, suddenly, after a few days, they withdrew. That wasn't a military decision—it was a political decision. . . . On the eve of the NAFTA vote, that withdrawal could not have been a mistake by the Federal Army. I'm convinced that it was a political decision coming from the very top. It couldn't have come but from the president of the republic."

58. De la Grange and Rico, 1998, 250.

59. Marcos attests to this, saying, "This is what Sedesol did, after May 1993; a lot of money came here in an effort to keep up appearances"; http://www.ezln.org/entrevistas/19941209.en.htm.

60. De la Grange and Rico 1998, 287–88.

61. Ibid., 287.

62. See Oppenheimer 1996/1998, 36: "The Salinas government had covered up widespread evidence of the guerrilla insurrection. In a system without checks and balances, where the government had always been able to buy off the most influential media and write history at its will, Salinas thought he could get away with describing any potential incidents of violence in Chiapas as isolated clashes stemming from age-old land disputes."

63. *Proceso*, no. 866, 7 June 1993, 18–21; *Proceso* 1993, 12, 13, and 15, respectively.

64. *La Jornada*, 2 August 1993, 1, 10.

65. *Proceso* 1993, 12–15; the news magazine's front cover read "Los grupos armadas en Chiapas."

66. Oppenheimer 1996/1998, 35, fn.

67. Interview with reporters from *Proceso, El Financiero,* and the *New York Times,* translated and reprinted in Autonomedia 1994, 198.

68. Published in Tostón 1995, 1–2.

69. On this process of selecting pseudonyms, see Le Bot 1997, 142.

70. Coote 1995, 15.

71. See Fuentes 1994/1997, 132: "Despite the ensuing publicity abroad, NAFTA was never publicly debated in Mexico." So too, Forbes (1995, 183–88) notes how the agreement was not constitutionally ratified in the United States, and that the Free Trade Commission and the various committees and regional commissions under it would be headed by people and boards that were not in any way democratically elected.

72. As Chomsky (1995: 177–78) observed, "A study by Mexico's leading business journal, *El Financiero,* predicted that Mexico would lose almost a quarter of its manufacturing industry and 14 percent of its jobs in the first two years after the enactment of NAFTA." A 1997 report from the Economic Policy Institute (1997) entitled "The Failed Experiment: NAFTA at Three Years," claimed the agreement had cost 2 million Mexican jobs, ruined 28,000 small businesses, and pushed 8 million Mexicans into poverty.

73. In a July interview with Bardach (1994, 132) Marcos denounced NAFTA as "a death sentence," arguing that "it leads to competition based on your level of skill, and what skill level can illiterate people have? . . . How can we compete with farms in California and Canada?" Hernández Castillo (2001, 189) observes that "for Mexican staple cereal producers, the end of guaranteed prices meant competing against highly technologized and subsidized American agriculture, whose low-cost products easily displaced local production." Harvey (1994, 13) emphasizes competing productivity levels, noting how the average per hectare yield for maize is 6.9 tons in the United States, but 1.7 tons in Mexico at large, and only 0.5 tons in the Los Altos of Chiapas.

74. Rosenthal 1993; sections 10–22 deal with Chiapas.

75. Quoted and translated in Russell 1995, 12.

76. See Womack 1999, 157–58; the region's indigenous had complained as early as the Indigenous Council (1974) of the lack of a hospital in the area. It had taken nearly two decades and the threat of guerrilla activity for the government to address this grievance.

77. Salinas's high-profile aid program was created in 1988 in an attempt to centralize the doling-out of public monies and works, thereby minimizing the siphoning off of funds by corrupt officials at the local level. However, although Salinas could boast a Pronasol budget of $1.7 billion in 1991, in reality social spending by 1993 had plunged to just 37 percent of what it had been in 1981; see Tangeman 1995, 77.

78. This was conceded by Colosio, who had been sent to Chiapas in August 1993

to distribute Solidarity funds: "Looking back and considering the levels of suffering and the demands of the people we found there, it's obvious that we arrived too late"; quoted in Oppenheimer 1996/1998, 36.

79. See Hughes 1994a, 15. See also Oppenheimer 2002, 58: "It was an $11 million state-of-the-art theatre and opera house . . . with 1,000 seats and a sunken pit for a 100-member symphony orchestra . . . to serve a city and several surrounding Indian towns that together had fewer than 100,000 residents, most of whom couldn't even afford the pair of shoes required to enter it. As if to drive home the contrast between rich and poor in Chiapas, the new theatre was going up right next to a crumbling government building where hundreds of homeless Indians from the nearby town of San Juan Chamula had taken refuge."

80. Benjamin 1989/1996, 235.

81. Ibid., 251: "The governor of Chiapas prior to 1994 controlled Solidarity disbursements and rewarded local political allies while bypassing politically independent communities and organizations."

82. Quoted in McCaughan 1995, 37.

83. Womack 1999, 212.

84. Hernández Castillo 2001, 196.

85. Cano 1994, 3f. Translated in Womack 1999, 217.

86. M. Benjamin (1995, 67).

87. Ibid. See also the interview with Marcos published in Bardach 1994, 128: "Marcos said that they had originally scheduled the assault for October 12, but that several days before that 'the army discovered our arms cache up in the mountains over there. Our forces were in position to attack the cities, but we had to pull them back.'"

88. De la Grange and Rico 1999, 83.

89. De la Grange and Rico (1998, 287) believe that the deal was that the Mexican government would allow the Church to play a more active role in Mexican society and would respect its clergy and refrain from meddling in ecclesiastical affairs, in return for the clergy practicing self-censorship and keeping silent concerning its criticisms of the new neoliberal policies that it was critiquing elsewhere, and which the Mexican government had so recently and completely embraced.

90. Chomsky 1995, 178–79.

91. Womack 1999, 42.

92. For more information on these campaigns, see http://www.amnesty.org/results/is/eng?queryType=0&searchIn=0&query=Fransisco+Gallardo+&start=1&num=10&max=25; http://hrw.org/update/2002/03.html#5; http://www.globalexchange.org/countries/mexico/news/gallardo.html; and http://www.pen.org/freedom/bulletin/gallardo.htm.

93. Posted on the Internet at http://www.humboldt.edu/~mc92/accionzap

atista/documents/nothingForOurselves/LongJourneyFromDespair
ToHope.pdf (translated by Cecilia Rodriguez).

94. M. Benjamin 1995, 67.
95. Autonomedia 1994, 155.
96. De la Grange and Rico 1999, 88.
97. Oppenheimer (1996/1998, 14) notes how president Salinas could not get confirmation of exactly what was happening in Chiapas during the early hours of 1 January "because top military officers in Chiapas were out celebrating the New Year." He also notes that "the army commander in Chiapas had gone with his family to visit the ruins of Palenque and had not been located."
98. See the interview with Marcos in Autonomedia (1994, 155): "If you check the press, three days before the whole country knew that a guerrilla group was in San Miguel (near Ocosingo), and everybody pretended not to know."
99. Oppenheimer 1996/1998, 17.
100. Marcos (in Vodovnik 2004, 634) writes: "Starting at dawn on the 29th, none of the vehicles entering [the town of San Miguel, Ocosingo municipality] left: all of them were 'borrowed' in order to mobilize the troops of the Third Regiment."
101. Ibid.
102. See Russell 1995, 26.
103. For what follows, see Vodovnik 2004, 634–35, and Le Bot 1997, 186–90.
104. In Vodovnik 2004, 634.
105. Ibid., 635.
106. In the surprise assault by the FMLN on San Salvador (November 1989), the guerrillas managed to infiltrate the capital with 1,500 troops entering the city via the sewage system and with 2,000 more making their way through the poor neighborhoods on the city's outskirts. Marcos was undoubtedly well acquainted with this offensive.
107. Lawrence 1999, 99–100. See also Oppenheimer 1996/1998, 19: "Hundreds of other Zapatista troops sneaked their way into town through the underground drainage system, whose tunnels—mostly dry at that time of year—led to various city suburbs."
108. In Vodovnik 2004, 634–35.
109. Tello Díaz 1995/2001, 232.
110. For Zapatista Radio announcements, see Bartolomé 1995, 18.
111. As Marcos (in Guillermoprieto 1994, 201) put it: "We will take Mexico City, although not necessarily in physical terms. Weren't we already there on January 2? We were everywhere, on the lips of everyone—in the subway, on the radio. And our flag was in the Zócalo."
112. Translated in Katzenberger 1995, i, and Clarke and Ross 1994/2000, 42; http://revolutionarydemocracy.org/rdvin2/marcos.htm.

113. This led Castañeda (1994b) to term the Zapatistas "armed reformists" only two days into the revolt. He argues that since the EZLN did not aim at taking state power, but merely employed arms to grab attention, they were not true guerrillas or revolutionaries.

114. Communiqué entitled "A Death Has Been Decided," July 2003; http://flag .blackened.net/revolt/mexico/ezln/2003/marcos/deathJULY.html.

115. Interview published in Bardach 1994, 128.

116. Ibid. See also Comandante Abraham, quoted in G. Ramírez (2003, 76): "We did not think that we were going to live; we thought that most of us would fall and that others would continue the struggle."

117. M. Benjamin 1995, 68.

118. For example, de la Grange and Rico (1998, 267) quote Lázaro Hernández, hardly an impartial witness, as saying that Marcos tricked (*engañaba*) the indigenous peasants under him into going to war by convincing them that an uprising was going to begin at the national and international level. So, too, Legorreta Díaz (1998, 237), who, being an advisor to ARIC, is also perhaps less than impartial, states that none of the indigenous cadres had sufficient access to information to properly evaluate the message being fed them by the EZLN leaders. She states: "They all believed what the EZLN leaders told them, that they would triumph militarily, that the entire country was preparing as they were, and that they would bring about an insurrection and a revolution at the national level. . . ."

119. As the nonagenarian Emetario Pantaleón, who fought alongside Emiliano Zapata in 1913, comments concerning the Zapatistas of the 1990s: "These muchachos are just boys. They don't think they are ever going to die"; quoted in Ross 1995a, 87.

120. See de la Grange and Rico 1999, 80.

121. Quoted in Autonomedia 1994, 63. See also Ross 1995a: "There are 1,056 settlements in the Cañadas [Zapatista heartland], 177 of them ejidos, a population of 65,000, 60% of whom are younger than twenty" (259), and "The bulk of the Zapatistas fighting force are 16 to 24 years old" (262).

122. Hernández Navarro 1994a, 58.

123. Womack 1999, 213.

124. Ovetz 1994a.

125. *La Jornada*, 7 February 1994; quoted and translated in Autonomedia 1994, 157.

126. For this figure, notably never contested by the government, see Subcomandante Marcos (1992). Marcos reiterates this in an interview posted at http:// revolutionarydemocracy.org/rdv1n2/marcos.htm in which he states: "The indigenous people of Chiapas suffer 15,000 deaths per year, that no one mourns. The great shame is that they die of curable diseases."

127. See Nash 2001, 121: "The Centre for Human Rights, 'Fray Bartolomé de

Las Casas,' recounted 56 incidents of violations of human rights, affecting a total of 1,036 people in the state of Chiapas, in the six months just prior to the uprising."

128. Kampwirth 2002, 41.

129. See also ibid., 12: "The poorest of the poor are the least likely rebels."

18 THE UPRISING

1. Red and black were originally the colors of the anarchists, but they were adopted by the Mexican labor movement in the 1910s and have been employed by it ever since. Red and black were also the Sandinistas's preferred colors.

2. In his communiqué entitled "Twelve Women in the Twelfth Year," dated 11 March 1996, posted at http://flag.blackened.net/revolt/mexico/ezln/1996/marcos_12_women_march.html.

3. Bañuelos 1995, 196.

4. For the application of the term "propaganda war" to the Chiapas revolt, see Labastida 1994. For the Zapatistas's propaganda war in the United States, see Asman 1994, 67.

5. Oppenheimer 1996/1998, 25.

6. Indeed, it is clear from Marcos himself, and from the actions of the Zapatistas at Ocosingo, that sparing the civilian population from an army onslaught and not using them as human shields was utmost in the guerrillas' preoccupations.

7. The standard procedure for six and one-half decades (and eleven previous presidential contests) in Mexico was that once an outgoing PRI president had named a presidential candidate—Mexicans call this *el dedazo* (the big fingerpoint)—and this candidate had been accepted by the party, that individual became de facto his successor.

8. See Oppenheimer 1996/1998, 144, 184–85.

9. As Oppenheimer 1996/1998, 8 notes: "Foreign investment in Mexico's stock market had risen by a whopping 98 percent in 1993 . . . the country could boast record international reserves of $24.5 billion, up 25 percent from the previous year. Inflation had dropped to 8 percent from a record 160 percent a year when Salinas had taken office . . . Forbes magazine's ranking of the world's wealthiest people had just included thirteen Mexicans—placing Mexico right after the United States, Germany, and Japan as the country with the most billionaires."

10. Oppenheimer 1996/1998, 22.

11. See *La Jornada*, 6 February 1994; retold in de la Grange and Rico 1998, 294, and Ross 1995a, 8.

12. Quoted in Oppenheimer 1996/1998, 22.

13. Published and translated texts of the Zapatista Declaration of War can be

found in Autonomedia (1994, 49ff); Subcomandante Marcos (1995a, 51ff); Womack (1999, 247ff); and Ponce de León (2001, 13ff).

14. Similarly, see the interview with Marcos dated 1 January and published in translation in Clarke and Ross 1994/2000, 42: "We want a transitional government and that this government hold new elections—but with a content that is genuinely egalitarian, offering the same opportunities to all political parties."

15. Translated in Womack 1999, 192–97, original emphasis. Similarly, see the FLN's Reglamento Insurgente (insurgent rules) drafted in 1985, which state: "The EZLN was created in order to conquer, by means of armed struggle, national liberation and our second independence, and not to suspend the struggle until we have installed in our country a political, economic and social regime of the Socialist type"; quoted in Tello Díaz 1995/2001, 264, 325, nn. 13, 15.

16. This point is also made by Womack (1999, 245) and by Tangeman (1995, 89). Tangeman notes the declaration is "devoid of much of the leftist rhetorical baggage usually accompanying Latin American guerrilla movements."

17. Oppenheimer 1996/1998 25, 28, 340. He cites his sources for this as being the "signed testimonies of the Salvador Morales Garibay (Subcommander Daniel), February 8, 1995, and María Gloria Benavides Guevara (Subcommander Elisa), February 9, 1995."

18. Quoted in de la Grange and Rico 1999, 82.

19. Tello Díaz 1995/2001, 267.

20. Ibid., 262–63.

21. Ibid., 262.

22. Communiqué published and translated in Ponce de León 2001, 149.

23. The other Pedro, who fell in 1994, was Subcommander Pedro, who died in Las Margaritas on 1 January.

24. Posted at http://flag.blackened.net/revolt/mexico/ezln/2001/ccri/yanez_feb.html.

25. Communiqué entitled "The Constitutional Reform in No Way Answers the Demands of the Indian Peoples of Mexico"; http://flag.blackened.net/revolt/mexico/ezln/2001/ccri/no_to_reform_apr29.html.

26. Entitled "We Are in Silence—And the Silence Is Not Being Broken"; http://flag.blackened.net/revolt/mexico/ezln/2002/marcos/silenceSEPT.html.

27. From Le Bot 1997, 164–67; translated into English in Womack 1999, 245.

28. For example, de la Grange and Rico 1998, 298: "The claims of the indigenous came as a second aim. In days following [the uprising], under the influence of a cover journalist who put the emphasis on the indigenous nature of the uprising, Marcos inverted the order of priorities in his discourse." So too Oppenheimer 1996/1998, 45: "The Zapatistas grew up as a traditional Marxist guerrilla group, which changed its rhetoric after the 1 January rebellion, when its media-savvy leader discovered the advantages of playing

up the Indian participation in his uprising—the one aspect of his revolt that had captured the world's imagination."

29. G. Ramírez 2003, 279.

30. Quoted and translated in Autonomedia 1994, 71. He also made specific reference to the Zapatistas as an indigenous movement in his interviews given on 1 January.

31. Estatutos de las Fuerzas de Liberación Nacional (6 August 1980). Article 5 (b), page 8, states that one of the FLN's goals is "to integrate the struggles of the urban proletariat with the struggles of the peasants and indigenous in the most exploited zones of our country." Article 7 (n), page 11, states that the FLN will fight until "the State guarantees to indigenous groups the right to recover their lands; to conceal and to conserve their cultures, dialects and customs, respecting their forms of social organization."

32. G. Ramírez 2003, 280.

33. Oppenheimer 1996/1998, 21.

34. Elsewhere, in Ponce de León (2001, 9), Marcos tells us that it was Elena, a "Lieutenant in the hospital unit" who "communicate[d]" to him that English-speaking people were asking questions which neither she nor the other indigenous troops present could comprehend.

35. Oppenheimer 1996/1998, 23.

36. Ibid., 22.

37. Ross 1995a, 17.

38. Ibid., 18. Marcos would later explain, "One of our main priorities will be to make sure that none of us becomes too much of a protagonist . . . we want to remain anonymous so that we won't become corrupt. . . . This man's name is Marcos here today, but tomorrow his name will be Pedro in the town of Las Margaritas, Josué in the town of Ocosingo, Alfredo in the town of Altamirano, or any other name"; quoted and translated in Oppenheimer 1996/1998, 21.

39. Originally quoted in *Proceso*, no. 897, 10 January 1994; see also Tello Díaz 1995/2001, 266. Similarly, when Oliver Stone met Marcos he exclaimed "what a showman!"; quoted in de la Colina 2002, 366.

40. Lawrence 1999, 102.

41. De la Grange and Rico 1998, 295–96.

42. As Oppenheimer notes (1996/1998, 23): "But reporters were already looking around for the more articulate, white-skinned Marcos."

43. Ibid., 23, fn. repeats military intelligence claims that Felipe "died a few months later, killed by a fellow Zapatista rebel in a fight in the jungle after a night of heavy drinking." This was denied by Marcos in Oppenheimer's subsequent interview with him. De la Grange and Rico (1998, 299) claim that Felipe "fell, shot-down, twenty four hours later during a skirmish near the Rancho Nuevo quarters."

44. Ross 1995a, 18–19.

45. Posted at http://nativenet.uthscsa.edu/archive/nl/9401/0307.html.

46. Ibid. See Kampwirth (2003, 236), who notes that because NAFTA came into effect on that date, "choosing 1 January as the birthday of the rebellion was more important for attracting international media coverage (which it did well)."

47. Ovetz 1994b. Ross (1995a, 22), describing the same scene, states that the audience merely comprised a "hundred or so hardy souls" and that Marcos told those present that they could leave after 7:30 A.M. the next morning, and then only westward to Tuxtla.

48. Ross 1995a, 22.

49. Ovetz 1994b.

50. Russell 1995, 56.

51. Interview on Radio UNAM, 18 March 1994.

52. For example, to name but a few, *Vanity Fair, Esquire, Cambio 16,* NACLA, *Le Figaro,* the *New York Times, Der Spiegel,* and the *San Francisco Chronicle* sent reporters into the jungle to interview Marcos in the days, weeks and months that followed.

53. Within a matter of weeks Octavio Paz (2002, 33) would write: "Thanks to his rhetoric and undeniable theatrical talent, Subcommander Marcos has won the opinion battle."

54. Quoted in de la Grange and Rico 1998, 301.

55. Quoted and translated in Autonomedia 1994, 157. Note that this contrasts strongly with another interview Marcos gave (Le Bot (1997, 187–88); my translation) in which he declared the aim of the attack to have been "not of taking the base, but of tying it down, obliging the soldiers to defend their base and not leave it."

56. Le Bot 1997, 157–58.

57. De la Grange and Rico, 1998, 302.

58. Tello Díaz 1995/2001, 248.

59. Le Bot 1997, 187–88; my translation.

60. For this information, see de la Grange and Rico 1998, 197.

61. Ibid., 190.

62. For Pedro's character, see the testimonies of his comrades Comandante Abraham, Subcomandante Marcos, Major Moisés, Captains Federico, Noé, Lucio, and Cornelio, Leiutenant Gabriela, and *compañeros* Gerardo and Raúl in G. Ramírez (2003, 35–54).

63. In Vodovnik 2004, 639.

64. De la Grange and Rico 1998, 300.

65. For the use of tear gas by the police, see Bartolomé 1995, 7, 22.

66. Recounted in de la Grange and Rico 1998, 303ff.

67. Bartolomé 1995, 22.

68. Ibid.

69. Ibid., 24, and de la Grange and Rico 1998, 304.

70. See Bañuelos 1995, 13–14, 24, for another such incident, also at Ocosingo, which involved seizing civilians—major landowner Don Enrique Solórzano and some of his male family members were taken hostage. Although elderly, he was subjected to a no-doubt terrifying mock trial and sham execution by Major Mario, before being released unharmed physically. See Weinberg 2000, 116, who observes that "in February, the governmental National Human Rights Commission (CNDH) announced it had received 218 complaints about the Federal Army, and twenty against the EZLN."

71. De la Grange and Rico 1998, 304.

72. Declaration of War, point three, in Autonomedia 1994.

73. Bañuelos 1995, 17. The judicial police (judiciales) had made themselves widely detested in Mexico. Paco Ignacio Taibo II (2002, 22–23) claims to have "overheard on the second day of January in the Mexico City metro: 'the judiciales aren't decent people; they aren't people.'"

74. Bartolomé 1995:27–28. He continues: "Images from San Cristóbal on the news . . . everything looks different there . . . no violence, no hostages, no attacks on civilians, no dead."

75. A recent communiqué entitled "In Memory of Those Who Fell" (14 February 2004) issued by the Clandestine Revolutionary Indigenous Committee—General Command lists the names and ranks of all those EZLN combatants who fell during the uprising. It is posted at http://www.ezln.org/documentos/2004/20040214.en.html.

76. Tello Díaz 1995/2001, 261.

77. Quoted and translated in Autonomedia 1994, 158.

78. Le Bot 1997, 188–89; my translation.

79. Ibid., 189–90; my translation.

80. Bartolomé 1995, 23.

81. Ronfeldt et al. (1998, 46–50) describe this turning away as a "shift from guerrilla warfare to social netwar."

19 "WAGING A MASTERFUL MEDIA WAR"

1. The title of this chapter derives from a quotation by Paco Ignacio Taibo II (2002, 29) describing Zapatista strategy.

2. Bartolomé 1995, 15, 20, 27–28.

3. In Spanish, "un usurpador y un vendepatrias," El Pais, 5 January 1994, 4.

4. See Romero 1994, 27.

5. Human Rights Watch 1997, 75–76.

6. Ibid., 75.

7. Strong 1992, 161–62, 165–66.

8. Rajchenberg and Héau-Lambert 1998, 23–24.

9. Interestingly, Salinas's presidential successor, Ernesto Zedillo, who was to

have just as much, if not more, trouble with the Zapatistas during his term of office, had also named his son Emiliano, after Zapata.

10. In 1979, the Mexican people organized mass demonstrations against the government's plans to move Zapata's remains from Cuautla (Morelos) to the Monument of Revolution in Mexico City, where, somewhat ironically, they would lie next to the corpse of his murderer, Venustiano Carranza. Harvey (1998, 132) describes this incident as a "struggle to retain popular control over the symbolic importance of Zapata."

11. *First Declaration of the Lacandón Jungle* (also known as The Declaration of War).

12. Interview with Dr. Robert Ovetz (1994a) in San Cristóbal.

13. Oppenheimer 1996/1998, 29.

14. Monsiváis 1996, 9–11.

15. Rajchenberg and Héau-Lambert 1998, 24; likewise noted by Castañeda 1995, 44.

16. In Autonomedia 1994, 144: "We had not planned to attack on the first of January . . . we tried many dates. . . . National politics were not central to the question of timing. . . . [We] began to take into account the logistical challenges of the uprising . . . for example, the uprising had to take place after the harvest when we could gather money."

17. See, for example, *Washington Post* (3, 4, 5 January); *New York Times* (3, 4, 5, 6 January); *Independent* (3 January); *Le Monde* (4 January); *Neue Zürcher Zeitung* (4 January); *Süddeutsche Zeitung* (4 January); *La Repubblica* (4 January); and *El Pais* (3–8 January).

18. See, for example, *La Jornada*, 19 January 1994, 6.

19. Let us not forget the Mexican government's track record in this area. In 1968, Mexico City witnessed soldiers and police shooting dead 325 student demonstrators. See also, specifically on Chiapas, the reports of Amnesty International (1986); Human Rights Watch (1991); Minnesota Advocates for Human Rights (1992).

20. Interestingly, the concept of civil society originated with the Italian communist Antonio Gramsci more than six decades earlier. As Womack (1999, 279) observes, the concept "had entered debates on the Mexican left in the 1970s" and so would have formed part of many of the lectures and discussions Marcos would have been exposed to during his years at UNAM and UAM. We know, after all, that Marcos had been influenced in those days by Gramsci's work on state apparatuses.

21. The statement is dated 4 March 1994; quoted by the Academia Mexicana de Derechos Humanos (1994).

22. Translation that of Autonomedia 1994, 77–78.

23. Ibid., 78–79.

24. Quoted and translated in Russell 1995, 26.

25. In addition to the two ministry of the interior reports cited above, on 5 January, President Salinas had already declared that "this is not an Indian uprising, but the action of a violent, armed group"; translated in Russell 1995, 26.

26. Translation that of Autonomedia 1994, 80.

27. The accusations concerning gross human rights abuses were supported by the National Human Rights Commission's unearthing of a mass grave at Ocosingo on 16 January; by an Americas Watch report from 1 February; and by the testimony of a Mexican army captain sent to Chiapas who claims he was told to kill "anyone who looked like a Zapatista"—the latter was subsequently granted political asylum in the United States after he fled there fearing retribution from his former military comrades.

28. In September 1960, Fidel Castro, in an act of solidarity with African-Americans, purposely elected to stay in the Hotel Theresa, in Harlem, as opposed to the Shelburne Hotel, in mid-town Manhattan, during his address to the United Nations in New York.

29. Indeed, so too the FLN's Statutes (article 29 [i], pages 20–21), printed on 6 August 1980, talk of "acting militarily against North American interests or their representatives, when imperialism attacks militarily against the Socialist countries or the people that fight for their liberation."

30. The translation here is that of Autonomedia 1994, 90.

31. Marcos brought attention to the United States's involvement in the repression of Zapatistas in point twenty-four of the CCRI-EZLN's list of demands issued on 1 March: "We also ask that the government of the United States of America withdraw its helicopters, because they are used to repress the people of Mexico."

32. "Drug Control: Counter-narcotics efforts in Mexico," GAO report (June 1996), 15, n. 5, posted on the Internet at http://www.gao.gov/archive/1996/ns96163.pdf.

33. See Monsiváis 2002, 127: "The news media are the front-line para-Zapatista army."

34. See, for example, La Jornada, front pages on Monday, 3 January, and Wednesday, 5 January; and, internationally, glossy but gory photographs in Newsweek 1994a, 31, and Time 1994a, 21. See also Paco Ignacio Taibo II (2002, 26): "I'm disturbed by the repeated sight of the bodies of campesinos, riddled with bullets, lying in ditches along the road. I see terrible images of a baby girl killed by a grenade fragment, her body lying in a cardboard box."

35. Ross 1995a, 97.

36. Final figures concerning the casualty rate vary. The National Commission for Human Rights (CNDH) gave the total as 159 dead; these included 16 Federal Army troops, 38 police, 67 civilians, and 38 unidentified persons. The International Committee of Jurists put the figure at much higher, stating

that there had been between two and three hundred fatalities. See Russell 1995, 23, for these and other figures and their sources.

37. *Reforma*, 5 January 1994, 5A. Quoted and translated in Russell 1995, 22.
38. Interview with reporters from *Proceso, El Financiero*, and the *New York Times*, translated and reprinted in Autonomedia 1994, 210.
39. De la Grange and Rico 1998, 382.
40. Gómez Peña 1995, 90.

20 A CEASE-FIRE

1. The public were also bombarded by academic publications and newspapers printing a host of statistics indicating the extent of the state's plight. For example, Vásquez Aguirre (1994, 27) ranked Chiapas as the worst state in Mexico for illiterates older than fifteen; population older than fifteen who have yet to complete primary school; population lacking electricity; population living in overcrowded domiciles; population making less than twice the minimum wage.
2. Kampwirth 1998, 16.
3. *La Jornada*, 13 January 1994.
4. For this, and the advice Salinas received from former Nicaraguan and El Salvadoran guerrillas urging him to declare a cease-fire, see Oppenheimer 1996/1998, 43.
5. For example, the aged, long-serving labor leader and ardent PRI supporter Fidel Velázquez who claimed the Zapatistas had "no justifiable complaints against the government," that they were led by fanatical foreign revolutionaries from Nicaragua, El Salvador, Peru, and Guatemala, and that therefore they should be "exterminated"; quoted and translated in Russell 1995, 26–27.
6. McLynn 2000, 76.
7. Namely that "on 16 January, 1994 at 11:30 A.M., approximately 35 military soldier-transport vehicles carrying 400 soldiers assaulted the municipal seat of Oxchuc."
8. As Russell (1995, 56) puts it, "Marcos very effectively kept media attention focused on Chiapas with his widely quoted sound bites."
9. Collier and Collier 2003, 246: "The Zapatistas played to the media from the beginning. Their willingness and ability to take their cause to the newspapers, television and Internet has often been portrayed as the most innovative aspect of their rebellion."
10. This translation is from Ponce de León 2001, 38–39.
11. *La Jornada*, 23 January 1994, 8; quoted and translated in Russell 1995, 30–31.
12. Marcos 1995a, 84–85.

13. The communiqué also rejects the notion that the Zapatistas are "the only true, honest, and revolutionary organization in Mexico or Chiapas" and instead emphasizes that "there are other honest, progressive, independent organizations of great value"; quoted and translated in Autonomedia 1994, III.

14. Interview with Le Bot 1997, 241; translated in Weinberg 2000, 189.

15. Ronfeld et al., 1998, 45.

21 THE CULT OF MARCOS

1. The Zócalo witnessed another mass mobilization only three days after the March for Peace on Saturday, 15 January.

2. Ross 1995b, 86–87.

3. Members of the foreign press, such as Tim Golden of the *New York Times*, brought press clippings from their own countries to show Marcos for him to react to. See interview with reporters from *Proceso, El Financiero*, and the *New York Times*, translated and reprinted in Autonomedia 1994, 210.

4. Translated and reprinted in ibid., 114–16. At 114, Marcos writes: "Well, finally, I have had the opportunity of a few hours in which to read some of the publications that someone was kind enough to send me."

5. Ronfeldt et al. (1998, 2) call him a "star-quality spokesman."

6. Urbina Nandayapa 1994, 143. Similarly, Ross 2000, 53: "By the end of February *Marcos Mania* was sweeping the land—the *subcomandante* stared out from every magazine cover and daily paper in Mexico"; and Weinberg 2000, 119: "A kind of Marcosmania prevailed."

7. McCaughan 2002, 73–74.

8. Transcript published in EZLN 1995, 69–70, and partially quoted and translated in Holloway 1998, 163. See also Durán de Huerta 1994, 28–29.

9. On the significance of masks in Mexican culture see Stavans 2002, 388. He writes: "Since pre-Columbian times Mexico has been enamored of the mask. . . . The mask is omnipresent in Mexico: in theatres, on the Day of the Dead, in *lucha libre*, the popular Latin American equivalent of wrestling. And among pop heroes like El Zorro, El Santo the wrestler, and Super Barrio, all defenders of *los miserables*, masked champions whose silent faces embody the face of millions." Similarly, de la Colina (2002, 364) notes that "a mask . . . [is] characteristic of the heroes in movies or comic strips (Zorro, Fantomas, Cruz Diablo, Batman, El Santo, El Mil Mascaras)."

10. Padgett 1996, 14. Berger (2001, 149) also identifies the phenomenon of "romantic guerrilla Marxism."

11. See Collier and Quaratiello 1994/1999, 4: "Guessing the identity of *Sub-Comandante Marcos* . . . suddenly became a popular obsession." De la Grange and Rico (1998, 336–37, esp. 459, n. 4) provide a long list, of the various people Marcos was alleged to be.

12. Russell 1995, 56.
13. Gómez Peña 1995, 92–93. She also notes the mass-merchandizing in the form of "an industry of Zapatista and Marcos-inspired souvenirs [that] flourished overnight" as a result of Marcos's popularity (92). They include T-shirts, post cards, posters, socks, dolls, key chains, and even condoms.
14. Translated and reprinted in Autonomedia 1994, 196–210; see in particular, 197 and 199.
15. Bardach 1994, 65, 66, 67.
16. Guillermoprieto 1994, 185–206.
17. Quoted in Ross, 1995a, 300.
18. Weinberg 2000, 126.
19. Ibid., 127.
20. This ploy clearly worked on Régis Debray (2002, 348), who wrote: "belonging to that odious species of temperate sleepers who can be content with four hours a night, Marcos, with the assistance of an electric lantern, conscientiously devours books and other printed matter, as in the good old days."
21. De la Grange and Rico 1998, 399–402.
22. Oppenheimer 1996/1998, 68.
23. Weinberg 2000, 118–27.
24. Womack 1999, 44.
25. See Castells 1997, 79; Cleaver 1998, 621–40; Group 2828 1997; Halleck 1994, 30–32; Ronfeldt et al. 1998; Stephenson 1995; Vincent 1996, 1; and Wray 1997.
26. T. Benjamin 1989/1996, 259.
27. Ross 1995a, 288.
28. Iliff and Corchado 2004.
29. See Ronfeldt et al. 1998, 88: "The fact that Marcos and the EZLN claim that they do not seek to seize state power, as would a traditional armed movement, takes the edge off their ambitions, making them seem less threatening."
30. See, for instance, an interview with Marcos as documented in Rosset 1994: "We do not want state power. It is civil society that must transform Mexico—we are only a small part of that civil society, the armed part—our role is to be guarantors of the political space that civil society needs."
31. Quoted in Monsiváis 1997, 138.
32. Abraham Guillen Press/Arm the Spirit (2002, 37) talks of Marcos's "transformation from FLN political and military leader to EZLN media darling."
33. Communiqué dated to 11 February 1994, translated in Autonomedia 1994, 176–82.
34. *Time* 1994a, 1994b, 1994c, 1994d.
35. *Newsweek* 1994a, 1994b, 1994c, 1994d, 1994e.
36. Katz and Eaton 1994.

37. Bardach 1994.

38. *Esquire* 1994, 72–78.

39. Quoted in Oppenheimer 1996/1998, 44, and Lawrence 1999, 114.

40. Quotation taken from Stan Gotlieb's article entitled "The New Kids on the Block," on his "Letters from Mexico" Web site at http://www.dreamagic.com/stan/index.html.

41. Sánchez Lira and Villareal 1995, 224–25.

42. De la Grange and Rico 1998, 382.

43. Zaid 1994, 22–34.

44. Concerning the latter, see López Vigil 1991, 107: "It was pointless to win great battles if the media didn't cover it. The point was to cause a scandal in the papers, to make the propaganda impact as great as the military one." Later in the text an example of the FMLN's interaction with the press in spring 1988 is related whereby the guerrillas "sat down to shoot the breeze with the journalists—one from NBC, one from the BBC, one from the *Washington Post*. . . . *Atilio* [Joaquín Villalobos] had already given interviews in '85 to the *New York Times, Le Monde* and other foreign media" (189).

45. De la Grange and Rico 1998, 381–82.

46. See, for example, Katz and Eaton 1994, which bears the subheading "Master Marketer," and J. Watson 2001. Stavans (2002, 389) writes: "He was a master at marketing."

47. Guillermoprieto 1994, 201.

48. Communiqué published and translated in Ponce de León 2001, 228. This verdict is not the sole preserve of Marcos; it is also shared by MacEoin (1996/2000, 101), who notes that this was ". . . the first time in history that a small, obscure group of rebels had in a few weeks been given de facto recognition as a social force by a sovereign government"; and by the 1988 presidential candidate Herberto Castillo, who argued in *Proceso*, no. 899 (24 January 1994, 47) that the EZLN had achieved more things more rapidly than any other group in Mexico since the revolution.

49. See Oppenheimer (1996/1998).

50. See Coote 1995 and Suchlicki 1996/2000. The Zapatistas were featured for three successive weeks in the *Economist* (January-February 1994).

51. See Human Rights Watch 1997; Centro de Derechos Humanos "Fray Bartolomé de las Casas" 1996.

52. Stephenson 1995; Gray 1997; and Ronfeldt et al. 1998.

53. Castells 1997.

54. T. Benjamin 1989/1996, 259.

55. As one interviewer comments, "Marcos seems happy to speak with strangers from the city, because even though Marcos now has plenty of people to write him letters, he is trapped, and far from what we call civilization"; interview dated 21 February with reporters from *Proceso, La Jornada*, and the *New York Times* (translated and reprinted in Autonomedia 1994, 202).

Marcos himself admitted to M. Benjamin (1995, 69) that his compulsion for writing arose from his having "so much built up inside me from these ten years that I've lived in this part of the country."

56. In the same interview (Autonomedia, 1994, 206) the interviewer again comments: "Marcos doesn't seem tired from talking so much and thinking about what he's saying . . . he gives the impression that he could keep talking throughout the day that is beginning, through nightfall." Similarly, Guillermoprieto (1994, 204–5): "We had been talking for hours, and Marcos showed no sign of retiring for the night . . . Marcos was not to be stopped"; and the interview with Bardach (1994, 66): "He paused, smiled, and agreed to talk 'for a few minutes.' More than four hours later, as darkness was falling, I turned off my tape recorder."

57. Guillermoprieto 1994, 201, 205.

58. Oppenheimer 1996/1998, 70.

59. After interviewing Marcos, Oppenheimer (1996/1998, 71) wrote: "Above all, he was desperately hungry for approval from Mexico City intellectuals." Oppenheimer also notes (ibid.) how, "when writer Elena Poniatowska asked him why he was so eager for the intellectuals' support, Marcos said, 'Because they are public opinion leaders.'"

60. Hence we find left-wing intellectuals such as Díaz Soto y Gama, Giraldo Magaña, and Abraham Martínez heading Emiliano Zapata's think tank and acting as his secretary and chief-of-staff, respectively.

61. Berger (2001, 149) observes that "more than any other rural insurgency in Latin America in recent years, their [the Zapatistas's] uprising has captured the imagination of activists and intellectuals around the world."

62. Quoted in Monsiváis 1997, x.

63. See Klein 2002, 120; there exist translations into English and at least thirteen other languages, including Japanese.

64. For example, Subcomandante Marcos 1995a, 1999a, 1999b, 1999c, 1999d, 2001a, 2001b; Clarke and Ross 1994/2000; Autonomedia 1994; Ponce de León 2001.

65. Womack 1999, 279.

66. Petras 1997, 42.

67. T. Benjamin 1989/1996, 259.

68. Quotation taken from Jim Tuck's "Mexico Connect" Web page at http://www.mexconnect.com/mex_/zapat1.html.

69. Montalbán 2000, 209.

70. Kapuściński 1992, 152.

71. Mexico's Nobel Laureate Octavio Paz (2002, 33), a highly conservative statesman who objects strongly to Marcos's politics and methods, nonetheless recognized the Subcommander's "imaginative and lively prose," which had "easily won the war of opinions."

72. These authors include Neruda, Whitman, Eliseo Diego, Fernando Pessoa,

Manuel Scorza, Mario Benedetti, Miguel Hernández, Paul Eluard, Antonio Machado, Pedro Salinas, Cesare Pavese, Ray Bradbury, John Berger, Hector Aguilar Camín, Edmond Rostand, Manuel Vázquez Montalbán, Julio Cortázar, Juan Rulfo, Umberto Eco, Emilio Abreu Gómez, Ernesto Sabato, José Luis Calva, J. Boltvinik, Adolfo Gilly, T. S. Kuhn, Dario Fo, and José Saramango.

73. Gilly et al. 1995.
74. Le Bot 1997.
75. Montalbán 2000.
76. Monsiváis 2001.
77. Báez 1998.
78. See, for example, Arm the Spirit 2002, 37, which calls Marcos "the consummate communicator." Ronfeldt et al. (1998, 23) call him "a superb media spokesman." Oppenheimer (1996/1998, 45) calls him the Zapatistas's "media-savvy leader."
79. See Burbach 2001, 117: "Marcos has certainly been the most notable figure of the movement, but this has been due to his literary and communication skills, which have caused the Mexican and the international media to focus on his personality."
80. Defined by Harvey (1998, 8) as "a type of leader who exercises undisputed control within popular movements."
81. *Proceso*, 21 February, 1994. Interview with reporters from *Proceso*, *El Financiero* and the *New York Times*, translated and reprinted in Autonomedia 1994, 210.
82. See, for example, Lawrence (1999, 102), who notes the media's concentration on Marcos and concludes that thus "the revolution died being born, but *Subcomandante Marcos* had just become larger than life."
83. This is reflected in his editing a school magazine, the type of poetry he included in it, his participation in school debates and oratorical competitions, and his liking for starring in and directing home movies.
84. De la Grange and Rico 1999, 83.
85. Weinberg 2000, 126.
86. Communiqué dated 5 May 1995, published by *La Jornada* (11 May 1995, 6) and translated and posted at http://flag.blackened.net/revolt/mexico/ezln/marcos_absence_exp_may95.html.
87. Guillermoprieto 1995a, 216.

22 PEACE TALKS

1. Kampwirth 1998, 16.
2. Castañeda 1995, 44: "In a country where treason abounds and loyalties are short-lived, the sensitivity to betrayal is always high. It rose to boiling

point a few days after the Chiapas rebellion exploded, as President Salinas de Gortari, either out of insensitivity or with deliberate symbolism, issued his proclamation of amnesty for the Chiapas insurgents in the Carranza Room of the presidential palace. He addressed the nation with a portrait of the white-haired, bearded coauthor of Mexico's constitution behind him. Zapata's self-styled heirs were being forgiven under the watchful gaze of the idol's murderer: a message not particularly comforting or subliminal."

3. Interview with correspondents from *La Jornada*, conducted 4–7 February, published 8 February, republished in Autonomedia 1994, 163.

4. Defense Minister General Antonio Riviello Bazan is the general who imprisoned General José Francisco Gallardo Rodríguez in November 1993 on a range of charges, including embezzlement and dishonoring the military.

5. Translated and posted at http://nativenet.uthscsa.edu/archive/nl/9402/0263 .html.

6. Ross 1995a, 209.

7. There were various reports issued around this time by human rights organizations documenting abuses by the Federal Army. For example, Canadian Catholic Organization for Development and Peace 1994; *Americas Watch Report* 1994; and Amnesty International 1994. The latter identified the Mexican Army as responsible for nine extrajudicial executions, fifteen suspicious killings, and numerous arbitrary detentions.

8. Autonomedia 1994, 126.

9. Ross 1995a, 209.

10. See Ross 1995a, 158, for more details of the general's record, including his alleged participation in the murder of an independent peasant organization's lawyer and a sociologist, which drew attention from Amnesty International and the Mexican Academy of Human Rights, respectively.

11. In the months following the general's release the remaining thirty-three were freed.

12. Ross 1995a, 186: "As late as June, anonymous trucks were still plying Zapatista villages, delivering sacks of rice and sugar to *campesinos*, the real price of the General's ransom."

13. As Russell (1995, 56) observes: "Almost 300 reporters were taken in 40 chartered minibuses to watch the release of the kidnapped former Gov. Castellanos Domínguez."

14. The eleven demands were work, land, housing, food, health care, education, independence, freedom, democracy, justice, and peace. For a translation of the speech, see Autonomedia 1994, 191–93.

15. Three concentric rings of security surrounded the venue where the peace talks were held: the first comprised 400 military police; the second, 300 civilian volunteers from the Red Cross; and the third, 400 individuals from local and national nongovernmental organizations.

16. See, for example, the communiqué dated 16 February: "While the CCRI-CG [General Command] of the EZLN decides whether or not to send me to the dialogue, I am very worried about what to wear. . . . Whatever happens, whether I go or not . . . the CCRI-CG has ordered me to silence"; and interview with reporters from *Proceso, El Financiero,* and the *New York Times,* "*Marcos* doubts that he will take part in the talks"; both the communiqué and the interview appear in Autonomedia (1994, 185–86, 207).

17. The delegation comprised Marcos along with six others who together represented the Zapatista's military structure and a further twelve members who represented the movement's political wing.

18. Communiqué to the press dated 16 February, translated in Autonomedia 1994, 185–86.

19. Gómez Peña 1995, 91.

20. Ibid.

21. See MacEoin 1996/2000, 101: "Four hundred Mexican and foreign journalists attested to the importance of the occasion."

22. Ross 1995b, 85. See also Ross 1995a, 230.

23. Translated and published in Autonomedia 1994, 227–34, esp. 230.

24. See Bonner 1999, 169.

25. See Castañeda 1995, 83: "From the revelations of Subcomandante Marcos in *Proceso* on 8 August, 1994, we learned that the government not only attempted to limit the matter to Chiapas, but also to its strictly financial aspects: it proposed giving money and public works in return for a few symbolic weapons."

26. See McLynn 2000, 247: "Zapata had only two demands, and they were nonnegotiable: Carranza had to retire so that there could be a genuinely representative interim government and then genuinely free elections; and the new regime must conform to the Plan of Ayala."

27. Marcos quite correctly perceived what others, such as Castañeda (1995, 83), knew to be true, namely, "that without a democratic transition in Mexico there could be no solution in Chiapas" and that "political reform in Chiapas [was] directly associated with genuine reform on a national scale." Similarly, see Hernández Navarro 1994a, 63: "Many of the reforms needed to resolve the conflict in Chiapas are also necessary for national modernization. . . . The worst possible reading of the events in Chiapas would be that the uprising stems from local causes which are not present in the rest of Mexico. . . . It is evident that this is really a national problem."

28. In the long run, however, as Castañeda (1995, 84) notes, although "the government never explicitly accepted Chiapas' inclusion within the national context, nor was it able, however, to dissociate Chiapas from the rest of the national agenda." He concludes, "There can be no greater proof of the [EZLN] movement's importance."

29. For Salinas's instruction to Camacho to be "generous," see Ross 1995a, 223.

30. For a day-by-day, fifteen-page account of the dialogues covering 1 February to 3 March, see *Proceso*, no. 956, 27 February 1995. For a full translation of these thirty-four points, plus the government's response to them, see Womack 1999, 269–77, and T. Benjamin 1989/1996, 263–69. Womack makes an important point at 268: "It is worth notice that unlike the Declaration of January 1, which made no reference to Indians or Chiapas, this statement was heavy on both such counts: 15 of its 34 demands were explicitly for Indians, six explicitly for Chiapas. (Four of them, nos. 4, 14, 16, and 17, all on Indian autonomy)."

31. This translation is that of Womack 1999, 277.

32. *Time* 1994d, 29.

33. Ross 1995a, 247.

34. Ibid.

35. Ibid.

36. This communiqué is quoted and translated in Autonomedia 1994, 115.

37. Ross 1995a, 358.

38. Hernández Navarro 1994b, 12.

39. Marcos was surely correct in his skepticism toward the government's plan to simply throw money at Chiapas's problems, and in particular using Pronasol and Solidarity to do so. Castañeda (quoted in Campa [1994, 17]) has observed that "the problems of poverty [in Chiapas] cannot be solved through money, because the problems are related to structures, not spending." See also Oppenheimer 1996/1998, 55, who talks of money being "squandered by a clique of corrupt PRI officials" and of "extravagant public works—aimed more at being captured in a picture that could be played on the front pages of Mexico City newspapers than at addressing the needs of the Indians"; and Russell 1995, 18: "[The government's] spending in Chiapas was characterized by: (1) corruption, (2) the rivalry between the traditional political elite and the new *Solidarity* bureaucracy, and (3) the overt political use of the program."

40. McCaughan 1995, 36.

41. For this quotation and what follows, see Bonner 1999, 114.

42. *Time* 1994d, 29. Similarly, in March, Marcos told one interviewer (McCaughan 1995, 36) that what the government had offered merely represented, as he saw it, "an attempt to influence them [the indigenous peasants] without resolving the fundamental causes, which are the lack of democracy, of freedom and of justice."

1. Bardach 1994, 128.
2. Translated in Bardach 1994, 129. Ross (1995a, 329) notes: "The prayers for peace resounded throughout Holy Week—there weren't many paeans for armed struggle."
3. For a detailed discussion on the origins, history, and development of civil society, see Esteva 2003, 248–52. A detailed description of the Zapatistas's definition of civil society can be found in their *The Fourth Declaration of the Lacandón Jungle* (1996), at http://www.ezln.org/documentos/1996/19960101.en.htm.
4. See, for example, Bardach (1994, 129), where "a week after Colosio's murder" Carlos Monsiváis told the reporter: "When there's a killing in Mexico, everyone thinks the government did it . . . we're calling it Colosio-gate"; the article goes on to state that "polls . . . five days after the assassination showed that 70 percent [of Mexicans asked] believed that the government would not tell the truth about the killing." See also Ross 1995a, 317–20; Oppenheimer 1996/1998, 62ff, 264–67; Fuentes 1994/1997, 117; de la Grange and Rico 1998, 44ff; and Guillermoprieto 1996, 281.
5. First published in Le Bot 1997, 216; translated in Womack 1999, 321.
6. King and Villaneuva 1998, 118.
7. From the video documentary *Zapatista Women* (1995).
8. McCaughan 1995, 36.
9. Russell 1995, 84, 95. He supplies a full list of these proposed projects on these same pages.
10. Oppenheimer 1996/1998, 75–76.
11. Ibid.
12. Collier and Quaratiello 1994/1999, 77. Subsequently, the Consejo Estatal de Organizaciones Indígenas y Campesinas (State Council of Indigenous and Peasant Organizations) coalition, always frail, split a month later, divided between those groups which had received government funding and who therefore opposed the Zapatistas's call for a National Democratic Convention and those who had not done so and were for the convention.
13. Russell 1995, 73–74. He also notes that "from January through May of 1994, the federal government spent $66 million in Chiapas, 129 percent more than during the same period in 1993" (73), adding that the government "wholeheartedly financed projects in an attempt to win Chiapans' hearts and minds . . . while rebels were surrounded by the Mexican army, spending for jobs, housing, social services, and infrastructure was concentrated in areas near but not in rebel-held territory" (84).
14. McCaughan 1995, 36.
15. Quoted in Reavis 1994, 28.
16. Subcomandante Marcos 1994.

17. Quoted in McLynn 2000, 120.
18. Quoted in Lawrence 1999, 113.
19. Communiqué dated 20 January, translated in Autonomedia 1994, 115.
20. The Zapatistas claimed to have consulted 64,712 people in their support base and that only 2 percent had voted to accept the terms offered by the government. See their two communiqués dated 1 June and 10 June, posted on the Internet at, respectively, http://palabra.ezln.org.mx/ (under the heading "Consulta Nacional Sobre la Propuesta de acuedos de paz"), and http://flag.blackened.net/revolt/mexico/ezln/ccri_Consult_results_jun94.html.
21. See Collier and Collier 2003, 246: "The Zapatistas won the media battle, however."
22. Russell 1995, 77.
23. *La Jornada* 13 June 1994, 10.
24. Harvey 1998, 204.
25. *Second Declaration of the Lacandón Jungle*: "We call for the realization of a Democratic Convention . . . the fundamental objective of a Democratic Convention is to organize civic expression and the defense of the popular will. . . . The Zapatista Army of National Liberation will recognize the National Democratic Convention as the authentic representative of the interests of the Mexican people in its transition to democracy"; translated in Womack 1999, 284.
26. Ross 1995a, 364.
27. McLynn (2000, 256) comments that the 1914 Aguascalientes convention "was a genuine cross-section of participants in the Revolution"; Marcos no doubt hoped that his Aguascalientes would comprise a genuine cross section of Mexican civil society or at least its more progressive elements.
28. See chapter 10; there had been, for example, in 1986, the three-day "El Encuentro" ("the meeting"), attended by Comandantes Elisa and Rodrigo, of workers, local *campesinos* and FLN cadres, in a newly made compound that contained a ceremony hall—named the "*Compañero* César Yáñez Hall" after Germán's brother—with two platforms and capacity for nearly one hundred people, complete with adjoining dining hall and a large tarpaulin sheet to keep off the rain.
29. For these figures relating to the press, see *El Financiero* 1994, 61.
30. De la Grange and Rico 1998, 346–47.
31. Ibid.
32. Oppenheimer 1996/1998, 142–43.
33. De la Grange and Rico 1998, 347.
34. Ibid.
35. See Oppenheimer (1998, 143) who quotes the governor as saying: "I decided to provide support for the meeting because if the Zapatistas concluded that the government was boycotting it, they would have had more reason to oppose the general elections. . . . I believed that a conciliatory attitude on

the part of the government would help the peace process"; and a presidential aid as echoing this: "Our biggest priority was to avoid violence during the elections . . . the convention was planning to adopt a wait-and-see stand about the elections. We naturally wanted to encourage that, because it would send a strong message to other hard-line leftist groups not to disrupt the voting."

36. Published and translated in Subcomandante Marcos 1995a, 243.
37. Quoted in Ross 1995a, 369.
38. The construction of the amphitheatre, the problematic fastening of the nylon rain canvas, and many other preparations for the convention can be seen on the video *Viaje al centro de la selva: memorial Zapatista* (1994), as can most of the Subcommander's speech and the Zapatista military parade.
39. Ross 1995a, 370. Chilangos are denizens of Mexico City. De la Grange and Rico (1998, 349), less charitably, call the attendees "a constellation of marginal groups who formed a kind of court of miracle workers of the Left."
40. See Fuentes (1994/1997, 93) who claims convincingly "that Subcommander *Marcos*, the Zapatista leader, has read more Carlos Monsiváis than Carlos Marx."
41. Womack 1999, 281.
42. Subcomandante Marcos 1995a, 242.
43. The quotation is from "Mexico Is Not Only Chiapas Nor Is the Rebellion in Chiapas Merely a Mexican Affair" at http://www.geocities.com/CapitolHill/Lobby/2379/tptg1.htm.
44. Ibid.
45. See Halleck 1994, 30–32.
46. Castells 1997, 79; italics in original. Also see page 80 for the history of the Internet in Mexico and in particular its use by nongovernmental organizations and women's groups.
47. See Klein 2002, 120.
48. The Zapatistas's Radio Insurgente (97.9 FM) no doubt took its inspiration from the FMLN's Radio Venceremos, which in turn had taken its inspiration from Fidel Castro's Radio Rebelde, which had begun broadcasting from the Sierra Maestra in 1958. Radio Insurgente broadcasts Zapatista communiqués, news about events, and a variety of music, ranging from traditional Mexican *corridos* to modern protest songs, from 4 A.M. to 9 P.M. Like Radio Venceremos, it broadcasts from a mobile radio station for security reasons.
49. Cleaver 1998, 81.

24 THE ELECTIONS AND THEIR AFTERMATH

1. See Castañeda 1995, 116, 78: "For its part, the Cardenista opposition believed the PRI would lose in clean elections, beyond a shadow of a doubt,"

adding, "no margin was left for a different hypothesis, even then the most plausible: that many people would vote for Cárdenas, but not enough to win or to feel robbed of a legitimate victory."

2. As Marcos himself put it: "We thought the PRI was going to win, but by a fraud so enormous that people would revolt. I'm not talking about taking up arms, but about a great protest movement. . . . There we fooled ourselves yet again"; from an interview with Le Bot 1997, 218–21; translated in Womack 1999, 322–23.

3. As Ross (1995a, 338) writes: "The PRI is not just a party—it is the government and has been so for six and a half decades. . . . The PRI doesn't just think it owns Mexico—it thinks it is Mexico. No other party is permitted to use the 'tri-color' of the country." Similarly, Castañeda (1995, 131) states "the umbilical cord between the PRI and the government has never been cut." One pertinent example of this blurring of the line between the PRI and the government is that Jorge Carpizo, the government's interior secretary, was simultaneously given the job of heading the Federal Electoral Institute.

4. See Oppenheimer 1996/1998, 169: "Its [the PRI's] share of the vote had been declining steadily ever since its creation in the late 1920s, when it used to run unopposed. . . . The PRI's share of the vote had fallen to 86% in 1964 to 80% in 1970 and 1976, 69% in 1982, 50% in 1988, and 48.8% in 1994."

5. See, for example, Castañeda 1995, 129ff; Harvey 1998, 206–7; Oppenheimer 1996/1998, 128–61, chapter 7, "The Cleanest Election," esp. 132f, 144f, 150ff, and 160–61; Ross 1995a, 386–94, 396–98; and Sánchez Lira and Villarreal 1995, 232ff.

6. Ross 1995a, 396.

7. Oppenheimer 1996/1998, 161.

8. Castañeda 1995, 130.

9. Sánchez Lira and Villarreal 1995, 232–33.

10. Ibid.

11. See Weinberg 2000, 135: "The PRI had spent about $72 dollars a vote nationally—a total of $1.25 billion, including government money, exponentially exceeding both the official $40 million cap on campaign spending and the sum spent by US President Bill Clinton to get elected two years earlier." Similarly, Ross 1995a, 387ff. So too, Oppenheimer (1996/1998, 144) adds: "According to PAN [Partido Acción Nacional (National Action Party)] estimates, the government spent about $4 billion in social development projects—mainly in opposition dominated areas—over the two months preceding the elections."

12. Ross 1995a, 388: "Civic Alliance . . . surveys indicated that Zedillo was assigned about 45% of all TV and radio newstime (more on Televisa's *24 Hours*)." See also Oppenheimer (1996/1998, 135, fn.): "Campaign coverage

was even more tilted toward Zedillo on radio stations than on television, according to the Federal Electoral Institute report. The study said that Zedillo got 50.1 percent of radio airtime, compared with 49.9 percent for the remaining eight candidates together."

13. See Castañeda 1995, 130, 134; Oppenheimer 1996/1998, 166; and Ross 1995a, 398 ff., for the belief that the PRI had won the 1994 election regardless of fraud.

14. Fuentes (1994/1997, 111–12) writes of "the unrepeatable traumas of . . . our year of living dangerously."

15. For example, Miguel Angel Rivera, in his daily political column for *La Jornada*, wrote that "the evil with which one is familiar [is] more inviting than the good one doesn't yet know"; quoted in Ross 1995a, 332.

16. De la Grange and Rico 1998, 30. See also Castañeda 1995, 96–97: "The PRI's . . . campaign succeeded thanks to one single element: fear. . . . Fear became the spearhead of the campaign. Voters were induced to ask themselves whether they wanted to live under an opposition government, with the ensuing chaos, violence and decomposition."

17. Ross 1995a, 400.

18. Sánchez Lira and Villarreal 1995, 231.

19. Oppenheimer 1996/1998, 130.

20. Castañeda 1995, 133.

21. Oppenheimer 1996/1998, 134–35.

22. Castañeda 1995, 153: "The meeting was immortalized in a photograph that appeared not only on the front pages of newspapers and on television screens, but also on posters later put up by PRD supporters—even in the middle-class areas of Mexico City."

23. Indeed, this perhaps represents a third consideration in the PRI victory, namely, that both opposition parties (the PRD and the PAN) committed serious errors that greatly weakened their chances of winning the election. For criticisms of Cárdenas's campaign see Castañeda 1995, 141–54, and Oppenheimer 1996/1998, 160.

24. Ross 1995a, 388.

25. Fuentes 1994/1997, 111.

26. Hernández Navarro 1994a, 63.

27. As Harvey (1994, 38) notes: "In a major speech, *Subcomandante Marcos* allayed fears of an imminent armed uprising following the national elections and instead called on the peaceful civic and popular movement 'to defeat us,' to make armed action unnecessary (*La Jornada*, 10 August, 1994)."

28. Fuentes 1994/1997, 80. Cf. Castañeda 1995, 101: "A hundred political activists from the opposition lost their lives during the government of Carlos Salinas."

29. See Ross 1995a, 377–82; Russell 1995, 92; and Weinberg 2000, 134–35.

30. Womack 1999, 288.
31. Avendaño was said to have polled 34.1 percent and the PAN candidate a mere 9.4 percent; for these figures, see Russell 1995, 93.
32. In an interview published in 1997, Marcos looked back at the election and commented: "Fraud was impossible to prove in the case of the presidential election, but for Robledo's election . . . really, it jumped right out before your eyes"; published in Le Bot 1997, 221; translated in Womack 1999, 323.
33. *La Jornada*, 5 October 1994, 24, and 15 October 1994, 15; *El Financiero*, 25 October 1994, 52; and *Proceso*, no. 940, 7 November 1994, 12–19.
34. Russell 1995, 93.
35. Ross 2000, 91.
36. See Russell (1995, 57–60) for other groups in other states following the Zapatistas's lead and pressurizing the government to address their grievances.
37. Van Cott 1996. T. Benjamin (1989/1996, 258) estimates the amount of land seized by spring as being 80,000 hectares outside the Zapatista zone of control and 100,000 within it. Harvey (1994, 41) claims that "during the first six months of the year some 340 private farms representing over 50,000 hectares were seized."
38. Russell 1995, 73. At the end of April, only four months prior to the election, the PRI mayor of Venustiano Carranza had been forced out of office by popular protest, while frustrated citizens set the town hall ablaze in Villa las Rosas after three sit-ins had failed to dislodge its PRI mayor. Further examples of mayors being ousted or deposed by the people they were supposed to have been elected by are cited by Nash 2001, 125.
39. *La Jornada*, 1994c, 5; quoted and translated in Russell 1995, 94.
40. See Russell 1995, 95, 120, n. 442.
41. On the assassination, see de la Grange and Rico 1998, 316; Oppenheimer 1996/1998, 187–214; and Weinberg 2000, 305–7.
42. Interview in *Proceso* 1994d, 15; translated in Russell 1995, 96.
43. Quoted in Ross 2000, 85.
44. Interview with *La Jornada's* Hermann Bellinghausen, quoted in Ross 2000, 85.
45. See Camp 1995.
46. Interview (23 July 1994) with Oppenheimer (1996/1998, 77). See also Marcos's comment in *Proceso* (1994a, 11) on 1 August: "I see Zedillo as very intolerant, very close-minded."
47. For example, Oppenheimer (1996/1998, 181) writes of Zedillo: "I got the hunch he would end up becoming a hard-line president. He had a short temper that could be taken for an authoritarian streak. . . . A no-nonsense technocrat with not much of a sense of humor and little political flair, he had the kind of personality that could lead him to become an autocratic

ruler." See, too, *Proceso*, no. 1069, 27 April 1997, the cover of which carried a photograph of the president with the headline, "La intolerancia de Zedillo," emblazoned across it.

48. Ibid., 121, fn.

49. Autonomedia 1994, 266. Also quoted in Ross 1995a, 343.

50. "I solemnly reject your invitation to a secret negotiation, behind the back of the nation"; Marcos's letter to Ernesto Zedillo, president of Mexico, 3 December 1994, at http://flag.blackened.net/revolt/mexico/ezln/marcos_zedillo_dec94.html and published in Ponce de León 2001, 70–79.

51. Quoted and translated in Russell 1995, 101.

52. Ross 2000, 85–86.

53. Marcos's letter to Ernesto Zedillo, president of Mexico. See also his interview on 9 December: "The number of troops has not decreased, it has increased. Their positions have changed, they have a base inside the jungle"; http://www.ezln.org/entrevistas/19941209.en.htm.

54. *Proceso*, no. 1105, 4 January 1998, 6–11; quoted and translated in Bonner 1999, 156.

55. Debray 2002, 344.

56. See Russell 1995, 98.

57. See Van Cott 1996: "On October 12, 1994 (not coincidentally, Columbus Day), a coalition of indigenous organizations issued a declaration establishing Indigenous Autonomous Regions throughout the state, which are intended to serve as a level of government between the municipal governments, indigenous communities and the state government. The indigenous organizations, in a document entitled 'Autonomy as a New Relationship Between the Indigenous Peoples and the National Society,' articulated a series of constitutional reforms that would create autonomous indigenous regions in all parts of the country where indigenous peoples are present, with broad local powers to govern political, administrative, and cultural matters. Leaders of the Autonomous Indigenous Regions demanded 'full respect and recognition of our irrefutable right to self-determination of our peoples and with that the recognition of our legitimate right to autonomy.' By late October, four autonomous regions had been established, including fifty-eight municipalities covering more than half the state's territory."

58. *Proceso* 1994c, 18; quoted and translated in Russell 1995, 97.

59. *New York Times* 1994a, A6.

60. Ross 2000, 86.

61. Collier and Quaratiello 1994/1999, 161. Ross (2000, 86–87) is equally as negative about the results of this convention.

62. Marcos himself talks of "the faltering of the civil movement" in an interview on 9 December.

63. See Collier and Quaratiello 1994/1999, 83; one of the EZLN's first cadres (possibly Jorge) was accidentally shot dead during a training exercise. He

was left-handed, and it is said that he is commemorated in the Zapatista left-handed salute.

64. Oppenheimer 1996/1998, 16–17. Oppenheimer, by writing that the ceremony "was carried out about four weeks before the Zapatista uprising," implies that the description he is giving is of the ceremony held one year earlier on 17 November 1993. However, it appears to me that his source, Bellinghausen (*La Jornada*, 19 November 1994), is actually giving a description of the 1994 ceremony (not the 1993 one), which he penned only two days after having attended it. (The 1993 ceremony, it should be remembered, was a highly clandestine affair, whereas that of 1994 was far more public.) Oppenheimer then is either confused, or else he is working on the (entirely plausible) hypothesis that the 1993 and 1994 ceremonies, being highly ritualized events, differed little from one another.

65. Ibid., 17. He continues, "In Mexico, a long history of deceptions had taught people not to trust words and to seal their commitments through symbols and rituals."

66. The text of this speech can be found in EZLN 1995, 131–39; all quotations from it are my translation, since there is, to the best of my knowledge, no translation into English of this important speech.

67. For Marcos's fondness for Pedro, see chapter 18. Marcos carried a photograph of Hugo—whose body was never found—around with him after his death and even dedicated several verses of Paul Eluard's poem "El Castillo de los pobres" ("The Castle of the Poor") to him in one of his subsequent communiqués (dated to 22 September 1994 and translated in Ponce de León 2001, 60–69).

68. In a communiqué dated to 28 May 1994 Marcos writes that "I just received a letter from the younger Antonio with his village's response to the government's proposals. He also wrote me that 'Old Antonio' had become very ill and that he died that night"; this translation from Autonomedia 1994, 312; also translated in Subcomandante Marcos 1995a, 209–15. Cf., however, Marcos's interview with Le Bot (1997, 135), where the Subcommander tells us "El Viejo Antonio muere en 1994, en junio."

69. For Carlos's death at age 38 of asphyxiation after an epileptic fit, an illness he had had since childhood, see de la Grange and Rico 1998, 64. Marcos was especially close to Carlos, who was only a year his senior and with whom he shared an apartment for three years while studing at Universidad Nacional Autónoma México.

70. This list of ethnic groups, the symbols, and their meanings is from Ross 2000, 88.

71. Letter to Ernesto Zedillo, president of Mexico, 3 December 1994. For example: "Your words today are the same ones we have had at the beginning of other administrations," and "You appoint a cabinet along the same lines as that man who buried the country in misery: Carlos Salinas de Gortari."

So too, Oppenheimer (1996/1998, 183–85) notes that "more than half of Zedillo's cabinet was made up of Salinas loyalists . . . [resulting in] a new government that looked largely like a continuation of the previous one."

72. Ross 2000, 91.

73. Quoted in Tangeman 1995, 115. On the theme of a divided Chiapas, see Hughes 1994b, 1.

74. Interview on 9 December, cited above (n. 53).

75. See Marcos's interview with Le Bot (1997, 221–22) where he places great importance on Zedillo's attendance at Robledo's inauguration: "It was a clear sign to us . . . From then the CCRI said that we had to do something so that they [the government] would remember we are here. . . . We wanted to call attention to ourselves, to say 'We are here, Zedillo, Listen to us!' "

76. Ibid.

77. The poll was published in the magazine *Reforma*, 11 December 1994, and quoted in Castells 1997, 79, n. 12.

78. As Marcos put it: "Nothing has happened—everything has remained the same . . . the same class structure is in place, the same racism, the same governmental structure, the same radical speeches and reactionary practices. . . . Chiapas in December of '93 and December of '94 [are] the same"; interview on 9 December, cited above (n. 53).

79. Ibid.

80. Tangeman 1995, 115. There are 111 Chiapan municipalities, so the Zapatistas now controlled roughly 34 percent of them. For a list of the thirty-eight municipalities, see EZLN 1995, 180.

81. Burguete Cal y Mayor 2003, 205. While noting that a desire for some semblance of autonomy had already been articulated during the February peace talks, she states that it was from December onward that the real push for autonomy and its realization began.

82. One such confused onlooker was Joel Padrón, a priest from the highland town of Simojovel; see Tangeman 1995, 115. Similarly, see Eaton 1995: "Residents in towns such as Simojovel said they saw townspeople changing into Zapatista clothes, putting on ski masks and marching around as if they'd just come in from the jungle."

83. Castells 1997, 81.

84. See, for example, Castañeda 1995, 190, 192–93; Fuentes 1994/1997, 130; Guillermoprieto 1996, 275–76; Oppenheimer 1996/1998, 229; and Ross 2000, 97.

85. The country's dollar reserves had been falling dramatically from the previous January, down from 13 billion to just 5 billion in less than a year—the lowest since 1988.

86. See Tangeman 1995, 115: "In an attempt to lay the blame for distasteful economic policy decisions on the Zapatistas, the Zedillo administration tried

to use the December 19 political turmoil as a cover for a relatively minor, yet much needed devaluation of the Mexican peso." Evidently some authors have been taken in by the government's attempt to link the crisis to the Zapatistas's recent campaign; for instance, Ronfeldt et al. (1998, 81). Castells (1997, 81) believes that although the Zapatistas were responsible for the crisis, it was "not that they deliberately sabotaged the economy." Others have seen through the government's ploy, such as Thomas Benjamin (1989/1996, 259), Fuentes (1994/1997, 130), and Ross (2000, 97–98, 283). More importantly, the Mexican public was clearly not fooled by Zedillo's ploy: a poll of 1,450 Mexicans showed that 48 percent blamed the government for the peso debacle, while only 18 percent blamed Subcommander Marcos; the poll is quoted in Oppenheimer 1996/1998, 99–100.

87. Tangeman 1995, 116. See also Oppenheimer (1996/1998, 313), who wrote that one year on, in late 1995, "interest rates . . . had reached 100 percent; car sales had plummeted by 70 percent; more than ten thousand businesses had closed down, and many more were threatened by a vicious circle of slumping sales and unpayable debts; more than one million people had been laid off, and the unofficial unemployment rate had reached a record 13 percent."

88. Burbach 2001, 42.

89. Barkin et al. 1997b, 24. Despite a hailed recovery in 1996, the average wage in Mexico lay somewhere between two and three minimum wages, at a time when an average urban family required 4.8 minimum wages to rise above the poverty line.

90. MacEoin 1996/2000, 54.

91. See, for example, Marcos's interview with Oppenheimer (1996/1998, 76): "The Salinas group had tried to present to the world the image of a stable and prosperous Mexico. It had also tried to convince Mexico that we were doing well, on our road to the First World. But, on 1 January, we brought the mask down and showed the country's real face to the world. People began to look at Chiapas, at Guerrero, at Oaxaca, and to realize that there is an underground Mexico, a basement of the country that was invisible in political, social, or economic terms, but that existed all along."

92. Mexico had twenty-three new billionaires in 1993—half of whom were created by Salinas's privatization of 252 state companies, including Telmex and major national banks; meanwhile, 41 million Mexicans lived below the poverty line. Moreover, as Tangeman (1995, 77) observes: "An estimated sixty thousand small businesses failed in 1990 alone . . . closed out of co-investment opportunities by the more lucrative partnership offers being pitched to foreign investors by Mexico's business elite, dominated by a group of thirty-seven Mexican moguls who controlled the country's top seventy corporations—an estimated 22 percent of Mexico's entire GDP and

some 60 percent of the shares of all Mexican companies listed on the national stock exchange." He adds, "From 1989 to 1993 wage earners saw their share of GDP fall by $165.9 billion in real terms" (ibid., 78).

93. Clinton had tried to secure a $40 billion financial rescue package for Mexico, but this required the consent of Congress, which was proving very hard to gain. In the end Clinton used $20 billion from his own presidential discretionary fund.

94. Fuentes 1994/1997, 144.

95. Ibid. See also Ross (2000, 102) who calls it "a 'bailout' that all but annexed Mexico to the U.S.," adding, "national sovereignty was at peril."

96. Communiqué published in *La Jornada*, 13 February 1995; http://flag.black ened.net/revolt/mexico/ezln/marcos_blood_loan_feb95.html.

97. Communiqué published in *La Jornada*, 11 February 1995; http://www.ezln .org/documentos/1995/19950202.en.htm.

98. Dated 13 January 1995; http://lanic.utexas.edu/la/region/news/arc/lasnet/ 1995/0109.html.

99. Quoted in Ross 2000, 98.

25 MARCOS UNMASKED AND RAFAEL REVEALED

1. See Associated Press 1995.

2. The PRI took advantage of a clause in the state constitution that allows a governor to take an eleven-month leave during his term and to be replaced in the meantime with another candidate.

3. Ross 2000, 101.

4. Ibid., 102.

5. For a detailed description of Daniel's correspondence and dealings with the Mexican Army's Second Section, see Oppenheimer 1996/1998, 235–36, 241–42. See, too, López y Rivas 2000, who, citing a source linked to the Mexican intelligence services, claims that "*Daniel* is today an official in the Mexican Army, with the rank of Second Captain . . . ," who works in an administrative capacity as part of a task force within military intelligence charged with combating armed groups threatening Mexico's national security.

6. Oppenheimer (1996/1998, 242) calls it: "A potentially precious chance for Mexico's beleaguered president to regain the upper hand in what had increasingly become a propaganda war the rebels seemed to be winning."

7. Ibid., 243.

8. Ibid., 245.

9. Ibid., 243.

10. McLynn (2000, 76–77) writes: "Business confidence in his regime had been severely dented by the revolt . . . [therefore] believing that only a decisive military victory would now restore confidence, Díaz sent an extra 5,000 troops to Chihuahua."

11. For this quotation and further details on the economic impact of the February offensive, see Nash 2001, 138.

12. For much of what follows, see Oppenheimer 1996/1998, 244–46, 248–49.

13. The case of Salvador Morales Garibay (Subcomandante Daniel) is very interesting. He is attested as having given his first declaration in February, and has not been questioned since, thereby failing to attend at least seven judicial summons to appear in court. Moreover, in Morales's initial 8 February statement he was read his rights under the federal Code of Penal Procedures by an agent of the public ministry, a standard procedure for a criminal held in custody. Morales's criminal status then appeared to be confirmed by a senior interior ministry official on 17 February, when he told foreign reporters that Morales was one of four top Zapatista comandantes. However, a volte-face was then effected in the Zedillo administration when, three days later, the attorney general denied Morales had been "detained," repeating this assertion on 27 March in Washington, D.C., at a meeting with various human rights groups. Moreover, as Human Rights Watch (1996, 9) observes, "Morales' 8 February statement does not indicate that authorities questioned him about his own activities as an alleged EZLN member, and it gives no reason for his alleged defection."

14. "President Zedillo's Address on the Chiapas Situation," Mexico City, 9 February 1995, translation circulated by the Embassy of Mexico, Washington, D.C.

15. Oppenheimer 1996/1998, 248.

16. Concerning the library, as Elena Poniatowska (2002b, 380) points out, "through collection drives, young people contributed several thousand books, and a number of university students traveled in caravans to the Lacandón jungle to work as librarians."

17. Communiqué at http://www.ezln.org/documentos/1996/19961023b.en. htm; also published in Ponce de León 2001, 136. See also Ross (2000, 107), who notes that "the entire space [Aguascalientes] was plowed under and re-seeded with fast growing pine and eucalyptus"—the intention was clearly to erase any trace of the site where the Zapatistas had met with civil society.

18. *Fourth Declaration of the Lacandón Jungle*; http://www.ezln.org/documentos/1996/19960101.en.htm. This seemingly senseless act of wanton vandalism prompted Poniatowska (2002b, 380) to ask: "What harm was there in a library? Why not leave it for the people of Guadalupe Tepeyac, to whom it belonged? Were they trying to erase a symbol, the symbol of the Zapatistas?"

19. Collier and Quaratiello 1994/1999, 189, n. 11.

20. Hernández Navarro 1998, 10.

21. Oppenheimer 1996/1998, 248

22. Quoted ibid.

23. Ibid., 249: "It soon became clear from neighbors and relatives that government forces had occupied both rebel hideouts [in Mexico City and Yanga, Veracruz] at least three hours before Morales [Daniel] had testified in court."

24. Human Rights Watch (1996, 1) claims: "During the operation, they [government forces] committed serious violations of Mexican and international human rights standards, including . . . the disregard of due-process guarantees." (So too, Human Rights Watch [1997, 89] states: "Federal and state prosecutors blatantly violated due process standards to make quick arrests." In particular, seven suspects were arrested in Yanga, Veracruz, with flagrant disregard for due process.) As the former Human Rights Watch report (1996) observes: "State judicial police entered their home using a warrant issued for three quite different suspects, living at a different address and wanted for a crime dating from August 1991." Comandante Vicente claims he was shown no arrest warrant and that he was denied access to a lawyer prior to questioning. On 1 November 1995, a judge, Fernando Andrés Ortiz Cruz, pronounced a full acquittal—appealed against by the Mexican government—of Elisa (Gloria Benavides) based on serious breaches in the arrest procedure: no warrant was shown to her, the police entered her house under the pretext of being friends of the family, and there were serious irregularities in the report of a witness, Odilón Hernández Flores, whose testimony that he was robbed by assailants outside Benavides's property and that the armed assailants subsequently entered her residence, provided the basis upon which the warrant was issued. Flores gave a false address and then could not be located.

25. Oppenheimer 1996/1998, 248. Oppenheimer (ibid.) also notes that "the Zapatistas had a sophisticated radio communications system in the jungle: because Chiapas was so poor and had so few telephone lines, the government and the Roman Catholic Church had long ago set up elaborate radio systems throughout the state to help bring Indian communities in the jungle closer to civilization." Similarly, Ross (2000, 105) asserts that Marcos was alerted by "the news coming in over the EZLN's radio communication system."

26. Bardach 1994, 128.

27. In reality, the only fatalities resulting from the government's offensive were one police officer shot dead in Cacalomacán during a shoot-out between 500 police officers and those in the safe house; and in Chiapas, the deaths of Colonel Hugo Manterola and a Zapatista from the village of La Grandeza.

28. MacEoin 1996/2000, 137.

29. Ross 2000, 110.

30. Cleaver 1998, 100, n. 11 provides the following examples: Robberson 1995,

A1; R. Watson et al. 1995, 36–40; TV Globo report (Sunday, 26 February 1995), rerun by CNN on their weekend World Report the same day.

31. Quoted in Cleaver 1998, 93, and again in Ronfeldt et al. 1998, 4.

32. Womack 1999, 295. Ross (2000, 110) lists the venues of these European demonstrations as Barcelona, Berlin, Madrid, Switzerland, and "all over Italy."

33. Interview with Le Bot 1997, 218–21; quoted and translated in Womack 1999, 325. Olesen (2004, 90) notes that Phase 2 (February 1995–summer 1996) of the transnational Zapatista solidarity network was "very intense . . . following the failed attempt by the Mexican Army to capture the Zapatista leadership in February 1995."

34. See, for example, Centro de Derechos Humanos "Fray Bartolomé de las Casas" 1995a and 1995b; Human Rights Watch 1996 and 1997.

35. Reuters 1995.

36. This photograph is reproduced in Oppenheimer 1996/1998, in the photograph section in the center of the book, and in Serrill 1995.

37. See Oppenheimer 1996/1998, 248: "'If we hadn't been one hundred percent sure of Marcos's identity, we wouldn't have allowed the president to make the announcement: We would have had the Interior minister or a lower-level official make it,' said one of Zedillo's top advisers, who personally checked the last details of Marcos's identity before the president went on the air. 'A mistake like that could cost us the presidency.'"

38. See de la Grange and Rico 1998, 23: "El procedimiento utilizado por las autoridades para desenmascarar al jefe del EZLN pretendía sin duda propinar un golpe psicológico a sus simpatizantes." See also Ross 2000, 107: "Ernesto Zedillo's unmasking of Marcos was designed to strip the Subcomandante of his power and mystique"; and Golden 1995.

39. De la Grange and Rico 1998, 344.

40. Communiqué dated 13 February 1995; http://flag.blackened.net/revolt/ mexico/ezln/marcos_blood_loan_feb95.html. See also Marcos's interview with Le Bot (1997, 320), where he complains that the uncovering had "ruined correspondence from women," adding, "I have to convince my adorers that I am not as ugly as that"; my translation.

41. Ross 2000, 109.

42. As Weller (2000, 96) observes, any attempt to unmask Marcos was a "feat of dubious and only vaguely interesting merit."

43. Oppenheimer 1996/1998, 242.

44. García Márquez and Pombo 2001, 79.

45. MacEoin 1996/2000, 138.

46. See chapter 24 for a poll which showed that 78 percent thought the Zapatistas's demands were justified on 9 December 1994. Indeed, as Kampwirth (2002, 111, n. 23) notes, "Support for the Zapatistas was to remain steady

over time: a nationwide poll conducted in August 1996 found that while almost 76 percent thought that the EZLN was doing the best it could to achieve peace through dialogue, only 22 percent thought that the government was doing the best it could."

47. T. Benjamin 1989/1996, 260.

48. Eaton 1995.

49. See Earle and Simonelli 2005, 267: "It is the threat of political instability or the perception of it brought on by an armed group of Indians in confrontation with Mexican authorities that keeps the government respectful of their right to resist." So too, Rubin 1994, 66: "This threat of violence in Chiapas will have to be maintained if the rebellion is to lead to significant reforms in the years ahead."

50. See, for example, Gordon McCormick, an expert in guerrilla warfare at the Naval Postgraduate School in Monterey, California: "We know Marcos has a popular following, but the relevant question is whether he can mobilize, whether he can put people in the field of battle. If he can't, he's not a threat"; quoted in Eaton 1995.

51. Ross 2000, 110: He adds: "Going to the gun would have brought the sky down on the Zapatista villages. The images of Vietnam with its flaming shards of napalm falling upon the civilian population, of Guatemala, the butchered Indians burnt alive in the churches, are powerful deterrents to guerrilla gung-ho."

52. MacEoin 1996/2000, 137.

53. Ibid.

54. Human Rights Watch 1997, 78. For details of such attacks on the Church at this time see Ross 2000, 112–13.

55. Quoted in McClintock 1998, 302. The Church was hardly a *vox clamantis in deserto*, however. The World Bank—as reported in the *Economist* (1996, 16)—had observed that between 1980 and 1995 in Latin America the percentage of the continent's population that was living in poverty had remained exactly the same. When population increase is accounted for, this means that whereas in 1980 there were 115 million people living in poverty, in 1995 the number had risen to about 160 million.

56. See Human Rights Watch 1997, 82, esp. n. 214.

57. Oppenheimer 1996/1998, 48; see, too, 248, which also listed "one of the rebel leader's black ski masks, several packages of tobacco, and his backpack full of medicine." Eaton (1995) identifies the brand of tobacco as being "Smoker's Choice."

58. Translated and posted at http://flag.blackened.net/revolt/mexico/ezln/marcos_retreat_sky.html.

59. De la Grange and Rico 1998, 54.

60. Oppenheimer (1996/1998, 259, 262) calls it a "comic adventure" and a "literary extravaganza."

61. Guevara 1994/1996, 261.

62. This point is noted by de la Grange and Rico (1998, 54), but they do not explicitly state that Marcos is simply imitating the story here. In any case, although Marcos would have undoubtedly been aware of this story, I believe his inspiration here was Che Guevara, as is shown by noting the similarities between Marcos's text and Che's.

63. Guevara 1994/1996, 195, under the earlier heading for 13 May 1967.

64. Ibid., 197, entry for 16 May 1967.

65. Translated and posted at http://flag.blackened.net/revolt/mexico/ezln/marcos_green_death_feb95.html.

66. Castañeda 1997, xvi, fn.

67. Communiqué dated 11 March; translated and posted at http://flag.blackened.net/revolt/mexico/ezln/marcos_ecuador_peru_mar95.html.

68. Guevara 1996, 126, under the entry for February 1957.

69. Ibid., 144.

70. See the following communiqués: http://flag.blackened.net/revolt/mexico/ezln/marcos_blood_loan_feb95.html; http://flag.blackened.net/revolt/mexico/ezln/marcos_retreat_sky.html; http://flag.blackened.net/revolt/mexico/ezln/marcos_green_death_feb95.html; and http://flag.blackened.net/revolt/mexico/ezln/marcos_ecuador_peru_mar95.html.

71. COCOPA comprised six federal senators and eight deputies from the four main political parties in Mexico (the PRI, the PAN, the PRD, and the PT [Partido del Trabajo, or Labor Party]), plus one representative each from both the executive branch of the government and from the Chiapas State Congress.

72. For examples of these acts, see Ross 2000, 115–16.

73. Reprinted in Ponce de León 2001, 241–45.

74. It was one thing for a PRI president to allow the signing of a peace treaty, as Salinas had done in 1992, between the FMLN guerrillas and the El Salvadoran government in Mexico City; it was quite another to afford Mexico's own guerrillas the same treatment.

75. For example, García Medrano (1997, 18) wrote: "A Manuel Camacho Solís . . . [Marcos] espetó la peregrina fábula de que las 'bases' del EZLN habían desautorizado a su delegación y que, por lo tanto, todo lo acordado con él quedaba sin efecto."

76. Weinberg 2000, 149.

77. Ross 2000, 138.

78. Nash (2001, 145) attributes this success to pressure put on the government by the Consulta: "The interest created in the plebiscite probably convinced the government to go back to the table and talk."

79. Ross 2000, 144.

80. Oppenheimer 1996/1998, 63.

81. Ross 2000, 138.

82. Ross 2000, 144.

83. Aubry (2003, 238–39, n. 7) observes how point four of the Zapatistas's 1994 demands pressed for "a new pact between the members of the federation that ends centralism and permits regions, indigenous communities, and municipalities to be self-governing, with political, economic, and cultural autonomy." Point sixteen similarly urged that "as the indigenous peoples that we are, let us be allowed to organize and govern ourselves with our own autonomy." So too, Burguete Cal y Mayor (2003, 204) notes that during the time of the peace talks Marcos expressed a desire "to enjoy an autonomy similar to the one existing in the Spanish regions of Catalonia and the Basque provinces" during an interview on Spanish television, and Marcos stated in an interview the same month (February) with *La Jornada* "that it is necessary to negotiate a statute of autonomy whereby the government recognizes our government, our administrative structure, so that we could co-exist without their interference in our affairs."

84. See Mattiace 2003b, 145: "The accord emphasized cultural rights (that is, recognition of Guatemala's multicultural composition, the legitimacy of using indigenous languages in official and public spaces, recognition and protection of Maya spirituality, and commitment to education reform), recognition of communal lands and the reform of the legal system, as well as indigenous political participation."

85. The stated aim, according to the United Nations, was to strengthen "international cooperation for the solution of problems faced by indigenous peoples in such areas as human rights, the environment, development, education and health"; http://www.unhchr.ch/indigenous/e2004–82.doc.

86. See Ross 2000, 143: "The huge absenteeism proved that the EZLN was the dominant political power in the state."

87. See Aubry (2003, 225): "In the first round (October 1995) the guests of the government joined those of the EZLN, which alarmed the official delegation."

88. Mattiace 2003b, 20–21. The notion of autonomy as an umbrella demand is repeated also on p. 157, n. 7, where Mattiace quotes anthropologist Héctor Díaz-Polanco, who served as advisor to the Sandinista government on the issue of indigenous autonomy, thus: "autonomy is the 'articulating demand'—the demand through which all other claims are fulfilled."

89. For full details of this incident and its aftermath, see *Proceso*, no. 991, 30 October 1995, which carried a photograph of Germán on its cover and devoted ten pages to the story.

90. See Mattiace 2003b, 120: "In a surprising move, the government uninvited its 'experts' on indigenous affairs from the National Indigenous Institute (INI) after the first phase ended. Critics claimed that the government became disenchanted with its INI because they had 'gone native,' openly supporting many of the demands expressed by the EZLN's invited guests."

91. See Aubry 2003, 234–35.

92. For these figures see Mattiace 2003b, 161, n. 2.

26 MAKING THE STRUGGLE NATIONAL AND GLOBAL

1. Civil interest in the Zapatistas abated during the run-up to the general election and remained muted even when Marcos accused the PRI of electoral fraud following its victory at the polls. See Womack (1999, 289f, 327ff) for a rather negative interpretation of the Zapatista's relationship with civil society and particularly the effectiveness of the FZLN in rousing Mexican civil society to action.

2. Quoted in Ross 2000, 155.

3. Mattiace 2003b, 120.

4. See Nash (2001, 149), who notes that at this event, "Subcomandante Marcos was the least seen member of the EZLN."

5. Ibid., 122: "The San Andrés Accords, signed in February, echo, to an astonishing degree, the conclusions reached at the National Indian Forum."

6. Quoted in Ross 2000, 160.

7. For a translation of the accords, see http://flag.blackened.net/revolt/mexico/ezln/san_andres.html.

8. This beleaguered president, whose first year in office had been tainted by a Zapatista maneuver that had broken the Federal Army's stranglehold, a badly mishandled devaluation of the peso, and a failed military offensive to capture the EZLN leadership, must have felt in dire need of a positive photo opportunity to flaunt while petitioning for Mexico's associate membership in the European Union—some of whose member states, notably Spain, Italy, and Germany, had strong pro-Zapatista support groups.

9. See Kampwirth 1998, 17: "At the request of the EZLN, photographers were not allowed at the official ceremony because the Zapatistas suspected that the government was more interested in the photo opportunity than in the content of the accords themselves." She continues: "Their suspicions proved correct. In subsequent months, the federal government refused to enact any of the legislation necessary to implement the accords, and paramilitary violence in northern Chiapas continued." This interpretation is shared by Ross (2000, 162–63), who adds, "Ernesto Zedillo would never forgive the Zapatistas for denying him his Kodak moment."

10. Harvey 1998, 222.

11. Ibid.

12. Interestingly, in an interview given with *La Jornada* (February 1994) in which the Subcommander discussed autonomy, Marcos chose as his points of reference not indigenous autonomy in Nicaragua, but rather "that of the Basques and Catalans"; quoted and translated by Burguete Cal y Mayor 2003, 204.

13. Womack 1999, 305. See also, Mattiace 2003b, 143: "In Nicaragua . . . on September 2, 1987, the Autonomy Statute was passed by the Sandinista legislature, which established two multi-ethnic Atlantic coast regions. . . . This statute included guarantees of equal citizenship for Atlantic coast indigenous peoples, as well as protection of their special rights. Under the agreement, the state recognized communal forms of landownership and indigenous people's right to 'provide themselves with their own forms of social organization and to administer their local affairs according to their traditions.'"

14. Ross 2000, 161.

15. For a full list of celebrities in attendance see Ross 2000, 167–69. They included writers, poets, film stars, rock idols, film directors, intellectuals, progressive politicians, radicals, union officials, environmentalists, human rights activists, and anarchists.

16. Padgett 1996, 14. So too, Britain's *Sunday Times* (Lang 1996, 17) treated Mitterrand's meeting with Marcos in detail.

17. Debray 2002, 347, originally published as "La guerilla autremont," *Le Monde*, 16 May 1996; "A demain, Zapata!," *Le Monde*, 17 March 1995. Translated into Spanish and published in *Proceso*, no. 959, 20 March 1995, 23–30.

18. Ross 2000, 170.

19. Quoted in De la Grange and Rico (1998, 75).

20. In San Cristóbal on 8 March 1996 (Women's Day), about five thousand indigenous marched through the city to demand the withdrawal of soldiers from their communities. One was quoted in *La Jornada* (9 April 1996, 12) as saying: "We want the army to leave. Our houses are used as brothels, the few classrooms available for our children are occupied by soldiers, sport fields are used as parking lots for war tanks and helicopters of that bad government"; translated in Hernández Castillo 2001, 207.

21. Weinberg 2000, 358, 357. He also notes (357) how a January 1996 issue of *Special Warfare* published by Fort Bragg, where many of these Mexican military officers were receiving training, openly stated that "particularly heavy emphasis is being placed on those forces that will be located in the states of Chiapas and Guerrero, where 'special airborne forces' will be set up."

22. Harvey 1998, 222–23.

23. Nash 2001, 189.

24. Mitterrand 1996, 58.

25. Elorriaga was formerly Comandante Vicente, head of the EZLN's ideological commission, and Comandanta Elisa's husband and the father of their child. During 1994 he had been instrumental in promoting the EZLN's propaganda, helping to distribute communiqués, faxing press releases (in Spanish and English), arranging interviews, raising funds, orchestrating events, and even helping broker a dialogue between the Zapatistas and President

Zedillo in January 1995. He had also co-produced a Spanish-language documentary video, *Viaje al Centro de la Selva* (*Journey to the Centre of the Jungle*) covering the first eight months of Zapatista actions, including the uprising and the peace talks in the Cathedral, and focusing in particular on the August National Democratic Convention at Aguascalientes. Bizarrely, the judge in Elorriaga's trial cited the latter's participation in this documentary as proof of his being guilty of terrorism. See *Proceso*, no. 1018, 6 May 1996, 28–30, and no. 1019, 13 May 1996, 16.

26. Echoing the feelings of many, see Ross 2000, 176: "The sentence was absurd. No credible crumb of evidence establishing that Elorriaga had participated in terrorist activities had ever been presented in court. Javier had been convicted of terrorism only because the President had said the Zapatistas were terrorists on television."

27. For an account of this high-profile campaign waged in the media by the Zapatistas, see ibid., 177.

28. Quoted in Weinberg 2000, 157.

29. For Elorriaga's arrest, trial, and release, see Ross 2000, 103–5, 114, 175–78.

30. Interview with Le Bot 1997, 218–21; quoted and translated in Womack 1999, 325.

31. Ross (2000, 191) lists some of the more illustrious attendees, including Uruguayan writer Eduard Galeano, Peruvian former guerrilla Hugo Blanco, Russian film producer Pavel Lungin, the rock group Rage Against the Machine, and French Latin American scholars Alain Touraine and Yvon Le Bot.

32. Ross 2000, 191. See also the words of another attendee: "We are here in our thousands. Mexico, Spain, France, Italy and Germany provide the largest groups. The U.S. delegation is unfortunately small, and smaller delegations have arrived from other European countries, Japan, and the rest of the Americas with a few from Oceania, Africa, Asia and the Caribbean. Our diversity is not just our continents and nations, or our gender (perhaps 40% women) or age (mostly young rather than veterans of the sixties), but our experience and ideas"; Midnight Notes Collective 2001, 46.

33. See Ronfeldt et al. 1998, 62: "The Zapatista movement writ large was a sprawling, swirling, amorphous collectivity—and in a sense, its indefinition was part of its strength." Similarly, Ross 2000, 191: "This indefinition was helpful to the Zapatistas. It made Zapatismo very plug-in-able all over the globe to fight local struggles."

34. The interview is reprinted in Autonomedia 1994, 289. See also Petras 1997, 40: "The indefinition of the EZLN leadership results in each group reading into the EZLN its own political concerns. For example, some French intellectuals praise the Zapatistas as the reincarnation of nineteenth-century republican citizens. Spanish anarchists see them in terms of Durruti's peasant armies."

35. From an interview with Le Bot 1997, 225–26; translated in Womack 1999, 325–26.
36. For the figure of $100 per day, see Bonner (1999, 154) drawing on *Mexico City Times* (19 August 1996).
37. On using donations from prestigious visitors for buying grain, see Ross 2000, 168, 205.
38. Rajchenberg and Héau-Lambert 1998, 20–21.
39. Alleged members of the EZLN seized during the government's February 1995 offensive in which it raided a bicycle repair shop in Yanga and found weapons and other incriminating evidence.
40. Human Rights Watch 1997, 93.
41. Human Rights Watch 1996, 3.
42. For some typical comments from Arturo, see Weinberg 2000, 280ff., esp. 299: "We do not consider that the state is invulnerable. We believe we can strike it and defeat it"; "We seek power. We won't carry on a dialogue with the murderous government"; and "Poetry cannot be the continuation of politics by other means."
43. Quoted in *La Jornada*, 3 September 1996.
44. See Ross 2000, 185: "By midsummer 1996, the press had turned its high beams on Guerrero. The *New York Times*, the *Washington Post*, and *Newsweek* all ran front-pagers, and the *Wall Street Journal* fretted about collateral damage to the stock market."
45. For a fuller history of the EPR and ERPI, see Weinberg 2000, 280–300.
46. Kampwirth 2002, 111, n. 23.
47. Quoted in Ross 2000, 200.
48. For a good summary of the COCOPA proposal, see Mattiace 2003b, 175–76, n. 13.
49. Ross 2000, 206. Kampwirth (1998, 17) also stresses that "the negotiating committee he [Zedillo] had assigned had drawn-up this latest version of the Accord itself."

27 A MARCH AND A MASSACRE

1. Posted on the Internet at http://flag.blackened.net/revolt/mexico/ezln/1997/ccri_why_reject_jan.html.
2. Posted on the Internet at http://flag.blackened.net/revolt/mexico/ezln/1997/ccri_response_gov_sa_jan.html.
3. Harvey 1998, 222–23.
4. Weinberg 2000, 164.
5. Ross 2000, 215.
6. Ibid., 210.
7. Quoted by Reuters, 23 January 1997.
8. Quoted in Aubry 2003, 222.

9. *La Jornada*, 4 March, 1997.

10. In the first two weeks of March land disputes took the lives of fifteen chiapanecos.

11. See Mattiace 2003a, 120: "In a public ceremony held in the ejido Plan de Ayala (Cañada Tojolabal) in 1988, leaders of the ejido union declared the formation of a regional government." (The *ejido* Plan de Ayala is located in what became Zapatista heartland, between Altamirano and Las Margaritas.) See also the introduction to Rus et al. (2003, 14): "The leaders of the RAP (Pluriethnic Autonomous Regions) movement are Tojolabal and Tzeltal Indians from Las Margaritas who have been working since the mid-1980s to develop regional governmental structures and to promote a pan-ethnic Indian identity in eastern Chiapas."

12. Quoted in Mattiace 2003b, 168, n. 2. Clearly Mattiace shares this view: "De facto autonomy was commonplace within Indian communities long before the Zapatista uprising . . . [but] the EZLN uprising provided a space for Indian and non-Indian activists and intellectuals to discuss and debate the issue of Indian rights and culture in Mexico" (21); and similarly at 89.

13. The state government had often shown its independence from the federal government, doing its utmost to oppose or negate centrally imposed measures it deemed inimical to its own interests. For this tension between the federal and state governments, see Mattiace 2003b, 125, 127, and Berger 2001, 162.

14. Oppenheimer 1996/1998, 327–28: "For the first time in recent memory, opposition parties won a majority, 261 seats, in the 500-seat lower house of Congress. . . . The PRI had won 239 seats, the centre-left PRD had won 125, the center-right PAN had 121, and other, smaller parties had 15."

15. Ibid., 328.

16. Ibid.

17. For an excessively negative assessment of this march see Ronfeldt et al. 1998, 87, and Castañeda 1996.

18. Human Rights Watch 1997.

19. See Ross 2000, 249.

20. See ibid., 235–38, for a catalogue of such acts.

21. See Collier and Quaratiello 1994/1999, 168, 172, esp. 191 n. 21; Hernández Castillo et al. 2001, 22–38; and Ross 2000, 239–50.

22. Oppenheimer 1996/1998, 335.

23. Quoted in Ross 2000, 246.

24. Bonner 1999, 159. Similarly, see G. Ramírez (2003, 150), who notes that "from 22 December 1997 (the day of the Acteal massacre) to the 13 January 1998 (a day after the assassination of Guadalupe Méndez, a member of the Zapatista support base), there had been mobilizations in 130 cities in 27 countries on five continents."

25. Ross 2000, 253–54.

26. Almost immediately after news of the massacre had been released the FZLN held a round-the-clock vigil in the center of Mexico City, at the Angel of Independence, collecting food and supplies for displaced Chiapan refugees, while a massive protest march wound its way through the capital, converging on the Zócalo on 12 January 1998.

27. The U.S. State Department, the Pope, the UN secretary general, France's prime minister, and the European Parliament all publicly condemned the Acteal massacre.

28 SPEEDY GONZALEZ BREAKS THE SILENCE

1. Quoted in Ross 2000, 231.
2. Womack 1999, 308.
3. Mattiace 2003b, 23.
4. For these comparisons, see Ross 2000, 264.
5. Aubry 2003, 241, n. 23.
6. Ross (2000, 264) notes this was a common refrain in television announcements produced by the Zedillo administration and aired on pro-government networks.
7. For example, to name but two, Pastors for Peace director Tom Hansen and French priest Michel Chanteau. For more details, see Chanteau 1999; Global Exchange 1999; Ross 2000, 257–61, 268f; and Weinberg 2000, 178–79.
8. Ronfeldt et al. 1998, 33.
9. Article 33 of the Mexican Constitution states that the executive branch of the government has the right to "force to leave national territory, immediately and without necessity of prior legal process, all foreigners whose stay in the country it deems undesirable." This contravenes, however, article 13 of the International Covenant on Civil and Political Rights (ratified 23 March 1981), article 22 (6) of the American Convention on Human Rights (ratified 24 March 1981), and the 1928 Convention on the Status of Foreigners (ratified 28 March 1931), all of which place emphasis on the due process that must be afforded to foreign nationals who have lawfully entered Mexico. See Human Rights Watch 1997, 20, esp. n. 14.
10. For more details, see Weinberg 2000, 179.
11. Burguete Cal y Mayor 2003, 218, n. 39.
12. Mattiace 2003b, 168, n. 1.
13. Quoted in Case 1998.
14. Ibid.
15. Weinberg 2000, 160–61.
16. Ross 2000, 280.
17. Weinberg 2000, 160–61.

18. Human Rights Watch Report 1999, 16.
19. See, for example, *Semana* 1998a, 6, entitled "¿Dónde está el subcomandante Marcos?"; and in the United States, the *New York Times* (1998) article entitled "Mexican Rebel Chief's 5-Month Silence Raises Doubts."
20. *Semana* 1998a, 6.
21. Ross 2000, 283. *Semana* (1998b, 8) called it an "enigmatic silence."
22. Quoted in Ross 2000, 294.
23. Ross (2000, 284) notes how "Speedy" had "achieved popular anti-hero status in Mexico in the 1970s"—a formative decade for Rafael Guillén. Both *Siempre!* (1998, 34) and *Semana* (1998b, 8) devoted an article to discussion of Marcos associating himself with Speedy Gonzalez.
24. Quoted in Ross 2000, 299.
25. Ross 2000, 293.
26. In 2005 the decision was given to grant Mexican nationals living abroad a postal vote for the coming 2006 election.

29 A CONSULTA, A STORY, AND A STRIKE

1. These figures derive from G. Ramírez 2003, 167.
2. Quoted in Ross 2000, 305.
3. Ibid.
4. *Guardian* 1999.
5. Ross 2000, 299.
6. Ibid., 306.
7. Communiqué posted on the Internet at http://www.ezln.org.documentos/ 1999/1990405a.es.htm.
8. "N.E.A. Couldn't Tell a Book by Its Cover," *New York Times*, 10 March 1999.
9. Quoted in Ross 2000, 308.
10. G. Ramírez 2003, 173.
11. Ibid., 175.
12. Ross 2000, 309.
13. See Marcos's closing speech at the National Encuentro in Defense of the Cultural Heritage (August 1999), translated in Hayden 2002, 293f.
14. Most notably, Ross 2000, 322.
15. Posted on the Internet at http://flag.blackened.net/revolt/mexico/ezln/ 1999/marcos_no_balkans_june99.html.
16. Posted on the Internet at http://flag.blackened.net/revolt/mexico/ezln/1999/ ccri_to_UN_july.html.
17. Ross 2000, 326.

1. In actual fact, the absence of a year zero in the Western calendar means that the third millennium began on 1 January 2001.
2. Kampwirth 2003, 233.
3. Human Rights Watch 1999, 5, 1. The report also singled out Jalisco, Morelos, Oaxaca, Tamaulipas, and Baja California for their nonpunishment of human rights abuses.
4. Bellinghausen 2000, 5.
5. See Oppenheimer 1996/1998, 67–68, 73. Demographics from the 1994 election had pointed to a future landslide. The Partido Acción Nacional (PAN, National Action Party) had won over many urbanites, the educated, the youth, and the private sector, each representing a rapidly expanding sector of Mexican society. Moreover, the fact that the PAN itself had always been seen as free from corruption, and that it had steadily built up its power base at the local level over many long years, made it an attractive prospect for many Mexican voters.
6. Kampwirth 2002, 84, n. 1. She continues: "Salazar, who like many opposition politicians in Mexico, had been a member of the PRI for most of his career (until 1999), was the first gubernatorial candidate from the opposition to ever be elected in the state of Chiapas." The coalition comprised eight opposition parties and won with 52 percent of the vote to the PRI's 46 percent, thus showing how determined an effort was required to wrest control of Chiapas from the PRI's hands.
7. That it was the Zapatistas themselves who had indeed largely helped achieve this aim is argued by Earle and Simonelli 2005, 276: "The PAN's victory was birthed in the Zapatista rebellion, in the courage to vote for change gained by the Mexican people because the indigenous and *campesinos* of Chiapas had the nerve to shout Basta!"
8. Collier and Collier 2003, 213.
9. Domby 2000. The article carries the subheading "The End Is Near for 'Marcos,' Whose Revolt Shook Mexico. Daniel Dombey Bids a Fond Farewell." The caption under a photograph of Marcos reads, "'Marcos' is facing consignment to history."
10. Quoted in Ross 2000, 324.
11. Sánchez Lira and Villarreal 1995, 229.
12. Ross 1995a, 331–32. Similarly, see Oppenheimer 1996/1998, 285–86.
13. Fuentes 1997, 77.
14. From Carmen Lira 1994, 1; translated in Oppenheimer 1996/1998, 49.
15. M. Benjamin 1995, 61.
16. In January 2003, Marcos, in a communiqué entitled "Durito on Trains and Pedestrians," tellingly wrote: "Durito says that in the dawn of the first of January of 1994 . . . a Zapatista indigenous put down his foot in order to

derail the all-powerful PRI train. Durito says that, 6 years later, the PRI was left lying in the bottom of the gully, and its remains are being fought over by those who yesterday mocked that indigenous who is, right now, carefully bandaging his foot, not because it hurts, but because he sees another train coming there, and another and another"; http://flag.blackened.net/revolt/mexico/ezln/2003/marcos/trainsJAN.html.

17. For example: "You chose, rather, the double strategy of feigning a willingness to dialogue and of continuing the path of violence. In order to achieve that, you tried to repeat the history of the Chinameca betrayal (February 9, 1995), you squandered thousands of millions of pesos trying to buy the consciences of the rebels. You militarized the indigenous communities (and not just in Chiapas). You expelled international observers. You trained, equipped, armed and financed paramilitaries. You persecuted, jailed and summarily executed Zapatistas (remember . . . June 10, 1998) and non-zapatistas. You destroyed the social fabric of the chiapaneco countryside. And, following the slogan of your putative child, the Red Mask paramilitary group ('We will kill the Zapatista seed'), you ordered the massacre of children and pregnant women in Acteal on December 22, 1997"; http://flag.blackened.net/revolt/mexico/ezln/2000/marcos_zedillo_nov.html.

18. For example: "Throughout this administration, your term of office has been a long nightmare for millions of Mexican men and women: assassinations, economic crises, massive impoverishment, the illicit and brutal enrichment of a few, the selling off of the national sovereignty, public insecurity, the strengthening of ties between the government and organized crime, corruption, irresponsibility, war . . . and bad jokes badly told"; ibid.

19. On Sunday 3 and Monday 4 December respectively.

20. Almost as soon as the Zapatistas appeared various journalists and academics have been predicting their imminent demise. In 1994 and 1995, following offensives by the Mexican Federal Army, many believed that Marcos and the EZLN would be annihilated militarily. When this failed to materialize, stagnation and public indifference were heralded as the bearers of their destruction. It is thus only to be expected that many viewed the PRI's defeat (and the PAN's victory) as sounding the Zapatistas's death knell.

21. E.g., Ross 2000; Vázquez Montalbán 2000.

22. E.g., Ponce de León 2001; Subcomandante Marcos 2001a and 2001b; Hayden 2002.

23. Collier in Foran 2003c, 213 notes that with the PRI ousted: "Now the Zapatistas have to regain the stage of support within Mexican society, which is probably why they're about to stage this march to Mexico City, the theatre that captures the popular imagination."

24. Ramonet 2002, 134.

25. Given that Fox had made much capital from this pledge on his way to the presidency, Marcos's sense of Schadenfreude possibly led him to enjoy see-

ing the president undergoing some uncomfortable moments on account of this boast.

26. Quoted in Ramonet 2002, 135.

31 THE ZAPATOUR

1. See Iliff (2001b), who quotes independent pollster Maria de las Heras as saying: "He is taking a risk, because he does not know how people in the cities are going to react."
2. Ibid.
3. Ibid.
4. The communiqué, dated 24 February, reads: "Fernando Yáñez Muñoz the architect . . . will be accompanying the zapatista delegation during their march to the federal district in the capacity of the EZLN's special guest"; http://flag.blackened.net/revolt/mexico/ezln/2001/ccri/yanez_feb.html.
5. Quoted in G. Ramírez 2003, 191.
6. Ibid.
7. Ramonet 2002, 135–36.
8. Ibid.
9. Ibid.
10. "La Mar" appears most in those communiqués that contain children's stories or scenes of domesticity. She can be found, in Subcomandante Marcos 2001b, 123, 126, 129, 156, 161, 164, 165, 167, 168, 174, 176, and 177, sleeping while romantic music plays quietly in the background; reading poetry by candlelight before falling asleep; listening to Marcos's stories by moonlight; carrying children on her shoulders; getting dressed by putting her shirt on over her head without undoing the buttons; exchanging meaningful looks with Marcos in silence; providing pencils for children to draw pictures; sleeping tight with Marcos in bed at night; being the "woman of the house"; playing "find-the-Sup" with a child on a Zapatista poster; hugging children, telling them stories, and combing the girls' hair; and generally joining in with the children's games.
11. Quoted and translated in Iliff 2001a. The identity of "La Mar" or "Mariana," however, remains uncertain. Most probably, she is the Mexican journalist Gloria Muñoz Ramírez, to whom Marcos recently has been romantically linked. She began her protracted stay in Chiapas in 1997, shortly after which time Marcos began writing of "La Mar"—the first reference to her appears in a communiqué dated Valentine's Day 1997. Certainly, Marcos's statement that Mariana "monitors the press for the rebel command" (Iliff 2001a) describes a role that would fit very well with the profile of Gloria Muñoz Ramírez.
12. Mitterrand 1996, 29–30.
13. In *Proceso*, no. 903, 21 February 1994, 7–15 (at 10), reprinted in Romero

1994, 38–41, and translated in Autonomedia 1994, 200. So, too, in Bardach (1994, 126), he states: "I think it was in the *Proceso* interview . . . I said that I didn't have a partner."

14. Iliff 2001a.

15. *Semana* (2001b, 7) notes that Marcos denies already having children, but quotes him as saying "le estamos echando muchas ganas para que pronto podamos tenerlo."

16. *Semana* (2001a, 10) published a story entitled "El subcomandante es papá," in which it quoted "un ex espía" who claimed "Marcos ya padre de un pequeño niño y además padeció hepatitis hace una semana."

17. Anderson 1992/1993, 230.

18. Quoted in Iliff 2001b.

19. Monsiváis 2002, 125.

20. Ibid., 125–26.

21. Ramonet 2002, 134.

22. *Washington Times* 2001.

23. G. Ramírez 2003, 193.

24. Monsiváis 2002, 130.

25. Quoted in ibid., 131.

26. Ibid., 132.

27. Ibid.

28. See Watson 2001; *San Francisco Chronicle* 2001; *Irish Times* 2001; and Buchanan 2001. Again, on Thursday, 8 March, the Zapatistas were featured on Japan's traditionally quite conservative NHK news at 10 P.M.

29. See, for example, the BBC's World Service Web page (Sunday 11 March, 23: 45 GMT), "Rebels Ride into Mexico City Centre": "Mexico's Zapatista guerrillas have arrived in triumph in the heart of the capital"; Fullerton 2001: "Zapatista rebel leader Subcommander Marcos made a triumphal entry to Mexico City's crowded main square on Sunday in the crowning moment of his journey"; Tricks 2001; Ignacio Ramonet (2002, 133): "Marcos made a triumphal entry into the Mexican capital."

30. Aridjis 2002, 142.

31. The claim of a lack of precedence, while strictly true, should perhaps be viewed rather as an attempt to avoid giving the world's media what it really wanted: the highly marketable photo opportunity of Marcos standing before the Chamber pleading his case.

32. Quoted in Ross 2002, 191.

33. In his speech to the people of Oventic (1 April 2001) reporting on the success of the Zapatour; http://flag.blackened.net/revolt/mexico/ezln/2001/march/report_back_marcos_apr1.html.

34. García Márquez and Pombo 2001, 71.

35. Ross 2002, 193.

36. García Márquez and Pombo 2001, 74.

37. Ross 2002, 193.

38. The vote was 220 in favor, 210 against.

39. Ross 2002, 193.

40. For the names of all the states (including those not voting), and which way they voted, see Mattiace 2003b, 177, n. 23.

41. Mattiace 2003b, 132. A more detailed discussion of the nature of these "controversies" and of the history behind them is found at 177, nn. 24–25.

32 MARCOS TODAY

1. See Earle and Simonelli (2005, 226f, 277) who describe a 22,000-strong Zapatista rally held in San Cristóbal on 1 January 2003. For continually updated information on Chiapas, see http://chiapas.mediosindependientes .org/. For the EZLN, see http://www.zeztainternazional.org/ and http:// enlacezapatista.ezln.org.mx/. For the FZLN, see http://www.fzln.org.mx/.

2. The magazine is posted on the Internet at http://www.revistarebeldia.org/.

3. Communiqués entitled "'No!' to the War in the Balkans" (June 1999); "No to War" (15 February 2003); and "The Attack on Iraq Is Just One Page in the Script of Terror" (April 2003); all posted at http://flag.blackened.net/revolt/ mexico/ezlnco.html.

4. See the following communiqués "The Basque Country: Paths" (7 December 2002) at http://flag.blackened.net/revolt/mexico/ezln/2002/marcos/ basqueDEC.html; and "I Shit on All the Revolutionary Vanguards of This Planet" (9–12 January 2003) at http://flag.blackened.net/revolt/mexico/ ezln/2003/marcos/etaJAN.html. So too, Earle and Simonelli (2005, 251): "International observers squabbled over the meaning of this harange, a diversionary tactic keeping the Zapatistas in international eyes while they hurried to complete the real work [of strengthening autonomy in local communities]."

5. In a series of communiqués throughout 2003 containing the names of successive Mexican states and the word "stele" in their title. They are translated and posted at http://flag.blackened.net/revolt/mexico/ezlnco.html.

6. Gillespie 1993, 195.

7. Translated into English by irlandesa and posted on the Internet at http:// www.ezln.org/documentos/2005/sexta1.en.htm. The declaration is signed in the name of the CCRI, but its style, I feel, betrays Marcos's authorship.

8. One such improvement is "the hospital Pedro: the first hope of the faceless ones," an autonomous clinic in rebel territory named in honor of the late Subcomandante Pedro.

9. In a 1995 interview given in the documentary video *Marcos: palabra y historia/Words and History*.

10. Reported in *USA Today*, "Zapatista Rebel Leader Jokes about Weight Gain,"

12 August 2005, at http://www.usatoday.com/news/world/2005-08-12-fatrebel-mexico_x.htm.

11. For example, "Look how all the politicians always have their nice houses and their nice cars and luxuries. And they still want us to thank them and to vote for them again. And it is obvious . . . that they are without shame. And they are without it because they do not, in fact, have a Patria, they only have bank accounts."

12. The following contain detailed accounts of these meetings' proceedings by those attending, including speeches by Marcos: http://www.narconews.com/Issue38/article1407.html; http://www.narconews.com/Issue38/article1416.html; http://www.narconews.com/Issue38/article1417.html; http://www.narconews.com/Issue39/article1447.html; and http://www.anarkismo.net/newswire.php?story_id=1190.

13. *Quien* 2005.

14. Danna Harman, "It Will All Be Made Clear in the Next Zapitista Memo," *Christian Science Monitor*, 2 August 2005; http://www.csmonitor.com/2005/0802/p01s04-woam.html. Harman cites a Latin America Intelligence Service Weekly Report (5 July 2005) as her source for the story; however, the report nowhere states that Ana María is no longer Marcos's spouse.

15. Posted at http://www.narconews.com/Issue39/article1454.html.

16. Brandon Sun Online, "Mexico's Zapatista Rebels' Spokesman Announces Plans for Nationwide Tour" (Saturday, 17 September 2005).

17. Interview with Alejandro Escalona 1997.

18. Quoted in Debray 2002, 348.

19. Landau 2002, 152.

20. Oppenheimer 2002, 52, 54. He both "questions . . . the sincerity of his [Marcos's] moderate, post-insurrection rhetoric" and labels him "a charismatic but marginal figure."

21. De la Grange and Rico 1998, 429. De la Grange and Rico then proceed (429–31) to blame Marcos for polarizing Chiapan society; causing a massive militarization of the state; bringing about a severe deterioration in the lives of indigenous people in the conflict zone; expelling dissidents and imposing terror in the EZLN-controlled areas; giving the Mexican army the excuse to increase both its budget and its interference in everyday life; aiding the PRI in its 1994 electoral victory by creating a climate of fear and chaos; and causing the paralysis of agricultural activity in and around the conflict zone due to fear of the military.

22. Quoted in Meyer 2002, 368.

1. See Debray (2002, 47) who writes that Marcos, "while still alive, has acquired a little of the kind of legend that posthumously hung around Che."
2. Gilly 1998, 312.
3. See Tello Díaz 1995/2001, 263: "Marcos had, from the start of the nineties, been a very enthusiastic promoter of computers. A considerable part of his expenses was dedicated concretely to buying the accessories and programs necessary to set-up Internet communication. He understood very well, in contrast to his comrades, above all the older ones, the possibilities offered by the telecommunications universe to the cause. From 1994 he exploited this with mastery."
4. Ross 2000, 196.
5. As Romero (1994, 17) puts it: "The new hero in the gallery of Latin American guerrillas." See also *Contenido* 2001, 54ff, which, although interesting, limits itself to providing an account of previous indigenous resistance movements in Mexico.
6. Ovetz 1994a.
7. See chapter 21 on the desire of Zapata and Marcos to court academics.
8. Castro was also interviewed by *Look* magazine (published 4 February 1958).
9. Castañeda 1994a, 92–93.
10. See the interview with Payeras (alias Comandante Benedicto) in Burbach and Flynn 1983, 63–67.
11. Castañeda 1994a, 92.
12. Ibid.: "His children's stories, published in Mexico in 1988, are a striking encounter of Indian folklore and children's fairy tales."
13. Villalobos 1989. Tellingly, the article was entitled "A Democratic Revolution for El Salvador," and in it he rejects dogmatism throughout, instead urging "flexibility" (116), and arguing for a fully participatory democracy "forged from above and below" (117–18).
14. Jonas 1991, 138.
15. Castañeda 1994a, 94.
16. Burbach and Flynn 1983, 95.
17. See Borge 1996, 81, and Zimmermann 2000/2004, 38, 45.
18. For these quotations concerning Fonseca, see Zimmermann 2000/2004, 6, 8.
19. For Guzmán, see Strong (1992); Palmer (1992); Castañeda (1994a, 119ff); and McClintock (1998, 261ff).
20. In Marcos's case it was smoking a pipe in a country where this is something of a rarity. In Guzmán's case it was smoking Winston Lights, the discovery of stubs of which in the garbage at one of the safe houses he frequented eventually led to his capture.

21. Sicilia (1997, 67) was one of the first to note the more profound similarities between Che and Marcos, writing that "Ambos son heroes románticos; ambos también tienen un exquisite y profundo sentido de la poesía."

22. See Landau 2002, 152: "Subcomandante Marcos . . . still belonged to the older Castro-Guevara tradition."

23. Anderson 1997, 753. Similarly, Jean Meyer (2002, 370) calls Marcos Che's "most recent reincarnation."

24. See Castañeda 1997, 192, where he notes "Che's indications regarding the ideal physical and psychological profile of the guerrilla fighter—down to the usefulness of smoking a pipe," adding, "nor could Che have foreseen that one of his later disciples, the Mexican rebel Subcomandante Marcos, would take the precept of the pipe to levels of international media fame that Guevara would never have imagined." (For Che's promotion of pipe smoking, see *Guerrilla Warfare* [1961/1998, 52]: "Pipes are useful because they permit using to the extreme all tobacco that remains in the butts of cigars and cigarettes at times of scarcity.")

25. For Che wearing two watches, see Anderson 1997, 723, 729, 742, and Ignacio Taibo II 1997, 570–72. For Marcos wearing two watches, see Oppenheimer 1996/1998, 64, and García Márquez and Pombo 2001, 75. De la Grange and Rico (1998, 193) note that both Che and Marcos wore two watches.

26. De la Grange and Rico (1998, 174) quote one source, "Tomás," as saying that when Marcos arrived in Chiapas he had told the *campesinos* that he had been a doctor, again like Che.

27. Le Bot 1997, 230–31.

28. Ibid., 230. See also Avilés and Minà 1998, 163–64, where Marcos similarly emphasizes Che's "gran formación cultural y fuertes convicciones morales."

29. Stavans 2002, 387.

30. Castañeda 1994a, 80.

31. From the communiqué entitled "We Are in Silence—And the Silence Is Not Being Broken" (September 2002); http://flag.blackened.net/revolt/mexico/ezln/2002/marcos/silenceSEPT.html.

32. In Burbach and Flynn 1983, 87.

33. Castañeda 1994a, 80.

34. See Ignacio Taibo 2002, 26: "In post-1968 Mexico, the forces of the new left opted to work for social organization among the masses. Thousands of students were mobilized by the union movement, the struggle in the slums, the slow work of assistance to *campesino* insurgent movements. A minority took up arms." Former UNAM student Stavans (2002, 393–94) writes of his (and Marcos's) generation that "friends would take time to travel to distant rural regions and live with the indigenous people. Most eventually returned, but many didn't—they simply vanished, adopting new identities and new lives."

35. Bardach (1994, 67) calls him "this unique creature"; and Bonner (1999, 154) writes that "Marcos is unique in many ways."
36. Castañeda 1995, 82, 85.
37. See Ignacio Taibo II (2002, 22) on Mexico's "Neanderthal Marxists."
38. Castañeda 1994a.

GLOSSARY

cacique	a leader/boss who controls social, political, and economic life at the local level. In this book, they are commonly associated with the PRI.
compa	abbreviated form of compañero
compañero	a word similar in political, military, and fraternal connotation to "comrade"
campesino	a peasant
cañada	a canyon
catechist	a Church lay worker
caudillo	a leader who uses strongman tactics
chiapaneco	an inhabitant of the state of Chiapas
Chol	one of Chiapas's many indigenous (Mayan) groups
consulta	a consensual decision-making process traditionally employed by village communities
dedazo	the "big fingerpoint"; a PRI ritual whereby the party's next presidential candidate is unveiled
ejiditario	a member of an ejido
ejido	communal agricultural lands that have been distributed through land reform
encuentro	a meeting
finca	a commercial farm
finquero	the owner of a finca
guardias blancas	White Guards or paramilitaries
jefe	a chief or leader
ladino	a Spanish-speaking non-Indian
latifundista	the owner of a latifundio (a large plantation)
Mams	one of Chiapas's many indigenous (Mayan) groups

mestizo	a person of mixed European-Indian ancestry (i.e., a non-indigenous Mexican)
municipio	municipality
palacio municipio	a town hall
pueblo	a village or hamlet
selva	tropical rain forest
sierra	a mountain range
Tojolabals	one of Chiapas's many indigenous (Mayan) groups
Tzeltals	one of Chiapas's many indigenous (Mayan) groups
Tzotzils	one of Chiapas's many indigenous (Mayan) groups
zócalo	central square or plaza in a town or city
Zoques	one of Chiapas's many indigenous groups

WORKS CITED

I have posted a comprehensive bibliography for *Subcommander Marcos: The Man and the Mask* on the Internet at http://www.angelfire.com/rebellion2/sub_marcos_bibliogra/Marcos_Bib/.

Abraham Guillen Press/Arm the Spirit. 2002. *A Commune in Chiapas: Mexico and the Zapatista Rebellion*. Montreal, Abraham Guillen Press; Toronto: Arm the Spirit.

Academia Mexicana de Derechos Humanos. 1994. *Special Bulletin Conflict in Chiapas*. Year 1, no. 8 (March 1–7). http://nativenet.uthscsa.edu/archive/nl/9404/0009.html.

Aceituno, Rafael. 1998. "Marcos: autoafirmación narcisista (Antonio Santamaría, siquiatra mexicano)." *Siempre!* 45, no. 2352 (16 July): 28–29.

Amnesty International. 1986. *Mexico: Human Rights in Rural Areas. Exchange of Documents with the Mexican Government on Human Rights Violations in Oaxaca and Chiapas*. London: Amnesty International.

———. 1991. *Mexico: Torture with Impunity*. London: Amnesty International.

———. 1994. *Amnesty International Delegation in Mexico Confirms Reports of Human Rights Violations during Chiapas Uprising*. AI Index: 41/WU 03/1994.

Anderson, Jon Lee. 1997. *Che Guevara: A Revolutionary Life*. London: Bantam.

———. 1992/1993. *Guerrillas*. London: Harper Collins.

Aridjis, Homero. 2002. "Indian Is Beautiful." In Hayden 2002, 142–45.

Asman, David. 1994. "Mexican Minefields." *Forbes Media Critic* (summer): 67.

Associated Press. 1995. "Zapatistas Celebrate Anniversary." *Dallas Morning News*, 2 January.

Aubry, Andrés. 2003. "Autonomy in the San Andrés Accords." In Rus, Castillo, and Mattiace 2003a, 219–41.

Autonomedia. 1994. *¡Zapatistas! Documents of the New Mexican Revolution*. New York: Autonomedia.

Avilés, Jaime, and Gianni Minà. 1998. *Marcos y la insurrección Zapatista*. Mexico City: Editorial Grijalbo.

Báez, René. 1998. *La disidencia en Disneylandia : el pensamiento político del Che Guevara, Agustín Cueva y el subcomandante Marcos: ensayo*. Quito, Ecuador: Eskeletra Editorial.

Bañuelos, Juan. 1995. "The Unfinished War." In Katzenberger 1995, 193–98.

Bardach, Ann Louise. 1994. "Mexico's Poet Rebel." *Vanity Fair* 57 (July): 68–74, 130–35.

Barkin, David, et al. 1997a. "Globalization and Resistance: The Remaking of Mexico." NACLA *Report on the Americas* 30, no. 4 (January/February): 14–27.

———, et al. 1997b. "Why the Recovery Is Not a Recovery." NACLA *Report on the Americas* 30, no. 4 (January/February 1997): 24–25.

Bartolomé, Efraín. 1995. "War Diary." In Katzenberger 1995, 5–28.

Bellinghausen, Hermann. 2000. "Hostilidad y prepotercia, Signos de la PFP en Chiapas." *La Jornada* (21 May): 5.

Benjamin, Medea. 1995. "Interview: Subcomandante Marcos." In Katzenberger 1995, 57–70.

Benjamin, Thomas. 1989/1996. *A Rich Land, A Poor People: Politics and Society in Modern Chiapas.* Albuquerque: University of New Mexico Press.

Berger, Mark T. 2001. "Romancing the Zapatistas: International Intellectuals and the Chiapas Rebellion." *Latin American Perspectives* 28, issue 117, no. 2 (March): 149–70.

Bonner, Arthur. 1999. *We Will Not Be Stopped.* New York: Universal Publishers.

Borge, Tomás. 1992. *The Patient Impatience.* Connecticut: Curbstone Press.

———. 1996. *Carlos, Now the Dawn's No Fond Illusion.* Translated by Dinah Livingstone. London: Katabasis.

Buchanan, Ronald. 2001. "Mexico Hails 'Rhinestone Rebel' on Peace Tour." *Telegraph,* 8 March, 15.

Burbach, Roger (interviewer), and Patricia Flynn (translator and editor). 1983. *Listen, Compañero.* California: Center for the Study of the Americas.

———. 2001. *Globalization and Postmodern Politics: From Zapatistas to High-Tech Robber Barons.* London: Pluto Press.

Burguete Cal y Mayor, Araceli. 2003. "The de Facto Autonomous Process." In Rus, Castillo, and Mattiace 2003a, 191–218.

Camín, Aguilar Héctor, and Lorenzo Meyer. 1993. *In the Shadow of the Mexican Revolution.* Austin: University of Texas Press.

Camp, Roderic Ai. 1995. *The Zedillo Cabinet: Continuity, Change or Revolution?* Washington, D.C.: Center for Strategic and International Studies.

Campa, Homero. 1994. "Castañeda: A New Threat of Violence." *World Press Review,* March.

Canadian Catholic Organization for Development and Peace. 1994. Press release, January. Montreal.

Cano, Arturo. 1994. "Lo más Delgado del hijo: Pronasol en Chiapas." *Reforma* (28 January): 3–7.

Carr, Barry, and Steve Ellner. 1993. *The Latin America Left: From the Fall of Allende to Perestroika.* Latin American Perspectives Series no. 11. Boulder: Westview Press.

Case, Brendan M. 1998. "Shootout May Intensify Chiapas Tension." *Dallas Morning News*, 14 June.

Castañeda, Jorge. 1994a. *Utopia Unarmed*. New York: Knopf.

———. 1994b. "The Chiapas Uprising." *Los Angeles Times*, 3 January.

———. 1995. *The Mexican Shock: Its Meaning for the United States*. New York: New Press.

———. 1996. "Chiapas War Ends in a Whimper." *Los Angeles Times*, 15 September.

———. 1997. *Compañero: The Life and Death of Che Guevara*. New York: Knopf.

Castells, Manuel. 1997. *The Power of Identity*. vol. 2 of *The Information Age: Economy, Society and Culture*. Oxford: Blackwell.

Castro, Yolanda. 1995. "Interview: Regional Union of Craftswomen of Chiapas." In Katzenberger 1995, 111–18.

Ceceña, Ana Esther, and Andrés Barreda. 1998. "Chiapas and the Global Restructuring of Capital." In Holloway and Peláez 1998, 39–63.

Centro de Derechos Humanos "Fray Bartolomé de las Casas." 1995a. *Informe preliminar de violaciones a los derechos humanos en Chiapas del 9 de febrero al 9 de abril de 1995*. Edited by Fray Bartolomé. San Cristóbal de las Casas.

———. 1995b. *Tortura: ¿Estado de Derecho?* Edited by Fray Bartolomé. San Cristóbal de las Casas.

———. 1996. *Ni paz ni justicia: Informe general y amplio acerca de la Guerra civil que sufren los choles en la zona norte de Chiapas*. Edited by Fray Bartolomé. San Cristóbal de las Casas.

Chanteau, Michel. 1999. *Las andanzas de Miguel: La autobiografía del padre expulsado de Chenalhó*. Edited by Fray Bartolomé. San Cristóbal de las Casas.

Chomsky, Noam. 1995. "Time Bombs." In Katzenberger 1995, 175–82.

Clarke, Ben, and Clifton Ross, eds. 1994/2000. *Voice of Fire: Communiqués and Interviews from the Zapatista National Liberation Army*. Revised edition. Berkeley: New Earth Publications.

Cleaver, Harry. 1998. "The Zapatistas and the Electronic Fabric of Struggle." In Holloway and Peláez 1998, 81–103.

Collier, George A., and Jane Collier. 2003. "The Zapatista Rebellion in the Context of Globalization." 242–52. In Foran 2003c.

Collier, George A., and Elizabeth L. Quaratiello. 1994/1999. *Basta! Land and Rebellion in Chiapas*. Revised edition. Oakland, Calif.: Food First Books, Institute for Food and Development Policy.

Contenido. 2001. "Los precursores de 'Marcos.'" 1 April, 54.

Coote, Belinda. 1995. NAFTA: *Poverty and Free Trade in Mexico*. Oxford: Oxfam.

Cornelius, Wayne, Ann L. Craig, and Jonathan Fox, eds. 1994. *Transforming State-Society Relations in Mexico: The National Solidarity Strategy*. U.S. Contemporary Perspectives Series no. 6. San Diego: University of California, San Diego, Center for U.S.-Mexican Studies.

Correa, Guillermo. 1996. "De la Grange, corresponsal de Le Monde: 'Con el veto en mi contra, Marcos se dio un tiro en la cabeza.'" Proceso, no. 1031 (4 August): 32–35.

Corro, Salvador. 1995. "Cesáreo Morales y Alberto Híjar evocan los años setenta, cuando se gustaba la insurrección." Proceso, no. 979 (7 August): 22–27.

Debray, Régis. 1967. Revolution in the Revolution? New York: Grove Press, Inc.

———. 2002. "A Guerrilla with a Difference." In Hayden 2002, 340–52.

de la Colina, José. 2002. "As Time Goes By: 'Marcos,' or The Mask Is the Message." In Hayden 2002, 363–67.

de la Grange, Bertrand, and Maite Rico. 1998. Subcomandante Marcos: la genial impostura. Mexico City: Aguilar.

———. 1999. "El otro subcomandante: Entrevista con Salvador Morales Garibay." Letras Libres, no. 2 (February): 76–83.

de la Vega, Miguel. 1998. "El silencio de Marcos vuelve aún más sombrío el ambiente en Chiapas." Proceso, no. 1129 (21 June): 6–11.

Delgado, Avaro. 1995. "Rafael Guillén, en la UAM-Xochimilco de los años 80: 'inteligencia filosa y certera,' 'humor privilegiado,' 'desmadrosos y chacotero.'" Proceso, no. 981 (21 August): 12–13, 16–19.

de Mora, Juan Miguel. 1995. Yo Acuso: A Los Gobiernos de Mexico y al EZLN! Edamex: Mexico City.

Del Muro, Ricardo. 1994. "Movimientos campesinos: la violenta lucha por la tierra." Macrópolis 98 (31 January): 16–23.

Dombey, Daniel. 2000. "Adiós Zapatistas." Weekend Financial Times (U.K.), 11 November, back page.

Durán de Huerta, Marta, compiler. 1994. Yo, Marcos. Mexico City: Milenio.

Earle, Duncan, and Jeanne Simonelli. 2005. Uprising of Hope: Sharing the Zapatista Journey to Alternative Development. Walnut Creek, Calif.: Altamira.

Eaton, Tracey. 1995. "Mexican Zapatistas' Threat Doubted: Despite Popularity, Some Question Rebels' Ability to Mobilize." Dallas Morning News, 19 February.

Eber, Christine. 2000. Women and Alcohol in a Highland Maya Town: Water of Hope, Water of Sorrow. 2nd edition. Austin: University of Texas Press.

———. 2003. "Buscando una nueva vida." In Rus, Castillo, and Mattiace 2003a, 135–59.

Economic Policy Institute. 1997. "The Failed Experiment: NAFTA at Three Years." 26 June. http://www.epi.org/content.cfm/studies_failedexp.

Economist (U.K.). 1996. "Latin America's Backlash." 30 November, 15–16, 19–21.

El Financiero. 1994. 8 August, 61.

Elorriaga Berdegué, Javier. 1997. "An Analysis of Evolving Zapatismo." In Motion Magazine January 6. Http://www.inmotionmagazine.com/chiapas1.html #anchor695207.

El Tiempo. 1994. 20 January, 3; 6 February, 3; and 11 February (a printing error means that this issue is dated 10 February), 3.

Escalona, Alejandro. 1997. "Carlos Fuentes: Novelist, Social Critic." *Chicago Tribune*, 3 August.

Esquire (U.K.) 1994. "On the Zapatista Trail." May. 72–78.

Esteva, Gustavo. 2003. "The Meaning and Scope of the Struggle for Autonomy." In Rus, Castillo, and Mattiace 2003a, 243–69.

EZLN (Ejército Zapatista de Liberación Nacional). 1985. *Reglamento insurgente.* Mexico City: EZLN.

———. 1994a. *La Palabra de los Armados de Verdad y Fuego: Entrevistas, Cartas y Comunicados del EZLN.* Mexico City: Editorial Fuenteovejuna.

———. 1994b. *Documentos y comunicados*, vol. 1. Mexico City: Ediciones Era.

———. 1995. *Documentos y comunicados*, vol. 2. Mexico City: Ediciones Era.

———. 1997. *Documentos y comunicados*, vol. 3. Mexico City: Ediciones Era.

Foran, John. 2003a. Introduction to Foran 2003c, 1–15.

———. 2003b. "Magical Realism: How Might the Revolutions of the Future Have Better End(ing)s?" In Foran 2003c, 271–83.

———, ed. 2003c. *The Future of Revolutions: Rethinking Radical Change in the Age of Globalization.* London: Zed Books.

Forbes, Jack D. 1995. "Native Intelligence: NAFTA Is Unconstitutional." In Katzenberger 1995, 183–88.

Foucault, Michel. 1984. "The Order of Discourse." In *Language and Politics*, edited by M. J. Shapiro. Oxford: Blackwell.

Fuentes, Carlos. 1970. *El tuerto es rey.* Edited by Joaquín Mortiz. Mexico City: Joaquín Mortiz.

———. 1994/1997. *A New Time for Mexico.* Berkeley: University of California Press.

Fuerzas de Liberación Nacional/Forces of National Liberation. 6 August 1980/ April 2003. *Estatutos de las Fuerzas de Liberación Nacional/Statutes of the Forces of National Liberation (FLN).* Toronto: Arm the Spirit/Mexico City: FLN.

Fullerton, Elizabeth. 2001. "Marcos Gets Rapturous Welcome in Mexico." *Reuters*, 11 March. Http://www.ainfos.ca/01/mar/ainfos00244.html.

Gane, M. 1983. "The ISAS Episode." *Economy and Society* 12 (4): 431–67.

García de León, Antonio. 1995. "Galloping into the Future." In Katzenberger 1995, 211–16.

García Márquez, Gabriel, and Roberto Pombo. 2001. "The Punch Card and the Hour Glass: Interview with *Subcomandante Marcos*." *New Left Review* 9 (May/ June): 69–79.

García Medrano, Renward. 1997. "No nos quiera tomar el pelo (la agenda política del *Subcomandante* Marcos, Rafael Sebastián Guillén Vicente)." *Siempre!* 43, no. 2283 (20 March): 18.

Gillespie, Richard. 1993. "Guerrilla Warfare in the 1980s." In Carr and Ellner 1993, 187–203.

Gilly, Adolfo. 1998. "Chiapas and the Rebellion of the Enchanted World." In Nugent 1998. 261–333.

————. 2002. "The Last Glow of the Mexican Revolution." In Hayden 2002, 323–40.

Gilly, Adolfo, Subcomandante Marcos, and Carlos Ginzburg. 1995. *Discusión sobre la historia*. Mexico City: Taurus.

Global Exchange. 1998. *On the Offensive: Intensified Military Occupation in Chiapas Six Months Since the Massacre at Acteal. Special Investigations Report*. San Francisco: Global Exchange. Http://www.globalexchange.org/countries/americas/mexico/OnTheOffensive.html.

————. 1999. *Foreigners of Conscience: The Mexican Government's Campaign Against International Human Rights Observers in Chiapas*. San Francisco: Global Exchange. Http://www.globalexchange.org/countries/americas/mexico/obervers/report/.

Golden, Tim. 1994. "The Voice of the Rebels Has Mexicans in His Spell." *New York Times*, 8 February.

————. 1995. "Mexico's New Offensive: Erasing Rebel's Mystique." *New York Times*, 11 February.

Gómez Peña, Guillermo. 1995. "The *Subcomandante* of Performance." In Katzenberger 1995, 89–96.

González, Mike. 2002. "The Zapatistas: The Challenges of Revolution in a New Millennium." In Hayden 2002, 430–51.

Goodwin, Jeff. 2001. "Is the Age of Revolutions Over?" In M. N. Katz 2001, 272–83.

Gosner, Kevin, and Arij Ouweneel, eds. 1996. *Indigenous Revolts in Chiapas and the Andean Highlands*. Amsterdam: CEDLA.

Gossen, Gary H. 1996. "Who Is the Comandante of *Subcomandante* Marcos?" In Gosner and Ouweneel 1996, 107–20.

————. 1999. *Telling Mayan Tales: Tzotzil Identities in Modern Mexico*. New York: Routledge.

Gotlieb, Stan. 1996. "New Kids on the Block." *Letters from Mexico* (Web site). Http://www.dreamagic.com/stan/index.html.

Gray, Chris Hables. 1997. *Postmodern War: The New Politics of Conflict*. New York: Guilford Press.

Greene, Graham. 1939/1981. *The Lawless Roads*. London: Penguin Books.

Group 2828. 1997. "Net—Which Net? Or, Our Collective Hammock. Or, the Net, Which Represents Us All. Or, Collectively We Are Stronger!" Http://www.eco.utexas.edu/homepages/faculty/Cleaver/wk1net.html.

Guardian (U.K.). 1999. "Millions Back Mexican Rebels in Referendum." 23 March.

Guevara, Ernesto "Che." 1996. *Episodes of the Cuban Revolutionary War 1956–7*. New York: Pathfinder Press.

————. 1994/1996. *The Bolivian Diary of Ernesto Che Guevara*. 2nd edition. New York: Pathfinder Press.

————. 1961/1998. *Guerrilla Warfare*. Nebraska: University of Nebraska Press.

Guillén Vicente, Rafael Sebastián. 1980 (October). *Filosofía y educación: prácticas discursivas y practícas ideológicas*. Tesis de licenciatura. Facultad de Filosofía y Letras. Mexico City: UNAM.

———. 1992. "El empresario del siglo XX y los retos de su circunstancia." *Ventas y Mercadotecnia*. Conferencia recogida por la revista de la Asociación de Ejecutivos de Ventas y Mercadotecnia de Tampico. 1st year, no. 4, April.

Guillermoprieto, Alma. 1994. "Zapata's Heirs." In Guillermoprieto 2002, 185–206.

———. 1995a. "The Unmasking." In Guillermoprieto 2002, 207–23; reprinted in Hayden 2002, 33–45.

———. 1995b. "Whodunnit?" In Guillermoprieto 2002, 239–54.

———. 1995c. "The Shadow War." *New York Review*, 2 March, 34–43.

———. 1996. "The Peso." In Guillermoprieto 2002, 275–85.

———. 2002. *Looking for History: Dispatches from Latin America*. New York: Vintage Books.

Haas, Antonio. 2001. "Marcos: Maestro de la teatralidad." *Siempre!* 47, no. 2491 (14 February): 37.

Halleck, Deedee. 1994. "Zapatistas On-Line." NACLA *Report on the Americas* 23, no. 2 (September/October): 30–32.

Harvey, Neil. 1994. *Rebellion in Chiapas: Rural Reforms, Campesino Radicalism, and the Limits to Salinismo*. No. 5 in the Transformation of Rural Mexico series. San Diego: University of California, Ejido Reform Research Project, Center for U.S.-Mexican Studies.

———. 1998. *The Chiapas Rebellion: The Struggle for Land and Democracy*. Durham: Duke University Press.

Hayden, Tom, ed. 2002. *The Zapatista Reader*. New York: Thunder's Mouth Press.

Hermosilla, Paulina, Hortensia Sierra, and Elizabeth Luis Díaz. 1995. "Testimonies." In Katzenberger 1995, 35–39.

Hernández Castillo, Rosalva Aída. 2001. *Histories and Stories from Chiapas: Border Identities in Southern Mexico*. Austin: University of Texas Press.

———. 2003. "Between Civil Disobedience and Silent Rejection." In Rus, Castillo, and Mattiace 2003a, 63–83.

Hernández Castillo, Rosalva Aída, Shannan Mattiace, and Jan Rus. 2001. "Before and After Acteal: Voices, Remembrances and Experiences from the Women of San Pedro Chenalhó." In *Other Word: Women and Violence in Chiapas Before and After Acteal*, edited by Rosalva Aída Hernández Castillo. Copenhagen: IWGIA, 22–38.

Hernández Navarro, Luis. 1994a. "The Chiapas Uprising." In Harvey 1994, 51–63.

———. 1994b. *La Jornada*, 15 September, 12.

———. 1998. "The Escalation of the War in Chiapas." NACLA *Report on the Americas* 31, no. 5 (March/April): 7–10.

Holloway, John. 1998. "Dignity's Revolt." In *Zapatista! Reinventing Revolution in Mexico*, edited by John Holloway and Eloína Peláez. London: Pluto Press, 159–98.

Holloway, John, and Eloína Peláez. 1998. "Introduction: Reinventing Revolution." In *Zapatista! Reinventing Revolution in Mexico*, edited by John Holloway and Eloína Peláez. London: Pluto Press, 1–18.

Huerta, Alberto. 1995. "Seeds of a Revolt." In Katzenberger 1995, 29–31.

Hughes, Sally. 1994a. "You Can't Eat Basketball Courts." *El Financiero International*, 24–30 January, 15.

———. 1994b. "Two Governors, Two Armies." *El Financiero International Edition*, 12–18 December, 1.

Human Rights Watch. 1990. *Human Rights in Mexico: A Policy of Impunity*. New York: Americas Watch Report.

———. 1991. *Unceasing Abuses: Human Rights in Mexico One Year After the Introduction of Reform*. New York: Americas Watch Report.

———1994. *Americas Watch Report*. Vol. 6, no. 3 (1 March).

———. 1994a. *Mexico: The New Year's Rebellion: Violations of Human Rights and Humanitarian Laws During the Armed Revolt in Chiapas, Mexico*. New York: Americas Watch Report.

———. 1994b. *Mexico at the Crossroads: Political Rights and the 1994 Presidential and the Congressional Election*. New York: Americas Watch Report.

———. 1995. *Mexico: Army Officer Held "Responsible" for Chiapas Massacre; Accused Found Dead at Defense Ministry*. New York: Americas Watch Report.

———. 1996. *Mexico: Torture and Other Abuses During the 1995 Crackdown on Alleged Zapatistas*. New York: Americas Watch Report.

———. 1997. *Implausible Deniability: State Responsibility for Rural Violence in Mexico*. New York: Americas Watch Report.

———. 1999. *Systematic Injustice: Torture, "Disappearance," and Extrajudicial Execution in Mexico*. New York: Americas Watch Report.

———. 2001. *Mexico: Military Injustice; Mexico's Failure to Punish Army Abuses*. New York: Americas Watch Report.

Ignacio Taibo II, Paco. 1997. *Guevara Also Known as Che*. Translated by Martin Michael Roberts. New York: St. Martin's Press.

———. 2002. "Zapatistas! The Phoenix Rises." In Hayden 2002, 21–30.

Iliff, Laurence. 2001a. "Rebels Romance Unmasked." *Dallas Morning News*, 15 February.

———. 2001b. "Zapatista Leader Launches March for Rights." *Dallas Morning News*, 25 February.

Iliff, Laurence, and Alfredo Corchado. 2004. "A Decade after Revolt, Zapatistas Strive for Autonomy." *Dallas Morning News*, 1 January.

Irish Times. 2001. "Cheers Greet Marcos and a Rattling Convoy of Rebels." 8 March.

Jonas, Suzanne. 1991. *The Battle for Guatemala: Rebels, Death Squads, and U.S. Power*. Boulder: Westview Press.

Joseph, Gilbert, and D. Nugent, eds. 1994. *Everyday Forms of State Formation: Revolution and the Negotiation of Rule in Modern Mexico*. Durham: Duke University Press.

Kampwirth, Karen. 1998. "Peace Talks, But No Peace." NACLA *Report on the Americas* 31, no. 5 (March/April): 15–19.

———. 2002. *Women and Guerrilla Movements: Nicaragua, El Salvador, Chiapas, Cuba*. Pennsylvania: Pennsylvania State University Press.

———. 2003. "Marching with the Taliban or Dancing with the Zapatistas? Revolution after the Cold War." In Foran 2003c, 227–41.

Kapuściński, R. 1992. *The Soccer War*. New York: Vintage.

Katz, Gregory, and Tracey Eaton. 1994. "Who Is That Masked Man?" *Dallas Morning News*, 7 February.

Katz, M. N. 1999. *Reflections on Revolution*. London: Macmillan.

———, ed. 2001. *Revolution: Internal Dimensions*. Washington, D.C.: Congressional Quarterly Press.

Katzenberger, Elaine, ed. 1995. *First World, Ha! Ha! Ha! The Zapatista Challenge*. San Francisco: City Lights.

Kincaid, Douglas. 1993. "Peasants into Rebels: Community and Class in Rural El Salvador." In *Constructing Culture and Power in Latin America*, edited by D. H. Levine. Ann Arbor: University of Michigan Press, 119–54.

King, Patricia, and Francisco Javier Villanueva. 1998. "Breaking the Blockade: The Move from Jungle to City." In Holloway and Peláez 1998, 104–25.

Klein, Naomi. 2002. "The Unknown Icon." In Hayden 2002, 114–23.

Krauze, Enrique. 1994. "Zapped: The Roots of the Chiapas Revolt." *New Republic*, 31 January.

———. 1997. *Mexico: Biography of Power*. New York: Harper Collins.

———. 2002. "Chiapas: The Indian's Prophet." In Hayden 2002, 395–417.

La Jornada. 1994a. *Chiapas El alzamiento*. Mexico City: La Jornada Ediciones.

———. 1994b. 13 June, 10.

———. 1994c. 31 August, 5.

———. 1996. 9 April, 12.

———. 1997. *Memorial de Chiapas*. Mexico City: La Jornada Libros.

———. 2001. *La caravana de la dignidad indígena: el otro jugador*. Mexico City: La Jornada Ediciones.

Labastida, Jaime. 1994. "Guerra de Propaganda." *Excelsior*, 20 January.

Landau, Saul. 1996. "In the Jungle with Marcos." Interview. *Progressive*, March, 25–30. Http://www.findarticles.com/p/articles/mi_m1295/is_n3_v60/ai_18049702.

———. 2002. "The Zapatista Army of National Liberation: Part of the Latin American Revolutionary Tradition—But Also Very Different." In Hayden 2002, 146–52.

Lang, Kirsty. 1996. "Mme Mitterrand in Jungle Tryst with Guerrilla Guru." *Sunday Times*, 7 July, 17.

Lawrence, Carl. 1999. *The Cross and the Sword: The Rebellion and Revolution in Chiapas, Mexico*. California: Shannon Publishers.

Le Bot, Yvon. 1997. *Subcomandante Marcos: El Sueño Zapatista: entrevistas con el subcomandante Marcos, el mayor Moisés y el comandante Tacho, del Ejército Zapatista de Liberación Nacional*. Mexico City: Playa y Janés.

Legorreta Díaz, Carmen. 1998. Religión, política y guerrilla en las Cañadas de la Selva Lacandona. Mexico City: Cal y Arena.

Leyva Solano, Xóchitl. 2003. "Regional, Communal, and Organizational Transformations in Las Cañadas." In Rus, Castillo, and Mattiace 2003a, 161–84.

Lira, Carmen. 1994. *"No Sería un Golpe Militar." La Jornada*, 25 August, 1.

López Vigil, José Ignacio. 1991. *Rebel Radio*. Translated by Mark Fried. London: Latin American Bureau; Willimantic, Conn.: Curbstone Press.

López y Rivas, Gilberto. 2000. *"Daniel*, de las filas del EZLN a las del Ejército." *La Jornada*, 25 March, 8.

Lorenzano, Luis. 1998. "Zapatismo: Recomposition of Labour, Radical Democracy and Revolutionary Project." In Holloway and Peláez 1998, 126–58.

MacEoin, Gary. 1996/2000. *The People's Church: Bishop Samuel Ruiz of Mexico and Why He Matters*. New York: Crossroad Publishing.

Majumdar, Margaret A. 1995. *Althusser and the End of Leninism?* London: Pluto Press.

Mancillas, Jorge. 2002. "The Twilight of the Revolutionaries?" In Hayden 2002, 153–65.

Markoff, John. 1997. "Really Existing Democracy: Learning From Latin America in the Late 1990s." *New Left Review* 223 (May/June): 48–68.

Marx, Karl. 1845. "Theses on Feuerbach." In *The Marx-Engels Reader*, 2nd ed. 1978. Edited by R. Tucker. New York: Norton, 145–47.

Mattiace, Shannan L. 2003a. "Regional Renegotiations of Space." In Rus, Castillo, and Mattiace 2003a, 109–33.

———. 2003b. *To See With Two Eyes*. Albuquerque: University of New Mexico Press.

McCaughan, Michael. 1995. "An Interview with *Subcomandante* Marcos." NACLA *Report on the Americas* 28, no. 1 (July/August): 35–37.

———. 2002. "King of the Jungle." In Hayden 2002, 72–75.

McClintock, Cynthia. 1998. *Revolutionary Movements in Latin America: El Salvador's FMLN and Peru's Shining Path*. Washington, D.C.: United States Institute of Peace.

McLynn, Frank. 2000. *Villa and Zapata: A History of the Mexican Revolution*. New York: Carroll and Graf.

Mergier, Anne Marie. 1995. "Los inicios de la UAM-Xochimilco, una experiencia inedita en la historia de la Universidad Mexicana: Raul Velasco Ugalde." *Proceso*, no. 981 (21 August): 14–15.

Meyer, Jean. 2002. "Once Again, the Noble Savage." In Hayden 2002, 367–72.

Midnight Notes Collective. 2001. *Auroras of the Zapatistas: Local and Global Struggles of the Fourth World War*. New York: Autonomedia.

Míguez, Alberto. 2001. "La verdadera historia del Dr. Guillén." *Epoca*, 11 March, 53.

Millán, Márgara. 1998. "Zapatista Indigenous Women." In Holloway and Peláez 1998, 64–80.

Minnesota Advocates for Human Rights. 1992. *Conquest Continued: Disregard for Human and Indigenous Rights in the Mexican State of Chiapas*. Minneapolis: Minnesota Advocates for Human Rights.

———. 1993. *Civilians at Risk: Military and Police Abuses in the Mexican Countryside*. Minneapolis: Minnesota Advocates for Human Rights.

———. 1994. *Codificando Represión: El Código Penal para el Estado de Chiapas*. December. Minneapolis: Minnesota Advocates for Human Rights.

Mitterrand, Danielle. 1996. *Ces hommes sont avant tout nos frères*. Paris: Éditions Ramsay.

Monsiváis, Carlos. 1996. "Fábula del país de Nopasando." *La Jornada Semanal*, 14 January, 9–11.

———. 1997. *Mexican Postcards*. Translated and with an introduction by J. Kraniauskas. London: Verso.

———. 2001. "Interview with *Subcomandante* Marcos." *La Jornada*, 8 January. Http://flag.blackened.net/revolt/mexico/ezln/2001/marcos_interview_jan .html.

———. 2002. "From the Subsoil to the Mask that Reveals." In Hayden 2002, 123–32.

Montalbán, Manuel Vázquez. 2000. *Marcos: El señor de los espejos*. Mexico City: Aguilar.

———. 2002. "Marcos: Mestizo Culture on the Move." In Hayden 2002, 472–83.

Montiel, Elsa. 1995a. "Living Conditions." In Katzenberger 1995, 33–34.

———. 1995b. "Land." In Katzenberger 1995, 131–32.

Moreno, Alejandra. 1996. *Turbulencia política. Causas y razones del 94*. Mexico City: Océano.

Nash, June C. 2001. *Mayan Visions*. New York: Routledge.

Newdick, Vivian. 1995. "Interview with Emiliano Zapata Campesino Organization." In Katzenberger 1995, 133–38.

Newsweek. 1994a. "Rage of the Zapatistas." 17 January, 30–33.

———. 1994b. "Let's Give Peace a Chance." 24 January, 28–29.

———. 1994c. "The Battle of the Soundbites." 7 February, 13.

———. 1994d. "The Marcos Mystique." 7 March, 25.

———. 1994e. "Keeping Ghosts at Bay." 14 March, 16.

New York Times. 1994a. 19 October, A6.

———. 1998. "Mexican Rebel Chief's 5-Month Silence Raises Doubts." 9 July.

Nodia, G. 2001. "The End of Revolution?" *Journal of Democracy* 11, no. 1 (January): 164–71.

Nugent, Daniel, ed. 1989/1998. *Rural Revolt in Mexico.* Expanded edition. Durham: Duke University Press.

Olesen, Thomas. 2004. "The Transnational Zapatista Solidarity Network: An Infrastructure Analysis." *Global Networks* 4: 89–107.

Oppenheimer, Andres. 1996/1998. *Bordering on Chaos.* Boston: Little, Brown.

———. 2002. "Guerrillas in the Mist." In Hayden 2002, 51–45.

Orwell, George. 1968/1994. "Shooting an Elephant." In *The Penguin Essays of George Orwell.* London: Penguin, 18–25.

Ouweneel, Arij. 1996. "Away from Prying Eyes: The Zapatistas Revolt of 1994." In Gosner and Ouweneel 1996, 79–106.

Ovetz, Robert. 1994a. "Interview (in English) with Subcommander Marcos (1 January)." Http://nativenet.uthscsa.edu/archive/nl/9401/0307.html.

———. 1994b. "They Came to Us." Http://nativenet.uthscsa.edu/archive/nl/9401/0305.html. Reprinted in *St. Cloud Unabridged* 8, no. 4 (January 2004): 8, 10–11.

Padgett, Tim. 1996. "The Return of Guerrilla Chic." *Newsweek,* 13 May, 14.

Palmer, David Scott. 1992. Introduction and conclusion to *Shining Path of Peru,* edited by David Scott Palmer. New York: St. Martin's Press.

Payeras, Mario. 1983. *Days of the Jungle: The Testimony of a Guatemalan Guerrillero, 1972–1976.* New York: Monthly Review Press.

Paz, Octavio. 1994. "El nudo de Chiapas." *La Jornada,* 6 January, 14.

———. 2002. "The Media Spectacle Comes to Mexico." In Hayden 2002, 30–33.

Pazos, Luis. 1994. *¿Porque Chiapas?* Mexico City: Editorial Diana.

Petras, James. 1997. "Latin America: The Resurgence of the Left." *New Left Review* 223 (May/June): 17–47.

Petrich, Blanche. 1995. "Voices from the Masks." In Katzenberger 1995, 41–54.

Pinchetti, Francisco Ortiz. 1995. "Los pasos de Rafael Guillén, 'El Mexicano,' por las montañas de Nicaragua, después del triunfo Sandinista." *Proceso,* no. 982 (28 August): 50–54.

Pizarro, Fernando Ortega. 1995. "Maestros y condiscípulos de Tampico recuerdan a Rafael Sebastián Guillén: inteligente, estudioso, culto, pero sobre todo, solidario," and "'La Raiz Oculta,' la revista que Rafael Sebastián Guillén dirigio en Tampico al final de la prepa." *Proceso,* no. 979 (7 August): 8–21.

Ponce de León, Juliana. 2001. *Our Word Is Our Weapon.* New York: Seven Stories Press.

Poniatowska, Elena. 1971/1994. *La noche de Tlatelolco.* Mexico City: Era.

———. 1995. "Women, Mexico, and Chiapas." In Katzenberger 1995, 99–107.

———. 2002a. "Women's Battle for Respect: Inch by Inch." In Hayden 2002, 55–57.

————. 2002b. "Voices from the Jungle: Subcommander Marcos and Culture." In Hayden 2002, 373–81.

Preston, Julia. 1999. "N.E.A. Couldn't Tell a Book by Its Cover." *New York Times*, 10 March.

Proceso. 1993. "Hay guerrilleros en Chiapas desde hace ocho años: grupos radicales infiltraron a la Iglesia y las comunidades." No. 880, 13 September, 12–15.

————. 1994a. "Guerra civil, si la Convención Democrática fracasa Zedillo, principal obstáculo para la paz: subcomandante Marcos." No. 926, 1 August, 6–13.

————. 1994b. "Un relato testimonial del Subcomandante Marcos." No. 927, 8 August, 60–62.

————. 1994c. "No permitiremos un gobierno que no sea el nuestro," advierte Marcos. No. 937, 17 October, 38–40.

————. 1994d. "'No podemos dialogar con los asesinos de Colosio y Ruiz Massieu; nos estamos preparando para la guerra': Marcos," No. 938, 24 October, 15.

————. 1995a. "Sea o no su hijo, El *subcomandante Marcos* ha revitalizado a Alfonso Guillén: 'camino mas aprisa, escribo mas rapido, las ideas me vuenen solas.'" No. 959, 20 March, 22–23.

————. 1995b. "De cómo el EZLN se organize, se armó y decidió iniciar en Chiapas la Guerra de liberación." No. 976, 17 July, 6–11.

————. 1996. "'Benigno' precisa: entrené guerrilleros mexicanos en 1971 y 1972; a Marcos lo conocíen México." No. 1018, 6 May, 44–51.

Puebla, Teté. 2003. *Marianas in Combat.* New York: Pathfinder Press.

Quien. 2005. "Marcos vive una intensa historia de amor." No. 99, 16 September, 40–50.

Rajchenberg, Enrique, and Catherine Héau-Lambert. 1998. "History and Symbolism in the Zapatista Movement." In Holloway and Peláez 1998, 19–38.

Ramírez, Jesus. 1997. "Rebel Leader *Marcos* says 'Che Lives On' in Mexico." *Reuters*, 28 August. Http://www.eco.utexas.edu/~archive/chiapas95/1997.08/msg00376.html.

Ramírez, Gloria Muñoz. 2003. *EZLN: 20 y 10 el fuego y la palabra.* Mexico City: Rebeldía//La Jornada Ediciones.

Ramonet, Ignacio. 2002. "*Marcos* Marches on Mexico City." In Hayden 2002, 133–41.

Reavis, Dick J. 1994. "Chiapas Is Mexico." *Progressive*, no. 5 (May): 28–33.

Reforma. 1994. "Lo más delgado del hilo: PRONASOL en Chiapas." 23 January, 3–7.

Rejai, Mostafa, and Kay Phillips. 1983. *World Revolutionary Leaders.* London: Frances Pinter.

Reuters. 1995. "U.S. Lawmakers Condemn Force in Chiapas." 14 February. Http://www.eco.utexas.edu/~archive/chiapas95/1995.02/msg00181.html.

Robberson, Tod. 1995. "Mexican Rebels Using a High-Tech Weapon: Internet Helps Rally Support." *Washington Post*, 20 February, A1.

Romero Jacobo, César. 1994. *Marcos: ¿un profesional de la esperanza?* Mexico City: Planeta.

Ronfeldt, David F., John Arquilla, Graham E. Fuller, and Melissa Fuller. 1998. *The Zapatista "Social Netwar" in Mexico.* Santa Monica: RAND.

Rosenthal, Eric. 1993. *Civilians at Risk: Military and Police Abuses in the Mexican Countryside.* North America Project Special Report no. 6. Minnesota Advocates for Human Rights and World Policy Institute, August.

Ross, John. 1995a. *Rebellion from the Roots: Indian Uprising in Chiapas.* Monroe: Common Courage Press.

—. 1995b. "Who Are They, What Do They Want?" In Katzenberger 1995, 81–88.

—. 1996. "Is Zapatista Rebellion Rooted in Oil?" *Earth Island Journal* 11, no. 2 (spring). Http://www.earthisland.org/eijournal/new_articles.cfm?article ID=387&journalID=59.

—. 1997. "Zapata's Children: Defending the Land and Human Rights in the Countryside." *NACLA Report on the Americas* 30, no. 4 (January/February): 30–32, 34–35.

—. 2000. *The War Against Oblivion: the Zapatista Chronicles 1994–2000.* Monroe, Maine: Common Courage Press.

—. 2002. "The Story of the Boot and the Chessboard." In Hayden 2002, 190–94.

Rosset, P. 1994. "Insurgent Mexico and the Global South." *Food First News and Views,* May. Newsletter of the Institute for Food and Development Policy.

Rovira, Guiomar. 1994. *¡Zapata Vive! La rebelión indígena de Chiapas contada por sus protagonistas.* Barcelona: Virus Editorial.

—. 2002. "Of Love, Marriage, Children, and War." In Hayden 2002, 452–71.

Rubin, Jeffrey W. 1994. "Indigenous Autonomy and Power in Chiapas: Lessons from Mobilization in Juchitán." In Harvey 1994, 64–69.

Rus, Jan, Rosalva Aída Hernández Castillo, and Shannan L. Mattiace, eds. 2003. *Mayan Lives, Mayan Utopias.* Maryland: Rowman and Littlefield Publishers.

Rus, Jan, and George A. Collier. 2003. "A Generation of Crisis in the Central Highlands of Chiapas." In Rus, Castillo, and Mattiace 2003, 33–61.

Russell, Philip L. 1994. *Mexico under Salinas.* Austin: Mexico Resource Center.

—. 1995. *The Chiapas Rebellion.* Austin: Mexican Resource Center.

Salmon, Catherine A., and Martin Daly. 1998. "Birth Order and Familial Sentiment: Middleborns are Different." *Evolution and Human Behavior* 19: 299–312.

San Francisco Chronicle. 2001. "Subcommander Marcos' Caravan Is Winning Hearts and Minds across Mexico." 8 March.

Sánchez Lira, Mongo and Rogelio Villareal. 1995. "Mexico 1994: The Ruins of the Future." In Katzenberger 1995, 223–34.

Selbin, Eric. 2001. "Same as It Ever Was: The Future of Revolution at the End of the Century." In M. N. Katz 2001, 284–98.

Semana. 1998a. "¿Dónde está el *subcomandante Marcos?*" Vol. 5, no. 281 (9 July): 6.

———. 1998b. "'Marcos' se cree 'Speedy González.'" Vol. 5, no. 283 (23 July): 8.

———. 2001a. "El *subcomandante Marcos* es papa." Vol. 7, no. 412 (19 January): 10.

———. 2001b. "La leyenda del *subcomandante Marcos.*" Vol. 7, no. 418 (2 March): 7.

Sereseres, C. 1985. "The Highlands War in Guatemala." In *Latin American Insurgences,* edited by G. Fauriol. Washington, D.C.: Georgetown University Center for Strategic and International Studies, 97–130.

Serrill, Michael S. 1995. "Unmasking Marcos." *Time Magazine,* 20 February, 32.

Sicilia, Javier. 1997. "El Che y Marcos." *Siempre!* 44, no. 2317 (13 November): 67.

Siempre! 1998. "El Subspeedy." 1998. Vol. 45, no. 2353 (23 July): 34.

———. 2001. "Marcos se cree Jesucristo." Vol. 47, no. 2492 (21 March): 6.

Simon, Joel. 2002. "The Marcos Mystery: A Chat with the Subcommander of Spin." In Hayden 2002, 45–47.

Snyder, R. S. 1999. "The End of Revolution?" *Review of Politics* 61, no. 1 (winter): 5–28.

Stavans, Ilan. 2002. "Unmasking Marcos." In Hayden 2002, 386–95.

Stephen, Lynn. 2002. *Zapata Lives! Histories and Cultural Politics in Southern Mexico.* Berkeley: University of California Press.

Stephenson, James. 1995. *The 1994 Zapatista Rebellion in Southern Mexico: An Analysis and Assessment.* Strategic and Combat Studies Institute, *The Occasional,* no. 12.

Strong, Simon. 1992. *Shining Path.* London: Harper Collins.

Subcomandante Marcos. 1992. *The South East in Two Winds.* (August). In Autonomedia 1994; Clarke and Ross 1994/2000; and Subcomandante Marcos 1995a.

———. 1994. Epigmenio Ibarra. "Interview with Subcomandante Insurgente Marcos." *La Jornada,* 9 December, 12–13." Http://www.ezln.org/entrevistas/19941209.en.htm.

———. 1995a. *Shadows of a Tender Fury: The Communiqués of Subcomandante Marcos and the EZLN.* New York: Monthly Review Press.

———. 1995b. "Carta a Adolfo Gilly." (22 October 1994). In Gilly, Marcos, and Ginzburg 1995.

———. 1995c. "Historia de Marcos y de los hombres de la noche." Interview with Carmen Castillo and Tessa Brisac. (24 October 1994). In Gilly, Marcos, and Ginzburg 1995, 131–42.

———. 1996. "The Reality." Excerpt from an address by Subcommander Marcos at the Inauguration Ceremony of the American Preparatory Meeting for the Intercontinental Encounter for Humanity and Against Neoliberalism. *Canadian Dimension* 30, no. 4 (1 July): 31–32.

———. 1999a. *The Story of Colors/La Historia de los Colores.* El Paso: Cinco Puntos Press.

———. 1999b. *Desde las Montañas del Sureste Mexicano.* Mexico City: Plaza y Janes.

———. 1999c. *Conversations with Durito.* AZ Editorial Collective.

———. 2001a. *Questions and Swords.* El Paso: Cinco Puntos Press.

———. 2001b. *Zapatista Stories.* Translated by Dinah Livingstone. London: Katabasis Press.

———. 2001c. "Marcos: Hope for a New Dawn in Chiapas." (Letter from *Subcomandante Marcos,* Zapatista Army of National Liberation to President Vicente Fox, Mexico). *Multinational Monitor* 22, no. 3 (1 March): 23.

Suchlicki, Jaime. 1996/2000. *Mexico: From Montezuma to NAFTA, Chiapas and Beyond.* 2nd edition. Washington: Brassey's.

Sulloway, Frank J. 1996/1997. *Born to Rebel: Birth Order, Family Dynamics, and Creative Lives.* New York: Vintage Books.

Tangeman, Michael. 1995. *Mexico at the Crossroads.* New York: Orbis Books.

Tello Díaz, Carlos. 1995/2001. *La rebelión de las Cañadas.* Segunda reimpresión corregia y aumentada. Mexico City: Ediciones Cal y Arena.

Time. 1994a. "Zapata's Revenge." 17 January, 20–22.

———. 1994b. "Strategic Retreat." 24 January, 28.

———. 1994c. "The Angry Youths behind the Masks." 7 February, 34–35.

———. 1994d. "Compromise Triumphs." 14 March, 29.

Tostón, Munda. 1995. "Overheard in the Marketplace." In Katzenberger 1995, 1–3.

Tricks, Henry. 2001. "*Marcos* Arrives to a Hero's Welcome." *Financial Times* (U.K.), 11 March.

Turok, Antonio. 1998. *Chiapas: The End of Silence/Chiapas: el fin de silencio.* Mexico City: Aperture Foundation.

Urbina Nandayapa, Arturo de Jesús. 1994. *Las razones de Chiapas.* Mexico City: Editorial PAC.

Van Cott, Donna Lee. 1996. "Defiant Again: Indigenous Peoples and Latin American Security." *McNair Paper* no. 53 (October). The Institute for National Strategic Studies and the National Defense University. Http://www.ndu.edu/inss/McNair/mcnair53/ mcnair53/mcnair53.pdf.

Vázquez Aguirre, David. 1994. "Algunas causas que explican el levantamiento armado en Chiapas." *El Cotidiano* 61 (March-April): 26–31.

Villalobos, Joaquín. 1989. "A Democratic Revolution for El Salvador." *Foreign Policy* 74: 103–22.

Vincent, I. 1996. "Rebel Dispatches Find Home on Net." *Globe and Mail* (Toronto), 11 June, 1.

Vodovnik, Žiga, ed. 2004. *¡Ya Basta!: Ten Years of the Zapatista Uprising.* San Francisco: A. K. Press.

Volman, Dennis. 1985. "Policies on Central American Issues Change." *Christian Science Monitor*, 31 October.

Washington Times. 2001. "Rebels Arrive." 12 March.

Watson, Julie. 2001. "Rebel Marcos Is Very Marketable." *Associated Press*, 28 February. Http://mailman.lbo-talk.org/2001/2001-February/003840.html.

Watson, Russell. 1995. "When Words Are the Best Weapon: Information Can Undermine Dictatorships, and the Faster It Flows, the More Trouble They're in. How Rebels Use the Internet and Satellite TV." *Newsweek*, 27 February, 36–40.

Weinberg, Bill. 2000. *Homage to Chiapas*. London: Verso.

Weller, Worth H. 2000. *Conflict in Chiapas: Understanding the Modern Mayan World*. North Manchester, Ind.: DeWitt Books.

Womack, J. 1999. *Rebellion in Chiapas*. New York: New Press.

Wray, S. 1997. "Looking for Ideas on Networks in Encuentro Documents." July. Http://www.thing.net/~rdom/ecd/looking.html.

Zaid, Gabriel. 1994. "Chiapas: la guerrilla posmoderna." *Claves*, no. 44 (July/August): 22–34.

Zimmermann, Matilde. 2000/2004. *Sandinista: Carlos Fonseca and the Nicaraguan Revolution*. Durham: Duke University Press.

USEFUL WEBSITES

http://flag.blackened.net/revolt/mexico/ezlnco.html. *An almost comprehensive translation of EZLN communiqués (1994–2005) into English.*

http://palabra.ezln.org.mx/. *An almost comprehensive posting of EZLN communiqués (1994–2005) in their original Spanish.*

http://www.ezln.org.mx/. *An unofficial EZLN Web page containing communiqués, interviews, news, etc.*

http://www.revistarebeldia.org/html/. *An EZLN magazine edited by leading former FLN, EZLN, and FZLN members.*

http://zeztainternazional.ezln.org.mx. *The EZLN's International Intergalactic Commission Web page.*

http://enlacezapatista.ezln.org.mx/. *Commission on the 6th Declaration of the Lacandón Jungle (with photographs and updates on* La Otra Campaña, *2006).*

http://www.radioinsurgente.org/. *The EZLN's Radio Insurgente.*

http://www.fzln.org.mx/. *Official home page of the FZLN.*

http://www.zapatistas.org/Links/links.html. *Directory of Zapatista-related Web pages.*

http://chiapas.mediosindependientes.org/. *Chiapas Independent Media Centre, for continually updated news, essays, photographs, and interviews related to Chiapas.*

http://www.narconews.com/otroperiodismo/. *Narco News (independent media coverage of* La Otra Campaña*).*

http://www.jornada.unam.mx/. La Jornada, *Mexican daily newspaper.*

http://www.proceso.com.mx/. Proceso, *leading weekly Mexican news magazine.*

http://www.nacla.org. NACLA, *North American Congress on Latin America.*

http://www.ezlnaldf.org/index.php. *Coverage of the 2001 "Zapatour."*

http://www.letraslibres.com. Letras Libres, *Mexican monthly magazine.*

http://www.inegi.gob.mex/inegi/default.asp. *Mexico's National Institute of Statistics, Geography and Information: 2000 Census and Housing.*

https://www.cia.gov/cia/publications/factbook/geos/mx.html. CIA World Factbook 2006: Mexico.

VIDEOS

Pictures from a Revolution: A Memoir of the Nicaraguan Conflict, by Susan Meiselas. GMR Films, 1991.

La Guerra de Chiapas, by Carlos Mendoza. Canal 6 de Julio, 1994.

Marcos, Marcos, by Oscar Mendez. Cine y Video Independiente, 1994.

Todos Somos Marcos. Canal 6 de Julio, 1994.

Viaje al centro de la selva: memorial Zapatista, enero-agosto 1994. Directed by Epigmeno Ibarra. Argos, 1994.

Marcos: historia y palabras / History and Words, by Cristian Calonico. Producciones Marca Diablo, 1995.

Chiapas, the unfinished story, by Cristian Calonico. Producciones Marca Diablo, 1995.

Zapatista Women. Abraham Guillen Press, 1995.

"Paz con justicia y dignidad para los pueblos Indios." Testimonios: Comandante Tacho y Major Moisés. Documentos de La Selva Lacandona III, vol. 1, parts 1 and 2a, by Rocio Reza. Medios del Sur, 1995.

El Sexto Sol: Rebelión Maya en Chiapas, by Saul Landau. Meridian Productions, 1997.

A Place Called Chiapas, by Nettie Wild. New Yorker Video, 1998.

Zapatista. Big Noise Films, 1998. The DVD version has a bonus Marcos interview.

Chiapas: la Guerra y la paz. Mexico Nuevo Siglo, 2001.

Storm from the Mountain. Big Noise Films, 2001.

EZLN: 20 y 10, el fuego y la palabra. Revista Rebeldía, 2003.

INDEX

Birth order, 15–17
Birth rate, 131
Bolivia, 27–28, 82, 113, 173, 234, 236, 289, 300, 305
Borge, Tomás, 26, 75, 109–10
Bosnia, 264, 307
Bravo, Douglas, 309

Cacalomacán, 282–83, 314
Caciques, 60, 95, 223, 252
Camacho Solís, Manuel, 77, 219, 250, 252, 267
Cama de Nubes Camp, 96, 159
Camín, Héctor Aguilar, 4, 106, 111
Cárdenas, Cuauhtémoc, 49, 114, 264, 273, 278–80, 304, 318
Cárdenas, Lazaro (president), 338
Carlos, Doctor (a.k.a. Gabriel Ramírez), 32, 40, 110, 117, 168–69
Carranza, Venustiano, 215, 247, 250
Casariego, Rocío (a.k.a. Mercedes), 32, 34, 40, 48, 117, 168–69
Castellanos Domínguez, Absalón, 60–62, 95, 111, 121, 248–49
Castro, Fidel, 13, 16, 25, 31, 33, 45, 85, 146, 229–30, 263, 273, 288
Catechists, 117, 119–21, 177
Catholic Church, 21, 62, 109, 117, 119, 120, 124, 228, 287
CCRI (Comité Clandestino de Revolución Indígena), 135, 152, 155, 163–65, 169, 171, 198, 271, 294, 301, 316, 328
CDLI (Comité de Defensa de las Libertades Indígenas), 142, 149
CEOIC (Consejo Estatal de Organizaciones Indígenas y Campesinas), 256, 268–69
Certificados de inafectabilidad, 61
Cervantes, Miguel de, 18, 21, 22, 237
César, Major, 135, 161, 168–69
Chamber of Deputies, 146, 179, 248, 318, 350

Chamber of Senators, 179
Chamula, 161, 178, 252
Chase Manhattan Bank, 276
Chenalhó, 216, 319
Chiapa de Corzo, 131, 185
Chiapas, 1, 2, 7, 8, 13, 21–22, 26, 34, 44, 48, 49, 51, parts 2–3 *passim*
Chicanos, 51, 104, 259, 309
Chihuahua, 117, 122, 186, 221, 226
Chile, 8, 45, 59, 113, 129
China, 125, 129, 231
Chinameca, 247
Cholera, 101, 133, 223
Chols, 82–83, 185, 217, 226, 270, 272
Chomsky, Noam, 182, 284
CIA (Central Intelligence Agency), 141
CIOAC (Central Independiente de Obreros Agrícolas y Campesinos), 393
Civic Alliance, 265, 294, 437–38 n. 12
Civil Society, 87, 188, 216, 220, 222, 225, 250, 253–61, 262, 265, 269, 274, 278–80, 284, 286, 291, 296–98, 301–2, 319–20, 326, 328, 333, 337, 347, 354, 355, 358
Clinton, William J. (president), 218, 276
CNC (Confederacíon Nacional Campesina), 61, 297
CND (Convencíon National Democrática), 88, 114, 257–58, 280, 291, 293–94, 301
CNN (Cable News Network), 213
COCOPA (Comisión de Concordia y Pacificación), 200, 290–91, 296–300, 302, 304, 307–8, 313–15, 322, 326–28, 341, 351–52
Coffee, 62, 85, 122, 126–27, 131, 223, 297, 320
Cold War, 5, 10
Colombia, 88, 119, 129, 158, 220, 234, 300, 340
Colosio, Luis Donaldo, 197, 253–54, 264, 266, 272, 302

FLN (Fuerzas de Liberación Nacional): anniversaries of, 72, 114–16, 128, 179–80, 186, 257, 402; Central Committee of, 163, 167; Cuba and, 40, 89; Declaracion de Principios del Partido of, 163; El Salvador and, 88–89; Las Escuelas de Cuadros (Schools for Cadres) of, 117; First Worker-Peasant Meeting of, 88; Monterrey network of, 51–52, 80; National Directive and, 163, 167, 410 n. 5; origins of, 44–45, 66, 72–73, 82, 115–16, 385–87, 402 n. 1; political bureau of, 51–52, 238; publications of, 38, 44, 67, 86, 98, 114, 117, 167, 186, 270, 380, 386; recruitment for, 30, 38, 44, 158, 167; safe houses of, 38, 50, 65, 68, 85, 115, 117, 150, 168–69, 282–83, 305; statutes of, 72, 167, 173, 199, 201; UAM and, 38, 44, 168; UNAM and, 38, 44, 168; University of Nuevo León connection of, 44; various fronts (e.g., "Central," "Villa") of, 50, 66, 69, 90, 149, 158, 167–68, 186–87. See also EZLN

Flores Magón (ejido), 323

FMLN (Frente Farabundo Martí de Liberación Nacional), 58, 79, 88, 100, 118, 125, 129, 146–47, 185, 188, 197, 217, 233–34, 363–64, 367

Foco, 4, 13, 57, 62, 66–67, 76, 79–80, 82, 84, 89–91, 107–8, 135, 138, 190, 363, 366

Fonseca, Carlos, 26, 36–37, 109, 234, 364–65

Foucault, Michel, 33, 36, 45, 230, 306

Fox, Vicente (president), 304, 340, 342–44, 348, 350, 353

Frank, 65–66, 77, 108, 139, 159–61, 167

Fray Bartolomé de las Casas Center for Human Rights, 122, 170, 182, 214, 291, 324

FSLN (Frente Sandinista de Liberación Nacional), 26, 39–42, 45, 100, 109–11, 129, 164, 197, 232–34, 303, 317, 364, 366

Fuentes, Carlos, 5, 18, 24, 233, 236, 276, 339, 359

FZLN (Frente Zapatista de Liberación Nacional), 150, 301, 308, 319, 321, 353

Gabino Barreda Award, 37, 364

Gabriela, 43–45, 69, 78, 89, 167–69, 174

Galeano, Eduardo, 236

Gallardo Rodríguez, José Francisco (general), 182

Gálvez, Andulio, 84, 87

García Márquez, Gabriel, 8, 18, 286, 349–50

Germán (comandante), 39–40, 44, 65–69, 75, 78–79, 82, 85, 88–92, 97–98, 102–3, 105, 108–9, 114, 116–17, 124, 130, 137, 139, 157–59, 163, 167–69, 173, 175, 186, 191, 199–201, 238, 271, 282, 290, 294, 299, 309, 342, 353

Gilly, Adolfo, 116, 156, 237, 334, 361

Global Exchange, 323, 339

Globalization, 1, 10, 145, 231, 235, 326, 359

Gómez, Abelardo, 175–76

Gómez, Francisco. See Hugo

González Garrido, Patrocinio (governor), 60–61, 121–22, 125–27, 139, 176–79

Gramsci, Antonio, 34

Greene, Graham, 58

Grenada, 45, 197

Guadalupe Tepeyac, 180, 229, 283, 257–59, 274, 278, 287, 296

Guatemala, 45, 57, 59, 61, 103, 118–19,

Montes Azules, 65–66, 288–89
Morales, Cesário, 33, 36
Morales Garibay, Salvador. *See* Subcomandante Daniel
Morelia, 97, 118, 124, 266, 267, 269, 283
Muñoz Ramírez, Gloria, 353, 358

NAFTA (North American Free Trade Agreement), 113, 126, 144, 146–48, 172, 176–77, 179, 182, 197, 205, 215, 235, 252, 262, 309
Ñancahuazú, 82, 173, 305
National Democratic Convention. *See* CND
National Indigenous Congress, 319,
National Indigenous Forum, 244, 309
National Indigenous Institute, 148, 297–98, 306
NEA (National Endowment for the Arts), 332
Neoliberalism, 113, 215, 239, 306, 310
Neplanta (magazine), 38, 67, 98, 114, 117, 270
Neplanta (safe house), 186
Neruda, Pablo, 22, 71, 230, 365
Newsweek, 197, 232, 305
NGOS (Non-Governmental Organizations), 66, 182, 248, 258, 271, 287, 291, 320–21, 323
Nicaragua, 26, 32, 36, 39–41, 45, 49–51, 79, 88, 104–5, 109–11, 118–19, 129, 146–47, 164, 189, 197, 229, 232, 234, 303, 320, 364
"Nightmare Camp," 67, 76, 79
Nuevo León, 4

Oaxaca, 95, 330, 346–47, 351, 362
OCEZ (Organización Campesina Emiliano Zapata), 122, 126, 131
Ochoa, Héctor. *See* Subcomandante Pedro
Ocosingo, 63, 65–66, 91, 113, 120, 124,

126, 131, 136–37, 139–41, 146, 148, 160, 163, 172–74, 178, 184–87, 197, 206, 209–12, 219, 267–68, 322, 333
Oil, 13, 59, 105, 172, 198, 276
Old Antonio, 80–81, 85, 152–53, 183, 271, 326
Olympics (Mexico City, 1968), 14
Orive, Adolfo, 34, 321
Orozco, Pascual, 221, 282
Ortega, Daniel, 234
Orwell, George, 156–57
Oventic, 124, 283, 307, 312
Oxchuc, 60, 139, 148, 184

Paco, 66, 79, 108
Padrón, Joel, 137, 140–41, 214
Palenque, 121, 142, 148–49, 185, 203, 211–12, 339
PAN (Partido Acción Nacional), 95, 279, 281, 298, 304, 327, 337–40, 351, 353, 354
"Papa Doc," 97
Paramilitaries, 7, 60, 83, 95, 108, 115, 140–41, 216, 268, 308, 316–17, 319, 325, 336–37
Paris, 13, 28, 33, 34, 51, 285, 305, 308, 320
Pastrana, Andrés (president of Colombia), 340
Payeras, Mario, 57, 75, 138, 234, 363–64
Paz, Octavio, 4, 6, 223, 233
Peace and Justice (paramilitary group), 108
Peace camps, 291
Pemex (Pétroleos Mexicanos), 65, 105, 184–85, 209, 211, 397
Penal Code (State of Chiapas), 60, 121–22, 149, 222, 250, 383
Peru, 44, 58, 113, 214, 264, 309, 365
PGR (Procuraduría General de la Repúblic), 2, 30–31, 282, 376
Piaget, Jean, 43

Nick Henck is a visiting associate professor at Keio University
in Tokyo. He is the author of several journal articles on the Late
Roman Empire, as well as a short monograph detailing how the
Zapatistas courted Mexican civil society and the global mass
media.

Library of Congress Cataloging-in-Publication Data
Henck, Nick
Subcommander Marcos : the man and the mask / Nick Henck.
p. cm.
Includes bibliographical references and index.
ISBN 978-0-8223-3978-6 (cloth : alk. paper)
ISBN 978-0-8223-3995-3 (pbk. : alk. paper)
1. Marcos, subcomandante. 2. Guerrillas—Mexico—Chiapas—
Biography. 3. Revolutionaries—Mexico—Chiapas—Biography.
4. Ejército Zapatista de Liberación Nacional (Mexico) I. Title.
F1256.M365H46 2007
355.02′18092—dc22
[B]   2006102427